Mobilizing for Human Rights

This volume argues that international human rights law has made a positive contribution to the realization of human rights in much of the world. Although governments sometimes ratify human rights treaties, gambling that they will experience little pressure to comply with them, this is not typically the case. Focusing on rights stakeholders rather than the United Nations or state pressure, Beth A. Simmons demonstrates through a combination of statistical analyses and case studies that the ratification of treaties leads to better rights practices on average. By several measures, civil and political rights, women's rights, the right not to be tortured in government detention, and children's rights improve, especially in the very large, heterogeneous set of countries that are neither stable autocracies nor stable democracies. Simmons argues that international human rights law should get more practical and rhetorical support from the international community as a supplement to broader efforts to address conflict, development, and democratization.

Beth A. Simmons is Clarence Dillon Professor of International Affairs at Harvard University and has also taught at Duke University and the University of California at Berkeley. Her book *Who Adjusts? Domestic Sources of Foreign Economic Policy During the Interwar Years, 1924–1939*, was recognized by the American Political Science Association in 1995 as the best book published in 1994 in government, politics, or international relations. Her article "International Law and State Behavior: Commitment and Compliance in International Monetary Affairs" won the Heinz Eulau Award for the best article published in the *American Political Science Review* in 2000. Her research also regularly appears in such journals as *International Organization*, *World Politics*, the *Journal of Legal Studies*, and the *Journal of Conflict Resolution*. She was elected to the American Academy of Arts and Sciences in 2009.

Dedicated to Robert O. Keohane – scholar, mentor, friend

Mobilizing for Human Rights

International Law in Domestic Politics

Beth A. Simmons
Harvard University

CAMBRIDGE
UNIVERSITY PRESS

CAMBRIDGE UNIVERSITY PRESS
Cambridge, New York, Melbourne, Madrid, Cape Town, Singapore,
São Paulo, Delhi, Dubai, Tokyo

Cambridge University Press
32 Avenue of the Americas, New York, NY 10013-2473, USA

www.cambridge.org
Information on this title: www.cambridge.org/9780521712323

First published 2009

Printed in the United States of America

A catalog record for this publication is available from the British Library.

Library of Congress Cataloging in Publication Data

Simmons, Beth A., 1958–
    Mobilizing for human rights : international law in domestic politics / Beth Simmons.
        p. cm.
    Includes bibliographical references and index.
    ISBN 978-0-521-88510-2 (hardback) – ISBN 978-0-521-71232-3 (pbk.)
    1. Human rights. I. Title.

K3240.S5446 2009
341.4'8–dc22   2008041979

ISBN 978-0-521-88510-2 Hardback
ISBN 978-0-521-71232-3 Paperback

Additional resources for this publication at http://scholar.iq.harvard.edu/bsimmons/
mobilizing-for-human-rights

Contents

List of Figures and Tables

Figures

Tables

Note: Appendixes can be viewed online at http://scholar.iq.harvard.edu/ bsimmons/mobilizing-for-human-rights.

Acknowledgments

Many colleagues, students, and institutions have helped to make this study possible. It began at the Center for Advanced Study in the Behavioral Sciences at Stanford University during the academic year 2002–3. The Center provided the intellectual environment in which my ideas for this project first took shape. Casual discussions with individuals and during seminars at the center were essential in sparking my interest in developing a book-length study of international law and human rights. I owe a special debt of gratitude to the Hewlitt Foundation for supporting financially my year at the CASBS.

A number of my friends and colleagues read parts of the draft and offered their critical insights. I am especially grateful to my colleagues and peers who attended a book conference sponsored by the Weatherhead Center for International Affairs at Harvard and offered me invaluable advice in a most comprehensive and constructive manner: William Alford, Bear Braumoeller, Jeff Frieden, Jack Goldsmith, Ryan Goodman, Daniel Ho, Robert Keohane, Lisa Martin, Kathryn Sikkink, and Richard Steinberg. Many other individuals read parts of the manuscript and gave me additional advice, including Philip Alston, Jacqueline Bhabha, Daniel Bodansky, Antonia Chayes, Jeff Checkel, Xinyuan Dai, Allison Danner, Andreas Føllesdal, Andrew Guzman, Emelie Hafner-Burton, Moonhawk Kim, Benedict Kingsbury, Charles Lipson, Paulette Lloyd, Dinah Shelton, Duncan Snidal, Sidney Tarrow, Geir Ulfstein, Jana von Stein, Joseph Weiler, and David Weissbrodt. I have also benefited from methodological discussions with James Alt and Gary King. Several scholars were generous in sharing data with me, including Emelie Hafner-Burton, Oona Hathaway, Kristian Gleditsch, Rachel McCleary, and Christine Min Wotipka. None of these persons are responsible for the mistakes and choices reflected in the final product.

Students have been essential to this project in a number of ways. They asked me the right questions at the right times: Why should we think that international law affects governments' human rights practices? They provided enthusiastic research assistance. More than two dozen students – graduates and undergraduates – have been involved to one degree or another in the research. I hope they have learned as much from participating in this project as I gained from their involvement. The University of California Berkeley's Undergraduate Research Apprentice Program provided me a well-qualified flow of undergraduate students willing to collect and code data, run to the library, and collect literature. It is a model program in which the faculty member mentors students in the ways of scholarly research for course credit. Through this program, I benefited from the research help of Meghana Acharya, Inbal Baum, Ivana Cingel, Nancy Jen, Karina Juarez, Mimi Kong, Olga Kotlyarevskaya, Brad LeVeck, Naz Modirzadeh, Nicole Skibola, Julia Stuart, Monica Swanson, Elena Virgadamo, Kay Vobis, and Debbie Won. I greatly enjoyed teaching students in this way, and my research has been strengthened as a result.

Several Harvard undergraduates assisted with research, often with WCFIA funding, including Tamar Ayrikyan, Jieun Baek, Merve Emre, Ashley Grand, Anika Grubbs, and Matthew Roller. Law students and graduate students at Harvard provided legal research. Asif Efrat researched Israeli Supreme Court cases, and Laura Pedraza did the same for Chile. Yevgeniy Kirpichevsky assisted with some Stata issues and discussed general concepts. I also had excellent summer assistance from a number of students, including Nicholas Fram, Edgar Morales, Koppel Verma, and especially Eugen Lamprecht, who spent three months collecting and coding original data on child soldiers for this project.

I am also exceedingly grateful to the large number of university departments, schools, and research centers around the country and beyond that invited me to present sections of my research in progress. I presented parts of the manuscripts at a number of law schools, including those at New York University, Harvard, the University of California at Berkeley, the University of Georgia, Georgetown, Columbia, and the University of California at Los Angeles. I was also fortunate to get feedback and comments from faculty and students in the social sciences at the University of Pennsylvania, Stanford, the University of Minnesota, Dartmouth, St. Louis University, the State University of New York at Buffalo, the University of Michigan, Oxford University, the University of Chicago, Tufts University, Arizona State University, and Indiana University. International scholars provided useful feedback on early drafts as well. These included scholars associated with the Royal Complutense College at Harvard and the Centro de Investigación y Docencia Económicas (CIDE), Mexico City; participants in the Kandersteg, Switzerland, Conference on Constitutionalism; and especially the Norwegian Center for Human Rights, Oslo, where Andreas Føllesdal arranged a two-day discussion of the manuscript draft. The book was also discussed at the annual meeting of the New England Political Science Association in 2006, where M. J. Peterson was the discussant, and at the International Studies Association meeting in 2007, where I received useful comments from Michael Byers, Charli Carpenter, and Claudia Dahlerus.

Harvard University has been an ideal environment in which to develop and complete this project. The Harvard Government Department generously supported my attendance at annual conferences, where I was able to present my research to the broader scholarly community. The Weatherhead Center for International Affairs directly supported my work in several ways: by sponsoring undergraduate research assistance, by providing the opportunity to present my work to Center affiliates and staff, and by organizing and financing the book conference mentioned previously. The WCFIA staff also supported me in innumerable ways and contributed to a setting where it is truly possible to concentrate on research. I received excellent assistance in the final preparation of the manuscript, index, and bibliography from Marina Ivanova. Thanks also to Amanda Pearson, who proofread the final page proofs. The most consistent long-term assistance I had on this project was from Alexander Noonan, who for four years assisted with every phase of the manuscript preparation, from research to editing to general discussion about the ideas. As I have said about five times a day for the past four years, "Thanks, Alex!"

Several people at Cambridge University Press were helpful in producing this book. I am grateful to Lewis Bateman for encouragement and advice on the manuscript. Helen Greenberg, copy editor, and Helen Wheeler, production editor, did excellent work converting the manuscript into the book.

My greatest personal debt, of course, is to my family: Bruce Jackan, Charles, Claire, Sara, and Grandy. They found every possible way to allow me to concentrate on this long-term task. I hope they are pleased with the result.

Finally, for all of his guidance over the past two decades, I am deeply grateful to Robert O. Keohane. His work inspired my interest in international institutions, and his dedication to intellectual rigor, collegiality, and principles of international justice and legitimacy continue to inspire me to this day. For being the best mentor ever, this book is dedicated to him.

Abbreviations

ACHR	African [Banjul] Charter on Human and Peoples' Rights
CAT	Convention Against Torture and Other Cruel, Inhuman or Degrading Treatment or Punishment
CEDAW	Convention on the Elimination of All Forms of Discrimination Against Women
CERD	Committee on the Elimination of Racial Discrimination
CIA	Central Intelligence Agency (United States)
COPACHI	Cooperative Committee for Peace in Chile (Comite de Cooperacion para la Paz en Chile)
CPT	European Convention for the Prevention of Torture and Inhumane or Degrading Treatment or Punishment
CRC	Convention on the Rights of the Child
CSW	Commission on the Status of Women
DEDAW	Declaration on the Elimination of Discrimination Against Women
ECOSOC	Economic and Social Council (United Nations)
EEOL	Equal Employment Opportunity Law (Japan)
EU	European Union
GAVI	Global Alliance for Vaccines and Immunization
GDP	Gross Domestic Product
IACPPT	Inter-American Convention to Prevent and Punish Torture
IADJ	International Association of Democratic Jurists
ICCPR	International Covenant on Civil and Political Rights
ICESCR	International Covenant on Economic, Social and Cultural Rights
ICJ	International Commission of Jurists
ILO	International Labor Organization
IMF	International Monetary Fund
MIR	Revolutionary Left Movement (Chile; Movimiento de Izquierda Revolucionaria)

NAACP	National Association for the Advancement of Colored People
NCW	National Commission for Women (India)
NGO	Non-governmental organization
OAU	Organization for African Unity
OECD	Organization for Economic Co-operation and Development
OP	Optional Protocol
OPCAC	Optional Protocol Relating to Children in Armed Conflict
PTA	Preferential Trade Agreement
UDHR	Universal Declaration of Human Rights
UN	United Nations
UNCHR	United Nations Commission on Human Rights
UNGA	United Nations General Assembly
UNHCHR	United Nations High Commissioner on Human Rights
UNICEF	United Nations Children's Fund
US	United States
USAID	United States Agency for International Development
USSR	Union of Soviet Socialist Republics
WTO	World Trade Organization
WWIN	Working Women's International Network

Part I

I

Introduction

Human rights underwent a widespread revolution internationally over the course of the twentieth century. The most striking change is the fact that it is no longer acceptable for a government to make sovereignty claims in defense of egregious rights abuses. The legitimacy of a broad range of rights of individuals vis-à-vis their own government stands in contrast to a long-standing presumption of internal sovereignty: the right of each state to determine its own domestic social, legal, and political arrangements free from outside interference. And yet, the construction of a new approach has taken place largely at governments' own hands. It has taken place partially through the development of international legal institutions to which governments themselves have, often in quite explicit terms, consented.

How and why the turn toward the international legalization of human rights has taken place, and what this means for crucial aspects of the human condition, is at the core of this study. From the 1950s to the new millennium, governments have committed themselves to a set of explicit legal obligations that run counter to the old claim of state sovereignty when it comes to protecting the basic rights of individual human beings. There was nothing inevitable about this turn of normative and legal events. Indeed, the idea that sovereign governments are not accountable to outsiders for their domestic policies had been presumed for centuries. But from its apogee in the nineteenth century, the idea of exclusive internal sovereignty has been challenged by domestic democratic movements, by international and transnational private actors, and even by sovereigns themselves. The result today is an increasingly dense and potentially more potent set of international rules, institutions, and expectations regarding the protection of individual rights than at any point in human history.[1]

---

1 See, for example, Power and Allison 2000.

So much is well known. What is less well understood is, why would individual governments – only a short time ago considered internally supreme – choose to further this project of international accountability? What disturbed the conspiracy of mutual state silence that prevailed until the second half of the twentieth century? And why would an individual government choose to commit itself internationally to limit its freedom of action domestically? The former question is related to broader processes of democratization, transnational social movements, and the creation of intergovernmental organizations that have pushed governments to take these rights more seriously. The latter question requires us to explore the choice a government faces to tie its hands – however loosely – with international human rights treaties. The choice to commit to, or to remain aloof from, international normative structures governing individual human rights is itself a decision that needs to be explained.

Whether treaty law has done much to improve rights practices around the world is an open question. Has the growing set of legal agreements that governments have negotiated and acceded to over the past half century improved the "rights chances" of those whom such rules were designed to protect? Attempts to answer this question have – in the absence of much systematic evidence – been based on naive faith or cynical skepticism. Basic divisions exist over who has the burden of proof – those who believe that international law compliance is pervasive and therefore conclude that it falls to the skeptics to prove otherwise[2] versus those who view international law as inherently weak and epiphenomenal and require firm causal evidence of its impact.[3] Supporters of each approach can adduce a set of anecdotes to lend credence to their claims. Yet, broader patterns and causally persuasive evidence remain illusive.

This book addresses this gap in our knowledge of the linkages between the international human rights treaty regime and domestic practices. I argue that once made, formal commitments to treaties can have noticeably positive consequences. Depending on the domestic context into which they are inserted, treaties can affect domestic politics in ways that tend to exert important influences over how governments behave toward their own citizens. Treaties are the clearest statements available about the content of globally sanctioned decent rights practices. Certainly, it is possible for governments to differ over what a particular treaty requires – this is so with domestic laws as well – but it is less plausible to argue that the right to be free from torture, for example, is not something people have a right to demand and into which the international community has no right to inquire; less plausible to contend that children should be drafted to carry AK-47s; and less plausible to justify educating boys over girls on the basis of limited resources when governments have explicitly and voluntarily agreed to the contrary. Treaties serve notice that governments

2 Chayes and Chayes 1993; Henkin 1979, 1995.
3 Downs et al. 1996; Goldsmith and Posner 2005.

are *accountable* – domestically and externally – for refraining from the abuses proscribed by their own mutual agreements. Treaties signal a seriousness of intent that is difficult to replicate in other ways. They reflect politics but they also shape political behavior, setting the stage for new political alliances, empowering new political actors, and heightening public scrutiny.

When treaties alter politics in these ways, they have the potential to change government behaviors and public policies. It is precisely because of their potential power to constrain that treaty commitments are contentious in domestic and international politics. Were they but scraps of paper, one might expect every universal treaty to be ratified swiftly by every government on earth, which has simply not happened. Rather, human rights treaties are pushed by passionate advocates – domestically and transnationally – and are opposed just as strenuously by those who feel the most threatened by their acceptance. This study deals with both the politics of treaty commitment and the politics of compliance. It is the latter, of course, that has the potential to change the prospects for human dignity around the world.

If it can be shown that government practices with respect to human dignity can be improved through the international legal structure, then this will have important consequences both for our theories of politics and, more importantly, for public policy and local and transnational advocacy. Respect for international legal obligations is one of the few policy tools that public and private members of the international community have to bring to bear on governments that abuse or neglect their people's rights. It is certainly not the case that such obligations can always influence behavior; certain governments will be very difficult to persuade in any fashion, and some will never significantly alter their practices. These are the unfortunate facts of life. But the evidence presented in this study suggests that under some conditions, international legal commitments have generally promoted the kinds of outcomes for which they were designed. This argues for a continued commitment to the international rule of law as a possible lever, in conjunction with monitoring, advocacy, and resource assistance, in persuading governments that they have little to gain by systematically violating their explicit rights promises.

WHY INTERNATIONAL LAW?

Human rights practices are never the result of a single force or factor. The first years of the twenty-first century may not provide the most convincing portrait of the importance of international law for ordering international relations or shaping governmental practices. Doubts abound regarding the ability of international law to constrain hegemonic powers from acting unilaterally at their pleasure or to alter the calculations of ruthless governments that would entrench and enrich themselves at the price of their people's dignity. Advances in human rights are due to multiple social, cultural, political, and transnational influences. Why are legal rules worth attention in this context?

The reason is simple. The development of international legal rules has been the central *collective* project to address human rights for the past 60 years. Whenever the community of nations as a whole has attempted to address these issues, it has groped toward the development of a legal framework by which certain rights might become understood as "fundamental." As I will discuss in Chapter 2, the progress of this collective project – its growing scope, sophistication, and enforceability – has been impressive, especially over the past 30 years. The international legal structure, and especially those parts to which governments have explicitly and voluntarily committed via treaty ratification, provides the central "hook" by which the oppressed and their allies can legitimately call for behavioral change.

This is not, of course, a view that is universally held. International law is viewed as little more than a shill for power relations by its critics. Maxwell Chibundu cautions that ". . . human rights claims are not less susceptible to capture by self-interested groups and institutions, and . . . when transposed from their lofty ideal to practical implementation they serve multifaceted goals that are rarely, if ever, altruistic. . . ."[4] David Kennedy is scathing in his critique of "law's own tendency to over-promise."[5] Susan Engle draws attention to the appeal to international law to justify particular policy interventions favored by the politically powerful while drawing attention away from the more critical problems facing oppressed groups.[6] To many taking a non-Western perspective, the dominant discourse that informs the global human rights movement – no less than the legal structure that supports it – is little more than a front for Western imperialist values.[7] Critical feminist legal scholars point to the essentially patriarchal and obsessively "public" nature of the international legal system.[8]

Even mainstream scholars increasingly warn of the dangers of too much legalization at the international level. A common theme is that international adjudication is a step too far for most governments and a problematic development for the human rights regime generally. Lawrence Helfer, for example, argues that supranational adjudication to challenge rights violations encourages some countries to opt out of treaty agreements.[9] Jack Snyder and Leslie Vinjamuri make the compelling case that zealous rights prosecutions – in the context of unstable political institutions – worsen rather than improve the chances for peace, stability, and ultimately justice.[10] In the context of the International Criminal Court, Jack Goldsmith and Steven Krasner have argued that this legal

---

4   Chibundu 1999:1073.
5   Kennedy 2004:22.
6   Engle 2005.
7   Anghie 2005; Mutua 2001.
8   Olsen 1992.
9   Helfer 2002.
10 Snyder and Vinjamuri 2003–4.

tribunal might actually increase rights violations by discouraging the use of force where necessary to halt and punish egregious violations.[11] These accounts reflect a growing skepticism that the world's idealists have thrown *too much* law at the problems of human rights, to the neglect of underlying political conditions essential for rights to flourish.

These views are not without merit, but they hardly deny the need to ask what effects human rights treaties have had on outcomes that many can agree are important aspects of individual well-being. Mutua's critique is helpful in this respect: We should harbor no naive expectations that a dose of treaty law will cure all ills. Political context matters. Once we understand the law's possibilities and its limits, we will be in a much better position to appreciate the *conditions* under which treaty commitments can be expected to have important effects on rights practices and the channels through which this is likely to happen. The theory I advance in fact does much to undermine what Mutua refers to as the "dominant discourse," which views oppressed groups as helpless "victims" and Western institutions and nongovernmental organizations (NGOs) as "saviors."[12] *Treaty commitments are directly available to groups and individuals whom I view as active agents as part of a political strategy of mobilizing to formulate and demand their own liberation.* Rather than viewing international law as reinforcing patriarchal and other power structures, the evidence suggests that it works against these structures in sometimes surprising ways.

But why focus on law, some may ask, rather than on the power of norms themselves to affect change in rights practices? Norms are too broad a concept for the mechanisms I have in mind in this study. The key here is commitment: the making of an explicit, public, and lawlike promise by public authorities to act within particular boundaries in their relationships with individual persons. Governments can make such commitments without treaties, but for reasons discussed in the following pages, treaties are understood by domestic and international audiences as especially clear statements of intended behavior. I am not referring here primarily to broad and continuous processes of socialization, acculturation, or persuasion that have pervaded the literature on the spread of international norms. The mechanisms discussed in these pages depend on the explicit public nature of making what might be referred to as a lawlike commitment. When such commitments are broadly accepted as obligatory, we call them "legal." My central contention is that commitments with this quality raise expectations of political actors in new ways. True, some agreements that are not strictly legally binding may also raise expectations in an analogous way (the much vaunted "Helsinki effect"). But legal commitments have a further unique advantage: In some polities they are in fact legally enforceable.

11   Goldsmith and Krasner 2003.
12   Mutua 2001.

In some respects, my focus on international law is fully consistent with the broader norms literature. International human rights law does, after all, reflect such norms to a significant extent. Norms scholars in fact often appeal to international law to discover the exact content of many of the norms they study.[13] But here I am interested in the effect of explicit commitment-making. For this reason, not every legally binding norm is relevant to this study. Customary international law governs the practice of torture but cannot, I argue, as effectively create behavioral expectations as a precise, voluntary, sovereign commitment.[14] Treaty ratification is an observable commitment with potentially important consequences for both law and politics. That ratification improves behavior is verifiable by dogged political agents and falsifiable in social science tests. That norms play a role is undeniable, but the point developed here is that under some circumstances the commitment itself sets processes in train that constrain and shape governments' future behavior, often for the better.

As will become clear, making a case for the power of legal commitment in improving rights chances is not the same as making a case for an apolitical model of supranational *prosecution*. Those who see international law as part of the problem are worried about the consequences of *overjudicialization*, not the consequences of the kinds of treaty commitments examined here. In this study, legal commitments potentially stimulate political changes that rearrange the national legislative agenda, bolster civil litigation, and fuel social and other forms of mobilization. Any model in which law *replaces* politics is not likely to bear much of a relationship to reality and is likely to give rise to misguided policy advice, as several of the preceding critiques claim.

I offer one final justification for the focus on international law. In my view, alternative levers to influence official rights practices have proved in many cases to be unacceptable, sometimes spectacularly so. Sanctions and force often cruelly mock the plight of the most oppressed.[15] Yet, social and political pressures alone sometimes lack a legitimizing anchor away from which governments find it difficult to drift. The publicness and the explicitness of international law can potentially provide that anchor. In a world of inappropriate or ineffectual alternatives, the role of international law in improving human rights conditions deserves scholarly attention.

---

13 See, for example, Legro 1997.
14 On the weakness of customary international law's effect on helping states make binding commitments, see Estreicher 2003.
15 Michael Ignatieff has written persuasively that "We are intervening in the name of human rights as never before, but our interventions are sometimes making matters worse. Our interventions, instead of reinforcing human rights, may be consuming their legitimacy as a universalistic basis for foreign policy" (Ignatieff 2001:47). Our own inconsistency with respect to humanitarian intervention "has led to an intellectual and cultural challenge to the universality of the norms themselves" (ibid.:48).

INTERNATIONAL LAW AND INTERNATIONAL RELATIONS: THE STATE OF KNOWLEDGE

At no time in history has there been more information available to governments and the public about the state of human rights conditions around the world. The dedicated work of governmental organizations and NGOs, of journalists and scholars has produced a clearer picture than ever in the past of the abuses and violations of human rights in countries around the world. The possibility now exists to make an important theoretical as well as empirical contribution to understanding the role that international law has played in influencing human rights practices around the world. Only within the past decade or two has it been possible to address this relationship in a wide-ranging and systematic fashion.

Theoretical obstacles to such inquiry are also on the decline. State-centered realist theories of international relations dominated the Cold War years and discouraged the study of norms, nonstate actors, and the interaction between international and domestic politics. Certainly, realism in international politics reinforced the idea that international law is not an especially gripping subject of inquiry. With some important exceptions,[16] realists have ignored international law, typically assuming that legal commitments are hardly relevant to the ways in which governments actually behave. One lesson some scholars drew from the interwar years and the humanitarian abominations of the Second World War was that the international arena was governed largely by power politics and that the role of law in such a system was at best a reflection of basic power relations.[17] International law's weakness, its decentralized character, and the remote possibility of its enforcement (outside of the normal course of power relations) demoted it as an area of scholarly concern. In policy circles, some viewed international law as a dangerous diversion from crucial matters of state.[18] The turn to the study of system "structure" reinforced by Kenneth Waltz's theory of international politics further denied the relevance of legal constraints as an important influence on governmental actions.[19] In this theoretical tradition, international law was viewed as epiphenomenal: a reflection of, rather than a constraint on, state power. And in the absence of a willingness to use state power to enforce the rules, adherence could be expected to be minimal.[20]

---

16 Krasner 1999.
17 Bull 1977; Carr 1964; Hoffmann 1956; Morgenthau 1985. These realists tend to agree with Raymond Aron that while "the domain of legalized interstate relations is increasingly large . . . one does not judge international law by peaceful periods and secondary problems" (Aron 1981:733). This perspective is tantamount to the claim that if international law cannot solve all problems, then it cannot address any, which Philip Jessup referred to as the fallacy of the "great issues test" (Jessup 1959: 26–27).
18 Kennan 1951.
19 Waltz 1979.
20 Krasner 1993.

The past decade has seen some interesting new ways to think about international law's effects on government actions and policies. Rational theorists have emphasized the role that law can play in creating institutions that provide information to domestic audiences in ways that help them hold their governments accountable.[21] Liberal theorists have argued that international legal commitments supplement domestic legal structures, and they view international human rights agreements as attempts to solidify democratic gains at home.[22] Constructivist theorists have come to view "... international law and international organizations [as] ... the primary vehicle for stating community norms and for collective legitimation,"[23] and some prominent legal scholars have explicitly incorporated such concepts as discourse, socialization, and persuasion into an account of transnational legal processes through which international law eventually puts down roots in domestic institutions and practice.[24]

The availability of new theoretical perspectives and new sources of information on rights practices has stimulated a range of research that was not possible only a decade or so ago. New empirical work has begun to illuminate and test theories generated by looking intensively at specific cases. Oona Hathaway's "expressive" theory of treaty ratification, Emily Hafner-Burton and Kiyoteru Tsutsui's theory of ratification as an empty promise created by institutional isomorphism, and Eric Neumayer's theory of civil society participation are all important efforts to put systematic evidence of treaty effects on the table.[25] These and other works illustrate that it is possible to test with quantitative evidence the proposition that the international legal regime for human rights has influenced outcomes we should care about.

Nonetheless, the study of international law and human rights is a minefield of controversy in several important respects. Here we are dealing with sensitive political, social, and even personal issues, in which the essentially human nature of our subject is central. People suffer, directly and often tragically, because of the practices examined in this book. Many readers will find it an effrontery to apply the strictures of social science to such suffering.[26] Others may have concluded that cultural relativism and the hegemony implied by the international legal order itself render uselessly tendentious any inquiry into international "law and order."[27] As alluded to previously, human rights issues are often

21 Dai 2005.
22 Moravcsik 2000.
23 Risse and Sikkink 1999:8.
24 Harold Koh (1999) argues that transnational interactions generate a legal rule that can be used to guide future transnational interactions. In his view, transnational interactions create norms that are internalized in domestic structures through judicial decisions, executive or legislative action, etc. The norms become enmeshed in domestic structures; repeated participation in this process leads nations to obey international law.
25 Hafner-Burton and Tsutsui 2005; Hathaway 2002; Neumayer 2005.
26 Some believe that the social sciences cannot be usefully integrated with legal studies generally. See, for example, Barkun 1968:2–3; Koskenniemi 2000; Stone 1966.
27 See, for example, Evans 1998.

highly "perspectived" in ways that are more obvious, diverse, and deeply felt than many other areas of social research.

There is no getting around the sensitive and subjective nature of the issues dealt with in this book. Yet, the question of international law's impact on state behavior and outcomes calls for a well-documented and consistent evidentiary approach. The research strategy that has dominated the literature in both international law and human rights studies has been the use of intensive case studies on individual countries.[28] These have been invaluable in generating insights into specific crucial episodes, but they leave open the question about the influence of international legal commitments on practices more broadly. I take a different tack, one that complements the rich collection of case studies in this area: I look for broad evidence of general relationships across time and space. To do this, it is necessary to categorize and quantify rights practices governed by the major treaties. To quantify is hardly to trivialize; rather, it is an effort to document the pervasiveness and seriousness of practices under examination.[29] It is fairly straightforward to quantify aspects of formal legal commitment. Data on which countries have signed and ratified the core human rights conventions, and when, are easily assembled. By further documenting the making of optional commitments (individual rights of complaint, the recognition of various forms of international oversight), reservations and declarations (which may be evidence of resistance to these treaties), and the willingness to report, we can get a good idea of the conditions under which governments sign on to a treaty regime.

Quantification of meaningful institutional and behavioral change is far more difficult.[30] It requires a systematic comparison across time and space and a willingness to compress many details into a few indicators. This is obviously not the only way to investigate human rights practices. It is just one way to view a complex and multifaceted set of problems. Clearly, there are limits to what this kind of approach can reveal. At the same time, the data do show some patterns that, to date, more detailed case studies have not brought squarely to our attention. The quantitative evidence is supplemented in Chapters 6 and 7 with detailed discussions of how treaties have influenced politics and practices in particular countries. My hope is that by being as transparent as possible about how the quantitative data are gathered and deployed and by providing qualitative examples of the potential mechanisms, I will persuade at least some readers

---

28 Among the best are Audie Klotz's study of apartheid in South Africa (Klotz 1995); Daniel Thomas's study of the effect of the Helsinki Accord on the rights movement in Eastern Europe (Thomas 2001); and Kathryn Sikkink's research on human rights coalitions in Latin America (Sikkink 1993).

29 On the difficulty of quantification in the human rights area, see Claude and Jabine 1986.

30 Scholars who point out how difficult it is to measure human rights practices/violations include Donnelly and Howard 1988, Goldstein 1986, Gupta et al. 1994, McCormick and Mitchell 1997, Robertson 1994, and Spirer 1990. In some quantitative studies of human rights, little attention has been given to whether or not "rights" are adequately conceptualized and measured (Haas 1994).

to add these findings to their store of impressions of how states engage – and are ultimately constrained by – the international legal system.

It is also important to be clear about the precise focus of this study. The primary theoretical and empirical contributions relate to the conditions under which international human rights treaties can influence the behavior of governmental and other actors in ways that accord with the contents of international agreements. Many studies take up the more primordial issue of what range of phenomena comprise human rights, how they can be justified philosophically, who has a claim to such a right, and who has a duty to recognize and protect such rights. These are important issues, but they have been ably discussed in a large number of existing studies.[31]

Finally, I want to dispel any impression of an inevitable teleology underlying my generally positive message of progress. Chapter 2 places the current human rights regimes in the broader context of a century of growing state accountability that has proved fecund for the development and observance of the rights under discussion. But within the general trend dwell pockets of resistance. There was nothing at all inevitable about the development of international human rights law. Were it solely up to the major powers (the United States, the United Kingdom, the Soviet Union) after World War II, the regime might have been limited to the nonbinding Universal Declaration of Human Rights (UDHR, 1948). While there has been general progress in the development of international human rights law and institutions, the flaws remain obvious and the gains have almost always been hard-fought.

THE ARGUMENT IN BRIEF

Treaties reflect politics. Their negotiation and ratification reflect the power, organization, and aspirations of the governments that negotiate and sign them, the legislatures that ratify them, and the groups that lobby on their behalf. But treaties also *alter politics*, especially in fluid domestic political settings. Treaties set visible goals for public policy and practice that alter political coalitions and the strength, clarity, and legitimacy of their demands. Human rights treaties matter most where they have domestic political and legal traction. This book is largely about the conditions under which such traction is possible.

Why should a government commit itself to an international legal agreement to respect the rights of its own people? The primary reason is that the government anticipates its ability and willingness to comply. Governments participate in negotiations, sign drafts, and expend political capital on ratification in most cases because they support the treaty goals and generally want to implement them. They tend to drag their feet in negotiating treaties they find threatening,

---

31   See, for example, Donnelly 1998:ch. 2; Føllesdal and Pogge 2005; Orend 2002; Reidy and Sellers 2005.

potentially costly, or socially alienating. Polities participate most readily and enthusiastically in treaty regimes that reflect values consonant with their own. In this sense, the treaty-making and ratifying processes "screen" the participants themselves, leaving a pool of adherents that *generally* are likely to support their goals. Were this not the case, treaty ratification would be empirically random and theoretically uninteresting – a meaningless gesture to which it would be impossible to attach political, social, or legal significance. If we expect treaties to have effects, we should expect them to be something other than random noise on the international political landscape.[32]

Treaties are not perfect screens, however – far from it. Motives other than anticipated compliance influence some governments to ratify, even if their commitments to the social purposes of the agreement are weak. The single strongest motive for ratification in the absence of a strong value commitment is the preference that nearly all governments have to avoid the social and political pressures of remaining aloof from a multilateral agreement to which most of their peers have already committed themselves. As more countries – especially regional peers – ratify human rights accords, it becomes more difficult to justify nonadherence and to deflect criticism for remaining a nonparty. Figuratively, a treaty's mesh widens as more and more governments pass through the ratification screen.

Treaties are also imperfect screens because countries vary widely in their treaty-relevant national institutions. Legal traditions, ratification procedures, and the degree of decentralization impact the politics of the treaty-acceptance process. Because governments sometimes anticipate that ratification will impose political costs that they are not ready to bear, they sometimes self-screen. Despite general support for the goals of a human rights accord, opposition may form in powerful political subunits (states or provinces) that have traditionally had jurisdiction in a particular area (e.g., the death penalty in the United States). Sympathetic governments may self-screen if the costs of legal incorporation are viewed as too high or too uncertain. They may also self-screen if the ratification hurdle is high relative to the value they place on joining a particular treaty regime. The point is this: Two governments with similar values may appear on opposite sides of the ratification divide because of their domestic institutions rather than their preferences for the content of the treaty itself. Treaties may act as screens, but domestic institutions can do so as well.

The most significant claim this book makes is that, regardless of their acknowledged role in generally separating the committed human rights defenders from the worst offenders, treaties also play a crucial constraining role. As in the case of their screening function, they constrain imperfectly but perceptibly. The political world differs in important ways on either side of the ratification act. The main reason is one that institutionalists have recognized since the

32 Simmons and Hopkins 2005.

publication of Robert Keohane's seminal work: Regimes focus actors' expectations. To be sure, the focus can begin to shift during the treaty negotiations.[33] Expectations can begin to solidify further as more governments express commitment to an emerging standard – the process of legitimation emphasized by scholars of international norms and their spread.[34] But expectations regarding a particular government's behavior change qualitatively when that government publicly expresses its commitment to be legally bound to a specific set of rules. Treaties are perhaps the best instrument available to sovereign states to sharpen the focus on particular accepted and proscribed behaviors. Indeed, they are valued by sovereign states as well as nongovernmental actors for precisely this reason.[35] Treaties constrain governments because they help define the size of the *expectations gap* when governments fail to live up to their provisions. This expectations gap has the power to alter political demands for compliance, primarily from domestic constituencies, but sometimes by the international community as well.

The three domestic mechanisms I explore in the following pages are the ability of a treaty to effect elite-initiated agendas, to support litigation, and to spark political mobilization. I think of these mechanisms as ranging from the most to the least elite of processes. In the simplest case, treaties can change the national agenda simply because they raise questions of ratification and hence implementation. International law raises the question: Do we move to ratify and to implement? In many cases, treaties insert issues into national politics that would not have been there in the absence of international politics. Governing elites can initiate compliance, with practically no public participation, if they value international cooperation on the issue the treaty addresses. Treaties are important in these cases, because the national agenda would have been different in the absence of international negotiations.

International treaties also provide a resource in litigation should the government be less than eager to comply. The availability of this mechanism depends on the nature of the domestic legal system and the quality of the courts. Litigation is a possibility where treaties have the status of law in the domestic legal system (or where they have been implemented through enforceable domestic statutes) and where the courts have a degree of political independence. Even in these cases, litigation cannot force compliance. It can only raise the political costs of government resistance by legitimating through indigenous legal institutions the demand to comply. In countries with a strong rule of law tradition, an adverse court ruling can add weight to the pressures a government will experience to comply.

---

33 Chayes and Chayes 1993.
34 Finnemore and Sikkink 1998.
35 See Chapters 2 and 3 for evidence that NGOs have spent scarce resources on codification and ratification campaigns because they believe that commitments support the campaign for better rights practices.

Finally, a public treaty commitment can be important to popular mobilization to demand compliance. Treaties provide political, legal, and social resources to individuals and groups whose goal is to hold governments to their promises. In these pages, I will argue that explicit legal commitments raise the expected value of social mobilization by providing a crucial tangible resource for nascent groups and by increasing the size of the coalition with stakes in compliance. What is more, this effect is greatest in countries that are neither stable democracies (where most rights are already protected and the motive to mobilize is relatively low) nor stable autocracies (where the likelihood of successful mobilization is low if the rights the treaty addresses are seen in any way as challenging status quo governing arrangements). Key here is the legitimating function of an explicit public commitment to a global standard. That commitment is used strategically by demandeurs to improve the rights in which they have an interest.

The central point is this: The political environment most (though not all) governments face differs on either side of the ratification divide. These changes are subtle, and they are often conditional. They involve changes that give relatively weak political actors important tangible and intangible resources that raise the political costs governments pay for foot-dragging or for noncompliance. These changes are not drastic, but they may be enough to encourage women's groups in Japan, supported by a few Diet members who otherwise might not have seized the cause, to press for legislation to address the most egregious forms of employment discrimination in that country. These changes are sometimes just enough to give a small rights interest group in Israel enough legal ammunition to argue before the Supreme Court that "moderate physical pressure" is not allowed under the Convention Against Torture and Other Cruel, Inhumane or Degrading Treatment or Punishment (CAT) and to turn the political tables by requiring the Israeli legislature explicitly (and, one can assume, to their embarrassment) to pass legislation to the contrary. No one, this author in particular, believes that signing a treaty will render a demonic government angelic. But under some circumstances, a public international legal commitment can alter the political costs in ways that make improvements to the human condition more likely.

The argument developed in this book is also conditional. Treaties vary by virtue of the rights practices they are attempting to influence. Some can directly impact the perceived ability of the government to maintain political control. The International Covenant on Civil and Political Rights (ICCPR) and the CAT are two examples that potentially have serious governing consequences for a ruling regime. Broad political rights can empower political opposition; the use of torture can be strategically employed to retain political control or to glean information from various enemies of the state. Governments are much more likely to disregard an international commitment if doing so is perceived in any way to endanger their grip on power or the "stability" of the broader polity. Other accords are less likely to threaten a government's political or security goals. The Convention on the Elimination of All Forms of Discrimination Against Women (CEDAW) and the Convention on the Rights of the Child (CRC) are much more important for their social impact than their direct political implications. Most governments – with the possible exception of theocracies whose doctrines embrace the political and social subordination of women – are far less likely to have a crucial political stake in assuring or withholding rights for women and children than they are to have the uninhibited freedom to oppress political opposition. The more a treaty addresses issues clearly related to the ability of the government to achieve its central political goals, the weaker we should expect the treaty's effect to be.

Finally, quintessentially political treaties, such as the CAT and the ICCPR, are likely to have their greatest mobilization effects precisely where the conditions exist to gain significant domestic political traction. Treaties alter politics; they do not cause miracles. They supplement and interact with domestic political and legal institutions; they do not replace them. Extremely stable domestic political institutions will not be much affected by a political human rights treaty commitment. On the one hand, in stable autocracies, they are largely irrelevant. Potential political actors simply do not have the resources to effectively demand change. Treaties may have effects if transnational coalitions are thereby empowered,[36] but the chain of demands is attenuated and likely to be weak. This obvious fact is what causes some scholars to conclude that human rights treaties do not have positive effects.[37] On the other hand, in stable democracies, treaties may be readily accepted, but they are often redundant. Because political rights are largely protected – and have been in living memory – treaty ratification adds very little political activity to that already established around domestically guaranteed protections. The point is that treaties have significant effects, but they do not have the same effects everywhere.

I argue that even the most politically sensitive human rights treaties have significant positive effects in those countries where political institutions have been unstable. Treaties alter politics through the channel of social mobilization, where domestic actors have the motive and the means to form and to demand their effective implementation. In stable autocracies, citizens have the motive to mobilize but not the means. In stable democracies, they have the means but generally lack a motive. Where institutions are most fluid, however, the expected value of importing external political rights agreements is quite high.[38] Rights beneficiaries have a clear incentive to reach for a legal instrument the content and status of which are unlikely to change regardless of the liberality of the current government. They also have a basic capacity to organize and to press for treaty compliance. In many cases, these more volatile polities have

36 Keck and Sikkink 1998.
37 Hathaway 2002.
38 Moravcsik 2000.

experienced at least a degree of political participation and enjoyed some modicum of democratic governance. It is precisely in these polities that we should expect ratification of the more political human rights treaties to influence political coalitions, demands, and ultimately government practices. One of the most significant findings of this book is that even the most politically sensitive human rights treaties have positive effects on torture and repression for the significant number of countries that are neither stable democracies nor stable autocracies. International law matters most where domestic institutions raise the expected value of mobilization, that is, where domestic groups have the motive and the means to demand the protection of their rights as reflected in ratified treaties.

ORGANIZATION OF THE BOOK

This book is divided into two parts. Part I is introductory, historical, and theoretical. Chapter 2 provides some historical context in which to understand the issues of treaty commitment and compliance that governments faced in the last third of the twentieth century. The idea of limiting state sovereignty in certain issue areas took root over the course of the twentieth century, setting the stage for the legalization of the human rights regime after World War II. This chapter explores the question: Why rights? Why a legal regime? And why at mid-twentieth century? The answers involve a mix of shock and horror in the wake of the Second World War, as well as a moral commitment to address the atrocities of the Holocaust. Cold War politics and decolonization played crucial roles as well. The former gave rise to the strategic deployment of rights discourse as a way to gain allies and the moral high ground in competition between the superpowers. The latter exposed the abuses of colonialism and tapped earlier Wilsonian ideas of self-determination of peoples in order to rid most of Africa of formal European rule. A coalition of nongovernmental actors and some of the smaller democracies have pushed along the project of legalization. As general trends in accountability have improved, these legal commitments have become plausible constraints on states' rights practices.

Chapter 3 is about the decisions of individual state governments to engage this growing body of law. How are we to understand the fundamental decisions each state faces about whether to participate voluntarily in the regime? The focus in this chapter is on the commitment issue. Treaties are theorized as consciously chosen, publicly deliberated, and legally ratified modes of communicating an official state intent to behave in ways consistent with the content of the agreement. The theoretical point of departure – the prime theoretical assumption – is that governments ratify treaties largely because they believe they can and should comply with them. Any other starting point is highly unsatisfactory both theoretically and empirically. But we know that there is not a perfect correspondence between ratification and compliance, so it is essential to theorize this discrepancy as well. Polities differ in their preferences for treaty content. Some governments are ambivalent but ratify to avoid the criticism associated with remaining outside of the regime. I refer to these cases as "false positives," and I argue that they tend to occur for externally motivated strategic reasons. Criticism is less concentrated when a small number of countries have ratified; it becomes more focused on laggards when greater numbers and especially regional peers have already ratified. Social and political pressure is a key explanation for ratification when governments are only weakly committed to the treaty's goal. Moreover, domestic institutions – constitutionally specified ratification procedures, decentralized public authority, legal traditions and structures – create incentives for a government to delay or withhold ratification even if the values reflected in the treaty are in fact closely held. I refer to these cases as "false negatives." Holding preferences constant, domestic institutions can raise the cost of ratification for some governments. The United States, for example, is often criticized for its egregious exceptionalism with respect to its human rights treaty ratification record. Arguably, its federal structure, supermajority ratification procedures, and highly independent and accessible courts go a long way toward raising the ex ante political costs of ratification.

These ideas are then tested on six of the most important multilateral treaties of the past 50 years.[39] The evidence suggests that treaty commitments clearly reflect underlying state and societal preferences. Democratic institutions, some cultural characteristics, and in some cases the political orientation of the government of the day affect the propensity to ratify. Domestic institutions (primarily the nature of the legal system, but also the height of the ratification hurdle) significantly reduce the probability of ratifying, producing some cases of false negatives. This chapter also shows that governments are greatly influenced by the commitments of other countries, especially the countries in their region. I argue that this reflects a desire to avoid criticism by taking ratification action typical of the region. A close look at the timing and incidence of regional clustering suggests a strategic logic rather than ratification behavior that reflects normative socialization. These findings are echoed in the patterns associated with reservation-making and the recognition of international authority as well. These dynamics account for at least some of the false positives – insincere ratifiers – upon which other quantitative studies have focused.[40]

Chapter 4 theorizes how treaties can be used by stakeholders to improve human rights practices. I argue that treaties influence outcomes by altering the political calculations of domestic actors. This chapter identifies three channels. The most "top-down" mechanism involves the effect an international treaty can

---

39 The ICCPR, International Covenant on Economic, Social and Cultural Rights (ICESCR), Convention on the Elimination of Racial Discrimination (CERD), CEDAW, CAT, and CRC.
40 Hathaway 2002.

have on the political agenda of governing elites. Individual governments simply cannot control the international agenda; for many governments, treaties are an exogenous shock to their national priorities, which many (but certainly not all) are willing to accommodate. Second, treaty commitments can inspire and facilitate litigation. A few citizens can leverage law in legal proceedings, and when they are successful, these actions can change the calculus of important political actors, including, potentially, the government itself. Third, treaties can provide resources and galvanize social mobilization. Unless a government is so firmly ensconced that it can ignore social movements, or so democratic that such movements barely have a motive to form in the first place, international human rights treaties can give rights movements a unique form of political ammunition that can help legitimate group demands.

Part II assesses the effect of treaties on state and state-sponsored behavior. Although I often use the language of compliance, this part is about behavioral or institutional changes that comport with the obligations contained in formal treaty commitments, whether or not that behavior constitutes full legal compliance with every aspect of the treaty. I am more concerned with measuring behavioral changes in the direction stipulated by the treaty than with coding whether a given country has fully complied. There are several reasons for this approach. First, improvements in practices and outcomes are of greater substantive interest than technical legal compliance. Even if it were possible to determine and to agree upon precise legal criteria for full compliance – which is not possible in the absence of a courtlike determination – we should be interested in evidence of substantive improvements in rights conditions rather than formal criteria. Furthermore, in many of the treaties examined here, there is room for what in the European context is referred to as a "margin of appreciation" that allows states to implement the treaty's purposes in a number of ways. Finally, many of the provisions in the treaties examined here contain clauses of permissible derogations, which try to balance different interests. The ICCPR, for example, allows for the derogation of certain of its provisions in the interest of national security, public safety, and public order.[41]

The first four chapters of Part II are the empirical climax of the study. Does a treaty commitment affect government behavior in ways that are required by the treaty? This is a crucial question, for it addresses the issue with which we all should be most concerned: the ability of legal conventions to improve the human condition. To demonstrate such a proposition is difficult for a number of reasons. First, there are obviously many explanations for the behaviors that are ostensibly governed by international treaty arrangements. It is important to do as much as possible to show that the legal arrangements themselves are likely influences on behavior. Compliance research has long been plagued by the difficult-to-disprove claim that the government would have behaved as we

---

41 See, for example, Article 4 of the ICCPR.

have observed *anyway*, whether or not it had committed itself to a particular treaty arrangement.[42] Chapters 5 through 8 show that there are reasons to believe that commitment does improve human rights behavior in ways that the treaties require. The empirical models leverage the findings about false negatives and false positives to develop instruments that can be used simultaneously to predict rights outcomes while holding the conditions associated with ratification itself constant. The idea is to "net out" the factors that explain both ratification and compliance, the better to draw inferences about the effect of treaty commitment itself on these outcomes. The inclusion of country fixed effects in these models (which control for many of the country characteristics that we cannot observe but that are likely to affect rights behaviors) raises confidence in the contention that the government in question was not simply a "natural" candidate for rights improvements. The inclusion of year fixed effects similarly raises our confidence that ratification and not some simultaneously experienced global event, such as a conference or another event, accounts for the observed effects.

These chapters demonstrate in a quantitative empirical study that human rights treaties have positive effects. Chapter 5 shows that countries that have ratified the ICCPR are in fact likely to reduce their interference with some civil liberties, such as free religious practice. Criminal justice shows much more variance, with ratification of the ICCPR mattering little in the provision of fair trials, but ratification of its Optional Protocol on the Death Penalty (OPDP) is strongly associated with the abolition of capital punishment. Chapter 6 shows that a government that has committed itself to CEDAW is much more likely to improve educational opportunities for girls, employment opportunities for women, and reproductive health care and autonomy for women, though effects were much stronger in secular states than those with an officially established religion. Chapter 7 shows that a commitment to the CAT lowers the probability that citizens living in all but the most stable democratic or autocratic regimes will be brutally tortured or abused by their own government while in its custody. Chapter 8 shows that child labor has been reduced and that governments have changed their military recruitment policies in an effort to comply with the CRC and its Optional Protocol Relating to Children in Armed Conflict (OPCAC). These effects tend to be stronger for compulsory than for voluntary conscription, a practice on which the treaty in fact takes a stronger stand. There is also some evidence that CRC ratification has been associated with a higher priority placed on childhood immunization for measles, at least in the middle-income countries, which is an important indicator of basic health care for children. These findings are robust to many alternative explanations, which are discussed in detail in these chapters. The statistical findings represent correlations (not strictly causation)

42 Downs et al. 1996.

between treaty ratification and outcomes. But to the extent that other explanations for observed improvements are controlled in the statistical design, the case for causation becomes stronger.

The emphasis in this book is on broad trends, but it is fair to wonder how treaty commitments work their way into policy change on the ground. As we should fully expect in a heterogeneous set of countries with varying political institutions and cultures, pathways to compliance vary. Chapters 6 and 7 provide detailed examples. The CEDAW has influenced Japanese employment policies, largely through its value in mobilizing women's groups to lobby the legislative branch for more equal treatment. It has also influenced Colombian women's rights groups to appeal to the treaty's provisions to demand constitutional change guaranteeing women's right to basic health care, which became a crucial argument in the 2006 landmark case that led to an exception to the illegality of abortion when the mother's life is at stake. The CAT has influenced Israeli interrogation practices because it was cited in the litigation leading to the famous Supreme Court ruling on interrogation practices. The CAT was also useful in Chile's struggle to end government-sponsored torture. These cases help to elucidate how treaties become useful in the hands of local rights stakeholders. Details obviously differ in each case, but in each, the international legal commitment stimulated and/or strengthened domestic change in policy and/or practice.

Conclusions are drawn in Chapter 9. It is here that I elaborate on the claim that international legal arrangements have an important role to play in creating an atmosphere in which human rights are increasingly respected. My conclusions are cautiously optimistic. They are cautious because treaties do not guarantee better rights; rather, they contribute to a political and social milieu in which these rights are more likely, on the whole, to be respected. The theory is probabilistic, not deterministic. Many of the countries examined here obviously have ignored their obligations in a most flagrant manner and will continue to do so regardless of their obligations under international law.

The conclusions are also cautiously optimistic, because while this study has considered many alternative explanations, these apparently do not overwhelm the influence of a public promise to one's citizens as well as to the international community to abide by specific human rights standards. The rigor of these tests suggests to me a causal relationship, but it is crucial to reiterate that the statistical evidence is, strictly speaking, no more than correlative. At a minimum, with very high confidence we can conclude that the ratification of human rights treaties is associated with improvements in outcomes that many of us care deeply about. It is not true, of course, that treaties are the most important explanation for rights improvements. Nonetheless, marginal gains in a very tough-to-influence arena under circumstances in which the international community's arsenal of tools is quite limited are important gains indeed. The study certainly suggests that the development and nurturing of the international legal system is wholly worthwhile for those who want to see improvements in official practices that affect basic human dignity. It suggests as well that private as well as official actors should continue to hold governments accountable for their international legal commitments. The international human rights regime deserves respect as an important way to improve basic human rights globally.

Why International Law? The Development of the International Human Rights Regime in the Twentieth Century

> It is difficult to restrain myself from doing something to stop this attempt to exterminate a race, but I realize I am here as an Ambassador and must abide by the principles of non-interference with the internal affairs of another country.
>
> Henry Morgenthau, U.S. ambassador in Turkey,
> to the U.S. secretary of state 11 August 1915[1]

The second half of the twentieth century was the first time in history that human rights were addressed in a systematic manner by the international community. Following the Second World War, official as well as nonstate actors worked together to address a broad range of rights – civil and political, economic and social, rights of nondiscrimination – and to finalize many of these in the form of legally binding covenants. The international legal edifice that thousands worked to shape has attracted criticism as well as praise; it has raised expectations as well as overpromised; it has aspired to universality yet still reflects some of the hegemonic ideas of the most powerful actors in the world polity. Most importantly, though, it has successfully challenged the unconditional assertion of national leaders that the way they treat their own people is exclusively a national sovereign concern. The idea that a government should have the freedom to treat its people as brutally as it wishes while others are helpless to intervene *because of its status as a sovereign state* is legally – and possibly, morally – untenable in the twenty-first century.

This chapter chronicles the evolution of a well-developed (though still contested and sporadically enforced) legal regime that spells out a broad range of individual rights and protections. The regime has been decades in the making and is related to broader developments such as the diffusion of democracy, the

---

1 Quoted in Kamminga 1992:6.

trend toward more accountability in international law generally, and the increasingly transnational organization of civil society. The fairly recent presumption that individuals have internationally protected rights that states are not at liberty to disregard in the name of sovereignty is profound. How did we move from a world in which a statement such as Morgenthau's reflected prevailing norms to one in which such a statement is hard to imagine a government official uttering publicly? Why have we ended up with a *legal* regime as the primary way human rights norms are expressed and implemented at the international level? How did international law designed to protect individuals come to invade the formerly nearly impenetrable space carved out for state sovereignty?

THE GLOBAL CONTEXT: THE INTENSIFICATION OF
STATE ACCOUNTABILITY IN THE TWENTIETH CENTURY

While the Second World War is considered the proximate setting, nothing as complex as the development of an international regime for individual rights could possibly be monocausal. If we want to understand why states might agree to limit their sovereignty through international legal agreements, it is useful to understand why accountability for individual rights through international law was even on the table in the 1940s. There were, after all, other possible answers to the litany of atrocities associated with World War II: Execution without trial, impunity, or the development of soft law arrangements to express collective outrage were some of the available options. But there have been at least three historical trends of reasonably long duration that have supported (not caused) the legalization of international human rights: the trend toward democratization, the elaboration of accountability in international law, and the growth in transnational civil society.

Democratization

It is difficult to understand both the development and the influence of the international human rights regime without acknowledging the crucial fact that over the course of the twentieth century governments increasingly became accountable to their own people. Democratization raises expectations that governments will respect a broad range of individual rights and freedoms, many of which are nearly synonymous with democratization itself. Additionally, establishing a democratic system increases the prospects for limitations on public authority imposed by the rule of law. Finally, of course, democracy provides the institutions – free elections, a relatively free press, relatively free speech – that hold governments accountable for their actions. From the ideas first expressed in the American and French Revolutions to the recent political liberalizations in the post–Cold War period, there has been widespread diffusion of the ideal of – and the mechanisms for – holding government leaders accountable to their citizens for their actions.

Democracies are the natural allies of human rights. The expansion of democratic accountability itself has been associated with the expansion of domestic rights protections. The rise of the bourgeoisie in the eighteenth century led to franchise extensions to this new social group and did much to secure their property and civil rights as well. The Industrial Revolution created a set of conditions under which workers were more able to organize to demand improvements in their working situations; the extension of the franchise to workers in several countries just before the Great War accelerated afterward as veterans demanded political representation in the nations for which so many had sacrificed. For the first time, social and economic rights were on the table in a number of countries as a result.[2] The defeat of fascism in World War II reestablished democracy in Western Europe, and gave rise to new constitutions[3] as well as regional structures[4] designed to ensconce rights in both domestic and international law. The illegitimacy and in some cases imminent breakdown of largely undemocratic imperial structures in the war's wake gave rise to demands for attention to rights from the nonviolent demonstrations of Ghandi in India to the anticolonial campaigns of Kwane Nkrumah in the region that became Ghana.[5] At the end of the twentieth century, the breakdown of the Soviet Union and its empire in Europe set these countries – however haltingly – on the road to political liberalization and gave rise to a new enthusiasm for participation in international human rights regimes (see Figures 3.2 and 3.3 in the following chapter).

The data on the spread of democracy to many parts of the world offer valuable insight into the connection between the development of an international human rights regime and political liberalization (Figure 2.1). The proportion of countries that can reasonably be called democratic increased fairly consistently from the mid-1800s to the outbreak of the First World War but plunged with the counterthrust of fascism during the interwar years. Despite a further downward turn in the early 1960s due to the proliferation of newly independent states (many of which were hardly democratic), by the late 1960s the number started to climb again. In the 1990s alone, the proportion of democratic countries around the world increased from about 30 percent to about 50 percent. By 2000, about 58 percent of the world's population could cast a

---

2 Ishay 2004.

3 The Japanese constitution, written largely by Westerners, contained some 31 articles out of 103 total outlining the rights and duties of the people. See generally the discussion in Kishimoto 1988. For an account that highlights the local popular contributions to Japan's postwar constitution, see Dower 1999.

4 Moravcsik 2000.

5 Gandhi 1957; Nkrumah 1957. Decolonization did not, of course, usher in a period of stable democracy in Africa, with a few exceptions such as Botswana, Mauritius, and until recently The Gambia.

Figure 2.1. Proportion of Democracies in the World. *Note:* Countries are counted as democratic if they score above 6 on the −10 to 10 Polity IV combined democracy–autocracy scale. Data supplied by Kristian Gleditsch.

meaningful vote in reasonably competitive and fair elections, though countries in the Middle East and Central Asia barely participated in this trend.[6] Accompanying this increase in democratic states is another striking trend: The international community is increasingly willing to monitor the quality of domestic accountability by monitoring the election process itself (see Figure 2.2).[7]

The point is this: International legal commitments are now increasingly made by governments that can be held accountable for their commitments by their own people. Xinyuan Dai has argued compellingly that democracy gives rise to constraints that make noncompliance with even weak international regimes potentially costly for governments.[8] As I will argue, even imperfect regimes that allow for the organization of rights demands and the use of law as a legitimating political resource are potentially fertile contexts for international law to influence official rights policies and practices.

---

6 The population share figure is from Freedom House; see "Democracy's Century: A Survey of Global Political Change in the 20th Century," http//www.freedomhouse.org/reports/century.html (accessed 9 September 2005). The literature on democratization is varied and cannot be reviewed here. Explanations include variations in regional levels of economic development (Lipset 1960), regionally specific cultural values (Almond and Verba 1963; Muller and Seligson 1994; Putnam et al. 1993), characteristic class relations (Rueschemeyer et al. 1992), and specific critical junctures and path dependence (O'Donnell et al. 1986). See also Huntington 1991.
7 In addition, for a complete list of all plebiscites, referenda, and elections held under the supervision or observation of the United Nations in Trust and non-self-governing territories, see Beigbeder 1994: table 4.1. For a discussion of trends in election monitoring, see Santa-Cruz 2005.
8 Dai 2005.

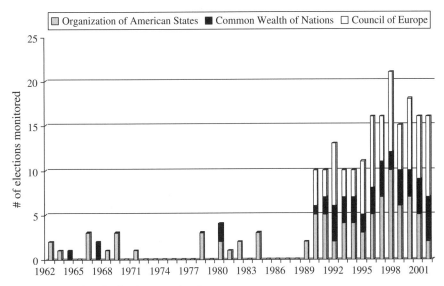

Figure 2.2. Regional Election Monitoring.

Accountability in International Law

Public international law itself has also undergone some important transitions over the course of the past century, and these changes are much broader than the development of human rights conventions that are the focus of this book. A close look at some key areas of law-governed interstate behavior reveals an evolving approach to sovereignty and accountability in governments' mutual relationships with one another. International human rights law is one area in which states have accepted new limits on their sovereignty, but it is not the only one. The trend to submit to monitoring, reporting, and surveillance mechanisms can be found in treaties in areas as diverse as arms control, the laws of war, trade and monetary relations, and dispute resolution and predates the elaboration of the human rights regime.[9]

9 Robert Keohane (1993) has argued that to the extent that these agreements represent incursions into state sovereignty, they are driven by the desire for reciprocal constraints on the actions of their peers. Some scholars have found it useful to distinguish three functional periods in international law development that roughly parallel the intensification of state-to-state accountability I develop here. Johnston (1997:111–13) distinguishes functional "periods" for international law: a "Classical" period up to World War I that concentrated on the containment of power abuse, facilitation of international trade diplomacy, communication, and settlement of interstate disputes; a "Neo-Classical" period (1919–mid-1960s) that institutionalized world society through intergovernmental organizations, promotion of the rule of law through codification, enhancement of human welfare through confirmation, and implementation of individual and social rights; and a "Post-Classical" period focused on correction of distributive justice, development of international regimes, and the transformation of international society from a nation-state system to a world community based on humanitarian ethics and cooperative behavior. See also Ku 2001.

Consider as an example an area that governments have long attempted to regulate through formal agreements: the control of armaments. Today few governments would consider negotiating an arms agreement that is unverifiable, yet the idea of including verification and monitoring mechanisms in arms control agreements is of fairly recent vintage. Documentary histories of nineteenth-century arms agreements reveal no efforts to hold signatories accountable to one another.[10] It was only after World War I, with the Treaty of Versailles and the creation of the League of Nations, that formal mechanisms of state accountability in arms control and disarmament were implemented.[11] The most important arms control agreement of the interwar years, the Washington Naval Treaty (1922), required the parties to "communicate promptly" plans for replacement tonnage;[12] it did not, however, provide for monitoring or verification of these reports.[13] By contrast, after World War II, practically no arms control efforts were considered that lacked monitoring, reporting, and verification.[14] The Cold War era inaugurated important superpower agreements in this regard, including the inspection regimes associated with the Anti-Ballistic Missile Treaty and two rounds of Strategic Arms Limitations Talks.[15] Similarly, governments with a broad range of ideological and cultural backgrounds agree

10 If arms control agreements were successful during that period, it is largely because they dealt with readily observable activities. For example, the American–British (Rush–Bagot) agreement of 1817 to reduce naval forces on the Great Lakes worked well without monitoring agreements (Blacker and Duffy 1984), likely because noncompliance was reasonably easy to detect.

11 Treaty of Versailles, 28 June 1919, Section IV: "Interallied Commission of Control," providing for inspections. Disarmament was addressed by the League of Nations (28 June 1919), which called for consultations and information exchange (Article 8 [4–6]). The Convention for the Control of the Trade in Arms and Ammunition, 10 September 1919, aimed at preventing arms trade in most of Africa and parts of Asia and required contracting parties to "publish an annual report showing the export licenses which it may have granted," with quantities and destinations, to be sent to the secretary general of the League of Nations (Ch. I, Article 5). Similarly, the Convention for the Supervision of the International Trade in Arms and Ammunition and in Implements of War, 17 June 1925, requires the parties to "undertake to publish within two months of the close of each quarter, a statistical return of their foreign trade during this quarter in the articles covered by categories I and II in Article I [of the convention]" (Ch. II, Article 6). They also had to publish information for each vessel of war constructed (Article 7) and the export of aircraft and aircraft engines (Article 9).

12 Washington Naval Treaty, 1922, Part 3, Sect. 1(b). Papers Relating to the Foreign Relations of the United States: 1922, Vol. 1, pp. 247–66; Treaty Series No. 671.

13 "Only the 1922 Washington Treaty Relating to the Use of Submarines and Noxious Gases in Warfare, which never came into force, had a clear enforcement mechanism. It provided that violations of its limitations on submarine attacks were to be treated as acts of piracy and prosecuted pursuant to the applicable universal jurisdiction" (Carter 1998:11).

14 On the early postwar acceptance of safeguards and inspections in principle, see Dupuy and Hammerman 1973. The slow start in postwar arms control was largely the result of difficulties in agreeing precisely how this principle of accountability should be implemented.

15 The ABM Treaty (Article XII [1]) provides for the use of "national technical means of verification ...," with which each agree not to interfere (Article XII [2]). The SALT I and II treaties have virtually identical provisions. See, e.g., SALT II Article XI [1–3]. http://www.dpi.anl.gov/dpi2/hist_docs/treaties/salt2.htm.

that the international community has the right to inspect national sites for weapons of mass destruction.[16]

Mechanisms of accountability also became integral to the laws of war-fighting over the course of the twentieth century. For the first time in history, governments agreed in the 1906 Geneva Conventions to exchange information on the condition of prisoners of war, though there was no real mechanism to enforce this commitment.[17] The idea of an independent agency, the International Red Cross, as a credible source of information to which the parties had an obligation to report, was ensconced in the accords on the Wounded and Sick in Armies in the Field (1929).[18] State and individual responsibilities under these conventions were further spelled out in the First Protocol (1949), which created an independent fact-finding commission to further secure belligerent states' – and their armies' – accountability.[19]

Peer accountability has also intensified in the economic realm. It was not until the founding of the Bretton Woods institutions that governments became legally accountable to their peers for their exchange rates.[20] While legal accountability for currency stability dissolved with the breakdown of the entire system in the 1970s, governments are still legally accountable to one another to maintain

16 The Nuclear Non-Proliferation Treaty provides for verifiable safeguards to ensure compliance with the appropriate use of fissionable materials (Article III). http://disarmament.un.org/wmd/npt/npttext.html. The postwar Chemical Weapons regime "provides for the most comprehensive and intrusive system of verification to date of any disarmament treaty applied globally (or in any other global treaty for that matter)" (Scott and Dorn 1998:88). The treaty requires detailed disclosure and on-site inspections by international civil servants (Article IV). http://www.defenselink.mil/acq/acic/treaties/cwc/cwc.htm. See also Goldblat 1982; Kessler 1995.

17 The 1906 Geneva Convention "enhanc[ed] compliance by further provisions for exchange of information on the sick and wounded. . . . A duty was imposed on the commanders-in-chief of belligerent armies now to provide the details of implementing the provisions of the convention. . . . In the same vein a requirement to make the provisions of the convention broadly known among not only the groups most directly affected but also the general population enhanced both knowledge and acceptance of the convention obligations" (Carter 1998:8).

18 The 1929 Geneva Convention for the Amelioration of the Condition of the Wounded and Sick in Armies in the Field. See especially Articles 77–88.

19 Geneva Conventions, Protocol I, Article 90. See Carter 1998. Article 91 provides that a party to a conflict that violates OP I's provision would in certain cases be liable to pay compensation for such violations and reiterates state responsibility for all acts committed by persons forming part of its armed forces. For a discussion of the "humanizing" of the laws of war since World War II, see Meron 2000.

20 As the Permanent Court of International Arbitration noted in 1929, the international community had quite clearly "accepted [the] principle that a State is entitled to regulate its own currency." Case of Serbian Loans, 1929, Permanent Court of International Justice, series A., nos. 20/21, p. 44. Cited by Gold 1984b:1533. The IMF statutes explicitly recognized for the first time that exchange rates were properly a matter of international concern. See IMF Articles of Agreement, Article IV, sect. 4. Furthermore, Article IV, sect. 2, provided that "no member shall buy gold at a price above par value plus the prescribed margin, or sell gold at a price below par value minus the prescribed margin." A central bank could not enter into any gold transaction with another central bank other than at par without one or the other violating the articles. On the public international law of money generally, see Schuster 1973.

convertible currencies[21] and are subject to regular on-site surveillance by staff members of the International Monetary Fund (IMF) to encourage members to follow "responsible" economic policies.[22] Accountability in the form of formal policy review has also intensified in the trade area, with regular (though voluntary) "trade policy reviews" under the auspices of the World Trade Organization (WTO).[23] These trends are consonant with the general direction of accountability that has developed over the past few decades.

Finally, states are increasingly accountable to their peers for the way they resolve disputes. Paul Jessup noted in his public lectures that up to the time of the Hague Conferences held at the turn of the twentieth century, even to tender an offer of mediation or good offices in a dispute among sovereigns was considered officious meddling.[24] That view was to change drastically over the course of the twentieth century. Figure 2.3 illustrates the phenomenal growth in international judicial and quasi-judicial institutions that have been created over the course of the past 100 years.[25] Some of these institutions involve individuals as defendants or complainants, but many resolve disputes between state parties, including the International Court of Justice and the Permanent Court of International Arbitration, the WTO's Dispute Settlement Mechanism, and the International Maritime Court, which handles disputes arising from the Law of the Seas Treaties.[26] While participation in these arrangements is typically voluntary, and while governments strive to maintain mechanisms of control over these adjudicative institutions,[27] Figure 2.3 illustrates the institutional instantiation of a growing norm of peer accountability.[28]

---

21 See Simmons 2000. IMF Articles of Agreement, Article VIII, sect. 2, para. (a), and sect. 3.

22 Gold 1983:474–5; James 1995:773, 775. Consultations with Article VIII countries were established in 1960 but were completely voluntary. De Vries and Horsefield 1969:246–7.

23 Marrakesh Agreement, April 1994, Article III (entry into force, 1995). According to the Marrakesh Agreement, "the function of the review mechanism is to examine the impact of a Member's trade policies and practices on the multilateral trading system." Annex III A(ii). http://www.wto.org/english/tratop_e/tpr_e/annex3_e.htm. On the Trade Policy Review Mechanism, see Abbott 1993; Blackhurst 1988; Curzon Price 1991; Forsythe 1989; Mathews 1997; Mavroidis 1992; Norris 2001; Qureshi 1990.

24 Jessup 1959.

25 Ad hoc arbitration procedures were used extensively toward the end of the nineteenth century (Mangone 1954:esp. 117), but these transient bodies can be contrasted with the permanent or semipermanent nature of the institutions discussed in this section. See also Gray and Kingsbury 1992; Grieves 1969; Nussbaum 1954:222–3. On the issue of compliance with these early institutions, see Nantwi 1966.

26 A series of studies have also documented the increased usage of the International Court of Justice. See, for example, Peck 1996; Rosenne 1989. Nonetheless, there is a clear tendency for "defendants" to contest the court's jurisdiction; see Fischer 1982. On the Dispute Settlement Mechanism of the WTO see Hudec 1999; Vermulst and Driessen 1995; on the International Maritime Court, see Charney 1996.

27 Reisman 1992.

28 Keohane et al. 2000; Romano 1999. Note that the proliferation of quasi-adjudicative institutions is not always an unalloyed positive development. For an argument that multiple institutions in the human rights area has led to forum shopping, which in turn has led to a certain degree of legal incoherence, see Helfer 1999.

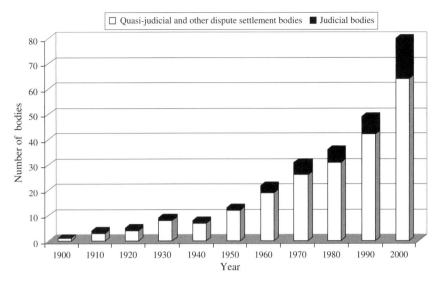

Figure 2.3. Growth in International Judicial, Quasi-judicial, and Dispute Settlement Bodies. *Source*: The Project on International Courts and Tribunals: The International Judiciary in Context, at http://www.pict-pcti.org/publications/synoptic_chart/Synop_C4.pdf (November 2004; accessed 11 August 2008).

In short, increasingly robust forms of state-to-state accountability were adopted over the course of the twentieth century. More treaties in a broader range of areas require consultations, reporting, verification, monitoring, and surveillance. Despite the obvious roots of these developments in the nineteenth century,[29] formal peer accountability structures in the contemporary period express the widely held view that sovereign governments are, and of right should be, consistently accountable to one another. The innovation of mid-century was not that governments should be held accountable for their legal commitments to one another. Rather, it was the idea that human rights – rights of domestic citizens – could be brought under this broader accountability trend in public international law.

International Civil Society

No discussion of the evolving context for international human rights law would be complete without mention of the growing role of international civil society. The details of the role of transnationally organized private actors in the

29 For an account of the history of international law and institutions that stresses continuity across the centuries, see Mangone 1954.

legalization and implementation of the human rights regime will be discussed in more detail later; here I stress the capacity of organized nonstate actors to influence policies more generally. There have, of course, always been groups of private citizens who have organized, often across national boundaries, to advocate public purposes of various kinds. But what has made these groups so central in the international public policy arena of the late twentieth and early twenty-first centuries is the drastic reduction in the start-up, organizational, and transactions costs they face to make their positions heard. This, in combination with states' (somewhat grudging) willingness to allow formal and informal access to official international decision-making venues has made NGOs far more influential than they have been in the past.

There is nothing new about civil society groups' efforts to influence issues of transnational or international public interest. Many have been recognized with the day's highest honors for their accomplishments. Antislavery and religious groups were active – and reasonably influential – in the nineteenth century, as Margaret Keck's and Kathryn Sikkink's research has emphasized.[30] Although much smaller in number than the welter of such groups today, transnational nongovernmental groups have long been active in the peace movement, in disarmament, and in issues related to human rights. As evidence of their perceived effectiveness, a number of NGOs were early winners of Nobel Peace Prizes, including the Institute of International Law (1904), the Permanent International Peace Bureau (1910), and the International Committee of the Red Cross (1917, 1944, and 1963).[31]

The influence of NGOs on a broad range of policy issues has increased significantly as start-up and operational costs for such groups have drastically fallen. The end of the Cold War also spurred the growth of civil society organizations in countries once dominated by communist parties.[32] As a result, there has been a rapid increase in the number and range of NGOs worldwide and a corresponding growth in opportunities for advocacy and policy influence.[33] Figure 2.4 provides a sense of how rapidly traditional NGOs have sprouted over the past five decades.

The explosion in the organizational capacity of transnational civil society can be traced directly to technological changes that have reduced drastically their costs of organization and operation. It now costs a fraction of what it once did for these groups to communicate and to disseminate information. In 1927,

---

30 Keck and Sikkink 1998.
31 Other NGOs that have more recently won a Nobel Prize for Peace include Friends Service Council and American Friends Service Committee (Quakers, 1947); Amnesty International (1977); International Physicians for the Prevention of Nuclear War (1985); Pugwash Conferences on Science and World Affairs (1995); International Campaign to Ban Landmines (1997); and Médecins sans Frontières (1999). For a complete list of recipients, see http://nobelprize.org/nobel_prizes/peace/laureates/ (accessed 28 November 2006).
32 For a discussion of the emergence of international civil society after the Cold War, see Otto 1996.
33 Boli and Thomas 1999; Otto 1996; Skjelsbaek 1971.

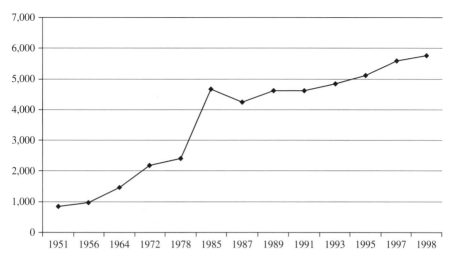

Figure 2.4. Total Conventional NGOs. *Source*: Union of International Associations, http://www.uia.org/statistics/organizations/ytb299.php. *Note*: Includes nonprofit NGOs (excludes multinational enterprises). All included bodies have members in at least three countries. Types of organizations include federations or "umbrella" organizations, universal membership organizations (involving members from at least 60 countries), and intercontinental and regional organizations (those whose members and purposes focus on a particular continent or subcontinental region). For a detailed description of included NGOs, see http://www.uia.org/uiadocs/orgtyped.htm#typet.

only about 2,000 transatlantic phone calls were placed, at a cost of around $16 for three minutes. From the United States, it is now possible to phone much of the rest of the world for 2 cents per minute.[34] The goals of traditional advocacy NGOs have been furthered significantly by the growth of, and growing access to, the Internet (Figure 2.5). It is hard to think of a communication medium that has done more to loosen governments' centralized control over information at such a low cost to small users than e-mail and the World Wide Web.[35] True, Internet access is quite uneven within and across regions[36] and is limited where

34 For rates associated with the first transatlantic cable, see http://en.wikipedia.org/wiki/ Transatlantic_telephone_cable. For current rates, see, for example, http://www.pennytalk.com/ (accessed 7 December 2006).
35 While observers generally acknowledge the greater difficulty governments have in controlling the Internet than they do other forms of media, the Internet has not proved impossible to control. See Sussman 2000.
36 In the Americas, for example, the United States at one extreme had 200 hosts per 1,000 persons in 2000 and the Dominican Republic had .003 host per 1,000. In Africa, as of 2000, South Africa had more Internet hosts than all of Africa combined, though other areas are gaining rapidly. Senegal's number of Internet hosts jumped more than 200% in a six-month period in the late 1990s, for example (Quarterman 1999).

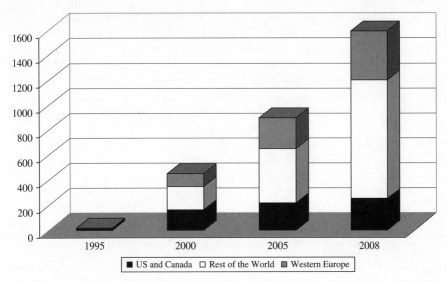

Figure 2.5. Number of Internet Users (Millions). *Source*: Nua, http://www.nua.ie/surveys/how_many_online/.

governments tend generally to suppress free communication (North Korea, Afghanistan, Iraq, Guyana, St. Helena, and Guinea-Bissau, to name a few).[37] Nonetheless, the net effect has been fundamentally to alter the ability of governments to maintain a monopoly on information. Most observers agree that relative to states, NGOs have been empowered disproportionately by cheap and decentralized information technology. This has a tremendous impact on the ability of NGOs to do practically everything mentioned in the preceding paragraph, from mobilizing coalitions to publicizing governmental policies and practices to participating in the enforcement of existing law.[38]

As a result of their greater ability to organize and communicate at drastically lower costs than was possible previously, NGOs have developed the capacity to hold governments accountable for their decisions.[39] Many NGOs have the potential to set behavioral or policy standards, to produce independent information, and to lobby governments to justify, clarify, and/or change their policies.[40] Some provide policy input in various governmental and intergovernmental organizations.[41]

---

37 http://www.matrix.net/publications/mn/mn1012_hosts.html (accessed 10 October 2002).
38 Mathews 1997; Norris 2001; Perritt 1998.
39 The NGO literature in the human rights area is vast and cannot possibly be reviewed here. On the importance of NGOs in this area, see Chinkin 2000; Clark 2001; Forsythe 1985; Korey 1998; Wiesberg and Scoble 1981. Regional studies are also plentiful. On the influence of NGOs in Latin America, see Burgerman 1998; Sikkink 1993; USIP 2001. On the influence of NGOs in Africa, see Welch 1995.
40 Forsythe 1989; Shepard 1981; Smith et al. 1998.
41 Charnovitz 1997; Otto 1996; van Boven 1989–90.

In 1968, NGOs were first permitted to participate in United Nations (UN) proceedings;[42] by the 1990s, their presence in that organization had become pervasive.[43] NGOs help hold governments accountable to existing laws by participating in and sometimes initiating litigation.[44] More broadly, they educate the public to demand greater accountability as well.[45] The new and decisive fact of the waning years of the past millennium was the presence of NGOs almost everywhere – in the halls of the UN, at major conferences, in capitals around the world, and in the headlines.[46]

The end result is that international politics have become more populist in nature,[47] if not more democratic.[48] Of course, there are valid arguments that these groups do not necessarily improve the quality of representation for most of the world's population. Many of these groups themselves are not clearly accountable to any constituency, or only to a fairly narrow one. But even if they do not represent a democratic improvement on state-centric representation, they have quite likely contributed to official accountability. By publicizing their version of public affairs and challenging governments to refute their information or to justify – or alter – official practices, these groups have challenged the official quasi-monopoly on information that many states enjoyed in earlier times. The growing role of NGOs certainly serves to break the state monopoly on information, standard-setting, and norm creation, even if it does not usher in a new era of democratic international politics.

The twentieth century saw at least three important contextual developments that were largely underway before any sustained effort to develop an international legal regime for human rights. The "Rights of Man" had begun to make its way into a growing number of states institutionalizing democratic forms of government. In their official relationships with one another, states were increasingly willing to acknowledge the rights of other states – or their agents – to monitor, verify, and practice surveillance, a trend that began prior to World War II but accelerated thereafter. Nongovernmental actors had long taken up various international causes, from slavery to peace to disarmament, but the

---

42 Resolution 1296 (XLIV) of the ECOSOC (23 May 1968). Prior to the adoption of the UN Charter, in only one international institution (the ILO) did NGOs have formal legitimacy and power (Korey 1998:52).

43 Christine Chinkin writes that, through the accommodation of NGO demands for inclusion in the international forum "the concept of civil society has infiltrated the formal structures of the international legal system" (2000:135). However, some scholars have noted how uncertain and irregular NGO involvement is in UN human rights activities; see Posner 1994.

44 Shelton 1994.

45 Ron et al. 2005; Tolley 1989; Wapner 1995.

46 For a discussion of NGO participation in major conferences, see Azzam 1993; Friedman et al. 2005; on NGO presence in capitals around the world, see van Boven 1989–90.

47 Johnston 1997. For a general discussion of nonofficial challenges to state authority, see Mathews 1997; Schachter 1997.

48 For an argument that these processes help to democratize the process of international standard setting, see van Boven 1989–90.

pervasiveness of these actors has undeniably intensified. Yet, none of these developments alone can adequately explain why the issue of human rights assumed central importance at mid-century or why governments agreed for the first time to fashion international legal agreements to bind their domestic policies and practices. In order to understand the international legalization of human rights, we need to understand the broader pattern of international conflict and domestic oppression in the twentieth century.

THE INFLUENCE OF WARTIME ON HUMAN RIGHTS

The most striking fact about the international law of human rights is its nearly complete absence prior to the end of World War II. To give the sense of a revolution in legal thinking in the rights area, Michael Ignatieff has noted, "In 1905, a leading textbook in international law concluded that the so-called 'Rights of Man' enjoyed no legal protection under international law, because it was concerned exclusively with the relations between states."[49] In fact, some have noted that international law served largely to denigrate human rights because it was often complicit in supporting imperialism, which in turn rested on wide-ranging forms of exploitation. At the same time, imperial law demanded institutional changes supportive of European freedoms – freedom of movement, religion, property, commerce, and dignity.[50] Nineteenth-century British legal scholars were apt to hold that "International law has to treat natives [of Africa, for example] as uncivilized. It regulates for the mutual benefit of the civilized states the claims which they make to sovereignty over the region and leaves the treatment of the natives to the conscience of the state to which sovereignty is awarded."[51] Martti Koskenniemi has written of the period that treatment of natives within European empires had, practically speaking, no implications in international law.[52] True, there were a number of international agreements in the nineteenth century with a "humanitarian" character,[53] but when it came to the rights of local subjects, respect for sovereignty typically provided a convenient pretext to remain aloof. Henry Morgenthau's quotation at the beginning of this chapter captures the tragic indifference international law displayed toward human rights early in the twentieth century.

The Great War provided the context to revisit the human rights issue – especially as it applied to the self-determination of peoples in the wake of the breakup of the Austro-Hungarian Empire and the last gasps of the Ottoman

---

49 Ignatieff 1999:313. The book he was referring to is A. H. Robertson and J. G. Merrils (1905), *Human Rights in the World*, 4th ed., Manchester: Manchester University Press, 1–23.
50 Anghie 2005:86.
51 Westlake 1896:143. Quoted by Koskenniemi 2002:127.
52 Koskenniemi 2002:128. Koskenniemi writes that the appeal to a broad civilizing mission as justificatory rhetoric for the imposition of European sovereignty was "the shadow of a disturbed conscience" (148).
53 Nussbaum 1954:198.

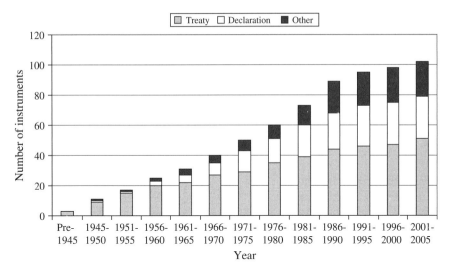

Figure 2.6. International Human Rights Instruments in Force. *Source*: UN, Office of the High Commissioner for Human Rights, http://www.unhchr.ch/html/intlinst.htm. "Other" includes a wide range of nonbinding instruments, such as proclamations, understandings, principles, safeguards, guidelines, recommendations, and codes of conduct.

Empire. Upon his arrival in France in 1918, American President Woodrow Wilson was seen as the harbinger of a new era,[54] his "Fourteen Points" ushering in "the principle of justice for all peoples and nationalities, and their right to live on equal terms of liberty and safety with one another. . . ."[55] Such lofty goals, however, were undermined by more traditional great power concerns, and while a few plebiscites were held to honor this vision of self-determination, the decisions on the boundaries of new states were for the most part made by the victorious powers.[56] Moreover, while the language appealed to a universal vision,[57] the major European powers favored only the independence of

---

54 See Manela 2006.
55 Woodrow Wilson, "The Fourteen Points Address," as quoted in Ishay 1997:303–4. Wilson's speech can also be found online at http://www.lib.byu.edu/~rdh/wwi/1918/14points.html (accessed 17 November 2006).
56 After World War I, plebiscites were held under international auspices, as provided by the peace treaties or by the Venice Protocol as follows: Schleswig, 10 February and 14 March 1920; Allenstein and Marienwerder, 11 July 1920; Klagenfurt Basin, 10 October 1920; Upper Silesia, 20 March 1921; Sopron, 14–16 December 1921. See the discussion in Beigbeder 1994:80–8.
57 Recent historical studies of the "Wilsonian Moment" examine how "the call for self-determination fired the imaginations of countless nationalists in the colonial world." Steigerwald 1999:98. See also Manela 2001. The Atlantic Conference had a similar effect during World War II.

nationalities in the Balkans and ignored independence claims from their colonies. Nor did the newly created League of Nations promote these claims, although it did oversee a system of mandates administered by the victorious European powers that was designed to move certain territories toward self-government. Racial and religious impartiality were written into the League Covenant,[58] but the mandate system was based on the assumption of "tutelage" rather than rights as such. The Polish Minority Treaty of 1919 and the Treaty of Riga, which brought a formal end to the Polish–Bolshevik war in 1921, contained provisions to protect Jewish, Ukrainian, Belarussian, and Lithuanian groups upon Polish independence.[59] These agreements had little effect as ethnic tensions intensified with the Great Depression and the rise of fascism.

The experience of the Great War touched other areas related to human rights as well. The war had empowered workers to a much greater extent than in the past. The International Labor Organization (ILO) was founded in 1919 to enforce better labor standards. It also called for a maximum working day and week, an adequate living wage, and the protection of various classes of workers against a range of risks and forms of employer abuse.[60] The war had orphaned thousands of children across Europe and beyond, concern for whom gave rise to new NGOs to defend children's rights. A terse Declaration of the Rights of the Child[61] was drafted by Eglantyne Jebb (founder of Save the Children Fund) in 1923 and adopted by the League of Nations in 1924. The war experience also provided an impetus to try to inject humanitarian considerations into the laws of war themselves. In Geneva in 1929, the major powers concluded an important agreement relating to the treatment of prisoners of war, which, among other provisions, was meant to protect such prisoners from being forced to provide information to captors and to guarantee them adequate food, shelter, and medical attention.[62] For the first time, warring states accepted neutral inspection of prison camps and the exchange of prisoners' names and agreed to correspondence with prisoners. Significantly, however, neither Japan nor the Soviet Union was to become a party. Nonetheless, these agreements represented "considerable progress" toward improving the rights of soldiers in wartime.[63]

Despite this progress, these efforts were far from a comprehensive approach to human rights. Treaties were concluded ad hoc, based on the salience of particular issues, but without serious institutional supports. Their geographical

---

58 Article 22 of the League Covenant says in part: "the Mandatory must be responsible for the administration of the territory under conditions which will guarantee freedom of conscience and religion, subject only to the maintenance of public order and morals. . . ." See http://www.yale.edu/lawweb/avalon/leagcov.htm#art22 (accessed 17 November 2006).

59 Some 15 or 16 treaties were concluded after the First World War on the issue of minorities. See, for example, the discussion in Burgers 1992:449–50; Claude 1955.

60 See relevant passages on the ILO in Endres and Fleming 2002.

61 The text can be found at http://www1.umn.edu/humanrts/instree/childrights.html.

62 The text can be found at http://www.yale.edu/lawweb/avalon/lawofwar/geneva02.htm.

63 Nussbaum 1954:267.

reach was limited, and important powers often opted out. Some were nonbinding. On the whole, these efforts paled in comparison to the challenges presented by the Great Depression, which intensified ethnic conflicts in many countries. Despite ardent liberal hopes to the contrary,[64] these accords were also trampled under the boots of the growing fascist movements in Europe and Japan. As Martha Minow summarizes this period, "Struggles to create new institutions to promote and secure respect for human rights, however impressive compared with their predecessors, produced more an idea than a practiced reality."[65] It is only a slight exaggeration to say that prior to the end of the Second World War, the state, with respect to the treatment of its own people, was a "moral black box."[66]

The turning point for the development of the rights regime was World War II. The turn came before the full revelations of Nazi atrocities; it began with the articulation of war aims themselves. The Allied powers – and especially the United States, which remained until December 1941 formally out of the war – needed a clear articulation of war aims behind which their publics could unite. For the United States, that statement was initially articulated by President Franklin D. Roosevelt in January 1941 in his famous "Four Freedoms" speech to Congress. By sketching a blueprint for a new world order founded on freedom of speech, freedom of religion, freedom from fear, and freedom from want, Roosevelt hoped to galvanize American support for the war effort but he also raised hopes about the nature of the new world order. In a ship anchored off the coast of North America, Roosevelt and Winston Churchill reiterated these values in the form of the Atlantic Charter. Whether these were genuine visions of the future of human rights or a way to get material support for the Allied cause,[67] these pronouncements had a singular impact on the hopes of oppressed peoples the world over. Not least was the effect among those within the United States itself. As Caroline Anderson has written, "For African Americans . . . the Atlantic Charter was revolutionary. It was something, as NAACP Board member Channing Tobias declared, that black people would be willing to 'live, work, fight and, if need be, die for.' "[68]

Exactly how these principles would be ensconced in the postwar multilateral architecture was a central issue in discussions framing the charter of the new UN. Despite the hopes they raised in 1941, neither the United States nor Great

---

64 See a maudlin contemporary plea for international law development in the early postwar years in Nippold and Hershey 1923.
65 Minow 2002:61.
66 Wenar 2005:286.
67 Universalizing human rights is interpreted as part of the U.S. hegemonic strategy for winning the war and assuming a central place in the new world order by Evans (2001:18–19). See also Loth 1988. For a brief historical treatment of the struggle between liberal ideals and realpolitik as it pertains to the Atlantic Charter – in particular, the shifting positions of Roosevelt and Churchill – see Olson and Cloud 2003.
68 Anderson 2003:17.

Britain was especially keen to give the new global institution much power to take action to protect human rights. In the United States, support for a formal role of the UN in enforcing rights ran up against the power of the southern Democrats in the Senate. Congressional leaders in the South were confronting a civil rights movement that had gathered steam during the war;[69] the last thing they wanted was a new international institution that would have the authority to meddle in the South's unique form of racial "justice."[70] Nor were the British especially enthusiastic to give the UN an expansive human rights mandate, given the restive state of some parts of their empire.

The problem was that the door to universal rights as an ordering principle of the postwar peace had been opened more than a crack by grandiose references to "Four Freedoms" and reinforced in the Atlantic Charter and elsewhere.[71] The full extent of the Holocaust was just in the process of becoming fully revealed to a world reeling from unspeakable atrocity on a massive scale.[72] Despite the clear absorption with realpolitik at the highest levels of the U.S. and British governments, grassroots movements demanding attention to human rights were cropping up around the world, not least within the United States itself.[73] Not to include *some* reference to human rights in the charter of the new global institution would have been almost impossible. At their meeting at Dumbarton Oaks in 1944 to discuss the outlines of the postwar peace, the United States, the United Kingdom, the Soviet Union, and China drafted a plan for a Security Council they would dominate, but the plan was harshly criticized by smaller powers for hardly addressing human rights.[74] These views were also expressed at the San Francisco conference in April 1945, to which prospective member states and NGOs were invited. One of the concerns of several Latin American countries – Chile, Cuba, and Panama in particular – was that the organization should more squarely address human rights. The initial great power proposal was condemned by anticolonial leaders, from Mahatma Ghandi to Carlos Romulo to Ho Chi Minh to Kwame Nkrumah, for disregarding the rights of

69 See Berman 1970:41.
70 According to Anderson (2003:44), "The Southern Democrats ruled the Senate. That was the bottom line. Circumventing the Constitution already required their eternal vigilance; the last thing they wanted was a UN Charter that provided yet another legal instrument that the NAACP and African Americans could use to break Jim Crow."
71 Borgwardt 2005.
72 While the horrors were being revealed to the world at large, there is considerable historical evidence that by 1942 – and earlier, by some accounts – the leading Allied figures had a fairly detailed knowledge of the plight of the Jews and still were late to act. Polish courier Jan Karski was smuggled into a death camp near Izbica, Estonia, and was able to provide a firsthand report to, among others, Anthony Eden and President Roosevelt. See Olson and Cloud 2003:208; Wood and Jankowski 1994. Slightly less well known, Roosevelt's response to the Katyn massacre – in which thousands of Polish officers were executed by Red Army personnel – was one of annoyance rather than concern over the violation of human rights. The "graves question," thought Roosevelt, "wasn't worth such a fuss . . ." (Olson and Cloud 2003:269–70).
73 Lauren 1998.
74 Waltz 2001.

indigenous peoples living under colonialism. Presentations were made by Frederick Nolde of the Council of Churches and Judge Joseph Proskauer, president of the American Jewish Committee. The World Trade Union Conference, the Provisional World Council of Dominated Nations, the West Indies National Council, the Sino-Korean People's League, and the Council of Christians added their voices calling for revisions to strengthen the UN's rights mandate.[75]

The major powers relented, eventually backing the NGOs' proposals. The charter's preamble would contain the statement that "We the people of the United Nations . . . affirm faith in fundamental human rights. . . ."[76] But in so conceding, the United States was careful to ensure that the UN itself would not have the authority to actually intervene in the domestic rights sphere in any important way. John Foster Dulles, wary of the constraints posed by the U.S. Senate, inserted an amendment into the charter that "nothing in the charter shall authorize . . . intervention in matters which are essentially within the domestic jurisdiction of the State concerned." This move drew opposition from a number of delegations, including those of Chile, Belgium, and Australia. Nonetheless, it was "abundantly clear that the domestic jurisdiction clause was America's price for allowing human rights to seep into the UN Charter."[77]

There was no denying the reality, however, that human rights *had* seeped into the consciousness of governments and individuals around the world as one of the most pressing issues of the new international order. Nazi atrocities – the extent of which were revealed fully only toward the war's end – provided the galvanizing outrage that motivated the drafting of the world's first formal commitment to universal human rights. The UDHR,[78] negotiated as practically the first piece of business of the new UN, has been interpreted as a nearly line-by-line response to the horrors the Nazi Third Reich had perpetrated. Johannes Morsink's documentary account of the negotiations over each provision of the declaration leaves little doubt that the negotiating delegations were motivated to declare rights that had been systematically violated by Adolf Hitler, his followers, and those of his ilk. "This shared outrage explains why the Declaration has found such widespread support."[79] The postwar consensus eventually gave rise to unanimous support for the declaration, with seven abstentions, including those of the Soviet Union, Saudi Arabia, and South Africa.[80]

---

75 Ishay 2004:214. William Korey (1998:29) argues that inclusion of human rights in the charter would not have been possible without the relentless pressures from these and other NGOs.

76 Preamble to the UN Charter; http://www.un.org/aboutun/charter/.

77 Anderson 2003:50.

78 Universal Declaration of Human Rights, adopted 10 December 1948, G.A. Res. 127A(III), UN GAOR 3d Session (Resolutions, Part 1), at 71, U.N. Document A/810 (1948). The UDHR, as well as the six core treaties discussed here, can be accessed in full at http://www.un.org/Overview/rights.html. For a history of the diplomatic discussions leading to the UDHR, see Glendon 2001; Korey 1998; Morsink 1999; Waltz 2001; Weissbrodt and Hallendorff 1999 (specifically on fair trials provisions).

79 See Morsink 1999:91. On this point, see especially ch. 2 (pp. 36–91).

80 Abstainers also included Ukraine, Belarus, Yugoslavia, and Poland.

TOWARD LEGALIZATION: PROGRESS AND HESITATION

The UDHR has been widely noted as a crucial milestone in the creation of the international rights legal regime. The declaration was a consolidation of liberal rights propounded in the seventeenth and eighteenth centuries, as well as (thanks largely to the contributions of Chile's Hernán Santa Cruz and other Latin Americans)[81] many of the social and economic rights that had gained adherents during the Industrial Revolution and more recently during the Great Depression. These rights were acknowledged as universal, in sharp contrast to those extended under imperialism. Its inclusiveness and breadth have made this document, according to Mary Anne Glendon, "part of a new 'moment' in the history of human rights."[82] For writers such as Norberto Bobbio, the unique value of the declaration was the consensus it represented; he terms it "the greatest historical test of the 'consensus omnium gentium' in relation to a given value system."[83] Asbjorn Eide represents a broadly held view that lauds the UDHR as having inspired "an unprecedented evolution of international standard-setting both at the global and the regional level."[84] Certainly, representatives of the world's states had never explicitly acknowledged such a broad range of rights in a multilateral setting at any other time in history. Eleanor Roosevelt, the U.S. representative to the UN Commission on Human Rights (UNCHR), herself triumphantly compared the UDHR to the Magna Carta, the French Declaration of the Rights of Man, and the American Bill of Rights in her speech before the General Assembly upon its passage.[85]

Putting on the Brakes: The United States and the Politics of Opposition to Legalization

This important milestone had one characteristic that was, ironically, essential to its acceptance: It was not legally binding. Even in the aftermath of as shocking an historical epic as World War II, the world's initial commitment to international human rights was in the form of a nonbinding declaration, not a legally binding treaty.[86] The United States, for one, would not have been comfortable with the document otherwise. For one thing, opposition formed against the panoply of economic rights that drafters of the declaration such as the Canadian John Humphrey, a social democrat (supported by much of Latin America), had

---

81 Glendon 2003:35.
82 Glendon 1998:1164.
83 Bobbio 1996:14.
84 Eide 1998:abstract.
85 Roosevelt 1947:867.
86 The weakness of the declaration – its lack of enforcement and institutionalization; the degree to which states had unanimously agreed on its nonbinding nature – signaled the triumph of mere symbolism over effective action, according to Hersch Lauterpacht, one of the major international legal scholars of the day. See the discussion of Lauterpacht 1950:397–421 in Koskenniemi 2002:395.

included. The United States, along with France, had opposed most of this language, but much remained prominently featured in the final document.[87] Even the commitment to civil and political rights provoked concerns among restive southerners in Congress about UN meddling in local affairs. In the end, the United States voted in favor of the UDHR, but precisely because it was "only" a statement of principle. Carol Anderson captures American sentiment well: "As John Foster Dulles later explained to a very wary and hostile [American Bar Association] the Declaration of Human Rights, for all that it was, was not a legal document. Rather it was more like America's 'Sermon on the Mount' in the 'great ideological struggle' between the United States and the Soviet Union."[88]

The gathering Cold War in fact had an important effect on the development of the human rights regime. Competition with the Soviet Union had a great deal to do with U.S. policy – both domestic and international – in the realm of rights. Domestically, the heating up of the Cold War gave urgency to civil rights reform in the United States, while internationally, it made the United States ever more wary of international authority to enforce rights. One early episode was especially telling in this regard. In October 1947, soon after the founding of the UN Commission on Human Rights, the Soviet Union supported a proposal to consider a petition by the National Association for the Advancement of Colored People (NAACP), drafted by the historian W. E. B. Du Bois, calling attention to the long history of cultural deprivation suffered by the African American.[89] The commission rejected the proposal that December, but from that incident many in the United States drew the lesson that the commission should be made as toothless as possible.[90] According to William Berman's compelling account, the embarrassment caused by the constant reminders during the human rights debates of the late 1940s and 1950s of "imperfections" in American democracy helped to build a fire under the Truman administration to confront racial injustice to a limited extent at home.[91] Much evidence suggests that the Truman administration was acutely conscious of the difficulty the

---

87 Irr 2003; Morsink 1999.
88 Anderson 2003:131. U.S. courts have consistently upheld the nonbinding nature of the declaration. See Connor (2001) on the unwillingness of the United States to accept international legal obligations (as opposed to declarations); see also Evans 1996.
89 "A Statement on the Denial of Human Rights to Minorities in the Case of Citizens of Negro Descent in the United States of America and an Appeal to the United Nations for Redress, Prepared for the NAACP," drafted by W. E. B. Du Bois, with the assistance of Milton Konvitz, Earl Dickerson, and Rayford Logan (Box 354 NAACP Papers, Library of Congress); cited by Berman 1970:66.
90 Eleanor Roosevelt, as the U.S. representative on the commission, also opposed a complaint submitted to the UNHRC charging South Africa with human rights violations associated with apartheid, concerned that "it would set a dangerous precedent that could ultimately lead to the United Nations investigating the conditions of 'negroes in Alabama'" (Anderson 2003:3).
91 This is the main theme of Berman's (1970) book; see also Dudziak 2000; Krenn 1998. Anderson (2003) cautions that the Cold War should also be understood to have undermined the ability of African Americans to claim social and economic rights, as these were characterized as inspired by and sympathetic toward Communism.

United States would have in credibly leading the "free world" when much of its own population was denied basic political rights and legal protections.

Just one day before the vote ratifying the UDHR, the UN General Assembly (UNGA) had adopted – also unanimously – its first legally binding multilateral treaty text, the UN Convention on the Prevention and Punishment of the Crime of Genocide. Adopted after relentless lobbying pressure from private groups and individuals such as Raphael Lemkin, a Polish émigré turned Duke University law professor,[92] no treaty could be a clearer response to the treatment of the Jews, Slavs, and other ethnic groups at the hands of the Nazis. The convention came on the heels of the Nuremberg trials (1945–46) and the Tokyo trial (1946), in which former Nazi and Japanese leaders were indicted and tried as war criminals, thus vindicating the persecuted and setting the precedent that national leaders were not immune from responsibility for such atrocities.[93] The Genocide Convention reinforced these rulings, making individuals – heads of state included – punishable for such crimes.[94]

The debates over the Genocide Convention revealed for the first time the difficulty that some states might have in ratifying a legally binding international human rights treaty. In the United States, the debate over ratification led to one of the most acrimonious discussions surrounding postwar foreign policy of the period. The Genocide Convention was opposed by conservative southerners in the Senate, who were concerned that its provisions might be used to hold individuals accountable in American or international courts for lynching and other forms of racial "justice."[95] Opponents of the convention raised the specter of federal power overcoming the rights of the American states in areas dealing with rights. The American Bar Association, and especially its Peace through Law Committee, led the charge in articulating these concerns: "If there is to be a succession of treaties from the United Nations dealing with domestic questions, are we ready to surrender the power of the States over such matters to the Federal Government?"[96] This group was largely responsible for making the arguments that converted a convention outlawing a heinous crime into "a subversive document undermining cherished constitutional rights. . . ."[97] The fight

---

92 Power 2002:51–76.
93 The effort to hold individuals accountable for war crimes has a longer history than this, including some roots in the fifteenth century. See, for example, Neier 1998. For a detailed discussion of the evolution of individual responsibility in international criminal law, see Ratner and Abrams 2001:ch. 1.
94 The convention provides (Article IV) that "Persons committing genocide or any of the other acts enumerated in Article III shall be punished, whether they are constitutionally responsible rulers, public officials or private individuals." The Genocide Convention entered into force in 1951. The text can be found at http://www.unhchr.ch/html/menu3/b/p_genoci.htm (accessed 21 November 2006).
95 See the discussion in Tananbaum 1988.
96 Carl Rix, American Bar Association Committee Through Law, quoted in Kaufman 1990:41. For a flavor of the constitutional arguments made at the time, see MacBride 1955.
97 Kaufman 1990:62.

in the Senate over the ratification of the Genocide Convention inspired John William Bricker of Ohio to offer an amendment to the U.S. Constitution that would have severely limited the ability of the federal government to enter into international treaties. It failed by only one vote. But the episode was important for the development of the international legal regime for human rights, which would have to be constructed largely without the leadership of the most power-ful democracy in the world.[98]

Meanwhile, the UN Human Rights Commission began to draft the first legal instantiation of the UDHR: a covenant to secure states' assent to the declaration's contents in legally binding form. The debate over the declaration proved prescient of the differences that were to develop over the contents of the first comprehensive human rights treaty. An early divide, aggravated by Cold War politics, opened up over civil and political versus economic rights, with the United States and some of its allies championing the former and the Soviet Union and much of the developing world the latter. The United States was an early advocate of separating the civil and political rights from the economic social and cultural rights in two distinct treaties.[99] Economic rights were "socialism by treaty," as far as Dwight Eisenhower was concerned.[100] On the other hand, the United States could enthusiastically endorse civil rights, such as free speech and expression and property rights, both of which dovetailed nicely with its opposition to the Soviet Union, and made these the centerpieces of its international rights campaign.

Yet, the bitter debate over the Bricker Amendment kept the Eisenhower administration from supporting even a free-standing ICCPR. The legacy of that debate, conjuring as it did threats to the U.S. Constitution and the intrusion of the UN into a cherished way of life, threatened U.S. participation in the international legal regime for decades to come. The Eisenhower adminis-tration's final decision to withhold support from the two human rights covenants was in the end not a difficult decision to make.[101] The United States proposed instead an "action program" that would focus on voluntary reporting of the status of rights to the commission.[102] Dulles, in his testimony to the U.S. Senate on the Bricker Amendment, asserted that the United States would work to influ-ence human rights through "persuasion, education, and example" rather than through binding treaties.[103] In 1953, Eisenhower opened his remarks to the UN with the comment that there were better ways of achieving respect for human rights than by drafting formal treaties on the subject.[104] For the remainder of the

98 Kaufman and Whiteman 1988. On the problem of lack of leadership, see Moskowitz 1974.
99 Kaufman 1990:92–3.
100 Eisenhower 1963:287.
101 See, for example, Pruden 1998.
102 Anderson 2003:229.
103 Anderson 2003:230.
104 Anderson 2003:236.

Cold War period, the United States would remain officially quite aloof to the legalization of international human rights,[105] leaving the initiative to draft and campaign for ratification to the smaller states and legally oriented NGOs.

Early Agents of Legalization

The immediate task of converting the UDHR into binding law was carried out by the UN Human Rights Commission, supported by a coalition of smaller democracies, newly independent states, and private individuals and groups. The commissioners continued to act in their capacity as experts, but they could not help but be influenced by developments in the United States and the world more broadly. The withdrawal from active support of the Eisenhower administration was a major setback. The British were also losing whatever enthusiasm they had had for the project of legalization, at least at the global level. In 1951 the Foreign Office had instructed British representatives to the UN to "prolong the international discussions, to raise legal and practical difficulties, and to delay the conclusion of the Covenant for as long as possible."[106] The "go slow" approach was reflected in the attitudes of the UN leadership at the top level. In 1953, Swedish diplomat Dag Hammarskjold became secretary general; surveying the political terrain, he told John Humphrey, the director of the UN Division of Human Rights, "There is a flying speed below which an airplane will not remain in the air. I want you to keep the program at that speed and no greater."[107] Citing budgetary problems, Hammarskjold reduced staffing at the division and support for the UN *Yearbook on Human Rights* between 1954 and 1956.[108]

Whatever leadership was to be had for treaties "with teeth" at this time was to come from individuals from the smaller democracies. Charles Malik of Lebanon and Max Sorenson of Denmark were in favor of tough binding accords and worked to influence the drafting in this direction. Several French citizens in their capacity as international civil servants were active supporters of a strong covenant as well, including Rene Cassin, who had been vital to the drafting of the UDHR, and Henri Laugier, assistant secretary-general for the UN Department of Social Affairs (resigned in 1951).[109] Perhaps the most consistent advocate

---

105 Quite clearly, this is not to say that the United States did not support human rights around the world in very material ways. One consequence of the Cold War was that the United States poured millions of dollars into Japan and Germany in order to shore up liberal regimes there. See, for example, Orend 2002:230.

106 As quoted in Lester 1984.

107 The original quote can be found in John Humphrey's diaries; see Humphrey et al. 1994:163–5. According to Humphrey's diary entry of 13 March 1954, Hammarskjold had instructed him to "throw the Human Rights Covenants out the window."

108 King and Hobbins 2003:348–50.

109 See Laugier 1950. Glendon (2001:209) notes that Cassin was by this time somewhat removed from the drafting process, given his other responsibilities and his involvement with the elaboration of the European human rights regime.

of the meaningful legal elaboration of the covenants was John Humphrey, who had a strong hand in moving the declaration along toward its legally binding form.[110]

These liberals had to make room for the demands of an emerging coalition of newly independent states with different priorities that can be summarized in two words: anticolonialism and development.[111] The new reality in the commission was the presence of new voices representing the views of individuals from former colonial societies whose primary interest was assuring the right of control over political development as well as natural and other economic resources necessary for national development. The Soviet bloc allied with these new countries, championing the inclusion of national self-determination rights in Article 1 of both covenants, to the delight of governments from Asia to the Arabian Peninsula to the Americas.[112] The move served ultimately to broaden legal protections for "peoples' rights," but it also inserted delay and further polarization into the official debate about the treaties.[113]

Much of the unofficial rights dialog was taking place outside of the UN Human Rights Commission. The Cold War was a competition not only for military supremacy, but also for symbols that could be used to recruit allies and political adherents. Human rights became one of these symbols. The "high ground" from which such critiques were launched was often the standard of law, with its undertones of legitimacy and neutrality. Both the United States and the Soviet Union used legal critiques of one another's practices in their global competition to win respect and adherents. The Soviets supported the work of the (purportedly nongovernmental) International Association of Democratic Jurists (IADJ),[114] which had been very critical of McCarthyism in the early 1950s.[115] Concerned that the Soviets had "'stolen the great words – Peace, Freedom, and Justice',"[116] venerable establishment figures in the United States such

---

110 Glendon 2001:ch. 11.
111 Charles Malik wrote in his diary of ". . . a new host of questions subsumed under the rubric of 'self-determination of peoples' . . ." (Glendon 2001:207). On the importance of economic rights to developing countries, see Vincent 1986:76–91.
112 The two covenants thus begin identically: "Article 1: 1. All peoples have the right of self-determination. By virtue of that right they freely determine their political status and freely pursue their economic, social and cultural development. 2. All peoples may, for their own ends, freely dispose of their natural wealth and resources without prejudice to any obligations arising out of international economic co-operation, based upon the principle of mutual benefit, and international law. In no case may a people be deprived of its own means of subsistence. 3. The States Parties to the present Covenant, including those having responsibility for the administration of Non-Self-Governing and Trust Territories, shall promote the realization of the right of self-determination, and shall respect that right, in conformity with the provisions of the Charter of the United Nations." See http://www.unhchr.ch/html/menu3/b/a_cescr.htm.
113 See, for example, Agi 1979.
114 Also sometimes translated as International Association of International Lawyers (IADL); see Tolley 1994.
115 Dezalay and Garth n.d.:24.
116 Dezalay and Garth 2006:234.

as John McCloy (high commissioner for Germany, 1949–52) and a small group of political lawyers (including Alan Dulles, president of the Council on Foreign Relations and deputy director of the Central Intelligence Agency [CIA]) formed the International Commission of Jurists (ICJ) in 1952. One of the original purposes of the ICJ was to take a law-based approach to countering the propaganda and policy moves of the Soviet Union: in Howard Tolley's words, to "mobilize the forces – in particular the juridical forces – of the free world for the defense of our fundamental legal principles, and in doing so to organize the fight against all forms of systematic injustice of the Communist countries."[117] In its earliest years, the ICJ did not concern itself directly with international law development; it did, however, articulate for a global audience Western conceptions of the rule of law that were to be reflected in the ICCPR, and to a much lesser extent in the International Covenant on Economic, Social and Cultural Rights (ICESCR).[118]

The ICJ became important for the legalization of the international human rights regime because of whom it mobilized and the strategy it developed for rights protection. First, it is important to point out that despite its funding from the CIA, its early members were true liberals who took rights seriously both nationally and internationally. Indeed, their passion in the Cold War was tied to these values. And these were *jurists*; they wanted to use *law* to influence governmental practices, especially in parts of the world where the Soviet Union was gaining influence. Moreover, many of the early members were from the liberal New York Bar Association,[119] not the more conservative American Bar Association that had fought the Genocide Convention. Despite CIA backing (which was exposed in 1967), as early as 1955 the ICJ came to criticize communist regimes as well as fascist ones.[120] It truly did become an equal opportunity critic of the exercise of arbitrary governmental power vis-à-vis the individual, investigating, analyzing, and exposing such practices not only in the Soviet Union and the new People's Republic of China, but also in Spain and South Africa.[121]

Some of the same individuals who had been active in the legal battles in the Cold War context brought the strategy of legalization to later initiatives in the human rights area. Yves Dezalay and Bryant Garth's recent work reveals the networks of individuals whose first international human rights experience was with the ICJ, who became invested in – and experienced with – legal approaches to human rights and then branched out to other activist organizations, such as Amnesty International and Human Rights Watch.[122] These

---

117 Tolley 1994:34.
118 The ICJ dealt with economic rights largely in an individual property rights framework, for example. See the declaration on economic rights passed at the Congress of Athens (Weeramantry 2000:19).
119 Tolley 1994:33.
120 Tolley 1994; Weeramantry 2000.
121 Tolley 1994:50–1.
122 Dezalay and Garth 2006.

individuals applied their legal experience to the campaigns of these and other human rights organizations, which in turn played an important role in negotiating the wave of new treaties over the course of the next two decades.

The coalition of smaller democracies, newly independent former colonies, and increasingly legal activists were the prime movers in codifying most of the provisions of the UDHR in treaty form over the course of the 1950s and 1960s. The ICCPR, the ICESCR (both of which opened for signature in 1966 and entered into force in 1976), and the Convention on the Elimination of Racial Discrimination (CERD) (opened for signature in 1966 and entered into force in 1969) were among the earliest products of this effort. The ICCPR is a global expression of the broadest set of civil and political rights articulated in binding treaty form, enumerating rights to be free from arbitrary arrest, detention, and torture; freedom of thought, religion, and expression; equality before the law, and others. The ICESCR provides for a right to work, to reasonable working conditions, to form trade unions, social insurance, an adequate standard of living, education, and various cultural rights.[123] The CERD was especially salient during the process of decolonization and the dismantling of systems of apartheid and entered into force in only three years' time (open for signature in 1966; entered into force in 1969).[124] It explicitly prohibited apartheid and provided for a host of rights to be provided equally and without respect to race.

THE 1970S AND BEYOND: THE ACCELERATION OF LEGAL DEVELOPMENT

The ideological competition of the early Cold War period eventually gave way to the more pragmatic approach of the Nixon administration. Human rights had settled into a fairly "well-defined consensus" that, in Evans's view, had "simpli[fied] the politics of human rights by reducing the debate to little more than an ideological struggle. . . ."[125] This struggle was subject to the ebb and flow of the foreign policies of the major powers, which under the Nixon administration had taken a distinctly pragmatic turn. More generally, as Kenneth Cmiel has noted, "as the Vietnam War wound down, human rights emerged as a new way to approach world politics."[126] The détente policy of Richard Nixon and Henry Kissinger had less use for a strident appeal to human rights – but also reduced the role that rights played in U.S. foreign policy.[127] For the first time since the late 1940s, it became possible to think of the project of human rights as only loosely coupled with the containment of Communism.

123 For a discussion on economic, social, and cultural rights, see Felice 2003.
124 Banton 1996.
125 Evans 2001:25.
126 Cmiel 1999:para. 7.
127 Boyle 1993.

While the policies of the Carter administration have drawn the most attention as reorienting global attention to human rights,[128] some of the most profound changes in this period with implications for the legalization of the regime preceded Jimmy Carter's election. One was the decision of the U.S. Congress, shocked by State Department support for dictators such as Augusto Pinochet and lobbied by a growing network of organizations,[129] between 1974 and 1976, to begin to tie U.S. foreign aid to rights performance. Whether or not the United States used this policy wisely or consistently, one consequence was the premium it placed on *information gathering*.[130] Once aid depended on it, once the topic was open to debate on the floor of the Congress, fledgling NGOs had much more incentive to collect the facts in a systematic and credible way. The political market for credible human rights information had begun to boom.

A number of entrepreneurial groups formed to meet the demand and to have a voice in shaping the direction of U.S. rights policy. New organizations included the Lawyers' Committee for Human Rights (1975), Human Rights Watch (1978), and the Human Rights Internet (1976). New funding sources opened up as well, notably the Ford Foundation, which decided in 1973 to begin to fund human rights advocacy groups.[131] In the 1970s, Amnesty International decided to shift its tactics from advocating exclusively for the release of individuals to exposing broader patterns of abuse and advocating broader policy positions as well.

These developments had a resounding impact on the legalization of the international human rights regime. The repressive turn in Latin American politics provided a focal point for Amnesty International and other organizations to fasten on issues of physical integrity and torture. Amnesty International launched a campaign against torture in 1973 that, through its constant lobbying efforts, led to a UNGA Declaration Against Torture (1975) and eventually to the legally binding CAT (1984). Many published accounts of the CAT emphasize the crucial role that NGOs – Amnesty International, the ICJ, and the International Association of Penal Law, among others – had in prodding governments to negotiate the treaty and their role in shaping it as well.[132] Nigel Rodley,

---

128 Jimmy Carter's human rights policies are discussed in Crockatt 1995; Garthoff 1994.
129 For a discussion and critique, see Farer 1988:88. "Direct bilateral U.S. aid [to Chile] rose from $10.1 million in 1973 to $177 million in 1975, despite indisputable evidence of mass murder and savage torture authorized at the highest levels of the Chilean government." Farer notes that in 1975, Chile received $57.8 million under PL480 (Food for Peace), while the rest of Latin America, with 30 times Chile's population, received only $9 million.
130 Cmiel 1999:para. 32.
131 Cmiel 1999:para. 11; Sikkink 1993.
132 On the growing importance of NGOs in the treaty-drafting process of the 1970s and 1980s, see Forsythe 1985; Korey 1998; Leary 1979; Tolley 1989; van Boven 1989–90:214. Tolley (1989) notes that by 1989 the ICJ had contributed significantly to several notable successes: the 1977 Protocols to the Geneva Conventions, the UN CAT, the European Torture Convention, the African Charter on Human and People's Rights, and several declarations of principles approved by the General Assembly.

Amnesty International's chief legal adviser, was an especially active lobbyist and publicist during the campaigns of the 1970s and 1980s.[133] The coalition for legalization was a now-familiar one of officials from the smaller democracies (on the CAT, the Swedish UN delegation as well as Dutchman Jan Herman Burger) working in cooperation with NGOs. Neither the United States (which supported universal jurisdiction but did not become a cosponsor and did not immediately sign the draft) nor the Soviet Union (which wanted to reduce significantly the power of the implementation committee) were among the leaders in the effort to ban torture in a dedicated multilateral treaty.[134] Nonetheless, Jack Donnelly's research supports the conclusion that these efforts contributed significantly to the institutionalization of legally binding accountability structures over the course of the 1980s and 1990s.[135] The CAT is the first internationally binding treaty to define torture, and to obligate parties to prohibit it and to investigate allegations of its practice within their jurisdictions.[136]

In the meantime, rules against discrimination against particular groups were strengthened as well. Women's political rights had been an early matter for legalization. As early as 1948, the UN Economic and Social Council (ECOSOC) had created a Commission on the Status of Women (CSW), though it would be decades before the commission would become active.[137] The early postwar mood was favorable in many countries; the Convention on the Political Rights of Women promised greater political participation, and women won the right to vote in France, for example, for the first time in 1944 thanks to General Charles de Gaulle's wartime decree.[138] Discrimination against women had been prohibited by Article 3 of the ICCPR,[139] and discrimination against women in the workforce was taken up by the ILO in the 1950s.[140] But there was hardly any legal development at the international level until the mid-1970s, when the

---

133 For Rodley's assessment of the legal and institutional accomplishments during this period see Rodley 1986.
134 See the discussion in Clark 2001:60–4.
135 Donnelly 1998:ch 1; Orentlicher 1994.
136 The CAT is one of "... a growing number of international instruments [that] generally require the state to punish those who commit human rights crimes, such as extra-legal killings, disappearances, and torture, and to assure that victims are afforded redress" (Orentlicher 1994:426). Increasingly, decisions of the Inter-American Court for Human Rights and the European Court for Human Rights reflect legal norms requiring states to punish those who commit atrocious crimes (Orentlicher 1994:431).
137 Hernandez-Truyol 1999:18.
138 French women obtained the right to vote by the ordinance of 21 April 1944 issued by the Comité Français de Libération Nationale (CFLN, French Committee of National Liberation). See James F. MacMillan, http://www.leedstrinity.ac.uk/histcourse/suffrage/coredocs/coredoc3.htm (accessed 17 January 2007).
139 Article 3: "The States Parties to the recent Covenant undertake to ensure the equal right of men and women to the enjoyment of all civil and political rights set forth in the present Covenant."
140 ILO Conventions No. 100, Equal Remuneration Convention (1951), and No. 111, Discrimination (Employment and Occupation) (1958). See Trebilcock 1999.

women's movement began to press for a treaty covering a broad panoply of rights for women.[141]

Women's issues gained international attention in 1975, which was proclaimed "International Women's Year." The first World Conference on Women was also held that year in Mexico City and was followed by the UN Decade for Women (1976–1985). The UN General Assembly adopted the most comprehensive treaty on women's rights in history with the passage of the CEDAW in 1979. The CEDAW defines and prohibits discrimination against women, and obligates parties to work to alter cultural patterns based on assumptions of women's inferiority and to provide women equal access to political rights, education, employment, and social benefits. The CEDAW did more than call for equal political and civil rights for women; as the result of input from the Women in Development (W.I.D.) lobby, it also acknowledged Third World perspectives in its preamble by making specific references to the rights of rural women to participate in development on a basis of equality with men.[142] The Second World Conference on Women, held in Copenhagen (1980), helped to maintain the momentum.

What certainly did *not* contribute to the momentum for international law to protect women's rights was the now familiar attitude of the U.S. Senate. The Clinton administration attempted to secure passage of the CEDAW in the 1990s but ran into many of the same concerns that human rights treaties had historically encountered, including the argument that the treaty would intrude on the balance of power between the federal and state governments.[143] In the face of opposition, the administration entered a series of fairly significant reservations, and in her effort to sell the treaty to the Senate Foreign Relations Committee, the State Department's deputy legal adviser earnestly noted, ". . . we are not talking about . . . changing U.S. law in any respect."[144] While U.S.-based women's groups were behind legalization, the United States, once again, decided to remain outside the formal treaty framework.

By the late 1970s, the international legal framework for protecting children's rights was still quite underdeveloped. The Polish government was the first to

---

141 Ashworth 1999:252.

142 Otto 1999:120.

143 In September 1994, the Senate Foreign Relations Committee reported favorably on the convention, and the Clinton administration announced at the 1995 Beijing Conference that ratification was one of its priorities. Two resolutions supporting ratification were referred to the House Committee on International Relations in 1997: HR Res. 96, 105th Congress, 1st Session (1997) and HR Res. 39, 105th Congress, 1st Session (1997). The newly Republican Senate took no action.

144 Halberstam 1999:147. Halberstam discusses U.S. reservations to exempt itself from obligations in four areas: private conduct (the obligation to enact legislation or take other action with respect to private conduct except as mandated by the U.S. Constitution); military service (the obligation to assign women to combat units); comparable worth (the obligation to enact comparable worth legislation; and maternity leave (the obligation to legislate to require paid or job-guaranteed maternity leave).

propose a comprehensive convention to address the needs of children and submitted a proposal to this effect to the UN Commission on Human Rights in 1978.[145] Poland's interest in this issue flowed from its experiences during the Second World War, when over 2 million Polish children were killed.[146] As was the case for the CAT and the CEDAW, NGOs played a significant role in both galvanizing states and developing an actual text. Several NGOs – Save the Children International,[147] the Polish Association of Jurists, the ICJ, and the International Association of Democratic Lawyers – were involved at various points early on. These and other organizations contributed to the working group set up by the UN Commission on Human Rights to address children's issues. By 1983, an alliance of 23 NGOs was participating in the drafting process. Some groups lobbied hard on specific issues; Rädda Barnen, the Swedish Save the Children Organization, for example, pressed hard for a provision making 18 years the minimum age for military service.[148] By most accounts, this alliance of NGOs had an important impact on the drafting of the convention: Their "imprint can be found in almost every article."[149]

The relatively swift and now nearly universal ratification of the CRC makes it easy to forget that there was actually quite a bit of resistance to the idea of a children's rights treaty in the late 1970s. Poland, several socialist allies, and many developing countries were supportive, but many among the Western developed countries were not convinced of the need and were wary of the timing. Representatives of the United States argued that few states had moved to implement provisions of the (nonbinding) 1959 Declaration on the Rights of the Child.[150] Canada's and Sweden's representatives called for a measured pace, noting that governments, specialized agencies, and other organizations needed time to express their views on the need for a convention. The United Kingdom's

---

145 The Rights of the Child, Fact Sheet No. 10 (Rev. 1). http://www.unhchr.ch/html/menu6/2/fs10.htm. Several histories discuss the history of the CRC negotiations. See, for example, LeBlanc 1995. For the history of specific articles, see Kaufman and Blanco 1999 (Article 27).

146 On the motives and role of Poland for the Children's Convention, see Cantwell 1992; Tolley 1987.

147 Established at the end of World War I in Geneva, this group had also drafted the 1924 declaration (Cohen 1990). The world's major NGO on children's issues, it now comprises 27 member organizations and operates in more than 110 countries. Information on the Save the Children Alliance can be found at http://www.savethechildren.net/alliance/index.html.

148 Rädda Barnen was not successful in its effort, however. The minimum age for children in armed conflict of 15, as laid out in the Geneva Protocol, was not raised to 18 in the CRC. One of the NGO group's major successes concerned juvenile justice protection. See Cohen 1990. More information on Rädda Barnen can be found at http://www.rb.se/eng/.

149 Cohen 1990.

150 The CRC had been preceded in 1959 by the Declaration on the Rights of the Child and in 1986 by the Declaration on Social and Legal Principles Relating to the Protection and Welfare of Children, With Special Reference to Foster Placement and Adoption Nationally and Internationally. According to Pais, "The prevailing consideration in this body of texts was that children should be cared for, protected, and guided by their parents within the unity, harmony, and privacy of the family" (1994:185).

representative also thought that the convention was not well justified and was premature.[151] Nonetheless, these countries (especially the European ones) were among the most active participants in the drafting process. Human rights – especially children's rights – were, after all, politically awkward to oppose. Ironically, the states that participated the most in the drafting process were not the quickest to ratify.[152]

With the exception of the ICESCR, five of the six "core" human rights treaties discussed previously – relating to civil and political rights, nondiscrimination on the basis of race, banning torture, eliminating discrimination against women, and protecting the rights of children – contain optional obligations that enhance the ability of the international community to scrutinize implementation and compliance.[153] For example, the ICCPR's first optional protocol gives states an opportunity to express their acceptance of the competence of the UN Human Rights Committee (UNHRC) to review and make recommendations on individual complaints alleging state violations of the treaty. Article 41 invites states to make an optional declaration that they accept the competence of the UNHRC to review and make recommendations on complaints of other state parties. The ICCPR's second optional protocol bans the use of the death penalty by those states that accept its provisions. The CAT provides that states may optionally declare that they recognize the competence of the Committee Against Torture to hear individual complaints arising from allegations of violations under the treaty (Article 22). The CERD has a similar optional provision (Article 14), as does the CEDAW in the form of an optional protocol. The CRC has optional protocols relating to child soldiers (OP I) and the sale of children, child prostitution, and child pornography (OP II).[154]

The legal regime has been supplemented with important institutional supports over the years as well, many of which go beyond these consensual treaty commitments.[155] Methods were devised to subject the most egregious cases of massive rights abuse to collective scrutiny, without the consent of the alleged violator, through what has come to be known as "1503 procedures."[156] At the instigation of groups such as Amnesty International and the ICJ, the fact-finding capacity of the UN was improved through the use of increasingly credible special rapporteurs convened in cases of egregious alleged abuses in the areas of arbitrary execution, torture, and religious intolerance and discrimination.[157] Many observers view the development of UN monitoring to be on a positive path, see growth in the authority and stature of monitoring bodies, and believe

---

151 LeBlanc 1995:19.
152 LeBlanc 1995:47.
153 For a balanced and policy-oriented discussion of the way these treaty-based oversight mechanisms work in practice, see Klein and Universität Potsdam. Menschenrechtszentrum 1998.
154 For a discussion of the monitoring mechanisms related to the CRC, see Cohen et al. 1996.
155 On the phases of the strengthening of the role of the UN, see Pace 1998.
156 Tardu 1980.
157 Rodley 1986; Weissbrodt 1986.

the UN is playing an important role in socializing states about global human rights expectations.[158] Others are highly skeptical that an institution that itself has been plagued with corruption, and some of whose members with enforcement roles themselves have poor rights records, can credibly oversee important improvements.[159] As I will argue, the true significance of the treaties has been neither in the willingness of the UN collectively to enforce them nor in the will of individual governments to do so. Rather, the impact of international commitments on domestic politics has been most significant in realizing actual gains in most cases.

CONCLUSIONS

The political environment in which states make international legal commitments has changed fairly drastically over the past half century. The presumption of state accountability on multiple levels places treaty-making in a new and dynamic political context. The most important change has been at the domestic level: The spread of democracy around the world has made governments accountable to citizen voters. Norms of peer accountability have also grown, as reflected in the significantly greater number of agreements of all kinds among states that explicitly call for surveillance, monitoring, and reporting. Finally, states are increasingly held to account by international civil society – private groups that position themselves to offer new information, alternative interpretations, and unofficial judgments about state policies and practices.

These were important structural changes that have taken a century or more to unfold. Together, they have made the choice to use international law as a tool to enhance individual rights seem plausible. But the death and destruction of the Second World War lent an undeniable urgency and legitimacy to the enterprise. The promise that the war was fought in the name of Four Freedoms raised hopes for the place for human dignity in the new world order. The decision to place human rights in the UN Charter and then to enumerate an officially and universally endorsed set of rights as the General Assembly's first order of business sent a message that in the end was difficult to amend, elide, or retract. The message had been heard loud and clear from Montgomery, Alabama, to the villages of Kenya. New governments were at the table for the first time, and they had an interest in legitimizing the decolonization process and assuring their national self-determination, free from external interference. Neither superpower wanted to be bound by international law to provide its people with

---

158 On the strengthening of the system of UN monitoring, see Myullerson 1992; Pace 1998; Szasz 1999. On the growth in the stature and authority of the Human Rights Committee (the implementation committee for the ICCPR), see Ghandhi 1986; McGoldrick 1991. On the general success of the UN's socializing functions, see Forsythe 1985.

159 For generally skeptical accounts of UN enforcement mechanisms, see Donnelly 1986; Robertson 1999; Weisburd 1999. For a highly critical account, see Robertson 1999.

human rights, but ideological competition made it hard to come out against the new legal approach. Each in fact sponsored "nongovernmental" organizations that operated transnationally whose purpose was to demonstrate how the rival power was not living up to international rights standards. The U.S. Senate refused to ratify the treaties that a coalition of public interest lobbies demanded and the smaller democracies championed, but the process was both difficult to oppose and not easily controlled. Once the move had been made to draw up the twin treaties that made the principles of the UDHR legally binding, a precedent had been set. The Cold War pushed human rights treaties to the background, but the thaw of the 1970s offered an opportunity to deal with issues such as women's rights and the brutal repression in several Latin American countries in new ways. The "advocacy revolution" of which Michael Ignatieff has written was a critical part of the story by that time.[160]

But what remains to understand is how governments decided – or not – to engage the formal set of rules that these forces had set in motion. This chapter has set the context for understanding the appeal of legalizing human rights internationally in the mid-twentieth century. It has discussed how the gears were set in motion to build an international legal edifice to address individual rights. But each government faces its own choice as to whether to commit itself fully to the agreements reached in the multilateral setting. The United States, as we have seen, chose to support the principles but to eschew the obligations. What about other countries? How can we understand the decision to take these treaties through the formal process of ratification? It is one thing to participate in this process – but why commit to the outcome? The next chapter presents a theory of human rights treaty commitment that discusses governments' preferences for rights, as well as the domestic institutional barriers some face in formally ratifying. It also theorizes the strategic behavior in which governments sometimes have incentives to engage. Major parts of the legal regime were put in place by the mid-1960s, but its ultimate success would depend on governments' willingness to explicitly commit to the rights project, which is the focus of the following chapter.

160 Ignatieff 2001.

3

Theories of Commitment

Why do states give us these whips to flagellate themselves with?

> Nigel Rodley, former legal adviser of Amnesty International and
> [at the time of writing] UN Special Rapporteur on Torture, 1993[1]

The international legal regime negotiated after World War II was the most ambitious effort in history to adopt new international legal standards for human rights. Historical circumstances – flowing from the war and from Nazi and other atrocities – were of such a nature and magnitude that for the first time governments joined in a cooperative effort under United Nations auspices to draft legal agreements to reduce the possibility of such tragedies in the future. Leaders in many parts of the developing world found that the rights framework resonated with self-determination in the project of decolonization. The Cold War encouraged leaders in both the United States and the Soviet Union to champion rights of differing kinds as a way to seize the moral high ground in their global competition for allies and adherents.

But as we have seen, the development of a successful legal regime was hardly a foregone conclusion. Chapter 2 discussed the domestic resistance within the United States to an enforceable rights regime internationally. The Soviet Union had withheld its support from the UDHR in 1948. The British took a decade to ratify the ICCPR, doing so the year it entered into force. The articulation and broad acceptance of a legal approach to international human rights was hardly assured in these years. But by the mid-1960s, governments around the world had to decide how they would engage the new internationalization of legal rights for the individual. They faced the decision of whether to participate in the growing system of treaties and, if so, which agreements they should ratify and with what

---

1 Clark 2001:4.

kinds of reservations. The legal regime gave each the opportunity to express support for specific rights clusters but also posed the potential risk of raising hopes by making commitments that under future circumstances might be difficult to honor.

This chapter shifts the focus from the historical context that gave rise to the development of the legal regime to each government's decision to ratify a particular treaty text. It raises a question the answer to which is not obvious: Why should a sovereign government explicitly agree to subject its domestic rights practices to the standards and, increasingly, the scrutiny of the rest of the world? Why do governments voluntarily hand over the figurative "whips," to use Nigel Rodley's colorful term, that then might be used by individuals, groups, courts, and peers to criticize their own policies and practices?

While the decision to ratify each of these agreements may be complex, the problem can be usefully simplified by thinking about three categories of governments. First are the *sincere ratifiers*: those that value the content of the treaty and anticipate compliance. Some may want to ratify in order to encourage others to do the same. Second are the group of governments that constitute *false negatives*: those that may be committed in principle but nonetheless fail to ratify. The United States seems rather consistently to provide a conspicuous example. For decades the United States refused to ratify the ICCPR, despite the strong resemblance of the covenant to its own Bill of Rights. The United States still has not ratified the CEDAW or the CRC, despite reasonably good protections for women and children's rights in domestic law. Governments may very well support the values a treaty represents but face daunting political and institutional challenges at home that make it difficult to secure ratification. Such barriers can influence the ratification decision by raising the political costs of ratifying, even for governments generally supportive of a treaty's purposes.

Finally, a number of governments are *strategic ratifiers*. They ratify because other countries are doing so, and they would prefer to avoid criticism. These governments trade off the short-term certainty of positive ratification benefits against the long-run and uncertain risk that they may face compliance costs in the future. They may ratify for relatively immediate diplomatic rewards, to avoid criticism, or to ingratiate themselves with domestic groups or international audiences. This strategy involves risks, since governments have only limited information about the future consequences of ratification and are likely to discount costs realized in the future. Moreover, assuming for a moment that any of these audiences cares more about rights than ratifications, strategic ratification makes sense only in contexts in which the likelihood that a government's commitment will be exposed as strategic is low. When the strategic nature of a commitment is exposed, it is likely to undermine any possibility for producing benefits. Governments with low time horizons may at times exploit the delay involved in exposing their strategic behavior in order to enjoy immediate benefits of ratification; they may also miscalculate the probability that their insincerity will be exposed or that their commitments will be enforced. When information is poor, for example, we should expect many more *false positives* – meaningless commitments – than when information about behavior and likely consequences is more abundant. As we will see, "emulation" of ratification behavior is in fact most likely to be strongest in regions where actual rights convergence is low and information is thin, suggesting a strategic decision to follow the decisions of peer governments. However, one consequence of the accountability revolution discussed in Chapter 2 is that strategic ratifications should be on the decline.

This chapter explains variance in the embrace of human rights treaties – across countries and over time – as a function of government preferences, domestic governing institutions, and varying incentives for some governments to ratify strategically. Like others, I argue that for democratic governments, human rights conventions are hardly problematic. But how can we advance and test propositions about the outliers, the false negatives and false positives? It is essential to theorize the domestic institutions in which these commitments are to be embedded, as well as identifying the conditions under which governments might expect few compliance pressures or miscalculate or discount the future compliance pressures they are likely to encounter. In short, ratification decisions reveal governments' best guess about the political and legal costs and consequences of explicit commitment to the international human rights regime.

WHY COMMIT? THE COMMON WISDOM

There are many ways to think about the influences on governments' commitments to international human rights treaties. One is to think of a treaty commitment as a low-cost opportunity to express support for a cooperative international endeavor. In this view, international legal arrangements are weak, enforcement is unlikely, and costs of noncompliance are low. Why *not* ratify and gain some praise from the international community for doing so? Oona Hathaway has proposed that governments ratify treaties because this allows a costless expression of support for the principles they contain. Those that ratify reap "expressive" benefits, that is, "rewards 'for positions rather than for effects'."[2] Because human rights agreements are not effectively monitored, the expressive benefits that countries gain from the act of joining the treaty will be enjoyed to some extent by all those who join, "regardless of whether they actually comply with the treaty's requirements."[3] The act of ratification, in this view, is driven by the potential benefits of signing an agreement that contains lofty principles but goes unmonitored. Proponents of this view expect

2 Hathaway 2002:2007.
3 Hathaway 2002:2006.

widespread ratification of these treaties, but with little impact on subsequent human rights behavior.[4]

Are such "expressive" benefits substantial? Are there really "rewards" for mere ratification? The logic of this position raises some questions. It is difficult to see how governments can enjoy much benefit from making obviously disingenuous expressions through treaty ratification. Such rewards might be a plausible explanation for ratification if no one cares about follow-up, but they are a poor fit for a world in which citizens, other governments, and assorted transnational advocacy groups value actual practices over mere ratification and have reasonably good information on the former. Moreover, expressive support does not occur in a political vacuum. It triggers political consequences by raising the consciousness of potential stakeholders and giving them a salient moral and legal claim on the realization of that right. In the absence of any intention of following through, the risks of such position-taking – the demands and expectations it is likely to stimulate – are likely to equal or perhaps even to exceed what can only be short-term benefits. It is possible that governments miscalculate the extent to which they will end up being held accountable (a possibility discussed later), but they run the risk of a political backlash in response to blatant inconsistency.[5]

Were treaty ratification universally costless (or even profitable?), the ratification of human rights accords would be immediate and universal. But this is patently not the case.[6] Figure 3.1 shows that ratification of these treaties has been quite gradual.

It took 10 years for the requisite 35 countries to ratify the ICCPR to bring it into force, and 35 years later, accession is still not universal. Support for the CERD was initially swift but then tapered off drastically toward the end of the decolonization period. The CAT has gleaned the fewest adherents of the treaties considered in this study. Slightly over half of the countries in the world have ratified it over the past 20 years.[7] With the possible exception of the CRC (which has weak enforcement provisions and many aspirational obligations), not all governments are in a rush to express even symbolic support for the six core human rights treaties.

Moreover, while these six core conventions are universal in principle, there are clearly important regional differences in governments' willingness to ratify

---

4 Some versions of this argument even claim that the ratification of human rights treaties worsens behavior. For example, Emilie Hafner-Burton and Kiyoteru Tsutsui have argued that "governments, armed with growing information that commitment to the regime would not lead to serious enforcement but would grant them legitimacy in the eyes of other states, were now free to hide domestic human rights practices behind the veil of international law" (2005:1384).
5 For a clear critique of this theoretical approach, see Goodman and Jinks 2003.
6 The United States, for example, is strongly criticized by NGOs as a laggard with respect to international human rights treaty ratification (Roth 2000).
7 For a detailed look at the Kaplan–Meier survival functions for ratification of each treaty, see Appendix 3.1 on the author's Web site.

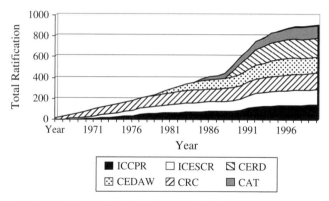

Figure 3.1. Cumulative Human Rights Treaty Ratifications.

them. Figure 3.2 shows that the European countries were, as of 2000, by far the most likely to commit to all six of these treaties. Figure 3.3 shows, additionally, that in the case of the ICCPR, for example, Europe (Eastern and Western) is the region most profoundly committed to this treaty, as indicated by a much greater tendency to accept optional obligations that give the treaty more potential enforceability. Governments in East Asia and the Pacific region are least enthusiastic about signing human rights treaties.[8] By 2000, states in that region were committed, on average, to only three of the six conventions. They have been especially reluctant to ratify the ICCPR and the CAT. Nor are optional ICCPR obligations typically taken on by eastern and southern African, Central Asian, or Middle Eastern governments. If treaty ratification is basically costless, what explains the variation in ratification across treaties, over time, and across regions of the world?

Treaties carry normative significance that it would seem should be an important part of the explanation of this variance. Treaty ratification may well reflect varied and changing notions of appropriate governmental behavior that may find its strongest expression among European states but that has had strong influences on much – though not all – of the world. Ratification patterns may be explained not by the calculating logic of rewards, but the normative logic of appropriateness. Sociologists have developed the concept of "world culture" to capture the idea that values, norms, and ideas of what constitutes proper behavior of a modern state diffuse in varying degrees globally. One way to interpret patterns of treaty ratification is to situate states in a global macrosociological context and view ratification as one instantiation of a diffusing logic of appropriateness that leads states to

---

8 Asia is the only region in the world that does not have a regional intergovernmental human rights regime (Muntarbhorn 1998:413).

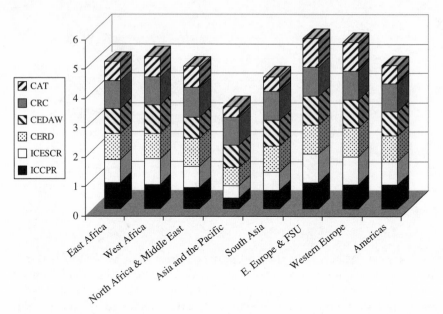

Figure 3.2. Average Ratification Rates (2004) by Region.

want to present themselves to the broader international community and to their own citizens as entities that affirm the basic rights of individuals. Ratification in this context can be thought of as an act of emulation in which states "enact" the values of a broader Western progressive culture in an effort to identify themselves formally as members in good standing of the modern society of states.[9] In the case of human rights treaty ratification, these standards of good standing are transmitted via international conferences, organizations, and the signals sent by the ratifications of peers.[10] Treaty ratification is one way to enact the "script" of modernity in this view.[11] The ratification of international human rights agreements may be a function of various socialization opportunities that in turn depend on the extent to which the nation-state is embedded in the structures of international society. This could explain why Europe is more staunchly committed to these treaties than are other regions of the world.

But if the diffusion of world culture explains ratification, we are faced with further ambiguities. What do we make of the ratification itself? Is it anything

9 On the idea that nation-states are influenced by world models of progress and justice set forth as universalistic scripts for authentic nation-statehood, see Anderson 1991; Meyer et al. 1997.
10 Berkovitch 1999; Boli and Thomas 1999.
11 Wotipka and Ramirez 2008.

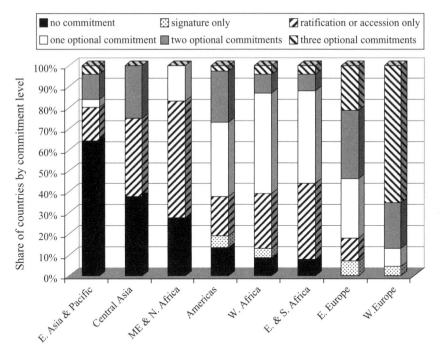

Figure 3.3. Depth of Commitment to the ICCPR (2004) by Region. United Nations General Assembly Resolution 2200A [XXI], 16 December 1966.

Optional commitments include:

- ratification of OP I, recognizing "the competence of the Committee to receive and consider communications from individuals subject to its jurisdiction who claim to be victims of a violation by that State Party of any of the rights set forth in the Covenant. No communication shall be received by the Committee if it concerns a State Party to the Covenant which is not a party to the present Protocol. . . ."
- ratification of OP II to the ICCPR, aiming at the abolition of the death penalty. (Adopted by General Assembly resolution 44/128 of 15 December 1989.)
- Article 41 declaration recognizing "the competence of the Committee to receive and consider communications to the effect that a State Party claims that another State Party is not fulfilling its obligations under the present Covenant. Communications under this article may be received and considered only if submitted by a State Party which has made a declaration recognizing in regard to itself the competence of the Committee. No communication shall be received by the Committee if it concerns a State Party which has not made such a declaration. . . ."

more than "isomorphism" – the adoption of superficially similar formal policies or structures among states? Alternatively, does it signal norm internalization that can be expected to influence more deeply ingrained behaviors and actual practices? Framing ratification with the concept of world culture implies formal convergence but a gradual unhinging of local practices from outward emulative displays. The risk is that we lose sight of how the global idea of rights interacts with very specific domestic political and social contexts to create expectations and demands with which leaders will eventually have to contend. No doubt brushing up against international society has some influence on governments' decision to ratify human rights treaties (treaty ratification is, after all, an aspect of a country's *foreign* affairs), but this approach privileges the global in ways that may not be fully justified. The mere availability of externally validated scripts does not provide much guidance as to why some governments find world culture alluring while others simply do not. Local cultures have in some cases resisted global trends fairly vigorously, yet this approach emphasizes the homogenizing influence, over time, of displays informed by dominant Western values.

A THEORY OF RATIONALLY EXPRESSIVE RATIFICATION

Building on these insights, one way to think about the ratification of human rights treaties is that such behavior is *rationally expressive*. Governments are more likely to ratify rights treaties they believe in and with which they can comply at a reasonable cost than those they oppose or find threatening. But ratification does not in practice always match a government's true devotion to rights. Some governments commit even if they are ambivalent to the treaty contents if they believe that the risk of facing compliance pressures is low enough. A few delay or withhold ratification of treaties they support in principle because domestic institutions create ratification costs. In most cases, though, governments sign treaties that they are willing to implement and ultimately comply with.[12] In short, treaty ratification is rationally expressive: It reflects a government's preferences and practices, subject to the potential net costs that ratification is expected to involve.

Government Preferences and Practices

One of the primary reasons governments commit themselves and their state institutions to international human rights treaties is that they genuinely support the content of those treaties. After all, governments are the principals that participate in the treaty-making process itself. Despite the influence of NGOs documented in Chapter 2, governments are likely to create legal institutions that

---

12 Of course, this preference-based selection process in the treaty regime will make it more difficult to infer a *causal* influence on compliance to the treaty commitment itself: It leaves our model potentially open to the criticism that parties to the treaty already tend to be good compliers, making it difficult to show what the treaty commitment adds on the margin. These methodological issues will be discussed in greater detail in the empirical chapters.

they can, in the end, accept.[13] A single text is open for signature, despite any remaining differences over its contents, and governments have to decide whether to put their political capital on the line by seeking national ratification.

The willingness to do so will largely reflect the values and practices of each individual government.[14] Treaty content will be quite close to the preferences of some governments (and the polities they govern), and highly threatening to others. It therefore should not be surprising that many states ratify fairly readily: They participated in the negotiation process and on the whole favor the treaty's contents. It makes sense, then, to assume that treaty commitments are not completely disingenuous: *Most* governments ratify treaties because they support them and anticipate that they will be able and willing to comply with them under most circumstances. To use the language of spatial models, *the nearer the treaty is to a government's ideal point, the more likely that government is to commit.* The reason is simple: The closer the contents of the treaty are to a government's ideal point, the smaller the required policy adjustments are likely to be.

Some straightforward expectations follow. Other factors being equal, we would expect governments with a deep historic commitment to democratic governance to be among the earliest ratifiers of human rights agreements. After all, these treaties to a great extent reflect the values of civil and political liberties, equality of opportunity, and individual rights upon which these systems are largely based. We might also expect that governments heading newly democratized systems would have a strong preference for international human rights treaties as a possible way to complement the domestic rule of law and "lock in" democratic gains, individual rights, and limited government. Andrew Moravcsik has noted that for the case of Europe, current governments may use rights treaties to constrain future governments.[15] Ratification will be resisted by authoritarian regimes that oppose the contents of the treaties.

Some of the strongest influences on a government's ideal conception of human rights and their place in modern society are cultural. The willingness to use law as a means to empower the individual vis-à-vis the government or society has roots in the Western European Enlightenment[16] and, we can

---

13 Chayes and Chayes (1993, 1995) stress the role that persuasion plays in the treaty-negotiating process, arguing that "jawboning" in the early phases of treaty development can have a positive impact on creating a consensus on the contents of the accord.

14 Cortell and Davis (1996) refer to the "domestic salience" of a particular norm as explaining its acceptance.

15 Moravcsik 2000.

16 Obviously, the linking of human rights to "European Enlightenment" is a gross simplification that has been exposed in several recent studies, including that of Muthu (2003), who notes that some ideas, such as opposition to European imperialism, for example, were absent from pre-eighteenth-century political thinking, bloomed during the eighteenth century among such philosophical giants as Diderot, Kant, and Herder, and then died out again in the nineteenth century. Muthu's work warns against the simplicity of linking the development of theories of human rights in a linear fashion to European Enlightenment thinking.

hypothesize, resonates most clearly and deeply within that cultural context. Modern international law itself has its roots in regulating rulers united by Christendom; moreover, according to Kung and Moltman, while the values contained in human rights treaties "are not exclusively Christian or European ... it was during the era of the Western Enlightenment that the formulations of human rights made their way into North American and European Constitutions, and it is through these constitutions that human rights have acquired world-wide recognition today."[17] If any governments find international human rights treaties palatable restrictions on their sovereignty, one would expect it to be those closely characterized by or linked to Western cultural mores and practices. This is not to suggest, of course, that Western Christendom has a lock on wisdom and moral insight into human rights issues. After all, as Leonard Swidler notes, it took Christians 1,800 years to come to the conclusion that slavery was not a natural situation for some humans.[18] It must be acknowledged that most of the major world religions have an understanding of the value of the individual as an expression of the Divine.[19]

The point about cultural proximity can perhaps best be made in its complementary form. From a range of non-Western perspectives, human rights may have different meanings and international law as a regulatory form is presumptively hegemonic.[20] One of the central debates in the philosophical literature on rights problematizes their content[21] and offers alternative cultural conceptions on the relative balance of rights and responsibilities, public and private spheres, and social versus individual perspectives. The critique of human rights treaties has come from many cultural quarters.[22] Most broadly, some scholars argue that

17 Küng and Moltmann 1990:120.
18 Swidler 1990.
19 "Most of the world's major religions – Judaism, Christianity, Islam, Hinduism, Buddhism, etc. – support in some form the idea that each human person, as the creation of some Divinity, has worth and value, and accordingly should be treated with a measure of dignity and respect" (Orend 2002:191); also see Robertson and Merrills 1993. Similarly, "There are traditions, including religious ones, in all nations which can be supportive of the acceptance of human rights ideas" (Mullerson 1997:77).
20 Brian Orend (2002:192) notes that Judeo-Christian traditions inscribe religious duties in a written, lawlike form, possibly making these religious traditions more acceptant of highly legalized forms of specifying appropriate human conduct.
21 There is a huge literature centered on the universality versus the cultural specificity of human rights. For arguments sympathetic to universality, see Booth and Trood 1999; Weston 1999. For arguments sympathetic to cultural sensitivity, see Ibhawoh 2000; Renteln 1990. For a moderate view, see the discussion in Donnelly 1998.
22 Individual rights have never resonated in many Asian cultures as they have in the West (Cook 1993). Scholars of Confucianism emphasize equitable social relations over individual rights. See the essays by Rosemont, DeBary, and Ames in Rouner 1988. Hindu scholars emphasize that rights exist in a context of duty that structures daily social interchanges; see the essay by Carmen in Rouner 1988. Buddhist scholars describe a philosophy of egoless "self-emptying" that is at odds in some ways with Western rights conceptions. See the essay by Unno in Rouner 1988. There is a large literature devoted to the distinctiveness of Islamic conceptions of human rights based on religious law (Shari'a) (Tibi 1994; Yamani 2000).

international human rights law reflects Western biases that are rightfully resisted in much of the non-Western world.[23] My point is not to stake a position on the general status of international human rights as "universal"[24] but simply to note that cultural propinquity to the values expressed in these treaties is one reason for their ready acceptance. The closer the contents of the treaty are to the ideals of the country in question, the easier it is for a political coalition to form and to persuade the government to ratify.

Finally, no matter a nation's history or its culture, preferences over rights can fluctuate over time. The long history of civil, political, and economic rights is reflected in the decades of struggle among the privileged few, the emerging bourgeoisie, and the working class. In recent times, preferences over rights have been reflected in changing political coalitions that differentially balance order versus dissent, property rights versus consumption rights, or ethnic/social privileges versus nondiscrimination and equality. When a country's governing coalition leans toward the rights that a specific treaty contains, it is much more likely to ratify. Ratification may well reflect a window of opportunity when a rights-based coalition comes to power and chooses to ratify in order to appeal to its broad coalitional base.

FALSE NEGATIVES AND FALSE POSITIVES

That liberal Western democracies support international human rights treaties is hardly news. The real puzzle is why some governments protect rights but eschew treaties, while others sign on with apparently little intention of complying. It is easy to think of cases in which governments that are generally sympathetic delay or even avoid ratifying a treaty. The United States, for example, has not ratified the CEDAW, despite having a fairly strong record of protecting the rights of women in domestic law. It is even easier to think of cases in which governments have committed their states to treaties that they show no signs of valuing. Burundi, Uzbekistan, and Cambodia have signed and ratified all six of the core treaties featured in this study, but we do not think of them as paragons of respect for human dignity. Why these anomalies?

Why Do Rights-Respecting Governments Refrain from Ratification?

The main domestic reason for making a treaty commitment is the expectation that it will be possible to comply at a reasonable cost. But broad value orientations are not the entire story. Governments face potential political costs whenever they attempt to integrate an external treaty arrangement – especially one

---

23 Mutua 2000.
24 See chapters 1 and 2 in Ishay 2004.

that potentially empowers their citizens against the state – into the domestic legal system. Ratification has implications for the *national* system of rules, customs, judicial decisions, and statutes. Unlike nonbinding political agreements, treaties may eventually be relevant to judicial outcomes in the countries that formally accept them. Admittedly, this is likely to be true only in countries in which the rule of law is generally taken seriously; nonetheless, for a large number of countries, it is essential to think through the implications of an international legal obligation for domestic law. In this section, I consider three kinds of legal integration costs: those stemming from executive–legislative relations, those stemming from the nature of the legal system, and those resulting from power-sharing in federal systems.

1. *Ratification Hurdles: Legislative Veto Players*

The first cost a government faces is the political one of domestic ratification. Treaties are not binding internationally,[25] nor are they a justiciable part of domestic law until they are ratified through whatever processes are locally legal and legitimate. These processes are a part of national law or custom,[26] and they vary in their stringency across countries. Ratification hurdles can be thought of as lying along a spectrum from least to most onerous. Governments face the fewest political costs when they closely control the ratification process. At the extreme, for example, ratification may be an executive prerogative in which the government or head of state has the sole right to negotiate *and to ratify* any treaty arrangement. Such a procedure provides practically no check on the executive; ratification follows virtually automatically from the signing of the text. Somewhat more constraining on the executive are rules (sometimes customs) that provide for parliamentary debate but no formal vote on the part of the legislative body. More constraining, and by far the most typical arrangement, is the need for a simple majority vote in a unicameral legislature. Bicameral approval and supermajorities are higher hurdles still.

The nature of the domestic ratification rules should impact the celerity, the intensity, and even the possibility of a treaty commitment. Higher hurdles pose the problem of more legislative veto players, which in turn raises the possibility that the government's externally negotiated agreement runs into domestic opposition. More significant legislative veto players may draw out the process of

---

25 However, according to the Vienna Convention on treaties, "A State is obliged to refrain from acts which would defeat the object and purpose of a treaty when: (a) it has signed the treaty or has exchanged instruments constituting the treaty subject to ratification, acceptance or approval, until it shall have made its intention clear not to become a party to the treaty . . ." (Article 18(a). http://fletcher.tufts.edu/multi/texts/BH538.txt) (accessed 11 August 2008).

26 Ratification processes are usually spelled out in a country's constitution. In some cases, customs surrounding the ratification processes have developed outside of the constitutional context. The "Ponsonby Rules" practiced in several Westminster systems are an example. See Appendix 3.2 on my Web site. Note also that ratification is not a sufficient condition for domestic enforceability, as the subsequent discussion of monist and dualist systems indicates.

domestic persuasion; their anticipated opposition can deter a government from submitting a treaty to ratification at all. Multiple veto players, as in the case of supermajorities or bicameral majority approval, can narrow the set of proposals that can be domestically ratified. Divided governments in presidential systems may have the same effect. In a bilateral negotiation, high domestic hurdles might strengthen the more constrained negotiator's hand in bargaining,[27] but in a multilateral setting, even the largest players will have difficulty wielding the threat of a ratification veto to much effect. Thus, we would expect that the higher the ratification hurdle, the less likely a government will be to ratify an international human rights agreement, even if it is sympathetic to its contents.

2. *Federal Political Systems: Subnational Players*

A federation is "a compound polity combining constituent units and a general government, each possessing powers delegated to it by the people through a constitution, each empowered to deal directly with the citizens in the exercise of a significant portion of its legislative, administrative, and taxing powers, and each directly elected by its citizens."[28] Highly federal governing structures tend to delay and sometimes to prevent international human rights treaty commitments because of the political costs associated with satisfying a larger number of quasi-veto players. Whether or not state or provincial representatives get a direct vote, as they do in the U.S. Senate, powerful local governments can create resistance that most central governments will have to take into account.

Treaty ratification raises political controversies in many federal polities. Political friction is likely to arise when treaties signed and negotiated by the national government encroach on the authority of the subnational unit. Many international regimes raise such concerns,[29] but none quite as intensely as do human rights agreements, which deal with the relationship of the individual to local political authority, the administration of justice, and discriminatory practices. Subnational governments can be expected to resist the encroachment on their prerogatives that a treaty implies. The death penalty, explicitly banned in the first optional protocol of the ICCPR,[30] has traditionally been left to the individual states of the United States.[31] Many subnational units have authority over

---

27 See, for example, the discussion in Milner 1997.
28 Watts 1998:121.
29 See, for example, the *Tasmanian Dam* case, involving federal intervention in traditionally local environmental and land use regulation in Australia. In 1983 the Australian High Court ruled that the federal government could intervene in this area because of its commitment to protect "World Heritge Sites" under international law; see Bzdera 1993.
30 On the "ban" of the death penalty in international law generally, see Schabas 2002.
31 The important U.S. Supreme Court ruling that invalidated the death penalty *as administered* in 40 states was *Furman v. Georgia*, 408 U.S. 238. This was really a series of cases challenging the death penalty in Georgia and Texas. For a brief history, see Zimring 2003.

educational and cultural issues, which are also central to obligations contained in the CERD and the CEDAW.[32] Switzerland, for example, made three reservations to the ICCPR, deferring to cantonal law.[33] Almost by definition, international human rights agreements that rest on universalistic principles are likely to come into tension with cultural specificities that federal systems are often designed to protect.[34] International human rights treaties can contain a range of proscriptions and prescriptions that are often within the competence of subnational governments in highly federal systems.

In some countries, federal political structures operate as a de facto ratification hurdle. The U.S. Senate, as a chamber representing states' interests, has functioned this way, as the effort to ratify the Genocide Convention illustrates (Chapter 2). Some central governments in federal systems have adopted customs or formal procedures to consult with provincial or state governments prior to submitting the treaty for ratification.[35] In 1996, in the face of local concerns that the federal government's treaty-making power would encroach on the authority of the provinces, Australia instituted new preratification procedures designed specifically to increase provincial input into the commitment decision.[36] Local governments have strong motives to insist on input at the preratification stage, for they tend to be much less successful at clawing back their authority in post-ratification litigation. The *Toonen* case,[37] in which the UN Human Rights Committee held that a local Tasmanian law outlawing consensual sexual relations between men was a violation of the ICCPR, was a wakeup call to the Australian provinces of the implications of international treaties. Nor is litigation in national courts sure to protect the rights of subnational governments when international treaties intrude into their areas of competency.[38] Studies suggest that federal courts tend to be nationalist rather than

---

32 Rights to maternity benefits, for example, vary across Australian provinces. See Australia's reservation to the CEDAW: http://www.unhchr.ch/tbs/doc.nsf/StatusfrsetP?OpenFrameSet (accessed 11 August 2008).

33 See http://www.unhchr.ch/html/menu3/b/treaty5_asp.htm (accessed 11 August 2008).

34 Carozza 2003.

35 For a comparative discussion of how the United States, Canada, Australia, and Switzerland have dealt with federal problems involved in international agreements, see Hendry 1955.

36 Emery 2005; Gelber 2001.

37 *Toonen v. Australia* (1994) was only the second homosexual rights case ever taken by an individual to the Human Rights Committee (a case from Finland was the first), and the first to be successful. Toonen argued that the ban on same-sex male acts in the Tasmanian Criminal Code violated his right to privacy and equality under the ICCPR (Articles 17 and 26). See Gelber 1999. It is notable that in this case the Australian government attached a brief on the side of the petitioner, with the attached Tasmanian government brief on the other side.

38 Francisco Martin (2001:249) notes in the conclusion of his exhaustive study of legal cases involving treaties in the United States that "State officials have no authority to ignore the U.S.'s treaty and customary international law obligations. . . . Unless they carefully follow international law developments, state authorities may well be facing enormous liabilities for violations of international law."

neutral in federal–provincial disputes,[39] which increases the motive for state and provincial political leaders to resist international treaties unless they are accompanied by clear understandings about the way they will affect subnational autonomy.

The result of these federal–state/federal–provincial struggles is to slow and sometimes even to deter ratification of human rights accords, even by central governments that in principle support the purposes of the treaty. By the mid-1990s, for example, only five countries had not ratified the CRC; of these, two were Western industrialized countries, and both were highly federal (the United States and Switzerland[40]). In many federal countries, the legal issues are getting sorted out[41] but the political issues remain and are reflected in an inordinate number of false negatives among the more highly federal political systems.

3. *Ex Post Legal Integration Costs: Judicial Institutions*

Finally, the incentives to ratify an international human rights treaty can vary across countries due to the nature of the local legal system. Treaty commitments have the status of law in most countries. So, it is important to understand what costs the legal system itself may generate for a government putting forward an international accord for domestic ratification. To the extent that ratification creates political resistance from the bar or the bench, or to the extent that governments cannot easily predict (or reverse) the outcome of judicial decisions involving a treaty commitment, governments should be very conservative in ratifying international agreements, even if they are generally sympathetic to their contents.

In this section, I argue that common law systems provide incentives for governments to go slow when it comes to treaty ratification, especially in the human rights area. Most of these costs flow from two features of common law systems: the emphasis they place on judge-made law through precedents and the power and independence from government of the judiciary. The existence of these costs is one reason why common law systems tend toward legal dualism: Not only is there a preference for involving the legislative branch in laws that affect citizens (through implementing legislation); there is also a preference to

---

39 Subnational governments can expect to be disadvantaged by what Bzdera refers to as the "nationalist" orientation of federal courts that are likely to rule on such issues. One reason this is true, he argues, is the way federal judges are appointed. See his study of eight federal systems: those of the United States, Canada, Germany, Belgium, Italy, Australia, Switzerland, and the EU (Bzdera 1993). For the U.S. case, see also ". . . the decisive interests of national uniformity which arise in the context of formal treaty obligations . . . mandate a different, and ultimately more accommodating, calculus for the interstitial lawmaking powers of federal courts within the scope of self-executing treaties" (Van Alstine 2004:Abstract).

40 Switzerland ratified in 1997. See http://www2.ohchr.org/english/bodies/ratification/11.htm (accessed 11 August 2008).

41 Swaine 2003.

shield local law from externally negotiated political agreements that are not likely to be a good match with organically grown precedent.

ADJUSTMENT COSTS. The first reason common law systems tend to take a cautious approach to international legal obligations is that treaties involve greater adjustment costs than is the case in civil law systems. Treaties are external political "deals" that challenge the very concept of organic, bottom-up local law designed to solve specific social problems as they present themselves. They are the philosophical and cultural antithesis of judge-made, socially adaptive, locally appropriate *precedent*.[42] The core quality of common law reasoning is its essentially evolutionary rather than revolutionary nature.[43] Treaties are more of a foreign substance in a common law system that values rules that evolve gradually from local problems and local judge-made solutions. Civil law systems are built on the civil code, a natural national analogy to the international "code," or treaty. Due to the legal culture these systems imply, treaties should meet with much greater resistance in common law than civil law systems.

The adjustments that treaty ratification implies in a common law setting are of two kinds. The first is merely perceptual. It involves the cognitive and emotional recognition that a code of largely external genesis has a rightful place among the legal concepts in a system that is largely local, organic, and experiential. To put it bluntly, integrating a treaty into a common law system requires more attitude adjustment than it does in the code-based civil law setting. Integrating a treaty into a common law system also requires greater adjustment to the prevailing mode of legal reasoning. Common law legal reasoning is *inductive*; it moves from the specific case to the general rule. Civil law legal reasoning is *deductive*; it involves the application of abstract principles to specific cases. Treaties – statements of general principles – are obviously much more in accordance with the prevailing form of legal reasoning in civil law settings than common law settings. An attachment to inductive legal reasoning can contribute to resistance in common law settings to the ratification of abstract treaty principles.

The second type of adjustment cost is tangible, and it is paid largely by the common law bar and bench. Common law judges and lawyers, relative to their civil law counterparts, have developed very specific assets in the interpretation

---

42 On the importance of precedent in a common law system, see Cappalli 1997; Darbyshire et al. 2001; Opolot 1981. Every primer in comparative law highlights this distinction between civil and common law systems, though there is disagreement over its significance. Glendon, Osakwe, and Gordon (1982), for example, note that civil law countries use precedent, too; it is more a matter of emphasis. See also Bogdan 1994. In an empirical study, La Porta et al. (2000:15) found that ". . . case law is a source of law in all [English legal origin] countries but . . . [French legal origin] countries occupy an intermediate position: case law is a source of law in 28.1% of th[ose] countries (many of them are Latin American countries which modeled their constitutions after the U.S. one." Some scholars trace the distinction to differences in the two systems between the role of the judge and of the legislature; in civil law systems, they argue, there is a strong assumption that the legislative body makes the law and the judges apply it (Tetley 1999/2000).

43 Zweigert and Kötz 1987.

of their common law precedents.[44] The civil law, on the other hand, tends to be more transparent, easier to research, easier to change, and more accessible than the more complicated system of precedents built up under a common law system; for this reason, practitioners in civil law systems tend to be generalists rather than specialists.[45] Actors with highly specific legal skills grounded in extant precedent are likely to resist the imposition of externally formulated rules on the local system of rules. The investment of legal actors in common law systems is likely to make them much more conservative with respect to treaty ratification than their civil law counterparts. Without their active support, and quite possibly because of their opposition, governments may decide that ratification is not worthwhile.

UNCERTAINTY COSTS. From a government's point of view, incorporating an international human rights treaty into a common law legal system creates more uncertainty than is the case in a civil law system. The greater certainty in the civil law system flows from the more constrained role of the judiciary in rule interpretation.[46] The strong presumption in a civil law setting is that judges are constrained to interpret rules narrowly and are barred from basing their decisions on expansive interpretations that border on legislation.[47] Moreover, judges in civil law systems tend to be educated in government civil service institutions, reinforcing their narrow legal discretion and reducing their independence from executive influence.[48] In the civil law system, the judge is a (relatively) low-status civil servant without independent authority to create legal rules.[49] This narrow conception of the judge's role is especially strong in France, but it is broadly characteristic of a civil law approach to judicial power.[50]

The relative independence and power of judges in the common law setting are accompanied by a much broader interpretive role.[51] As a result, the government in a common law setting faces a wider range of possible treaty effects; a

---

44 Cappalli 1998.

45 Adriaansen 1998; David and Brierley 1978. Glendon, Osakwe, and Gordon (1982:32) claim that "The *Code civil des francais* was meant to be read and understood by the citizen."

46 Mirow (2000) argues, for example, that civil law has historically been used to centralize in Latin America, creating greater governmental judicial dependence.

47 In the civil law tradition, the legislated code controls judicial action, which was initially conceived as mechanistic application of law to fact (Tunc 1976). The French Civil Code is explicit that judges are forbidden to lay down general and regulatory rules, and with only a few exceptions it has its equivalent in all the law of the Romano–Germanic family (David and Brierley 1978). Continental civil law systems hold in common the underlying principle that the judge should not play the role of legislator.

48 This tradition of a judiciary narrowly focused on law application is reinforced by the way judges are trained and appointed in most civil law systems (David and Brierley 1978).

49 Mahoney 2001.

50 See, respectively, Glendon et al. 1982; David and Brierley 1978.

51 Some scholars have argued that the presence of interest groups that attempt to influence judicial decision making is an endogenous consequence of such judicial independence (Landes and Posner 1975).

greater range of interpretative possibilities from a highly independent judiciary makes it more difficult to know ex ante how any particular treaty will be interpreted. True, common law judges are bound by precedent, but importing an external obligation raises questions of interpretation that a government can less easily predict in a common law setting.[52] Add to this the greater independence and prestige of the judiciary in a common law system, and it is clearly possible that governments may balk at committing to new rights obligations the consequences of which are less predictable. The fact that governments in common law settings are much more likely to require extensive compatibility studies to ascertain the degree of concordance between the treaty obligation and the local body of (largely case-based) law[53] is a manifestation of this much greater preratification uncertainty.

A concrete example straight from the pen of a government official in a common law country helps to illustrate these points, particularly the problem of ex ante uncertainty regarding treaty interpretation. In 1992, Michael Duffy, Australia's attorney general, tried to explain to a (generally) pro-rights national audience why the Australian government had taken such a long time to ratify the ICCPR. One of the government's key concerns reflects the uncertainty costs discussed previously. Referring to the broad interpretive power of Australian courts, Duffy noted that "Some of their decisions have appeared to give very broad and generous meaning to some of the expressions and to adopt interpretations which the government itself may not consider appropriate. Faced with this position, the government has recently announced that it will legislate to provide guidance as to the meaning of certain of the convention terms [referring in this case to refugee conventions] such as 'well founded fear' and 'persecution.'" Betraying the government's uncertainty over how Australian courts might interpret such treaties, he noted that "The government considers it important that it retain some control of the meaning that is to be given to its international obligations in this area."[54] Referring to the problem of treaty interpretation in Australia courts, Duffy declared, ". . . it is important that governments assume burdens that are known."[55] "[G]overnments will feel increasing disenchantment with International Law," the Australian attorney general concluded, "if they feel their

---

52 Because the consequences of legislative change are less easy to predict, David and
    Brierly view common law systems as inherently more conservative: "In [common law]
    countries where the law is judicially created, there is sometimes hesitation about abolish-
    ing or changing a rule because the consequences in relation to the whole of the law are
    not clear. In countries of the Romano–Germanic system, such reforms are more easily
    accepted because it is more evident which rules will be affected and which unchanged"
    (1978:93).
53 Heyns and Viljoen 2001:497.
54 Duffy 1992:18.
55 Duffy 1992:21.

consent to particular obligations is then being used by . . . courts . . . to seek to impose different unforeseen burdens."[56]

In short, governments in common law legal systems face a much greater ex ante dispersion of possible treaty interpretations than is the case in a civil law system; by comparison, the dispersion of possible interpretations will be more "spiked," or closely clustered, in a civil law system, as illustrated in Figure 3.4. The power of the judiciary to interpret the nature of the rights obligation generates uncertainty for governments in common law systems and may create incentives to resist or delay and add reservations at the time of treaty ratification.

IRREVERSIBILITY COSTS. Finally, civil and common law systems differ systematically with respect to rule irreversibility and enforceability. Several structural features of the common law system tend to make it more difficult than in a civil law system for the government to escape the obligations in domestic law that the treaty envisions. First is the greater structural independence of the judiciary in most common law systems, where judges tend to be independent policymakers occupying high-status offices. Second is the competence of courts to review administrative actions and to hold governments accountable for their infractions of constitutional or treaty-based human rights, making it harder to go back on a commitment. Third is the role of precedent, which creates a way for treaties to make a deeper footprint in local jurisprudence than is the case in code-based legal systems.

Compared to common law systems, courts in civil law systems are much less able systematically to check government actions and policies. Mahoney writes, "The fundamental structural distinction between the common law and civil law lies in the judiciary's greater power to act as a check on executive and legislative action in a common-law system."[57] In some civil law systems, ordinary courts typically have no power to review government action. France's administrative courts do have this power, but these courts are closely super-vised by the executive branch of government.[58] The courts in civil law systems tend to display a much weaker tendency to review the constitutionality of government policies and to intrude in the administration's "pursuit of the public interest."[59]

---

56 Duffy 1992:21.
57 Mahoney 2001:507.
58 Mahoney notes that administrative court judges "are trained at the administrative schools alongside the future civil servants whose decisions they will oversee" (2001:512).
59 Mahoney 2001:512. Other scholars note the relatively weak ability of courts in civil law systems to review the constitutionality of policies taken by their governments (Glendon et al. 1982:59): ". . . in France . . . courts are not competent to sanction violations of individual constitutional rights. . . ." [which is not true in Germany]. "Despite the independence and prestige of the Council of State, some French observers have expressed concern that a court which is, at least theoretically, part of the executive branch has the exclusive power to review the legality or constitutionality of the acts of the executive" (ibid.:62).

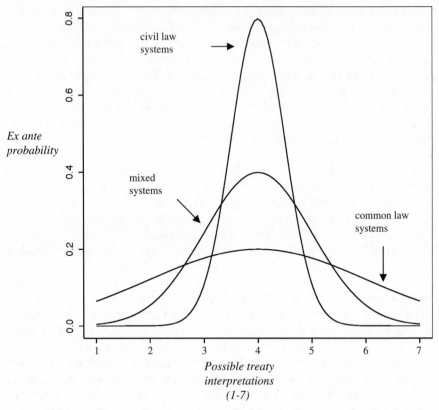

Figure 3.4. Ex Ante Probability of Possible Treaty Interpretations: Civil Compared to Common Law Systems.

The structural ability of judges to provide a stronger check on government power is manifest in other ways as well. Studies have demonstrated that in civil law countries, supreme court judge tenure is significantly shorter than in common law countries. One study found that all countries of English legal origin had lifelong tenure for supreme court judges, while fewer than three-quarters of those of French legal origin had this practice.[60] The importance of precedent in the common law system is also a way for judges to guard their independence from government interference.[61] Indeed, were a common law

---

60 La Porta et al. 2002:14.
61 "Because the power of precedent restricts the ability of the government to influence judges, it too serves as a useful measure of judicial independence" (La Porta et al. 2002:9). However, judges in civil law countries do pay attention to precedent (Damaska 1986:33; Glendon et al. 1982:132–4; La Porta et al. 2002:9).

government to want to void its obligations under a particular interpretation of a human rights treaty simply by terminating its adherence, to the extent that the treaty has left its footprint in domestic legal precedent, it may be difficult to do so.

The upshot of these structural differences in the ability of courts to check central government actions is that the contents of a human rights treaty are much more likely to be enforced vis-à-vis the government in a common law than in a civil law country. Independent and powerful judiciaries are important players in the domestic realization of human rights. To the extent that governments can neither predict nor easily avoid enforcement of judicial determinations of their obligations under treaty law, they will be especially hesitant to ratify an international human rights treaty.[62]

Why Do Rights-Abusing Governments Sometimes Ratify?

In the previous section, I argued that some domestic institutions could help create false negatives – countries that seem to value the contents of the treaty but that have not ratified. In this section, I argue that we also need a theory of false positives – a reasonable explanation for why a government might decide to ratify without having a strong normative commitment to the contents of the treaty. The answer must be that, given their circumstances, they believe ratification is worth it. The expected value of ratifying must exceed the costs the government expects to incur. Insincere ratifiers gamble that the consequences will not overwhelm the benefits of ratification, at least within the time frame relevant to the decision maker.

Motives for Insincere Ratification: Expected Benefits

There may be a number of reasons governments ratify human rights treaties without fully expecting to comply. One is that they are enticed to ratify by the promise of some benefit offered by promoters of the human rights regime. While there is no reason to believe that ratification alone produces significant tangible benefits for a government, it can produce good press or an improved image with audiences both at home and abroad. That governments enjoy the positive publicity associated with treaty ratification is indicated by their tendency to publicize their actions, often on Web sites oriented toward

---

62 Some scholars have argued that the distinction between common and civil law systems has eroded over time, but this argument may apply more to Britain and France than to their former colonies and other "legal transplants." Tetley (1999–2000:20) notes that "Since most legal systems duplicated the law administered in another jurisdiction (e.g., former British colonies duplicated British law), major legal traditions tend to be associated with the original legal system as it then existed rather than as it exists today." Any convergence that has taken place is likely to have been primarily in Europe, where intensive interactions and a deliberate program of legal integration may have caused a degree of convergence.

international audiences.[63] The Web sites of nongovernmental human rights organizations add positive reinforcement by mentioning in a positive light governments that have ratified the treaties they support.[64]

Insincere ratification may be further encouraged if governments are offered tangible benefits for ratification. Some intergovernmental organizations may expect human rights treaty ratification as a condition for membership. Some states may hold out the possibility of improved access to trade or aid for countries that ratify these agreements. Governments may think that investors will be impressed by their willingness to ratify human rights treaties, believing ratification will convince investors of the strength of domestic rule of law or the government's long time horizons.[65] Less tangibly, one of the primary reasons governments may ratify even if they do not have sweeping plans to comply is the desire to glean praise and to avoid criticism, often from external audiences of peers or activists organized transnationally. The thinner the information environment, the harder it is for peers and NGOs to expose inconsistency; given poor information, it might be possible for a government to enjoy positive buzz from ratification for a longer period of time.

Uncertainty over Consequences

Ratifying a human rights treaty is a gamble because governments cannot be certain about the broader social and political consequences. I assume that governments are fairly sophisticated in assessing these risks. But it is possible that there are some circumstances under which governments actually miscalculate (or fail fully to appreciate) the consequences of their actions at the time of ratification. They may ratify human rights treaties to enjoy whatever immediate social and political benefits may flow from formally supporting the treaty regime, but they find that (contrary to their initial expectation) the costs are greater and they are incurred sooner than the government had anticipated. In short, governments may ratify insincerely because they underestimate the probability that they will be pressured to live up to their international treaty commitments in the years to come.

---

63 Turkey, for example, has publicized its recent flurry of treaty ratifications on its embassy Web sites around the world. See, for example, the posting on the Web site of its embassy in Ottawa at http://www.turkishembassy.com/II/O/InternationalHumanRightsUpdate.htm (accessed 11 August 2008).

64 To provide but a few examples, Amnesty International's Web site advocates the need to ratify the Protocol on the Rights of Women in Africa and announces approvingly those governments that have ratified; see Public Statement, AI Index: AFR 01/002/2005 (Public) News Service No.: 204, 29 July 2005 at http://web.amnesty.org/library/Index/ENGAFR010022005?open&;of=ENG-375 (accessed 11 August 2008). Countries have been praised by Human Rights Watch for their ratification of the statutes of the International Criminal Court; see http://www.hrw.org/english/docs/2000/12/11/german645.htm (accessed 11 August 2008).

65 Farber 2002.

A good example of such miscalculation is found in Thomas Risse's and Kathryn Sikkink's notion of "tactical concessions" that governments make to domestic pressure groups demanding adherence to particular norms. "When they make these minor concessions," Risse and Sikkink write, "states almost uniformly underestimate the impact of these changes, and overestimate their own support among their population. They think the changes are less costly than they are, and they anticipate that they have greater control over international and domestic processes."[66] They note that governments can get trapped in their own rhetoric and are often surprised by the impact of an apparently small concession to human rights norms, such as ratifying a treaty. Risse and Sikkink argue that when entering the "tactical concession phase," governments "cannot be expected to know the extent of pressures" they would face substantially to improve rights practices.[67]

But why is it that governments sometimes make faulty forecasts when they have every incentive to "get it right"? The main reason is that conditions change in ways that governments simply do not expect at the time of ratification. Unanticipated political or social shocks occur in ways that governments cannot anticipate years in advance. Few could have anticipated the end of the Cold War a decade prior, but that development had a momentous impact on demands for rights protections in many parts of the world, from Eastern Europe to Latin America. Few could have predicted the growing political support for the legal doctrine of universal jurisdiction for those accused of torture. Certainly Pinochet did not fully appreciate the consequences when in 1988 his government ratified the CAT, the very convention under which he was extradited and prosecuted a decade later.[68] Miscalculation is possible – even likely – when political conditions rearrange the stakes in ways that run against prevailing assumptions and past practice. Some governments are willing to gamble on ratification for tangible or intangible benefits if they (sometimes incorrectly) believe they will never be held to account.

Short Time Horizons

Finally, insincere ratification may be rational if a government has especially short time horizons. Governments that discount the future highly are likely to be tempted by whatever short-term benefits result from ratification, and they are likely to discount the compliance demands they may have to face in the future. Since benefits are likely to dissipate as soon as a government is revealed

---

66 Risse and Sikkink 1999.
67 Risse and Sikkink 1999:27.
68 Phillippe Sands has quoted Pinochet's human rights adviser at the time as saying, "It never occurred to us that the torture convention would be used to detain the senator." *San Francisco Chronicle*, 13 November 2005. The article can be viewed at http://www.sfgate.com/cgi-bin/article.cgi?f=/c/a/2005/11/13/INGUPFLGKJ1.DTL (accessed 11 August 2008).

as strategic, only governments that place a premium on immediate gratification are likely to ratify insincerely. Moreover, uncertainty over future compliance demands increases over time. Governments are typically much better able to gauge net treaty costs in the short term than they are in the long run. Uncertainty over the outcomes of ratification increases over time, while the benefits of insincere ratification fall as other actors discover that ratification was strategic.

Why might a government ratify a human rights treaty even if it does not expect to comply? The answer I have suggested here is the desire for some short-term benefit, whether tangible or intangible, for which the government is willing to take the gamble of ratification. Ratification appears to be a good bet where the expected benefits are highly valued, where potential benefactors cannot confirm actual behavior, where a government anticipates (although with uncertainty) little future demand for compliance, and where a government seeks immediate rewards while discounting future costs. In these circumstances, it makes sense to gamble on ratification. Support for this theory of commitment to human rights treaties is tested empirically in the following section.

THE EVIDENCE: EMPIRICAL PATTERNS OF TREATY COMMITMENT

To what extent is this theory of rationally expressive ratification borne out in actual governmental behavior? This section examines the evidence that treaty commitment reflects preferences, can be hampered by domestic institutions, and can be encouraged under some circumstances by strategic moves to benefit in the short run. I examine three areas of treaty engagement: treaty ratification, reservation making, and the making of optional commitments that deepen the obligations in the main text of the treaty, often through quasi-enforcement mechanisms. Data have been gathered for every country possible. For ratification and optional commitment-making, observations are yearly and extend back to the date at which the treaty was open for signature wherever data availability makes this possible.

For ratification and optional commitments, I use event history models, which focus on the spell of time until the event of interest occurs (in this case, the making of a human rights treaty commitment). Event history models (also known as "hazard models") are appropriate in this case because they capture the accumulation of "risks" over time that affect the decision to commit.[69] Specifically, I employ a Cox proportional hazard model to examine the effects

---

69 In this respect, the hazard model is more general than a panel probit in that it allows for the underlying probability of committing to a given treaty to change each year. In addition, the structure of the data (all os and a single switch to 1 at the point of each country's commitment) is analogous to "death" in the epidemiological studies in which such models are frequently employed.

of both constant and varying conditions on the decision to ratify. The Cox model estimates a "hazard rate"[70] for a treaty commitment event (such as ratification or an optional commitment) at a particular point in time. This hazard rate is modeled as a function of the baseline hazard (h_0) at time t – which is simply the hazard for an observation with all explanatory variables set to zero.[71] The idea is to analyze the factors expected to affect the probability over time that an uncommitted government will decide to ratify. The influence of each factor is reflected in the hazard ratio: A ratio greater than 1 increases and a ratio of less than 1 reduces the likelihood of a commitment in any given year for which a commitment has not already been made. Once a country ratifies, it is dropped from the analysis. While post-ratification behavior is central to understanding treaty effects (see Chapters 4–6), it is of no practical interest here because in fact no government has ever formally reversed or voided its treaty commitment. Since reservations are entered at the time of ratification, I use a simple probit model that estimates the likelihood that a particular factor is associated with reservation-making. In general, the simplest and most robust results are reported in the tables.[72]

Ratification

1. *Preferences and Ratification*

Suppose we begin with the least controversial of the claims made previously: Governments with preferences closest to the contents of the treaties are most likely to ratify. If this is true, we should expect democracies to be among the first and strongest supporters of the six core treaties. Furthermore, we might expect governments of the left – most often associated with equality and civil and political protections for the less advantaged – to be among the most enthusiastic supporters. Finally, we might expect Western nations to throw their support early and often to legal agreements to protect human rights. I use the dominant religion as an indicator of Western civilization. These indicators are decent proxies for preferences, reflecting as they do each government's political history, its current political complexion, and its cultural context. (For exact data measures and sources, see the data appendix at the end of the book.)

---

70 The hazard rate is defined as: $h(t)$ = probability of committing between times t and $t + 1$ (probability of committing after time t).

71 In this case, we have set all variables to their minimum value in order to avoid interpretations based on deviations from unobserved values of the explanatory variables.

72 More extensive tests involving a wider range of controls can be found in Appendix 3.3 on my Web site. A detailed data appendix, which describes the definition and source for each variable, can be found at the end of this book.

Democracy certainly increases the probability that a government will commit itself to a human rights treaty, an unsurprising result that reflects its preferences over rights. The positive and highly significant hazard ratio – the proportion by which the explanatory variable is estimated to raise or lower the probability of ratification – reported in Table 3.1 shows with a high degree of certainty that democratic governance has facilitated international human rights treaty ratification.[73] The hazard ratios are straightforward to interpret: For the ICCPR, for example, a one-point increase along the polity scale (a measure of democratic governance emphasizing free and fair elections, political competition, and constraints on executive authority, ranging from –10 to 10) increases the probability of ratifying the ICCPR by a little over 11 percent (the hazard ratio is 1.11). Democracy has mattered least to ratification of the CRC, but it is estimated to have increased the chances of ratification by almost 4 percent each year in which the treaty had not yet been ratified. There is little question that if we use the continuous polity scale as our metric for democracy, there is a strong linear relationship between regime characteristics and ratification.

Another way to capture the effects of regime type is to define categories rather than use the continuous scale. If we look at the influence of various *categories* of democratic governments, we can see a similar pattern. Rather than replicate the models contained in Table 3.1, Table 3.2 compares the effect of mature, young, and emergent democracies on ratification behavior (using a similar battery of controls, which are not reported).

The evidence is strong that the long-term, stable democracies – those that have been consistently democratic since World War I – have been swiftest to ratify the two documents often referred to as the "International Bill of Rights" (the ICCPR and the ICESCR). For the ICCPR and the ICESCR, the proportional hazard ratios indicate that democracies stable since World War II were two to three times more likely to ratify than were countries that have never been democratic. Newly transitioned but currently stable democratic governments were over two times more likely to ratify than were all other governments. For these two treaties, the results are almost certainly linear (the more mature and more stable the democracy, the more likely the government is to commit).[74] The results in Tables 3.1 and 3.2 point to a positive relationship between the quality and durability of a country's democratic institutions and the propensity to ratify.

The straightforward relationship between democracy and ratification does not hold up as well for the three later treaties – the CAT, CEDAW, and CRC. In fact,

---

73 Note that this is a reduced form version of a model with far more extensive controls. See Appendix 3.3 on the author's Web site. Controls that were never significant are omitted from the analyses presented in Table 3.1.
74 See the arguments made by Moravcsik 2000.

Table 3.1. Influences on the Rate of Treaty Ratification

Cox proportionate hazard model (reduced-form models; see Appendix 3.3 on the author's Web site for robustness results)
Hazard ratios, probabilities

Explanatory Variable	ICCPR	ICESCR	CERD	CAT	CEDAW	CRC
Indicators of preferences						
Democracy	1.11***	1.17***	1.06***	1.04**	1.13***	1.039***
	(p = .000)	(p = .000)	(p = .001)	(p = .035)	(p = .001)	(p = .000)
Democracy^2	—	—	—	.990***	.994**	—
				(p = .007)	(p = .034)	
Protestant	4.51***	2.65**	—	1.93*	—	—
	(p = .000)	(p = .030)		(p = .059)		
Catholic	3.02***	2.56***	—	—	—	—
	(p = .000)	(.001)				
Islam	—	—	—	—	.463***	—
					(p = .000)	
Left executive	—	1.75**	1.77*	—	—	—
		(p = .030)	(p = .053)			
Domestic Institutions producing false negatives						
Common law legal tradition	.326**	.338***	—	.395***	.510***	.507***
	(p = .049)	(p = .000)		(p = .000)	(p = .001)	(p = .003)
Presidential system	—	—	.648***	—	—	—
			(p = .010)			
Ratification process	1.01	.776	—	—	1.03	.847
	(p = .940)	(p = .140)			(p = .879)	(p = .191)
Ratification barriers in democracies	.970	.959**	—	—	.947***	—
	(p = .130)	(p = .037)			(p = .010)	
Federalism	—	.868*	—	1.11**	—	.955
		(p = .098)		(p = .049)		(p = .250)

(continued)

83

Table 3.1 (continued)

Explanatory Variable	ICCPR	ICESCR	CERD	CAT	CEDAW	CRC
Strategic behavior potentially producing false positives						
Regional ratifications	1.01*	1.00	.996	1.01**	1.01	1.01**
	($p = .073$)	($p = .710$)	($p = .578$)	($p = .025$)	($p = .120$)	($p = .029$)
Alternative explanations: World culture						
Embeddedness	—	1.23***	—	1.12**	1.20***	—
		($p = .002$)		($p = .033$)	($p = .001$)	
Average regional political rights	1.43***	—	—	—	—	—
	($p = .008$)					
Regional norm for government role in market	—	.482***	—	—	—	—
		($p = .001$)				
Alternative explanations: Coercion						
Log of GDP/capita (wealth)	.733***	—	—	—	—	.847***
	($p = .008$)					($p = .003$)
Log of GDP (size)	1.11	—	—	—	.916*	—
	($p = .130$)				($p = .086$)	
Overseas development assistance/GDP	—	—	—	.008***	—	—
				($p = .005$)		
Use of IMF credits	.440**	.478***	—	—	.690	—
	($p = .013$)	($p = .003$)			($p = .123$)	
# of countries	117	113	73	138	129	131
# of ratifications	93	83	54	97	118	129
# of observations	1,663	1,438	858	1,430	1,206	450
Prob >χ^2	0.000	0.000	0.000	0.000	0.000	0.000

* Significant at the .10 level; ** significant at the .05 level; *** significant at the .01 level.

Table 3.2. Influences on the Ratification Rate

Cox proportionate hazard model
Hazard ratios, probabilities

Explanatory Variable	ICCPR	ICESCR	CERD	CAT	CEDAW	CRC
Democratic since World War I	2.97* (p = .070)	3.14** (p = .028)	2.83** (p = .048)	.542 (p = .143)	.650 (p = .223)	1.21 (p = .490)
Democratic since World War II	3.14*** (p = .009)	2.83** (p = .015)	3.19*** (p = .004)	.911 (p = .798)	.914 (p = .700)	1.05 (p = .840)
Newly transitioned democracy	2.63** (p = .020)	2.66*** (p = .001)	2.57*** (p = .001)	1.32 (p = .209)	1.58** (p = .035)	1.49** (p = .048)

Note: Analyses include but do not report the same covariates included in Table 3.1, substituting democratic categories for polity and polity.[2]
* Significant at the .10 level; ** significant at the .05 level; *** significant at the .01 level.

the hazard rate decreases and falls below 1 (indicative of a negative effect) for the mature democracies in two of these cases. For the CAT, CEDAW, and CRC, newly transitioned democratic polities are most likely to ratify sooner (see the statistically significant negative result for the nonlinear term "democracy²" in Table 3.1).[75] These treaties were largely ratified once the third wave of democratic transitions was underway. Table 3.2 also indicates the more ready acceptance of the CEDAW and the CRC among newer democracies.

Dominant religion[76] is an imperfect indicator of cultural orientation, but the results of its inclusion also fit expectations reasonably well. Christian countries have tended to ratify these arrangements relatively quickly, although the effect declines for the CAT and disappears for the CERD, CRC, and CEDAW. Results for Catholic countries were in every case in the expected direction (see the complete report of results in Appendix 3.2 on my Web site) but were only statistically significant for the ICCPR and the ICESCR. Protestant countries were two to three times more likely to ratify the ICCPR compared to all other non-Catholic and non-Islamic countries. Muslim countries apparently do not differ much from other cultures, with the almost certain exception of women's rights, which they are significantly slower to support.

Government preferences are also reflected to a limited extent in the ideological orientation of the government actually responsible for ratification. Left governments in each case produced positive hazard ratios, and in two cases, reported in Table 3.1, the ICESCR and the CERD, left governments were consistently statistically significantly more likely to do so.[77] In the case of both the CERD and the ICESCR, left governments were approximately 75 percent more likely than other governments to preside over treaty ratification (hazard ratio of 1.75) and nearly 80 percent more likely to ratify the CERD (hazard ratio of 1.77).[78] Arguably, these results support the notion that governments willing to address nondiscrimination and economic rights – programs often associated with left-wing parties – are in fact most likely to support these treaties.

2. *The Legal System, Institutions, and Ratification*

What is the evidence that domestic institutions might make it difficult or costly for a government to ratify, thus increasing the chances of a false

---

75 Squaring the democracy term tests the hypothesis that the *middle* of the distribution behaves differently than either extreme; the negative relationship in this case means that countries at the extremes of the distribution have a proportionately reduced risk for ratifying.

76 I use the religion practiced by the largest sector of the society.

77 It was necessary in the case of the CERD to use a coding for socialist system rather than the left party measure used in the other specifications. This is because CERD ratification accelerated quite early and the data for the party of the chief executive do not begin until the mid-1970s.

78 In Table 3.2 I eliminated left government from the CERD model even though it is highly statistically significant because data limitations reduce the observations to about half.

negative – a rights-respecting country that delays or refuses to ratify? The most consistent result with respect to domestic institutions' impact on the propensity to ratify human rights treaties is without doubt the nature of the legal system into which the instrument is potentially to be integrated. For five of the six core treaties under consideration here, there is strong evidence that common law countries ratify at a much lower rate than do civil law countries and other legal systems. In the cases of the ICCPR, ICESCR, CAT, CEDAW, and CRC, the effect is highly statistically significant.[79] The effects of the nature of the legal system are substantively significant as well. In the case of the ICESCR, common law countries were about 66 percent less likely to ratify than were countries with other legal systems (the hazard ratio is .338). In the case of the CRC, common law countries were about half as likely to ratify as were civil law countries, according to Table 3.1. These are notable effects, which survive the inclusion of other governmental institutions typically associated with British political culture (parliamentary government and the ratification process, colonial heritage, for example; see Appendix 3.3 on my Web site).[80] The evidence points fairly convincingly to an independent negative effect of common law systems on the likelihood of early treaty ratification.

There is also fairly good evidence that ratification procedures make it much harder for a government that might support a treaty in principle actually to ratify. The requirement of a supermajority or a majority in two chambers apparently has slowed ratification considerably in the cases of the ICESCR and the CEDAW. The interaction term indicates that constitutional hurdles become more constraining where legislatures actually have meaningful input into policymaking in general. This may reflect the fact that legislative advice and consent exact a much higher political cost for a chief executive in countries where that input is most meaningful. Other domestic institutions that might have been expected to reduce the likelihood of ratification – federalism and presidentialism, which introduce subnational veto players and the possibility of divided government – performed far less consistently. Governments in federal systems have been much less likely to ratify the ICESCR, although, surprisingly, they have apparently been more likely to ratify the CAT. One might speculate that the ICESCR's obligations tend to impinge much more on subnational prerogatives (often precisely in the social, economic, and cultural areas) than do the focused prohibitions of the CAT. In one case, the CERD, presidentialism is convincingly associated with a reduced likelihood of ratification. This is consistent with the assumption that parliamentary governments generally face weaker legislative veto players.

---

79 The one exception is the *positive*, though statistically insignificant, effect of the British common law heritage in the case of the CERD.

80 See also Appendix 3.4 on my Web site, which indicates the correlation and degree of overlap between common law and other British-like institutions and associations, including status as a British colony since World War I, parliamentarism, and the nature of ratification hurdles.

3. Strategic Ratification

Finally, consider the evidence of strategic ratification. I have argued that one observable implication of strategic behavior is that governments may tend to ratify these rights agreements late in their terms. It turns out that there is little unconditional evidence of legacy ratifications, and the number of years in a government's term is omitted from Table 3.1. However, a closer look at the data is warranted. There is no reason for legacy ratification to be especially attractive for governments in general, but rather only for those that do not intend to make a significant effort to comply. This suggests that we should see legacy ratifications primarily among governments at the apex of nondemocratic regimes, which are least likely to be willing to make significant institutional and policy changes to implement rights treaties, especially those that empower potential political opponents. To see if this is the case, I examined the effect of the length of time in office with a dummy variable for countries that had never experienced democracy during the entire post–World War II period. The hazard ratios are graphed in Figure 3.5. With the exception of the CERD, which runs in the opposite direction, most of the treaties ratified by nondemocratic countries were more likely to be ratified later in the government's tenure in office. The front bars indicate the hazard rate for a nondemocratic country whose leader is in his or her first year of power. The bars behind indicate the estimated influence on ratification of each additional year in power. With the exception of the CERD and the CAT (for which additional years in power apparently make no difference), autocratic governments are more likely to ratify as their term progresses. This suggests a pattern among nondemocracies of legacy ratification, falling time horizons, and a desire to gain short-term praise while leaving the political consequences to the next government. No such pattern is detectable among democracies.

Regional emulation may also provide a possible explanation for false positives (insincere ratifiers). I have argued that one way to avoid criticism is to practice "social camouflage": Select policies that do not differ significantly from those of surrounding neighbors. Local ratification trends are important because the fewer the holdouts, the more nonratification is interpreted as resistance to the substance of the treaty in question. Local ratification density is also important because the fewer the holdouts, the more focused the pressure campaign to ratify is on the remaining few. On the other hand, nonratification by a large number of countries creates only very diffuse pressure to ratify. Indeed, the expectation of public adherence may be so diffuse as to constitute no social or political pressure at all.

Social camouflage is a rational response to perceived social pressure in a normatively charged situation. It is rational because, for governments that are nearly indifferent with respect to treaty ratification, it can lower the expected costs associated with social criticism. This is not because the signing fools

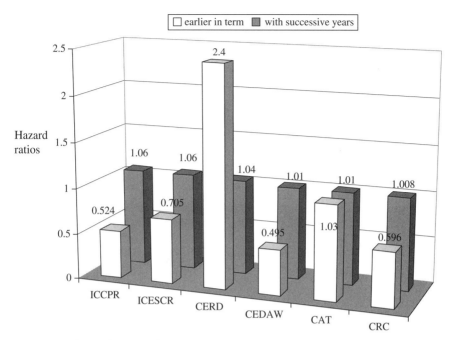

Figure 3.5. The Probability of Nondemocratic Ratification.

anyone about behavior. Rather, it is because moving with the crowd reduces the increment of criticism that can be directed at any particular country.[81] If NGOs have fixed resources and if peer governments are willing to expend a fixed amount of diplomatic effort to influence rights commitments, it is much better to be 1 of 50 countries that have not ratified a treaty rather than 1 of 5. In most cases, the benefits of socially motivated ratification will not be great enough to overcome domestically generated preferences, but at the margins it could produce false positives. The more some crucial reference group ratifies a particular treaty, the greater the pressure for any individual government to do so.[82]

---

81 One possible analogy in the natural world is the phenomenon of fish traveling in schools. This is a highly successful strategy for protection from predators. Swimming in schools makes it difficult for a predator to concentrate on catching any particular fish; the predator's effort is dissipated and the schooling fish have improved their chances of survival.

82 Research in sociology suggests that conformity-seeking behavior is strongest among middle-status actors. For example, concerning the practices of Silicon Valley firms, see Phillips and Zuckerman 2001.

Exactly what constitutes a "crucial reference group" is open to much debate.[83] In the human rights area, I would argue that the region in which a country is situated is theoretically most relevant to the decision to make a treaty commitment. For one thing, conditions at the regional level foster the kind of cooperation that helps to keep group members in step with one another. Regional organizations – the European Union (EU) and the Organization of American States (OAS), for example – create the structures in which governments have repeat transactions over economic issues, security issues, and social issues. In some regions, dense and long-term interactions are encouraged through a multiplicity of overlapping regional associations of various kinds. These structures facilitate intensely shared common knowledge, which further improves the ability of states in the region to coordinate. In addition, the majority of NGOs are either region-ally focused[84] or, if they are global, have regional "desks" or "watches."[85] If the social pressure is regionally organized, as it tends to be in the human rights area, regional camouflage is rational governmental behavior.

The ratio of countries within one's own region that have ratified the treaty in question is therefore a reasonable proxy for pressures governments may feel to coordinate their ratification behavior with that of nearby governments. By this measure, there is some evidence of regional pressures to ratify. Ratification of the ICCPR, CAT, and CRC (and possibly the CEDAW as well) clusters in a significant way by region. The ratio of regional ratifications in these cases is positively signed and statistically significant. I have theorized these patterns as strategic in nature – that is, as resulting from a logic of consequences rather than a logic of appropriate-ness – but the unconditional proportionate hazard rates for the density of regional ratifications alone cannot easily distinguish strategic from more normative behavior. A cautious norms scholar might look at these regional clustering results and warn of premature theoretical closure: After all, the correlation is consistent with models of normative cascades and socialization within regions as well.

4. Regional Clustering: Strategic Behavior or Localized Socialization?

By taking the context of this regional clustering into account, we can draw some inferences about whether regional clustering is driven primarily by normative or

---

83 See, for example, the discussion in Simmons and Elkins 2004.
84 Skjelsbaek 1971.
85 Human Rights Watch is a quintessential example. See http://www.hrw.org/. The examples, of course, extend beyond the human rights area. For example, the International Campaign to Ban Landmines (ICBL) targets particular regions in their campaign for ratification of the Landmine Treaty of 1997. In 2000, the focus was on Africa. See "Ratification Campaign: Urge African Countries to Ratify the Landmines Treaty by 1 March 2000!!!!" http://www.icbl.org/action/africaim2000.html (accessed 23 December 2003). The Persian Gulf states as a group were tar-geted by their campaign for ratification in 2003. See "Gulf States Urged to Do More to Eradicate Landmines," Sharjah, 8 December 2003, ICBL Web site, http://www.icbl.org/ (accessed 23 December 2003).

strategic behavior. One way to do so is to ask whether reasonable prerequisites are in place for regional socialization to take place. With relatively little evidence, we want to infer what is driving the regional ratification influences discussed earlier. Context matters here: If you hear animal hooves in Wyoming, you should guess their source is horses; in the Serengeti, if you hear similar sounds, you should guess zebras. Our exercise here is similar: There are some contexts in which regional ratification clustering is more likely to indicate strategic behavior, and there are others where it is more likely to indicate genuine social convergence. Where the conditions that support socialization are strong, these correlations are likely to represent true normative behavior, the result of regional interactions that foster learning, persuasion, and internalization. But if positive regional correlations are strong under conditions that socialization theory suggests *are not* conducive to socialization, the same positive correlation should be interpreted as something else: strategic behavior.

First, regionalization is more likely where regional human rights standards are clearest. Socialization theory suggests that governments are more likely to become socialized if the normative standard in question is relatively clear. Where actual human rights practices are highly divergent, it is difficult to know what the standard is, let alone to feel the persuasive pull of that standard. This suggests that we look directly at the degree of normative convergence in the region over time. I use the Political Rights indicator created by Freedom House and take the *variance* (standard deviation) on this measure by region, by year. For ease of interpretation, I invert the measure (so that higher numbers indicate normative convergence within the region) and normalize the lowest value to zero. This measure is then multiplied by the density of regional ratifications. This interaction captures the influence of regional ratifications on the decision to ratify as actual practices converge. The socialization hypothesis predicts a *positive* coefficient, because socialization behavior should increase as values within the region converge. Strategic behavior, on the other hand, should not be especially sensitive to the degree of normative convergence within the region. The interaction of regional normative convergence and regional ratification behavior should be zero.

Second, regional socialization is more likely where socialization opportunities are high. We should expect regional clustering to reflect socialization where governments have frequent persuasive opportunities to convince other governments to take seriously a particular moral position. Such opportunities create interactions that can be important in the process of norm internalization. *If we observe regional effects in a highly socialized milieu, the observed effects can reasonably be interpreted as normative rather than strategic in nature.* As the world culture literature emphasizes, every conference on human rights can be thought of as a socialization opportunity. One indicator of an environment rich in socialization opportunities is the number of human rights treaties that already exist in the region. By most accounts, the process of treaty drafting, negotiation, and bargaining creates persuasive opportunities that play an important role in eventual norm internalization.[86] If we observe strong and positive regional effects in such contexts, a case can be made that ratification behavior reflects the normative consensus that tends to emerge from such processes.

For each region, I created a count of the number of resolutions, treaties, statutes, and other legally relevant instruments relating to human rights under regional designations listed by the University of Minnesota Human Rights Library Web site.[87] This count variable (representing the density of normative opportunities within the region) is interacted with the regional ratification density for each treaty. As such, it captures the effect of regional ratifications as socialization becomes more intensive within the region. A positive coefficient – greater influence at the regional level as persuasive opportunities increase – would be more indicative of socialization than strategic behavior.

A third way to pry apart strategic from normative behavior is to look at regional effects over time. Socialization takes time. Strategic behavior can be practically instantaneous. Therefore, the passage of time should produce two very distinct consequences for normative versus strategic behavior. On the one hand, we should expect regional ratification behavior that reflects socialization to intensify over time as values within the region begin to converge. The opposite should be true of strategic behavior, which should diminish over time. The reason is that better information about governments' true intentions is more likely to be revealed over time, reducing the typically ephemeral payoff to strategic ratification to virtually nothing. As time passes, the information environment about human rights practices within a region more closely resembles complete information, reducing any benefit a government might expect from insincere ratification. The intuition is that socialization takes time, whereas strategic ratification loses its value over time, as it is revealed for what it is. This idea can be tested by grouping the yearly data into separate observation periods. These periods can then be interacted with regional ratification behavior. *If positive regional effects are stronger in the earlier period, they should be interpreted as strategic.* If they are stronger in the later period, they are much more likely to be the result of normative convergence.

Finally, we can assess the hypothesis that regional mimicry is strategic by examining the information environment directly. Normative socialization should thrive where information flows most freely. Strategic ratification makes sense only when it is hard to detect. Where information is thin and it is difficult to distinguish the sincerity of the commitment, it may be possible to gain short-term benefits from strategic ratification. If regional effects are strongest in countries with a press that is free from government control, socialization

---

86 See, for example, the discussion in Chayes and Chayes 1993.
87 The treaties were downloaded from http://www1.umn.edu/humanrts/instree/ainstls1.htm (accessed 11 August 2008). The Americas and Africa are self-evident descriptions, but Europe is not obvious. I take the region "Europe" to include all the members of the Council of Europe.

may indeed be the explanation. But where the press is muzzled, the government may have incentives to follow the region and ratify strategically. By interacting an average measure of press freedom for each region with the density of regional ratification, we can measure the effects of ratification by others in the region as the information environment improves. If regional emulation is strongest where information is better, the emulation itself is more likely to reflect socialization than strategic ratification. Therefore, strategic behavior is more consistent with positive regional clustering in regions where press freedom tends to be low.

The results of these tests are shown in Figure 3.6. Here I compare graphically the hazard ratios for regional influences by context (based on models developed in Table 3.1). The evidence that regional ratification effects reflect normative socialization is weak at best. The strongest evidence against the socialization hypothesis is depicted in Figure 3.6a. Surely socialization theory should expect regional mimicry to be stronger when there is actually more convergence on values within the region. Genuine regional socialization should be much more difficult when governments in the region have widely divergent practices. But that is almost certainly not the implication for ratification of the ICCPR and the CAT, at least. When regional norms (measured as actual political rights practices) are most *dispersed* (rear bars), the hazard ratio for regional ratifications of these two treaties is strong and positive, which is much more consistent with a strategic than a normative explanation for ratification. The interaction term suggests that regional ratifications have a negative effect when norms are converging (front bars) – a finding not predicted by socialization theory.

More doubt is cast on the socialization hypothesis by Figure 3.6b. Socialization should be highest in regions that have more conferences and reach more agreements about human rights. The evidence for all six treaties is fairly clearly to the contrary. Regional effects are much stronger where socialization opportunities as measured by regional human rights agreements are zero (the rear bars). As regional socialization opportunities become more intense, regional emulation tends to be nonexistent or even negative (the front bars). These findings should encourage us to interpret regional effects as largely strategic in nature rather than the result of processes of socialization.

Throwing the socialization account into further doubt are the findings with respect to the passage of time. The socialization hypothesis predicts stronger positive results in later periods. Strategic theory predicts the opposite: As information improves, insincere ratifiers are revealed, and incentives to ratify strategically decline. The results graphed in Figure 3.6c suggest just the opposite. Regional effects are positive and strong before 1989 (hazard ratios represented by the rear bars) and strong and negative thereafter (front bars), with the exception of the CRC. This temporal pattern of early regional similarities followed by a reversal in regional effects is much more likely to be a reflection of the

a

Regional effects, by degree of normative convergence

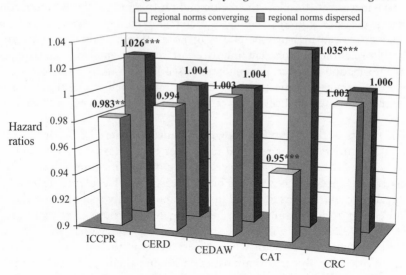

b   ### Regional effects, by varying levels of regional socialization opportunities

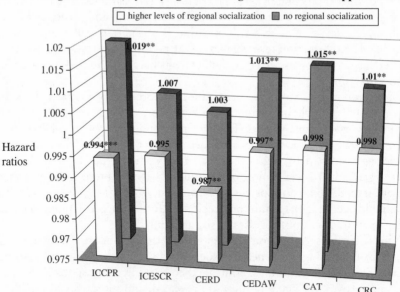

Figure 3.6 a–d. Regional Effects: Socialization or Strategic Behavior? * Significant at the
.10 level; ** significant at the .05 level; *** significant at the .01 level. *Note*: analyses
include but do not report the same covariates for each treaty included in Table 3.1.

c

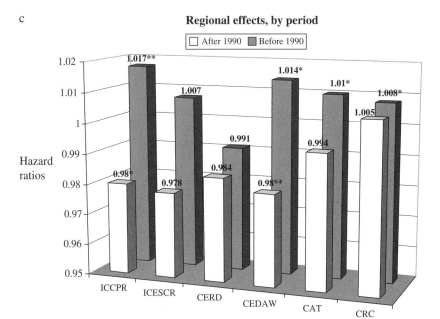

Regional effects, by period

d **Regional effects, with differing levels of information**

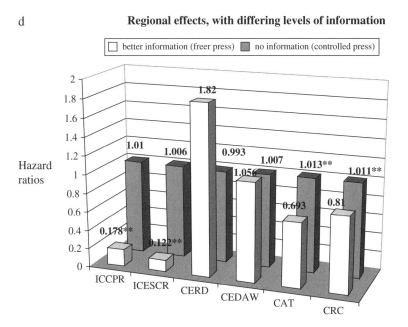

Figure 3.6 a–d. (*continued*)

breakdown of strategic behavior as accountability mechanisms improved rather than a reflection of regional socialization.

Information seems to play a fairly systematic role in the strategic ratification behavior of governments as well. Figure 3.6d shows that with the stark exceptions of the CERD and the CEDAW, governments that control the press (rear bars) are much more likely to follow regional ratification trends than are those that allow press freedom (front bars). In the case of the ICCPR and the ICESCR, regional effects are strongly negative when information flows the most freely. The cases of the CRC and CEDAW fit expectations best: Strategic ratification is apparent when information is thin but it dwindles as information improves.

To conclude this section: A close look at the context suggests that regional ratification "emulation" is much more likely to be strategic than normatively driven. Like the sound of hooves, the indicator is crude, but the context is quite revealing. It is far more likely that the regional effects displayed in Table 3.1 reflect the strategic calculations of states rather than their genuine conversion to higher human rights standards. This point should be placed in its broader perspective, however. Governments ratify human rights treaties primarily because they value their contents and plan to abide by their provisions, as indicated by the strong positive findings on democracy, some cultural indicators (religion), and government ideological orientation (left-leaning governments). However, this analysis has also successfully identified reasons for false negatives (domestic institutions) and false positives (strategic behavior). The fact that treaty ratification is not a perfect reflection of preferences is a crucial point: It provides an opportunity to identify compliance models (Chapters 5–8) that allow for the theoretical possibility that treaties constrain behavior as well as screen out parties that are not interested in trying to comply.[88]

5. How Robust? Alternative Explanations for Ratification

Many other conditions could have an influence over the ratification decision, but the basic findings discussed here are robust to a wide range of alternatives. Rather than discussing one possible confounding factor after another, it is useful to think in terms of theoretically coherent clusters of conditions that could potentially influence governments' ratification decisions. One possibility is suggested by sociology: the idea of the spread of world culture, which leads governments to make similar institutional choices as they worship at the feet of a globally appealing concept of modernity. In the human rights area, scholars with a world culture perspective have claimed that dominant Western ideals can be transmitted through international meetings, normative discussions of

---

88 Simmons and Hopkins 2005.

the kind alluded to previously, and other forms of unchanneled global influences. To address these possibilities, I test for the independent impact of the density of global ratifications, the timing of meetings of UN-sponsored meetings of particular import (e.g., the Women's Conference in Beijing, 1995; for a list of conferences see Appendix 3.6 on my Web site), and a measure of treaty "embeddedness." The last measure is meant to absorb a "culture of legalization" that may be perceived to be an important part of modern Western culture. It is the sum of each country's ratification status on preferential trade agreements and memberships, three multilateral environmental treaties, and status as a party to the Vienna Convention on Treaties. After all, it is possible that some governments ratify human rights treaties because they have bought nto the "script" that holds up the legalization of agreements in treaty form as the most modern form of international interaction. The findings on these variables are in Appendix 3.3 on my Web site[89] and the most important influences are recorded in Table 3.1. Only the legal embeddedness measure performs as world culture theory suggests it should; none of these variables disturbs the basic findings about government preferences, institutions, and strategic behavior. While these tests are barely more than lip service, they do serve to increase confidence that the basic findings are quite stable across specifications.

Another concern could arise from that mainstay of international relations, coercion. It is difficult to think of a good reason that one state would want to coerce another into a human rights treaty. As I will argue, these agreements gain their political legitimacy largely because they are thought to be commitments freely made. Moreover, coercion is not costless, and forcing a state to enter into a treaty encounters the same kinds of collective action problems (to be discussed in Chapter 4) as treaty enforcement itself. Nonetheless, the asymmetries inherent in international relations make it prudent to examine at least some plausible channels of coercive influence. Smaller, poor states, especially those dependent on the favors of wealthier patrons, may be most vulnerable to such pressures. Former colonies may in theory be vulnerable to the suggestions of their erstwhile colonizers or may be (unduly?) influenced by the commitment of the mother country itself, but the data never bore this out. Indicators meant to capture such vulnerabilities performed poorly. Where they do produce results, the direction tends to be counterintuitive from a coercion perspective. The finding that larger countries may ($p = .15$) have tended to ratify the ICCPR more readily than smaller ones, as well as the finding that governments that take aid from the IMF or other donors tend to delay or eschew ratification, does not fit a theory that postulates a coercive regime into which the most vulnerable are corraled by the powerful.

---

89 http://scholar.iq.harvard.edu/bsimmons/mobilizing-for-human-rights.

Customized Commitments: Reservations

Treaty ratification is not the end of the commitment story. Governments have options to "customize" their commitments through the use of reservations and declarations. The nature of the reservations they make can have a significant impact on the precise nature of the legal obligation each government commits to undertake.[90] Reservations are an important way to reconcile an international obligation with domestic law. They also allow a government to join in a multi-lateral endeavor while registering a set of preferences or constraints that may differ somewhat from those elaborated in a treaty obligation, subject to the limitation of remaining consistent with the basic purposes of the agreement as a whole.[91]

Reservations, understandings, and declarations (or "RUDs," as they are sometimes referred to in the legal literature) are typically made at the time of ratification. Reservations are usually not accepted after ratification has taken place, and only occasionally are they removed. Parties to each agreement have an oppor-tunity to protest a state's reservations, though, in effect, a very small number of countries take on this policing role.[92] Reservations are important because they have a bearing on a country's legal commitment and because, in some cases, they are a clue to the politics of commitment.

Since sovereign governments have the option to enter reservations to these six treaties, one might suspect that the practice is rampant.[93] However, most governments that ratify treaties do not enter reservations of any kind. The countries listed in Section a of Table 3.3 have signed all six treaties and have not registered any objections to *any* of the 226 separate articles to which they have committed their polity. The countries in Section b of the table have ratified four or five of the six core treaties and similarly have not entered reservations in an attempt to sculpt their obligations. Nonreservers are concentrated in Africa and Latin America. Among wealthy Western countries (for example, those that are members of the Organization for Economic Co-operation and Develop-ment [OECD]), only Portugal has signed a majority of the treaties without reserving any of its rights.

Reservation making can provide further information about the nature of treaty commitment behavior.[94] Granted, it looks as though the making of reservations has

90 Reservations have been studied extensively in the legal literature, largely in order to explicate and clarify the rules of treaty law and, in some cases, to make recommendations about how it is to be applied. Studies exist on the reservations made to each of the treaties examined here. For example, on the CEDAW, see Arat 2002.

91 Vienna Convention on the Law of Treaties, Section 2, Article 19(c).

92 The Nordic countries are consistently active in protesting reservations they believe to be con-trary to the meaning and purpose of the treaty. See Klabbers 2000.

93 Many scholars of reservations are worried that they will weaken the treaty commitment as a whole. See, for example, Lijnzaad 1995.

94 The literature on why states enter reservations is sparse and quite speculative. See Coccia 1985:18–22; Shelton 1983.

Table 3.3. Nonreservers

a. Countries that have signed all six core human rights treaties but have never entered reservations or made declarations

Africa	Central Asia	East Asia	Europe	Latin America/ Caribbean
Benin	Armenia	Cambodia	Albania	Bolivia
Burkina Faso	Azerbaijan	Philippines	Estonia	Colombia
Burundi	Kyrgyz Republic		Georgia	Costa Rica
Cameroon	Tajikistan		Latvia	Honduras
Cape Verde	Turkmenistan		Lithuania	Peru
Chad	Uzbekistan		Moldova	St. Vincent
Cote d'Ivoire			Portugal	Uruguay
Gabon			Yugoslavia	
Malawi			Macedonia	
Namibia				
Nigeria				
Senegal				
Seychelles				
Sierra Leone				
Togo				

b. Countries that have signed four or five core human rights treaties but have never entered reservations or made declarations

Africa	Central Asia	East Asia	Europe	Latin America/ Caribbean
Angola	Kazakhstan	Solomon Islands	San Marino	Dominican Republic
Central African Republic				Dominica
Congo (Zaire)				Grenada
Eritrea				Haiti
Guinea-Bissau				Nicaragua
Somalia				Paraguay
Sudan				Surinam
Tanzania				
Zimbabwe				

a good deal to do with state capacity. But controlling for basic developmental conditions, we should expect reservations largely to support the theoretical claims about preferences, domestic institutions, and regionally conditioned behavior. That is, in most cases, reservations should reflect values and culture. They might also reflect the difficulties associated with domestic legal integration: Common law systems should be expected to display evidence in their reservation-making of the struggle to make the treaty compatible with local law, for example. If states continue their strategic behavior to shape social meanings, we might also expect a high degree of regional similarity in the kinds of reservations made.

Consider first the threshold question of what influences the probability that a state will enter one or more reservations when it ratifies one of these six treaties.[95] Pooling the information across all six treaties, Table 3.4a reports the factors associated with reservation-making (conditional on ratifying the treaty). The unit of analysis here is a "country ratification episode." In Model 1, ordinary least squares regression is used, and the dependent variable is the log of the total number of articles against which a country has reserved. In Model 2, logistical regression is used, and the dependent variable is whether or not a ratifying country has entered at least one reservation or reservation-like understanding or declaration. Note that in contrast to the hazard models used previously, the coefficients reported here take on positive as well as negative values.

The results of these tests are striking. First, while treaty ratification could never be shown to be consistently linked to a country's developmental status, reservation-making much more clearly is. The higher a country's per capita gross domestic product (GDP), the more likely it is to enter a reservation upon ratification. This most likely reflects the fact that combing through a treaty to search for conflicts with domestic law requires both resources and expertise that many of the poorer countries do not have or cannot spare. It is possible to conclude from this that reservations are, in practical rather than legal terms, the prerogative of the rich. Poor countries are far less likely to exercise their sovereign right to reserve than are their wealthier counterparts.

---

95 Of course, the six human rights treaties under examination here differ with respect to governments' reservation patterns. More than half of the 147 governments that have ratified have made at least one reservation to the ICCPR, while about a third of the much larger number that have ratified the CEDAW, CERD, and CRC have entered reservations. There is also evidence, however, that normative convergence differs across these treaties. Where specific articles are mentioned, it is possible to calculate just how much agreement there is among governments that obligations under these articles should be accepted or conditioned. For example, conditional upon making any reservation at all, the chances that any two governments will make reservations concerning the same article are about 68% for the ICCPR. Appendix 3.5 on my Web site shows that most of these reservations have to do with Art. 14, which relates to fair trials. At first blush, the concentration of reservations looks higher for both the CAT (.71) and the CEDAW (.95), but reservation concentration falls drastically if one disregards a single lightning rod for disagreement in each of these (dispute settlement to be handled by the International Court of Justice). When such a dispute settlement clause is excluded from the calculations (along with the governments for which it was their sole reservation), the ICCPR emerges as the treaty with the highest concentration of reservations, while the reservations made in the case of the CERD and the CRC demonstrate the highest degree of heterogeneity. The fact that reservations for these two treaties tend to be "all over the map" may be taken as an indicator of a higher degree of normative divergence with respect to these treaties' obligations.

Table 3.4a. Reservations

Ordinary least squares and logistical regression, probabilities based on robust standard errors

Explanatory Variable	Model 1: OLS Regression. Dependent Variable: Log of the Number of Articles Specifically Affected by Reservations		Model 2: Logistical Regression. Dependent Variable: Whether or Not a Government Made a Reservation at All	
Constant	−.298 ($p = .197$)	−.329** ($p = .032$)	−4.61*** ($p = .000$)	−4.73*** ($p = .000$)
GDP per capita, logged	.079** ($p = .023$)	.083*** ($p = .000$)	.229* ($p = .090$)	.431*** ($p = .000$)
Density of regional reservations	.807*** ($p = .005$)	.762*** ($p = .000$)	4.42*** ($p = .000$)	4.00*** ($p = .000$)
Common law legal tradition	.172*** ($p = .006$)	.164*** ($p = .001$)	.654** ($p = .022$)	.448* ($p = .052$)
Islam	.123* ($p = .080$)	.076** ($p = .041$)	.959*** ($p = .008$)	.231 ($p = .357$)
Democratic	−.025*** ($p = .001$)	−.011** ($p = .022$)	−.072 ($p = .127$)	−.082** ($p = .013$)
Rule of law	.064*** ($p = .001$)	—	.378*** ($p = .001$)	—
# of observations	413	694	413	694
R^2	.28	.21	.25	.17

Note: All models include but do not report treaty fixed effects. All models are conditional on having ratified the treaty.
* Significant at the .10 level; ** significant at the .05 level; *** significant at the .01 level.

Second, we see continued evidence that treaty behavior reflects state preferences. In most models, the more democratic the ratifying country, the less likely it was to enter a reservation. Moreover, the evidence in Table 3.4a suggests that this is because democracies tend to prefer the contents of the treaty, not simply that they are more law-oriented. Having a reputation as a rule-of-law state independently *increases* the probability of adding reservations upon ratification. This is not very surprising: After all, polities that place a very high value on the rule of law are likely to be especially careful about the precise nature of the legal obligations into which they enter.[96] But this renders the net effect of democratic governance especially telling: Once we have controlled for the cautiousness flowing from the likelihood that the law will in fact be enforced, democracies still are less likely to customize their treaty commitments. This provides further evidence that democracies tend to favor the *contents* of these treaties, and their reservation behavior reflects this preference.

Muslim countries also have an especially high tendency to add reservations to their ratifications. Once again, this supports a preference-oriented explanation of treaty behavior. In important ways, respect for Shari'a has made these agreements more difficult to ratify without fairly widespread reservations, as has been noted by a number of scholars, especially with respect to women's rights (see Chapter 5). But the results in Table 3.4a suggest that even when we control for the nature of the treaty (systematic differences between treaties are controlled for in these models with a series of treaty dummies; not reported here), predominantly Muslim countries are more likely to enter reservations to human rights treaties than are countries that are not predominantly Muslim. This reflects the fact that these governments are not simply posturing for international kudos, but are to some degree trying to make their international commitments fit their cultural conceptions of justice.

Finally, there is very strong evidence of the influence of common law systems on treaty behavior. Previously, we saw that common law countries were much slower than others to ratify these treaties. I argued that this is because of the costs that actors in common law countries associate with importing an externally negotiated political agreement into the local precedent-based system. Table 3.4a displays evidence consistent with this mechanism. Common law countries spend a great deal of time and effort customizing their treaty commitment to fit their local largely case-based law. The results of that effort show up in their reservations, which tend to far outnumber those of other legal systems. That the common law result remains once we have controlled for regime type, developmental level, rule

---

96 This is a point made by, among others, Arthur Rovine during his tenure as legal adviser to the U.S. Department of State. See Rovine 1981:fn. 57.

of law, and regional practices makes it far more believable that it is the nature of the legal system itself that produces both tardy and highly conditioned treaty commitments.

Of course, not all reservations are of the same nature, and it is important to know whether these results are an artifact of a simple count of the affected articles. Accordingly, each country's reservations were read and coded for *breadth*, effect on *enforceability*, and claims relating to *capacity* to comply. The basic story holds up in very convincing ways when analyzing specific *kinds* of reservations (Table 3.4b).

Cultural preferences show up in the strong tendency for Muslim-dominated countries to make reservations of every kind (especially with respect to the CEDAW) *except* those based on capacity. Reservations by these governments tend to be principled rather than expedient. We can see the effort by more highly developed countries to carefully compare treaty commitments with various aspects of their national law: Wealth was associated with the most specific form of reservation-making, both in the form of specific exceptions and with specific references to national codes. The common law effect shows up across all reservation types, but because common law countries are more concerned with how treaties fit into their body of case law, there is practically no relationship to reservations referencing specific national codes.

Finally, the regional effects persist to a remarkable extent. The results reported in Table 3.4b indicate that one of the most important influences on the type of reservation a country makes is the *density of that specific type of reservation in the region*. This is likely true of specific reservations and likely ($p = .148$) true of broad reservations as well. It is almost certainly true of reservations that attempt to reduce the ability to enforce the treaty or certain of its provisions. Governments have the clearest incentive to follow prevailing cultural norms in this regard if they are less than enthusiastic about the overall contents of the treaty. The more other countries in the region have opted for reduced enforceability, the more likely a particular country is to do so as well. This kind of behavior is precisely in line with the social camouflage that I have argued could lead to false positive commitments to a treaty regime in the first place.

Beyond Ratification: Recognizing International Authority

When governments decide to commit themselves to an international treaty regime, ratification of the basic treaty is the primary concern. However, four of the conventions under examination – the ICCPR, CERD, CEDAW, and CAT – have optional protocols by which governments precommit to recognize the authority of an international implementing authority to hear complaints brought by individuals and to express official views on whether the state party's

Table 3.4b. Types of Reservations

Dependent variable: whether or not each country has entered at least one reservation of the following type
Logistical regression, probabilities based on robust standard errors

Explanatory Variable	Model 1: Broad	Model 2: Specific	Model 3: National Code	Model 4: Capacity	Model 5: Reduce Enforcement
Constant	-8.31*** (p = .000)	-9.60*** (p = .000)	-6.59*** (p = .000)	-5.09*** (p = .006)	-6.81*** (p = .000)
GDP per capita, logged	.437* (p = .060)	.765*** (p = .000)	.544** (p = .013)	-.223 (p = .465)	.249 (p = .184)
Density of regional reservations	2.03 (p = .148)	2.78* (p = .079)	-.086 (p = .967)	-.686 (p = .741)	4.32*** (p = .000)
Islam	2.78*** (p = .000)	1.06* (p = .074)	1.08** (p = .038)	-.200 (p = .824)	1.47*** (p = .007)
Common law legal tradition	1.002** (p = .023)	.919* (p = .014)	-.091 (p = .806)	2.74*** (p = .000)	.806** (p = .050)
Democracy	-.014 (p = .830)	-.031 (p = .590)	-.022 (p = .702)	.082 (p = .389)	-.035 (p = .548)
Rule of law	.099 (p = .583)	.350** (p = .030)	.305** (p = .033)	.543** (p = .049)	.160 (p = .272)
# of observations	413	413	413	341	350
Pseudo R^2	.29	.37	.23	.25	.28

Note: All models include but do not report treaty fixed effects. All models are conditional on having ratified the treaty.
Types of reservations are defined as follows:

1. *Broad reservations.* These include such things as broad references to religious law or national constitutions. They also include broad statements about the domestic status of the treaty (e.g., that it is not self-executing).

2. *Specific reservations.* These make reference to specific obligations under the treaty, usually mentioning an article or a subclause. They carve out a specific arena in which a national practice, should it be interpreted by others to conflict with a specific clause of the treaty, would be construed as consistent with or excepted from the article or clause in question.

3. *National code reservations.* These refer to specific sections of the national code or specific elements of the constitution. These kinds of reservations are similar to specific reservations in that they make a clear effort to name and delimit the excepted practices. In this case, however, they do so with very specific references to elements of the national code or constitution.

4. *Capacity reservations.* In some cases, governments justify reservations based on a claimed inability to implement the obligation in question. Often these reservations are based on resource limitations. Sometimes capacity reservations make general references to the "impracticality" of implementing a particular reservation under "current circumstances."

5. *Enforcement reducing reservations.* These reservations are designed to reduce the possibility that the obligation will be enforced in a domestic court of law or by an international tribunal or other authority.

* Significant at the .10 level; ** significant at the .05 level; *** significant at the .01 level.

practices in fact constitute treaty violations.[97] Only the ICCPR contains the further option of committing to allow other *states* to lodge violation complaints with the UN Human Rights Committee (though it has never been exercised).[98] By examining governments' willingness to take on commitments that progressively expose them to greater authoritative external scrutiny, we can get a clearer picture of what factors contribute to high commitment levels.

The first column of Table 3.5 shows that it is very hard to get empirical traction on why states agree to give their peers a right of complaint. But the evidence suggests that, as has been the case whenever civil and political rights are involved, mature democracies may be more likely to make commitments ($p = .11$). They are more than two times more likely to commit to the ICCPR state complaint system than are autocracies, and are probably much more willing to allow foreign sovereign complaints than are newer democracies. Religious culture weakly follows the basic patterns we have seen elsewhere, in this case with the strongest impact associated with Protestant countries, which are more than

97 OP I of the ICCPR, for example, specifies that "A State Party to the Covenant that becomes a party to the present Protocol recognizes the competence of the Committee to receive and consider communications from individuals subject to its jurisdiction who claim to be victims of a violation by that State Party of any of the rights set forth in the Covenant. No communication shall be received by the Committee if it concerns a State Party to the Covenant which is not a party to the present Protocol. . . ." Optional Protocol to the International Covenant on Civil and Political Rights, G.A. res. 2200A (XXI), 21 U.N. GAOR Supp. (No. 16) at 59, U.N. Doc. A/6316 (1966), 999 U.N.T.S. 302, *entered into force* 23 March 1976. For a discussion of how this mechanism works, see De Zayas et al. 1985. The OP of the CEDAW provides that "A State Party to the present Protocol . . . recognizes the competence of the Committee on the Elimination of Discrimination against Women . . . to receive and consider communications . . . submitted by or on behalf of individuals or groups of individuals, under the jurisdiction of a State Party, claiming to be victims of a violation of any of the rights set forth in the Convention by that State Party." Articles 1 and 2, Optional Protocol to the Convention on the Elimination of Discrimination against Women, G.A. res. 54/4, annex, 54 U.N. GAOR Supp. (No. 49) at 5, U.N. Doc. A/54/49 (Vol. I) (2000), *entered into force* 22 December 2000. In the case of the CERD, a similar option is spelled out in Article 14, which reads: "A State Party may at any time declare that it recognizes the competence of the Committee to receive and consider communications from individuals or groups of individuals within its jurisdiction claiming to be victims of a violation by that State Party of any of the rights set forth in this Convention. . . ." Article 14, International Convention on the Elimination of All Forms of Racial Discrimination, 660 U.N.T.S. 195, *entered into force* 4 January 1969. Similarly, the CAT contains a provision for optionally establishing such an obligation. According to Article 22: "A State Party to this Convention may at any time declare under this article that it recognizes the competence of the Committee to receive and consider communications from or on behalf of individuals subject to its jurisdiction who claim to be victims of a violation by a State Party of the provisions of the Convention." G.A. res. 39/46, annex, 39 U.N. GAOR Supp. (No. 51) at 197, U.N. Doc. A/39/51 (1984), *entered into force* 26 June 1987.

98 This option is contained in Article 41: "A State Party to the present Covenant may at any time declare under this article that it recognizes the competence of the Committee to receive and consider communications to the effect that a State Party claims that another State Party is not fulfilling its obligations under the present Covenant. Communications under this article may be received and considered only if submitted by a State Party which has made a declaration recognizing in regard to itself the competence of the Committee. No communication shall be received by the Committee if it concerns a State Party which has not made such a declaration. . . ." G.A. res. 2200A (XXI), 21 U.N. GAOR Supp. (No. 16) at 52, U.N. Doc. A/6316 (1966), 999 U.N.T.S. 171, *entered into force* 23 March 1976.

Table 3.5. Recognition of International Authority to Rule on Complaints

Dependent Variable: declaration or ratification accepting optional obligations under the following articles or protocols
Cox proportionate hazard model
Hazard ratios probabilities

Explanatory Variable	State-to-State Right of Complaint		Individual Right of Complaint							
	ICCPR Art. 41.		ICCPR OP I		CERD Art. 14		CAT Art. 22		CEDAW OP	
Democratic since World War I	2.55	($p = $ .110)	3.58**	($p = $ .026)	6.34**	($p = $ .032)	2.95	($p = $ .170)	3.00	($p = $ .107)
Democratic since World War II	.976	($p = $ .973)	2.28**	($p = $ .089)	4.45**	($p = $ .04)	1.51	($p = $ .550)	3.06	($p = $ .054)
Newly transitioned democracy	1.58	($p = $ .482)	3.28***	($p = $ .000)	1.90	($p = $ .353)	4.88***	($p = $ .005)	2.28*	($p = $ .046)
Common law legal tradition	.529	($p = $ .181)	.509*	($p = $ .065)	.119***	($p = $ .001)	.458*	($p = $ .081)	.617	($p = $ .302)
Left executive	—		2.03***	($p = $ .007)	—		1.72	($p = $ .170)	—	
Log GDP	1.16	($p = $ .147)	.806***	($p = $ .004)	1.07	($p = $ .613)	1.21*	($p = $ .062)	1.01	($p = $ .830)
GDP/capita	1.00	($p = $ .920)	1.00	($p = $ .260)	.999	($p = $ .168)	1.0001*	($p = $ .056)	.999	($p = $ .111)
Protestant	3.31**	($p = $ .038)	1.44	($p = $ .473)	3.42*	($p = $ .067)	1.15	($p = $ .830)	2.20	($p = $ .157)
Catholic	1.15	($p = $ .782)	1.90**	($p = $ .041)	1.83	($p = $ .258)	.850	($p = $ .756)	2.45**	($p = $ .015)
Islam	.488	($p = $ .346)	.602	($p = $ .182)	.802	($p = $ .791)	1.14	($p = $ .847)	1.67	($p = $ .262)
Regional ratifications	1.02*	($p = $ .095)	1.018***	($p = $ .002)	1.34**	($p = $ .016)	1.04*	($p = $ .09)	1.04***	($p = $ .000)
# of countries	149		134		144		149		154	
# of ratifications	37		70		29		35		45	
# of observations	3,677		2,097		3,465		1,854		569	
Prob >χ^2	0.000		0.000		0.000		0.000		0.000	

* Significant at the .10 level; ** significant at the .05 level; *** significant at the .01 level.

three times more likely to ratify Article 41 (signifying their willingness to accept the authority of the UN Human Rights Committee to hear state complaints) than are governments of other non-Christian and non-Muslim societies. The power of regional practices once again is noticeable: Ratifications of Article 41 in a region almost certainly have a strong positive effect on a given country's ratification. A 1 percentage point increase in the proportion of countries ratifying in the region raises the probability that another country in that region will do so by perhaps 2 percent (hazard ratio 1.02). Several indicators that could reflect other external influences, such as relative size, a high degree of dependence on foreign aid, and a high-visibility UN conference on a related topic had no effect.[99]

When governments accept optional obligations to allow individuals to complain about violations before an authoritative body of the international community, they expose themselves to even further scrutiny. Individual standing is potentially an important mechanism for helping to hold a state accountable for its treaty compliance.[100] Four of the treaties under examination have such optional mechanisms, though a minority of parties to each treaty have actually agreed to be thus bound. Unlike the state complaint mechanism discussed previously, individuals have been far less reticent to complain about the practices of their own governments.

The final four columns of Table 3.5 document a now familiar pattern. With the very interesting exception of the CAT, stable democracies have been the most willing to ratify these optional agreements to give individuals a right to complain to international authorities about their own state's violations. Democracies of every description – mature and newly transitioned – were much more likely to do so than were nondemocracies (with varying degrees of certainty). This is true despite the fact that a significant proportion of mature democracies, the European countries in particular, have an individual right of complaint within their regional grouping.[101] The CAT is a very interesting exception. For this convention, there are traces of evidence that potentially support a nonlinear relationship consistent with democratic lock-in arguments.[102] Newly transitioned democracies were by far the most eager to commit to external scrutiny when it came to the problem of torture. They were almost five times more likely to do so than nondemocracies

99 The latter two are not reported here, but in robustness checks, foreign aid scaled to GDP had zero impact and a UN conference, if anything, seemed to have a negative impact on Article 41 ratification. See Appendix 3.6 on my Web site for a list of conferences relating to each treaty.

100 Legal scholars have identified an individual right of complaint as a key ingredient in rendering any quasi-adjudicative institution more "courtlike." See Helfer and Slaughter 1997.

101 Hefferman notes that European countries were slightly slow to commit to the ICCPR's first OP because of the regional alternative. She also shows that individuals are much more likely to petition the European Court of Human Rights than the UN Human Rights Committee, despite the fact that findings of inadmissibility are staggeringly high in the regional institution (Heffernan 1997:81).

102 Moravcsik 2000. But compare Goodliffe and Hawkins (2006), who find no such effects with a different specification.

and approximately half again as likely as were mature democracies. These strong systematic differences are fairly clear indications that governments tend to commit at much higher levels to agreements that reflect their preferences as well as their specific historical contexts.

The effect of the nature of the legal system on accepting international authority to hear individual complaints was always in the anticipated direction, with common law countries tending to be reluctant to give individuals access to external courts. In the case of the ICCPR, CERD, and CAT, the effect was strong and significant. The government of a common law country is estimated with a high degree of certainty to be about 90 percent less likely to declare itself bound by the CERD's Article 14 (hazard ratio .119). With somewhat less certainty, such a government is also likely to be much less willing to ratify the ICCPR's first OP. This accords with all of our earlier findings regarding the incentives governments face in common law systems. One issue that likely discourages some governments from ratification is that of how the views of external authorities such as the UN Human Rights Committee fit into the structure of local case-based jurisprudence.

Once again, there is overwhelming evidence of the influence of regional practices on the decision to allow authoritative review of individual complaints. For individual complaint procedures in all cases, the rate of regional ratifications is highly significant and in the positive direction.

CONCLUSIONS

Why do state actors commit themselves to international human rights treaties? After World War II, a consensus had seemed to form – at least as expressed in the UDHR – that the rights of individuals were a proper concern of international society. Chapter 2 discussed the range of actors, especially small democracies sometimes joined by newly independent countries and urged on by private individuals and groups, that took the lead in drafting legal agreements in treaty form. The strong presumption was that states should sign these instruments, and as we have seen, many did. For some governments, commitment to these agreements was hardly problematic. Some governments enthusiastically joined, secure in the knowledge that for the most part they were willing and able to comply. This is not to say that these agreements would not require policy adjustments – improving legal procedures to ensure fairer trials, improving access of racial minorities to jobs and education, raising the minimum age for military service – but these were changes some governments were in principle not opposed to implementing.

That governments ratify because they intend to comply is one of the most robust findings of this chapter. The evidence presented here shows that governments ratify when their preferences line up with the contents of the treaty. Democratic governments were the most likely to ratify treaties that replicate the kinds of rights they already tend to have in place, namely, strong civil and political rights. Democracies were also less likely to enter reservations to such treaties and to commit to higher levels of external scrutiny through optional protocols that give individuals the right to complain about treaty violations to the various oversight committees. The converse of these findings is quite telling: Nondemocratic governments – polities that never experienced much democratic participation and accountability at any point in their histories – have been systematically reluctant to commit themselves to the contents of legal arrangements that declare the importance of civil and political rights for the individual. Similarly, governments of polities that hold social values that fit quite uneasily with the values reflected in these treaties are also systematically unlikely to commit, as is especially clear in the case of predominantly Muslim societies' reluctance fully to embrace the CEDAW. These are not patterns that fit easily with a theory of costless commitment-making. Were there something to gain from costless ratification – and were there no attendant risks – even the most stable autocracies might have jumped on the human rights treaty bandwagon, washing out the main findings of this chapter.

But it is equally clear that prevailing values alone are not the entire explanation for the pattern of treaty commitment we observe. Some governments may value the contents of the treaty in principle but delay or fail to ratify because domestic institutions raise barriers or otherwise create disincentives to do so. Federal political structures and ratification procedures could in theory produce false negatives, but there is only weak systematic evidence of their effect in this chapter. What is clearer, however, is that the nature of the legal system has a significant and highly consistent effect on governments' commitment patterns. Governments in common law settings are systematically more reluctant to ratify most of these treaties. They enter far more reservations of every kind, which provides striking evidence of the care with which they think through the adjustment, uncertainty, and irreversibility costs their commitments imply. Governments in common law countries are also less likely to go the extra mile with optional commitments giving individuals the right to lodge complaints with the appropriate international authorities, though this result is statistically significant only in the case of the CERD. One of the most important findings of this chapter is that the nature of the legal system itself can create resistance against the ready acceptance of the international human rights regime. Though this has rarely been noted in the literature, it is an understandable consequence of the uncertainties associated with trying to import externally negotiated political agreements into a locally and organically grown system of precedent, where judges wield broad powers of interpretation, with consequences that will be difficult to reverse. My argument is that the nature of the legal system can account for some of the false negatives – supportive but uncommitted states – we have witnessed over the past few decades.

The most profound puzzle is why governments sign international human rights agreements even though they have no intention of implementing them. The evidence presented in this chapter suggests an explanation. Under some circumstances, governments have incentives to ratify strategically. In order to understand why this might be, it is useful to recall the conditions discussed in Chapter 2. The UDHR had placed all governments at the time (except the seven abstainers) on record for supporting a broad set of individual rights. The Cold War placed rights at the center of an ideological struggle that paid lip service to their protection but at the same time discouraged enforcement, especially against a political ally. Information on actual rights practices was fairly thin, as few organized groups had much capacity to collect information systematically. Many states had an interest in keeping the UN enforcement regime weak as they pursued other aims on the plane of high politics.

With this in mind, it is clear that some governments have had incentives to engage in opportunistic ratification. But the evidence certainly implies that governments are savvy about when to make an insincere commitment. I have argued that there may be some short-term benefits to ratification: A sense of joining the world's law-abiding states, the desire to avoid criticism as a nonratifying outlier, a bit of international praise, a stronger claim to a right to participate in future international rights discussions, and the support of some domestic constituency are possible positive benefits. But it is important to realize that these benefits are likely to materialize only in the short run. Patently insincere ratification is likely to be revealed, making it risky as a long-run strategy.

One of the striking findings of this chapter has been evidence that identifies strategic ratification with particular conditions. The finding that governments in countries that have never been democratic tend to ratify international human rights treaties later in their terms in office suggests a legacy motive consistent with short time horizons. The later a dictator ratifies, the more immediate the gratification and the more limited the likely repercussions. No such behavior could be detected for governments in democracies, which are much more likely to be among the sincere ratifiers in the first place.

Perhaps the most interesting finding of this chapter is the extent to which governments apparently take cues from the decisions of other governments in their region. This is a central and increasingly important dynamic of the international human rights legal regime. It is startling to see the extent to which regional effects surface in practically every measure of commitment – from ratification to reservation-making to the acceptance of OPs. Even some *types* of reservations made have strong regional counterparts. This is very likely to reflect the self-conscious coordination of human rights activities on the part of many countries for the reasons discussed in this chapter. Governments appear to time their ratifications – even coordinate their reservations – largely to keep in step with their regional peers. Especially telling are the conditions under which regional emulation is likely to take place. With only a few exceptions, regional emulation was strongest before 1989, in regions with few regional rights commitments, and in countries with government-controlled presses. These are precisely the conditions under which it might make sense to ratify a universal agreement strategically simply to avoid the criticism of being an outlier: When information on true intentions is thinnest and enforcement is least likely to be forthcoming. These strategic opportunities are likely to produce at least some false positives as rights-oriented countries pull their less enamored neighbors along in their wakes.

This chapter has provided evidence that governments ratify human rights treaties for both sincere and strategic reasons. They calculate the costs versus the benefits in the context of their values, region, national institutions, and time horizons. The next four chapters turn to the question of compliance with treaty obligations. As we will see, treaties are more than scraps of paper: They can become powerful instruments in the hands of rights claimants to hold governments to their promised behavior.

4

Theories of Compliance

I believe the decision by totalitarian states to formally (if not practically) recognize these shared values results in part from the international program of support for human rights movements around the world. These legal commitments serve both as the encouraging fruit of efforts to force observance of human rights and as a useful tool by which to transform totalitarian governments into more democratic ones.

> Leonid Romanov, member of the St. Petersburg Legislative Assembly and chairman of the parliament's Commission on Education, Culture, and Science[1]

Human rights have been one of the most powerful normative concepts of the past half century. They have been championed by groups and individuals disgusted by the oppression of which some governments have shown themselves capable. They have been supported by governments genuinely eager to set a pro-rights example as well as by cynical governments for purposes of international posturing. Cynical ratification was theorized to be rational only under certain narrow conditions – for instance, when information is thin and autocratic leaders' time horizons are short. Much of the evidence presented in the previous chapter followed patterns consistent with these expectations. Democracies have tended to be at the forefront in the process of ratification, while nondemocratic regimes have fairly consistently lagged behind. There is also evidence of strategic ratification in the form of social camouflage, but really only during the Cold War years, where the news media were under the governments' tight control, and in regions with wider dispersions in actual rights practices. In these cases, governments with little intention of actually improving their practices might rationally have assumed that they could avoid criticism while enjoying the approval of the international community in the short run.

---

[1] Power and Allison 2000:64.

But what happens after the making of a formal commitment? Improved behavior is far from an instant or even a consistent result of treaty ratification. A ratifying government may have intended to comply, but an election could inaugurate leadership with differing priorities. Coups, sectarian or class violence, and civil wars have even more serious consequences for rights protections. Unanticipated events – from terrorist attacks to serious economic crises – could further disrupt progress toward the implementation and observance of agreements. Nor is it a foregone conclusion that governments that were essentially false positives at the time of ratification will never reform or be replaced. Pinochet did not anticipate that the CAT, which his own government ratified, would be used by future governments to hold him accountable a generation later. The totalitarian states referred to in the quote by Leonid Romanov may have underestimated in the 1970s and 1980s the extent to which formal agreements might become a "useful tool" of political liberalization.

This chapter continues the argument developed in Chapter 3. One of the major themes developed there is that some governments ratify human rights agreements sincerely, fully intending to comply with their commitments, while others ratify strategically, hoping for credit or relief from criticism at least in the short run. Certainly, we should expect the former group to have better rights practices than the latter. But in order to argue that the ratification of international treaties affects policy and rights practices, we need a theory of how treaties might matter in the politics of both willing and resistant states. In both cases, treaties potentially influence domestic politics. Even among the sincere ratifiers, treaties can change the priorities of governing leaders, the reasoning of courts, and the demands of groups of potential rights beneficiaries. Among the more resistant ratifiers (plausibly among the false positives discussed in Chapter 3), treaties will have their most important influences through the effects they may have on political mobilization. Mobilization, in turn, is a function of both the *value* that potential rights claimants place on the rights in question and the *likelihood* that mobilization will succeed in realizing them. The central argument developed here is that ratified treaties can influence agendas, litigation, and mobilization in ways that should be observable in government policies post-ratification. *Treaties change politics* – in particular, the domestic politics of the ratifying country. While their enforcement internationally tends to create collective action problems that state actors have few incentives to overcome, the consequences locally can be profound.

This chapter begins by justifying a theoretical focus on the domestic consequences of treaty ratification. Despite the fact that governments toward the end of the twentieth century have accepted a higher degree of peer accountability than ever before, they are still largely reluctant to enforce international human rights agreements in all but the most egregious cases, and only when it serves their broader political purposes. Moreover, in stark contrast to agreements based on mutual gain and state-to-state reciprocity, international human rights agreements are essentially not self-enforcing. So, how should we construct a robust theory of compliance? By thinking about the influence of treaties on domestic politics. Treaties influence the national policy agenda, they influence legal decisions, and they influence the propensity of groups to mobilize. These three mechanisms in the aggregate should lead us to expect at least some positive impact to the making of a treaty commitment on human rights outcomes – a proposition that is tested in the following four chapters.

INTERNATIONAL TREATIES AND INTERNATIONAL POLITICS

Scholars of international relations are often pessimistic about the ability of international law to influence human rights practices because they are largely looking in the wrong direction: *outward* at interstate relations rather than *inward* at state–society relations. The interstate vantage point does not provide a lot of reason for optimism. The international legal system – while improving – is still one of the most underdeveloped legal systems in the world. Despite the proliferation of treaties and monitoring mechanisms, there is no central lawmaking body, no international tribunal broadly accepted as a legitimate interpreter of legal obligations, and no global "law enforcement" corps to enforce the rules. Many commentators have even wondered whether we should speak of the international legal system as such. What (if anything) drives compliance in such an effete legal environment?

The Common Wisdom

The most common answer is simply state power and state interests. Treaties reflect the power and the interests of the states that take part in their negotiations and add little to an understanding of why governments behave the way they do post-ratification. Governments may comply with agreements only because the treaty does not engage a national interest, or if it does, only if the treaty is consistent with that interest. Compliance against the grain of interests is interpreted as the result of coercion on the part of more powerful states or other actors.

These views are well represented among academic realists.[2] Even as Eleanor Roosevelt and the new UN Human Rights Commission sought to elaborate international rights principles, a spate of extended critiques of international law appeared in response to the legal idealism perceived to have pervaded the inter-war years. The decentralized nature of the international legal system was typically presented as its prime defect. International agreements lacked restraining power, as Hans Morgenthau argued, since governments generally retain the

2 See, for example, Bork 1989/90; Boyle 1980; Mearsheimer 1994–5.

right to interpret and apply the provisions of international agreements selectively. While Morgenthau was ready to admit that "during the four hundred years of its existence international law ha[d] in most instances been scrupulously observed," he thought that this could be attributed either to convergent interests or prevailing power relations.[3] Governments make legal commitments cynically and "are always anxious to shake off the restraining influence that international law might have upon their foreign policies, to use international law instead for the promotion of their national interests. . . ."[4] The suggestion of the British school – that all law rested ineluctably on politics and international law on the balance of power – did little to encourage inquiry into the role of law in ordering international politics.[5] The analytical move by neo-realists to strip the essential political structure down to the bare bones of power relationships among states[6] set the study of international law and institutions back a further decade. Certainly, neo-realism has done much to fuel skepticism that international institutions have much influence on important international policy decisions and outcomes.[7]

Realists have primarily provided a critique of international law as a way to enhance international peace and stability, but their arguments have a direct parallel in the human rights area: *Governments will not honor international human rights treaties when it is not in their interest to do so.* Some domestic settings approximate international anarchy: competitive and brutal, with little but power to back government policies. Governments have no incentive under these conditions to hand rights to their political or cultural opponents. And in the absence of an international will to enforce these rights, the domestic balance of power – with whatever regime of repression that implies – will hold sway. For most rights violations, international enforcement simply will not be forthcoming. Foreign governments face severe collective action problems when it comes to paying the military, economic, or diplomatic costs of enforcement. Each government will be driven by its own political agenda, firmly tethered to its particular understanding of its nation's interest.[8] In most cases, such an

---

3 Morgenthau 1985:295.
4 Morgenthau 1985:299. In the realm of high politics, realists have been especially skeptical about the rule of law and legal processes in international relations (see Bulterman and Kuijer 1996; Diehl 1996; Fischer 1982; Fisher 1981). Raymond Aron (1981:109) put it succinctly: "International law can merely ratify the fate of arms and the arbitration of force." For the most part, realist perspectives have focused on the fundamental variables of power and interest, rarely feeling compelled to inquire further into states' compliance with international agreements.
5 Bull 1977; Carr 1964.
6 Waltz 1979.
7 Mearsheimer 1994–5.
8 George F. Kennan (1951) and other "applied" realists made the normative case that this was the only way to properly formulate foreign policy, as have current government officials. John Bolton (2000:9), for a short time George W. Bush's ambassador to the UN, has written that any claims that international law had binding and authoritative force ultimately ring either hollow or unacceptable to a free people.

understanding will not include pressing for the prosecution of paramilitary personnel for extrajudicial killings in Colombia, ridding the Sudanese military of children, or intervening to improve the treatment of prisoners and detainees in Turkey.

The key realist insight comes down to this: Treaties have little purchase over government behavior because they are not likely to be meaningfully enforced. "High compliance rates" should not be mistaken for important treaty effects, since most treaties just reflect the easy commitments governments were willing to implement even in the treaty's absence.[9] Treaties "screen" but they do not constrain;[10] they separate willing compliers from resistors, without much effect on either. Or alternatively, they are signed symbolically or even cynically in the anticipation that external enforcement will not be forthcoming,[11] often resulting in "radical decoupling" of principle and practice.[12] Jack Goldsmith and Eric Posner represent the mainstream realist view: "Most human rights practices are explained by coercion or coincidence of interest."[13] If we are looking for empathetic enforcement from other countries, we will be looking in vain for a long time.

Self-Enforcing Agreements

If the key explanation for compliance is enforcement, it raises the question of *how* and *when* agreements are enforced. The lack of central authority or the fickle application of brute power is not the end of the story. Many international agreements are self-enforcing: They rely on the interests of the parties themselves or the international community to keep the cooperation coming.

A self-enforcing agreement is one in which two or more parties adhere to the agreement as long as each gains more from continuing the agreement than from abrogating it. These types of agreements are not without sanctions; rather, the sanctions they do involve flow from the nature of the agents' interaction itself. Self-enforcing agreements do not depend on third parties to enforce their terms: The nature of the agreement itself provides incentives for the actors to stick to it even in the absence of external enforcement mechanisms. The expected long-term benefits outweigh the present value of violating the agreement. The agreement is "enforced" by shutting down or reducing that future flow of benefits.

The most obvious mechanism of self-enforcement is for a treaty partner to quit the agreement and refuse future cooperation in that issue area. *Reciprocity* is thus a key aspect of self-enforcing agreements. The risk that another player or players will exit the agreement rather than tolerate cheating can deter a

9 Downs et al. 1996.
10 Von Stein 2005.
11 Hathaway 2002.
12 Hafner-Burton and Tsutsui 2005.
13 Goldsmith and Posner 2005:134.

would-be violator from cashing in on the short-term benefits of defection if that actor places enough value on future interactions. *Reputation* is an additional mechanism for self-enforcing agreements. Quite aside from the specific issue and party involved in a given incident, a reputation as an unreliable treaty partner can potentially influence the willingness of others to negotiate mutually beneficial agreements in a broader range of issue areas. Self-enforcing agreements can be bolstered by community sanctioning, which would raise even further the costs of noncompliance. Enforceable levels of cooperation may vary over time, but they can be altered by the possibilities for reciprocity and the importance of reputation.

Much of the early thinking of cooperation theorists relied on the logic of self-enforcing agreements. The transactions costs literature explains the demand for cooperative international arrangements, but once in place, these rules were theorized as largely self-enforcing. In Robert Keohane's formulation, governments comply with their agreements because they want to benefit from ongoing cooperation. Accordingly, he cites "reasons of reputation, as well as fear of retaliation and concern about the effects of precedents" as the major reason egoistic governments follow the rules and principles of international regimes, even when it is in their short-term interest to renege.[14] As long as the parties expect the cooperative arrangement to extend long enough into the future (the discount factor is low), self-interest can result in a high degree of agreement compliance.[15]

Self-enforcing agreements are stable over time because they imply costs of abrogation that counterbalance any short-term temptation to deviate unilaterally from the terms of the agreement. The rules regarding trade provide a good example. The market access rules of the WTO are largely respected, arguably, even in the absence of WTO enforcement power, because the parties basically have an ongoing interest in free trade. Reciprocity means that a government's violation or compliance will be returned in kind. The prospect of being denied market access by a trade partner lessens the temptation to defect now. The risk that others will infer from the observed infraction that a state is an unreliable trade partner strengthens the self-enforcing nature of the contract.

There are limits, of course, to the ability of reputational considerations to support self-enforcing agreements. Reputational considerations will not be very important among parties that barely interact with each other and within communities that the would-be violator does not much value. A reputation is difficult to establish in those cases where the behavior in question is difficult to observe. Reputations may be somewhat easier to establish where behaviors are transparent and in more homogeneous communities where the behavior of

14 Keohane 1984:106.
15 Telser 1987.

individuals is common knowledge.[16] Moreover, the ability of actors to regulate the exact message they want others to infer from their behavior may be limited, as governments often cultivate multiple reputations.[17] In trade, for example, a government may want to cultivate a domestic reputation for responsiveness to constituency interests but an international reputation for cooperativeness. Finally, "reputational sanctions," like any other kind of sanction, may be sub-optimal if the community does not find a way to overcome collective action problems in its supply.[18] There is simply no guarantee that non-third-party enforcement can generate reputational costs that exceed the present value of opportunism.

Compliance with agreements is explained in this approach by the ability to structure incentives in such as way as to make noncompliance too costly to consider *in the absence of third-party enforcement.* Hence the attractiveness of this approach: Self-enforcing agreements would seem to be the only stable agreements in an anarchic setting. Many people who have never uttered the word "realism" would come to conclusions similar to those outlined previously: In the absence of external enforcement, an agreement must be self-enforcing – neither party has any incentive to defect – if it is to have any credibility. Compliance with self-enforcing agreements – unsurprisingly – should be high. Compliance with all other agreements will be problematic.

Treaties as Commitment Devices

What most discussions of self-enforcing agreements do not do, however, is to answer the question, *why treaties?* International treaties are one of the oldest forms of communication among sovereigns, and some 3,000 multilateral and 27,000 bilateral treaties are in effect today.[19] It is hard to imagine why this is the case if they do not perform some kind of useful function among sovereign governments that is difficult to achieve in some other way. What do formal legal agreements add to the calculus to defect that we have been exploring? Why do states use this kind of instrument to support their international cooperation, and what difference – if any – does it make to outcomes we might care about?

One possibility is that treaties support higher levels of international cooperation by enhancing states' ability to make credible commitments to one another, even if they have incentives to misrepresent their true intentions. If states are able to send costly signals of their intentions, the messages they send should ultimately be far more credible. Two kinds of costs are distinguished in the literature: ex ante (or "sunk") costs that have the effect of credibly

16 Landa 1981.
17 Keohane 1997.
18 Guzman 2002.
19 John Gamble, based on Wiktor's Calendars, Rohn's indices, and *Treaties in Force.*

distinguishing a sincere government from an opportunistic one and ex post costs that are paid if a violation takes place.[20] High ex ante costs send a credible signal of intentions: No rational government would pay a high "down payment" on a cooperative enterprise if it did not intend to abide by the agreement. When a government pays high ex ante costs, others can reasonably draw the conclusion that this government will follow through with its agreement. High ex ante costs screen governments by type, revealing their true nature. Their interest in ex post compliance does not change; rather, they signal how much the government values compliant behavior in the first place.

Costs paid ex post work in a different way. If ex ante costs can screen, then ex post costs can *constrain*. Ex post costs are simply the consequences of non-compliance, which can range from trivial to monumental. When ex post costs are high enough, they can effectively tie a government's hands; noncompliance can in some cases be too costly to contemplate. The seriousness of these consequences has the effect *of changing* a government's interest in compliance. In the absence of consequences, the government might have preferred to defect; ex post costs make defection much less attractive. Essentially, we are back in the world of enforcement, broadly understood. Credible commitments that involve ex post costs increase the range of self-enforcing agreements with which the parties have an incentive to apply.

How do *treaties* assist governments in making credible commitments to behave – or refrain from behaving – in particular ways? Let's begin with the sunk costs that allow a government to signal credibly its intent to comply. In many polities, treaties are unique among interstate agreements in that they require domestic ratification. In contrast to other forms of international agreement – memoranda of understanding, executive agreements, or other political announcements – treaty ratification generally involves the assent of a legislative or at least a cabinet-level body. As discussed in Chapter 3, ratification procedures are usually spelled out in a country's constitution, and can range from executive approval to legislative majority to legislative supermajority to national referendum.[21] These procedures require varying levels of government effort to secure domestic political support for the agreement in question. In some countries, there is practically no political difference between ratifying a treaty and signing an executive agreement. But in a great many others, the government has to expend significant political capital to assemble a coalition in favor of treaty ratification. The more hawkish the legislature in these cases, the greater the political resistance the government can expect to ratification and the less likely such a government would be to pay these ex ante ratification costs.[22]

---

20 Fearon 1997.
21 See my Web site at http://scholar.iq.harvard.edu/bsimmons/mobilizing-for-human-rights.
22 Evans et al. 1993; Milner 1997.

The ratification process helps governments to send a credible signal primarily because of the screening effects of relatively high ratification hurdles. In the face of high up-front domestic political costs, the willingness of a government to expend political capital on ratification sends a credible signal that the government in question attaches a high value to the contents of the treaty.[23] Committed types are likely to secure ratification, while uncommitted types are not. In these cases, treaty ratification can be thought of as a separating equilibrium, in which only the committed are likely to pay the steep political costs of ratification.

Ratification is the only clear ex ante cost associated with treaty making. A much more varied set of arguments has been developed that treaties – in comparison to other kinds of international agreements – impose significant ex post costs in the event of breach. All of these arguments are consistent with viewing treaties as enhancing the self-enforcing qualities of the agreement. Moreover, practically all of these arguments extend the reputational analysis of self-enforcing agreements discussed previously. Andrew Guzman captures the logic of all of these arguments very well when he writes that treaties "represent the complete pledge of a nation's reputational capital."[24] Treaties somehow *put it all on the line in the diplomatic world.* The ex ante cost of violation, in this context, is a severe loss of diplomatic stature and credibility as a contracting party.

The first reason many offer for the credibility of a treaty commitment is its status as law. Among all forms of international agreement-making, treaties have a fairly unique feature: They are clearly embedded in a broader system of interstate rule-making, normatively linked by the principle of *pacta sunt servanda* – the idea that agreements of a legally obligatory nature must be observed. Unlike political or other kinds of agreements, treaties are not freestanding; they gain status from their mutual recognition as legally binding. The link to the underlying principle of good faith fulfillment leverages the commitment made in any one case by linking it with other agreements of a similarly obligatory stature. By embedding an agreement in a broader principle of good-faith compliance, treaties allow actors to draw better inferences about the law-abiding nature of other governments. Normative linkage justifies the inferential round trip from specific violations to the broader reputation for legality back to expectations about future compliance with otherwise unrelated treaty commitments. Violating a legal agreement, in this view, provides information on both the government's attitude toward the contents of the treaty and respect for law itself.

The notion that treaties are embedded in the broader international legal *system* (weak though that system may be) informs a good deal of legal thinking

---

23 Martin 2000. Lisa Martin tests this argument for the United States by comparing treaties with executive agreements. She finds that U.S. presidents typically choose the treaty form for high-value agreements, which is necessary to assure other countries that the United States intends to comply. See http://www.wcfia.harvard.edu/node/815 (accessed 12 August 2008).

24 Guzman 2002:65.

on the compliance question. This linkage implies that a country can develop a good reputation for law-abiding behavior that has value and meaning across issue areas. Oscar Schachter, for example, has written about a country's "reputation for legality" and suggests that treaty violations are costly to this reputation, even for powerful states.[25] Roger Fisher uses a similar logic to argue that treaty violations are generally deterred by governments "engaged in an expensive effort to create a favorable opinion."[26]

Arguably, treaties also allow for a more complete reputational commitment because of their capacity for clarity. They can be used as a mechanism to enhance the precision of a commitment, making it clearer just what compliance requires. Treaties are well suited to focusing expectations by reducing ambiguity about what behavior is required, permitted, or proscribed. Precision reduces the scope for plausible deniability of violation; it "narrows the scope for reasonable interpretation" of the parties' intentions.[27] Of course, when drafting a treaty, governments are faced with familiar problems of incomplete contracting, or the difficulty of foreseeing and clarifying every conceivable contingency. This is why there has been a strong move to codify rules for treaty interpretation,[28] which further narrow the range of agreed-upon responses when governments disagree over the substance of their treaty obligations. Although precision is neither inherent in nor unique to treaty agreements, when governments want to be precise about the nature of their obligations, treaties are typically the instrument of choice.[29]

Normative as well as rational theorists have explored the quality of law precision as an influence on compliance. In a normative vein, Thomas Franck has theorized that precision, or "coherence," increases the legitimacy of a rule and increases its "compliance pull."[30] In James Morrow's rationalist interpretation of the laws of war, the relative precision of treaty arrangements supports reciprocity between warring states by clarifying prescribed and proscribed behaviors and by limiting the permitted range of responses to violation.[31] In both accounts, compliance is enhanced, ceteris paribus, by rules that are clear – or can readily be clarified – to all parties concerned.

Human Rights Treaties: A Continuing Theoretical Puzzle

None of these theoretical approaches are very satisfying for understanding treaty compliance in the human rights area. Many of the realist insights are

---

25 Schachter 1991:7.
26 Fisher 1981:133.
27 Abbott et al. 2000.
28 Vienna Convention of the Law of Treaties. Part III, section 3, Arts. 31–33.
29 Lipson 1991.
30 Franck 1990.
31 Morrow 2002.

correct (although, as I will argue, they reach the wrong conclusion): Governments are quite unlikely to comply with their international treaty obligations with respect to human rights if it is not in their interest to do so. Governments are likely to repress political opposition when opponents pose a challenge to national "peace and stability" (or, more likely, the ruling coalition's hold on political power). Governments are likely to engage in various forms of coercive interrogation if they want intelligence from individuals who are considered threats. They are likely to turn a blind eye to the use of child soldiers if that is what it takes to raise a fighting force during wartime.

Furthermore, skeptics are right that peer enforcement is likely to be weak.[32] Foreign governments simply do not have the incentives to expend political, military, and economic resources systematically to enforce human rights treaties around the globe. Even if they value respect for the international legal system and human integrity, states face tremendous collective action problems in organizing potential enforcement efforts. Governments would face these collective action problems even if enforcing international human rights were their top foreign policy priority, but, of course, in most cases it simply is not. Punishing foreign governments for their human rights violations is likely to come into conflict with other foreign policy objectives. For a number of reasons, international punishment is quite likely to be underprovided compared to some optimal level of enforcement.

Governments will have especially weak incentives to enforce international human rights agreements involving their important trade partners, allies, or other strategically, politically, or economically important states. Empirical studies of U.S. foreign policy, especially during the Cold War period, support the point that U.S. administrations have tended to provide aid on the basis of foreign policy exigencies rather than human rights performance.[33] A few studies have drawn similar conclusions for the United Kingdom.[34] The targets of these enforcement efforts are generally small countries whose sanctioning imposes no important costs for the would-be enforcer. For example, countries that are the target of trade–human rights linkage are typically *much* smaller markets than those that are not: Countries with preferential agreements including human rights clauses in 2000 were on average less than a quarter of the size of those

---

32 See, for example, Dai 2005.

33 In an early study, Schoultz (1981) found that U.S. aid was disproportionately distributed to countries with repressive governments. Carleton and Stohl (1985) similarly found that human rights were ignored by policymakers during the Cold War. Blanton (2005) has found that the amount of military assistance the United States provided during the Cold War was unrelated to political rights, though there is some evidence that this situation has changed since the end of the Cold War.

34 Barratt (2004:59) found that "When all potential recipients were examined together, states with worse human rights records were actually more likely to receive aid than the ones with better human rights records. ... UK policymakers only take human rights into account in the case of potential recipients with which they will not be endangering and [sic] important export market."

without such linkage clauses.[35] Multilateral institutions also have serious political biases when it comes to the enforcement of human rights standards. The UN Human Rights Commission, for example, has traditionally been one of the most politicized institutions with the authority to officially denounce a government's human rights policy. In terms of the supply of external enforcement, then, we should expect it to be undersupplied as well as "inappropriately" (that is, highly politically) supplied.

Whether theories of self-enforcing agreements and credible commitments greatly increase our understanding of international human rights compliance is also doubtful. In crucial ways, this family of theories is simply an uncomfortable fit for explaining human rights compliance. We can begin with the opening assumption of contracting for *mutual* gain.[36] In the human rights area, of course, a country can generally realize its desired level of rights without the cooperation of any other state. Why contract at all?[37] In fact, from the government's point of view, it would be most efficient to determine the optimal level and type of rights unilaterally. Joint gains from this perspective would predict a conspiracy to mutual silence. The contracting approach is misplaced from the outset: If a government places a high value on the protection of its citizens' rights, it is hardly necessary to contract with other states to do so.

The external enforcement mechanisms implied by rationalist theories are also an awkward fit for the human rights area. The most common mechanism of self-enforcement that these theories posit is responding to violation by terminating the treaty – a mechanism that is not realistically available in this context. Human rights regimes do not involve *reciprocal* compliance (as is the case with trade agreements).[38] No government is likely to alter its own rights practices to reciprocate for abuses elsewhere. Short of a policy of linkage (better rights for economic aid, for example), reciprocity is difficult to invoke.

35 Based on data provided by Emilie Hafner-Burton. See Hafner-Burton 2005. The 125 countries that had some form of human rights linkage built into their preferential trade agreements in 2000 had an average GDP of only about $102 billion, while the 44 countries that had no such riders in their trade agreements had an average GDP of $469 billion. The difference in mean GDP is highly statistically significant ($p = .007$).

36 Mutual gain is an assumption made by all functional theories of international regimes and international law that credit the value governments place on reciprocal compliance by other governments and the expected future stream of benefits with overcoming the temptation to defect from an international agreement in the short run (Keohane 1984).

37 One possibility is that poor rights elsewhere create negative externalities via refugee flows, as in the case of Haitian flows to the United States in the early 1990s.

38 Canada respects its North American Free Trade Agreement (NAFTA) trade commitments with the United States because the expected value of future cooperation between these two countries is so high. Were Canada to repeatedly violate the agreement, it would risk the United States doing the same, and potentially would make it more difficult to conclude other potentially valuable agreements with the United States and possibly trade agreements with other countries.

Nor is it as straightforward to identify the consequences of a bad reputation with respect to human rights treaty compliance as it is in other areas of interstate contracting.[39] First, compliance with human rights treaties takes place domestically, and despite the widespread development of the accountability mechanisms discussed in Chapter 2, many violations are truly difficult to detect, to observe, and even more difficult to verify. In all but the most headline-grabbing cases, it is likely to be too costly for outside actors to collect, assess, and disseminate the kind of information that can inform strong reputational judgments.

Second, even if it is possible to get the right kind of information, it is not obvious why a government would be too concerned to develop a positive international reputation in the human rights area in the first place. What is the instrumental value of such a reputation? What do governments infer from a state's compliance or noncompliance with international human rights treaties? Does noncompliance in human rights make a government an unreliable trade partner or military ally? George Downs and Michael Jones argue that unless whatever compliance costs have led to noncompliance in one issue area are correlated with noncompliance in another issue area, there is no good reason for other countries to draw reputational inferences for other issue areas.[40] There is no reason to suspect that a country that violates a human rights agreement will break out of an arms control treaty. Downs and Jones view the costs of complying with human rights agreements as very weakly correlated with the costs associated with compliance in other issue areas. From this they conclude that, "reputation promotes compliance with international law most in trade and security and least in environmental regulation and human rights."[41] In practice, reputations are highly segmented; a reputation for respect for law is difficult, if not impossible, to develop across issue areas with very different logics of cooperation.

Third, enforcing reputational consequences is subject to collective action problems in the same way (though possibly not to the same degree) as are other kinds of sanctions.[42] States may disagree in their assessment of the gravity of the violation; they may also differ in the value they place on a positive relationship with the alleged violator. On the one hand, if official criticism is publicly issued, it is likely to inject some resentment into two countries' relationship. On the other hand, costless criticism cannot provide effective enforcement. Costly criticism is just that, and many governments will wait for others to step up and provide it.

---

39 In the monetary area, see Simmons 2000.
40 Downs and Jones 2002.
41 Downs and Jones 2002:S112.
42 On collective action problems in sanctioning, see Martin 1992. Andrew Guzman (2002) argues that for this reason, reputational sanctions are likely to be undersupplied.

"Joint gains" and "reciprocity" (as these terms are usually understood) are fairly beside the point for interstate interactions in the human rights area. Reputation works – at best – very weakly in this area as well. For these reasons, "signaling" theories are also orthogonal to the analysis of human rights compliance. Signaling theories are interesting only because they allow actors to realize joint gains that they cannot easily reach because of the risk of defection by the other party. International human rights agreements, I have argued, do not produce such joint gains. Hence, there is no reason to send a signal of one's type to other governments in the first place. Moreover, signaling theories predict but do not explain compliance. Ratification procedures, for example, may impose ex ante costs that only a compliance-prone government would pay. But if we observe such a government refraining from torture, we are likely to agree with George Downs and others that it was likely to have complied anyway. Signaling is superfluous to an understanding of human rights treaty effects. In the absence of joint gains, there is simply no reason to send a signal in the first place.

For a number of reasons, a theory of compliance with international human rights treaties is difficult to develop purely in the context of international politics. States (and their agents, intergovernmental organizations) have very little interest in enforcing these agreements, which tend to impose costs on the enforcers without hope of commensurate gains. Many of our theories of international cooperation – self-enforcing agreements, credible commitments – fall flat because these agreements do not involve either joint gains or reciprocity. Reputations are difficult to develop because information is largely internal (although this is changing), because it remains difficult to draw useful behavioral inferences across issue areas, and because even reputational punishment is fraught with collective action problems.

This does not mean that international human rights treaties are useless. It just means that international relations theorists have been analyzing their effects with the wrong analytical tools.

A DOMESTIC POLITICS THEORY OF TREATY COMPLIANCE

If international human rights treaties have an important influence on the rights practices of governments that commit to them, it is because they have predictable and important effects on domestic politics.[43] Like other formal institutions, *treaties are causally meaningful to the extent that they empower individuals, groups, or parts of the state with different rights preferences that were not empowered to the same extent in the absence of the treaties.* I have argued that external enforcement mechanisms – whether material or reputational – are likely to be undersupplied and quite weak in securing compliance with

---

43 For an excellent study that privileges domestic international law enforcement primarily through electoral mechanisms, see Dai 2005.

international human rights accords. Peers cannot act as reliable enforcers of the regime. They have incentives to ignore violations, either because they are essentially unaffected by practice elsewhere, or because other foreign policy objectives swamp the concerns they have in a particular case, or because they hope that someone else will pay the costs of enforcement. *The real politics of change is likely to occur at the domestic level.*

International human rights treaties have a singularly unusual property: They are negotiated internationally but create stakeholders almost exclusively domestically. In the human rights area, intergovernmental agreements are designed to give individuals rights largely to be guaranteed and respected by their governments. Treaties of this kind have a potentially dramatic impact on the relationship between citizens and their own government, creating a huge pool of potential beneficiaries if the treaty is given effect. State–society relations, or "the relationship between governments and the domestic and transnational social context in which they are embedded,"[44] should be the most important context for shaping compliance. By sharp contrast, international human rights treaties engage practically no important interests among states *in their mutual relationships with each other*. Most of these agreements simply do not have the capacity to alter international politics in important and predictable ways. The same is not true of politics at home.

This section suggests three theoretical mechanisms through which treaties can influence domestic politics in very positive ways. These are theories that privilege domestic political actors as agents in their own political fate. External actors can certainly facilitate some of these processes, but in principle, they are all possible without the contributions and the interference of outside actors. This approach is an important complement to many others that have emphasized transnational actors as primary change agents.[45] The mechanisms to be discussed view local actors not as voiceless victims to be rescued by altruistic external political actors, but as agents with some power selectively to choose tools that will help them achieve their rights goals. My argument is that for each of the mechanisms to be discussed, an official commitment to a specific body of international law helps local actors set priorities, define meaning, make rights demands, and bargain from a position of greater strength than would have been the case in the absence of their government's treaty commitment. Treaties are potentially empowering, and both those who would use them to repress and to achieve liberation should be assumed to have a good appreciation of this potential.

The following discussion is organized from the perspective of actors who may want change in rights policies and practices. I consider the role of the executive, the judiciary, and citizens.

44 Moravcsik 1997:abstract.
45 Keck and Sikkink 1998.

Executive Powers: Treaties and Agenda-Setting Influences

Treaties can have important influences in countries even when governments are basically supportive of their purposes. Some might object that these are the conditions under which treaty-consistent behavior cannot be attributed to the treaty itself, but rather to underlying preferences. To the extent that governments adopt policies that are treaty consistent, some would conclude that such behavior would easily have occurred in the absence of an external commitment.[46] The conclusion often drawn is that positively disposed governments would have complied in the absence of the treaty. The treaty itself has no independent effects on behavioral outcomes.

As a general rule, this conclusion is too hasty. It ignores the power of an internationally negotiated treaty to alter the domestic agenda and to empower particular branches of national policymaking.[47] Even when treaties reflect the preferences of particular governments, they can be independent influences on outcomes (laws and practices) by influencing a country's policy agenda.

For most countries, an internationally negotiated treaty is an exogenous event in the flow of national policymaking and legislation. Very few countries have both the political power and the will to fashion an international human rights agenda that matches exactly their own legislative agenda. Not only are concessions made to other countries, but as the following chapters demonstrate, priorities are critically shaped by international bodies and nonstate actors with an interest in the substance of particular human rights agreements. It would be an amazing coincidence were a treaty that emerged from global political processes to match exactly the legislative agenda of any particular government. This is not to say that these governments oppose the treaty; rather, it is to appreciate the extent to which the timing and precise content of global treaties are exogenous to most individual countries' policy agendas.

The need to consider ratification can therefore rearrange a country's priorities, if not its preferences.[48] A sympathetic government might not have wanted to spend the political capital to raise the issue of the death penalty, but the existence of the second optional protocol of the ICCPR raises the question of whether the government wants to go on record in this regard. A government might wish to join in an international ban on the use of children in the military, but would not have made this a high priority were the CRC's Optional Protocol Relating to

---

46 Downs et al. 1996.
47 Christina Davis (2004) argues that treaty negotiations have largely empowered foreign relations officials over special interest groups that otherwise might dominate trade talks. She argues that this has had an important effect on the agenda of the international trade regime.
48 While this is an elite-focused argument, it differs significantly from more constructivist arguments about the conditions under which elites become persuaded and change their preferences; see Checkel 2001. I am not arguing, of course, that elites cannot be persuaded to change their minds about the value of rights protections. Rather, this argument focuses on how the institution of treaty-making can empower an executive to initiate reform given constant preferences.

Children in Armed Conflict (OPCAC) not presented for consideration by the international community. One way to think about this issue is by considering the costs associated with delayed rights reform. Arguably, these costs are higher on the margin when a treaty that the government has participated in negotiating is on the table than when it is not. It is one thing not to *initiate* policy change on the national level and quite another not to *respond* once a particular right is made salient through international negotiations. Silence is ambiguous in the absence of a particular proposal, but it can easily be interpreted as opposition in the presence of a specific accord. The ratification decision affects the set of policy options facing a government, potentially shifting rights reform to a higher position on the national agenda than it might otherwise have occupied.

Treaties can influence national legislative priorities in both parliamentary and presidential systems. In the former, a prime minister may be encouraged by international negotiations (and externally generated expectations) to ratify and implement the agreement in good faith. The party in power might simply decide to insert the item into the normal flow of legislative business, over which the government has fairly clear institutional control. In presidential systems, treaties can have even more significant independent agenda-setting effects. As other scholars have noted in very different substantive contexts, in presidential systems in which legislatures have more power to initiate the lawmaking process, treaty-making uniquely empowers an executive vis-à-vis the legislature.[49] Practically every constitution in the world gives the prerogative to negotiate international treaties to the executive branch of government.[50] This gives an executive an important way to take the initiative with respect to the legislative agenda. Where legislatures have strong institutional agenda-setting powers – the United States, for example – the ability of an executive to insert an externally generated agenda item can be especially significant.

Treaties also influence the national agenda by creating a focal point to minimize the problem of legislative cycling. A particular political party might have a general preference for rights reform but might be hampered in making legislative progress by multiple proposals over which legislators have intransitive preferences. A treaty gives the executive a fairly clear proposal to discuss as an alternative to the status quo. Despite the fact that most treaties can be implemented in a number of ways, the existence of an authoritative text reduces the range of options and reduces the possibility of cycling through votes on a number of reform programs – none of which may gain a legislative majority – by

---

49 See, for example, Rachel Brewster, who argues in the U.S. context that one important thing international law does is to give significant agenda control to the executive: "The executive can oversee the development of substantive rules internationally and then use international organization decisions to constrain subsequent legislative action and oversight" (2003:4). She develops this argument for the case of trade policy liberalization.

50 For example, U.S. Constitution Article II(2). See http://www.law.cornell.edu/constitution/constitution.articleii.html#section2 (accessed 13 August 2008).

giving the executive a clear set of guidelines for proposing policy changes. The treaty itself reinforces the executive's ability to set the agenda under such circumstances.

If treaties really do influence national politics through their agenda-setting capacity, then we should expect the strongest positive treaty effects in domestic institutional settings that tend to privilege legislatures. This argument implies that treaties should have their greatest impact where governments are otherwise constrained in their ability to initiate legislative reforms to protect rights. Note that this is not an argument that executives have stronger preferences for rights than do legislatures. Rather, it is an argument that because the conduct of foreign policy (including the ratification of treaties) typically resides in the executive branch of government, treaty ratification provides a unique opportunity for the executive branch of government to place what otherwise might have been a legislative item on the national policy agenda. To be sure, legislatures could decide to legislate rights protections, and many, of course, do. In such cases, the influence of the treaty per se may be minimal. But the more constrained a national executive is in proposing legal innovations, the more important the agenda-setting power associated with the foreign policy prerogative implied by the power to conclude treaties is likely to be.

The ability of treaties to impact national agendas is a highly conditional claim. It operates on the margins within some states with a proclivity to embrace rights anyway. This is a mechanism that is available only within the sincere ratifiers. It is also only a claim that international treaties can change national *legislative* agendas; it does not speak as such to deeper problems of implementation or enforcement on the ground. Still, it is not trivial. It implies that pro-rights legislative changes may be taken that would not have been in the absence of the exogenously generated legislative agenda shuffle.

If the agenda-setting function of treaties is important, then some observable implications should follow. It should be possible to turn up cases in which the rights issue was not otherwise on the national agenda, but a legislative debate to change national law was prompted by the need to consider treaty ratification. Furthermore, it might be possible to infer that treaty effects are related to shifts in agenda control if positive change in rights legislation is greater in systems where the executive tends to be more constrained vis-à-vis the legislature. We might, for example, expect more legislative innovation upon ratification in presidential systems than in parliamentary ones. It is in the former that treaties significantly enhance the power of the executive to propose legislative rights reforms.

Courts: The Leverage of Litigation

The potential agenda-setting influence of treaties has a subtle influence on relationships between the executive and legislative branches of government, redistributing the power of initiating legislation to the former. Ratified treaties also have implications for the role of the judiciary. In many instances, international legal obligations form an important part of the body of law on which judicial decisions may (or must) be based.

Litigation based on international law is certainly nothing new. "[L]awyers have been trying for over a century and a half to utilize international law material in human rights cases," according to Roger Clark.[51] In the United States, in the early nineteenth century, Francis Scott Key appealed to foreign and customary international law to free the humans imported aboard the *Antelope* (1820); John Quincy Adams did likewise in the *Amistad* case (1841). The rise of explicit treaty law has made awkward appeals to customary international law and foreign practice much less necessary.[52] Increasingly, individuals and groups who use the courts and explicit treaty commitments to leverage their rights claims are holding governments accountable for their human rights behavior. The possibility of litigation changes a government's calculation with respect to compliance. Interfering with or ignoring a ruling of a duly constituted national tribunal greatly raises the political costs of noncompliance. Subject to several important caveats, treaties raise the costs of noncompliance when the international legal system is used to authenticate an individual's complaint.

Treaties make litigation possible because they are (or they give rise to) domestically enforceable legal obligations. In monist legal systems – those that do not distinguish between international and domestic law – ratified treaties are an integral part of the domestic legal system. In such systems, international law has a primary place in a unitary legal system, whether or not national lawmakers take steps to implement international law through specific domestic legislation. In such systems, international legal obligations are directly enforceable in domestic courts. The constitution of the Netherlands, for example, not only recognizes treaties as part of national law; it also states that whenever a statute conflicts with a treaty obligation, the former is void.[53] There is a good deal of variance across countries, but in systems that are monist in conception, there is a strong presumption that international law is directly enforceable in national courts.[54] Many postcommunist countries' constitutions, for example, include provisions incorporating treaties as enforceable domestic law and as superior in constitutional status to statutory and administrative law.[55] In other legal

---

51 Clark 2000:191.

52 In common law systems, customary international law has typically been assumed to have direct effects on national law (consistent with the evolutionary approach to law that these systems evince; see Chapter 3; see the discussion in Ginsburg et al. 2006). The awkwardness in common law systems is not the status of international rules but, as always, determining precisely the content of international custom itself.

53 See the discussion in Ginsburg et al. 2006:4–7. Possibly for this reason, the Netherlands tends to enter a lot of reservations to its treaty ratification. See also Goodman 2002:547.

54 Ginsberg, Elkins, and Chernykh (2006) note that systems can vary in their treatment of treaty law versus customary international law and have developed a number of approaches to conflict-of-law issues.

55 Ryan Goodman (2002:541) lists Armenia, Bulgaria, the Czech Republic, Estonia, Georgia, Kazakhstan, Moldova, Poland, Romania, Russia, Slovakia, and Tajikistan as examples.

systems, typically referred to as "dualist," the influence of international law on the legal system involves the additional step of passing implementing legislation. In these countries – often, though not exclusively, common law countries concerned to preserved parliamentary supremacy and the development of localized legal precedent, as discussed in Chapter 3 – international legal obligations must be "translated" into domestic law in order for their provisions to be enforced in domestic courts.[56] Whenever treaties have direct effects or give rise to implementing legislation, they can provide new tools for litigation that might not have existed in the absence of treaty ratification.

Litigation in national courts is one of the best strategies available for creating homegrown pro-rights jurisprudence.[57] Treaties can be an especially helpful element in this regard. If treaties are cited in a legal case, judges have to think about how they are to be interpreted. One place they may look for interpretive guidance is the reports of the UN implementing committee designed to oversee treaty implementation. Another is decisions of other countries whose courts have already cited the treaty in their decisions. Litigation over rights contained in international treaties increases the opportunity for national courts to engage in the (rather elite) process of transjudicial dialog described by several international legal scholars.[58] Cases with international legal components provide opportunities for judges to import international norms into domestic jurisprudence. In the United States, for example, courts have made a concerted effort to interpret federal statutes in a fashion consistent with U.S. international treaty obligations.[59]

The existence of a tool does not guarantee that it will be used, of course. The availability of treaty law certainly does not ensure that litigation will take place.

---

56 Local implementation does not, however, affect the nature of the *international* legal obligation (the obligation to other states to observe treaty commitments). Some countries are neither monist nor dualist, but have more complicated rules that specify whether a treaty is automatically incorporated into the domestic legal system or whether, to be enforceable in domestic courts, it must be implemented through domestic law. In the United States, for example, some treaties are considered self-executing, and hence enforceable in U.S. courts, while others are considered non-self-executing and requiring implementing legislation to be enforceable in this way. For a discussion of U.S. law in this area see Stone 2005:332. In some cases, the United States has explicitly tried to reduce the possibility of domestic enforcement by entering reservations upon ratification that specify particular articles as non-self-executing. In the case of the ICCPR, the United States stipulated its understanding that Articles 1–27 of the convention were in fact non-self-executing (Article III(1)). U.S. reservations to the ICCPR can be found at http://www1.umn.edu/humanrts/usdocs/civilres.html (accessed 12 August 2008). According to some eminent scholars, the monist/dualist distinction does not matter for the way states actually engage international law. Louis Henkin claims that "Differences between monism and dualism, I emphasize, were theoretical, conceptual; they appear not to have inspired significant differences between states in their application of international law" (1995:65).
57 Osofsky 1997. On transnational public law litigation generally, see Koh 1991.
58 See, for example, Slaughter 1995.
59 Brewster (2003:21) discusses in the U.S. context "rules that construe other federal law to be consistent with our treaty obligations," citing the case of *Murray v. the Schooner Charming Betsy* (1804).

Potential litigants must be aware – or be made aware – of their rights under international law (or under the implementing legislation it has inspired). A certain degree of "legal literacy" is required if individuals are to access the courts. Rights organizations are crucial actors in this regard. Sally Engel Merry has recently documented many efforts of various rights organizations to enhance legal literacy and encourage individuals to cast their complaints in terms of legally enforceable rights. In Fiji, for example, the local women's rights movement has worked since the early 1990s on legal literacy campaigns, focusing on CEDAW and women's rights.[60] Legal literacy has been an important part of certain NGOs' strategy to encourage women to claim their rights in Africa,[61] suggesting the possibility of converting cultural resistance into a rights framework potentially pursuable in the courts.

The existence of a new legal tool also does not mean that it will be fairly employed. One of the most important conditions for litigation to be a potentially useful strategy to enforce rights is judicial independence. For courts to play an important enforcement role, they must be at least somewhat free from political control.[62] The government or one of its agencies, representatives, or allies is likely to be the defendant in rights cases, and unless local courts have the necessary insulation from politics, they are unlikely to agree to hear and even less likely to rule against their political benefactors. Anticipating futility, individuals or groups may decide to avoid the courts altogether.[63]

It is important to put these limitations on litigation in their proper perspective. Certainly, thousands of violations go unlitigated because individuals do not have the resources or the information to mount a court case. Undoubtedly, law operates in its traditional fashion only by institutions prepared to interpret and apply it fairly and independently. But as I will argue, much research suggests that litigation's power resides not so much in its ability to provide every victim with a decisive win in court. Litigation is also a *political* strategy, with the power to inspire rule revision and further to mobilize political movements. It can often be used strategically not only to win cases, but also to publicize and mobilize a cause.

Examples of litigation involving rights guaranteed by ratified treaties can be found in every region of the globe. Human rights litigation is burgeoning in some parts of the developing world, notably in Latin American countries with fairly recent histories of severe rights abuses.[64] Several African countries have

---

60 Merry 2006:172.
61 Hodgson 2003.
62 Frank Cross (1999) finds judicial independence to be crucial to the enforcement of domestic human rights, such as freedom from unreasonable search and seizure. La Porta et al. (2004) find that countries with greater judicial independence also have higher levels of freedom.
63 See, for example, the model developed by Powell and Staton 2007.
64 Lutz and Sikkink 2001.

used international treaties to shape their own jurisprudence on civil and political rights. Namibian courts have referred to the ICCPR to provide guidance in the determination of national discrimination law.[65] Botswanian courts have made reference to international instruments to determine reasonable criteria for a fair trial.[66] The Russian court has used international law to support its decisions in criminal justice cases as well, instructing the rest of the judiciary to apply the ICCPR over domestic legislation in cases involving petitions about the lawfulness of detentions.[67] In Japan, women have used the courts to realize their right not to be discriminated against in employment, and in Israel, the Supreme Court has ruled that certain interrogation practices do, in fact, constitute torture as understood by the Committee Against Torture.[68] Cases filed in the Indian Supreme Court in 1994 "asked the Court to order the government to show what steps were being taken to end discrimination in the personal laws consistent with the principles of CEDAW," thus effectively forcing the government to articulate the extent of its compliance with its 1993 ratification commitment.[69]

Litigation has grown in importance in many countries because of a growing network of "cause lawyers" with the interest and the expertise to push human rights cases through the courts. Cause lawyering – or legal work that is "directed at altering some aspect of the social, economic, and political status quo"[70] – is traditionally associated with the litigation campaigns of the NAACP in the case of the civil rights movement of the United States. In many parts of the developing world, it has evolved into a broader conception of "alternative lawyering," which Stephen Ellman describes as legal work emphasizing "working with and organizing community groups rather than simply taking a random set of individual cases," at times even deemphasizing litigation in favor of working with governmental agencies and using alternative dispute resolution methods, but almost always emphasizing legal literacy at the grassroots level.[71]

The question remains whether litigation is an effective way to achieve a real improvement in rights practices. Certainly, a strategy of using courts has its limits. Because it proceeds on a case-by-case basis, the absolute number of cases one could cite to illustrate this mechanism is bound to be small. Even where judiciaries are relatively independent, as in the United States, rules that restrict

---

65 Tshosa 2001:110.
66 Tshosa 2001:172.
67 Danilenko and Burnham 2000:43.
68 These and other examples of successful litigation based on human rights treaties are collected by a variety of NGOs. See, for example, http://madre.org/articles/int/hrconv.html (accessed 12 August 2008).
69 Merry 2006:167.
70 Sarat and Scheingold 1998:4.
71 Ellmann 1998:359.

access to the courts have been shown to be important barriers to successful legal mobilization.[72] Courts typically do not have the resources to enforce their decisions against branches of government – including a conservative bureaucracy – determined to resist.[73] Gerald Rosenberg views litigation as a "hollow hope" for furthering social change, even in the United States, where courts tend to be independent and legal resources relatively plentiful.[74] He argues that litigation contributed marginally to the civil rights movement in the United States. The movement was succeeding in any case, Rosenberg argues; winning in court was not decisive in influencing rights outcomes.[75] Some researchers conclude that litigation is such a cumbersome way to proceed that some social movements are better off pursuing other, less status-quo-preserving tactics.[76]

A spate of research (largely centered on litigation in the U.S. civil rights case) has hotly contested Rosenberg's conclusion, noting that litigation influences the way issues are "conceived, expressed, argued about, and struggled over."[77] By mechanisms familiar to constructivist theorists, litigation contributes to the reframing of political demands in the legitimizing framework of rights. Moreover, litigation can be mounted with relatively few participants, thus helping to overcome the collective action problems[78] that often make it difficult to mobilize a broad coalition for "justice." Thus, Robert Glennon's analysis of the history of the U.S. civil rights movement concludes that successful litigation provided a "shot of adrenaline" during the Montgomery, Alabama, bus boycott that helped to consolidate the gains resulting from direct protest.[79] Alan Hunt holds out the "possibility that [even] litigation 'failure' may, paradoxically, provide the conditions of 'success' that compel a movement forward."[80] Social movement leaders often choose to litigate strategically,[81] and often *after* favorable laws have been passed, precisely in order to sustain the movement and to ensure favorable interpretation and enforcement.[82]

---

72 Frymer 2003:486–8. On the potential for human rights litigation in the United States, see Tolley 1991. The point is that the potential exists, but it is relatively limited. Individuals' access to courts varies greatly. The Supreme Court of India, for example, has decided that cases can be taken up on behalf of those in poverty who are unable to file for themselves and that such cases can be initiated simply by letter. See Ellman 1998:358.
73 James Spriggs (1996) finds, for example, that a number of parameters influence the ability and willingness of administrative agencies effectively to overturn U.S. Supreme Court decisions.
74 Rosenberg 1991.
75 See also Rosenberg's response to his critics (1992). With a similarly skeptical view that "legal mobilization" has a decisive impact on social movements or the rights they have espoused, see Brown-Nagin 2005.
76 On the case of the environmental movement, see Coglianese 2001–2.
77 Hunt 1990:320.
78 Zemans 1983:698.
79 Glennon 1991:61–2.
80 Hunt 1990:320.
81 Including somewhat "fringe" groups, such as animal rights groups in the United States. See Silverstein 1996:227.
82 Burstein 1991; Burstein and Monaghan 1986.

International treaties, as part of domestic law, provide another opportunity for individuals (usually in cooperation with activist legal advisers) to claim, define, and struggle over a right that might not have a well-defined or well-tested counterpart in domestic law. The risk, of course, is that litigation risks loss and potential delegitimation, but even a loss can be useful publicity to a movement under some circumstances. A favorable ruling by an authoritative judicial body carries a great deal of weight in many countries. Such decisions can be ignored, but at a greater political cost than would be the case in their absence. Legislatures can often craft or recraft rules that denigrate the rights treaties are designed to protect, but this comes at a price as well. The Israeli Supreme Court, for example, ruled that interrogation practices allowing for moderate physical pressure contravened that country's obligations under the CAT, but the court also held that the Knesset was free to legislate a specific intent to override those obligations. Were it to do so, however, the Knesset would have to endure criticism for making Israel, in Stanley Cohen's words, "the only country in the world to legislate torture."[83] Bureaucracies, too, may resist. No one believes that a court victory alone produces permanent rights changes. Rather, the point is that availability of litigation – and the crucial role of a *treaty commitment* rather than customary international law (which is harder to establish empirically) or a mere norm – is a crucial legitimating lever and can interact positively with political mobilization generally. Especially when treaties have direct effects in countries with independent judicial systems and broad respect for the rule of law, litigation is potentially an important mechanism for compliance.

Group Demands: Rights and Mobilization

A third mechanism by which international human rights treaties can influence rights outcomes is through their strategic use as a tool to support political mobilization. This section begins with a discussion of the mobilization process and then argues that ratified treaties can interact with such processes to enhance the likelihood that individuals will mobilize to claim the rights the treaties contain. I first consider the social mobilization process itself and ask, under what conditions can citizens be expected to mobilize to claim a set of human rights from their political leaders? Second, I argue that international treaties influence the probability of mobilization. They do this in two principal ways. International human rights treaties influence the value individuals place on the right in question (the value of succeeding), and they raise the likelihood of success. Given the proper political opening, international human rights treaties can have a significant impact on domestic politics at the mass level.

---

83 The quote can be found in an interview located at http://www.abbc2.com/historia/zionism/torture.html (accessed 12 August 2008).

Why Mobilize? Theories of Social Mobilization

Before discussing the role of international human rights law, it is useful to discuss why it is that individuals form or join groups to demand social or political change at all. The underlying issues are complex, but for individuals, we can think of mobilization as a function of two basic assessments: the *value* they place on the rights in question and the *probability that they will be successful* in their demands. The willingness to mobilize – to formulate a set of demands and to organize to press for them – can be thought of in terms of an individual's "expected utility," or the value of the outcome scaled by the likelihood that it can be realized. Individuals are much more likely to demand their rights when there is a perceived "rights gap" (there is much, potentially, to be gained), as well as a reasonable likelihood of success (a political and social environment that is relatively tolerant to such demands). The expected value of mobilization is highest when *the interaction* of these conditions is at its maximum.[84] People can hardly be expected to make a rights demand when there is practically no chance of succeeding, as in the case of immediate, harsh government repression. On the other hand, the motivation to demand is also low when the perceived value of the right demanded is marginal. Where rights are already well supplied and protected, the motive to demand more is fairly weak.

One reason people organize to demand political or social change is the sense that something is seriously wrong or unjust in their society. The concept of "grievance" has long been a central part of sociological theories of mobilization and plays a central role in many, if not most, accounts of social movements. Grievances can have many sources, depending on the nature of the society in question. Traditional explanations for grievances have emphasized sudden "structural strains" caused, in turn, by rapid social or economic change, by changes in power relations, or by structural conflicts of interest.[85] On the other hand, more "entrepreneurial" accounts suggest that given a basic latent discontent based on major interest cleavages, it is possible for energetic movement entrepreneurs to act without the rise of a significant new grievance. The point is not that grievances are manufactured de novo by such entrepreneurs but that they are able to tap into existing discontent, raising the chances of mobilization even in the absence of an abrupt structural upheaval.[86] To a large extent, we can

---

84 Cost–benefit calculations of this kind are a central theme in what some scholars have dubbed the "second wave" of social movement theory. See, for example, Zirakzadeh 2006:235–6. The logic advanced in this section is related to the logic discussed in the literature on political violence and repression. This literature emphasizes that mild political openings in a formerly repressive regime can lead some groups to make their political demands violently and for the government to counter with redoubled political repression. See, for example, Buena de Mesquita et al. 2005; Fein 1995; Gurr 1986; Muller 1985.

85 See, respectively, Gusfield 1968; Korpi 1974; plus McCarthy and Zald 1977 and Zald and McCarthy 1979.

86 McCarthy and Zald 1977.

think of discontent as structural, arising from the existing political, social, and economic relationships within a given society. In some cases, of course, grievances may be sharpened and focused by leaders who may have their own interest in stimulating the rights demands of aggrieved individuals or groups.

The most significant *variable* – or conditions subject to change and manipulation in the fairly short-term – in explaining mobilization is the probability that demanding a right will, in fact, turn out to be *successful*. The probability of success can turn on exogenous change in the existing political space; mobilization stands a much better chance as authoritarian regimes begin to come under greater challenge generally, for example. The probability of success is also influenced by shifts in the power and influence of the social movement itself. "Resource mobilization theory" emphasizes that movement success is influenced by tangible resources (money, facilities, and means of communication) as well as intangible resources (legitimacy, experience, various forms of human capital or skills, etc.).[87] One of the most important resources for a movement's success has been found to be support from actors who are not direct beneficiaries of the movement's goals. As Alan Hunt has written, ". . . one of the most important features of any such strategic project is the concern to find ways of going beyond the limited expression of the immediate interests of social groups . . . such that they connect up with and find ways of articulating the aspirations of wider constituencies."[88] Although there has been a good deal of debate over exactly which resources strengthen a group's political position, generally the greater a nascent movement's access to tangible and intangible resources, the better its chances of success.

The question of how such groups overcome collective action problems is still an issue. How do "the aggrieved" form an effective political force, considering that "justice" by definition is a collective good? The problem is compounded if the potential group of aggrieved individuals is geographically dispersed; it is mitigated somewhat if they are in relatively close geographical proximity.[89] One answer lies in cultivating group solidarity – strengthening group identity so that individuals incorporate outcomes for the groups into

---

87 Freeman 1979.
88 Hunt 1990:315–16. The campaign to ban child soldiers, for example, would never have gotten off the ground had it depended on the political voice of the world's children to express demands for protection. Resource mobilization includes the ability to garner resources and political support from individuals and groups that sometimes end up speaking for rather than working with the aggrieved groups.
89 Geography has been important for political mobilization of a broad range of latent political forces. In political economy, Busch and Reinhardt (2000) have found that protection is higher for geographically concentrated industries. In the rights area, studies have found that urbanization provided the geographical proximity helpful in organizing the southern black population in the United States (Wilson 1973). See also Handler (1978:16–18) who emphasizes the distribution (dispersed versus concentrated) of both costs and benefits in the likelihood of social mobilization.

their individual utility function.[90] Another answer lies in selective incentives. Divisible benefits are traditionally weak in the human rights area, although some have theorized the role that such incentives as career opportunities or individually bestowed moral approval may play for the entrepreneurial leaders themselves.[91] While notions of group solidarity, moral commitment, and intangible rewards can take us some way toward understanding human rights mobilization, it is generally the case that resources for human rights organizations are likely to be undersupplied.

In short, the formation and success of social and political movements are often linked to political, legal, organizational, or social changes that reduce the costs of mobilization and improve the likelihood of success.[92] International human rights treaties can prove to be an important resource in this regard. Such treaties are potentially important resources in domestic mobilization because, under some conditions, *they raise the expected value of mobilizing* to make a rights demand. As I discuss in the following two sections, they can change the value individuals place on succeeding as well as the probability of success.[93] In this way, treaties change the complexion of domestic politics in ways that make a net positive contribution to rights practices in many – though not all – countries around the world.

This is a "bottom-up" account of treaty effects that contrasts state-centered approaches prevalent in the international relations literature. When international relations scholars think of treaty effects, they are far more likely to have in mind the effects of an international agreement on states than on their citizens; on elites rather than on civil society. Martha Finnemore's work emphasizes international organizations as the normative teachers of *state elites*. Harold Koh's theory of transnational judicial process stems from transnational interactions among *judicial elites*, which generate rules for future interactions, which are eventually internalized. Jon Pevehouse's theory of democratization from the outside in and Iain Johnston's account of Chinese socialization focus on the role that face-to-face elite interactions in regional organizations can play in sensitizing *bureaucratic elites* to their interests in democratization and regional cooperation.[94] Possibly for very good reasons, citizens play no role in these accounts. They must play a central role, however, in the diffusion of values for the

---

90 Jenkins 1983.

91 Jenkins 1983:536.

92 Jenkins 1983.

93 This formulation draws on both of the major strands of legal mobilization literature: that of legal behavioralism, which tends to "identify law primarily in instrumental, determinate, positivist terms" and interpretive approaches, which focus on "the intersubjective power of law in constructing meaning." See the review of these literatures in McCann 2006. (Quotes from page 21.)

94 See Finnemore 1993; Johnston 2002; Koh 1999; Pevehouse 2002. See also Checkel 2001, who argues that Ukraine's elites' attitudes toward nationality policy were subject to persuasion by European elites.

protection of individual rights. *Rights treaties affect the welfare of individuals.* If there is any international issue area in which socialization at the nonelite level is important, this should be it.[95]

In the politics of social mobilization, law can play an important role. "Legal mobilization" is the term sociologists and other scholars have given to the act of invoking legal norms to regulate behavior. The law can be mobilized quite outside of the litigation processes described in the previous section. The law is mobilized whenever "a desire or want is translated into a demand as an assertion of one's right."[96] The making of claims based on legal rights is an especially effective way of asserting a political or social demand, because it grounds one's claims in the legitimacy of law, on which most governments claim that their own legitimacy is based. Legal mobilization can be thought of as a form of political participation, not necessarily as a form of conflict containment or resolution. Indeed, scholars of legal mobilization have long recognized that law can be used as a political resource. Agents vie for control of this resource as they would for any other, sometimes leading to conflicts among groups (women and men; gays and straights; ethnic groups; dominant groups and dissidents) and between a group and a government.[97] Quite aside from the benefits (and risks) associated with litigation, legal mobilization in the broader sense of appealing to legal rights promotes movement organization and claim-making.[98]

International human rights treaties are useful in this mobilization process. I argue that they are useful in two ways. They can be useful in introducing rights claims to potential claimants, helping them to imagine themselves as bearers of such rights and encouraging them to value the substantive content of the treaty in question. Treaties can increase the value that potential rights demanders place on a set of rights. Ratified treaties can also increase the likelihood of a movement's eventual success in realizing its rights demands. The availability of international treaty law can thus increase agents' expected value of social/political mobilization, in turn increasing pressure on governments to live up to their legal obligations. These treaty effects are discussed in the following two sections.

Treaties, Rights Demands, and the Value of Succeeding

Legal frameworks are important resources in social mobilization because they have a powerful influence over how individuals and groups understand their identity and define their interests. One of the most powerful treaty effects is the introduction of a new set of rights and a new understanding of rights claimants into the local political setting. Treaties are externally negotiated agreements,

---

95 Jeffrey Checkel (1997) develops a framework in which the role civil society groups play is conditioned by the nature of domestic institutions, whether liberal, corporatist, or statist.
96 Zemans 1983:700.
97 Turk 1976:284.
98 McCann 1994.

which are *potentially* a source of great influence in local polities. They often introduce ideas and conceptions that are foreign, new, or at least not well articulated in a given local setting. This is the source of their potentially radical power but also, ironically, of their irrelevance. The transformative potential of externally negotiated law depends importantly on the success of "translating" external norms for local audiences, a condition I address in greater detail subsequently.

A growing body of research seems to indicate that legal frameworks have a significant impact on how individuals understand their interests and even their identities. Part of the "educative role of law," according to early work by Frances Zemans, is its ability to "change the citizenry's perceptions of their interests."[99] According to Patricia Ewick and Susan Silbey, legal frameworks are an important source of cultural schemas "that operate to define and pattern social life"[100] and, as such, exert a powerful influence over how people think of their rights and interests. New research on social movements focuses on such identity-formation processes and has found that people's actions are structured by deeply held beliefs,[101] which in turn respond, at least in part, to social conventions as reflected in legal arrangements.

Much of the evidence for these claims comes from studies of the influence of domestic legal frames on how people think about issues that concern them. Anna Maria Marshall's research shows that women use legal frames as a criterion for understanding their experiences of sexual harassment on the job.[102] Willima Eskridge, Jr.'s, research on equality in the United States found that "law contributed to group consciousness and motivation to seek greater equality by people of color, gay people, women, and people with disabilities. . . ."[103] He argues that law that discriminates or tries to end discrimination between or among groups is especially influential in hastening group identity formation. The process of using legal rights to enhance political mobilization and identity formation was crucial to identity formation of the U.S. civil rights movement. According to Elizabeth Schneider, civil rights activists "asserted rights not simply to advance [a] legal argument or to win a case, but to express the politics, vision, and demands of a social movement, and to assist in the political self-definition of that movement. We understood that winning legal rights would not be meaningful without political organizing to ensure enforcement of and education concerning those rights."[104] Drawing on these and other studies, Alan

---

99 Zemans 1983:697.
100 Ewick and Silbey 1998:43.
101 Zirakzadeh 2006:235.
102 Marshall 2003.
103 Eskridge 2001–2:451.
104 Schneider 1986:605. See also Francesca Polletta's (2000) recent study of the civil rights movement in the southern United States. She concludes that legal mobilization, including victories inside and outside of the courtroom, was a significant factor in overcoming the collective action problems of the movement.

Hunt advances a "Gramscian" perspective on rights that highlights their potential to change the discourse and thus to contribute to the political struggle.[105]

International human rights agreements have the potential to influence domestic politics because they suggest new ways for individuals to view their relationship with their government and with each other. The ICCPR suggests that individuals have a clear sphere of freedom for participating in political life; the CERD suggests to racial minorities their right to participate equally in the social and political life of their community and country; the CEDAW suggests to women that they are men's equals and entreats them to start viewing themselves in that light. In some societies, these suggestions will be superfluous (Scandinavian women may already view themselves as men's equals). In others they will be resisted; no doubt the very act of framing a practice as a right will resonate to differing degrees in different cultures.[106] But in many cases, human rights accords will contain highly attractive principles for a quite receptive mass audience segment.[107] Some citizens may not have thought of a particular practice in rights terms at all. Others may have questioned the appropriateness of thinking that way. When this is the case, international legal agreements are important because they can "condition actors' self-understandings, references, and behavior. . . ."[108] William Eskridge's perspective is apt: "A social group defined and penalized by [local] legal stigmas will not have an incentive to organize so long as most of its members view their stigma as justified, acceptable, or inevitable."[109] International legal standards that explicitly provide otherwise are useful alternative frameworks by which the oppressed gain a sense of political identity, legitimacy, and efficacy.

New research in social anthropology helps us to understand the processes by which international legal rights can influence the way local people form their identity as rights claimants and understand their interests. Sally Engle Merry's study on translating international human rights into local justice is especially helpful in this regard. Merry focuses on the critical role of local individuals who are deeply rooted in a particular local social and political context but with extensive connections to international and transnational communities in translating human rights from the "universal" to the "local vernacular." These actors – which in her case study of gender violence include national political elites, human rights lawyers, feminist activists and movement leaders, social workers and other social service providers, and academics – play a crucial role in bringing transnational cultural understandings to local settings.

105 Hunt 1990.
106 Cook 1993.
107 "A social group defined and penalized by legal stigmas will not have an incentive to organize so long as most of its members view their stigma as justified, acceptable, or inevitable" (Eskridge 2001–2:439).
108 Reus-Smit 2004:3. The influence of international law can be especially significant in this regard in transitioning countries. See, for example, Teitel 2000.
109 Eskridge 2001–2:439.

Transnational programs and ideas are translated into local cultural terms by these agents, but Merry notes that in doing so, they "retain their fundamental grounding in transnational human rights concepts of autonomy, individualism, and equality."[110] Merry's study suggests that individuals do not abandon their earlier values/perspectives; they layer new transnational human rights perspectives over them.[111] With the help of cultural translators, for example, indigenous women in Hong Kong developed a sustained critique of their problems in claiming property rights based on human rights as outlined in the CEDAW, and were much more successful in articulating and realizing their rights when they did compared to a frame that allowed the women's plight to be interpreted as a mere family squabble.[112]

The strategy of using treaties to raise rights consciousness is observable in the activities of many groups and organizations. NGOs have often specifically positioned themselves to educate people about the rights contained in documents their own governments have signed. Relatively new rights organizations, such as those of the disabled rights movement, view treaties as an important way to raise public consciousness about rights issues in this area.[113] The Coalition to Stop the Use of Child Soldiers "campaigns for all governments to adhere to international laws prohibiting the use of children under the age of 18 in armed conflict" in the context of its advocacy and public education functions.[114] The newly negotiated International Convention for the Protection of All Persons from Enforced Disappearance (2005) is viewed by transnational rights organizations as "an extremely important development in the fight against forced disappearances and for the protection of victims and their families,"[115] and these organizations advocate ratification as a tool for explicitly recognizing and educating people regarding a right not to "be disappeared" as a way to hold governments accountable. Francesca Polletta's research on the U.S. civil rights movement cautions that such innovative rights framing is most likely to occur and to be effective ". . . in settings where social institutions (legal, religious, familial, economic) enjoy relative autonomy, and when organizers are at some remove from state and movement centers of power."[116] But in many cases, organizations are positioned to advertise the existence and contents of a treaty commitment that, if taken seriously, turns out to be inconvenient for the government and other power brokers, providing identities and rights models that run counter to commonly held conceptions.

110 Merry 2006:177–8.
111 Merry 2006:180.
112 Merry 2006:202.
113 Disability 2002.
114 See the Web site of the coalition at http://www.child-soldiers.org/coalition/what-we-do (accessed 12 August 2008).
115 See Human Rights Watch: http://hrw.org/english/docs/2005/09/26/global11785.htm (accessed 12 August 2008).
116 Polletta 2000:369.

Human rights treaties, in short, may contain persuasive new information and ideas that can influence the values and beliefs of a public for whose benefit the agreement was ostensibly designed. They can put local cultural or political practices in a more universalistic perspective, suggesting a right to which some might not have previously considered themselves entitled. *Ratified* treaties reveal new information regarding a government's formal complicity in the rights enterprise, signaling for domestic audiences the legitimacy of pursuing rights in this specific cultural and political context. Treaties can inform interests and change values. Admittedly, the meaning of rights contained in international conventions is hardly determinative, and there is much room for contention and struggle over just what it means to be a legitimate rights claimant.[117] Nonetheless, treaties express collective intentionality,[118] the full meaning of which cannot easily be controlled by local power brokers. The fact that one's own government may have participated in and assented to this collective project legitimates it as an acceptable set of values in the local context. Officially acknowledging a set of rights – publicly and possibly for the first time – can affirm its value in the public consciousness.

This view of law as framing new interests and even identities (as legitimate claimants) stands in contrast to several other perspectives. In contrast to the view of Jack Goldsmith and Eric Posner,[119] I argue that moral/legal talk cannot be assumed to be costless, for it risks changing the values, identities, and interests of potential beneficiaries. Now, it could be that for the reasons alluded to in the previous chapter (short time horizons or poor information, which encourage strategic ratification), governments do not expect to bear the cost of new rights demands, but this does not prevent the potential for the educative or framing function of law described previously. This account is also distinct from the information role of international institutions, though information – about the existence of a public obligation, the nature of the rights at stake, and the rectitude of demanding compliance – is relevant. International institutions are not just a source of information in this account, as they are in Xinyuan Dai's analysis of monitoring regimes with weak enforcement; they are a source of new ideas as well.[120] "Information" in this conception is not exclusively about

---

117 A lot of new research on legal mobilization emphasizes that "The indeterminate meaning of rights . . . provides the [political or social] movement with space in which to shape its own identity" (Silverstein 1996:232). It also opens up the possibility, even the likelihood, of a conservative effort to delimit new understandings consistent with the interests of the dominant social and political power holders.

118 Collective intentionality is a key concept in much constructivist thought. See the discussion in Ruggie 1998.

119 See the discussion in Goldsmith and Posner 2002. The primary "rational" explanation for moral talk in international relations is that it is costless. Since to refrain from moral (or legal) talk might be interpreted as amoral (or a-legal), Goldsmith and Posner (2002) argue that there may be some benefit but little downside risk to making moral arguments.

120 Dai 2005.

objective realities that may be hidden from voting publics. It is also about conceptual frames that may serve to animate the demands of those whose ability, regularly and at low cost, to turn their leaders out of office is much less secure. Treaties matter because they potentially change the ideas that inspire political organization and activity. Ironically, this treaty effect may be stronger – because it is more radical – in repressive regimes than in those that are already quite free.

Mobilization Success

The preceding argument is about the recognition of *values* that people are convinced are worth organizing to demand. This section is about the *resources* a ratified treaty can bring to the fight. As social movement theorists have recently emphasized, legal rules and institutions are themselves a type of political opportunity structure that enables and constrains social movements.[121] Here I argue that a ratified treaty can do four things to improve the chances of successful mobilization. First, it precommits the government to be receptive to the demand; second, it may increase the size of the coalition; third, it enhances the intangible resources available to the coalition; and fourth, it expands the range of strategies the coalition may employ to secure the realization of their demands. Each of these effects will be discussed in turn.

Let us begin with one of the unique features of a ratified treaty compared to a broad international norm. A ratified treaty *precommits* the government to be receptive to rights demands. Ratification is not just a costly signal of intent; it is a process of domestic legitimation that some scholars have shown raises the domestic salience of an international rule.[122] In most countries, governments are required to submit international treaties to the legislature and to secure at least a majority vote. Some countries have even higher ratification barriers: The United States requires treaties to be ratified with the advice and two-thirds consent of the Senate. In a few countries, ratification requires a majority vote in both of two legislative chambers. Westminster parliamentary systems traditionally have not required a formal vote of the parliament, but have evolved norms that ensure that that body basically approves the treaty before the executive formally ratifies. Obviously, in some countries, ratification is a meaningless political gesture, just as all votes of the legislature are meaningless. But where the legislature has any independent stature at all, ratification engages its reputation for meaningful political activity. This does not mean, of course, that a ratified treaty will be promptly and unproblematically implemented into domestic law. It does mean, however, that individuals or groups with demands consistent with a ratified treaty are more likely to encounter a legislature "primed" – because they are precommitted – seriously to consider their demands. Ratification increases the probability that the legislative body itself may be – or at least contain – important political allies.

121 Pedriana 2004. See also Gamson and Meyer 1996:289; O'Brien 1996:32.
122 Cortell and Davis 1996:456.

Ratification precommitment has a subtle effect on the politics of rule implementation. Precommitment makes it harder for a government that has secured
domestic ratification to plausibly deny the importance of rights protection in
the local context. Even ratification that could be mere lip service has an important influence on domestic politics. Kathryn Sikkink has written that "The
passage from denial to lip service may seem insignificant but suggests an important shift in the shared understandings of states that make certain justifications
no longer acceptable."[123] The domestic act of ratification has even clearer implications for domestic understandings. As I have repeatedly argued, a citizenry
has an even stronger motive than the international community to demand consistency in their government's behavior; after all, they live with the consequences of this behavior on a daily basis. Disingenuous governments will face
inconsistency costs and thus risk loss of a degree of domestic legitimacy to
the extent that their populations expect commitments to correspond at least
in a very broad way to policies and practices. Ratification of important human
rights treaties has the potential to raise governments' consistency costs at home
and thereby to erode their domestic political support.

Rights demanders and their advocates work assiduously to expose the
inconsistencies between precommitment and post-ratification behavior in
countries around the world. Advocates for Tibetan rights include in their literature a list of the "relevant" human rights instruments that the People's Republic of China has signed (and presumably violated) in that country's treatment of
ethnic Tibetans.[124] The Baha'i International Community refers to the ICCPR as
one of "various international covenants on human rights that the government
has freely signed" to legitimate its demands for religious freedom for the Baha'i
living in Iran.[125] Groups that allege that the U.S. government has violated the
privacy of U.S. citizens frame their complaints in terms of treaty violations for
similar reasons.[126] Governments and even individual legislators who want to
avoid apparent inconsistencies in their ratification position and post-ratification
program are potential allies of a nascent rights movement.

The availability of legislators as allies leads directly to the next point: Ratified treaties offer opportunities to increase the size of the pro-rights coalitions in
ways that would be less available without the ratified treaties. One of the most
important insights of resource mobilization theories of social movements has
been to point to the importance of out-of-group supporters in joining the initial
cause – white students joining the civil rights movements of the 1960s, for

---

123 Sikkink 1993:415.
124 See, for example, Appendix 4 to the 2004 Annual Report of the Tibetan Centre for Human
Rights and Democracy at http://www.tchrd.org/publications/annual_reports/2004/appendices/
4_ratifi.html (accessed 12 August 2008).
125 See their Web site at http://denial.bahai.org/004_5.php (accessed 12 August 2008).
126 See, for example, a 21 December 2005 press release of the Meiklejohn Civil Liberties Institute,
Berkeley, California; posted at http://www.uslaboragainstwar.org/article.php?id=9849 (accessed
12 August 2008).

example. The ratification of a treaty has the potential to bring in a broader range of allies to join the core beneficiaries in demanding rights implementation. One group might be individuals who oppose or want to constrain the government for reasons that do not relate explicitly to their own individual current rights struggles. Government opponents might decide to seize on the rights issue – playing up the inconsistency discussed previously – to embarrass or even bring down a government they oppose on other grounds. A ratified treaty could serve as a focal point for tactical support of a pro-rights coalition by a broad range of government opponents.

Second, as a form of law, ratified treaties are more likely than international norms or treaties the government has rejected to engage the interest of the legal profession. The mechanism here may be of two kinds. Legal interest groups may take a new interest in the issues covered by the treaty, debating, publicizing, and interpreting its meaning within the local legal system. Additionally, legally trained individuals – strongly motivated by selective incentives – may decide to lend their professional expertise to the nascent rights movement, providing the legal, technical, and advocacy skills that many students of social movements have noted are critical to their success.[127]

"Internationalists" – individuals or organizations that have strong material interests in maintaining good public relations with the outside world – may also have an incentive to support a local pro-rights movement. After all, treaty ratification is also an international commitment. I have argued that it is an international commitment that is unlikely to be enforced reliably, but even a small probability of enforcement is a serious worry for domestic groups that depend heavily on good political relationships with the outside world. In some countries, the pro-rights group will be supported in their quest by pro-internationalist groups that believe they have more to gain from their government's rights cooperation than from its intransigence. While they may be only mildly committed to rights per se, internationalists may support their demands *in the presence of a ratified treaty* as an insurance policy against the small probability that to renege could introduce political friction into their external relations – their foreign trade, travel, or investments. In this way, a treaty can change a *pro-rights* coalition into a *pro-compliance* coalition. The latter is almost by definition larger than the former. In short, a ratified (but unimplemented) treaty provides an opening for governmental opponents, actors with legal expertise, and actors with international interests to ally with a nascent rights movements for tactical reasons that may be orthogonal to those of rights claimants themselves.

Third, a ratified treaty provides *intangible resources* to a nascent rights coalition. The most important of these is legitimacy, which in turn can be

---

127 Note, however, that there is a debate in the legal mobilization literature that legal tactics divert movement resources to lawyers and away from grassroots mobilization, to the detriment of the movement. See, for example, Brown-Nagin 2005; McCann 1986; Rosenberg 1992; Scheingold 1974.

parlayed into further political support. Treaties are especially useful in establishing the legitimacy of a claim because they represent global agreement on "best practices" and as such offer a fairly clear statement of the nature (and limits) of the demands the group is making. In the Russian context of the early 1990s, for example, Gennady Danilenko writes that "The legitimacy attributed to international human rights standards was . . . based on the general perception that they expressed 'universal human values' shared by the majority of the international community."[128] This is particularly important when local rights standards are new, in question, or in flux.[129] In these cases, treaties play crucial roles in providing benchmarks, focal points, and models. As a benchmark, they provide standards against which both the demands of the populace and the actions of the government can be assessed. The treaty provides reassurance to citizens that their rights demands are not unreasonable, making them more willing to mobilize. As a focal point, a ratified treaty can also help to coordinate and prioritize the efforts of the coalition. In India, for example, the National Commission for Women (NCW) was set up in 1990 to safeguard women's interests by reviewing legislation, intervening in individual complaints, and undertaking remedial actions, but they seized on India's 1993 ratification of the CEDAW to pressure the Indian government to implement specific programs.[130] Finally, ratified treaties provide a resource as models for domestic legislation. Sally Engle Merry's study of India and China reveals the extent to which the CEDAW has effectively been imported into a number of important legislative protections for women.[131]

Finally, treaty ratification increases the range of strategies a social movement can use to secure policy change. To circle back to the point developed previously with respect to litigation, a ratified treaty has in many countries the status of law and thus offers a unique point of entry into an important indigenous branch of local governance – the courts. And to reiterate the point stressed earlier, such cases are politically important for rights movements even if they do not result in a decisive legal win.

Treaty ratification also provides a political opening for rights demanders in polities where the courts are unlikely to be accessible or reliable. The voluntary assent of a government to a legal standard of behavior creates room for strategies of "rightful resistance," or the ability of individuals and nascent social movements to use officially sanctioned levers in pressing their rights claims. In Kevin O'Brien's useful formulation, "Rightful resistance is a partly institutionalized

---

128 Danilenko 1994:459.
129 These are the conditions under which Jeffrey Checkel (2001) argues that international norms become most "persuasive."
130 Merry 2006:170–1.
131 Merry cites the Indian 2001 draft domestic violence law, which mentions CEDAW; she also notes that the Law of the People's Republic of China on the Protection of Women's Rights and Interests is based on CEDAW (2006:167).

form of popular action that employs laws, policies, and other established values to defy power holders who have failed to live up to some ideal or who have not implemented a popular measure." The fact that some government official or officials participated in the act of ratification opens the possibility of exploiting divisions among the powerful. As O'Brien notes, "When receptive officials, for instance, champion popular demands to execute laws and policies that have been ignored, unexpected alliances often emerge and simple dominant–subordinate distinctions break down. On these occasions, popular resistance operates partly within (yet in tension with) official norms."[132] Rightful resistance employs the rhetoric and commitments of the powerful to curb political or economic power. Treaty ratification contributes to this strategy by providing a lever to critique the government with its own commitment. Whether a government is sensitive to this critique or not depends on its ability to insulate itself from rights-based popular demands.

To summarize: The ratification of international treaties influences the chances of successful social mobilization. I have provided reasons to expect this influence to work in a positive direction – toward more effective mobilization as expectations of success increase. But these claims are about broad tendencies based on expected influences in domestic politics. In common with other mobilization theorists, I recognize that these kinds of claims can stimulate counter-reactions and conservative opposition. There is nothing inevitable about the triumph of treaty commitments over domestic practices, any more than it is inevitable that all rights appeals will prove irresistible.[133] On balance, however, ratified treaties provide a political opening for rights demanders that is more favorable than is the case in their absence. In combination with their educative function, ratified treaties tend to enhance the motive as well as the means for group mobilization. They tend to increase the expected value of such mobilization.

EXPECTATIONS

The three mechanisms through which treaties might have effects in domestic politics – altering the national agenda, leveraging litigation, and empowering political mobilization – suggest some fairly precise expectations for empirical research. First of all, they suggest that treaty ratification should *generally* have positive effects on various measures of government behavior associated with the obligations contained in ratified treaties. However, none of these mechanisms suggest that international law has a homogeneous effect across all polities. Each mechanism suggests that treaties can be more or less influential *under particular institutional or political conditions.* The purpose of this section is to make this

132 O'Brien 1996:iii and 32.
133 Hunt 1990.

point explicitly for each of the channels through which treaties potentially influence domestic politics (recognizing, of course, that these channels are not at all mutually exclusive).

Altering the National Agenda

I have argued that treaties can have an important influence on national politics simply because they alter the substantive priorities of the legislative agenda compared to what it would have been in the absence of an exogenously presented treaty obligation. This is a modest but not a trivial mechanism. It does not posit a change in the information, preferences, or resources of any domestic political actor. It simply notes that treaty effects – especially legislative changes – can result from a relatively uncontroversial international commitment. Nevertheless, these changes would not have occurred in the absence of the intrusion of international politics into the domestic legislative space.

Agenda effects of the kind described here should be most noticeable in indicators of legislatives output and harder to detect in indicators of changes in actual practice. Moreover, agenda effects should be most noticeable in countries that are most likely to have been among the sincere ratifiers discussed in the previous chapter. The prime candidates for the agenda-setting effects of international legal agreements are expected to be the Western democracies. Finally, agenda-setting effects are likely to be most pronounced in polities in which legislatures tend to have relatively greater control over the national legislative agenda. On the one hand, we might expect greater impact to a treaty negotiated and introduced by the executive if this gives him or her unique agenda-setting power vis-à-vis the legislature. This would lead us to expect a greater treaty agenda-setting impact in presidential systems. If this pattern prevails, we might infer a greater tendency for treaties to empower a president relative to the legislature.

On the other hand, once a treaty has been introduced for ratification (once again, emphasizing that this is a prerogative of the executive), the ability to get legislation passed in compliance with treaty obligations is higher where the government faces no important resistance to placing related legislative reform on the legislature's agenda. If simply altering the national agenda is an important mechanism by which legislative compliance is observed, we might expect ratification to lead to legislative changes more often in systems where legislatures exert fewer effective constraints on the executive. The result in the aggregate is likely to be ambiguous, since agenda changes are likely to be larger but fewer in presidential systems and smaller but more frequent in parliamentary ones, where the government already has a stronger legislative agenda-setting role (making change from the status quo less significant but also more frequent). Overall, *the ideal typical case where we might expect strong agenda-setting effects from treaty ratification is in a highly democratic parliamentary or presidential system.* These are hardly, of course, difficult cases for human rights treaty compliance, but they may nevertheless constitute evidence of an important mechanism by which international norms are imported into domestic law.

Leveraging Litigation

In many if not most cases, the political consensus for compliance and implementation may not be as strong as in the agenda-altering scenario previously described. Ratified treaties may encounter resistance flowing from incompetence to inattention to downright opposition from the government of the day to the permanent bureaucracy to various societal powerbrokers. But in contrast to norms and even international custom, treaties are explicit statements of a legal obligation to comply with their terms. Treaties are laws in most countries. Under a circumscribed set of conditions, they can be used to litigate in national courts, which, I have argued, can influence the further development of rights jurisprudence, alter the political costs of noncompliance, and, equally important, stimulate the politics of rights mobilization going forward.

Litigation can be expected to enhance treaty compliance only under a limited set of circumstances. Specifically, for litigation to be an important compliance mechanism, treaties have to be enforceable in domestic courts and litigation itself must be meaningful. If litigation – or the potential for meaningful litigation – accounts for changes in rights protection, then we should expect treaties to have their most significant impact where respect for judicial decisions is likely to be highest. *Evidence that treaties have stronger effects in countries with more independent judicial systems would be consistent with the litigation mechanism.* Where courts are relatively free from political interference, treaties as legal instruments should have their greatest potential to influence policy.

Empowering Political Mobilization

Treaties can change values and beliefs and can change the probability of successful political action to achieve the rights they promulgate. I have argued that a ratified treaty can effectively raise the expected value to potential rights holders of mobilizing to demand their government's compliance. For these reasons, we should expect treaty effects to show up in countries' compliance behavior. Consider first the *value* a nascent group is likely to place on the contents of a human rights treaty. A treaty dealing with civil or political rights would likely duplicate a number of existing guarantees in a stable democracy. The treaty itself would likely add very little to the rights already enjoyed in such a polity. The marginal value of an additional right in a rights-rich environment is likely to be small. On the other hand, an individual's welfare gain associated with the realization of even basic civil and political rights in a highly repressive regime or even basic recognition of equality in a highly discriminatory one is potentially

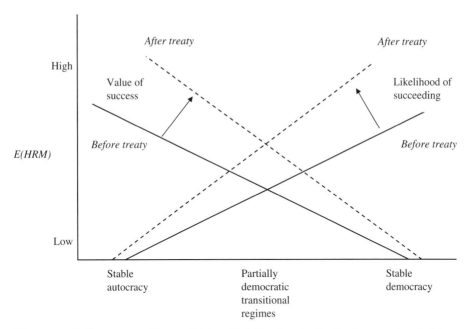

Figure 4.1. Influences on Human Rights Mobilization in Stable Autocracies, Stable Democracies, and Partially Democratic or Transitional Regimes.

very high indeed. The value of securing treaty compliance is much higher in a repressive or discriminatory setting than in a liberal democracy, which has a wide variety of domestic guarantees already in place. This is depicted as a downward-sloping relationship in Figure 4.1.

At the same time, the probability of *successfully* demanding a civil or political right is likely to be low in a highly repressive environment. Such demands are likely to be met with repression in stable autocracies or regimes rooted in discrimination. Democracies tend to be highly responsive to citizens' demands. The presumption is not only that individuals have basic civil and political rights and equality before the law; if they request it, they are also likely to get a ballot in their native language, be able to register to vote when they renew their drivers' licenses, and get a ride to the polls. All the accoutrements of freedom – a free press, free assembly, free speech and expression – increase the likelihood that a demand will be given a fair hearing.[134] Thus, the probability is relatively high that potential demanders will succeed in their rights claims. The probability of succeeding is depicted as upward-sloping in Figure 4.1.

134 Eskridge notes in his study of the civil rights movement in the United States that the broad range of civil and political freedoms contributed to the "massness" of the movement and its ultimate success (2001–2:452).

The treaty effects via social mobilization are illustrated with the dashed lines. A ratified human rights treaty can increase the value an individual places on succeeding in securing a policy change, often by framing the issue itself in rights terms. We should expect treaty effects to be minimal in a stable democracy, where international agreements contribute little to prevailing beliefs and understandings. Citizens in stable democracies are already apprised of their rights and do not need a treaty to shore up these beliefs and values. The situation in autocracies is fundamentally different. Individual civil and political rights are existentially denied, brutally repressed, and delegitimated constantly. Citizens identify much more readily as subjects of the state than as individuals with an autonomous right to participate in the political and social life of the country. The potential for value reorientation is much greater in an autocracy, and a ratified treaty suggests that *even my government agrees – formally and publicly – that I can legitimately claim some individual rights vis-à-vis the state.* When this happens, treaty effects show up as a steepening of the line representing the value an individual places on succeeding in a rights demand.

I have argued that treaties can also influence the expected value of mobilization by increasing the chances of success. But it is very possible that this influence varies across regime types as well, at least for civil and political rights. The mechanisms I have outlined by which treaties increase the likelihood of a successful mobilization are more likely to prevail in a democracy than in an autocracy.[135] Take the strategy of litigation as one example. The political control typically exerted over the judiciary in autocratic polities forecloses litigation as a realistic alternative. Treaties have played a much more important role in litigation in the highly democratic and newly democratic countries – from Canada to Australia, from Argentina to Israel – than they have in autocracies. As legal instruments, they are a much greater resource in countries where law can be used in the courts to constrain political actors. Treaties have institutional traction in democratic polities (relative to autocracies); the effect is to steepen the line representing the likelihood of success.

When we combine these arguments, some interesting expectations emerge. Figure 4.2 graphs the expected value of mobilizing to demand a right (value of succeeding times probability of success) with and without a ratified treaty obligation. Rights mobilization is low in autocracies because people are afraid of the consequences. Treaties may instill a new identity as a rights holder, but individuals run up against "brute facts" and are deterred from making much of a demand. Rights mobilization is relatively low in democracies as well: Even though democratic governments tend to be responsive (increasing the

---

135 Much of the law and society literature has come to recognize the conditional nature of the power of legal mobilization. According to Michael McCann, "Legal mobilization does not inherently disempower or empower citizens. How law matters depends on the complex, often changing dynamics of the context in which struggles occur" (2004:519).

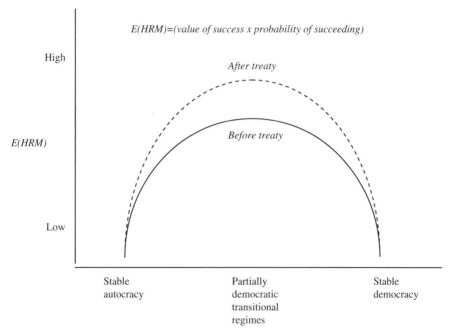

Figure 4.2. The Expected Value of Human Rights Mobilization in Autocracies, Democracies, and Partially Democratic/Transitional Regimes.

probability of success), it is hard to get excited about mobilizing where the *n*th right is of decreasing marginal utility. International human rights treaties are largely redundant.

Where we are likely to see the most significant treaty effects – at least with respect to civil and political rights – is in the less stable, transitioning "middle ground." In these countries, individuals have both the motive and the means realistically to press their governments to take international human rights treaties seriously. Treaties can still play a legitimating function, reassuring a nascent coalition that their demands are legitimate and solidifying their identity as individuals with a moral and legal case to make vis-à-vis their government. Mobilizing is meaningful, even exciting, but not nearly as dangerous as in stable autocracies that tolerate no opposition. Treaties create additional political resources for pro-rights coalitions under these circumstances; they resonate well with an embryonic rule of law culture and gather support from groups that not only believe in the *specific* rights at stake, but also believe they must take a stand on rule-governed political behavioral in general. The courts may be somewhat corrupt, inexperienced, or even incompetent, but they are not nearly as likely to execute the government's will as loyally as in a stable autocracy. International human rights treaties may be in their most fertile soil under such circumstances. As we shall see, the consequences for rights compliance can be profound.

CONCLUSIONS

To the question "why – or under what conditions – do governments comply with their international human rights treaty commitment?" this chapter has proposed that we look closely at domestic mechanisms. None of the international explanations for international human rights compliance are particularly plausible. Globally centralized enforcement is a chimera; despite the rise in state-to-state accountability chronicled in Chapter 2, states simply do not have a strong and consistent interest in enforcing human rights agreements in other countries. The assumptions underlying theories of self-enforcing agreements are suited for issues involving mutual gains and reciprocity – two assumptions that are a stretch, if not completely inappropriate, in the human rights area. Theorists also underestimate the collective action problems associated with reputational sanctions; governments have typically been reluctant to impose costs of any description on all but the most egregious rights abusers. In the absence of such costs, it is difficult to view international human rights treaties as costly commitments to the international community of states. Nor are international signaling models very helpful. They see treaties as screens but not *constraints* on state action. High ex ante costs lead to an interpretation that only the highly committed are likely to sign the treaty in the first place. This is interesting when a costly signal is necessary in order for two or more states to realize a joint gain, but it is less relevant if we are looking for treaty effects on an individual government's behavior.

I have advocated a theoretical reorientation of the compliance problems premised on the highly plausible stipulation that nobody cares more about human rights than the citizens potentially empowered by these treaties. No external – or even transnational – actor has as much incentive to hold a government to its commitments as do important groups of its own citizens. Citizens mobilize strategically. But these strategic calculations are influenced by what they value (or come to value) as well as the probability of succeeding in realizing these values. An international treaty regime has the potential to influence both the ideational and strategic components of mobilization's expected value. Treaty ratification will be shown in the next four chapters to improve rights practices and outcomes around the world. As we will see, certain civil rights, women's equality, the protection of children from exploitation, and the right of individuals to be free from officially sanctioned torture have improved once governments have explicitly made relevant treaty commitments. This chapter has made a case for the power of domestic mechanisms – new agendas, litigation, and especially social mobilization – in harnessing the potential of treaties to influence rights practices. These effects should not always be thought of as unconditional. At least in the case of civil and political rights, a treaty's greatest impact is likely to be found not in the stable extremes of democracy and autocracy, but in the mass of nations with institutions in flux, where citizens potentially have both the motive and the means to succeed in demanding their rights. The following four chapters examine the data and cases and find a good deal of hard evidence for the positive impact of international law across several indicators of human rights.

Part II

5

Civil Rights

I promise you this: everyone who lives on a dollar a day in Zimbabwe will be able to afford a PalmPilot in five years. Will I be able to get a fair trial in Zimbabwe in five years? If I can get a fair trial in Zimbabwe in five years, I can assure you – even if nobody there has a PalmPilot – Zimbabwe will do just fine. If I cannot get a fair trial in Zimbabwe in five years, they can give everyone there a PalmPilot and all the bandwidth they can consume and it will not make a dime's worth of difference.

Thomas L. Friedman, "Foreign Affairs" columnist for the *New York Times*, UCLA, 17 January 2001

Civil rights are those personal rights granted by governments that individuals enjoy as a matter of citizenship within their state's territorial jurisdiction. The UDHR (1948) and the legally binding ICCPR (1966) define a set of such liberties that are well accepted in Western political culture and assert their connection with "the inherent dignity of the human person."[1] As discussed in Chapter 2, the preamble of the ICCPR itself echoes the language – "freedom from fear and want" – that rallied the Allies and much of the world to oppose fascism during World War II. Though many people believe that governments ratified the ICCPR and other agreements with little intention of actually implementing the treaty's provisions at the time of ratification, the central argument of this book is that treaties can affect rights outcomes by influencing the nature of political or social demands citizens are willing to make, the legal framework within which courts make decisions, and the agenda of governments themselves. If the theory advanced in Chapter 4 has any purchase on the politics of human rights, then we should expect ratification of the ICCPR to improve at least some aspects of civil rights over time.

---

1 Friedman 2001. ICCPR Preamble, available at http://www.hrweb.org/legal/cpr.html (accessed 8 May 2008).

This chapter explores whether there is any evidence of civil rights improvements over time associated with ICCPR ratification. Demonstrating treaty effects in the area of civil rights during the second half of the twentieth century is fraught with difficulties. The past three decades have been an era of widespread democratization, and international law probably played a bit role in those broader social and political processes. Since many of the rights contained in the ICCPR are practically synonymous with democracy, it is difficult to show that practices are influenced – at least in part – by an international treaty commitment as distinct from these broader processes. For example, Article 25 of the ICCPR provides a right "To vote and to be elected at genuine periodic elections which shall be by universal and equal suffrage and shall be held by secret ballot, guaranteeing the free expression of the will of the electors. . . ."[2] Such a right is so intimately connected – practically by definition – with democratic transitions that it makes little sense to test it as an empirical outcome of a treaty commitment.

The question this chapter tries to answer is whether, and under what conditions, a commitment to the ICCPR has improved important aspects of civil rights that can vary across countries with roughly similar degrees of participatory democracy. The challenge in answering this question is to choose civil rights about which the ICCPR is fairly explicit but that are not *by definition* a part of the process of democratization. In the following sections, I test for the impact of ratification of the ICCPR on three clusters of civil rights: freedom of religion, fair trials, and the right to life, as reflected in abolition of the death penalty. While rightly considered an "Enlightenment right," the freedom to practice one's own religion and the unconditional right to life are not quintessentially aspects of democratization and, as we will see, do not vary directly with regime type. A similar point applies to the quality of criminal justice more broadly. Since most citizens will never brush up against the criminal justice system, this is an area that could easily lag behind the broader processes of democratic development. Yet, how a society deals with persons accused and convicted of serious crimes is a central civil rights issue.

Ratification of the ICCPR, as it will become clear, is not associated with improved practices across all aspects of civil rights or across all kinds of governing regimes. One of the most interesting findings of this research is the importance of being able to observe and verify treaty compliance. Fair trials and the death penalty provide a very useful contrast in this regard. Since public law and practice is easy to observe with respect to capital punishment (in contrast to the details of trials, and certainly in contrast to torture, which will be analyzed in Chapter 7), it is much easier for interested groups to detect noncompliance with international legal commitments with respect to capital punishment. The easier it is to observe the behavior or behavioral outcome that treaties try to regulate,

---

2 ICCPR, Article 25(b).

the easier it will be to detect, publicize, and mobilize against noncompliance. As we will see, ratifiers are unambiguously more likely to abolish the death penalty than are nonratifiers, in contrast to fair trial guarantees, where ratification makes virtually no difference in the prospects of actually receiving a fair trial in stable autocracies and stable democracies. Fair trials and freedom of religion are much more likely to improve in partially democratic countries, where domestic actors are much more likely to organize to demand compliance.

Would civil liberties have improved over the past three decades in the absence of the treaty commitment these states have made? There is little doubt that the struggle for civil rights is multicausal. Many factors affect the choices public authorities make with respect to civil rights. The quantitative evidence can only be suggestive of a causal relationship. The following tests attempt to control for many of the obvious explanations that are certainly available – for example, that civil liberties begin to improve as violent civil conflicts are resolved, or that abolition of the death penalty is simply a consequence of democratization, or that both of these outcomes are simply emulative behaviors that flow from copying other states' policies and practices. Certainly, treaties can be important in those emulative processes (a treaty commitment may in part explain one state's commitment, which is then taken into account by others). Quite likely, by controlling for the policies of other countries in one's own region, I am *underestimating* the effects that international law has actually had on civil rights outcomes.[3] Nonetheless, even controlling for other countries' practices and a wide range of other factors, there is some evidence consistent with the proposition that international legal commitments elicit behavioral changes in favor of better human rights practices.

In order to address these issues, the first section of this chapter provides some background and discusses the place of civil rights in international law. Sections two (on religious freedom), three (on fair trials), and four (on the death penalty) test the proposition that treaty ratification – focusing on the ICCPR and its optional protocol relating to the death penalty – have had a significant "commitment effect." The pattern of evidence supports the idea that this effect is conditional. It is strongest where domestic groups have both the motive and the means to make civil rights demands of their government. Furthermore, it is strongest in cases in which the right in question is centrally violated and relatively easy to detect and monitor. The key finding is that international legal obligations make an important and positive difference to practices in these three areas, but the greatest differences are to be found where citizens have the capacity and motivation to mobilize to demand rights that they can observe and monitor at reasonable cost.

---

3 Technically, I am focusing on the *direct effects* of treaty ratification rather than the broader influences of international law, which are likely to work through a range of other mechanisms, including regional influences, pressures from international organizations, and the acceptance of certain of these rights as a part of customary international law.

CIVIL RIGHTS AND INTERNATIONAL LAW

Background

Civil and political rights were one of the first areas to be addressed by the international human rights treaty regime that was negotiated in the mid-1940s. Along with economic and social rights, they were the central core – the first 19 articles – of the UDHR, passed unanimously by the UNGA in 1948. But for reasons that have been discussed in Chapter 2 – foot dragging, notably by the major powers – it took 18 years to agree upon a binding treaty covering civil and political rights and then to negotiate its contents (despite the fact that most of its provisions were already contained in the UDHR itself).[4] At the insistence of the United States, a move was made to bifurcate the social and economic rights on the one hand from the civil and political on the other. The ICESCR contains the codification in treaty form of the former, while the latter are encoded in the ICCPR. The ICCPR, along with the ICESCR and the UDHR, are often referred to collectively (if loosely) as the "International Bill of Rights."[5]

The ICCPR is the primary global treaty devoted to what people have come to call "first-generation" human rights.[6] These are the complex of "Enlightenment rights" that in their day were crucial in overthrowing feudalism and shattering the uncontested divine right of kings.[7] Infused with Enlightenment notions of individualism and laissez-faire, this first generation of rights, with their focus on the rights of the individual vis-à-vis political authority, has come largely to be thought of as a set of "negative rights," or rights that require government to abstain from denigrating (rather than requiring governments to intervene on behalf of) human dignity.

In large part, the emphasis on "negative freedoms" can be seen in the ICCPR's Part III, which contains the treaty's substantive obligations.[8] Individuals have a right to their lives (Article 6), to be free from torture or degrading treatment (Article 7), to be free from slavery or servitude (Article 8), to liberty and security of person (Article 9), to free movement (Article 12), to a fair trial (Article 14), to freedom of religion and thought (Articles 18 and 19), and to peaceful assembly and free association (Articles 21 and 22). Rights of political participation are guaranteed in Article 25, while equality before the law and minority rights are protected in Articles 26 and 27. But the treaty suggests positive rights of individuals as well. "Each state Party to the present convention," according to Article 2(1), "undertakes

---

4 See Articles 3–21 of the UDHR. Many scholars also hold that at least some of the obligations found in the ICCPR reflect customary international law. See Henkin 1995.
5 Henkin 1995.
6 The delineation of civil and political rights as "first-generation" human rights has become standard terminology. See, for example, *Encyclopaedia Britannica* 2007; Ishay 2004:3.
7 Ishay 2004:7.
8 The text of the ICCPR can be accessed at http://www1.umn.edu/humanrts/instree/b3ccpr.htm (accessed 8 May 2008).

to respect and to ensure to all individuals within its territory and subject to its jurisdiction the rights recognized in the present convention, without distinctions of any kind. . . ." The treaty thus contains an affirmative obligation for states to organize civil and political life in ways that make the enjoyment of the rights contained in the treaty possible.

The drafters of the treaty did not, however, envision that these rights would be absolute; both the ICCPR[9] and the UDHR[10] recognize that these rights may need to be limited when necessary to protect certain public interests.[11] Many states reinforce and specify their rights of derogation through the use of reservations.[12] Some – China with respect to freedom of religion is an outstanding example – provide for the civil freedoms contained in the ICCPR in their domestic law, but then take back the guarantee with domestic derogations that are much broader than the ICCPR itself allows.[13] Many civil rights – citizens' rights vis-à-vis the state – raise culturally sensitive controversies about the proper relationships between the individual, society, and the state.[14] Ideological differences drove the East and West to spar over civil rights during the Cold War. Today, civil rights are among those most likely to be dismissed as "Western."

In order to facilitate enforcement of these obligations, the ICCPR established the UN Human Rights Committee (Article 28),[15] whose main purpose is to enhance the mechanisms of accountability through its authority to monitor and receive state reports that are due on a regular basis. The committee is also empowered by the convention to consider complaints of one state against another (Article 41), although this process has never been used. The committee is also empowered through the first optional protocol to consider individual complaints against one's own government.[16] Although the UN Human Rights Committee was established expressly as a committee of experts rather than a court, analysis of its recent practice reveals that it is becoming increasingly "court-like."[17]

---

9 ICCPR, Article 4.
10 UDHR, Article 29(2).
11 In 1985, the ECOSOC negotiated a set of principles defining the conditions under which derogation of ICCPR treaty obligations are in fact allowed. See United Nations, Economic and Social Council, Siracusa Principles on the Limitation and Derogation Provisions in the International Covenant on Civil and Political Rights, U.N. Doc. E/CN.4/1985/4, Annex (1985); http://www1.umn.edu/humanrts/instree/siracusaprinciples.html (accessed 8 May 2008).
12 The North African countries tend to make "states of emergency claims" for purposes of derogation; see Allain and O'Shea 2002:90.
13 Kolodner 1994:484.
14 The "Asian values" debate is pertinent in this regard. On the idea that the global civil rights regime may not be compatible with Southeast Asian notions of statehood, see Mohamad 2002.
15 Forsythe (1985), for example, prefers to think of the activities of the UN Human Rights Committee as "socialization" rather than enforcement.
16 For a legal analysis of the individual right of petition before the UN Human Rights Committee, see De Zayas et al. 1985; Ghandhi 1986; Heffernan 1997; McGoldrick 1991; Myullerson 1992. For an example of a Human Rights Committee communication process that had an impact on government practices in the case of New Zealand, see De Zayas et al. 1985.
17 Helfer and Slaughter 1997. For a review of the literature on the effectiveness of the UN Human Rights Committee, see Donnelly 1998; Keith 1999.

The ICCPR is not the only treaty to have addressed civil and political rights, but it is certainly the most central. Many of these rights have also been developed at the regional level, and in Europe with accompanying institutions with real enforcement power.[18] The first 18 Articles of the European Convention for the Protection of Human Rights and Fundamental Freedoms (1953) anticipates the civil and political rights covered by the ICCPR, and Section II establishes a regional court to ensure enforcement.[19] All of the first-generation civil rights covered in the ICCPR are also detailed in the American Convention on Human Rights, bookended by guarantees of juridical personhood and judicial protection of the rights contained in the treaty.[20] The African Charter on Human and Peoples' Rights (1981) contains, in a more limited and contingent form, some of the civil rights found in the ICCPR, including liberty and security of a person, a right to a trial, freedom of conscience, free practice of religion, the right to disseminate one's opinion, and free assembly and association.[21] Practically the entire panoply of civil rights has been exported from the ICCPR to other international conventions aimed at protecting specific groups, including racial minorities by the CERD[22] and children by the CRC.[23]

Social scientists have begun to research the conditions conducive to improvements in civil rights.[24] Few, however, have inquired into the relationship between international law and rights improvements. Case studies that have

18 Furthermore, specific civil rights relating to criminal justice have been elaborated in a growing body of nonbinding international legal instruments that spell out "standards" and "codes of conduct" for the official treatment of persons being held by the state. These accords cover issues that range from nonbinding minimum standards on the treatment of prisoners (1955) to an optional protocol to the CAT, authorizing external visits to detention centers (2002). See Appendix 5.1 on my Web site for a list and graph of these (primarily nonbinding) global agreements over time.

19 Convention for the Protection of Human Rights and Fundamental Freedoms, 213 U.N.T.S. 222, *entered into force* 3 September 1953.

20 American Convention on Human Rights, O.A.S. Treaty Series No. 36, 1144 U.N.T.S. 123, *entered into force* 18 July 1978. See the extensive list in Chapter II (Articles 3–25).

21 African [Banjul] Charter on Human and Peoples' Rights, adopted 27 June 1981, OAU Doc. CAB/LEG/67/3 rev. 5, 21 I.L.M. 58 (1982), *entered into force* 21 October 1986. See generally Articles 6–14.

22 International Convention on the Elimination of All Forms of Racial Discrimination, G.A. res. 2106 (XX), Annex, 20 U.N. GAOR Supp. (No. 14) at 47, U.N. Doc. A/6014 (1966), 660 U.N.T.S. 195, *entered into force* 4 January 1969. See especially Article 5(a–d).

23 Among other things, guaranteeing children a right to religious freedom and free conscience, peaceable assembly, and civil rights when accused of crimes (CRC, Articles 14, 15, and 40, respectively).

24 The major finding of this literature is not very surprising: More authoritarian governments tend to be among the worst guarantors of civil rights, and democracies are among the best. See Landman 2005:ch. 5; McKinlay and Cohan 1975, 1976. For a study that focuses on the negative association between ethnic diversity and civil rights, see Walker and Poe 2002. Other studies have situated the provision of civil and political rights in the nature of external political and economic interdependence (Stohl and Lopez 1984). See also Meyer (1998), who argues that civil and political rights in the cases of Chile, India, and Mexico were positively influenced by foreign direct investment, high levels of external debts, and high levels of development aid (though not military aid) from the United States. See also Richards et al. 2001.

examined the impact of the ICCPR on specific countries have turned in rather mixed reviews. In Japan's case, Kenneth Port has found that rules that are cast as immediate prohibitions have had little impact on a country such as Japan, where the local culture favors incrementalism and voluntary goals.[25] Lawyers are likely to approach the "influence" question in terms of the incorporation of international human rights law into domestic constitutional law, on the assumption that incorporation is a necessary step toward effectiveness;[26] by this standard, even countries with relatively good rights practices – such as the United Kingdom, the United States, and Australia – are judged to fall short.[27]

Increasingly, scholars have tried to test for the impact of an ICCPR commitment on actual civil rights practices using quantitative indicators. Linda Camp Keith's was one of the earliest efforts to control for a broad range of factors that influence the provision of civil rights. Using civil and political rights indicators from Freedom House between 1976 and 1993, this study found that a commitment to the ICCPR was not among them.[28] On the other hand, using a different model specification, Todd Landman's more recent study does suggest a relationship between ratification of the ICCPR and better performance on the same Freedom House civil liberties and political rights scale.[29]

The studies just discussed hardly converge on a single message regarding the impact of the ICCPR on various kinds of civil liberties. Nor do they adequately control for the endogeneity of the treaty commitment itself. Treaty effects can be under- or overestimated if we ignore the conditions that gave rise to the treaty commitment in the first place. Moreover, my point of departure is that treaty ratification contributes to compliance via enhanced political mobilization. Table 5.1 suggests that this is a plausible mechanism for treaty consequences. It shows that ratification of the ICCPR has given rise to a significant increase in local membership in international NGOs one to four years after ratification. Ratification appears to stimulate membership in civil society organizations even when we control for external aid, population growth, wealth, and a time trend. It is therefore at least plausible that the treaty effects discussed previously have much to do with the organization of civil society's demands for

25 Port 1991.
26 According to Shany, ". . . incorporation of IHR standards into domestic law (directly or through elaboration of analogous domestic standards) goes a significant way towards ensuring their effectiveness" (2006:350).
27 Shany 2006.
28 Camp Keith (1999) controls for level of democracy, population (logged), civil war, international war, ex-British colony, military government, left-socialists, and GDP per capita.
29 Landman uses a two-stage estimation, in which he uses instrumental variables first to explain treaty ratification and then the effect of ratification on civil and political rights. The actual instruments he uses, however, are highly problematic. The two-stage least squares (2SLS) strategy requires instruments for ratification that themselves do not explain human rights behavior, except via ratification. It is hard to imagine that democracy and GDP per capita, which he uses as instruments (2005:136–7), do not directly affect civil rights, as practically every study ever done finds, including Landman's own.

Table 5.1. Effect of ICCPR Commitment on Local Memberships in
International NGOs

Dependent variable: logged INGO memberships
Ordinary least squares regression model
Coefficients, *p*-values, based on robust standard errors

Explanatory Variable	Model 1: No Fixed Effects	Model 2: Country Fixed Effects
Logged INGO memberships, $t - 1$	.776*** $(p = .000)$	—
ICCPR commitment, $t - 1$	.054*** $(p = .000)$	−.044 $(p = .155)$
ICCPR commitment, $t - 2$	—	.011 $(p = .592)$
ICCPR commitment, $t - 3$	—	.033** $(p = .030)$
ICCPR commitment, $t - 4$	—	.034*** $(p = .010)$
ICCPR commitment, $t - 5$	—	−.027 $(p = .175)$
Overseas development assistance/GDP, $t - 1$	−.027 $(p = .488)$	.488*** $(p = .001)$
Logged total population, $t - 1$	.075*** $(p = .000)$	.528** $(p = .022)$
Logged GDP/capita, $t - 1$	.072*** $(p = .000)$	.135 $(p = .180)$
Change in civil liberties, $t - 1$	—	.007 $(p = .408)$
Civil liberties, $t - 1$	.023*** $(p = .000)$	—
Year trend	.005*** $(p = .000)$	.042*** $(p = .000)$
Constant	−10.07*** $(p = .000)$	—
# of countries	173	173
# of observations	3,646	3,757
R^2	.975	.218

Note: Country fixed effects are included in Model 2 but are not reported here. Because of the fixed effect, the lagged dependent variable (which functions as a baseline for change) is omitted.
Results based on robust standard errors, clustering on country.
While inclusion of a time trend does not disturb these results, year fixed effects increase the standard errors on ICCPR ratification.
* Significant at the .10 level; ** significant at the .05 level; *** significant at the .01 level.

compliance. This interpretation is consistent with a host of case studies that describe treaties as an important tool in drawing attention to the civil rights violations of governments.[30] In the following sections, I test the proposition that ratification of the ICCPR has influenced government respect for civil rights in ways that are consistent with the mobilization of domestic audiences theorized in Chapter 4.

30 For a discussion of how NGOs such as Human Rights Watch and the American Civil Liberties Union use the ICCPR to criticize, for example, the United States, see Shapiro 1993.

RELIGIOUS FREEDOM

Religious rights were among the first set of rights accorded to groups and later to individuals through international legal agreements.[31] Governments have been concerned about the practice and protection of religion over the centuries because it has implications for their political legitimacy and authority. Confessional differences were one of the earliest areas of social difference among groups – a signal distinction that was quite salient until well into the eighteenth century.[32] As John Hall has written, "Religions deal in ultimate meanings that bear a claim to exceed merely secular authority. Thus, they remain a potent basis for contesting political legitimacy both within and beyond nation-states. . . ."[33] Governments have often feared that their authority could be undermined by spiritual claims that transcend their temporal and territorial domain. Sociologists have discovered that political movements with religious roots typically ". . . originate in social strata that are negatively privileged politically and economically, or socially ascendant but blocked from power."[34]

Governments are motivated to regulate religious beliefs because religion can and historically has served to mobilize political opposition in ways that dominant social classes or regimes view as threatening. Religious fervor and religious intolerance have historically been prime ingredients in episodes and even eras of violent conflict.[35] More mundanely, governments might choose to repress even relatively powerless religious movements or individuals in order to "reinforce general norms of cultural conformity."[36] Often, restrictions on religious organizations and practices involve calculated efforts to balance political control with personal freedom. The Communist Party of China's effort carefully to control certain religious practices while accepting others can be viewed as an attempt to grant limited personal autonomy while trying to guard the political legitimacy of the regime,[37] which is typically justified in the name of maintaining "social harmony."[38]

Religion has always been a social force with which governments have had to reckon. Recent surges in various indicators of religious fervor have made the issue more pertinent than ever. Throughout the former Soviet Union, in the past 30 years approximately 100 million people joined religious groups for the first time.[39] According to Ronald Inglehart, scholar and chairman of the World

---

31 Humphrey 1984:176; Partsch 1981:209; Sieghart 1983.
32 Hannum 1991.
33 Hall 2003:367.
34 Hall 2003:367.
35 Some studies suggest that religious nationalism has had an especially strong association with violent conflict since the 1980s. See Fox 2004.
36 Hall 2003.
37 Potter 2003.
38 Kolodner 1994:466.
39 Froese 2004:57. Froese notes that this has led not to a proliferation of religious faiths but to the unprecedented growth in religious monopolies associated with orthodox Christianity and Islam.

Values Survey, ". . . unequivocally . . . there are more people alive today with traditional religious beliefs than ever before in history, and they're [sic] a larger percentage of the world's population than they were 20 years ago."[40]

Modern states have come up with legal mechanisms for handling issues of religious freedom and its limits. Western perspectives typically assume that religious tolerance is the basis for peace;[41] the separation of church and state is an oft-advocated formulation. Today, as many as one-third of the world's states include formal guarantees of church–state separation in their constitutions.[42] Even the constitutions of communist countries guaranteed freedom of religious belief and practice as long as religions were not "misused" politically for opposing the (socialist) constitution.[43]

Religious Freedom and International Law

Modern international law has had several responses to the issue of religious freedom. During the interwar years, Article 22 on the League of Nations Covenant imposed upon Mandatory Powers the duty to guarantee freedom of conscience and religion.[44] The UDHR, though not legally binding, stipulates in Article 18 that "Everyone has the right to freedom of thought, conscience and religion; this right includes freedom to change his religion or belief, and freedom, either alone or in community with others and in public or private, to manifest his religion or belief in teaching, practice, worship and observance."[45]

The ICCPR contains a number of articles that obligate state parties to respect the right of individuals to believe and practice their own religion.[46] Article 2 prohibits discrimination against the rights enumerated in the covenant on the basis of, among other things, religion, and Article 24 extends protection against discrimination to children explicitly.[47] Article 20(2) calls on states parties to prohibit "Any advocacy of national, racial or religious hatred that constitutes incitement to discrimination, hostility or violence. . . ."[48] The most important guarantee of religious freedom is spelled out in Article 18, which provides that

---

40 Ronald Ingelhart, "Is There a Global Resurgence of Religion?" Speech before the National Press Club, 8 May 2006. Transcript available at http://pewforum.org/events/index.php? EventID=116 (accessed 8 May 2008).
41 See studies by the United States Institute of Peace, discussed in Little 1996:75.
42 Davis 2002:223. On Latin American constitutional provisions, see Sigmund 1996.
43 Riis 1999:24. Frequently, of course, a state seeking to suppress religious freedoms characterizes the activities of religious groups and leaders as impermissible political action or subversion. See Ribeiro 1987.
44 Lerner 1996:84.
45 UDHR, G.A. Res. 217A (III), U.N. GAOR, 3d Sess., U.N. Doc. A/810 (1948).
46 Generally, see the discussion of ICCPR provisions in Lerner 2006; Tahzib 1996:82. Religious toleration was excluded from earlier binding accords, such as the CERD, because of opposition from the socialist countries at the time (Taylor 2005:9).
47 ICCPR, Article 2, para. 1; Article 24 para. 1; see also Article 26.
48 ICCPR, Article 20, para. 2.

"Everyone shall have the right to freedom of thought, conscience and religion. This right shall include freedom to have or to adopt a religion or belief of his choice, and freedom, either individually or in community with others and in public or private, to manifest his religion or belief in worship, observance, practice and teaching."[49] According to Article 4(2), Article 18 is one of the provisions of the treaty that is nonderogable, even in a declared national emergency.[50] Interestingly, the ICCPR's Article 18 does not reiterate the UDHR's language specifying a right to *change* religions – a provision that was opposed by Saudi Arabia and other conservative Muslim countries.[51]

Several regional agreements also contain provisions about religious freedom.[52] Article 9 of the 1950 European Convention almost replicates Article 18(3) of the ICCPR. The Organization on Security and Cooperation in Europe's Principle VII of the Helsinki Final Act refers to freedom of thought, conscience, religion, and belief for all without distinction as to race, sex, language, or religion.[53] The 1960 American Convention on Human Rights provides for freedom of conscience and religion (Article 12) and proclaims the right to maintain and to change one's religious beliefs.[54] Article 8 of the African Charter guarantees free conscience and the free practice of religion.[55]

Islamic agreements referring to religious freedom are much more circumspect. While agreeing to the principle of freely chosen religious commitments, they evince a real concern with conversion from Islam to other belief systems. The Cairo Declaration on Human Rights (1990) prohibits "any form of compulsion on man or to exploit his poverty or ignorance in order to convert him

---

49 ICCPR, Article 18, para. 1. The right to practice one's own religion is also guaranteed in Article 27. There are permissible limitations on the right to "manifest" one's religious beliefs. See the discussion in Taylor 2005:292–338.
50 ICCPR, Article 4, para. 2.
51 "The Saudi Arabian representative argued that explicit recognition of freedom to change one's religion or belief would foster discrimination in favour of religions possessing highly organized proselytizing institutions, particularly in the case of a state with a proselytizing state religion" (Tahzib 1996:85). To quote the Saudi delegate, "Men could in fact be induced to change their religion not only for perfectly legitimate intellectual or moral reasons, but also through weakness or credulity." UN Doc. A/C.3/SR.1021, para. 27. See also Taylor 2005:29–34.
52 These are discussed in Lerner 2000:40–50.
53 The Final Act of the Conference on Security and Cooperation in Europe, 1 August 1975, 14 I.L.M. 1292 (Helsinki Declaration); text at http://www1.umn.edu/humanrts/osce/basics/finact75.htm (accessed 8 May 2008). Furthermore, "The monitoring of human rights by the Council of Europe, the OSCE, and the EU has produced significant case law with respect to religious rights" (Lerner 2000:42). For a comparison of international and European law on religious freedoms, see Taylor 2005.
54 Statute of the Inter-American Commission on Human Rights, O.A.S. Res. 447 (IX-0/79), O.A.S. Off. Rec. OEA/Ser.P/IX.0.2/80, Vol. 1 at 88, Annual Report of the Inter-American Commission on Human Rights, OEA/Ser.L/V/11.50 doc. 13 rev. 1 at 10 (1980), text at http://www1.umn.edu/humanrts/oasinstr/zoas4cms.htm (accessed 8 May 2008).
55 African [Banjul] Charter on Human and Peoples' Rights, adopted 27 June 1981, OAU Doc. CAB/LEG/67/3 rev. 5, 21 I.L.M. 58 (1982), *entered into force* 21 October 1986; excerpted text at http://www1.umn.edu/humanrts/instree/z1afchar.htm (accessed 8 May 2008).

to another religion or to atheism" (Article 10).[56] Article 22 allows freedom of expression as long as it is exercised in a manner that is not contrary to the principles of Shari'a.[57] According to some scholars, religious freedom is sharply curtailed in certain Islamic theologies by the view that conversion from Islam to another religion is tantamount to treason and potentially punishable by death.[58]

More than a decade after the ICCPR opened for signature, the UNGA passed a (nonbinding) resolution that filled out some of the details of the religious clauses of the ICCPR. In 1981, the UNGA adopted by consensus the Declaration on the Elimination of All Forms of Intolerance and of Discrimination Based on Religion or Belief. Its main purpose is to give more concrete content to the general norms of the UDHR and the ICCPR.[59] UN-based law on religious freedom is also reiterated in the CRC, which acknowledges children's "freedom to manifest [their] religion or religious beliefs" (Article 14), although this is the most reserved-against provision of that convention.[60]

Despite these international legal obligations, it is not at all obvious that governments have taken practical measures to improve religious freedom within their jurisdictions. In 1986, a study of UN members' constitutions found that most had in fact provided for the protection of religious freedoms in their national constitutions and guarded against religious discrimination in their penal codes – though very few countries were judged to have implemented these measures in a satisfactory way in practice.[61] State control over religious groups in Communist China has long been notoriously tight and treatment of many religious groups especially harsh.[62] Some countries, such as Russia, have ratified the ICCPR but have also recently implemented domestic laws on religious freedom that are noticeably more restrictive.[63] In fact, as Peter Beyer has noted, ". . . maintenance of some kind of religious hegemony is the rule all across global society . . . unfettered freedom of religion or genuine religious pluralization is correspondingly rare, if it exists anywhere."[64] Even liberal democracies such as Germany and

---

56 Cairo Declaration on Human Rights in Islam, 5 August 1990, U.N. GAOR, World Conf. on Hum. Rts., 4th Sess., Agenda Item 5, U.N. Doc. A/CONF.157/PC/62/Add.18 (1993) [English translation]; Article 10. Text at http://www1.umn.edu/humanrts/instree/cairodeclaration.html (accessed 8 May 2008).

57 Cairo Declaration, Article 22.

58 Talbi 1986:182.

59 Article 1 affirms the right to freedom of thought, conscience, and belief and the right to manifest one's religion or belief. Article 2 prohibits discrimination on the basis of religion or belief. Neither provision defines "religion" or "belief," nor are these terms defined elsewhere in the declaration. See the discussion in Sullivan 1988. See also Lerner 2000:20–8; Odio Benito 1989: 48–50.

60 For a discussion of religious rights of children, see Brems 2006.

61 Odio Benito 1989:22–30.

62 Evans 2002.

63 Durham and Homer 1998. Some scholars characterize the restrictive 1997 law as a return to religious restrictions during the Stalin era. See Froese 2004:69.

64 Beyer 2003:abstract.

France have taken actions that to some extent discriminate against or suppress religious groups and practices.[65] Richard Lillich has concluded that ". . . one is forced to acknowledge that the right of religious freedom is one of the weakest – from the point of view of its recognition and its enforcement – of all the rights contained in Articles 3–18 of the Universal Declaration."[66] Does it matter for the enjoyment of religious freedom that governments have committed themselves to the ICCPR?

Data and Methods

While no society can be characterized by the perfectly free practice of religion – even the hyperliberal United States curtails religious practices considered immoral or a public danger – it is reasonable to expect governments that have committed themselves to the ICCPR to move in the direction of a relatively more liberal approach to religious belief and practice. In order to test this proposition, it is necessary to measure the relative liberality of official *practices*. Data collected by David Cingranelli and David Richards provide one such measure. Their religious freedom indicator measures "the extent to which the freedom of citizens to exercise and practice their religious beliefs is subject to actual government restrictions. Citizens should be able to freely practice their religion and proselytize (attempt to convert) other citizens to their religion as long as such attempts are done in a non-coercive, peaceful manner."[67] This variable is dichotomous; that is, countries are coded as either restrictive or free. Governmental practices that count as restrictions include prohibitions on proselytizing; prohibitions on clergy's political participation; arrest, detention, or violence toward religious officials; citizen conversions forced by government officials; citizen arrests; harassment and/or intimidation for religious beliefs and practices; and so forth.

The worldwide average relationship between this measure and ratification of the ICCPR is depicted in Figure 5.1. There appears to be no clear relationship between ICCPR ratification, which has trended upward over time, and this average measure of religious freedom worldwide. Religious freedom worldwide seems to take a dive between 1985 and 1987 and then improves slightly in the earliest post–Cold War years, only to drift downward over the course of the 1990s and early 2000s. Obviously, more than international legal developments are at play here. But the question is, given the broad range of pressures on governments to accommodate or to repress free religious practices, how, if at

---

65 On Germany, see Editorial 1998; On France's "Anti-Sect" Bill, see http://www.cesnur.org/testi/fr2K_july4.htm (accessed 12 August 2008).

66 Lillich 1984:60.

67 See the description at http://ciri.binghamton.edu/documentation/ciri_variables_short_descriptions.pdf (accessed 8 May 2008).

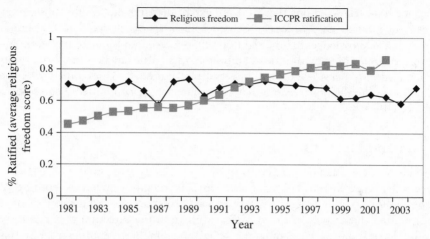

Figure 5.1. ICCPR Ratifications and Religious Freedoms. *Note*: Includes ratifications and accessions.

all, has ratification of the main binding global instrument – the ICCPR – influenced actual practices?

In order to address this question, I use a two-stage regression model in which ratification in the region, the common law legal system, and ratification procedures are used as instruments for ratification. These variables make good instruments because, as we have seen in Chapter 3, they were found to be significantly associated with ratification of the ICCPR (as well as other human rights treaties), yet they do not themselves directly influence a country's human rights practices. Country fixed effects – dummy variables that pick up many constant features of the countries we are analyzing but about which we are not specifically theorizing – are included as controls but to conserve space their coefficients are not reported. Year fixed effects are also included to reduce the likelihood of attributing improvements in religious freedom to some simultaneously experienced shock, such as the end of the Cold War. A lagged dependent variable is also included so that we are in effect modeling *improvements* in religious freedom within countries from year to year. The results are based on robust standard errors with a correction for clustering on countries.

A number of control variables are included to reduce the risk of drawing inappropriate inferences about ICCPR commitment. An indicator is included to capture the extent to which the state has a constitutionally established relationship with an official religious organization. I distinguish those states that established an official religion between 1970 and 2000 from those that disestablished an official religion in the same time period. My expectation would be that establishment would be associated with more government interference in free religious practices, while disestablishment would be associated with a liberalizing trend. I also distinguish states that were stable with respect to the establishment of a state religion between 1970 and 2000, although I do not expect to find clear trends in their repression. After all, there is no reason to expect religious repression/freedom in a country to change much where relations between church and state are fairly stable.[68]

One of the most important conditions for which to control is the extent of societal homogeneity with respect to religious culture. In societies characterized by a high degree of homogeneity, state repression will hardly be necessary to achieve a consensus on basic value and social issues. But where many religious groups vie for social or cultural space, politicians may decide to use repression to advantage their religious supporters and quash culturally based opposition. The greater the degree of religious fractionalization, the greater we might expect religious repression to be.

I also control for the dominant religion within each country. Certainly, no particular religious orientation has a monopoly on repressive tactics, whether for political or spiritual reasons. Yet, it remains true that certain of the world's major religions are "universalistic" in orientation; in Ole Riis's words, they "claim to contain the whole spiritual truth, [while] particularistic religions have more specific aims and only claim partial access to that truth."[69] Riis goes on to contend that "While the former confront the individual with a fundamental choice and demand total commitment from their members, the latter are less demanding and may even be combined in functional mixtures, which, for the universal religions, would be perceived as eclecticism, syncretism and heresy. As a consequence, religious pluralism seems to be less problematic when particularistic religions are involved."[70] For these reasons, I include indicators for predominantly Protestant, Catholic, and Islamic countries. If Riis's observation can be generalized, we might expect countries dominated by these faiths to be relatively intolerant of, and possibly even repressive toward, religious minorities.

External pressures could also account for some episodes of liberalization toward religious belief and practice. Some of the wealthiest countries in the world are the most democratic and among the staunchest supporters of rights worldwide. Some of these governments are likely to use their aid strategically to oppose minority repression of all kinds; ensuring religious freedom would be only one among many of these governments' goals. In addition, foreign aid in some countries – the United States in particular – may have been influenced by religious Christians intent on punishing governments that take a harsh stance

---

68 Ironically, the motive behind establishment of a particular state religion usually is to strengthen that religion, but the effects are ultimately to undermine the vitality of the established religion. Establishing a state religion tends to reduce actual religious attendance. See North and Gwin 2004.

69 Riis 1999:23.

70 Riis 1999:23–4.

against Christian churches and missionaries.[71] Aid given by external actors could easily be conditioned – whether implicitly or explicitly – by demands that recipients honor the religious rights of their local citizens and of foreign missionaries. The more important such aid is as a proportion of GDP, the more we might expect an improvement in religious freedom, quite independent of the demands associated with treaty ratification.

Findings: ICCPR Ratification and Religious Freedom

The results of these analyses are displayed in Table 5.2. One thing is quite clear: There are many factors that impact government policies with respect to religious freedom other than the ratification of the ICCPR. Models 1–3 indicate that ratification is positively associated with minimal governmental restrictions on religious freedoms, although the result is statistically significant on average only five years after ratification. Models 3–5 run similar analyses on subsets of countries: transitioning countries, stable democracies (since World War II), and stable autocracies. These tests show that the transitioning group – countries that at some point since World War II have experienced a modicum of democratic governance – accounts for the most convincing share of the effects of ICCPR ratification. (For a precise definition and list of these transitional and partially democratic countries, please see the Data Appendix at the end of this book.) According to Model 3, we can be fairly sure that among partially democratic and transitioning countries, ratification of the ICCPR is associated with an 11 percent increase in the average religious freedom score. If anything, ICCPR ratification is associated with a slight deterioration in freedom in stable democracies ($p = .165$, which is below standard levels of statistical significance), while in stable autocracies, the standard error is far too high to draw any inferences at all. Ratification of the ICCPR is most convincingly associated with improvements in religious freedoms in countries in transition. These results are robust to the inclusion of country and year fixed effects, a year trend, the actual degree of democracy in each year, and the average degree of religious freedom in the region.[72]

Of course, much else explains governments' efforts to control religious beliefs and practices in their jurisdictions. The changing relationship between church and state over time appears to be quite important, but its significance varies across subgroups by regime type. Establishment and disestablishment were associated with greater governmental restrictions on religion in general, but not within stable democracies, where these changes seem to make no systematic difference to religious freedoms. Generally, in countries with a high degree of religious fractionalization, there tends to be much more official state

71 Martin 1999.
72 For brevity, these results are not shown here.

Table 5.2. The ICCPR and Freedom of Religion

Dependent variable: religious freedom
Instrumental variable least squares regression model
Coefficients, probabilities based on robust standard errors

Explanatory Variable	Model 1: All Countries		Model 2: All Countries		Model 3: Transitional/ Partly Democratic Countries Only		Model 4: Stable Democracies Only		Model 5: Stable Autocracies Only	
ICCPR commitment (lagged 5 years)	.080*	$(p = .055)$	.073*	$(p = .089)$	.111**	$(p = .018)$	−.023	$(p = .165)$	.081	$(p = .402)$
State religion, 1970–2000	.600*	$(p = .052)$	.749***	$(p = .000)$	—		—	—	−.614	$(p = .179)$
Establishing states, 1970–2000	−.033*	$(p = .092)$	−.305***	$(p = .009)$	−.709***	$(p = .000)$	−.091	$(p = .329)$	.787**	$(p = .012)$
Disestablishing states, 1970–2000	−.518***	$(p = .001)$	−.416**	$(p = .016)$	.056***	$(p = .000)$	.321	$(p = .304)$	.930*	$(p = .074)$
Religious freedom, $t − 1$	.466***	$(p = .000)$	.464***	$(p = .000)$	.471***	$(p = .000)$	.426***	$(p = .000)$	.456***	$(p = .000)$
Religious fractionalization	−.0002***	$(p = .000)$	−.0002***	$(p = .000)$	.597***	$(p = .010)$	—		−.00006***	$(p = .000)$
Overseas development aid/ GDP, $t − 1$	.476***	$(p = .004)$	.480***	$(p = .006)$	.311*	$(p = .091)$	.669	$(p = .351)$	.541**	$(p = .018)$
GDP per capita, logged	−.097*	$(p = .052)$	−.093*	$(p = .090)$	−.126*	$(p = .106)$	−.027	$(p = .666)$	−.155*	$(p = .092)$

(continued)

Table 5.2 (continued)

Explanatory Variable	Model 1: All Countries		Model 2: All Countries		Model 3: Transitional/ Partly Democratic Countries Only		Model 4: Stable Democracies Only		Model 5: Stable Autocracies Only	
Islam	-.032**	$(p = .015)$	-.18	$(p = .306)$	.149	$(p = .122)$	—		-.055**	$(p = .030)$
Catholic	.454***	$(p = .000)$	.463***	$(p = .000)$	-.382*	$(p = .063)$	-.073	$(p = .405)$	.856***	$(p = .008)$
Protestant	.108***	$(p = .000)$	.241*	$(p = .055)$	-.061	$(p = .274)$	.165	$(p = .483)$	1.27**	$(p = .013)$
Democracy	—		.002	$(p = .336)$	—		—		—	
GDP growth	—		.0004	$(p = .760)$	—		—		—	
Trade openness	—		-.0005	$(p = .336)$	—		—		—	
Civil war	—		.023	$(p = .527)$	—		—		—	
Interstate war	—		.019	$(p = .620)$	—		—		—	
Country fixed effects?	yes		yes		yes		yes		yes	
Year fixed effects?	yes		yes		yes		yes		yes	
# of countries	147		144		55		32		59	
# of observations	2,691		2,556		1,022		661		1,038	
R^2	.700		.702		.701		.343		.644	

Instrumented: ICCPR obligation.
Instruments: All explanatory variables above, plus ratification procedures, common law legal tradition, regional ICCPR obligation density, a counting vector of years without ICCPR ratification, three cubic splines, and a year time trend.
* Significant at the .10 level; ** significant at the .05 level; *** significant at the .01 level.

oppression than in more religiously homogeneous societies, but the stable autocracies account for most of the repression in this case. For an autocrat, religious opposition might well represent a perceived political threat, "justifying" a crackdown on the religious followers of political rivals.

Foreign aid also seems to work, as expected: As aid increases as a proportion of the recipient's GDP, governments tend to remove restrictions and take a more liberal approach to religious freedoms. This result is especially strong for autocracies, though, as we might expect, weak to nonexistent within stable democracies. A strong possibility is that aid is given selectively, that is, to countries that already have fairly strong respect for religious freedoms. It could also indicate a form of soft conditionality if aid providers extend assistance on the understanding that rights practices with respect to religious freedoms are expected to improve. Surprisingly, a country's level of development seems to be negatively associated with religious freedoms: Controlling for differences between countries and focusing only on effects within them, greater wealth per capita is associated with more governmental interference with religious freedom.

As the major religious cultures span many countries, I have tested for differences in practices with respect to religious freedom for predominantly Protestant, Catholic, and Islamic states. No predominantly Islamic countries were among the stable democracies, but neither branch of Christianity had any significant impact on religious freedoms in stable democracies. Predominant religious culture in the transitioning countries and stable autocracies displays contrasting results, with Islam associated with greater religious freedoms among transitioning countries and Christianity associated with greater religious freedom among stable autocracies.

For our purposes, the major result is the weak but noticeable influence of the ICCPR within five years of ratification for all regime types, with a clear concentration of the treaty's liberalizing effects within countries that have had at least some postwar experience with a moderate level of democratic governance. This is consistent with a theory that predicts the strongest treaty influences in countries in which individuals and groups have both the motive and the means to demand treaty adherence. It is also consistent with anecdotal evidence of the weight that at least some religious groups attach to ratification of the ICCPR as a way to enhance their ability to operate freely in many locations throughout the world.[73] Indeed, the ability to organize and to draw from the strength of faith-based communities with dense social networks may be one of

---

73 Among U.S. religious and church organizations, the more liberal – often those whose organizational provenance can be traced to the antiwar movement of the Vietnam era – tend to support the ratification of the ICCPR and other covenants, while more conservative religious organizations, such as the National Association of Evangelicals, are distinctly cool to the UN approach to rights. See the discussion in Livezey 1989. For more on the follow-up of religious as well as secular NGOs, see Tahzib 1996:245 and generally the discussion on pp. 223–45. See also Roan 1996.

the key reasons that the ICCPR's religious guarantees are more difficult for governments to ignore than other aspects of the treaty. A fairly sharp comparison can be drawn with civil rights touching on criminal justice, which is explored in the following sections.

FAIR TRIALS

The right to a fair trial has deep historical roots that extend back as far as the Magna Carta (1215).[74] The idea of that document – and many to follow with successively greater elaboration and expansion – was to prevent the arbitrary exercise of sovereign power to arrest, detain, and convict individuals for various infractions and misdeeds without basic provisions for the due processes of law.

So, why do some states fail to provide their populace access to a fair trial? One cluster of explanations resides in the generally repressive nature of governance on which some regimes rely. Denying access to justice for groups ranging from political opponents to common criminals is one way for an oppressive state to maintain its arbitrary control over social and political developments. Demands for fair treatment before the law have historically been associated with a break with arbitrary or authoritarian rule. Fair trials were central among the liberties that distinguished the colonial rights of Englishmen in the New World on the eve of the American Revolution.[75] Fair trials were also a centerpiece of the democratic transition in former communist countries, such as the Czech Republic, Hungary, Poland, Lithuania, and Romania, and made their way prominently into the new postcommunist constitutions in these states.[76] A right to a fair trial was not included in the South African constitution until apartheid was brought down in 1994; such a right as existed in common law in that country could be overridden legislatively according to principles of parliamentary sovereignty.[77] The concept of popular sovereignty historically has fueled demands for legal reforms that reflect the basic civil right to due process of law for individuals accused of crimes.[78]

There may be other reasons for weak due process in practice. Some observers associate a breakdown in the fair delivery of criminal justice with a broad

---

74 "No free man shall be seized or imprisoned, or stripped of his rights or possessions, or outlawed or exiled, or deprived of his standing in any other way, nor will we proceed with force against him, or send others to do so, except by the lawful judgment of his equals or by the law of the land." Magna Carta, Article 39. Text can be accessed at http://www.fordham.edu/halsall/source/magnacarta.html (accessed 8 May 2008).

75 See Bodenhamer 1992:19.

76 See the articles by Hollander, Vasilescu and Trocsanyi, Staciokas, Oniszczuk and Horvath in Council of Europe 2000.

77 Skeen 2000:110.

78 Sung 2006.

incapacity of organs of justice more generally.[79] In particular, some countries are plagued with judicial incompetence and poor police training.[80] The provision of a fair trial may be limited not only for political purposes of despotic states, but can also flow from bureaucratic incapacities that stem from broader resource deficiencies.

Fair Trials in International Law

The Universal Declaration of Human Rights was the first modern multilateral document to articulate a right to a fair trial. Fair trials were somewhat less controversial than the provision of religious freedom, though debates did ensue about the exact parameters of this guarantee. The United States was eager to articulate postwar principles of civil and political rights, and provided the first proposal containing some of the substantive fair trial provisions for the UDHR.[81] The United Kingdom drafted provisions for protections from arbitrary arrest.[82] Delegations from Cuba, Chile, and Mexico were also especially active in the drafting of fair trial provisions and were insistent on their inclusion. As a result of these efforts, fair trials feature prominently in the UDHR: Article 8 provides for remedies for violations of the right to a fair trial; Article 9 deals with arbitrary arrest; Article 10 expresses the basic right of the individual to a fair trial in both civil and criminal proceedings; and Article 11 refers to a presumption of innocence and the prohibition of ex post facto laws and penalties.[83]

The ICCPR was negotiated concurrently with the UDHR, and the UDHR's Articles 8–11 were made legally binding in Articles 14 and 15 of the covenant. "All persons shall be equal before the courts and tribunals. In the determination of any criminal charge against him, or of his rights and obligations in a suit at law, everyone shall be entitled to a fair and public hearing by a competent, independent and impartial tribunal established by law," according to Article 14.[84] Article 15 guarantees a presumption of innocence and prohibition of ex post facto laws and is one of the seven articles specified as nonderogable in Article 4.[85] The ICCPR also addresses some events leading up to and following the trial proper, including arrest, detention, interrogation, and punishment.[86] According

---

79 See the rambling and disorganized discussion in Asian Human Rights Commission 2000.
80 As an example, see the statistics regarding Nepal cited in Sangroula 2000.
81 These provisions, though developed specifically for the UDHR, were eventually adopted in the ICCPR's Article 14, to the development of which the United States was decidedly cool. See Weissbrodt 2001:44.
82 Weissbrodt 2001:44.
83 See UDHR, Articles 8–11.
84 Article 14. On the origins and drafting history of Article 14, see Weissbrodt and Hallendorff 1999.
85 See the discussion in Weissbrodt 2001:93–110.
86 See Articles 4, 6–11, 17, and 26.

to the UN Human Rights Committee, the object of these provisions – especially Articles 14 and 15 – is to ensure that no one is subject to arbitrary prosecution, conviction, or punishment.[87]

Fair trials are also mentioned in several regional human rights agreements. The nations in the Americas were among the earliest to institutionalize a right to a fair trial on a regional basis. The 1948 American Declaration of the Rights and Duties of Man mentions a fundamental right to access the courts "to ensure respect for his legal rights,"[88] while the American Convention on Human Rights provides for a liberal list of "minimal guarantees" for "[e]very person accused of a criminal offense. . . ."[89] Article 6 of the 1953 European Convention for the Protection of Human Rights and Fundamental Freedoms (as amended), which preceded the ICCPR, specifies a right to a fair trial and describes this right in much the same way as does the ICCPR.[90] The League of Arab States' Charter on Human Rights (as revised, 2004) also contains guarantees with respect to fair trials.[91] Article 7 of the African Charter includes the rights to be presumed innocent, to defense and counsel of the accused's choice, and to an impartial trial within a reasonable period of time and protection from ex post laws, but it does not contain many of the other components of a fair trial specified in the UDHR and the ICCPR.[92] The right to a fair trial is also addressed under international humanitarian law, in particular the Geneva Conventions (1949) and their 1977 protocols.[93]

---

87 Accordingly, they have interpreted the provisions as applying to both general and specialized courts (e.g., military tribunals) that try civilians, and view fair trial provisions as pertaining to violations at any stage of the proceedings. Human Rights Committee General Comment 13(21) (adopted in 1984), UN Doc. HRI/GEN/1/Rev.2 (1996). Text located at http://www1.umn.edu/humanrts/gencomm/hrcom13.htm (accessed 10 May 2008). For a discussion of the various fair trial provisions of the ICCPR, see De Zayas 1997; Jayawickrama 1997; van Dijk 1983.
88 American Declaration of the Rights and Duties of Man, O.A.S. Res. XXX, adopted by the Ninth International Conference of American States (1948), Article XVIII. Text at http://www1.umn.edu/humanrts/oasinstr/zoas2dec.htm (accessed 10 May 2008).
89 American Convention on Human Rights, O.A.S. Treaty Series No. 36, 1144 U.N.T.S. 123, *entered into force* 18 July 1978, Article 8, paras. 1 and 2. Text available at http://www1.umn.edu/humanrts/oasinstr/zoas3con.htm (accessed 10 May 2008). For a discussion of cases heard by the Inter-American Commission on Human Rights and the Inter-American Court of Human Rights, see Augusto Cancado 1997; Kokott 1997.
90 Convention for the Protection of Human Rights and Fundamental Freedoms, 213 U.N.T.S. 222, *entered into force* 3 September 1953, *as amended by* Protocols Nos. 3, 5, 8, and 11, which *entered into force* 21 September 1970, 20 December 1971, 1 January 1990, and 1 November 1998, respectively. See http://www1.umn.edu/humanrts/instree/z17euroco.html (accessed 10 May 2008). See the discussion in Leigh 1997; Matscher 2000.
91 See Articles 13 (paras. 1 and 2), 14 (para. 5), 16, 17, and 20 (para. 2). League of Arab States, Revised Arab Charter on Human Rights, 22 May 2004. Text available at http://www1.umn.edu/humanrts/instree/loas2005.html (accessed 10 May 2008).
92 African [Banjul] Charter on Human and Peoples' Rights, adopted 27 June 1981, OAU Doc. CAB/LEG/67/3 rev. 5, 21 I.L.M. 58 (1982), *entered into force* 21 October 1986. See the discussion in Badawi El-Sheikh 1997:328.
93 Swinarski 1997.

The ICCPR remains the most important universal treaty to guarantee a right to a fair trial. What has the ratification of the ICCPR contributed to the actual provision of a fair approach to criminal justice? The strategy for answering this question is discussed in the following section.

Data and Methods

If the ICCPR has an influence on the civil rights of accused persons, then we should see actual practices guaranteeing fairness improving among ratifiers. Oona Hathaway has developed a sophisticated measure of fair trials, using international legal texts – primarily the ICCPR – as her guide and State Department reports for the raw material from which her index is coded.[94] The index considers the extent to which trials are carried out by independent and impartial tribunals; whether an accused person has a right to counsel (and, if necessary, an interpreter) and to present a defense; whether there is a presumption of innocence; and whether the trial is held publicly, in a timely fashion, and with a right to appeal. In addition, Hathaway coded for prohibitions on ex post facto laws and the right to have charges presented with prior notice.[95] This index captures well the international norms embodied in the ICCPR.

Figure 5.2 illustrates the worldwide average of the fair trial score each year from 1982 to 2002. We only have data since 1982, but the trends are toward a slight deterioration in the mid-1980s and again in the late 1990s. On the face of it, it would appear that there is very little relationship between average global ratification of the ICCPR and the average on this scale, in contrast to the broader civil liberties measure examined previously. Of course, many factors influence the will and capacity to provide individuals accused of a crime with a fair trial. What, if anything, does ratification contribute?

In order to answer this question, it is again important to construct a model that accounts for ratification endogeneity, constant characteristics of countries, shocks specific to particular years, and a host of alternative explanations. As was done in the models analyzing religious freedoms, the models reported in Table 5.3 pool countries over time and employ two-stage least squares, and they endogenize the decision to ratify the ICCPR as described previously.[96] They all contain country fixed effects, so that constant characteristics of particular countries do not drive results, as well as year fixed effects to control for the

---

94 On the quality of State Department reports, see De Neufville 1986.
95 For the original coding justification, see Hathaway 2002.
96 Unfortunately, in this case, the common law variable is unlikely to make a good instrument. According to some legal scholars, the idea of a fair trial for those accused of crimes is a contribution of the common law tradition, with its emphasis on fair play. See, for example, Matscher 2000:10. Thus, identification in this case depends almost exclusively on regional ratification density in the previous period.

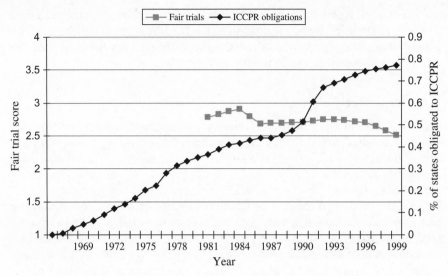

Figure 5.2. ICCPR Ratifications and Fair Trials. *Note*: Includes ratifications and accessions. *Source*: fair trial score: Hathaway 2002 (updated, interpolated, and inverted so that high values represent better practices).

possibility that some common external shock jolts all countries to alter their policies at given points in time. To account for policy inertia, the dependent variable lagged three years is included, as are average regional trial practices to account for the possibility of socialization or mimicry toward regional norms. Since we do not want to confuse the effects of ICCPR ratification with the general processes associated with democratization, variables to capture both democratic levels and change are included. Since it is reasonable to assume that fair criminal justice is more likely to be suspended during national emergencies, civil and international wars are included. Fair trials could also be a function of development level (GDP/capita) or external influences, such as development assistance; both of these are controlled in what follows. In addition, I control for extraordinary efforts to improve government accountability with respect to human rights practices with controls for truth commissions and criminal trials aimed at prosecuting officials for criminal human rights violations. As previously, the results are based on robust standard errors with a correction for clustering on countries.

Oona Hathaway pioneered research in this area and found that ratification of the ICCPR had little effect on state practices with respect to a fair trial. Quite the contrary: Some analyses of her evidence suggest that rights practices worsen once a treaty commitment has been made. However, I am interested not only in the aggregate effects of the ICCPR with respect to fair trials, but also in *the*

conditions under which we might expect ratification to have its strongest impact.
Theoretically, there are strong reasons to suspect that fair trials are already
provided in stable democracies, and there is little reason for ratification of the
ICCPR to stimulate new political demands in that regard. Nor should we expect
the ICCPR to make much difference in stable autocracies, where potential
demanders can anticipate costly state resistance. Ratification should matter
most where local groups have both the motive and the means to demand compliance. This is the case in countries characterized by some degree of regime
transition.

Findings: ICCPR Ratification and Fair Trials

The results for the influence of ICCPR treaty commitments are reported in
Table 5.3. With one exception, in every version of the model, ICCPR ratification
is weakly associated with improvements in fair trial practices. However, when
all countries are included in the sample, the result does not meet traditional
standards of statistical significance. Interesting variation emerges, however,
when we look at subgroups of countries. Ratification of the ICCPR appears
to have no discernible effects in countries that were never democratic during the
post–World War II period or in stable democracies over those years. But if we
run a similar test for countries that had had some experience with democratic
politics – transitional countries in the sense that they had passed a moderately
high democratic threshold at some point in the postwar years – ratification of
the ICCPR is quite likely to be associated with fairer domestic trials from year
to year, at least in the short run. When we look for the impact five years after
ratification, the ICCPR effect becomes swamped by other factors. Nevertheless, there is some evidence that for the 55 countries coded as transitional,
ratification has contributed to better practices – fairer trials for individuals than
would have been the case had the treaty not been ratified at all.

Ratification of the ICCPR is, of course, not the only influence on fair trials,
and the control variables tested here reveal some important influences on legal
practices. The usually strongly positive lagged dependent variable indicates that
countries with poor ratings were likely to have poor ratings in the next period,
indicating that the fairness of trials is marked by a high degree of institutional
inertia. The most consistent external influence across all categories of countries is
the nature of the practices in the region in which the country is situated. Across
all subgroups and the sample as a whole, fair trial practices in the region were a
strong predictor of fair trial practices in a specific country. This effect appears to
be the strongest among the moderately democratic and transitional countries,
though it is statistically significant in every model. This pattern could be
explained by shared cultural patterns or even regional socialization or mimicry.
Another external influence that is strongest in transitional countries is the positive influence of overseas development assistance. But it is important to note

Table 5.3. Effects of an ICCPR Commitment on Fair Trials

Dependent variable: fair trial practices
Instrumental variable least squares regression model
Coefficients, probabilities based on robust standard errors

Explanatory Variable	All Countries	Trans. Only	Trans. Only, with Controls	Never Democratic Only	Stable Democracies Only	Trans., ICCPR 5 Year Lag
ICCPR commitment	.168	.314*	.348*	.094	-.076	.055
	($p = .175$)	($p = .086$)	($p = .087$)	($p = .674$)	($p = .509$)	($p = .763$)
Fair trials ($t - 3$)	0.163***	.152**	.148**	.110	.206	.174**
	($p = .002$)	($p = .024$)	($p = .047$)	($p = .125$)	($p = .220$)	($p = .027$)
Regional fair trial average ($t - 2$)	.163***	.909***	1.00***	.647*	.362***	1.01***
	($p = .001$)	($p = .000$)	($p = .000$)	($p = .054$)	($p = .001$)	($p = .000$)
Democracy (level)	-.004	—	-.004	-.008	.278***	.0003
	($p = .635$)		($p = .70$)	($p = .570$)	($p = .001$)	($p = .978$)
Democratic change	-0.019***	-.017**	-.020**	-.014	.134*	-.019**
	($p = .006$)	($p = .019$)	($p = .017$)	($p = .211$)	($p = .050$)	($p = .018$)
Military government	-.144	-.267**	-.243*	.054	—	-.236*
	($p = .148$)	($p = .020$)	($p = .052$)	($p = .650$)		($p = .067$)
Truth commission	.436**	—	.349*	.105	.299	.360
	($p = .025$)		($p = .083$)	($p = .558$)	($p = .263$)	($p = .116$)
Criminal trials	.023	—	.038	.079	.223**	.037
	($p = .814$)		($p = .717$)	($p = .649$)	($p = .018$)	($p = .734$)
Total fractionalization, logged	.440*	—	.061	-.097	3.97***	-.243
	($p = .089$)		($p = .932$)	($p = .837$)	($p = .001$)	($p = .731$)

GDP per capita, logged	−.235 (p = .354)	—	.111 (p = .811)	−.598* (p = .069)	−.386 (p = .217)	.169 (p = .731)
Total population, logged	−.845* (p = .055)	—	.019 (p = .983)	−.189 (p = .884)	−1.92*** (p = .001)	.413 (p = .648)
Overseas development assistance/GDP	.372 (p = .600)	—	1.35* (p = .096)	−.045 (p = .962)	−10.32*** (p = .001)	1.37* (p = .085)
Civil war	−.207** (p = .044)	—	.006 (p = .960)	−.237* (p = .065)	−1.04*** (p = .000)	.038 (p = .757)
Interstate war	−.255** (p = .034)	—	−.021 (p = .809)	−.521*** (p = .000)	.090* (p = .097)	−.005 (p = .953)
Rule of law	1.83** (p = .020)	—	−.631 (p = .643)	.340 (p = .557)	.497 (p = .158)	−.217 (p = .871)
Country fixed effects?	yes	yes	yes	yes	yes	yes
Year fixed effects?	yes	yes	yes	yes	yes	yes
# of observations	1,890	746	684	756	434	684
# of countries	140	55	51	59	28	51
R^2	0.767	0.724	.725	0.580	0.881	0.715

Instrumented: ICCPR Commitment. Instruments: All explanatory variables above, plus ratification procedures, common law legal tradition, regional ICCPR ratification density, a counting vector of years without ICCPR ratification, three cubic splines, and a year time trend.
* Significant at the .10 level; ** significant at the .05 level; *** significant at the .01 level.

that the effects of the ICCPR are noticeable among the transitional countries even when controlling for their regional context and foreign development aid.

One of the most important influences on fair trial practices is the nature of the domestic political regime, but the results hold some surprises in this regard. A country's extent of democracy at the time of observation does not have the positive effect on fair trials one might expect (except among those countries that have been stable democracies since World War II). Even more surprising, democratic change tends to lead to worse fair trial practices in the following year, and this result is especially robust for the 55 transitional countries. What these results suggest is that in practice, fair trials do not improve in lockstep with democracy and democratic improvements. Protecting the legal rights of the accused requires something more than encouraging participatory democracy. More in line with expectations, civilian governments are more likely to be associated with fair trials. Legal fairness appears to deteriorate significantly, especially for countries in transition governed by military leaders. (Note that there were no military governments among the stable democracies, so the variable drops out of that model.) There is also some evidence that governments especially committed to exposing the crimes and abuses of earlier regimes through the use of truth commissions also improve their trials in the following year. Unsurprisingly, countries that score high on the rule of law scale also tend to provide fairer trials for accused persons. The inclusion of these variables helps to control for a domestically generated commitment to improve human rights practices and increases our confidence that the ICCPR ratification variable is not simply reflecting a set of domestic legal innovations.

There is little evidence that fair trial practices are driven by what might broadly be considered developmental or local social factors. While it undoubtedly takes resources to hold fair trials – providing the defense with qualified attorneys and educating independent judges are not low-cost options – it is not the case that wealthier countries conduct fairer trials, all else equal. In fact, there is some suggestion that the opposite is true, at least for the more authoritarian regimes. Countries that are more varied in terms of religion, language, and ethnic groups may tend to have somewhat better practices as well, but this result seems to be driven by the stable democracies, such as Belgium. A burgeoning population may contribute to deteriorating practices if social and other problems worsen, though in this case the effects seem to be concentrated in the stable autocracies. Overall, however, it is hard to say that there is a clear social or developmental country profile associated with fair trials.

Far clearer is the role that violent conflict plays in the administration of justice for the accused. The expectation that violent periods of "national emergency" are often used as reasons to short-circuit normal rights protections in the name of national security is borne out in these tests. Both civil wars and interstate wars returned the expected negative coefficient for the sample of countries as a whole, but the most consistent deterioration in rights associated with war is concentrated in the countries that were never democratic during the postwar years. The effect is apparently contradictory for stable democracies, with civil wars associated with worse practices and international wars with fairer trials. In the transition countries, wars – whether civil or international – are not associated with clear trends in fair trials in either direction.

Overall, the influence of ICCPR ratification on fair trials is highly conditioned by the nature of the regime. There is a mild positive but statistically insignificant association across all countries, but the analysis of subgroups indicates that the positive effects are concentrated largely in neither the stable democracies nor the stable autocracies, but rather in those polities that have had some experience with democratic government, however fleeting. The statistical strength of the relationship is not very strong – we can only be 91–92 percent confident that the relationship is not due to chance alone – but it does offer some evidence that ratification is associated under the right political circumstances with actual improvements in fair trials, as required by the ICCPR.

CRUEL AND INHUMANE PUNISHMENT: THE DEATH PENALTY

A final area to consider governed by the ICCPR, and especially its Optional Protocol on the Death Penalty (OPDP), is that of cruel and inhuman punishment. Specifically, this section will inquire into compliance with international legal commitments to abolish capital punishment, or the penalty of death for the commission of a crime.

The death penalty is one of the oldest forms of criminal punishment. Laws providing for the death penalty date from the eighteenth century B.C.E. in Babylonia. In seventh-century B.C.E. Athens, the Draconian Code made death the only punishment for all crimes. In a less absolute form, capital punishment became part of Roman law in the fifth century B.C.E. and has been used throughout much of the world for most of recorded history.[97] The death penalty is referred to in sacred texts from the Bible to the Koran. Some anthropologists count capital punishment as a "universal cultural trait" alongside families and religion, viewing it as common at some point in time to all known cultures.[98]

Enlightenment thought represented a trend toward greater circumspection regarding the death penalty. The most influential work of the period was penned by the Italian criminologist Cesare Beccaria, who emphasized both its futility and its inhumaneness.[99] By the nineteenth century, governments began to view the practice much more critically. There were practical reasons to curtail

---

97 For a concise historical overview, see the introduction to Schabas 2002.
98 For a discussion of the death penalty in early rabbinical and Christian thought, see Berkowitz 2006. Otterbein 1986:37–45 makes the broader universalistic claim.
99 Beccaria 1963.

the widespread practice of execution as well. Many a poor British citizen was hung in London in the eighteenth century, though the main reason Britain had to curtail public hangings is alleged to be not a humanitarian concern, but the problem of numbers.[100] Soon, developments in long-distance transportation made it possible to export rather than execute offenders – an option embraced by abolitionists in England.[101] Opposition to the death penalty began to develop elsewhere in the Western Hemisphere as well. Michigan became the first jurisdiction to abolish the practice permanently, in 1864.[102] Venezuela was one of the first countries to remove the death penalty for all crimes (1863), and several countries in Latin America and Europe followed by eliminating the death penalty at least during peacetime – Portugal being the first country in Europe to do so in 1864.[103]

The movement to abolish the death penalty gained momentum after World War II. What distinguishes this period of abolition from the past (when it was considered an internal matter) is the largely European-driven effort to use international treaties to bring about abolition.[104] As discussed in further detail later, since 1983 the Council of Europe has banned the death penalty, and accession to that ban is a condition for joining the EU.[105] In Europe, the discourse of "civilization" and human dignity has framed the death penalty debate.[106] Largely as a result of this frame, Europe was a "de facto death-penalty-free continent" by the year 2000.[107] Among democracies, the United States stands out as the most important country to oppose the European effort to eliminate the death penalty worldwide.[108]

Outside of Europe, the death penalty remains widespread, in law and in practice. It continues to be used in countries as culturally diverse as China, Islamic countries, and the United States.[109] By some accounts, the abolitionist movement reached a plateau by the late 1990s.[110] In some cases, there have even been reversals (in The Gambia, Kansas, and New York, for example). As Roger Hood has written, there is nothing inevitable about the process of abolition.[111]

---

100 Gatrell 1994; Linebaugh 1991.
101 Ekirch 1987.
102 On the historical background, see Davis 1957.
103 On the abolition of the death penalty in Europe, see Ancel 1962:8–14. On the history of death penalty abolition in the Americas, see Bowers et al. 1984:146.
104 Boulanger and Sarat 2005; Hood 2001:337.
105 See http://ec.europa.eu/external_relations/human_rights/adp/index.htm (accessed 10 May 2008).
106 Boulanger and Sarat 2005:32.
107 Puhar 2005:55.
108 For an interesting discussion of U.S. attitudes toward the death penalty, see Zimring 2003:42–64. See also Baumer et al. 2003.
109 See the discussion in Wyman 1997. Hood notes that it is misleading to speak of "the" United States in this regard since the death penalty is largely regulated by the states (2001:343).
110 Radzinowicz 1999:293.
111 Hood 2001:333–5.

A range of theories have been advanced to explain the retention of the death penalty. Some scholars emphasize its role in consolidating political legitimacy,[112] while others link it with religious beliefs about the inappropriateness – or the moral necessity – of earthly retribution.[113] One thing does seem apparent: While numerous studies have shown that repressive governments are more likely than liberal ones to have and use capital punishment,[114] there is no necessary link between democracy and the decision to abolish the death penalty. Stable democracies from the United States[115] to Jamaica to Japan[116] as well as some of the most oppressive autocracies from China to Iran to Tajikistan retain the death penalty for ordinary crimes.[117] And it is quite clear that the demand for abolition is not typically linked to popular democratic forces. In 1975, some 85 percent of Britons polled said that they favored the death penalty in their country, even though it had been repealed a decade earlier.[118] In much of Eastern Europe the death penalty was repealed, despite the fact that public opinion often supported it;[119] in many cases, change was wrought through constitutional courts rather than parliamentary decision.[120]

This ironic situation – abolition often against prevailing public preferences – is one of the most intriguing aspects of this issue area. Democratic governments are often willing to abolish capital punishment, despite fairly broad public support for it in many cases. Despite the moral argument that can be made against the death penalty,[121] broad swathes of democratic publics are likely to accept the utilitarian notion that the death penalty deters crime[122] and to believe

112 Miethe et al. 2005; Otterbein 1986:37–45; 73; Ruddell 2005. For a comprehensive review and tests of the determinants of the death penalty, see Anckar 2004.

113 Jacobs and Carmichael 2004; Miethe et al. 2005; Potter 1993; Soss et al. 2003.

114 Miethe et al. 2005; Ruddell and Urbana 2004.

115 Some authors have emphasized U.S. harshness in the area of criminal justice, in growing contrast to a relatively milder approach in continental Europe. See Whitman 2003. For a review of public opinion on the death penalty in the United States, see Atwell 2004.

116 Johnson attributes Japanese retention largely to the U.S. occupation of that country, where unlike in Germany, "abolishing capital punishment was nowhere on this agenda . . ." (2006:259). Capital punishment in contemporary Japan tends to be shrouded in secrecy, a legacy of the Occupation's policy of "censored democracy" (Johnson 2006:260). On the cultural aspects of the American commitment to the death penalty, see Garland 2002.

117 Of course, it is difficult to know the exact extent of state executions in many highly repressive countries; in the Soviet Union, for example, that information was a state secret (Puhar 2005:59).

118 Zimring 2003:10.

119 This was the case in Poland, for example. See Fijalkowski 2005:157.

120 Puhar 2005:83.

121 Perry 2007:37–51.

122 Palmer and Henderson 1998; Wynarczyk 1999. Studies that conclude that the death penalty deters crime include Ehrlich 1975; Wolpin 1978. Support for the death penalty as a deterrent to crime is also strong in (nondemocratic) China, despite the lack of any government propaganda to influence public opinion (Ho 2005:280–1). There is also good evidence that the demand for capital punishment increases as the seriousness of the crime in the respondent's location increases (Cameron 1993).

that it appropriately respects the interests of victims and/or their families for "closure."[123] "Tough on crime" rhetoric can be used to deflect incipient concerns regarding the morality of capital punishment and mobilize popular consent for the death penalty.[124]

The Death Penalty in International Law

The death penalty has been addressed in international law only since World War II. It was discussed by the UN Human Rights Commission while debating the contents of the UDHR, but no clear consensus could be reached. Article 3 provides that "Everyone has the right to life, liberty and security of person," while Article 5 requires that "No one shall be subjected to torture or to cruel, inhuman or degrading treatment or punishment."[125] No specific mention is made of the death penalty. Negotiation of the ICCPR provided another opportunity to be explicit about banning the death penalty in international law. This time the opportunity was taken, but a clear compromise was struck. The covenant reiterated an affirmative right to life.[126] It also provided that *for countries that had not already abolished the death penalty,* it should be used only for the most serious crimes and that the provision should not be used to justify delay of abolition.[127] An explicit ban was opposed by the United States as well as the majority of predominantly Muslim countries.[128] While there may have been some assumption of an eventual ban by many countries, continuing disagreement led to compromise language.

In contrast to fair trial guarantees, which are rarely opposed in principle by any government, state opponents of the death penalty are often explicit in their opposition. Among the strongest opponents to the abolition of the death penalty in UN debates have been Singapore and Egypt, which have led the charge against several EU efforts to universalize and strengthen international law on the death penalty.[129] Several governments have made clear reservations or declarations to the ICCPR, indicating their understanding that it does not prohibit the use of capital punishment. Both the United States' and China's reservations to the ICCPR, for example, explicitly exempt them from provisions regarding the death penalty.[130] In debates before the UN, Sudan has claimed that "Capital

---

123 Dunér and Geurtsen 2002:10.
124 Garland 2001.
125 Articles 3 and 5 of the UDHR text at http://www.un.org/Overview/rights.html (accessed 10 May 2008).
126 ICCPR, Article 6, para. 1.
127 ICCPR, Article 6, para. 2.
128 Wyman 1997. The only outright ban on the death penalty contained in the ICCPR is in the case of minors, against which the United States entered a reservation, and pregnant women (Article 6, para. 5).
129 Bantekas and Hodgkinson 2000.
130 Albrecht 2000:99.

punishment is a divine right of some religions. It is embodied in Islam and these views must be respected."[131] While some scholars have claimed that the ban against the death penalty has hardened into a custom in international law,[132] it seems unlikely that this view would be broadly accepted outside of Europe and possibly Latin America.

The countries of Europe were determined to proceed with law development against the death penalty, despite opposition from the United States and the Middle and Far East. Crucial in Europe was the reframing of the death penalty as a human rights issue rather than as an issue of criminal justice. After 30 years of domestic legal change effectively banning capital punishment at the national level, the most important regional legal change came with passage of the 1983 Protocol No. 6 of the European Convention on Human Rights.[133] Like the multilateral optional protocol that was to follow, this regional accord banned the death penalty unequivocally, though allowing for reservations preserving the option for the most serious crimes during wartime.[134] A year later, the UN's ECOSOC adopted a resolution that acknowledged the gravity of the issue without broaching the question of a ban by adopting a resolution to protect the rights of persons facing the death penalty.[135]

The general prohibition in international law on executions came in the form of an optional protocol to the ICCPR.[136] Adopted by the UNGA in 1989, the OPDP bans executions outright.[137] Like European Protocol No. 6, this agreement abolishes the death penalty in all situations, including war, unless a country specifies otherwise through reservation at the time of ratification.[138] The second optional protocol to the ICCPR is the clearest obligatory multilateral document to ban the death penalty under virtually all circumstances. The next section considers the extent to which countries have complied with their legal obligations in this area by looking at actual patterns of death penalty abolition.

---

131 This was a 1994 statement, as quoted by Hood 2001:341.
132 Ohlin 2005.
133 Protocol No. 6 to the 1950 European Convention for the Protection of Human Rights and Fundamental Freedoms, E.T.S. 114, *entered into force* 1 March 1985. See text at http://www1.umn. edu/humanrts/euro/z25prot6.html (accessed 10 May 2008).
134 Protocol No. 6, Articles 1 and 2.
135 Safeguards guaranteeing protection of the rights of those facing the death penalty Adopted by Economic and Social Council resolution 1984/50 of 25 May 1984. See text at http:// www.unhchr.ch/html/menu3/b/h_comp41.htm (accessed 10 May 2008).
136 Second OPDP to the ICCPR, aiming at the abolition of the death penalty. Adopted and proclaimed by UNGA resolution 44/128 of 15 December 1989. Text at http://www.unhchr.ch/ html/menu3/b/a_opt2.htm (accessed 10 May 2008).
137 Second OPDP to the ICCPR, Article 1, para. 1.
138 Second OPDP to the ICCPR, Article 2, para 1. See the discussion in Dunér and Geurtsen 2002:7. They note that very few countries make such a reservation upon ratification (p. 9).

Data and Methods

If the ICCPR, and especially the OPDP, have had any influence on states' practices, we should expect the propensity to remove the death penalty to correspond with ICCPR and OPDP ratification. Of all of the civil rights we have examined in this chapter, we should expect the results to be the strongest: Abolition is a public policy, and execution is generally a public act taken by the central government in large part for its deterrence value. It is relatively easy to monitor cases of capital execution – at least in comparison with torture and the fairness of a criminal trial.[139] We should expect compliance to be clearly associated with commitment to the ICCPR and especially to the OPDP once we have accounted for the factors that lead countries to ratify these agreements in the first place, as well as a host of alternative explanations (discussed later) for reliance on the death penalty itself.

The dependent variable in the first instance is whether or not the central government *has* the death penalty; the second is whether or not a state *removes* the death penalty within its jurisdiction. The latter is indicated by the first year capital punishment is banned. In both cases, I use a pooled time series for this test and two-stage least squares for whether or not the death penalty is in place and for death penalty removal[140] (endogenizing ICCPR and OPDP ratification in both cases). I expect ratification to reduce the incidence of the death penalty (a negative coefficient) and increase the likelihood that the death penalty will be abolished (a positive coefficient).

Before proceeding, it is useful to note that the use of the death penalty is on the decline on average worldwide. Figure 5.3 charts the upward trend in the number of countries that have abolished the death penalty completely, the decrease in the number of countries that have abolished it for ordinary crimes, and the nearly constant number of countries that retain the death penalty for extraordinary crimes (such as treason during wartime). The figure also shows the upward trend in the number of countries that have ratified the OPDP since 1989.

The empirical problem is to estimate the influence that ratification has had on actual practices. In addition to endogenizing the treaty commitment itself, a battery of controls are included to reduce the chance that alternative explanations wash out the effect of making an international legal commitment. Because

139 Use of the death penalty may, however, be correlated with violence, torture, and extrajudicial killings. See Miethe et al. 2005.
140 A probit model would have been more appropriate here given the dichotomous nature of the data, but the full model could not converge with the proper range of controls as well as fixed effects, and so 2SLS was used. As a robustness check, I test whether or not a country uses the death penalty, looking at a single year (2000). The results support the general conclusions reported here. See the robustness results in Appendix 5.2 posted on my Web site at http://scholar.iq.harvard.edu/bsimmons/mobilizing-for-human-rights.

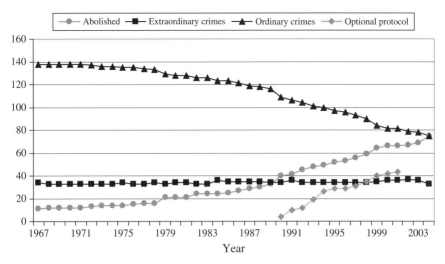

Figure 5.3. Number of Countries with the Death Penalty. *Source*: Amnesty International, http://web.amnesty.org/pages/deathpenalty-countries-eng.

many theories of the death penalty view it as a mechanism of social control, and because ethnic diversity is sometimes construed as a threat to such control, one might expect the death penalty to be much more widespread in societies with a high degree of ethnic fractionalization.[141]

Domestic political conditions are also likely to be a major explanation. Although democracy per se is not an obvious correlate (as discussed previously), I control for regime type and changes in regime type on the hypothesis that the trend to abolish the death penalty is a reflection of the waves of liberal reform sweeping much of the world. Previous research has noted that military governments are more likely to retain the death penalty, as are conservative or right-wing governments,[142] and so I control for military control of the government as well as government partisanship. At least in the United States, federalism is largely responsible for the retention of the

141 Existing research suggests that the death penalty is associated with societies in which dominant ethnic groups feel threatened by significant minorities or subordinate majority groups. See, for example, Ruddell 2005; Soss et al. 2003; Turrell 2004.

142 Research suggests that right-wing parties are much more likely to crack down on crime through greater imprisonment than are left-wing parties, even controlling for rates of crime and unemployment (Sutton 2000). In the United States, more vigilant law enforcement is associated with Republican Party governance (Jacobs and Helms 1997). States that have higher numbers of people identifying as Republicans are more likely to legalize the death penalty (Jacobs and Carmichael 2002), and to impose it as well (Jacobs and Carmichael 2004). On the history of the partisan fight in the British Parliament, see Block and Hostettler 1997. For a discussion that connects attitudes on the death penalty to ideas of personal responsibility often espoused by conservatives, see Lakoff 1996.

death penalty; these tests control for the degree of decentralization of government in each case.

The security environment is also a likely contributor to the decision to impose or lift the death penalty. The option to make reservations allowing for the death penalty in wartime signals the importance states have given to issues of national security. I hypothesize that the death penalty is more likely to be retained in states facing civil or international wars.[143] Some analysts have noted that capital punishment is an instrument of state consolidation.[144] To account for this possibility, I include the logged years since each state's independence. The longer it has been since independence, the less the imperative to maintain capital punishment for purposes of consolidating state authority.

Finally, it is obvious that the international environment has been important in fueling the abolition movement.[145] The most important factor in this area has been the role that Europe has played in trying to persuade governments around the world that capital punishment violates basic human rights and ought to be banned. The Council of Europe has made elimination of the death penalty a requirement for joining the council and a criterion of "democracy."[146] The EU has campaigned for universal abolition of the death penalty in all circumstances; in fact, since 1998, abolition of the death penalty has been a formal condition of membership, which has clearly influenced the policies of some new member states, such as Estonia.[147] By comparison, the Inter-American regime – the only other regional organization to have an explicit position on the death penalty – freezes current practices but does not abolish capital punishment.[148] I therefore include indicators that should reflect a country's anticipation of joining the Council of Europe (membership three years in the future), the density of regional death penalty states, and a dummy variable for Europe itself (East and West). If patterns of abolition are primarily due to European socialization (or pressure), these indicators should be associated with a reduction in the death penalty and an increase in the probability of banning the practice.

Findings: The ICCPR, the OPDP, and Abolition of the Death Penalty

The results are displayed in Tables 5.4 and 5.5. The primary result is strong support for the proposition that countries that ratify the ICCPR and the OPDP are clearly associated with abolition of the death penalty in their jurisdiction. In

---

143 Dunér and Geursten look at simple percentages and find that countries experiencing recent war have ratified a death penalty protocol fewer times than those enjoying peace (2002:12).
144 Turrell 2004.
145 Zimring 2003:39.
146 Bantekas and Hodgkinson 2000:23; Fawn 2001; Puhar 2005.
147 Puhar 2005:103.
148 Some have therefore judged it "symbolic." See Dunér and Geurtsen 2002:7.

Table 5.4. The ICCPR, the OPDP, and the Death Penalty

Dependent variable: de jure death penalty
Instrumental variable least squares regression model
Coefficients, p-values based on robust standard errors

Explanatory Variable	Model 1: Basic		Model 2: Domestic Political Controls		Model 3: Security Controls		Model 4: Regional Influences	
ICCPR commitment	−.036	(p = .456)	−.082***	(p = .008)	.081	(p = .157)	−.018	(p = .741)
OPDP ratification	−.09***	(p = .010)	−.112**	(p = .027)	−.100***	(p = .008)	−.073*	(p = .096)
Death penalty ($t − 1$)	.853***	(p = .000)	.817***	(p = .000)	.850***	(p = .000)	.861***	(p = .000)
Years since last execution	.040***	(p = .005)	.048***	(p = .008)	.030*	(p = .019)	.039***	(p = .004)
Ethnic fractionalization	.141**	(p = .011)	.009	(p = .576)	.071***	(p = .008)	−.026	(p = .517)
Trade openness	−.0002	(p = .117)	−.0002	(p = .151)	−.00007	(p = .515)	−.0002	(p = .209)
Democracy	—		.0007	(p = .454)	—		—	
Yearly change in democracy	—		.0004	(p = .574)	—		—	
Military government	—		−.017*	(p = .090)	—		—	
Federalism	—		−.003	(p = .423)	—		—	
Left executive	—		−.014	(p = .205)	—		—	
Civil war	—		—		−.007	(p = .456)	—	
Civil war experience	—		—		.090***	(p = .006)	—	
Interstate war	—		—		.0004	(p = .930)	—	
Logged years since independence	—		—		.002	(p = .767)	—	
Membership in Council of Europe ($t + 3$)	—		—		—		−.002	(p = .938)
Regional death penalty density ($t − 1$)	—		—		—		.039	(p = .312)
Europe	—		—		—		.0007	(p = .992)
Islam	—		—		—		−.035	(p = .559)
Country fixed effects?	yes		yes		yes		yes	
Year fixed effects?	yes		yes		yes		yes	
# of observations	4,598		3,033		4,444		4,598	
# of countries	170		149		169		170	
R^2	.94		.94		.95		.94	

Instrumented: OPDP and ICCPR commitment.
Instruments: all preceding explanatory variables, plus ratification procedures, common law legal tradition, regional ICCPR commitment, and regional OPDP density.
* Significant at the .10 level; ** significant at the .05 level; *** significant at the .01 level.

Table 5.5. Death Penalty Abolition

Dependent variable: first year of death penalty abolition
Instrumental variable least squares regression model

Explanatory Variable	Model 1: Basic	Model 2: Domestic Political Controls	Model 3: Security Controls	Model 4: Regional Influences	Model 5: Full Set of Controls
ICCPR commitment	.078 ($p = .181$)	.065 ($p = .195$)	.114 ($p = .127$)	.080 ($p = .180$)	.084** ($p = .050$)
OPDP ratification	.315** ($p = .048$)	.524* ($p = .092$)	.333* ($p = .051$)	.317* ($p = .057$)	.558 ($p = .126$)
Years since last execution	—	—	-.023 ($p = .116$)	—	-.041** ($p = .036$)
Ethnic fractionalization	—	-.249*** ($p = .000$)	—	—	-.271*** ($p = .002$)
Religious fractionalization	—	—	—	—	-.843*** ($p = .000$)
Language fractionalization	—	—	—	—	.672*** ($p = .000$)
Trade openness	—	—	—	—	.0004* ($p = .078$)
Democracy	—	-.0005 ($p = .616$)	—	—	-.002* ($p = .053$)
Yearly change in democracy	—	-.001 ($p = .405$)	—	—	-.002 ($p = .162$)
Military government	—	.014 ($p = .138$)	—	—	.0057 ($p = .499$)
Federalism	—	.003 ($p = .414$)	—	—	.0008 ($p = .826$)
Left executive	—	.017 ($p = .246$)	—	—	.022 ($p = .215$)
Civil war	—	—	.005 ($p = .675$)	—	.004 ($p = .735$)

Civil war experience	—	—	−.020 (p = .157)	—	−.123*** (p = .000)
Interstate war	—	—	.003 (p = .702)	—	.008 (p = .245)
Logged years since independence	—	—	.003 (p = .724)	—	−.011 (p = .691)
Membership in Council of Europe (t + 3)	—	—	—	.0006 (p = .986)	.011 (p = .860)
Regional death penalty density (t − 1)	—	—	—	−.066 (p = .548)	−.124 (p = .498)
Europe	—	—	—	.047 (p = .399)	—
Islam	—	—	—	.019 (p = .318)	.262*** (p = .000)
GDP per capita, logged	—	—	—	—	.005 (p = .788)
Year	—	—	−.003 (p = .120)	—	—
Country fixed effects?	yes	yes	yes	yes	yes
Year fixed effects?	yes	yes	yes	yes	yes
# of observations	5,048	2,695	4,293	4,883	2,298
# of countries	165	134	159	164	123
R^2	.020	.084	.007	.003	.097

Instrumented: OPDP and ICCPR commitment.

Instruments: All preceding variables, plus ratification procedures, common law legal tradition, regional ICCPR commitment, and regional OPDP density.

Note: Conditional on having the death penalty at the beginning of the observation period.

* Significant at the .10 level; ** significant at the .05 level; *** significant at the .01 level.

Table 5.4, ratification of the OPDP reduces the likelihood that a state will have the death penalty by anywhere from 7 to 11 percent. This is an effect that is estimated to be directly attributable to the OPDP, net of the factors that led the government to ratify it in the first place, net of ICCPR ratification, and net of all of the control variables included in the various specifications. Moreover, ratification of the OPDP is associated with a 30 to 50 percent greater chance that a country will abolish the death penalty. Given that many countries abolish in *anticipation* of ratification, this is a significant impact. This is one area of human rights commitment in which governments commit and follow up with a very high probability.

Several other factors have a strong relationship with death penalty practices as well. Across all specifications, there is strong evidence that ethnic fractionalization is associated with maintenance of the death penalty. The presence of many ethnic groups makes it likely that a state will have the death penalty and much less likely that it will be removed. The domestic political variables that one might have thought would be associated with the death penalty hardly contribute to the explanation at all, and when they do, they are not in the direction one would expect (military governments are slightly *less* likely, according to Table 5.4, to preside over the death penalty). As one would expect, the death penalty is much more likely to exist and much less likely to be removed in countries that have had recent civil war experience, although not necessarily embroiled in civil conflict at the moment.

As noted previously, the ICCPR itself does not ban the death penalty. Ratification of the ICCPR alone is associated with a much weaker effect on death penalty practices than is the OPDP. In only one model – the one with domestic political controls – was there a convincing statistical relationship between ICCPR ratification alone and existence of the death penalty. Only in one model of death penalty repeal did ICCPR ratification have a statistically stronger relationship with repeal than did the OPDP. In each of these cases, the substantive significance of the OPDP far outweighs the substantive impact of ICCPR ratification. The substantive effect of the OPDP on repeal of the death penalty was four to seven times larger than that for the main treaty. This evidence is consistent with a theory of international law that associates commitment with a serious effort to comply. In the case of capital punishment, characterized by centralized policies that are reasonably easy to monitor, states do not ratify until they are certain that they will be willing and able to comply. Ratification matters in these cases precisely because it is straightforward to monitor, observe, and criticize potential violations.

CONCLUSIONS

The development of international human rights law has been one of the most significant projects of the past 60 years. Statesmen, activists, legal scholars, and organizations have committed a great deal of effort to fashioning a legal regime by which individuals might claim a broad array of civil rights vis-à-vis their own governments. Many have boldly labeled the central documents reflecting these efforts as "The International Bill of Rights" and have touted these instruments as the closest thing the international community has to a global constitutional statement of the civil rights of humankind. There is little doubt that the UDHR and the ICCPR represent normative aspirations of a good number of well-intentioned individuals, but it is also necessary to take stock of the effects of these documents and ask, what have they contributed to the actual realization of the rights they proclaim?

This chapter has been a modest step toward exploring and trying to answer this question. It has gone beyond claims that treaty ratification is largely symbolic and has taken seriously the idea that domestic rights demanders have strong incentives to use whatever tools are available to them – including international treaty commitments – to claim the rights these treaties express. One surprise has been that ratification has mattered at all to civil rights practices, given the prevailing assumption that such commitments are close to meaningless and largely unenforced by external actors. It is also surprising to observe systematic ratification effects, given the stringency of the models developed here. It is not easy to claim, given these analyses, that in broadening religious freedom, making trials fairer, and abolishing the death penalty governments are simply mimicking others, that this is just a residual consequence of the process of democratization, or that the government would have changed its behavior even in the absence of the treaty commitment. These claims do not ring true, because they are largely controlled for by the nature of the tests performed. The methods I use do not prove a causal relationship between treaty ratification and improved practices, but they do eliminate many alternative explanations that one might have initially thought would be a more powerful explanation of official civil rights choices. Nor do I claim that treaty commitment is the only or even the most important reason for the improvements we do observe. The claim is rather that such commitments have made an important contribution to rights practices, and that scholars and practitioners have not to date been able or willing to recognize this contribution.

Why should treaty ratification matter? The mechanisms are potentially myriad, but one is especially plausible: Treaty ratification matters because it stimulates domestic organization and mobilizes locals to claim the rights the treaty contains. We have seen that ICCPR ratification is followed by a burst of civil society organization, consistent with the idea that citizens view the post-ratification period as a time to organize to demand the kinds of rights the treaty promises on paper. Of course, not all kinds of issues elicit identical kinds or degrees of domestic mobilization. This research shows that there is a real payoff to breaking out different kinds of civil rights and comparing the treaty impact across issue areas. This is important because the politics differ across different civil rights areas in ways relevant to the mechanisms of treaty compliance. Compare religious freedom with fair trials, for example. The domestic demands for compliance are likely to be much stronger for religious freedom than for fair trials. In many cases, religious freedom will be demanded by organized religious groups that have the organizational capacity to press the government to allow them to worship and practice their religion freely. The primary demanders of fair trials may not only be political opponents of the government, but also an unsavory array of criminals. Not only is it difficult for such groups to organize themselves, it is also often difficult to assemble a broad coalition for fair trials because to do so can be framed as being soft on crime. Unsurprisingly, ratification has a less convincing impact on fair trials. This does not mean, however, that a treaty commitment is meaningless where mobilization is weak. It may mean that other methods must be found to enforce compliance. In Egypt, for example, the high court has used the ICCPR to craft rulings that improve the fairness of trials.[149]

One of the most striking results is the evidence of stronger treaty effects in countries experiencing regime instability or transition. This was found to be the case with respect to both religious freedom and fair trials. The theoretical discussion provided a good reason to suspect that treaty ratification would have the least impact in stable democracies (where rights are already very well protected) and in stable autocracies (where people anticipate harsh repression were they ever to demand treaty compliance). The evidence analyzed here is quite consistent with these expectations. With respect to religious freedom, the ICCPR has apparently had practically no impact in stable democracies or autocracies, but has had a positive impact in countries with some prospect of or experience with moderately responsive government. The evidence was weaker with respect to fair trials, but the basic pattern was similar: much more convincing positive ratification effects in the transition countries than in the stable extremes.

Death penalty compliance contrasts with both fair trials and religious freedom. For starters, governments have often been ahead of their publics on the issue of death penalty abolition. In countries from the United Kingdom to Estonia to Poland, European elites have tended to lead their mass publics toward abolition. Capital punishment also contrasts with other forms of government repression in that it is centrally carried out in a publicly authorized fashion. As a result, it is easy to monitor – much easier than most other government rights practices, including not only fair trials, but also torture, the use of child soldiers, or a range of other rights violations that are carried out in a more decentralized fashion and are extremely difficult to observe. The ability of other governments, domestic governmental officials, groups, and citizens to monitor capital punishment makes this an especially crucial area for a government to ratify a binding obligation only

---

149 See, for example, Sharif 2000.

if it is committed to compliance. The strong positive association between ratification and abolition of the death penalty supports this interpretation.

These results suggest a modest but important conclusion: International treaty commitments quite likely have made a positive contribution to civil rights practices in many countries around the world. Of course, ratification of the ICCPR does not guarantee good practices. It certainly cannot overcome the stresses of a conflict-ridden polity governed by a succession of despots. Ratification has had little impact in stable autocracies, where governments have few incentives to liberalize. The Chinese government's relative intransigence with respect to true religious freedom may be a case in point.[150] It may not even be as important as the examples (good and bad) provided by other governments elsewhere in the region. But ratification does seem to support civil rights improvements on the margins. It does this most consistently where people have both the motive and the means to mobilize to demand compliance and where the practice in question can be monitored at reasonable cost. This finding contrasts with those of previous scholars, who have viewed treaty commitments as cheap opportunities for governments to score public relations points with few risks that they will be expected to improve the behaviors the treaty regulates.[151] The evidence reviewed here indicates that the case for mere symbolic ratification is far from open and shut. Rather, it is consistent with a theory that views ratification as a political opportunity – depending on the anticipated costs – to mobilize to demand civil rights guarantees from one's own government. The next chapter extends this argument to the arena of women's rights, and provides statistical corroboration as well as case study evidence that international treaties are useful tools in stakeholders' hands for securing improvements in individuals' and groups' rights chances.

150 According to some observers, there has been practically no effect of international standards on China with respect to religious freedom "when political push comes to political shove" (Fu 1997:88).
151 Hathaway 2002; Keith 1999.

6

Equality for Women: Education, Work, and Reproductive Rights

Recognition of the inherent dignity and of the equal and inalienable rights of all members of the human family is the foundation of freedom, justice and peace in the world.

UN Universal Declaration of Human Rights[1]

CEDAW is an international agreement that will change the relationship between labor and employers and women and men in Japan. If we do not have the agreement, Japanese society will not move toward change.

Editorial, *Yomiuri Shimbun*, 27 July 1984[2]

The legal regime for international human rights has always been conceived as universal – that is, as applying to every human being. As time passed, however, it became clear to specific groups of activists how it would help their cause were these rights to be institutionalized for specific vulnerable groups. Racial minorities, women, and children were to be protected by waves of obligations that not only formalized earlier treaties, such as the ICCPR and ICESCR, but also addressed concerns specific to these groups. This chapter asks whether and how the CEDAW[3] has improved the rights chances of women around the world.

In the previous chapter, the ICCPR was shown to be associated with improvements in the delivery of civil and political rights, though these findings were hardly uniform. The strongest effects were found not in the stable autocracies or the stable democracies, but rather in those countries in which

1 Preamble, UDHR, adopted and proclaimed by General Assembly Resolution 217 A (III), 10 December 1948.
2 Quoted by Flowers 2002.
3 Adopted and opened for signature, ratification, and accession by UNGA resolution 34/180 of 18 December 1979; *entry into force* 3 September 1981.

only moderate levels of democracy exist or that experienced a transition (whether liberal or illiberal). The strongest effects were also found in areas in which individuals could be expected to overcome their collective action problems and actively lobby for their freedoms (the case of religious freedom compared with fair trials) and in policy areas in which it was relatively easy to observe central government compliance (abolition of the death penalty – again, compared with fair trials). The ICCPR fostered rights realization where groups were most willing and able to organize to demand government compliance.

This chapter turns to a problem that is often deeply rooted in a local culture: the discriminatory treatment of female citizens. Attitudes toward women often frustrate the efforts of the most sincere governments to improve significantly women's rights chances. But as we shall see, an international legal commitment may play an important role in helping girls and women achieve better access to education and jobs and secure better control over their repro-ductive future. When governments publicly announce that they are bound by the contents of treaty arrangements, women and their advocates tend to mobi-lize to realize the rights that those treaties address. International legal commit-ments to protect the rights of women have had important consequences in many cases.

Chapter 4 developed the argument that international treaties can play an important role in changing rights outcomes when they impact domestic politics in certain ways. By altering the national policy agenda, by providing ammuni-tion for litigation, and especially by mobilizing citizens to demand their rights, treaties can lead to real improvements. The task of this chapter is to provide empirical evidence that international law has influenced women's realization of their rights in appreciable ways. The first section of this chapter discusses the situation of women in recent decades. In much of the world, severe inequalities have traditionally existed – and continue to exist – between women and men. Differences in legal rights, family rights, nationality rights, and access to the means of self-betterment, employment, health care, and education have stymied the status of women around the world. The CEDAW is the world's premiere legal response to these inequalities, yet enforcement of this agreement has been highly decentralized. The second, third, and fourth sections of the chapter provide evidence that ratification of CEDAW has improved the treatment of women in three fundamental ways: It tends to improve their access to basic education, to modern forms of family planning, and to employment opportu-nities. The findings are remarkably robust: International legal commitments improve the legitimacy of women's demands for equality and help to elicit social change. The fifth section of the chapter explores some possible domestic mechanisms for these results, using more detailed accounts from Japan and Colombia, and finds evidence that the CEDAW has altered national agendas and enhanced nondiscrimination through litigation. The CEDAW has been most influential where the incentives for women's rights groups to mobilize exist (or, more precisely, where the *disincentives* to mobilize are not overwhelming). The basic conclusion of this chapter is: International law plays a crucial supporting role for women who demand improvements in their rights prospects.

WOMEN'S RIGHTS AND INTERNATIONAL LAW

By almost any measure, women's rights globally have largely been subordinated to those of men. In 1979, the year that the CEDAW was open for signature, a Report on the State of the World's Women found that "Women and girls constitute one-half of the world's population, and one-third of its labor force. They perform two-thirds of the world's work hours. They earn, by one estimate, only one-tenth of the world's income. They own less than one-hundredth of the world's property. Worldwide, women attend school half as often as men. Two out of every three illiterates are female."[4] By the turn of the millennium, women were still largely in dire straits compared to men. According to the World Health Organization, 70 percent of the 1.2 billion people living in poverty are female. There are twice as many women as men among the world's 900 million illiterates, and the growth in female illiteracy seems to be outstripping that of men. Millions of women lack protection against unwanted pregnancies: Including unmarried women, 122.7 million women have an "unmet need" for contraception.[5] Economically, women continue to face a clear gender disadvantage: On average, women are paid 30 to 40 percent less than men for comparable work. In a number of ways, then, women face important disadvantages worldwide.[6]

The Role of International Law

Attempts have been made to address these inequalities through multilateral legal instruments. The rights outlined in the founding human rights agreements discussed in Chapter 2 and analyzed in Chapter 5 were explicitly intended to apply equally to men *and* women.[7] Yet, for a number of reasons that have been the subject of much feminist analysis,[8] women's rights had for many years not been seen as central to the main body of human rights broadly understood.

The 1970s were a propitious period for change. Two broad conditions helped to facilitate the further elaboration of women's rights in international law.

---

4 Langley 1988:39–45.
5 Ross and Winfrey 2002.
6 World Health Organization, Fact Sheet No. 251, June 2000. http://www.who.int/inf-fs/en/fact251.html (accessed 8 July 2003).
7 A general right of nondiscrimination on the basis of sex is guaranteed in Article 2 of the UDHR, Article 1(3) of the UN Charter, Article 2(1) of the ICCPR, and Article 2(2) of the ICESCR.
8 See, for example, Charlesworth et al. 1991.

Without a doubt, the more important one was the rise of women's movements within and across states. In 1966, the National Organization for Women was founded in the United States and lobbied for an Equal Rights Amendment to the U.S. Constitution, which was passed by Congress in March 1972 but failed to be ratified by the requisite number of states. Two months later, Congress passed Title IX of the Education Amendments of 1972, banning sex discrimination in schools. Change was afoot in Europe as well. In France, the efflorescence of the feminist movement was one of the most important legacies of the student uprisings of the spring of 1968.[9] Transnational organizations concentrating on women's issues have a history stretching back to the nineteenth century,[10] but in many parts of the world they formed a "second wave" in the 1960s and 1970s that some scholars see cresting in 1985, the final year of the International Women's Decade.[11] The women's movement was at its height between 1965 and 1985, which gave impetus to the elaboration of women's rights in international law.

A second important context is the détente between the Soviet Union and the United States in the early 1970s. The Cold War had largely frozen multilateral negotiation in the human rights area in the late 1960s and early 1970s. With the major powers at odds over the content of rights (recall the separation and politicization of civil/political rights, on the one hand, and social/economic/ cultural rights, on the other) and the strategic use of rights language to gain the moral upper hand in the Cold War competition characteristic of the 1950s and 1960s, it came as a refreshing surprise to find the United States and the Soviet Union largely in agreement over the content of the Women's Treaty in the late 1970s. Indeed, the *travaux preparatoire* of successive drafts of the CEDAW reveal close cooperation between East and West. In fact, the critical third draft of the treaty was a product of close cooperation and cosponsorship between the Soviet Union and one of the United States' closest allies in the developing world, the Philippines.[12] The period of détente turned out to be a propitious time to make international progress on women's legal rights.

Moreover, the 1970s provided a window of opportunity for advancing women's rights prior to the resurgence of various forms of religious traditionalism that would blossom in many parts of the world in the 1980s and after. Mark Jeurgensmeyer has written persuasively about the decline of secular nationalism – "the ideological partner of what came to be known as nation-building"[13] and the rise of movements of religious nationalism that have come to the fore in the Middle East, South Asia, and many parts of the postsocialist world. Richard

9 Jenson 1996.
10 See Rupp (1997) on the histories of the International Council of Women, the International Alliance of Women, and the Women's International League for Peace and Freedom, founded in 1888, 1904, and 1915, respectively; and see Anderson (2000) on the first stirrings of transnational feminist cooperation in the first half of the nineteenth century.
11 Moghadam 2005:1.
12 See Rehof 1993.
13 Juergensmeyer 1993:28.

Antoun documents and analyzes the rise of Jewish, Christian, and Islamic "fundamentalism" (his word choice) as an affective orientation toward the world whose hallmarks include resistance to change and selective modernization.[14] Ronald Inglehart and Pippa Norris have recently provided an evidentiary basis to suppose that strongly religious individuals and societies have a marked tendency to resist embracing norms of female equality associated with secularism.[15] Had the CEDAW not been negotiated in the 1970s, the world's women might have had to wait decades for a more propitious moment. In short, the 1970s were a window of opportunity for the elaboration of international norms of equality for women. Cold War competition had been mitigated by détente; women's groups were in the ascendancy; and the resurgence of religious fundamentalism as a political force had barely begun outside of Iran, whose 1979 revolution coincided with the year the CEDAW was to open for signature.

The CEDAW was the culmination of a series of multilateral negotiations on women's issues after World War II. In 1952 the UNGA had adopted the Convention on the Political Rights of Women.[16] Yet, it would be years before states would again address women's issues in treaty form. Early in 1967, the UN's Commission on the Status of Women (CSW) began drafting a nonbinding Declaration on the Elimination of Discrimination Against Women (DEDAW), which was adopted by the UNGA in November of that year.[17] The ECOSOC and CSW worked on strategies for implementing the declaration over the next several years. One tactic was to ask states to submit reports on their implementation efforts voluntarily, but this request elicited very little cooperation.[18] By the mid-1970s, the CSW was working on a draft of a comprehensive and legally binding instrument, and by 1976 it began to garner the comments of governments and specialized agencies. The International Year of the Woman was declared for 1975 and opened the Decade of the Woman from 1976 to 1985, which helped to focus global attention on women's issues. A series of working groups finalized the agreement throughout 1979, and the CEDAW opened for signature the next year.

In contrast to the divisions over civil and political versus social and economic rights, the CEDAW negotiations displayed little evidence of old Cold War politics. As mentioned previously, one of the most "Western" of the Asian developing countries, the Philippines, worked closely with the Soviet Union to

---

14 Antoun 2001. On similar themes, highlighting the subordination of women in various "fundamentalist" religions, see Howland 1999.
15 Inglehart and Norris 2003.
16 Opened for signature and ratification by UNGA resolution 640(VII) of 20 December 1952; *entry into force* 7 July 1954. Text available at http://www.unhchr.ch/html/menu3/b/22.htm (accessed 13 August 2008).
17 Proclaimed by UNGA resolution 2263(XXII) of 7 November 1967. Text available at http://www.unhchr.ch/html/menu3/b/21.htm (accessed 13 August 2008).
18 Rehof 1993:7.

propose an influential third draft.[19] Under President Jimmy Carter, the U.S. government was more cooperative than in the 1950s and 1960s, when many in official circles were obsessed with opposition to all projects containing the merest whiff of socialism. But the CEDAW negotiations revealed a number of controversies as well. One was over just how much protection ought to be given to women in employment based on their physiological roles as (expectant) mothers. The Soviets argued for rather more protection, but several European countries noted that this position undermined the principle of equality.[20] The question of whether the treaty should require "reverse discrimination" stimulated some controversy, with both France and Britain vehemently opposed.[21] Countries that were predominantly Muslim played their most active role in the discussion of Article 16, which deals with marriage and family relations. In particular, Pakistan, Bahrain, and Egypt forewarned their peers that national rules in this area were governed by the religious law of Shari'a.[22] Despite complaints that the treaty had been rushed and was not well vetted by the legal offices of the UN,[23] negotiators met their goal of having an authoritative draft ready for ceremonial signing at the Copenhagen World Conference in July 1980.

Interest in women's rights picked up over the course of the 1990s. Women's rights were on the agenda of the UN World Conference on Human Rights held in Vienna in 1993 and were mentioned fairly prominently in the "Declaration and Programme of Action" adopted at that conference.[24] In 1994, a Special Rapporteur on Violence Against Women was appointed by the UN Commission on Human Rights[25] belatedly taking a place alongside similar machinery to address such problems as disappearances and freedom of religion.[26] That same year, the UNGA passed the Declaration on the Elimination of Violence Against Women.[27] World

---

19 Rehof 1993:43. While the Philippines took the most active role of any developing country, its draft contained no implementation provisions whatever (Rehof 1993:209).

20 A series of studies by the UN and the ILO had also begun to question the extent of women's need for protection in work. See McKean 1983:186–7; Oosterveld 1999:375.

21 Peters 1999:261; Rehof 1993:68.

22 Rehof 1993:168–87.

23 Donner 1993–4; McKean 1983:193.

24 The Declaration and Programme of Action (1993) is available at http://www.unhchr.ch/huridocda/huridoca.nsf/(Symbol)/A.CONF.157.23.En?OpenDocument (accessed 12 August 2008). See especially Part A, sections 18, 28–30; Part B, sections 36–44; and Part D, section 81.

25 1994/45. Question of integrating the rights of women into the human rights mechanisms of the UN and the elimination of violence against women, 56th meeting, 4 March 1994; see paragraph 7. Resolution creating the Special Rapporteur for Violence Against Women is available at http://www.unhchr.ch/Huridocda/Huridoca.nsf/2848af408d01ec0ac1256609004e770b/34a30d007de68b3d8025672e005b0410?OpenDocument#45 (accessed 12 August 2008).

26 For a recent list of special rapporteurs on human rights set up under the UN Human Rights Commission, see http://www.unhchr.ch/html/menu2/7/b/tm.htm (accessed 12 August 2008).

27 UNGA resolution 48/104 of 20 December 1993, A/RES/48/104, 23 February 1994. The declaration can be accessed at http://193.194.138.190/huridocda/huridoca.nsf/(Symbol)/A.RES.48.104.En?Opendocument (accessed 12 August 2008). For a discussion of the role of the UN in improving women's rights, see Pietilä and Vickers 1994.

attention on women's issues reached its apex at the 1995 World Conference on Women, sponsored by the UN and held in Beijing.[28]

The Women's Convention (as the CEDAW is commonly known) is widely viewed as "the starting point for delivery of justice for women."[29] It is quite an ambitious convention. Not only did it purport to provide women with equal political and civil rights; it was apparently intended to eliminate *all forms* of discrimination against women. Article 1 is quite sweeping; it defines discrimination as ". . . any distinction, exclusion or restriction made on the basis of sex which has the effect or purpose of impairing or nullifying the recognition, enjoyment or exercise by women, irrespective of their marital status, on a basis of equality of men and women, of human rights and fundamental freedoms in the political, economic, social, cultural, civil or any other field."[30] All measures that are discriminatory against women are forbidden – even if governments did not intend them to be.[31] The treaty even obligates governments to "modify the social and cultural patterns of conduct of men and women, with a view to achieving the elimination of . . . practices which are based on the idea of the inferiority or the superiority of either of the sexes or on stereotyped roles for men and women. . . ."[32]

Still, resistance to explicit international legal machinery to support women's rights is fairly widespread. Despite its swift entry into force (the CEDAW was opened for signature in December 1979 and entered into force less than two years later), reservations have been broad and numerous – this despite the fact that many commentators at the time noted that the CEDAW was largely "promotional" and "programmatic" in nature.[33] The most common reservation has been against jurisdiction by the International Court of Justice (a provision introduced, ironically, by the United States).[34] A number of parties – particularly Islamic countries – have placed exceptionally broad reservations on their acceptance of CEDAW obligations.[35] Though the Women's Convention came into force with a comparatively weak monitoring committee,[36] the stature and powers of the implementation committee were addressed in 1999 with the UN Commission on the Status of Women's adoption of a no-reservations-allowed

---

28 Documents related to the 1995 Women's Conference are available at http://www.un.org/ womenwatch/confer/beijing/reports/plateng.htm (accessed 12 August 2008).
29 Freeman and Fraser 1994:124.
30 CEDAW, Article 1.
31 CEDAW, Article 2.
32 CEDAW, Article 5(a).
33 See, for example, McKean 1983:193; Peters 1999:260. The United States has not ratified. The Carter administration was supportive, but the Reagan and first Bush administrations were not. For a discussion of U.S. reservations to the treaty, see Halberstam and DeFeis 1987:61–3.
34 Article 29. See Rehof 1993:239.
35 On the general issue of reservations against the CEDAW, see Clark 1991. On reservations by governments of Islamic countries, see Mayer 1995, 1999.
36 For a comparison of the CEDAW with the CERD, concluding that the former is much weaker, see Donner 1993–4. For an assessment that concluded early in the treaty's existence that the complaint and oversight systems were flawed, see Galey 1984.

optional protocol. Entering into force in December 2000, the optional protocol gave individuals and groups of individuals a right to complain about their government's violation of the treaty provisions.[37]

For all of the legal machinery that has been developed over the past two decades to address women's issues, we know very little about its effects on the actual realization of women's rights because research has been limited. Dorothy Stetson has attempted to explain governments' policies toward women using scores on a "feminist policy scale" that addresses laws relating to abortion, woman battery, rape, and prostitution.[38] She found in bivariate tests for a cross section of 23 European countries (plus the United States) in the 1980s that acceptance of human rights documents was one of only four predictors to be correlated with higher scores on the scale.[39] Appropriately, nowhere does she claim a *causal* interpretation running from legal commitments to feminist policies; indeed, the causal relationship could just as easily run in the opposite direction. In a more elaborately controlled study that looked specifically at changes over time, Oona Hathaway found no statistically significant relationship between ratification of the Convention on the Political Rights of Women (1954)[40] and the proportion of females in national legislatures.[41] Yet a recent study by Gray, Kittleson, and Sandholz has uncovered some evidence that CEDAW ratification is associated with some measures of improvement in women's living conditions.[42] Once again, the scant literature has barely addressed the nexus between international legal obligation and rights outcomes.[43] The studies that have been done to date remain inconclusive.

Before proceeding, it is useful to note that there is some plausibility to the argument that CEDAW ratification has had an influence on domestic politics by stimulating formation of women's organizations, at least in some cases. Table 6.1 shows that there is some evidence that memberships in women's organizations have increased post-ratification. A closer look by regime type shows that the

---

37 Optional Protocol to the Convention on the Elimination of All Forms of Discrimination against Women, Article 17. The OP to the CEDAW can be found at http://www.bayefsky.com/treaties/cedaw_opt.php (accessed 12 August 2008).

38 Stetson 1995.

39 Acceptance of human rights documents coded for ratification of the ICCPR, the ICCPR's OP I, ICESCR, and acceptance of jurisdiction of the International Court of Justice.

40 Convention on the Political Rights of Women, opened for signature 27 March 1953, U.S.T. 1909, 193 U.N.T.S. 135 (*entered into force* July 1987).

41 Hathaway 2002.

42 Gray et al. 2006.

43 There is more literature that tries to explain the provision of women's rights without considering treaty effects. Steven Poe, Karl Ho, and Dierdre Wendel-Blunt used a 1994 cross section of scores on women's political and economic rights around the world based on U.S. State Department reports to show, using bivariate tests, that the more economically advanced countries (measured by GDP per capita) tended to have a better record on women's rights than less economically developed countries (Poe et al. 1997). Clair Apodaca has demonstrated that an index that she terms the Women's Economic and Social Human Rights (WESHR) – an amalgam of indicators meant to capture the right to work, the right to an adequate standard of living, the right to health and well-being, and the right to an education – is positively associated with per capita GNP (Apodaca 1998).

Table 6.1. Effect of CEDAW Ratification on Local Memberships in Women's International NGOs

Dependent variable: logged women's INGO memberships
OLS regression model
Coefficients, probabilities based on robust standard errors

Explanatory Variable	Model 1	Model 2	Model 2, by Regime Type		
			Stable Democracies	Stable Autocracies	Transition/Partially Democratic Countries
Women's INGO memberships, $t-3$	—	.912*** ($p = .000$)	.945*** ($p = .000$)	.951*** ($p = .000$)	.807*** ($p = .000$)
CEDAW commitment	-.701 ($p = .280$)	.393 ($p = .207$)	.87 ($p = .893$)	.910 ($p = .145$)	-.005 ($p = .988$)
CEDAW commitment, $t-1$	.498*** ($p = .001$)	.159 ($p = .512$)	-.063 ($p = .878$)	-.177 ($p = .706$)	.601* ($p = .061$)
CEDAW commitment, $t-2$	.802*** ($p = .000$)	.474** ($p = .025$)	.438 ($p = .194$)	.483 ($p = .334$)	.443* ($p = .057$)
CEDAW commitment, $t-3$	.785*** ($p = .000$)	-.394* ($p = .063$)	.066 ($p = .888$)	-.722* ($p = .061$)	-.361 ($p = .212$)
CEDAW commitment, $t-4$	3.16*** ($p = .000$)	.131 ($p = .501$)	-.053 ($p = .875$)	.000 ($p = 1.000$)	.486 ($p = .158$)

Overseas development assistance/GDP, $t-1$	−20.06*** ($p = .000$)	4.56*** ($p = .002$)	−10.27 ($p = .444$)	−3.21* ($p = .063$)	−4.04 ($p = .129$)
Democracy	−.004 ($p = .951$)	.004 ($p = .881$)	.686** ($p = .027$)	.046 ($p = .272$)	−.011 ($p = .712$)
Log of GDP, $t-1$	−21.63*** ($p = .000$)	−5.14*** ($p = .000$)	−7.15*** ($p = .000$)	−2.15 ($p = .193$)	−7.88*** ($p = .004$)
Log of GDP/capita, $t-1$	22.48*** ($p = .000$)	5.09*** ($p = .000$)	8.3*** ($p = .002$)	2.37 ($p = .137$)	7.23*** ($p = .006$)
Year trend	1.51*** ($p = .000$)	−5.14*** ($p = .000$)	.374*** ($p = .000$)	.268*** ($p = .000$)	.550*** ($p = .000$)
Country fixed effects?	yes	yes	yes	yes	yes
Year fixed effects?	yes	yes	yes	yes	yes
# of countries	151	151	29	66	56
# of observations	3,929	3,629	847	1,423	1,359
R^2	.94	.98	.98	.96	.97

* Significant at the .10 level; ** significant at the .05 level; *** significant at the .01 level. Robust standard errors, clustering on country.

positive effects of CEDAW ratification on the growth in women's organizations are concentrated not in the stable democracies or the stable autocracies, but rather in the transitional countries. Even when controlling for country and year fixed effects, a time trend, and a lagged dependent variable, there is significant evidence that membership in women's international NGOs grew in the first and second years *after* CEDAW ratification. The treaty has given women a stronger stake in organizing to demand nondiscrimination and basic rights, due at least in part to its influence on expectations and mechanisms (e.g., reporting requirements) that invite these groups to critique government policies.

What Rights? Education, Reproductive Health, and Employment

Few studies to date have looked at the effects of the global legal centerpiece for guaranteeing women's equality: the CEDAW itself.[44] A central difficulty is that the CEDAW contains broad obligations that are difficult to define precisely and even more difficult for governments to guarantee effectively. In a fashion comparable to the analysis of the ICCPR in Chapter 5, the strategy here is to choose some of the most basic rights, which are mentioned in explicit form, and to test the proposition that governments that have committed themselves to the CEDAW will make an effort to design policies to address the exercise of these rights. The rights examined in this chapter relate to government policies with respect to girls' education, policies to enhance reproductive health and autonomy, and policies to enhance women's participation in the workplace. The evidence suggests that at least under some conditions, committing to the CEDAW has had some effect on spurring governments to take women's rights seriously.

EDUCATIONAL OPPORTUNITY

Education is fundamental to a whole range of other rights that the CEDAW envisions women should equitably enjoy. Access to education influences the exercise of a broad range of social and political rights and, more generally, is one of the primary determinants of the gender gap.[45] A mother's level of education

44 Studies have taken up related themes, such as the role of international socialization in addressing issues of violence against women (Hawkins and Humes 2002) and the extension of the franchise to women (Ramirez et al. 1997). The 2006 study by Gray et al. does not consider indicators that capture the gap between women and men, i.e., policy *discrimination*.

45 Wils and Goujon 1998. Decades of recent research have confirmed that educating girls, especially at the primary through secondary school levels, has a large positive impact on women's earnings (relative to those of men); see, for example, Knowles et al. 2002. For a review of the research on the greater return to female than to male education, see Psacharopoulos 1994. For household survey-based research that reaches similar conclusions in Taiwan, see Spohr 2003; and in India, see Duraisamy 2002. On the importance of female literacy to the health, well-being, and mortality of children under age five, see the literature reviewed and evidence presented in Drèze and Sen 2002:245–56.

can have important consequences for her own well-being and for that of her family. In 20 developing countries, mortality of children less than five years of age was found to be significantly related to a lack of maternal education.[46] Education is one of the important factors found to influence contraceptive use,[47] which, as will be discussed, contributes to a reduction in female and child mortality and morbidity.

The CEDAW addresses educational equality head on. Article 10 requires that "States Parties shall take all appropriate measures to eliminate discrimination against women in order to ensure to them equal rights with men in the field of education. . . ."[48] Governments are also required to provide education of comparable quality for girls and boys in all types of schools, in rural as well as urban areas, and in preschool, general, technical, professional, and higher technical education, as well as in all types of vocational training.[49] Moreover, girls are to have a right to the same curricula, the same examinations, teaching staff with qualifications of the same standard, and school premises and equipment of the same quality.[50] They are to have equal access to scholarships and educational grants.[51] Governments that become party to the CEDAW are required to address the literacy gap between men and women and to put programs in place to address the problem of female retention in school.[52]

If governments have moved to implement the educational guarantees of the CEDAW, we should be able to observe change from year to year in the ratio of girls to boys attending elementary and secondary schools.[53] As this ratio rises, it is possible to infer a much greater government effort to provide a free and widely available opportunity for families to send their daughters to school. Obviously, this ratio alone does not capture all of the detailed requirements of the subparagraphs of Article 10,[54] but it is a good start for examining governments' commitment to the crucial first step: getting girls out of the house, the field, or the factory and into the classroom. Figure 6.1 graphs the raw ratio over time. Apparently, on a global scale, girls' educational opportunities have by this

---

46 World Health Organization, Fact Sheet No. 251, June 2000. http://www.who.int/inf-fs/en/ fact251.html. For a general discussion linking the well-being of children to a society's policies of gender neutrality, see Sen 1999.
47 Ainsworth et al. 1996; Sai 1993.
48 CEDAW, Article 10.
49 CEDAW, Article 10(a).
50 CEDAW, Article 10(b).
51 CEDAW, Article 10(d).
52 CEDAW, Article 10(e and f). For a general discussion of the potential for international law to address issues of girls' education, see Van Bueren and Fottrell 1999.
53 Data are from the World Bank's World Development Indicators.
54 Admittedly, equal numbers in school need not mean equal education. Mai Yamani gives a poignant example: "[in Saudi Arabia] the first school opened in 1903 was named Falah ('success'). This school was only for men. The first school of an equivalent nature opened in Jeddah only at the beginning of the 1960s, with the name Dar al-Hanan ('house of tenderness'). The objective of dar al-Hanan was to produce better mothers and homemakers through Islamically guided instruction" (Yamani 2000:141).

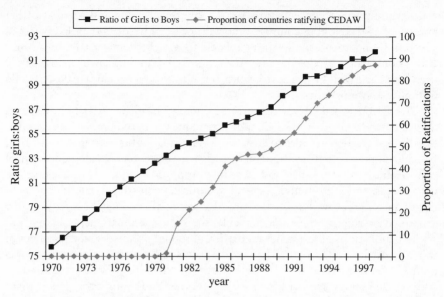

Figure 6.1. CEDAW Commitments and Girls' Education (Global Averages). Ratio of girls to boys enrolled in elementary and secondary education.
Note: Includes ratifications and accessions.

measure improved over the past two decades.[55] Indeed, the data suggest that the upward trend began prior to the year in which the CEDAW was open for signature. The question we need to answer, however, is whether the public commitment to the CEDAW has *contributed* anything to this upward trend.

If signing the CEDAW treaty encourages governments to do more to ensure girls' equal access to education, then we should observe a positive correlation between the ratio of girls to boys in school and the making of a CEDAW commitment, other contributing factors held constant. In order to draw firm inferences about potential causal impacts, it is crucial to develop a stringent series of models that make it less plausible that the treaty commitment is coincidental with broader trends that could explain the improvements as well. First, it is clear, especially in the case of equal access to education, that there has been an improvement over time and that this improvement began prior to the signing (indeed, the existence) of the CEDAW. It is essential, therefore, to control for the effects of time alone. In all of the models explaining gender ratios in schools, a "year" variable is included in order to eliminate any explanation that might be linked to natural improvements over time.

---

55 World expenditures on education are up drastically over the past couple of decades. See the discussion of the UN Educational, Social, and Cultural Organization's (UNESCO's) estimates in Galey 1999.

Additionally, year fixed effects are included to absorb commonly experienced external influences that might account for changes in these ratios across a number of countries. In order to minimize the confusion of cause and effect, all explanatory variables – including the CEDAW commitment – are lagged one period.[56] Furthermore, there are many other explanations at the national level that could explain the outcomes with which we are concerned.[57] In order to avoid baseline bias, I use country fixed effects to reduce the possibility that some unobserved effect that existed prior to the treaty commitment made the country a "natural candidate" for improvement in girls' education. Finally, all models include in the selection equation a lagged dependent variable, or a baseline from which to measure improvements.[58] In the case of education, I use the absolute ratio in the period three years prior to the observed period. Every model reported, therefore, includes a time trend, fixed effects, and models change from a baseline.

The problem of the endogeneity of ratifying the CEDAW is handled as in Chapter 5: two-stage estimation using instrumental variables to predict ratification itself. This approach helps to address the statistical problem that ratification and compliance are largely explained by the same factors. As in Chapter 5, the key instruments are previous CEDAW ratification in the region and the nature of the legal system, both of which influence the ratification decision but do not *directly* influence women's rights. By endogenizing the treaty commitment in this fashion, the probability of attributing explanatory power to the treaty when the explanation is really the conditions that gave rise to the treaty's ratification in the first place is greatly reduced.

A series of control variables are included to isolate the impact of making a treaty commitment. The most obvious alternative explanation is that educating girls depends on the availability of resources associated with higher levels of development. The tests that follow control for development level by including GDP per capita and GDP growth, as well as child labor practices. Child labor could certainly have an effect on gender ratios in school, especially if there is a gender disparity in the tendency to enter the workforce at a young age, and could provide information on economic development generally. The tests also control for basic demographic characteristics, such as the youth of the

---

56 All reported results generally hold up when lagging all explanatory variables for three periods, with the exception of those for the transitional countries, which become statistically insignificant. In fact, the coefficient on the CEDAW commitment increases to 6 ($p = .014$) when Model 1 is estimated with a three-year lag. This specification recognizes that it probably takes time – bureaucratically, politically, and logistically – for the influences discussed here to have effects on the outcomes in which we are interested. Yet, they are already detectable in the first year after ratification.

57 With respect to population policies, see Lush et al. 2000.

58 In this case, including the lagged dependent variable in the *output* equation destroyed the significance of *all* explanatory variables, including the CEDAW, because of its overwhelming explanatory power. The lagged dependent variable is included in the input equation.

population (share of the population under 14 years of age) and the proportion of the country's population living in urban areas.[59] Furthermore, the tests that follow control for political conditions that may have an independent effect on policies. One might hypothesize that democratic polities are much more likely to demand gender equality and female empowerment; after all, countries that empower women to vote generally receive a higher polity score than countries that systematically exclude women. I also control for the effects of military conflict. Civil and interstate wars can be expected to draw boys out of the classroom and into battle; this may have a positive effect on the ratios we are examining, though it is hardly an acceptable solution to the problem of ensuring girls' educational rights.

These tests also control for the pervasiveness of women's international NGOs operating within each country over time. One of the central findings in much of the case study research in the area of women's rights has been the crucial role of women's international NGOs as a driving force not only for construction and interpretation of international law, but also for maintaining compliance pressures. Margaret Keck and Kathryn Sikkink found that the transnationally organized women's movement was important to the spread of suffrage and the crystallization of women's rights over the course of the past century.[60] A host of authors have noted that women's advocacy groups have been central to the formation as well as the enforcement of the CEDAW.[61] These tests will help to determine whether they have been influential in changing government practices as well. Along with CEDAW ratification, the rise of memberships in women's organization has been endogenized in these tests.

Finally, all of these tests control for the average ratios of other countries in the region. Other studies have found regional dummies to have substantial impacts on women's rights.[62] Inserting a regional measure is likely to absorb developmental and cultural factors common to a particular region. But unlike a dummy variable, the regional measure – which changes from year to year as neighboring governments change their practices – also captures mounting pressure within the region to behave in ways that are consistent with those of comparable nearby countries. We have found in earlier chapters that there are

---

59 For robustness, I also tested for share of GDP value-added accounted for by agriculture, which was never significant in any specification.

60 Keck and Sikkink 1998.

61 Freeman and Fraser 1994. Christine Chinkin writes that the international women's movement has engaged the human rights movement "to create networks that confront the global subordination of women. . . . This has challenged the boundaries, concepts, and structures of human rights law, and forced changes in the international legal regime" (Chinkin 2000:133). On the importance of women's organizations for framing the issues from a rights perspective, see Coomaraswamy 1996; Joachim 2003. On the importance of objective data from NGOs, see Cook 1993b.

62 Apodaca 1998.

exceptionally strong regional effects both when governments commit to treaties and in their compliance patterns. We should control for any such influences if we want to isolate the specific influence of making a legal commitment to the CEDAW.

Table 6.2 provides the results of the analysis for factors contributing to an improvement in the ratio of girls to boys in primary and secondary education. Model 1 tests the impact for all countries, while Models 2–7 explore the impact of a CEDAW commitment across different subsets of countries of theoretical interest. Model 1 demonstrates that, net of many other influences, ratification of the CEDAW has a positive and statistically significant effect, with a 95% confidence interval. The effect of the CEDAW treaty is significant despite the fact that all models include a time trend, and despite the inclusion of country dummies that should help to account for any natural country-specific tendency to improve girls' education over time and year fixed effects that absorb common shocks. In fact, a CEDAW commitment is estimated to improve this ratio by almost 5.5 percent (Model 1).

The tests reveal something else: Despite its positive average influence, the CEDAW has not had the same effects everywhere. We can assess the plausibility of the domestic mechanisms discussed in Chapter 4 by looking more closely at the *conditions* under which the CEDAW has had important positive effects. Models 2 and 3 distinguish the transition countries from the stable democracies and stable autocracies. The CEDAW's ability to facilitate improvements in girls' access to education is apparently much greater in the countries that are neither stable democracies nor stable autocracies. In transition countries, the effect of ratifying the CEDAW was statistically distinguishable from zero; ratification is associated with more than a 6 percent increase in the ratio of girls to boys in school. By contrast, in the stable extremes, the impact was perhaps about half as much (though the effect cannot be measured very precisely). This result is understandable if we believe that women's groups in democracies are already largely satisfied with their access to education and women in autocracies are largely deterred from organizing to demand better access.

Perhaps even more insightful is the difference we can observe across those countries in which religion has played a more important role in public life compared to those in which it has played a less official role. Models 6 and 7 present the same model run separately on those countries that have a state religion (any faith) and those that do not. This allows us to look more closely at the (dis)incentives women might face to organize to demand better education for themselves and their daughters. Assuming for a moment that the existence of a state religion is an indicator of the importance of religious influences in a society or, at a minimum, that it represents the solidarity of an alliance between the dominant religious establishment and the state, we might expect much more conservative attitudes toward females in states with established and officially

Table 6.2. Effects of a CEDAW Commitment on Girls' Education

Dependent variable: ratio of girls to boys in elementary and secondary schools
Instrumental variable least squares regression models
Coefficient, probabilities based on robust standard errors

Explanatory Variable	Model 1: All Countries	Model 2: Stable Democracies, Autocracies	Model 3: Partial/Transitional Countries	Model 4: Low Rule of Law Countries	Model 5: High Rule of Law Countries	Model 6: State Religion	Model 7: No State Religion
CEDAW commitment	5.45** (p = .023)	3.11 (p = .376)	6.23*** (p = .003)	−.652 (p = .737)	5.09* (p = .092)	3.17 (p = .438)	7.22* (p = .052)
Women's INGOs, logged	39.35** (p = .021)	45.02** (p = .032)	6.25 (p = .257)	−17.57** (p = .016)	41.79** (p = .030)	40.15** (p = .093)	47.91 (p = .102)
Year	−1.61** (p = .013)	−2.03** (p = .030)	−.450 (p = .504)	.548* (p = .082)	−2.12** (p = .043)	−1.74* (p = .072)	−2.77 (p = .109)
Regional enrollment ratios	0.465* (p = .085)	.287 (p = .487)	.124*** (p = .001)	.868*** (p = .001)	−.227 (p = .541)	.004 (p = .994)	.330 (p = .501)
Catholic	−75.63* (p = .068)	15.92 (p = .624)	1.48 (p = .950)	80.00** (p = .033)	−100.2** (p = .025)	−36.63 (p = .438)	.437 (p = .981)
Islam	−1.15 (p = .865)	68.43 (p = .161)	−15.93 (p = .803)	−5.74 (p = .322)	−113.9** (p = .044)	13.90 (p = .803)	−21.91 (p = .529)
Overseas development aid/GDP	9.34 (p = .395)	7.72 (p = .536)	20.61* (p = .073)	−1.79 (p = .737)	18.89 (p = .650)	32.88 (p = .150)	−2.70 (p = .857)
Democracy	−.238 (p = .227)	−.641 (p = .152)	−.084 (p = .451)	.075 (p = .472)	−.386 (p = .274)	−.111 (p = .694)	−.491 (p = .135)

Left executive	1.73 (p = .376)	−.507 (p = .810)	−1.15 (p = .646)	−1.88 (p = .371)	.245 (p = .871)	2.29 (p = .417)	1.89 (p = .519)
GPD per capita, logged	1.30 (p = .805)	−1.17 (p = .865)	−1.17 (p = .865)	.456 (p = .887)	.456 (p = .128)	9.51 (p = .298)	−10.18 (p = .194)
GDP growth	.009 (p = .895)	.003 (p = .974)	.010 (p = .825)	−.008 (p = .803)	−.199* (p = .054)	.036 (p = .684)	.026 (p = .795)
% of population urban, logged	−29.64* (p = .080)	−29.73 (p = .197)	−36.02** (p = .049)	24.39* (p = .058)	−39.21** (p = .030)	−38.49 (p = .320)	−12.23 (p = .376)
% of population under 14, logged	.673 (p = .965)	−1.03 (p = .962)	4.94 (p = .742)	7.66 (p = .648)	12.06 (p = .452)	39.01 (p = .103)	−55.99 (p = .191)
Child labor	.212 (p = .776)	.750 (p = .470)	−.187 (p = .137)	−.681* (p = .051)	−.890 (p = .178)	−1.53 (p = .246)	1.23 (p = .420)
Civil war	2.93 (p = .279)	2.49 (p = .659)	1.99 (p = .150)	2.69* (p = .099)	13.89* (p = .066)	.552 (p = .882)	9.74 (p = .114)
Interstate war	.567 (p = .792)	−.567 (p = .792)	−1.87 (p = .402)	−1.45 (p = .325)	2.22 (p = .179)	2.31 (p = .435)	3.41 (p = .402)
Country fixed effects?	yes	yes	yes	yes	yes	yes	yes
Year fixed effects?	yes	yes	yes	yes	yes	yes	yes
# of observations	2,232	1,434	798	1,146	1,086	1,030	1,202
# of countries	134	83	51	73	61	61	73
R^2	0.70	0.54	.95	.92	.65	.64	.69

All explanatory variables lagged one period.
Instrumented variables: CEDAW commitment, women's INGOs. Instruments: common law heritage, average regional CEDAW commitment, two splines, official development assistance/GDP, and ratio of girls to boys in elementary schools $(t − 1)$.
* Significant at the .10 level; ** significant at the .05 level; *** significant at the .01 level.

sanctioned religions.[63] Women might be much less willing to demand equal educational access in such societies, anticipating that their state – and society – will be unwilling to respond favorably. The results reported in Models 6 and 7 are consistent with such an interpretation. The CEDAW appears to have a much stronger impact on women's access to education in countries without a state religion for the duration of the period (1970 to the present) than in countries with a state religion. We can be fairly confident that the CEDAW is associated with improvements in girls' access to education in secular states – increasing the ratio of girls to boys in primary education on average more than 7 percent – but the impact of ratification in states with established religions is statistically indistinguishable from zero. This is consistent with the claim that the CEDAW has had more impact in societies where women have fewer societal and official disincentives to demand that their government live up to its legal obligations.

Finally, consider the evidence that the CEDAW's effects may be realized through the courts. While data on litigation in every ratifying country do not currently exist, it is possible to infer the plausibility of this mechanism from the patterns of improvement across countries. As discussed in Chapter 4, a necessary condition for meaningful litigation is that groups and individuals have incentives to use the courts to secure their rights. Where the legal system is not perceived as efficient and independent, litigation is not a plausible mechanism. If litigation – or the threat of litigation – is a potentially important mechanism, we should see much more significant effects of CEDAW ratification in countries with a strong rule of law tradition than those with weak, inoperable, or politically controlled court systems.

The proxy used here for judicial independence is a measure of the rule of law collected by the World Bank. This proxy measures "perceptions of the extent to which agents have confidence in and abide by the rules of society, and in particular the quality of contract enforcement, property rights, the police, and the courts, as well as the likelihood of crime and violence."[64] Conceptually, this is much broader than we might like, since it combines perceptions of a *society's* commitment to the rule of law, and not just that of the government. And while it includes perceptions of the strength of the courts, it also includes perceptions of noninstitutional factors as well. Even the more "institutional" aspects of this measure are somewhat too heavily influenced by the enforcement of economic transactions. Moreover, the indicator does not exist for many countries in which investors are the least interested, such as those in much of Africa. Finally, we

---

63 Admittedly, many of the established Protestant religions hardly reflect this claim (e.g., the Church of England no longer exerts a profound influence over British society), but in general, it is likely to be the case among Catholic and Islamic societies. For a number of reasons, some scholars have observed that religious considerations can interfere with the education of girls. See, for example, the discussion in Van Bueren and Fottrell 1999:133–5.

64 Kaufmann et al. 2008:10. See the description at http://papers.ssrn.com/sol3/papers.cfm?abstract_id=1148386.

should remember that it is an indicator of perceptions – including those of experts, investors, and think tanks. It is not an objective account of how truly independent and strong courts are in each country. Nonetheless, this proxy provides one (noisy) cut at the question of whether the CEDAW is more likely to matter in countries where the courts are more likely to be respected.

Our expectations for treaty effects seem to be borne out in the data. Models 4 and 5 compare countries with a strong positive reputation for the rule of law with those with a weak reputation.[65] CEDAW ratification is associated with a moderate but statistically detectable impact on the ratio of girls to boys in school: The difference between ratifiers and nonratifiers for countries in the high rule of law group was about 5 percentage points. But the difference between ratifiers and nonratifiers in low rule of law countries was practically nil. The fact that the law may be enforced through the courts could well help to explain behavioral improvements associated with CEDAW ratification.

Some of the other domestic political variables were surprisingly impotent. The level of democracy in a given year never had an impact on gender ratios in schools. This is the case for all countries taken as a whole as well as within the categories of stable versus transitional regimes. Gender equality in education apparently does not march in lock step with traditional indicators of participatory democracy. Furthermore, the political complexion of the government of the day does not strongly influence these ratios. The political orientation of the party of the executive of government does not systematically influence gender equality in education. Much deeper forces seem to be at work. For example, the prevalence of Islam in high rule of law countries had a strong negative impact on the ratio. Where Islamic law is strictly enforced (in Saudi Arabia, for example), girls are much less likely to be educated to the standard of boys. A similar pattern holds for Catholicism among high rule of law countries. Conservative laws and mores strictly enforced are likely to reduce girls' educational opportunities.

On the other hand, the presence of women's international NGOs had a consistently positive impact on getting girls into school, with the flagrant

---

65 This measure is the average rule of law score assigned by the World Bank for each country between 1996 and 2004. Source: World Bank. http://info.worldbank.org/governance/kkz2004/ indicator_report.asp?indicatorid=5. The low rule of law countries are Afghanistan, Albania, Algeria, Angola, Armenia, Azerbaijan, Bangladesh, Belarus, Benin, Bhutan, Bolivia, Bosnia and Herzegovina, Brazil, Burkina Faso, Burundi, Cambodia, Cameroon, Central African Republic, Chad, China, Colombia, Comoros, Congo, Cote d'Ivoire, Cuba, Democratic Republic of Congo, Djibouti, Dominican Republic, Ecuador, El Salvador, Equatorial Guinea, Eritrea, Ethiopia, Fiji, Gabon, The Gambia, Georgia, Guatemala, Guinea, Guinea-Bissau, Guyana, Haiti, Honduras, Indonesia, Iran, Iraq, Jamaica, Kazakhstan, Kenya, Kyrgyz Republic, Laos, Liberia, Libya, Macedonia, Madagascar, Malawi, Maldives, Mali, Marshall Islands, Mauritania, Mexico, Moldova, Mozambique, Myanmar, Nepal, Nicaragua, Niger, Nigeria, Pakistan, Papua New Guinea, Paraguay, Peru, Philippines, Romania, Russia, Rwanda, Sao Tome and Principe, Senegal, Sierra Leone, Soloman Islands, Somalia, Sudan, Surinam, Swaziland, Syria, Tajikistan, Tanzania, Togo, Tonga, Turkmenistan, Uganda, Ukraine, Uzbekistan, Vanuatu, Venezuela, Vietnam, Yemen, the former Yugoslavia, Zambia, and Zimbabwe.

exception of the case of low rule of law countries. For the most part, the presence of active international women's organizations was associated with a growth in the girl:boy enrollment ratio in the next year. But it is interesting to note that CEDAW effects do not depend on these memberships in international organizations. There is still much room for a story that emphasizes *domestic* political strategies and organization around implementation of the CEDAW. Furthermore, the influence of the policies of other countries is highly uneven as well. Regional enrollment ratios seem to exert a positive impact overall (Model 1), but this external effect seems to be highly concentrated in the low rule of law countries (Model 4) and, to a much lesser extent, the transition countries (Model 3). Surprisingly, these regional effects tell a more consistent and statistically significant story than the national level developmental indicators. Neither GDP growth nor GDP per capita appears to have a significant impact on change in the ratio of girls to boys in school. Large urban populations were sometimes associated with a reduction in this ratio. But the prevalence of child labor – another developmental indicator – had little impact, with the possible exception of low rule of law countries. The relative size of the population under 14 made no difference. Neither civil nor international war had any statistically significant effects either.

The bottom line is that countries that have made a CEDAW commitment have higher ratios of girls to boys in primary school overall (Model 1),[66] and that the strongest positive results are to be found in transition or moderately democratic countries, secular states, and countries reputed for their well-developed rule of law institutions. Not only does the CEDAW influence these ratios in the first year after ratification, the effects are important for at least five years into the future. Women's organizations also make a significant contribution in this regard. Figure 6.2 illustrates the estimated effects of a CEDAW commitment on the ratio of girls to boys in school over time. It graphs the coefficients of Model 1 estimated with up to a five-year lag between explanatory variables and the outcomes ratio. There is a slight tendency for the effect of CEDAW ratification to degrade over the years, but the rate of degradation is comparable to that of an increase in women's organizations, for example.

REPRODUCTIVE HEALTH

Reproductive health is another fundamental right that is central not only to basic autonomy, but also to the enjoyment of other rights as well. The growing

---

66 This is true even when controlling for the earliest commitment to nondiscrimination in education, the Convention against Discrimination in Education, Paris, 14 December 1960. Negotiated some 20 years earlier, this agreement addressed educational discrimination "based on race, colour, sex, language, religion, political or other opinion, national or social origin, economic condition or birth . . ." (Article 1). For ratifications see http://portal.unesco.org/la/convention.asp?KO=12949&language=E&order=alpha (accessed 12 August 2008).

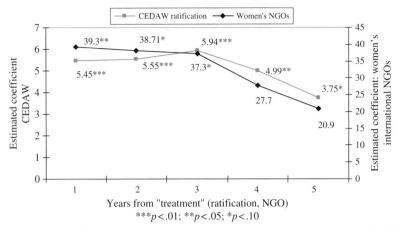

Figure 6.2. Effect of CEDAW and Women's Organizations on the Ratio of Girls to Boys in Primary and Secondary School.

(though imperfect) consensus of the international community is reflected in the words of the UN, which concluded almost three decades ago that "the ability to regulate the timing and number of births is one central means of freeing women to exercise the full range of human rights to which they are entitled."[67] In 1994, the UN International Conference on Population and Development reiterated and solidified a rights-based approach to reproductive health,[68] marking a shift from emphasis on population control to women's empowerment more generally.[69] Reproductive health has increasingly been cast as an issue of fundamental human rights. As such, it refers to the ability to reproduce, to regulate fertility, and to carry reproduction to a successful and healthy outcome. Services to promote reproductive health include providing appropriate sex education counseling, the means to prevent unwanted pregnancies, and to prevent and treat sexually transmitted diseases and infertility.[70]

Central to reproductive well-being is the ability to control one's fertility. When women are denied the means to do this, study after study shows that their health – and that of their growing family – is at risk.[71] Conversely, when

67 *Status of Women and Family Planning*, 1975, UN Doc. E/CN.6/575/Rev.1.
68 Documents relating to this conference can be found at http://www.iisd.ca/linkages/cairo.html (accessed 12 August 2008).
69 Lane 1994. Follow-up to the Cairo meeting included a Special Session of the UNGA that met at UN headquarters in New York, 30 June–2 July 1999. Statements from this meeting are reproduced in [Anon.] 1999b. Progress on implementation of the Cairo agreement was followed up at an intergovernmental forum convened by the UN Population Fund in The Hague, 8–12 February 1999. The Hague Forum was preceded by related meetings of nongovernmental organizations, representatives of youth groups, and of parliamentarians; see [Anon] 1999a.
70 Cook 1993a. On the concept and measure of reproductive health, see Sadana 2002.
71 Winikoff and Sullivan 1987.

contraceptives are available, maternal and infant health improves significantly.[72] The effects of uncontrolled fertility are compounded in conditions of poverty. Poor families tend to be larger than richer ones and adolescent pregnancy tends to be much more common, which increases the reproductive and caring burden on women.[73] Overall, epidemiological data demonstrate life and health risks from pregnancies that come too early, too late, too often, or too close together in a woman's reproductive years.[74] Since the alternative to contraception in much of the world is unsafe abortion, some scholars have argued for access to preventive and emergency birth control on the basis of a right to life itself.[75]

The drafting of the CEDAW revealed a good bit of controversy over a women's right to reproductive freedom. Representatives from the Philippines proposed a specific reference to education in family planning (which had been articulated in principle in the DEDAW but had never found its way into a binding instrument). Several countries, including Sweden and Austria, were wary of making access to family planning information and services part of a women's treaty, noting the shared nature of the responsibility in this area. A number of Muslim states, as well as the United States (this was, after all, the late 1970s) and the International Planned Parenthood Federation, were keen that the treaty make reference not only to information and advice, but to services as well. During drafting, Colombia opposed the idea that the treaty should address family planning at all.[76] But as we shall see, the reproductive health elements of the treaty would indeed have a significant impact on access to modern forms of birth control in this conservative country, thanks to CEDAW-induced constitutional innovations and the extraordinary activity of the Colombian judicial system.

The CEDAW provides the legal basis for a woman's right of access to the means to control her own reproduction.[77] Article 10(h) provides for "access to specific educational information to help to ensure the health and well-being of families, including information and advice on family planning."[78] Article 12(1) obligates governments ". . . to eliminate discrimination against women in the field of health services, including those related to family planning."[79] Article 16(1)(e) stipulates a right "to decide freely and responsibly on the number and spacing of their children and to have access to the information, education, and means to

---

72 Diaz 1998; Miller and Rosenfield 1996; Schenker and Eisenberg 1997.
73 World Health Organization, Fact Sheet No. 251, June 2000. http://www.who.int/inf-fs/en/fact251.html.
74 Royston and Armstrong 1989.
75 Cook and Dickens 2003; Teklehaimanot 2002.
76 See the discussion on the *travaux preparatoires* in Rehof 1993:120–1.
77 Cook 1993a.
78 CEDAW, Article 10(h).
79 The travaux preparatoires indicate that during drafting, several countries were opposed to the mention of "family planning services" because they feared it would reduce some states' willingness to ratify. See Rehof 1993:145. The accepted wording was proposed by Finland, India, and Iran. Note that Article 14(2)(b) guarantees a similar right specifically to rural women.

enable them to exercise these rights."[80] According to one scholar of reproductive rights, "The goal [of these CEDAW provisions] is the reduction of maternal mortality and morbidity and enhancement of the dignity of women and their reproductive self-determination."[81] In this regard, the CEDAW is a unique international instrument; according to the UN Population Fund, "CEDAW is the *only* human rights treaty that affirms the reproductive rights of women" (emphasis added).[82]

The indicator of compliance with the right of women to make basic choices about their reproductive future is the extent to which government policy facilitates general access to contraception. Since 1976, the UN Population Division's Department of Economic and Social Affairs has periodically surveyed governments to ascertain their practices with respect to access to family planning technologies. Governments' responses fall into one of four categories: a policy of limiting access; a policy of providing no support for access; a policy of providing indirect support; and, finally, a policy of providing direct family planning support (see Figure 6.3).[83]

Governments that provide direct support for family planning, other things being equal, are doing much more to give women the right to make their own reproductive choices.[84] Note that the focus here is on *government policy*; it is not on contraceptive uptake. A woman might still feel a good deal of personal or social pressure to have children based on the desires of her partner, the demands of her farm, the practices in her village, or the mores of her religion.[85] Governments are in a position to enhance a woman's control over her reproduction – and hence a significant aspect of her future – by providing free and widely available access to modern forms of contraception. I am interested in analyzing government policies with respect to these issues, which brings us closest to the compliance question.

80 CEDAW, Article 16(1)(e).
81 Cook 1993a:75.
82 See the UN Population Fund, http://www.unfpa.org/rights/women.htm (accessed 12 August 2008).
83 Surveys relate to 1976, 1986, 1996, and 2001. UN Population Division, Department of Economic and Social Affairs, http://www.un.org/esa/population/publications/npp2001/doc/nppdownload. htm (accessed 12 August 2008). Note that these data do not indicate what kinds of family planning measures have been implemented. A study by Cook, Dickens, and Bliss suggests that there has been some liberalization toward legal abortions during this period (1999). For a broad historical account of family planning practices over the course of the past half century, see Caldwell et al. 2002.
84 For a critique of the extent to which these programs are really empowering, or even voluntary for women (at least in the case of India in the mid-1970s), see Nair 1992. For a broader critique of narrow "family planning" programs, see Claudia Garcia-Moreno and Amparo Claro, "Challenges from the Women's Health Movement: Women's Rights Versus Population Control," http://www.hsph.harvard.edu/rt21/globalism/CLARO.html.
85 Sai 1993.

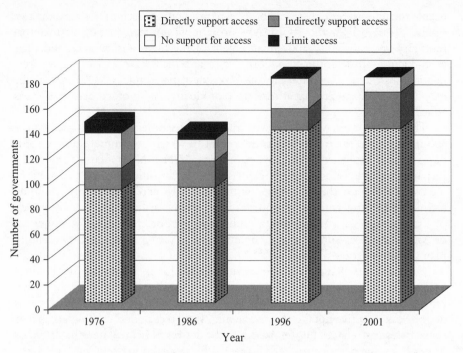

Figure 6.3. Government Policies on Contraceptive Access.

The model used to assess the impact of the CEDAW on women's reproductive rights is similar in structure to the model presented previously on education.[86] In this case, I use dummies for the primary religion practiced within the country.[87] This seems like a good alternative, since religion can in theory have a tremendous impact on population practices within a society.[88] While I control for the dominant religion, I specifically test for the penetration of religious ideas

86 Because the dependent variable in Model 1 is an ordered category, an ordered logit model would have been preferable, but it would not converge using two-stage estimation procedures and fixed effects. As an alternative, I interpolate the data, making for more of a continuous measure and allowing for more degrees of freedom in estimation, proceeding with two-stage instrumental variable regression.

87 The inventory of religions includes Sunni Muslim, Shi'a Muslim, Ibadhi Muslim, Judaism, Ukrainian Greek Catholicism, Roman Catholicism, Hinduism, Mahayana Buddhism, Theravada Buddhism, Tibetan Buddhist Lamarism, Shinto, Confucianism, Taoist, Alawis, HaoHao, Cao-Dai, Native/traditional/indigenous/local, Protestant, Wesleyan, Anglican, Church of England, Baptist, Evangelical Protestant, Lutheran, Presbyterian, Evangelical Lutheran, Church of Ireland, Calvinist, Methodist, Orthodox, Eastern Orthodoxy, Russian Orthodox, Greek Orthodox, Armenian Orthodox, Bulgarian Orthodox, Georgian Orthodox, Ukrainian Orthodoxy, Ethiopian Orthodox Christian, Animist, and other.

88 For a discussion of the tensions between religious beliefs and internationally encouraged standards of reproductive health that emerged over the course of the 1990s, see Freedman and Isaacs 1993.

into the public policy arena by looking at the nature of church–state relationships. As earlier, I control for previous policies; in the case of access to contraception, I use the "initial policy" reported by the government in 1977. Including year in the specifications also controls for any potential time trend.

Several of the control variables discussed previously are included here (regional policies, women's advocacy groups, GDP per capita, the pervasiveness of child labor, the relative youth of the population). In addition, it is important to control for some variables that may influence policies for family planning access more specifically. Most importantly, there is an obvious need to control for population policies. State policies of access to contraception have traditionally been aimed at controlling aggregate population growth, though there is some evidence that justifications are shifting in many countries to broaden the rationale to encompass women's empowerment.[89] But if we are to interpret access to birth control as a woman's right, we should see a CEDAW effect *above and beyond whatever general goals the government has with respect to population growth.* All of the specifications control for governments' stated population policies: whether they favor a population increase or a decrease (the excluded category is noninterference, the category to which coefficients on indicators of population policy orientation are compared). It is also vital to control for important demographic conditions by including a measure of the youthfulness of the population (the share of the total population under 14 years of age). Especially young demographic structures could certainly influence governments' policies on access to contraception. Finally, all models control for overseas development assistance as a proportion of GDP. Many studies emphasize the extent to which international aid donors, such as the World Bank, have influenced governments to put population control programs in place.[90] It is important to distinguish these incentives from the treaty commitment itself.

With a few interesting twists, the results of these analyses of government contraceptive policies tell a highly consistent story. Table 6.3 demonstrates that once again, under highly stringent specifications, making a CEDAW commitment makes it much more likely that a government will support access to modern methods of contraception. Both models that include all states (Models 1 and 2) suggest that we can be at least 93 percent confident that, on average, CEDAW ratification has had a positive effect on such access. Because all models include fixed effects based on the *religion of the majority of the population,* rather than the country itself, results should be interpreted as net of any

---

89 Ollila et al. 2000. The 1994 International Conference on Population and Development held in Cairo was especially important in this regard. A "new paradigm" in population policy emerged from the conference that shifted emphasis from a macro concern with rapid population growth to individual rights concerning sexuality and reproduction (DeJong 2000). For case studies on the generally successful implementation of a more rights-based approach to family planning in Latin American and the Caribbean region, see Helzner 2002.

90 Luke and Watkins 2002; Nair 1992.

Table 6.3. Effects of a CEDAW Commitment on Access to Modern Family Planning

Dependent variable: government policy with respect to family planning access
Instrumental variable least squares regression model
Coefficients, probabilities based on robust standard errors

Explanatory Variable	Model 1: Basic Model, All Countries	Model 2: Controls, All Countries	Model 3: States with Stable State Religions	Model 4: States without State Religions	Model 5: States with Church–State Relations in Flux
CEDAW commitment	.148* (p = .068)	.176** (p = .043)	.011 (p = .924)	.243** (p = .030)	.493 (p = .248)
Year	—	.009 (p = .419)	—	—	—
Initial contraceptive policy	.369*** (p = .000)	.436*** (p = .000)	.510*** (p = .000)	.362*** (p = .000)	.852*** (p = .000)
Policy of population increase	–.118 (p = .130)	–.018* (p = .059)	–.223** (p = .026)	–.019 (p = .867)	–.332 (p = .179)
Policy of population reduction	.149*** (p = .002)	.178*** (p = .004)	.101* (p = .095)	.191* (p = .052)	.225 (p = .308)
Average regional access to modern family planning	.561*** (p = .000)	.677*** (p = .000)	.313 (p = .187)	.863*** (p = .000)	–.320 (p = .623)
Overseas development assistance (% of GDP)	.472 (p = .141)	.315 (p = .528)	.287 (p = .536)	.347 (p = .456)	1.99** (p = .027)
% of population under 14	–.501** (p = .019)	–.890** (p = .011)	–1.09*** (p = .004)	–.254 (p = .463)	–1.45 (p = .495)
GDP per capita, logged	–.175*** (p = .000)	–.202** (p = .017)	–.159 (p = .108)	–.084 (p = .376)	.221 (p = .189)
Democracy	.014*** (p = .003)	.012** (p = .011)	.011 (p = .174)	.020* (p = .097)	–.041 (p = .193)

	(1)	(2)	(3)	(4)	(5)
Women's INGOs, logged	—	-.247 (p = .290)	—	-.255 (p = .856)	—
Child labor	—	.001 (p = .765)	—	—	—
GDP growth	—	.004 (p = .179)	—	—	—
Civil war	—	-.132 (p = .131)	—	—	—
Interstate war	—	-.112 (p = .406)	—	—	—
% of population urban, logged	—	.044 (p = .778)	—	—	—
Trade openness	—	.0005 (p = .688)	—	—	—
Left executive	—	-.066 (p = .428)	—	—	—
Dominant religion fixed effects?	yes	yes	yes	yes	yes
Year fixed effects?	yes	yes	yes	yes	yes
# of observations	2,478	2,249	1,023	1,142	207
# of countries	132	126	48	84	20
R^2	.613	.567	.793	.491	.794

Note: All explanatory variables lagged three periods.

Data on dependent variable are interpolated.

Instrumented variable: CEDAW commitment and women's international nongovernmental organizations. Instruments: common law heritage, average regional CEDAW commitment, three splines, baseline contraceptive access (all lagged one period).

* Significant at the .10 level; ** significant at the .05 level; *** significant at the .01 level.

influences that might flow from particular religious beliefs (although the official relationship between the state and the dominant religion is a distinct issue and will be discussed later). This time, there is no detectable time trend ("year" is insignificant). There is, unsurprisingly, a highly significant baseline effect: Governments that had policies of high accessibility in 1976 were likely also to have highly accessible policies in succeeding years. In effect, then, we should interpret all coefficients – including the CEDAW commitment – as the *additional* probability of supportive access policies above and beyond those in place at the beginning of the observation period.

Once again, it is clear that the CEDAW's impact is muted in highly religious states. Controlling for the specific dominant religion in each country, it remains clear that the CEDAW has had the strongest positive consequences where women have some incentive to demand such access: secular states. While the units are somewhat arbitrary (fractions of the categories described earlier), the direction of CEDAW ratification in these countries is clear. Secular states that have ratified are much more likely to encourage women's access to modern forms of birth control – controlling for their overall population policy – than are secular states that have not ratified. Note well the nature of the finding. Not only do secular states have better access overall, but *among secular states*, the CEDAW has made a real difference in access policy. Contrast this with the finding for states with stable state religions or relationships in flux. There is absolutely no indication that the CEDAW has mattered in states with stable state religions. For those in which these relationships have changed over the period (from 1970 to 2000), the estimated effect is almost twice as high as in secular states. The possible impact in these transitional cases is perhaps quite large, but it is hard to estimate with any precision.

Several other variables have a consistent effect on access policies. Highly significant (in most cases) is the government's general desire to reduce the rate of population growth. The general desire to *increase* the rate of population growth (or, in some cases, to halt decline) was signed in the expected direction, away from encouraging broad access, and was marginally significant in Model 2. Interestingly, it was also significantly negatively signed for states with stable state religions, possibly reinforcing these governments' preferences with regard to religious values. The inclusion of these controls facilitates an interpretation of the CEDAW commitment as a principled, rights-based policy rather than simply as a pragmatic response to population pressures.

As in the case of education, when analyzing all states (Models 1 and 2) there is an undeniably strong regional influence on contraception policies. Some of this result may be due to similar developmental conditions or cultural influences, although the inclusion of the battery of developmental indicators and the fixed effects based on religion makes such an explanation less likely. These regional effects could have much more to do with localized learning or regional socialization than with developmental factors alone. Regional influences appear to be strongest among the more secular states. For our purposes, however, it is important to note that treaty commitment survives the inclusion of a regional context, though admittedly, the latter is highly statistically significant.

The remainder of the control variables perform roughly as one might expect, but not with a high degree of consistency. In general (Models 1 and 2), the more democratic a country, the more it encourages women's access to modern forms of birth control, but rising incomes reduce the state's commitment. States with an especially young population are less likely to encourage access. Overseas development assistance improved access only for countries whose church–state relationships were in flux. The remainder of the control variables had practically no impact on women's access to modern forms of birth control.

Once again, ratification of the CEDAW has been shown to be associated with important consequences for women. The impact can be seen across all countries on average, but the positive effects are undeniably concentrated in societies that are not characterized by the deep penetration of religious values into official public policy. One interpretation of these results is that women face strong barriers to organizing and demanding sexual autonomy in such societies, even if we control for the dominant religion itself (which all of these models do with fixed effects). But *where they have both the motive and the means* to recover control over reproductive choices, the CEDAW provides a justification for doing so.

EMPLOYMENT

Despite some improvement in the 1990s, when compared to their male counterparts, women face far more discrimination in entering the workplace and holding a job.[91] There are only 11 countries where women are roughly equal to men with respect to paid employment in industry and services.[92] Globally, women earn 20–30 percent less than men. More and more women are entering the workforce, but more jobs do not necessarily mean *better* jobs. Half of the world's workers are in gender-stereotyped occupations, with women dominating those occupations that are the lowest paying and least protected.[93] Part-time

---

91 This is the case, for example, in Latin America, where, on average, women receive 50% of the salary earned by men in the same position (Julieta Lemaitre, Luisa Cabal y Mónica Roa, Cuerpo y Derecho: legislación y jurisprudencia en América Latina, Editorial Temis, Colombia, 2001, http://www.whrnet.org/docs/issue-sexualrights.html).

92 Source: UN Development Fund for Women (UNIFEM), 1 June 2000, http://www.unifem.undp.org/progressww/pr_progress1.html.

93 A study by the ILO notes that the information, communications, and technology revolution has only very partially addressed these disparities. There remains a "digital gender gap" within many countries, as women often find themselves occupying lower-level ICT jobs while men rise to higher-paying, more responsible positions. International Labor Organization, Press Release, "ILO's World Employment Report 2001: Despite Improved Employment Outlook, Digital Divide Looms Large," 24 January 2001 (*ILO*/01/03) http://www.ilo.org/public/english/bureau/inf/pr/2001/03.htm (accessed 30 July 2003).

work and work in the informal sector remain the norm. It is estimated that, were the value of the unpaid, invisible work done by women – approximately US$11 trillion per annum – included in the total, global output would be almost 50 percent greater. Those women who do find paying jobs face a much higher risk than men of a drastic drop in living standards when they retire.[94]

The CEDAW protects women's right to nondiscrimination in the workplace explicitly in Article 11(1): "States Parties shall take all appropriate measures to eliminate discrimination against women in the field of employment in order to ensure, on a basis of equality of men and women, the same rights. . . ."[95] Governments are bound by the terms of the treaty to ensure that women have the right to the same employment opportunities,[96] the right to a free choice of profession and employment, the right to promotion, training, job security and benefits,[97] equal pay for equal work,[98] equal access to unemployment, retirement, and sick pay benefits,[99] and a right to a safe working environment.[100]

Has the CEDAW improved the lot of women with respect to equal employment opportunities? In answering this question, we face the same difficulties as we did in testing for the impact of the CEDAW on educational opportunities. Governments are responsible for providing a range of guarantees, and employment figures alone cannot attest to the true quality of opportunities afforded women in the workplace. Moreover, the government is not directly responsible for the exact terms of employment in the private sector, though it is, of course, responsible for enforcing the laws on the books, including relevant international legal commitments. However, there is a way to see if governments are making a good-faith effort to reduce job discrimination: by examining employment patterns in the *public sector*. The public sector provides the most direct indicator that governments are meeting their obligations under international law equitably to employ women.[101] Furthermore, public sector jobs often provide the best benefits (job security, sick pay, pensions), to which the subclauses of Article 11 say women are equally entitled. The indicator of compliance with Article 11 of the CEDAW is therefore the share of women employed in the public sector. If the treaty has any effect on government policies with respect to nondiscriminatory employment, it should show up in this share. Figure 6.4 shows the average growth in this ratio across countries since the mid-1980s.

---

94 ILO, GENPROM. http://www.ilo.org/public/english/employment/gems/about/ (accessed 30 July 2003).
95 CEDAW, Article 11(1).
96 CEDAW, Article 11(1)(b).
97 CEDAW, Article 11(1)(c).
98 CEDAW Article 11(1)(d).
99 CEDAW, Article 11(1)(e).
100 CEDAW, Article 11(1)(f).
101 Public sector discrimination can include prohibitions or numerical limits on women taking civil service exams, for example, as was the case in Japan until after CEDAW ratification. See Yamashita 1993:70.

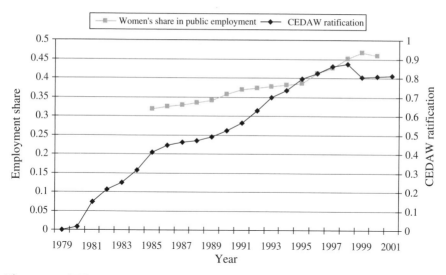

Figure 6.4. CEDAW Commitments and Women's Average Share of Public Employment. *Note*: Includes ratifications and accessions.

The model used to assess the impact of the CEDAW on the public sector is similar to the two-stage ordinary least squares regression used to assess educational opportunity and access to modern forms of birth control. Once again, I use country and year fixed effects, a lagged dependent variable, and control for any potential trend over time. However, the data available on public employment by gender are much more limited than those on school enrollment. The earliest observations are for 1985, and many countries had already ratified the CEDAW by that time. Moreover, data are available for only between 45 and 55 countries. Data are almost completely unavailable for African countries. Surprisingly, data were quite sparse for the most highly developed OECD countries as well. Most consistently represented in the tests that follow are the middle-income countries of Latin America, Asia, and parts of Europe.

The effect of CEDAW affects on public employment are reported in Table 6.4.

The first point to notice is that, as for education and access to contraceptives, there is (in this case a marginally) statistically significant effect of the CEDAW on the share of women in public employment. Ratification of the CEDAW is associated with an increase of almost 3 percent in the ratio of women:men in public employment three years after ratification (Model 1). But once again, we see a very uneven distribution of this ratification boost across different kinds of states. This time, it is not the transition regimes that display the most significant effects; their CEDAW ratification effect on women in public employment is

Table 6.4. Effects of a CEDAW Commitment on the Share of Women in Public Employment

Dependent variable: share of women in total public employment (lagged three periods)
Instrumental variable least squares regression model
Coefficients, probabilities based on robust standard errors

Explanatory Variable	Model 1: All Countries		Model 2: Stable Regimes		Model 3: Partial/Transitional Regimes		Model 4: High Rule of Law Countries		Model 5: Low Rule of Law Countries	
CEDAW commitment	.028*	($p = .085$)	.021	($p = .171$)	.023	($p = .285$)	.105***	($p = .000$)	.009	($p = .433$)
Women's INGOs (log)	.070	($p = .164$)	.048	($p = .715$)	.047	($p = .138$)	.022	($p = .253$)	−.013	($p = .705$)
Women's share of public employment ($t - 1$)	.687***	($p = .000$)	.540***	($p = .000$)	.470***	($p = .000$)	1.04***	($p = .000$)	.239	($p = .455$)
GDP per capita, logged	.046	($p = .228$)	.013	($p = .732$)	.011	($p = .681$)	.151	($p = .216$)	.012	($p = .635$)
Interstate armed conflict	.0003	($p = .960$)	.002	($p = .767$)	.009	($p = .129$)	−.004	($p = .209$)	.005	($p = .128$)
GDP growth rate	.00002	($p = .970$)	.001	($p = .260$)	.0002	($p = .658$)	−.003*	($p = .095$)	.0008	($p = .320$)
% of population under 14, logged	−.059	($p = .111$)	−.014	($p = .862$)	−.338**	($p = .043$)	.034	($p = .353$)	−.006	($p = .941$)
Use of IMF credits	.422***	($p = .004$)	−.123	($p = .487$)	1.53**	($p = .049$)	.104*	($p = .100$)	−.239	($p = .665$)
% of population urban, logged	−.0009	($p = .976$)	.018	($p = .562$)	.023	($p = .817$)	.327*	($p = .076$)	−.070	($p = .139$)
Civil war	.015	($p = .299$)	—		.015	($p = .159$)	—		.007	($p = .533$)
Year	−.003	($p = .167$)	−.001	($p = .752$)	−.009	($p = .126$)	−.016**	($p = .045$)	.004	($p = .260$)

Average regional women's share of public employment	-.276	$(p = .210)$	.009	$(p = .932)$	-.273	$(p = .337)$	-.168	$(p = .491)$	-.068	$(p = .651)$
Overseas development assistance/GDP	-.034	$(p = .383)$	-.245	$(p = .124)$	-.082	$(p = .180)$	10.70	$(p = .214)$	-.004	$(p = .911)$
Country fixed effects?	yes		yes		yes		yes		yes	
Year fixed effects?	yes		yes		yes		yes		yes	
# of observations	347		158		161		101		246	
# of countries	50		19		26		13		37	
R^2	.99		.99		.99		.99		.99	

All explanatory variables lagged three periods; regional female:male ratios lagged one period. Instrumented variable: CEDAW commitment. Instruments: common law heritage, average regional CEDAW commitment, three splines, ratio of women to men in public employment, and a year trend (all lagged one period).

* Significant at the .10 level; ** significant at the .05 level; *** significant at the .01 level.

nearly identical to that for stable regimes, whether democratic or authoritarian. The big difference this time is between countries in which women might reasonably expect to access the courts – the high rule of law states – to enforce their rights, including rights contained in a treaty commitment. While we are now dealing with a very small number of countries (13), in this case it looks like the most plausible mechanism for CEDAW consequences might be litigation – or the threat of possible litigation – alleging that women are not being treated fairly in the employment arena.

None of the other variables used as controls performed especially well in explaining increases in the ratio of women to men in public employment, with the exception of drawing on IMF credits. Moreover, the direction of the estimated effect is the opposite of what one might have expected. Drawing on IMF credits, at least in some cases, is associated with an increase in the ratio of women to men in public employment. This is counterintuitive, since the IMF expects reductions in public budgets, and if women are being discriminated against, one might have expected this ratio to fall rather than rise. None of the other controls seem to tell a systematic story about women's employment. In contrast to other findings, there is not even evidence of regional emulation. This could be the result of the sparseness of the data on public employment. Even a measure of democracy did nothing to budge the ratio (not reported).

Modeling the proportion of women in public employment has turned out to be a difficult task. Data limitations blow up standard errors, so it is difficult to have confidence in many of the explanations tested in Table 6.4. Still, the estimates for a commitment to the CEDAW treaty were in the hypothesized direction and were within a 90 percent confidence interval for the models that endogenize the treaty commitment itself. This is consistent with the results for girls in school and for policies regarding access to contraception. But when it comes to employment, women may turn to the courts to realize their rights.

A CLOSER LOOK AT MECHANISMS

CEDAW ratification has an important effect on policies and outcomes that the treaty is designed to influence, but through what mechanisms does the CEDAW actually have an effect? Statistical analysis can take us only so far in trying to answer this question. In this section, I explore two cases of the politics the CEDAW has unleashed in countries that one might have expected to be highly resistant to certain of the treaty's provisions: Japan with respect to employment policy and Colombia with respect to reproductive health and autonomy. In each case, women mobilized in order to capitalize on significant legal changes ushered in by their countries' ratification of the CEDAW, and in both instances women's rights improved as a consequence.

Japan: CEDAW, Women, and Employment Policy

Japan provides an interesting case by which to examine the potential role of the CEDAW in influencing discrimination in employment. Despite the fact that for the past 60 years it has been a stable industrialized democracy with a well-developed respect for law, Japan is quite a difficult case for the penetration of international law on women's issues. Among industrialized countries, Japan "is often regarded as representing an extreme case of sexual inequality. . . ."[102] The debates over equality versus gendered specialization – men at work, women in the home – though hardly new in the late 1970s and 1980s,[103] were often cast in culturally apocalyptic terms.[104] At the extremes, the debate over women's equal access to employment, promotion, and benefits was framed as a threat not only to Japan's (at that time) successful economic model based on male lifetime employment and extreme job devotion, but also to Japanese culture itself. The CEDAW demanded quite different standards of equity in employment than those reflected in law and practice in Japan.[105] In short, Japan in the 1970s and 1980s was not a natural candidate for the adoption of equal employment policies between the sexes.[106]

Unsurprisingly, then, the Japanese government was not enthusiastic when the UN turned its attention to drafting a treaty on women's rights as the legal capstone to the International Women's Decade (1976–85). Japan's efforts during negotiations were minimal, and were largely directed toward softening the treaty's language and reducing its scope. Most of these proposals were rejected, and initially it appeared that the Japanese negotiators would in fact refuse to sign the draft treaty,[107] citing how difficult it would be to alter domestic legislation in education, nationality law, and employment.[108] When this prospect was reported in Japanese newspapers only weeks before the signing ceremony,[109] a coalition of female Diet members, the media, NGOs such as the International Women's Year Liaison group, and, perhaps most importantly, women from

---

102 Lam 1992:7, 14–19.
103 Japanese women's groups had for decades joined the debate about the proper relationship between home and work for women. See Buckley 1994.
104 Upham 1987:150. Multiple sources emphasize the extent to which the entry of women into the male-dominated workforce was perceived as a threat to stable social and economic relationships. See Knapp 1995:85; Liu and Boyle 2001:394.
105 Liu and Boyle (2001:391) argue that there was a "real tension in Japan between the traditional gendered division of labor and international standards of equality."
106 Iwasawa notes that the Human Rights Committee of the ICCPR had criticized Japan's reports heavily in 1981, 1988, and 1993 for its treatment of women (1998:207). The areas singled out were nationality law, employment, and participation in public life (1998:210).
107 Iwasawa 1998:207–9; Rehof 1993:442.
108 Kobayashi 2004:104. According to Kobayashi, both the Ministry of Education and the Ministry of Justice pled difficulty in adjusting the existing laws to conform to the CEDAW at a 28 March 1980 meeting of the Budget Committee of the House of Councilors.
109 *Asahi Shimbun*, 10 June 1980.

within the Ministry of Labor bureaucracy, lobbied the government hard to change its mind.[110]

Eventually, and in time to attend the signing ceremony, the pro-treaty coalition prevailed. The argument that appears to have won over the Japanese government was the claim that having participated in the negotiation, it would be shameful for Japan not to sign the draft.[111] In a 27 June 1980 meeting, each administrative vice minister of government agreed to work toward the required legal reforms, and on July 15 – just one day before the signing ceremony at the UN – the cabinet officially decided to sign the Women's Convention and ratify it by July 1985, which was the deadline for ratification.[112]

Pressure from women's groups, the media, and members of the bureaucracy did not let up after signature; on the contrary, it increased as the Japanese government began drafting a plan to come into at least minimal compliance with the CEDAW. Much of the pressure focused on the necessity of drafting new legislation, required as a good-faith effort to change domestic law prior to ratification. Not to do so would bring shame on Japan in the eyes of the international community, these groups alleged. The publicity attached to signature and preparation for ratification gave the government little choice but to pursue the legal changes it knew would be required in order to ratify the CEDAW.[113]

Such pressure hardly led to a national consensus on gender equality, however. Deep divisions characterized Japanese society even as negotiations over equal opportunity legislation began. The major divide was represented by the positions of labor and management, which were at odds over the role of protections for women in employment versus true equality of treatment. Labor wanted the continuation of gendered protections, especially those relating to maternity, but employers wanted to eliminate these protections if they were to accept the general principle of equality. The form of a compromise began to take shape in March 1984, when the Japanese Federation of Employers Associations sent a memo, reported in the press, to the Ministry of Labor asking point blank what the minimum conditions were for an equal employment opportunity bill that could be construed as in compliance with the CEDAW. The ministry

---

110 *Asahi Shimbun*, 22 July 1980. In the secondary literature, see Flowers 2002:126; Iwasawa 1998:209.
111 This was the position of the Liaison Group, led by Ichikawa Fusae, in particular. See, for example, the discussion in Kamiya 1995:40; Kobayashi 2004:105.
112 *Asahi Shimbun*, 15 July 1980. Parkinson 1989:616, fn. 40; Upham 1987:149. See also Flowers 2002:126; Lam 1992: 89–90. After that date, states would have to accede to the agreement, and while the legal status of the commitment is the same, those who ratify are viewed as among the original supporters of the agreement.
113 Buckley 1994:163; Flowers 2002:159; Iwasawa 1998:215. Flowers's study of the local editorial pages between 1984 and 1986 notes that they were largely favorable to both ratification of the CEDAW and passage of domestic equal opportunity legislation and, most importantly, these articles tended to explicitly recognize the connection between instituting the EEOL and ratifying the CEDAW; the former had to be completed before the latter could take place.

responded that the least Japan could do would be to prohibit dismissal from a job based on marriage or pregnancy and discrimination based on a woman's marital status.[114]

The existence of CEDAW standards on this question gave pro-equality bureaucrats in the Women's Bureau of the Ministry of Labor a chance to broker a deal that, in its grossest terms, would trade broad gender protections (with the exception of those relating to maternity) for the principle of equality.[115] With time to the ratification deadline short and consensus lacking, the Ministry of Labor crafted a bill that was closer to the position of business than that of labor. While unsatisfactory from the perspective of the labor unions, they had little choice if they wanted progress in time to ratify the treaty.[116] The Deliberative Council of Women's and Minors' Problems approved the bill formulated by the Women's Bureau on 9 May 1984, and it was approved by the full cabinet four days later.

The debate in the Diet reflected these broader societal concerns. In introducing the Equal Employment Opportunity Bill, the prime minister tried to reconcile international standards with particular Japanese values and practices. "...[W]hile bearing in mind the ideals of the Convention, we came up with the [Equal Employment Opportunity Law] EEOL proposal based on the reality of our country's socio-economic situation; this proposal is the appropriate step based on that reality."[117] There was some obvious resentment among legislators of the values – not to mention the tight schedule – imposed by the essentially Western CEDAW agreement.[118] On the one hand, conservative legislators raised questions about the compatibility of CEDAW provisions with Japanese culture and values. On the other, the socialists were concerned that the policies under debate would in fact repeal the protections women had enjoyed, leaving them worse off in some ways.[119] But there were also those who thought that the CEDAW had exposed important contradictions in Japanese society and offered an opportunity to address them. The views expressed in the Diet regarding

114 Kobayashi 2004:109–14.
115 Kobayashi 2004:104; Lam 1992:96–8. Note that the CEDAW discourages but does not prohibit gendered employment protections, as this was a contentious issue in the original negotiations. Article 11(1)(a–f) calls for equality in employment protections for men and women, with allowances for maternity (Article 11(2)(a–d)). Article 11(3) requires that "Protective legislation relating to matters covered in this article shall be reviewed periodically in the light of scientific and technological knowledge and shall be revised, repealed or extended as necessary." Thus, the CEDAW's presumption is against the need for special employment protections (e.g., regarding hours, types of work, etc.) based on gender.
116 Kobayashi 2004:113.
117 Flowers 2002:134.
118 Upham 1987:151.
119 MP Takako Doi, popular leader of the Socialists, thought that in order to be consistent with the CEDAW, Japan must pass a law that "protects women's basic rights as employed workers," which she did not think the proposed EEO bill did. Lower house debates, 26 June 1984, as discussed in Flowers 2002:133.

CEDAW were articulated in a very similar way in the discussion of the EEO bill as well.[120]

The EEOL passed – in the last possible Diet session before the 17 July 1985, CEDAW ratification deadline – and became law in April 1986.[121] The Japanese government ratified the convention in June 1985, without reservations, despite the fact that, worldwide, the CEDAW is one of the most reserved-against human rights treaties.[122] This "clean" ratification may have reflected the demand of societal groups in Japan for a commitment without exceptions.[123]

Two points should be made concerning Japan's first-ever effort to legislate gender equality in employment. First, it was undeniably connected to the ratification of the CEDAW. No available secondary source account argues that Japan would have passed legislation to address some of the most egregious aspects of discrimination against women in employment had not the question of Japan's position on the CEDAW come up. Clearly, this was a case in which an externally negotiated agreement changed the country's legislative agenda, placing issues of women's equality much higher on the list of legislative priorities than would have existed had Japan not been faced with the issue of what to do about the CEDAW. To be sure, women's equality had its domestic supporters, but they were clearly in a minority and somewhat isolated politically and bureaucratically. They were hardly a match for Japan's powerful business interests that wanted to maintain the status quo. Second, the existence of the CEDAW increased the size of the coalition that was to support the EEOL. The Ministry of Foreign Affairs, for example, would not normally weigh in on domestic legislation on equality in women's employment, but they did in this case because they wanted Japan on board with this major UN initiative.[124]

The result was domestic legislation – the first of its kind in Japan[125] – that likely would not have existed were it not for the external negotiation of the CEDAW. This is overwhelmingly the assessment of the literature on this episode. Yuji Iwasawa, for example, notes that many significant gender-based laws have been introduced in Japan, "but by far the most important have been those that were brought about by the ratification of the Convention in 1985."[126] Alice Lam similarly notes that "... the EEO law is an outgrowth of internal

---

120 See the discussion in Flowers 2002:132–4.
121 Knapp 1995:107.
122 Noted by Iwasawa 1998:209.
123 Flowers 2002:136.
124 Kobayashi (2004:106) discusses the Japanese MOFA's motives toward the UN in greater detail.
125 The EEOL of 1985 was the first law addressing discrimination in private sector employment. Other laws, such as the National Public Service Law of 1947 and the Local Public Service Law of 1950, cover only public employment. Article 14 of the Japanese constitution, stipulating non-discrimination on the basis of, among other things, sex, had never been interpreted to apply to private relations. Furthermore, the Labor Standards Law applied only to "wages" and exempted gender from its list of groups not to be discriminated against with the longer list of rights (working hours and other working conditions). These are discussed in Iwasawa (1998:213).
126 Iwasawa 1998:212.

socio-economic changes and external pressures from the international community, not the result of an indigenous women's movement."[127] Petrice Flowers also concludes that the EEOL was the direct result of the ratification deadline for CEDAW.[128] Both the minister of labor and the director of the Bureau of Women's and Young Workers' Affairs have stated that the EEOL was drafted and passed specifically so that Japan could qualify to ratify the CEDAW.[129]

There is far less consensus on how beneficial the EEOL was for Japanese working women. While the law was unprecedented in Japan, it was, by most accounts, still quite weak – certainly weaker than the standards set by the CEDAW. Rather than fully embracing CEDAW's obligation to end gendered stereotypes, the EEOL's very purpose, stated in Article I, was to help women (not men) reconcile their work and home roles and responsibilities.[130] Most of the important concessions in formulating the law were made by the supporters of gender equality, with very few important ones made by management.[131] The EEOL sought to eliminate discrimination in recruitment and hiring; job assignments and promotion; training; fringe benefits; and mandatory retirement age, retirement, and dismissal. But it did establish the notorious "two-track system" distinguishing clerical from managerial positions, with little opportunity to move between the two tracks.[132] These provisions left the door wide open for discrimination.[133] As passed in 1985, the law contained no penalties for discrimination; instead, it relied on voluntary procedures, administrative guidance, and so on. Furthermore, the 1985 EEOL provided neither a private cause of action nor criminal sanctions, so it was hard to use it in litigation.[134]

The EEOL very likely did have some positive consequences, however. Barbara Molony notes that at least during the "bubble economy" of the late 1990s, the EEOL could be credited with higher enrollment for females in four-year colleges and an increase in hiring of female college graduates, which on balance increased the pool of women potentially available for managerial positions.[135] Soon after its passage, there was a noticeable equalization in starting salaries for women as many companies began revising their rules of employment in light of

---

127 Lam 1992:6.
128 Flowers 2002:139.
129 Parkinson 1989:616, fn. 40.
130 Knapp 1999:161.
131 Upham 1987:153–4. Upham termed the 1985 law "a major victory for management" (1987:152). He noted that off the record, managers often said that the EEOL strengthened their hand vis-à-vis female employees rather than weakening it (1987:153). For an equally critical assessment, see Knapp 1999; for a more balanced assessment, see Flowers 2002:139–41.
132 Knapp 1995:123.
133 Iwasawa 1998:220.
134 Kamiya 1995:68; Knapp 1995:117.
135 Molony 1995:298. She notes, however, that the effects on job assignment and promotion were minimal. The hortatory provisions on recruitment and hiring turned out to be better observed than the prohibitory provisions on training and benefits.

the legislation.[136] However, a government White Paper released in March 1989 noted that while employment opportunities for women had improved, women still earned significantly less than men. The same paper reported that the government itself was unlikely to meet its goals for female hiring for advisory positions.[137] And as the economy began to slow down in the early 1990s, women began to drop out of college and the professional job market.[138] A 1992 survey of nonfarm employment found that although 19.3 million Japanese women worked outside the home, they were mainly in jobs at significantly lower levels than men.[139] On balance, the EEOL seems to have made some important changes in the opportunities of working women, though these were hardly revolutionary strides forward.

But what the EEOL and the CEDAW did inspire was increased mobilization and litigation. Thanks to CEDAW ratification, Japan was obliged to report to the Committee on the Elimination of Discrimination Against Women, and it received some fairly harsh feedback in its 1994 report. Ten years after the initial legislation, the wage gap between women and men remained stubbornly wide – and well publicized in the press in Japan and abroad.[140] Pressure mounted to improve the weak EEOL. At least in part, the move to amend and strengthen the EEOL in 1997 reflected the Japanese bureaucracy's interaction with the CEDAW. The 1997 amendment moved away from the narrow problem of direct discrimination[141] and began to address issues that indirectly discriminated against women in the workplace. The 1997 amendment also prohibited employers from discriminating against women, replacing the earlier language that they should "endeavor" to not discriminate. The law was strengthened again in 2003. In these ways, the initial impetus of the CEDAW increasingly stiffened domestic Japanese law to deal with the problem of gender discrimination in employment.[142]

Ratification of the CEDAW also improved women's chances of successful litigation when faced with discrimination,[143] even though litigation is not an especially welcome method for achieving change in Japanese society.[144] Japanese women had started to use the courts in the 1960s to improve their access to equal

---

136 Parkinson 1989.
137 Kyodo News Service, Japan Economic Newswire, 24 March 1989. Lexis-Nexis.
138 The *Daily Yomiuri* (23 February 1991, Lexis-Nexis) reported that women were dropping out and were no longer trying for managerial positions; they were not as interested in trying to compete in a man's world. The point of the article is that the society has not changed significantly.
139 *Nihon keizai Shimbum*, the *Nikkei Weekly*, 19 April 1993. Lexis-Nexis. For a report on women quitting because of the menial and dead-end nature of their jobs, see *Nihon Keizia Shimbum*, the *Nikkei Weekly*, 30 November 1992.
140 "Japan Beginning to Bolster Discrimination Laws," *New York Times*, 18 December 1996.
141 Liu and Boyle 2001:397.
142 Iwasawa 1998:217.
143 Gelb 2002:12.
144 Knapp 1995:102. Knapp argues further that law in general has not been an effective agent for social change in Japan.

employment opportunities, but for the most part they did not have very strong legal protection.[145] Furthermore, like disadvantaged groups elsewhere, most women did not have the time or money to litigate. Ratification of the CEDAW has had two effects on litigation. First, it has encouraged women's groups to file cases, focusing on some of the largest industrial conglomerates in Japan. For example, in the mid-1990s, the Working Women's International Network (WWIN), mainly comprised of professional women, launched lawsuits against Sumitomo companies – a strategy aimed at generating publicity by focusing on a single large corporation.[146] Initially, several of these cases were unsuccessful. The case against Sumitomo Chemicals ended with a ruling that gender-specific career tracks did not violate the norms prevailing in the 1970s; another one, against Sumitomo Electric alleging the illegality of gender-based career tracking, was lost in 2000. However, rulings began to change thereafter – largely as the result of amendments to the EEOL that had been inspired by interactions with the CEDAW over the course of the 1990s and beyond. In 2002, a lower court ruled that Nomura Securities Company's two-track system discriminated by putting male workers on a career track and females on a noncareer track, in violation of the EEOL. A settlement was reached several years later out of court. In March 2005, the Osaka District Court ordered Sumitomo Metal Industries to compensate four female employees, though it took nearly 10 years for the court to find that "The company took measures that discriminated between men and women in terms of promotions and wages based on internal personnel rules that are not made clear to the employees. . . . This goes against public order and is illegal."[147] The groups that helped to launch these cases, the WWIN in particular, have been explicit about their intention of holding the Japanese government to CEDAW standards through a strategy of litigation and the crucial role of the CEDAW committee in assisting in this regard.[148] According to observers, success in this and other cases would not have been possible without the standards of the CEDAW to which to appeal.[149] Yuji Iwasawa is blunt about the role that

---

145 Iwasawa 1998:214.

146 Weathers 2005:81.

147 *Japan Times*, 29 March 2005. http://www.k2.dion.ne.jp/~sumikins/en/jptime.html (accessed 12 August 2008).

148 Liu and Boyle (2001:395) cite a 1994 letter from the Japanese Women Circle to the CEDAW Commission as well as a pamphlet issued by the Working Women's Network entitled, "Why Is It Equal When Women Are Paid Half of Men's Wages? Sexual Discrimination by Big Corporations and the Responsibility of the Ministry of Labor" 1997) that both make this point.

149 According to a 4 January 2005 editorial in the *Japan Weekly*. "In Japan, efforts to eliminate discrimination against women have been made on the basis of the UN convention. Female workers at Nomura Securities and at Sumitomo Electric Industries won an out-of-court settlement in which their claims for promotion were accepted, thanks to the UN convention and other international arrangements as well as the movement in Japan and abroad calling for the discrimination to be eliminated." See http://www.japan-press.co.jp/2005/2413/women.html (accessed 12 August 2008).

the CEDAW played in this regard: "... Japanese women had to wait for the advent of international human rights law, especially the Women's Convention, before such law actually materialized."[150] According to Liu and Boyle, these female litigants "went directly to CEDAW for legitimation of their claims."[151]

The case of women's efforts to overcome employment discrimination in Japan does not demonstrate that Japanese women have achieved equality in employment with men, nor does it suggest that the CEDAW has significantly altered broader cultural patterns in that country. Illustrating the claims made earlier, ratification of the CEDAW made it possible to make more progress in Japan's employment policies than would likely otherwise have been the case. And the law that was a direct response to ratification was used strategically by those with a stake in its application to further their rights claims. I am not claiming that Japan would never have acknowledged greater appreciation of women as employees had it not been for the CEDAW; Alice Lam notes that Japan may have faced some economic pressure for change in its employment practices in the absence of the treaty.[152] But CEDAW did alter the "political opportunity structure" in ways that are difficult to imagine in its absence.[153] There is no reason to think that Japanese bureaucrats would have decided that the early 1980s was the opportune moment to tackle this serious social and economic issue (or even have viewed it as serious), were the treaty not forced onto their agenda by a vote of the UN in 1979. But once it was there, the treaty – and the perceived duty to implement it – provided opportunities to persuade both employers and unions about gender equality.[154] Once the CEDAW was signed, activists and some bureaucrats – including unlikely partners in the Ministry of Foreign Affairs – were able to frame the prospect of nonratification as a shameful act.[155] The first EEOL – weak as it was – was a clear effort to implement an international legal obligation. Even some of its staunchest critics recognize that the EEOL has significantly changed perceptions in Japan about what it means to be a working person.[156] It encouraged women's groups – politically isolated though they were – to use the weak domestic law and the stronger

150 Iwasawa 1998:215.
151 Liu and Boyle 2001:397.
152 Lam 1992.
153 This is the central argument in Kobayashi 2004. Liu and Boyle (2001:400) conclude that CEDAW was important for political mobilization.
154 Kobayashi 2004:29, 104.
155 Kobayashi 2004:121.
156 Kamiya 1995. According to Kamiya, "The major effect of the Act was that it made the career path to the top more visible to the majority of the society, and hence more acceptable. . . . Thus an unintended effect of the Act has been a rise in expressions of concern for all workers to be able to live decent lives" (1995:64–6).

international obligation to eventually move judges and improve the law itself.[157] The result has by no means been revolutionary, but on the margins it has meant important improvements in the employment prospects of millions of Japanese women. As Akamatsu Ryoko declared, "without the international convention, the amendment to the Japanese Nationality Act, the enactment of the Equal Employment Opportunity Law, and coeducation in the homemaking curriculum would not have been. There is no international treaty that imparts as much influence on our lives as the Convention on the Elimination of Discrimination Against Women."[158]

Colombia, CEDAW, and Women's Reproductive Autonomy

Like Japan, Colombia is not the first country that comes to mind when thinking about the vanguard of women's rights. Yet, this nation provides another unlikely example of the role that international legal norms, and specifically the CEDAW, have had in institutionalizing women's rights. As Japanese women found in their efforts to reorient Japanese law and society, Colombian women have also found the CEDAW philosophy and obligation a crucial hook for their demands to provide women access to the safest and most effective reproductive health services. For a number of reasons, Colombia is not an obvious case for illustrating the useful role of international legal commitments for securing human reproductive rights: Traditionally, it was one of the most conservative Catholic countries in the Western Hemisphere (although the Catholic Church has lost some of its influence over public policy in the past couple of decades), it has been racked by extreme civil violence for the past four decades,[159] and it is not known for its highly responsive governmental bureaucracy. Yet, the CEDAW inspired Colombian women to demand that gender equality be included in the constitutional changes of the early 1990s.[160] Along

---

157 Improvements in the EEOL have continued to very recent times. A further amendment in 2006 strengthens bans on indirect discrimination such as setting unnecessary physical conditions, including weight or appearance, as criteria for hiring or promotion. It also makes it illegal for employers to urge pregnant workers to quit or accept other positions. See "Japan Tightens Laws Against Sex Discrimination," Agence France Presse, 15 June 2006. Lexis-Nexis. However, Knapp 1999 notes that Japan has always taken a gradualist approach to social problems; this case is no exception.

158 Speech at the 10th anniversary symposium of the adoption of the convention held by the Japanese Association of International Women's Rights on 24 June 1989; as quoted by Yasuko (1993:78).

159 Civil violence has subjected Colombian women to high levels of sexual violence, sexually transmitted disease, and unwanted pregnancy. Some 58% of the more than 2 million persons fleeing civil violence in the last couple of decades have been women, and the movement has largely been from rural to urban areas, placing a significant strain on the provision of women's reproductive and health services generally. See Plata and Guy 2000.

160 Colombia is one of a handful of countries whose constitutions explicitly guarantee reproductive rights. See http://www.savingwomenslives.org/factsheet_human_rights.htm.

with the domestic institutional changes the new constitution brought about, the women's treaty was central to the gender reorientation that took place in Colombia in the 1990s and has continued to unfold over the past few years.

Somewhat surprisingly, Colombia was, early on, near the forefront in the developing world in the provision of modern forms of birth control. Despite opposition from the Catholic Church, an active coalition consisting of Colombian medical schools, the Health Ministry, and a very active local affiliate of Planned Parenthood International, Profamilia (founded in 1965), helped to make Colombia an early model among developing countries struggling with high rates of population growth.[161] In the early years, access to modern forms of birth control was largely viewed as a development issue rather than a human rights issue.[162] The politicization of birth control practices was furthered by U.S. policy under the Reagan administration, which for the first time threatened to undermine population control policies in developing countries by withholding United States Agency for International Development (USAID) funding from groups supporting abortion or "coercive" methods of birth control. Abortion was illegal in Colombia, but since Profamilia did receive support from Planned Parenthood International, U.S. threats had to be taken seriously.[163]

Despite the controversies the family planning community encountered, NGOs, especially Profamilia, continued to work and prosper during the 1970s and 1980s. According to the group's executive director, Maria Isabel Plata, Profamilia started distributing contraceptives at a time when pharmacies would not carry them and when the Catholic Church vehemently opposed them. The government, on the other hand, was something of a silent partner, leaving the group the space and initiative to serve women whose demand for access to quality reproductive care and birth control was growing, but leaving them to absorb the heat from the social controversy their growing service provision engendered.[164]

The CEDAW provided an interesting opportunity for the community of family planning organizations. The Colombian government ratified the treaty quite early – in 1982 – and within a very short time, family planning organizations began to use the treaty to further their work among women. Taking the lead in 1986, Profamilia started its Legal Services for Women program, with two initial objectives:

161 See, for example, Bravo 1973; Ott 1977.
162 With a heavy emphasis on sterilization, especially of females, detractors publicly criticized the practice as "castration and mutilation" – and these practices would certainly fall under the umbrella of human rights. See "Battleground in Colombia: Birth Control," *New York Times*, 5 September 1984, Section A, p. 2, column 3.
163 "Battleground in Colombia: Birth Control," *New York Times*, 5 September 1984, Section A, p. 2, column 3.
164 Interview with Maria Isabel Plata, http://www.unfpa.org/icpd5/press/rhrt5.htm.

- "to use and publicize the Convention on the Elimination of All Forms of Discrimination Against Women as a means to improve women's condition and secure for them equal access to family planning services;
- to publicize the new rights of women in the family environment by means of educational material and by direct and personalized legal orientation."[165]

Over the course of the next few years, Profamilia's legal outreach – the centerpiece of which was the CEDAW itself – led to the establishment of legal clinics in family planning centers in five cities, the explicit purpose of which was to "educate women on their rights." Not only that; these clinics were set up to provide "legal services, including legal representation in the area of domestic and family law, to both women and men attending family planning clinics."[166] The Legal Service for Women program was an explicit strategy to raise consciousness in Colombia about women's reproductive rights, and activists could and did point to a public governmental commitment to these rights in the form of CEDAW ratification only a few years earlier. Profamilia's silent partner had handed them a legal commitment to elevate population policy to the level of human rights, and the NGO community leveraged this commitment to legitimate their work in providing women with access to reliable and reasonably priced modern forms of birth control.

In fact, CEDAW ratification provided a strong stimulus to women's organizations across Colombia more generally. This can be seen in the degree of organization in internationally affiliated local women's NGOs in Colombia over time. Figure 6.5 demonstrates a noticeable upward increase in the slope of the line documenting the number of such organizations in Colombia, with a pivot upward almost exactly on the year of CEDAW ratification. Even more stunning is the pivot point on the year 1991 – the year in which Colombia adopted a new and far more socially and politically inclusive constitution. This is crucial for women's rights because parts of the CEDAW were imported directly into the new constitution, including an explicit reference to reproductive rights. It is therefore important to understand how the CEDAW fed into debates over the constitution and the ways in which the new constitution furthered women's rights in Colombia.

The constitutional debate that took place in the second half of the 1980s was an opportunity for the CEDAW to make an impact on Colombian society and politics. Unlike other countries in the region, in Colombia the constitution had been in place for about a century. It was a conservative document, which gave a majority of legislative seats to rural interests despite the fact that, by the late 1980s, about 70 percent of Colombia's population lived in urban areas.[167] Presidents had tried for decades to wrest power away from the Congress, which was

---

165 Profamilia, http://www.ippf.org/charter/guidelines/legal.htm.
166 Profamilia, http://www.ippf.org/charter/guidelines/legal.htm.
167 Nielson and Shugart 1999:316.

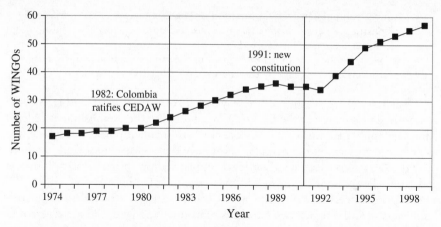

Figure 6.5. Colombia, WINGOs, and the CEDAW.

dominated by rural interests. Eventually, what Nielson and Shugart termed a "crisis of urbanization"[168] drove a presidential effort to bypass the Congress and seek popular support for constitutional reform – a tactic that was narrowly supported by the country's judiciary.

The most profound voice to counter the availability of contraceptives in Colombian society was, of course, the Catholic Church. It enjoyed almost complete control over Colombian social life in the 1950s and early 1960s but saw its power wane over the course of the 1970s and 1980s.[169] In Colombia's case, part of the decline in the church's influence was due to its close identification with the conservative oligarchy. Over the course of the 1980s, its power and influence steadily waned until Catholicism was disestablished by Article 19 of the constitution that would be promulgated in 1991 – making Colombia an officially secular state.

For Colombian women's groups, the debate over constitutional reform was an opportunity not to be missed, and they seized on the availability of the CEDAW to make a series of proposals designed to advance women's social and legal standing while improving their access to political participation. Even though they were vastly underrepresented in the Constitutional Assembly,[170] women's groups, working through the Women and the Constituent Assembly National Network, used the CEDAW as a model for what it means to eliminate discrimination against women.[171] As a result of these efforts, the ways in which the new constitution resembles the CEDAW is quite striking. The 1991

168 Nielson and Shugart 1999:322.
169 Dix 1987:7; Hartlyn and Dugas 1999; Levine 1981.
170 For a discussion of the nature of the constitutional assembly that led to the far more inclusive constitution, see Uprimny 2003:52.
171 Landsberg-Lewis 1998.

constitution recognizes both the equal rights of women and the state's obli-
gation to promote conditions of equality. Consonant with CEDAW, the new
constitution provides for measures to ensure women's equality (Article 13).[172]
The new constitution's Article 40 obligates the state to guarantee adequate
political representation for women, while Article 42 directly addresses
CEDAW's Article 16 prohibition on violence in the family and CEDAW's
Article 12 on women's health and reproductive autonomy.[173] Moreover,
Articles 93 and 94 of the new constitution import all international human
rights treaties ratified by Colombia into domestic law.[174]

The Women's Network for Sexual and Reproductive Rights (a coalition of
some 20 Colombian women's organizations) succeeded in their effort to influence constitutional drafting concerning the recognition of reproductive rights.
They advocated sex education in schools and a national women's health program, which was eventually addressed in the constitution. Strong Catholic
mores led to the failure of their efforts to decriminalize abortion, however. Still,
this coalition succeeded in making Colombia's constitution one of the few
worldwide that addresses reproductive rights. By all accounts, the Ministry of
Health has interpreted these constitutional provisions, as well as the CEDAW
itself, to require domestic health policy to pay special attention to gender in the
provision of health services and to include a right of access to modern forms of
birth control.[175] The Committee on the Elimination of Discrimination Against
Women (the international CEDAW oversight body) praised the turn toward
guaranteeing gender equality in the new constitution.[176]

How was it possible for a country as conservative as Colombia to adopt a
constitution with such an expansive vision of women's rights? The existence of
the recently ratified CEDAW was crucial in this regard. According to María
Isabel Plata and Adriana de la Espriella, of Profamilia, "The strengths of the
proposals advanced by the Women and Constitution Network lay not only in
their recognized support by the women's organizations, but in the fact that they
emphasized that *the principles embraced in their proposals were mandates contained in international human rights instruments, such as CEDAW. They won
legitimacy by being framed as internationally recognized human rights*

---

172 Morgan 1998:268–9.
173 Landsberg-Lewis 1998.
174 Article 93 provides: "International treaties and conventions ratified by the Congress that recognize human rights and that prohibit their limitation in states of emergency have priority in
the internal order. The rights and duties consecrated in this Charter will be interpreted in
accordance with international treaties on human rights ratified by Colombia." Article 94 provides: "The enunciation of rights and guarantees contained in the Constitution and international conventions in effect should not be understood as a negation of others which, being
inherent to the human being, are not expressly contained in them." Translated by Morgan 1998.
175 See the discussion in Cook 1993a. especially ca. p. 80, where she discusses various changes in
domestic Colombian law that reflect this interpretation.
176 Concluding Observations of the Committee on the Elimination of Discrimination against
Women: Colombia, 31/05/95, A/50/38, para. 608.

provisions. In this case, the use of international human rights language proved to be an effective strategy for introducing women's rights into the constitution, taking advantage of the fact that Colombia is a country that is constantly scrutinized by the international community for its compliance with human rights principles" (emphasis added).[177]

Women's rights, as reflected in the constitution of 1991, might have been empty promises were it not for another important aspect of the institutional overhaul: the strengthening of and improved access by ordinary citizens to the judiciary. The 1991 constitution created a new Constitutional Court, which "dramatically improved access to justice for ordinary people and has had a decisive impact in shaping and influencing major aspects of public policy."[178] The constitution also inaugurated the writ of protection, known in Spanish as *"tutela,"* which enables individuals to invoke judicial protection when their fundamental rights are threatened or violated. The *tutela* system has made it relatively easy for individuals to claim their rights and for the courts to enforce them. As an indicator of their perceived usefulness, *tutela* filings in Colombian courts rose from about 10,000 in 1992 to over 141,000 in 2002 – more than a 14-fold increase in a decade.[179] The Constitutional Court, which has earned a reputation for independence and a progressive attitude toward individuals' rights,[180] has the power to review the constitutionality of legislation and the *tutela* decisions of lower courts.[181] These legal innovations have greatly enhanced the importance of rights on paper; since 1991, they are much more likely to be enforced, and the cause of women's rights has quite often been the beneficiary of the court's orientation.[182] In the view of some analysts, the new constitution has therefore "opened the judicial system to women and other marginalized groups who before had little reason to consider using Colombia's courts as a means of social redress."[183]

Over the course of the 1990s, Colombia made policy changes and resource decisions that reflected the gender-sensitive commitments inspired by the CEDAW and reflected in its 1991 constitution. In 1993 the Colombian government initiated a wholesale reform of the health care system with its Law 100, which provides universal health care coverage and managed public–private provider competition. The approach to reproductive health services is comprehensive

---

177 Quoted by Landsberg-Lewis 1998:2.
178 Faundez 2005:758.
179 Faundez 2005:759.
180 Uprimny (2003:62) attributes the court's activism to various institutional arrangements that enhance its power and independence, but also to the weakness of Colombian social movements and exclusionary politics.
181 Faundez 2005:758.
182 Faundez 2005:759–60.
183 Morgan 1998:262.

and includes health care, contraceptives, counseling, clinical consultations, and treatment.[184] After 1994, an explicitly rights-based approach was adopted, and women's groups have continued to press for full implementation and to expose inconsistencies and violations.[185] Over the objection of the Catholic Church, emergency contraception is now widely available from both public and private providers,[186] but condoms have become the most commonly used method as awareness of and concern about human immunodeficiency virus/ acquired immune deficiency syndrome (HIV/AIDS) has spread.[187] As a result of Colombia's sustained attention to these programs, fertility rates have fallen sharply in comparison to the rest of the region and the abortion rate has declined.[188]

Yet, in one area, Colombia's policies relating to reproductive health have lagged for many years: Until quite recently, Colombia was one of only three countries in Latin America in which abortions were illegal *under all circumstances*, even in cases of rape or where the mother's health and life were at risk.[189] In the government's 2005 report to the CEDAW, Colombian officials noted that judges were allowed to reduce or waive criminal penalties under certain circumstances (for example, in cases of pregnancy as the result of force). They also defended the policy as the result of the legitimate legislative processes of a democratic country.[190] Nonetheless, the CEDAW committee criticized Colombia's provisions on abortion as a "violation . . . of the rights of women to life and health and of Article 12 of the Convention" and has called repeatedly for reform.[191]

With efforts at legislative reform repeatedly blocked by Congress, the courts were the only realistic option for women's groups determined to address Colombia's ultra-strict laws against abortion. In 2005, Monica Roa, director of the Gender Justice Program at Women's Link Worldwide, filed a court case challenging the highly restrictive provisions of the Colombian penal code. Her brief argued for legalization of abortion on the basis of Article 13 of the Colombian constitution, guaranteeing equality and nondiscrimination (discussed

---

184 Heimburger et al. 2003:155. See also "A Third World Effort on Family Planning," *New York Times*, 7 September 1994, Section A, p. 8, column 4.

185 Heimburger et al. 2003:156.

186 Heimburger et al. 2003:156.

187 Ali et al. 2003:671.

188 Singh and Sedgh 1997; Jayne and Guilkey 1998; Parrado 2000.

189 Colombia – 2005 Country Report to CEDAW, sections related to Article 12. The full text is available at http://www.bayefsky.com/reports/colombia_cedaw_c_col_5_6_2005.pdf. The other two countries are Chile and El Salvador.

190 Colombia – 2005 Country Report to CEDAW, sections related to Article 12. The full text is available at http://www.bayefsky.com/reports/colombia_cedaw_c_col_5_6_2005.pdf.

191 Concluding Observations of the Committee on the Elimination of Discrimination Against Women: Colombia, 04/02/99, CEDAW/C/1999/I/L.1/Add.8; see especially paragraphs 57 and 58; http://www. acpd.ca/compilation/CEDAW_C_1.htm#COLOMBIA. The CEDAW has made a general recommendation that abortion be decriminalized. See General Recommendation #24 (20th session, 1999), paragraph 31(c); http://www.un.org/womenwatch/daw/cedaw/recommendations/recomm.htm# recom18.

previously as a philosophy directly imported from the CEDAW); the right to life, health, and integrity; and the right to reproductive autonomy (including references to Article 42 of the constitution, implementing CEDAW's Article 16 obligations). In May 2006, after 13 months of considering Roa's two legal briefs, the court reached a 5–3 decision to legalize abortion in cases of danger to a woman's life, when the fetus has an illness that would restrict its ability to survive outside the womb, or in cases of rape and incest.[192] As if to underline the urgency of the matter, rather than turning the issue over to Congress for further debate and legislative reform, the judges invoked their special authority to make their decision effective immediately.[193]

It is important to recognize how ratification of the CEDAW enabled this recent liberalization of abortion laws in Colombia. The rights contained in the national constitution upon which the case was based were clearly domestic responses to Colombia's obligations under international law.[194] International law itself was becoming more available to Colombian courts, as Rao explained: "In the past 10 years two relevant legal developments have occurred that make this challenge viable and irrefutable. On one hand the Colombian constitutional court has recognized the legal value of international human rights arguments and has used them to solve constitutional challenges in other areas. On the other hand the international human rights arguments that frame illegal abortion as a violation of women's rights have become clearer and stronger."[195] The conscious effort to use international legal norms and obligations in domestic litigation has been an important part of a strategy in Colombia to improve women's access to modern forms of birth control and, finally, to reduce the risks to their lives and health in the case of a dangerous or involuntary pregnancy.

The increasing emphasis on the right to reproductive and sexual health that has been articulated in the CEDAW is changing the way family planning services are devised and provided. Colombia is a good example of these trends. As citizens of a generally quite conservative polity, with a broad range of challenges flowing from four decades of civil war, women in Colombia have benefited from their government's ratification of the CEDAW in 1981. Increasingly, women who need reproductive health services have access to advocates who can educate them about their rights and counsel them if these rights have been violated.[196] Both men and women now have good access to a wide range of modern forms of birth control, from condoms to surgery to emergency contraception. This is not, of course, to

---

192 "Abortion Adds to Colombia's Election Turmoil," Nicole Karsim, Women's eNews, Inc., 25
      May 2006. http://www.womensenews.org/article.cfm/dyn/aid/2752/context/archive.
193 "Abortion Adds to Colombia's Election Turmoil," Nicole Karsim, Women's eNews, Inc., 25
      May 2006. http://www.womensenews.org/article.cfm/dyn/aid/2752/context/archive.
194 "Colombians Push Abortion Onto National Agenda," Women's eNews, Inc., 22 December
      2005. http://womensenews.org/article.cfm/dyn/aid/2577/.
195 Interview with Monica Roa. http://www.whrnet.org/docs/interview-roa-0507.html.
196 http://www.un.org/ecosocdev/geninfo/women/womrepro.htm.

claim that all issues of reproductive health and autonomy have been resolved – there are still hundreds of thousands of pregnancies that are unwanted to one degree or another[197] and an acknowledged unmet demand for contraceptives among youth and rural populations[198] – but it is to claim that the CEDAW has improved the prospects for a large number of women in Colombia to gain control over their reproductive health in ways that would have been much less conceivable in the absence of the treaty.

CONCLUSIONS

The CEDAW has been the most serious international legal effort to deal with one of the world's gravest inequalities: that prevailing between men and women. It is an extraordinarily ambitious agreement, setting out an agenda that even its staunchest supporters envisioned would require a generation or more to implement. This treaty deals with sensitive social and family issues, and as such has drawn a broad range of reservations from state parties. Social and religious beliefs can be difficult barriers to the full implementation of the CEDAW, despite the fact that many countries ratified it quickly.[199] Indeed, one of the most consistent findings of this chapter is that women's rights are highly conditioned by the strength and nature of a polity's religious commitments. The statistical tests reveal that ratification of the CEDAW has consistently led to the most important improvements in more secular polities (in the area of girls' access to education and women's access to modern forms of birth control); in countries experiencing some degree of regime transition during the time period (access to education); and where the rule of law was well enough developed to make the courts a reasonably good bet for rights enforcement (girls' access to education and women's share of public employment).

Of course, the CEDAW is far from the only influence on the realization of women's rights. Women's NGOs have made a significant contribution to increasing the ratio of girls to boys in schools, especially in stable democracies with strong respect for the rule of law. Family planning provisions are almost certainly driven *primarily* by the aggregate population policies of the government. Women's access to plum jobs in the public sector is apparently supported in at least some countries by at least some forms of foreign aid, as the surprisingly positive

---

197 Plata and Guy 2000.
198 Colombia – 2005 Country Report to CEDAW, sections related to Article 12. The full text is available at http://www.bayefsky.com/reports/colombia_cedaw_c_col_5_6_2005.pdf.
199 See, for example, Sundstrom 2002 on the case of Russia. On the point that women's rights have to do with broader issues of the subordination of women within the family structure, see O'Hare 1999.

IMF indicator suggests.[200] In the case of school enrollment and access to modern forms of contraception, regional influences appear strong in some instances. There is no denying that we are looking at a multiplicity of explanations for the fate of women's rights over the past few decades.

Nevertheless, there is good reason to believe that the legalization of women's rights in treaty form was worth the effort, and these treaties continue to be worth the vigilance required to ensure continuing compliance. The CEDAW is a promissory note that the world's women and their sympathetic partners have used to leverage social change in a broad range of cases. The data point reasonably clearly and consistently to the positive impact of ratification. CEDAW ratification is associated with a growing effort to get girls out of the field and home and into the educational mainstream. CEDAW ratification is also associated with the growing recognition that women cannot control their life chances unless they can better control their reproductive capacities: Net of any policy to increase or reduce population in the aggregate, governments that have ratified the CEDAW are more likely to encourage women's access to modern forms of birth control. We have seen how CEDAW has influenced demands and policies in the case of Colombia, where the decision to import CEDAW obligations directly into the constitution has had profound effects on what women have come to demand and what the government and courts have been willing to provide in the area of reproductive health and autonomy. With respect to employment, the results of CEDAW ratification were generally positive, but were especially concentrated in countries with a strong rule of law tradition. Women in Japan have been able to leverage the legal system, cultural mores notwithstanding, in ways that have made their terms of employment somewhat more equitable.

Importantly, gender equality is not an automatic outcome of either democratization[201] or development.[202] It involves political agency and demands for change, and arguably the CEDAW has strengthened the prospects for meeting those demands in many countries around the world. Yet, it is crucial to

---

200 Other studies have linked backsliding with respect to women's rights more broadly to the retrenchment required by the IMF's structural adjustment conditionality. See, for example, Freeman and Fraser 1994:119, citing "Engendering Adjustment for the 1990s: Report of a Commonwealth Expert Group on Women and Structural Adjustment," London: Common Wealth Secretariat, 1989. On the effect of structural adjustment on government spending and human rights generally, see also Fields 2003.

201 For example, democratization in some Eastern and Central European countries resulted in the rollback of some rights and privileges won by women as nationalist patriarchal discourses resurged. See Eglitis 2000. Similarly, Einhorn and Sever (2003:abstract) conclude that in Poland and Yugoslavia, for example, "the transformation from socialism to democracy and a market economy met the ideological constraints of religious traditionalism and nationalism respectively." See also Gal and Kligman 2000. Similarly, in Latin America, some research suggests that dictatorships were more progressive on women's rights than democratically elected governments. See Htun 2003.

202 See the discussion in Drèze and Sen 2002:245.

acknowledge the limits of the argument. Ratification has made little difference in countries where the conditions do not exist for mobilization[203] or litigation.[204] CEDAW effects could never be shown to exist in countries with established, stable official religions or in countries with nonperforming judicial systems. Women mobilize strategically,[205] as the theory developed in Chapter 4 suggests. Where they have both the motive and the means to use international law to improve their rights chances, the CEDAW has proved to be a powerful tool in their hands.

203 See http://archive.idea.int/women/parl/annex1a.htm. International Institute for Democracy and Electoral Assistance: "It is vital that parliamentarians have a comprehensive understanding of these legally and non-legally binding instruments. They offer additional arguments to MPs raising issues regarding women's situation and concerns. They also raise the issue of the obligations undertaken by states that have ratified relevant conventions or that have otherwise made commitments in international meetings and fora. The role of NGOs in this area should not be underestimated. The importance of the links of MPs with women's grass-roots groups has already been emphasized in the handbook. National NGOs could inform female MPs about specific problems that women face in their countries, update them about the progress of international legislation, help them to lobby, inform other colleagues in parliament, and initiate relevant amendments in national legislation."

204 In India, for example, where the constitution explicitly provides that India is bound by the contents of all international treaties it has ratified, the Supreme Court has ordered parliament to come up with suitable legislation in conformity with the principles outlined in the CEDAW in order to address sexual harassment in the workplace (Nussbaum 2001:217). In Botswana, a court of appeals declared the 1987 Citizenship Act, which stripped Botswana female citizens married to foreigners of their right to pass on their Botswana citizenship (and thus political rights, such as the right to vote) to their children, unconstitutional. The act was successfully challenged in *Atty Gen v. Unity Dow*, and the court relied heavily on Botswana's CEDAW commitment in reaching its decision. The case also led to an enactment of the Citizenship (Amendment) Act No. 14 of 1995, Section 4(1), which extends citizenship to the children of Botswana women married to foreigners (Tshosa 2001:185–6). In Japan, women had attempted to use the courts to improve employment protections since the 1960s, but were not successful until the legal environment improved with the passage of the CEDAW (Iwasawa 1998:213–26).

205 On the importance of mobilization and organization of women's movements, especially in areas relating to employment terms and opportunities, see the essays in Naples and Desai 2002.

7

Humane Treatment: The Prevalence and Prevention of Torture

> We know from historical experience that when human beings have defensible rights –
> when their agency as individuals is protected and enhanced – they are less likely to be
> abused and oppressed. On these grounds, we count the diffusion of human rights
> instruments as progress even if there remains an unconscionable gap between the
> instruments and the actual practices of states charged to comply with them.
>
> Michael Ignatieff[1]

Cruelty is perhaps the most difficult human interaction to regulate. Whether inflicted on alleged criminals, ethnic minorities, political opposition, or enemies of the nation, torture and inhumane treatment involve relationships of power and vulnerability that frequently resist external intervention. Torture is often one despicable act in a broader, frequently violent, political drama. Perpetrators sometimes view their actions as justified when placed in their broader context. What hope is there for international legal commitments to influence the torture and inhumane treatment of detainees held by public authorities? Does the diffusion of treaties banning torture really count as progress, as Michael Ignatieff implies, or is the "unconscionable gap" so wide as to make a mockery of efforts at legal prohibition?

The previous chapters have demonstrated that international legal agreements have had a positive, though limited, effect on the human rights practices of some governments. The crucial difference between gender or children's issues (discussed in the next chapter) and torture is that the latter is often perceived to have a critical bearing on the ability of the government to maintain order, security, and its own political power. This chapter will examine whether, and under what conditions, international legal commitments can influence governments' most repressive and coercive tactics to achieve political goals. As we shall see, this is

1 Ignatieff 2001:4.

256

an area in which even the most democratic governments have preferred to retain a degree of discretion, though the ban in international law is absolute.

This chapter is organized as follows. The first section discusses the problem of torture. Unfortunately, torture is widespread and, for reasons to be discussed, extremely difficult to detect and eliminate. The next section discusses international legal efforts to address this problem. While the prohibition against torture is now widely considered a part of customary international law, one global treaty in particular – the Convention Against Torture and Other Cruel, Inhuman or Degrading Treatment or Punishment (the CAT) – defines and *categorically proscribes* the kinds of practices with which we are concerned here. The third section reviews what researchers now know about the scourge of officially sanctioned or permitted torture. Thanks to data that have been systematically gathered by such NGOs as Amnesty International and by some government agencies (the U.S. Department of State,[2] for example), it has been possible to research the coercive tactics that most governments would prefer to keep hidden from the broader international community.

The centerpiece of this chapter is an empirical investigation of what role, if any, international law has played in conditioning governmental use of torture. Few scholars or practitioners would expect an external legal obligation to have much leverage over a government intent on coercively cowing its own people into submission by employing extreme physical or psychological cruelty. But the findings of this chapter are surprising in this regard. As many skeptics would assume, there are certainly conditions under which treaty commitments matter not a (statistically detectable) whit to the governments that use these horrific political practices. But probing deeper reveals something quite interesting: Governments of polities that are partially accountable or in democratic transition are much less likely to use torture if they have made a public CAT commitment than similarly situated governments that have not. This process is examined in the context of Chile, where a brutal regime ratified the CAT before an election and then discovered just how powerful a tool it could be in the hands of activists. I then turn to the case of Israel, a democratic country but one embattled and conflicted over the issue of how to treat individuals held in detention by state security forces. In both of these cases, the evidence suggests that explicit international legal commitments can provide a mechanism allowing citizens to grasp their rights when their governments might prefer harsh repression. International law has its most important consequences in those – by now quite numerous – polities that have had at least a taste of democratic accountability and refuse to allow their governments to turn back.

---

2 Some of the practices that the State Department reports have condemned in other countries have, ironically, been approved by the United States in the interrogation of alleged terrorists. See Malinowski 2005.

TORTURE AND INTERNATIONAL LAW

The Nature of the Problem

Without a doubt, the use of torture by state officials is one of the most horrify-ing human rights violations imaginable.[3] The use of severe physical or psycho-logical coercion can be sensational but more often it is insidious, as officials deny or minimize and justify their practices in the name of a higher national or political purpose. Despite offending states' efforts to obscure such practices, the right to be free from torture is often listed as one of the physical integrity rights most commonly violated.[4] By some accounts, despite a decade-long campaign by NGOs to expose such practices, by the early 1990s torture continued to be practiced in more than half of the world's countries.[5] The fates of torturers' victims are not usually well known. Some are (intentionally) made to disappear; others remain at a vicious government's mercy for years. Some survive to see a new regime that effectively renounces such policies. Others flee, looking for sanctuary in a new location. By some estimates, 5 to 35 percent of the world's 20 million refugees have experienced torture.[6] And lest we imagine torture to be limited to a few brutal areas of the world, it is important to note that no region is immune. Appalling photos from the Abu Graib prison in Iraq have reminded Americans of the crucial importance of vigilance against the insidious abuse of prisoners. Even Europe, with the strongest legal regime of any region, still presents some surprisingly disturbing cases.[7]

The practice of torture is centuries old[8] and calls for explanation. Torture is broadly understood to mean the deliberate infliction of violence involving severe mental or physical suffering. The purpose of torturing an individual can vary: Jack Donnelley and others have noted that such explanations range from sadism to national security.[9] Psychologists and social psychologists con-centrate on the immediate environmental and personal conditions that stimulate individuals to intentionally inflict pain on others. Social psychologists have analyzed the use of torture as they do other forms of human aggression, noting that stress, risk, group conflict, physical discomfort, and the belief that cher-ished values are at stake are conditions that can provoke the use of intentional pain on detainees.[10] Sociologists have analyzed torture as an institution used to "deculturate" a society by silencing the dominant group's cultural enemies and

---

3 Several books provide an account of the history of torture; see, for example, Dunér 1998.
4 Cingranelli and Richards 1999a.
5 Basoglu 1993.
6 Baker 1992; Kane and Peterson 1995.
7 Cassese 1996.
8 See Ross 2005.
9 Becker and Becker 2001; Donnelly 1998; Worden 2005.
10 Dunér 1998.

breaking down rival cultural identities.[11] Perhaps this is why some studies suggest that physically harsh repression is more prevalent in culturally and racially diverse societies than in more homogeneous ones.[12] Political scientists have tended to analyze torture as a practice used to achieve particular political or governing goals, especially as a means of maintaining order, security, or power by cowing political opposition. In the United States, torture has most recently been discussed as a way to "exploit [detainees] for actionable intelligence"[13] essential to the country's national security.[14] Social scientists have tried to explain why torture is appallingly widespread and to model the conditions under which it can become increasingly sadistic.[15]

The use of torture is a very difficult phenomenon to study in an objective and systematic way. Given the negative connotation modern societies attach to the use of intentionally painful coercive practices, completely frank discussions about official torture are extraordinarily rare. Even governments that have accepted the obligation under the CAT to report to the Committee Against Torture hardly expose their shortcomings gladly; more complete disclosures are usually left to "shadow reports" submitted by various nongovernmental human rights organizations.[16] Simply put: Every government has an incentive to minimize the seriousness of their own abuses; ironically, it is the most open governments that are most likely to allow the kind of access from which the more highly critical shadow reports can be written.[17] Furthermore, even if we can all agree that torture is abhorrent, people differ over exactly what it is. Whether a particular practice constitutes "maltreatment," "abuse," or is serious enough to be termed "torture" can be highly contentious in all but the most extreme cases.

Controlling the practice of torture – even among governments willing to do so – is quite difficult because of the highly decentralized way in which it is carried out. Certainly, torture is more likely to be systematic and widespread

---

11 Sironi and Branche 2002; Slaughter 1997.
12 Walker and Poe 2002.
13 Article 15–6, Investigation of the 800th Military Police Brigade, paragraph 6. Text of the report, investigated under the direction of Maj. Gen. Antonio M. Taguba, can be found at http://www.msnbc.msn.com/id/4894001/ (accessed 30 June 2008).
14 Danner 2004.
15 Wantchekon and Healy 1999.
16 The United Kingdom's report to the Committee Against Torture is criticized by Amnesty International for not acknowledging that authorities had "violated the prohibition against the use of statements obtained through torture as evidence in any proceedings, except against a person accused of torture." See http://web.amnesty.org/library/Index/ENGEUR450292004? open&;of=ENG-GBR (accessed 30 June 2008). The U.S. report to the Committee Against Torture, for example, is criticized by the World Organization for Human Rights USA for "side-step[ping] and downplay[ing] the reality that as a matter of official policy the United States has been encouraging the use of torture of detainees on a systematic and widespread basis, and seeking to justify these major violations of international human rights standards as a necessary tool to combat terrorism." See http://www.humanrightsusa.org/modules.php?op=modload& name=News&file=article&sid=32 [inactive link].
17 Goodman and Jinks 2003.

where governments encourage or condone such practices. But even when they do not, even when official policy actively opposes torture, the act of torture itself may be carried out in innumerable police stations, detention centers, or prisons around a country. It can be very difficult to make official policy effective in such highly decentralized settings. In their study of Latin American transitions, Ellen Lutz and Kathryn Sikkink found that although torture was explicitly prohibited by treaty and implemented in domestic legislation, eliminating such practices lagged behind progress in other, less legalized but more public areas, such as democratic elections. They point precisely to this problem of decentralization, noting that even a government that *wants* to comply with legal prohibitions against torture may find it difficult to control the actions taken in multiple police precincts across a country.[18]

International Legal Efforts to Prohibit Torture

The prohibition against torture has been a part of the international human rights regime since its post–World War II inception. The UDHR addressed torture in Article 5, which states, "No one shall be subjected to torture or to cruel, inhuman or degrading treatment or punishment."[19] But because the declaration is a broad statement of principles, it neither defines torture nor provides any hint of enforcement. The first treaty to mention torture in peacetime was the ICCPR, whose Article 7 provides that "No one shall be subjected to torture or to cruel, inhuman or degrading treatment or punishment." In light of Nazi practices in the 1930s and 1940s, Article 7 went on to provide that "In particular, no one shall be subjected without his free consent to medical or scientific experimentation." As discussed in Chapter 5, the ICCPR created the Human Rights Committee and, for the first time, began a system of oversight (largely through state reporting). The ICCPR did not enter into force until 1976, however, and by that time, a concerted effort was underway, led by Amnesty International, to draft and promulgate a convention specifically designed to eliminate torture.[20]

From 1972, Amnesty International was a central advocate for, and ultimately an influential architect of, the international legal regime to ban torture.[21] Amnesty's campaign focused on key national legislatures (for example, the U.S. Congress), as well as the UN, in essence urging these bodies to take the problem much more seriously. Amnesty succeeded in arranging a joint UN–NGO Conference for the Abolition of Torture in 1973, which by most

18 Lutz and Sikkink 2000.
19 UDHR, Article 5.
20 For a discussion of the development of the UN regime with respect to torture, see Clark 2001:37–69.
21 On the role of NGOs in drafting the CAT, see Baehr 1989; Burgers 1989; Burgers and Danelius 1988; Clark 2001; Korey 1998; Lippman 1994; Tolley 1989. Korey describes this campaign as ". . . one of the most successful initiatives ever undertaken by an NGO" (1998:171).

accounts was successful in publicizing the issue.[22] Soon thereafter, the governments of Sweden and the Netherlands took an especially active role, urging the UNGA to pass the Declaration on the Protection of All Persons from Being Subjected to Torture and Other Cruel, Inhuman or Degrading Treatment or Punishment in December 1975.[23] The first article contained, in embryonic form, the definition of torture that would eventually make its way into the world's first binding treaty devoted to the subject. This declaration also proclaimed torture to be unjustifiable under any circumstances[24] – language that eventually became enshrined in treaty law.

The CAT is without doubt the premiere universal effort on the part of the international community to guarantee individuals a right to be free from torture and to ban its practice. On 4 February 1985, the convention was opened for signature at UN headquarters in New York City. Representatives of twenty-five states signed early that year.[25]

The CAT is the first international and legally binding effort to define torture. Article 1, paragraph 1 says:

> Torture means any act by which severe pain or suffering, whether physical or mental, is intentionally inflicted on a person for such purposes as obtaining from him or a third person information or a confession, punishing him for an act he or a third person has committed or is suspected of having committed, or intimidating or coercing him or a third person, or for any reason based on discrimination of any kind, when such pain or suffering is inflicted by or at the instigation of or with the consent or acquiescence of a public official or other person acting in an official capacity. It does not include pain or suffering arising only from, inherent in or incidental to lawful sanctions."[26]

Article 2 makes it clear that the prohibition contained in the treaty is absolute. The convention is aimed at *official* or *officially condoned* or permitted torture.[27] Torture cannot be justified under any circumstances, including war,

---

22 See, for example, Leary 1979.

23 UNGA 9 December 1975 (resolution 3452 [XXX]). Text can be found at http://www.unhchr.ch/html/menu3/b/h_comp38.htm (accessed 23 August 2005).

24 CAT, Article 3.

25 Afghanistan, Argentina, Belgium, Bolivia, Costa Rica, Denmark, Dominican Republic, Ecuador, Finland, France, Greece, Iceland, Italy, Luxembourg, Netherlands, Norway, Panama, Portugal, Senegal, Spain, Sweden, Switzerland, United Kingdom, Uruguay, and Venezuela.

26 CAT, Article 1, para. 1.

27 On the other hand, the Tokyo declaration, adopted by the World Medical Association in 1975, defines torture as ". . . the deliberate, systematic or wanton infliction of physical or mental suffering by one or more persons acting alone or on the orders of any authority, to force another person to yield information, to make a confession, or for any other reason." World Medical Association Declaration Guidelines for Medical Doctors Concerning Torture and Other Cruel, Inhuman or Degrading Treatment or Punishment in Relation to Detention and Imprisonment (Declaration of Tokyo). Adopted by the 29th World Medical Assembly, Tokyo, Japan, October 1975.

internal political instability, or any other public emergency,[28] nor can it be justified by orders from a superior public authority.[29]

Like the other core treaties examined in this book, the CAT sets up an oversight committee, the Committee Against Torture, to which the state parties are required to report shortly after ratifying and every four years thereafter, for purposes of informing the committee of progress made with respect to treaty implementation.[30] As with other treaties we have examined, the committee may make comments or suggestions (which are not legally binding), to which the reporting government may respond.[31] Official governmental reports are typically fairly unrevealing, but they do give the committee a chance to go on record about what constitutes torture, a practice that has had important political consequences in some countries, as we will discuss. Article 20 of the CAT allows the committee to initiate investigations into allegations of torture if credible evidence of widespread abuse exists, though this authority has been used rarely.[32]

The CAT takes three approaches to enforcement. First, it establishes universal jurisdiction for the crime of torture. Article 5 of the treaty requires nations either to extradite or to prosecute alleged torturers within their boundaries, *regardless of where their crimes took place.*[33] In theory, this means that torturers have no place to hide; they can be held legally accountable for their actions if they enter the jurisdiction of any party to the treaty. Article 5 was successfully used in Pinochet's prosecution, for example, illustrating that heads of state are not immune from the CAT's provisions.[34] In practice, of course, governments may be reluctant to prosecute torturers for political reasons, especially if they are former heads of state.[35] Nonetheless, most analysts have hailed universal jurisdiction as an important and innovative way to enforce the treaty's provisions.[36]

The CAT also contains two optional enforcement mechanisms. First, any state party may declare under Article 21 that it "recognizes the competence of the Committee to receive and consider communications to the effect that a State Party claims that another State Party is not fulfilling its obligations under this

---

28 CAT, Article 2.2. Text of the CAT can be found at http://www.hrweb.org/legal/cat.html.
29 CAT, Article 2.3. For a defense of the nonderogable nature of this prohibition, see Lukes 2006.
30 CAT, Article 17.
31 CAT, Article 19.
32 Turkey (1993), Egypt (1996), Peru (2001), Sri Lanka (2002), and Mexico (2003). See http://www.unhchr.ch/tbs/doc.nsf (accessed 30 June 2008). For a discussion of the investigatory power of the CAT, see Schou 2000.
33 CAT, Article 5. Sweden and a group of NGOs – notably the International Association of Penal Law and the ICJ – were especially influential in including universal jurisdiction language in the CAT. See Burgers and Danelius 1988; Hawkins 2004; Rodley 1999.
34 Bosco 2000.
35 See Solomon 2001.
36 On the importance of universal jurisdiction in the CAT, see Boulesbaa 1999; Hawkins 2004; Rodley 1999.

Convention." The committee is directed under Article 21 to handle such complaints in a dispute settlement rather than an enforcement mode. Its decisions are not binding on either party. Despite the fact that 53 states have to date made an Article 21 declaration,[37] this procedure has *never* been invoked.

The second optional enforcement mechanism is for state parties to declare themselves bound under Article 22 ". . . to recognize the competence of the Committee to receive and consider communications from or on behalf of individuals subject to its jurisdiction who claim to be victims of a violation by a State Party of the provisions of the Convention."[38] Such a declaration, in effect, gives individuals standing to complain about a state's behavior to the Committee Against Torture. Some 56 states have made such a declaration, and as of April 2004, the committee has received 241 complaints. Sweden, Switzerland, and Canada head the list of countries complained against, indicating that this provision may be most relevant to those individuals already in possession of a fairly strong sense of their rights.[39]

The State of Research

Relatively little cross-national research has been done to try to explain the prevalence and patterns of state-sponsored torture, and attention to the role of international legal commitments has been even more scant. Research did begin in the mid-1980s on the theme of "state violence" and "state terrorism," which focused on broader forms of state terror aimed at the systematic repression of domestic populations.[40] While not explicitly focusing on torture, several studies associated the broader repressive policies of governments with developmental level (including "dependent development"), Cold War conditions and alliances, and a country's mode of integration into the capitalist world economy.[41] Many of these early studies did not survive more systematic evidentiary scrutiny. Some researchers have shown that (nonmilitary) U.S. aid takes human rights into account,[42] and they have failed to confirm the Cold War as a major facilitating condition for widespread abuses.[43] And rigorous tests of the proposition that dependence on the capitalist world economy is associated with repression have not sustained such claims. In fact, some researchers have found a

---

37 Declarations can be found at http://www.unhchr.ch/html/menu2/6/cat/treaties/convention-reserv.htm (accessed 30 June 2008).
38 CAT, Article 22.
39 Statistics (current as of 30 April 2004) on individual complaints under Article 22 can be found at http://www.unhchr.ch/html/menu2/8/stat3.htm (accessed 30 June 2008).
40 See, for example, Stohl and Lopez 1986.
41 See, for example, the essays collected in Lopez and Stohl 1989.
42 Cingranelli and Pasquarello 1985. For a series of exchanges challenging and reestablishing the contention that U.S. aid policy is sensitive to human rights issues, see Carleton and Stohl 1987; Mitchell and McCormick 1988; Poe 1992. For case studies examining U.S. aid policy as a means to influence flagrant human rights abuses in Latin America and Africa, see USIP 2001a, 2001b.
43 Cingranelli and Richards 1999b.

positive relationship between foreign economic penetration and respect for individuals' physical integrity rights.[44] The most consistent findings about the conditions associated with violation of physical integrity rights are not very surprising. Democracies have a better record than do more autocratic states. Civil and international wars are associated with deterioration in rights and the spread of abuses.[45] Constitutional provisions have mixed effects, with only one due process provision – namely, the right to a fair trial – positively associated with improved personal integrity rights.[46]

Only two studies have addressed the role of international law in affecting governments' physical integrity rights violations, and only one of these deals specifically with torture. Linda Camp Keith's study of the ICCPR found differences across signatories and nonsignatories, but found no improvement in physical integrity rights among signatories before and after treaty ratification.[47] The only study to directly examine the effect of the CAT on practices that are specifically banned by that convention is that of Oona Hathaway. Her work does not support the proposition that making a commitment to the CAT has much effect on the propensity to torture. Quite the contrary: She concluded her study by noting that "the torture and genocide conventions appear to have the smallest impact on human rights practices of all the universal conventions."[48] This is the most careful work to date modeling torture and by far the best effort anyone has made to match the coding of practices with those behaviors specifically banned by international treaties. Because the dependent variable is so carefully constructed, it is worthwhile to extend Hathaway's data in time and reassess the evidence using a more revealing and theoretically satisfying model of the key relationships.

Hathaway's explanation for the CAT's null effect is that governments ratify human rights conventions to express their symbolic support for their principles as well as to reduce criticism attendant upon remaining formally outside the conventions. But compliance theorists have noted the logical oddities in such an argument, at least as a general explanation. The single most puzzling problem is why any government would sign an international treaty thinking that this would be sufficient to deflect criticism from their practices.[49] As I have argued in Chapters 3 and 4, the empirical record with respect to treaty ratification seems to suggest a completely different dynamic: NGOs have campaigned hard for ratification (notably Amnesty International in the case of the CAT)[50] because

---

44 Richards et al. 2001.
45 See, for example, Poe and Tate 1994; Poe et al. 1999. For a discussion of the use of torture in fighting insurgencies, see Robin 2005.
46 Keith 2002.
47 Keith 1999.
48 Hathaway 2002:1988.
49 Goodman and Jinks 2003.
50 A point made by many observers of NGO priorities and the CAT ratification record; see Claude and Weston 1992; Forsythe 1985; van Boven 1989–1990.

they believe it will give them greater moral, legal, and political leverage over states than would have been the case otherwise. The evidence does not seem to support the contention that ratification alone satisfies antitorture groups that their mission has been accomplished.

A more reasonable expectation is that an international commitment to eschew the practice of torture is effective under some conditions and not under others. *Some* governments may ratify the CAT for expressive purposes; these are likely to be those polities already quite committed to the treaty's provisions. They do not need an international commitment to influence their policies: A credible commitment to abstain from torture can be generated from within the domestic political system itself. The Swedens, Netherlands, and Costa Ricas of the world may sign as an expression of their commitment to humane treatment and their desire to influence others to do the same,[51] but so many internal checks on torture are in place that an international treaty is superfluous. On the other hand, *some* governments may believe (wrongly in many if not most cases) that ratification will earn them some cheap credit with the international community. In both cases, ratification should not be expected to alter behavior significantly: Those with the best records will continue to eschew torture, while the few looking for cheap international kudos will continue to behave badly. Under these conditions, the motives for signing and the propensity to torture will differ radically, but the behavioral observation – no apparent treaty effect – will be the same.

Many governments are neither stable compliers nor cynical signers. They rule polities with *some* experience with democratic principles and human rights. Their populations have in many cases had *some* exposure to the rule of law, as well as a degree of governmental accountability, and value international obligations as a way to help secure greater human rights guarantees. As I have argued in Chapter 4, international legal instruments can mobilize individuals and groups to demand their rights under the treaty's provision. This is especially true in the case of torture. Experiences of pain and loss cut to the core of everyday lives, and when such suffering is the result of torture, these feelings can occupy a prominent place in the domains of public opinion and issue activism.[52] Civil society is *provokable* in these countries, and citizens have enough freedom to be able to act according to their values and in their perceived interests. In these cases, one might expect a convention against torture to have real effects on government practices.

There are good theoretical reasons to take another look at the effect of ratification of the CAT, specifying clearly the conditions under which we might expect it to have real consequences for the polity. Torture is about political and

---

51 See, for example, the discussion regarding the desire to influence others to sign as a motivation in Ratner 2004.

52 Jennings 1999.

social control. The CAT should have its strongest positive effects in places where control is contested – where politics are most unstable and precarious for the governing elite. Neither stable democracies nor complete autocracies fit this description. Rather, we should expect a commitment to the CAT to matter most where political regimes are in flux. The next section tests this idea and reveals treaty effects that earlier studies have obscured.

DATA AND METHODS

The Dependent Variable: Torture Scale

As defined by the CAT, torture is the intentional and coercive inflicting of severe pain or suffering by a government authority acting in his or her official capacity on another person or persons. The CAT specifically excludes pain or suffering caused by "lawful sanctions." Two sources have long collected information useful in developing a torture measure: NGOs (Amnesty International, in particular) and the U.S. Department of State. Oona Hathaway's work depended on the latter, which does not differ significantly from information collected by nongovernmental sources. Indeed, the Department of State to a large extent bases its own reports on information supplied at least in part by NGOs.[53] Since her measure is designed specifically to tap compliance with the CAT, I have extended Hathaway's data through 2002.

The dependent variable is a five-category measure that captures the pervasiveness of the practice of torture by government officials.[54] The worst cases (Category 1) are those in which torture (including severe beatings) was considered "prevalent" and "widespread."[55] The next category (Category 2) includes cases in which torture was considered "common," there were widespread reports of beatings to death, or other beatings and other forms of abusive treatment were quite routine. The third category involves those cases in which there was some reference (without specified frequency) to maltreatment, or common beatings or isolated reports of severe beatings (e.g., to death). The fourth category includes those cases in which abuses were occasional or there were

---

53　For a discussion of how the U.S. Department of State reports are compiled, see De Neufville 1986; Valencia-Weber and Weber 1986.

54　For a detailed discussion of the criteria used, see Hathaway 2002. These categories are greatly preferable to counting instances of torture or abuse, which several researchers have noted give a false sense of accuracy; see Goldstein 1986; Stohl et al. 1986. The use of this scale comports with Thomas Pogge's notion of individuals' right to institutions that secure access to a particular right. Pogge asserts, for example, that whether an individual enjoys the human right against torture turns not on whether the individual is actually tortured, but rather on the probability that that individual will be tortured under the prevailing social conditions, which are roughly what this scale captures (2002:65).

55　Hathaway's (2002) coders also looked for terms such as "repeated," "methodical," "routine," and "frequent."

possible cases of beatings (though never to death). And finally, the fifth category involves the best cases, those in which serious abuses were never reported, though isolated cases of a less serious nature were on rare occasions reported and responded to with disciplinary action. Table 7.1 summarizes the criteria used for the torture scale.

Figure 7.1 gives a sense of how torture practices have compared with CAT ratification since 1985. Apparently, the number of treaty adherents has increased even as the global average of torture practices has deteriorated. The question addressed here, though, is whether committing to the CAT improves practices among the committed or whether there are any conditions under which commitment improves practices, controlling for other explanations and influences. If governments are influenced by their international legal commitments, we should see a positive relationship, indicative of improvement, when countries ratify the CAT.

Conditioning Effects: Regime Type and Judicial Institutions

The central hypothesis of this chapter is that human rights treaties need at least some domestic political traction to have significant positive effects. They are not likely to change behavior in countries with stable dictatorships or in countries that reliably ensure the political accountability of leaders and other agents of the state. Legal constraints are largely ignored in the former and are redundant in the latter. As in the preceding chapters, I distinguish three kinds of historical regime experiences. First, I distinguish countries that have been stable democracies for the entire post–World War II period or, if newly independent since 1945, democratic for their whole independent existence. I code them as "stable democracies" if their democracy score never goes below 8 in the polity dataset during the post–World War II period. Next, countries are never democratic if they have never had a democracy score above 5. I would expect a treaty commitment to have very little effect in either of these cases. That leaves the unstable, transitionally or partially democratic "middle" – a category that includes a large number of countries (see the Data Appendix at the end of the book). Many of these are countries transitioning toward democracy; a smaller number are moving in the opposite direction. A few are fairly stable partial democracies. I run additional tests later to see whether volatility or partial democracy seems to account most fully for the observed effects of the CAT in this cluster of regimes.

The Statistical Models

One of the most serious problems associated with trying to estimate treaty effects accurately is that, with a few exceptions, the same factors that lead to ratification are likely to explain compliance (Chapter 3). Thus, it is important to use a statistical model that endogenizes the ratification choice itself and to

Table 7.1. Torture Prevalence: The Dependent Variable

Note: In each case, at least one of the following must be true:

Type of Activity	Category 1	Category 2	Category 3	Category 4	Category 5
Psychological mistreatment		Frequent, often	Used without reference to frequency	Sometimes, occasional	Isolated reports with disciplinary response
Rough handling, other abuse		Frequent, routine	Regular brutality, severe maltreatment of prisoners	Sometimes, occasional	Isolated reports with disciplinary response
Beatings		Frequent, routine	Common (or not uncommon), numerous reports	Allegations or indications (any reported – regardless of redress)	Isolated reports with disciplinary response
Torture	Prevalent, widespread, repeated, methodical	Common, several reports, numerous allegations	Some, occasional (unless redressed)	Unsubstantiated; unlikely true; isolated, with redress	None
Abused to death	Common, frequent, many, widespread	Some, occasional incidents, several reports	Isolated reports	None	None

Note: This presentation inverts the original scale so that higher scores represent better practices.
Source: Hathaway 2002.

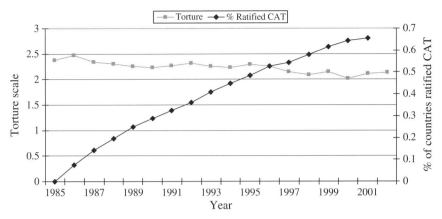

Figure 7.1. CAT Ratifications and the Torture Scale. *Source*: Ratification status for the CAT: Office of the UN Commission for Human Rights, http://www.ohchr.org/english/countries/ratification/9.htm. Torture Scale (measuring torture prevalence): Hathaway 2002 (inverted scale).

"identify" the model with instruments that can help distinguish ratification from compliance. Two of the most reliable factors that influence ratification, as we have seen, are the nature of the legal system[56] and treaty ratification of other states in the region. These are the two variables I use to explain ratification in the first equation of a two-stage least squares model. The second-stage equation tests the hypotheses for the CAT's influence that were developed previously. I expect the CAT to improve torture practices; hence, we should expect a positive relationship between the CAT and the torture scale. Furthermore, in order to control at least in part for various constant but unmeasured national characteristics that may affect both the commitment decision and the compliance outcome, I use country fixed effects in all models presented later. And because torture practices are admittedly hard to change, and are likely affected by a great deal of institutional and cultural inertia, I include a lagged dependent variable to better account for *changes* from past practices. In order to guard against picking up trends in the dependent variable not directly linked to the treaty obligation, I include a time trend wherever it was found to be statistically significant. One possible explanation for the downward drift in the torture index is that it reflects better information or changing norms about what constitutes torture (e.g., various forms of physical and psychological deprivation or

---

56 Common law countries are much less likely to ratify a human rights treaty (Chapter 4), but they are no more or less likely to engage in torture. In fact, common law countries average 2.3 on the torture scale, while all other countries average 2.2 – a statistically indistinguishable and substantively insignificant difference.

manipulation from which an individual might eventually recover). If reporting standards evolve slowly over time, the year trend will be useful in absorbing these effects to a certain extent. Finally, there is little doubt that observations across time within countries are not independent, which can reduce standard errors and unjustifiably increase confidence in our estimates. In order to address this, results based on robust standard errors are reported, which take into account clustering by country.

Controls

A series of control variables are included in all specifications to reduce the possibility of erroneously attributing causal significance to ratification of the CAT. Certainly, the basic causal explanations for the prevalence of torture are not likely to be an international legal commitment, but rather institutional and social features of each country, as well as each government's perceived threats to national security or to its hold on political power. No one should expect international law to overcome these basic conditions; rather, the question is, once we control for these conditions, does a treaty commitment make any difference to the prevalence of torture on the margins?

A first set of controls speaks to the country's domestic institutions. The primary hypotheses have to do with degree of democratic accountability and the rule of law, but other domestic institutions could matter as well. Most important here are institutions that make it difficult for a government to torture its citizens without some resistance. Besides regime characteristics, accountability could plausibly be influenced by a free press. Torture is much less likely to be widespread in countries in which the press can expose and criticize the government without censorship or fear of reprisals or harassment. A free press can both expose abuse and remind a people that its government is violating international accords to which it is legally committed.[57] It might also be easier to control government agents in a more unitary political system; hence, I control for the degree of federalism as well. The following tests also control for the existence in each country of the death penalty, since some authors claim that polities with more violent forms of punishment are also likely to mete out harsh treatment during interrogation and detention.

National truth commissions can be used in exceptional circumstances to try to address the widespread use of torture and related rights abuses. A truth commission is a domestically generated effort to come to terms with an oppressive and violent past. The creation of such a commission presumably signals a commitment to acknowledge past abuses, set the record straight, and place the country on a more just path. Truth commissions can certainly be aimed at injustices other than torture, but they are frequently set up specifically to

57 On the role of the press generally in exposing human rights abuses, see Husarska 2000.

address egregious human rights abuses.[58] If they are successful, we might expect torture practices to be ameliorated once a commission is established. Including a truth commission also allows us to take note of a government's intense commitment to improve human rights practices, thus reducing the risk that we will assign to international law causality that belongs more immediately in the domestic sphere. Another way potentially to tap into the degree of a government's commitment is to look at whether the making of an Article 22 declaration gives individuals within countries a "private right of action" before the Committee Against Torture. One might expect that a government willing to make such a commitment would also be firmly committed to improving its own standards for treatment of individuals held in detention.

The second set of controls relate to a country's security situation. One of the classic justifications for using coercive tactics against detainees is either to silence or to wrench information from various groups or individuals the government considers its or the country's enemies. War also gives rise to physical and social conditions that are linked to individual aggression.[59] Even countries that eschew torture under normal circumstances can find justifications for its use when the nation is at war.[60] Practically every study on human rights notes that they deteriorate during wartime.[61] We should therefore expect the use of torture to spread and become more intense during a violent conflict. Indicators for both international and civil wars are therefore included in the following analysis. Leadership of a military government was also included in several tests, but as it was never significant and significantly reduced the sample size, it was ultimately dropped and not reported. I have also attempted to capture the potential for other forms of group conflict, testing for the significance of religious, ethnic, and language fractionalization to be found within societies.[62]

A third set of controls relate to potential external levers of influence over a country's torture practices. Countries that receive large amounts of foreign aid or that trade extensively with wealthy democracies could be discouraged from using brutal interrogation practices if these partners publicize these practices and/or threaten sanctions. I therefore include overseas development aid as a proportion of GDP and the total number of preferential trade agreements as potential sources of external leverage over rights practices.

Among potential external levers, the international community working through the UN has developed mechanisms to investigate, expose, and embarrass governments about their repressive practices. Three major UN mechanisms

---

58 Bronkhorst 1995; Hayner 1994, 2001.
59 Sironi and Branche 2002.
60 For an excellent book on the French use of and justification for torture during the Algerian War, see Maran 1989.
61 See, for example, Apodaca 2001; Haas 1994; Hamburg 2000; Ignatieff 2001; Poe and Tate 1994; Poe et al. 1999.
62 Only religious fractionalization had any systematic effects, and it is the only one of these to be reported later.

could potentially have an influence on a country's propensity to torture.[63] The first is the UNGA's use of specific resolutions criticizing a country by name for some aspect of its human rights record. These resolutions are relatively rare; they are not formally binding and are not enforceable in any way. But they do express a sense of concern from the UNGA regarding a serious human rights situation in a given country. Unfortunately, they do not specifically mention torture, even if torture is in fact widespread in the country being named. Nonetheless, it is possible that the shame of being named by one's peers as a country whose human rights practices are problematic could cause a government to take stock and try to address some of the most serious issues, among which we should expect the widespread use of torture to be one.

The second mechanism the international community has at its disposal for influencing countries' most egregious human rights practices is what is known as a 1503 Investigation. Established by the ECOSOC in 1970 (by Resolution 1503), this procedure deals with communications relating to practices that amount to a pattern of gross violations of human rights. Official acts of torture are among the complaints the Human Rights Commission considers, along with systematic discrimination, arbitrary killings or detentions, and violent political repression. Complainants must have exhausted domestic remedies; that is, they must demonstrate that they have done everything possible to resolve the problem within their own country. If considered admissible, communications – whether from individuals or groups – are reviewed by a working group of the Commission on Human Rights. Communications remain confidential unless and until the commission decides to make recommendations to the ECOSOC. The whole process is political rather than judicial. Its aim is to identify countries in which serious abuses are occurring rather than provide a remedy for those complaining of human rights violations.[64]

Third, since the 1980s, the special rapporteur on torture has been available to provide visits to countries that evidence indicates have indulged in torture on a systematic basis. Country visits are supposed to "provide the Special Rapporteur with a firsthand account of the situation concerning torture, including institutional and legislative factors that contribute to such practices."[65] Unlike either of the mechanisms discussed previously, such visits are essentially voluntary. Governments must "invite" the special rapporteur, though they are sometimes asked to do so by the rapporteur's office itself. Also unlike the mechanisms discussed previously, this one is aimed *specifically*

63 For a discussion of these and other "enforcement" mechanisms, see Donnelly 1998. Legal scholars have considered these mechanisms "international secondary soft law"; see Shelton 1997.

64 For a general discussion of these mechanisms, see Tardu 1980. For a case study that provides some evidence that debate and resolutions adopted by the Human Rights Commission under these procedures has had some influence on China, see Kent 1999.

65 Description on the Web page of the Office of the High Commissioner for Human Rights: http://www2.ohchr.org/english/issues/torture/rapporteur/visits.htm (accessed 30 June 2008).

at torture as defined by the CAT. The special rapporteur meets with government officials, representatives of NGOs, and alleged victims and their families and writes a report "intended to assist Governments in identifying factors which may contribute to torture, and provide practical solutions to implement international standards," according to the UNHCHR.[66] Since these visits are at least nominally voluntary, they are not especially adversarial in nature. The reports are nonbinding. The special rapporteur generally (though not always) follows up within five years of the initial visit. The special rapporteur for torture has investigated some 26 countries since its establishment in 1985. Cases in which individual countries are mentioned by name in a UNGA resolution for human rights abuses, 1503 investigations, and special rapporteur visits are listed in Appendix 7.1, posted on my Web site.

Finally, I control for a country's developmental level, as measured by its GDP per capita, the size of its population (a large population could explain Amnesty International's ability to tally up large numbers of torture cases), and average regional trends (average torture score in the region in the previous period). Regional practices are considered an important influence on the pervasiveness of torture. To some extent, this variable controls for commonly shared values within a region. But it may also reflect a high degree of social influence, as nearby governments can have a crucial effect on a country's own practices.

STATISTICAL FINDINGS

Partially Democratic/Transition Regimes

The first point that these analyses confirm is that committing one's state to honor the CAT does not have a positive effect on torture practices in all kinds of regimes. *The CAT does not have unconditional effects.*[67] In fact, in a lightly controlled model (Table 7.2, Model 1), the CAT appears to be mildly *negative* (though not significantly so). But if ratifying the CAT appears to have no positive effect across the board, it does seem to have important effects *under certain political conditions.* Whereas we might not expect a CAT commitment to have much of an effect in a stable democracy – with well-developed and highly stable channels of political accountability – and while it may not be realistic to expect an international legal obligation to matter much in a polity that has never experienced any degree of political accountability, we can test the proposition that *ratifying the CAT helps significantly to reduce torture in polities with some experience with or prospect for a degree of political accountability.* These are

---

66 http://www2.ohchr.org/english/issues/torture/rapporteur/visits.htm (accessed 30 June 2008).
 For a general discussion of the role of UN special rapporteurs, see Rodley 1986; Weissbrodt 1986.
67 This confirms the reported findings in Hathaway 2002.

Table 7.2. Effects of a CAT Commitment on the Prevalence of Torture

Dependent variable: torture prevalence (see Table 7.1)
Instrumental variable least squares regression
Coefficients, probabilities based on robust standard errors

Explanatory Variables	Model 1: All Countries, Basic Model	Model 2: All Countries, Controls	Model 3: Partial/Transitional Regimes, Basic Model	Model 4: Partial/Transitional Regimes, Controls	Model 5: Stable Democracies, Controls	Model 6: Never Democratic, Controls
CAT commitment	−.034 (p = .698)	.180 (p = .328)	.282** (p = .039)	.395* (p = .060)	.237 (p = .814)	.003 (p = .990)
Torture prevalence, $t − 1$	.371*** (p = .000)	.338*** (p = .000)	.343*** (p = .000)	.331*** (p = .000)	.376*** (p = .000)	.300*** (p = .000)
Year	−.023*** (p = .001)	−.011 (p = .646)	−.037*** (p = .004)	−.031 (p = .475)	.023 (p = .669)	−.028 (p = .319)
Truth commission, $t − 3$	.184* (p = .090)	.183 (p = .125)	.167* (p = .059)	.154 (p = .109)	.131 (p = .550)	.139 (p = .680)
Free press	.204*** (p = .000)	.210*** (p = .000)	.178*** (p = .006)	.165** (p = .016)	.256 (p = .284)	−.330*** (p = .003)
Rule of law	.357*** (p = .000)	.000 (p = 1.00)	.425*** (p = .000)	.145 (p = .913)	1.07 (p = .696)	1.21 (p = .518)
Religious fractionalization	−2.74*** (p = .000)	.459 (p = .946)	−.673*** (p = .000)	1.17 (p = .802)	10.88 (p = .633)	−2.13 (p = .484)
GDP per capita, logged	.278** (p = .018)	.189 (p = .207)	—	.054 (p = .888)	−.286 (p = .767)	.241 (p = .159)
Preferential trade agreements, with HR provisions	—	.005 (p = .768)	.040 (p = .645)	−.017 (p = .605)	−.002 (p = .940)	.032 (p = .259)
Article 22 declaration	—	−.578 (p = .397)	—	−.458 (p = .580)	−.686 (p = .640)	−1.74 (p = .212)

Average regional torture prevalence	.161 (p = .143)	—	.142 (p = .537)	.328 (p = .232)	.131 (p = .459)
Democracy	-.004 (p = .776)	—	-.004 (p = .829)	-.052 (p = .750)	-.009 (p = .709)
PTAs with hard HR conditions	-.009 (p = .898)	—	.117 (p = .377)	-.198 (p = .323)	.166 (p = .173)
Overseas development assistance/GDP	.475 (p = .195)	—	.988 (p = .227)	-3.01 (p = .473)	.555 (p = .214)
Civil war	-.117 (p = .256)	—	-.078 (p = .666)	-.291 (p = .334)	-.099 (p = .453)
Interstate war	-.177 (p = .261)	—	-.100 (p = .635)	.223** (p = .026)	-.475* (p = .083)
Death penalty	.048 (p = .322)	—	.041 (p = .609)	.048 (p = .683)	.220*** (p = .002)
Federalism	.039 (p = .377)	—	.004 (p = .957)	.298 (p = .175)	-.035 (p = .546)
Total population, logged	-.284 (p = .731)	—	.000 (p = 1.000)	-1.26 (p = .615)	.508 (p = .523)
UN 1503 investigation, t − 3	-.024 (p = .764)	—	.045 (p = .625)	-.162 (p = .676)	.034 (p = .795)
UNGA HR resolution, t − 3	.126 (p = .400)	—	.035 (p = .899)	.074 (p = .751)	.227* (p = .092)
Visit, special rapporteur on torture, t − 2	-.067 (p = .660)	—	-.055 (p = .791)	—	-.058 (p = .757)
Country fixed effects?	yes	yes	yes	yes	yes
Year fixed effects?	yes	yes	yes	yes	yes
# of observations	2,228	795	766	448	857
R^2	.71	.71	.68	.72	.71

Instrumented variables: CAT commitment and CAT Article 22 commitment (where included). Instruments: common law heritage, average regional CAT commitment, and two splines (all lagged one period).

* Significant at the .10 level; ** significant at the .05 level; *** significant at the .01 level.

the regimes in which domestic groups and stakeholders have both the motive and the means to organize to demand compliance with the CAT.

The tests reported in Table 7.2 suggest that the CAT may indeed have an important impact on the severity of torture practices for countries with only moderately accountable institutions. Table 7.2 shows there is practically no influence of ratifying the CAT in stable democracies (those *never below* 8 on the polity scale since World War II; Model 5) and countries that have never been democratic (Model 6). It is fairly clear that ratifying the CAT does not help much in stable democracies or stable autocracies. For the most part, there is no significant difference within these categories between ratifiers and nonratifiers.[68] In fact, for countries that have never been democratic, the model with a full set of controls suggests that ratification likely has no effect whatsoever. Evidently, these are the governments most likely to believe that they can ratify the CAT strategically.

The results for countries in transition provide a sharp contrast. For these countries, it is fairly clear that those that ratify the CAT are much more likely to improve their practices (reduce their incidence of torture) than transitional countries that do not. Statistically speaking, we can be fairly confident (about 94 percent confident) that among transitional countries, CAT ratifiers' practices become much better than those of nonratifiers. Ratification of the CAT is associated with almost a 40 percent increase in the likelihood that a country will improve by one category on the torture scale. Among the control variables, the only consistent explanation appears to be the importance of information, as indicated by the strong positive effect of a relatively free press. The use of truth commissions may also be associated with future reductions in the use of torture, increasing the chances of moving from one category on the scale by about 15 percent. Surprisingly, neither international nor civil wars mattered significantly in these specifications for the transition countries. Nor did any of the UN mechanisms have much impact in these countries.

Partially Democratic Regimes and Regional Mechanisms

The CAT is not the only agreement designed to prohibit torture; three regional agreements contain similar provisions. The Inter-American Convention to Prevent and Punish Torture (IACPPT)[69] was adopted in 1985 and

---

68 It is important to note, though, that stable democracies still tend to be at the very good end of the torture scale: about 85% of stable democracies' torture observations were in the top two categories. Among stable democracies, not a single observation fell in the worst category. Lithuania, Jamaica, and Israel were the only stable democracies to have had more than one observation in the second to the lowest category. Neither Lithuania nor Jamaica had ratified the CAT; Israel, on the other hand, had.

69 OAS Treaty Series No. 67, *entered into force* 28 February 1987; *reprinted in* Basic Documents Pertaining to Human Rights in the Inter-American System, OEA/Ser.L.V/II.82 doc.6 rev.1 at 83 (1992); available online at http://www1.umn.edu/humanrts/oasinstr/zoas9tor.htm.

entered into force in 1987. Sixteen of 34 members of the Organization of American States (OAS) have ratified and deposited their instruments of ratification with the OAS.[70] The convention is similar to the CAT in many ways: It defines torture in similar terms,[71] it prohibits torture by public servants or with their acquiescence,[72] and it allows no justifications.[73] The IACPPT does not create a specific oversight committee, as does the CAT, but rather requires the state parties to inform the Inter-American Commission on Human Rights of their implementation progress, and for the commission to review and analyze that progress in its annual report.[74] The IACPPT does not mention the Inter-American Court of Human Rights specifically, but it does provide that "After all the domestic legal procedures of the respective State and the corresponding appeals have been exhausted, the case may be submitted to the international fora whose competence has been recognized by that State."[75]

The European Convention for the Prevention of Torture and Inhuman or Degrading Treatment or Punishment,[76] which entered into force in February 1989, is the major international instrument prohibiting and monitoring torture in Europe. The treaty itself does not define torture. The major innovation is that this agreement provides for inspections, ensuring impartial medical review of the conditions of detainees.[77] The treaty obligates signatories to "permit visits, in accordance with this Convention, to any place within its jurisdiction where persons are deprived of their liberty by a public authority."[78] The findings of periodic visits are not generally made public, but the monitoring committee may decide to make its views public if it fails to get cooperation from a state party.[79] Parties can denounce the treaty by giving notification (none have), but reservations are not allowed.[80]

Africa does not have a treaty devoted exclusively to the prohibition and prevention of torture. However, the African [Banjul] Charter on Human and Peoples' Rights (ACHR),[81] adopted 27 June 1981, by members of the Organization

---

70 For ratification, see http://www.oas.org/juridico/english/Sigs/a-51.html (accessed 30 June 2008).
71 Although the coverage of the Inter-American Convention is somewhat broader, adding, "Torture shall also be understood to be the use of methods upon a person intended to obliterate the personality of the victim or to diminish his physical or mental capacities, even if they do not cause physical pain or mental anguish" (Article 2).
72 IACPPT, Article 3.
73 IACPPT, Article 5.
74 IACPPT, Article 17.
75 IACPPT, Article 8, para. 3.
76 E.T.S. 126. Text of the European Torture Convention can be found at http://www1.umn.edu/humanrts/euro/z34eurotort.html (accessed 30 June 2008).
77 For a discussion, see Harding 1989. For a generally positive assessment of the inspection regime, see Evans and Morgan 1997.
78 European Torture Convention Article 2.
79 European Torture Convention Article 10.
80 European Torture Convention Articles 21 and 22.
81 OAU Doc. CAB/LEG/67/3 rev. 5, 21 I.L.M. 58 (1982). Excerpts of the text can be found at http://www1.umn.edu/humanrts/instree/z1afchar.htm (accessed 30 June 2008).

for African Unity (OAU), does prohibit torture in general terms: "All forms of exploitation and degradation of man, particularly slavery, slave trade, torture, cruel, inhuman or degrading punishment and treatment shall be prohibited."[82] The charter creates a commission[83] to which state parties are required to report every two years.[84]

If regional agreements have the same kinds of effects as do international agreements prohibiting torture, we should expect to see patterns similar to those we saw with respect to the CAT: In highly accountable but stable states, these agreements should be expected to be redundant; in unaccountable stable states they should be irrelevant. But once again, when states have some degree of regime accountability, these regional treaties should be expected to provide a degree of protection against torture that clearly repressive and clearly democratic polities do not enjoy.

Table 7.3 reports on the effects of these regional agreements. Because we are using subsets of the data regionally, it is not feasible to perform the tests used earlier on distinct subsets of regime types; the number of observations would be too small. In this case, tests were performed by region, interacting treaty ratification with the transitional regime category. Similar controls were used as in the previous tests, but for simplicity of presentation they are not reported here. The first thing to notice in these cases is that ratifying a regional human rights agreement in stable countries is generally associated with a negative coefficient. Certainly, there are plenty of countries that sign regional conventions to prevent torture whose practices actually *deteriorate* with ratification. It is also interesting to note, however, that in every case the coefficient for transitional countries that have not signed is always much more negative than that of the transitional countries that have committed to a regional torture agreement. As the bottom four lines of the table show, the difference is statistically significant. Model 2, which endogenizes *any* regional treaty ratification itself and includes fixed country and regional effects, reinforces the point. Transitional countries that had ratified any one of these three regional treaties were much more likely to improve their torture practices than transitional countries that had not, controlling for statistically significant factors included in Table 7.2. The difference between ratifiers and nonratiferiers in these countries is statistically distinguishable with more than 95 percent certainty ($p = .049$).

It is natural to wonder, what drives the "transitional" result: the fact that the country is partially democratic, and thus individuals and groups have both the motives and the means to demand greater respect and protection from their government? Or is it that they are unstable, and treaties – especially treaties

---

82 African [Banjul] Charter Article 5.
83 On the operation of the African Commission for Human Rights, see Ankumah 1996; Evans and Murray 2002.
84 African [Banjul] Charter Article 62.

Table 7.3. Effect of Regional Torture Conventions on Torture Prevalence in Transitional Countries

Dependent variable: torture prevalence
Instrumental variable least squares regression
Coefficients, probabilities based on robust standard errors

Explanatory Variable	Model 1 (endogenizes CAT ratification)		Model 2 (endogenizes regional ratification)	
CAT commitment	−.274	($p = .371$)	—	
Transitional/partial democracies	−.678***	($p = .004$)	—	
CAT commitment for transitional/partial democracies	−.089	($p = .498$)	—	
European CPT	−.064	($p = .665$)	—	
European CPT commitment for transitional/partial democracies	.344	($p = .530$)	—	
African Charter commitment	−.142	($p = .433$)	—	
ACHR commitment for transitional/partial democracies	.185	($p = .464$)	—	
Inter-American CPT	−.217	($p = .391$)	—	
IACPPT commitment for transitional/partial democracies	.860	($p = .124$)	—	
Any regional commitment	—		−1.03***	($p = .006$)
Any regional commitment for transitional/partial democracies	—		1.60**	($p = .023$)
Pseudo R^2	.687		.663	
# of observations	2,442		2,462	

Probability that transitional countries that have signed the following agreements have the same propensity to torture as other transitional countries

CAT	$p < 0.069$	—
European convention	$p < 0.034$	—
African Charter	$p < 0.0005$	—
Inter-American convention	$p < 0.006$	—
Any regional convention	—	$p < .049$
# of observations	2,242	2,462
R^2	.687	.687

Note: Each regression contains all control variables listed in Table 7.2 (basic model). For brevity, results on the controls are not reported here. Model 2 contains both country and regional fixed effects.
** Significant at the .05 level; *** significant at the .01 level.

guaranteeing a right not to be tortured – are a way to stabilize antitorture norms? In order to get at the mechanism involved, we can implement two further tests. The first tests for the hypothesis that the CAT has most traction under moderate levels of democratic accountability. I created an interaction term for moderate levels of democracy and interacted it with CAT ratification.[85] Moderate democracies thus defined were much more likely to improve their torture practices than moderate democracies without such a commitment ($p = .074$, using the basic set of controls in Table 7.2). The same relationship did not hold for either full democracies or full autocracies. On the other hand, there was no systematic difference in the effect of ratification between countries that were more volatile (as measured by the standard deviation of their polity score) and those that were relatively stable.[86]

The Courts: Possibilities for Litigation

The data suggest – they of course do not prove – that when a government makes a formal and public commitment to abide by the provisions of the CAT, under certain conditions it is likely to do so. The conditions under which CAT ratification was most likely to affect actual practices were conditions of partial democratization. I have theorized that these are the conditions under which groups and individuals have both the motive and the means to mobilize to demand that their rights be respected.

A second mechanism discussed in Chapter 4 was litigation. Treaties are law in most countries; as such, they are available at least in theory as a way to make a legal case against practices state agents use to hold "dangerous" persons while in custody. This should be true, however, only if a country's courts are not a sham. If they are politically controlled by the government, no citizen or activist would consider it worthwhile to launch a case to try to get the CAT enforced against a brutal government able to pull all judicial strings.

It is possible to test for the plausibility of litigation as a mechanism by examining the relationship between CAT ratification, torture practices, and judicial independence. The proxy used here for judicial independence is the same as that described in Chapter 6. It is a measure of the rule of law collected by the

---

85 For purposes of this test, moderate democracies are those years scoring between 3 and 8 on the polity scale, inclusive. Full autocracies are those that scored 1 or 2, and full democracies are those that scored 9 or 10.

86 Forty-six countries had no change whatsoever in their polity score during the time period under observation (1967–2002). Twenty-four of these were completely nondemocratic (perfectly stable 0 score) and 21 were completely stable democracies. Only one was at neither extreme: Singapore, with a perfectly stable score of 2. All other countries are assigned the standard deviation of their democracy score for the period as a whole. Spain, Portugal, Hungary, Poland, Uruguay, Mongolia, and The Gambia have experienced the greatest regime volatility by this measure. For tests that specifically address the question of regime volatility, see Appendix 7.2 on my Web site at http://scholar.iq.harvard.edu/bsimmons/mobilizing-for-human-rights.

World Bank broadly reflecting perceptions of the quality of judicial institutions as well as law and order in each country. While we should be cognizant of its weaknesses as a measure of judicial independence, this proxy provides one (noisy) cut at the question of whether the CAT is more likely to matter in countries where the courts are more likely to be respected.

A certain degree of judicial independence, competence, and credibility is necessary if the courts are to be a mechanism available for the enforcement of international treaty commitments. To be sure, countries with the most highly developed rule of law norms are unlikely to be among the worst torturers in the first place. If we see large improvements in torture practices in countries with the weakest court systems, we should seek the explanation outside of the court system itself. If the courts are an important enforcement mechanism, we should see the top tier and possibly the middle tier of high-scoring rule of law countries making improvements after ratification.[87]

Table 7.4 shows that ratification is associated with significant improvements in torture practices – but not universally. It uses an interaction term, as in Table 7.3, to determine the influence of ratifying the CAT conditional on whether a country's rule of law score is high, low, or somewhere in between.[88] Among countries with very weak legal systems, ratification makes no difference whatsoever (compare lines 4 and 5 in columns 5 and 6; the difference between these values is never significant). Similarly, there is not much difference within high rule of law countries between those that have ratified and those that have not (compare lines 2 and 5 in columns 1 and 2). In fact, if anything, it looks like nonratifiers have better torture records among high rule of law states than nonratifiers, but the relationship is inconsistent and not statistically reliable. The picture is very different among the mid-level set of countries (listed in the Data Appendix at the end of the book). Where the rule of law is reasonably well developed and the courts are fairly independent of governmental control, chances are good that CAT ratification has indeed served to improve practices on average and controlling for many other alternative explanations. In the basic model, the probability that ratifiers in this mid-level category perform better than nonratifiers is estimated with about 85 percent confidence. In the model with more controls, the probability of a positive difference is 98 percent ($p = .023$). As in the previous models, freedom of the press, per capita GDP, and preferential trade agreements were also associated with torture practices, but few of the other controls contribute anything to the explanation.

---

87 Kaufmann et al. 2008:10. See the description at http://papers.ssrn.com/sol3/papers.cfm?abstract_id=1148386.

88 There are 7,068 observations on the rule of law variable. The median score is −.022457; the standard deviation is .9665798; the minimum is −1.912 and the maximum is 2.138. For purposes of this analysis, "low" is defined as any country below −1 and "high" is defined as any country above 1. All other countries fall within the medium range.

Table 7.4. Effects of a CAT Commitment on the Prevalence of Torture Conditional on the Rule of Law

Dependent variable: torture prevalence
Instrumental variable least squares regression
Coefficients, probabilities based on robust standard errors

Explanatory Variable	Strong Rule of Law	Strong Rule of Law	Mid-Level Rule of Law	Mid-Level Rule of Law	Weak Rule of Law	Weak Rule of Law
CAT commitment for strong rule of law	-1.76 (p = .122)	-1.96* (p = .071)	—	—	—	—
CAT commitment for moderate rule of law	—	—	2.45* (p = .085)	2.52** (p = .049)	—	—
CAT commitment for weak rule of law	—	—	—	—	-7.81 (p = .227)	-.486 (p = .906)
CAT commitment in all other countries	.012 (p = .955)	.176 (p = .607)	-2.20* (p = .055)	-2.15** (p = .038)	.133 (p = .646)	-.367*** (p = .007)
No CAT commitment for rule of law type	-.384** (p = .027)	1.97 (p = .494)	-1.60 (p = .260)	-.793 (p = .200)	5.20 (p = .377)	2.18 (p = .670)
Torture prevalence, $t-1$	.373*** (p = .000)	3.59*** (p = .000)	.366*** (p = .000)	.355*** (p = .000)	.359*** (p = .000)	.363*** (p = .000)
Free press	.208*** (p = .000)	.188*** (p = .000)	.197*** (p = .000)	.181*** (p = .000)	.191*** (p = .000)	.217*** (p = .000)
GDP per capita, logged	.416*** (p = .002)	.435*** (p = .004)	—	.386** (p = .025)	—	.289 (p = .147)
Total preferential trade agreements	-.118*** (p = .000)	-.097*** (p = .003)	—	-.106*** (p = .005)	-.100** (p = .026)	-.094*** (p = .001)

Overseas development assistance/GDP	.159 (p = .609)	—	.232 (p = .486)	—	−.040 (p = .906)
Civil war (since 1968)	.013 (p = .987)	—	2.75 (p = .237)	—	1.28 (p = .430)
Interstate war	−.146 (p = .361)	—	−.145 (p = .382)	—	−.176 (p = .227)
Regional torture prevalence	.074 (p = .382)	—	.038 (p = .680)	—	.081 (p = .423)
Federalism	−.001 (p = .988)	—	−.040 (p = .542)	—	−.010 (p = .906)
Truth commission	.043 (p = .738)	—	.012 (p = .926)	—	.134 (p = .347)
Total population, logged	−.465 (p = .351)	—	−.553 (p = .296)	—	.250 (p = .462)
UN 1503 investigation	.069 (p = .324)	—	.036 (p = .690)	—	.042 (p = .697)
UNGA HR resolution	−.112 (p = .520)	—	−.093 (p = .599)	—	−.202 (p = .287)
Visit, special rapporteur on torture	−.065 (p = .750)	—	−.107 (p = .576)	—	−.038 (p = .858)
Country fixed effects?	yes	yes	yes	yes	yes
# of observations	2,187	2,187	2,149	2,332	2,149
R^2	.66	.65	.65	.49	.70

Instrumented variables: CAT commitment and CAT commitment*regime type. Instruments: common law heritage, average regional CAT commitment, and two splines (all lagged one period).

* Significant at the .10 level; ** significant at the .05 level; *** significant at the .01 level.

Thus, there may be some basis to conclude that the CAT has had an important impact on a considerable subset of countries in which stakeholders and other activists have the motive and the means to mobilize politically to demand compliance with the CAT and to use the CAT in domestic legal struggles over the meaning and use of torture. The following section discusses two examples of how this treaty became important in domestic law and politics, eventually contributing to the amelioration of torture practices on the part of government agents.

CHILE AND ISRAEL: EXPERIENCES WITH THE CAT

To illustrate the kinds of political and legal dynamics that could be behind the broad trends documented previously, it is useful to look at an example of how the CAT has made its way into domestic politics and litigation. The case of Chile illustrates the role that this convention can play in a partial or transitional democracy. First, it shows that human rights activists strategically deployed international legal norms to gain adherents and to strengthen the legitimacy of their opposition to Augusto Pinochet's military regime. However, they were hobbled in this early effort by a paucity of ratified treaties and the uselessness of litigation by a conservative, regime-controlled court system. Second, it illustrates that rights activists did want international legal commitments to bind their government. In fact, by the mid-1980s, several groups were specifically and publicly demanding CAT ratification – often at significant personal risk. Third, the CAT was highly relevant to local law development well into the transition period and beyond. Once the courts were reformed (circa 1997), and particularly once the CAT's power was demonstrated by the arrest and extradition of Pinochet himself, litigation involving the CAT grew significantly. Furthermore, there is some evidence that torture practices in Chile were ameliorated at around this time as well. Overall, the case is useful in suggesting the importance of both the mobilization and litigation mechanisms discussed earlier.

Israel, of course, is a fairly stable democracy, and activists were motivated almost immediately upon Israel's ratification to use the CAT to bolster court cases alleging the use of torture and to embarrass the government by pointing to the treaty as an authoritative statement regarding the definition and the unconditional prohibition of torture. Crucial here was the Committee Against Torture's official view that many of the practices used in detention did in fact constitute torture. Once the Supreme Court of Israel rendered its landmark decision (1999) incorporating this view, the ball was back in the Israeli politicians' court: They could choose to legalize those practices, but at the peril of making Israel the only country in the world to legalize torture. In both of these cases, the treaty was important in changing the way in which individuals held in government detention were treated.

Chile: Democratic Transition, Judicial Reform, and the Legal Empowerment of the CAT

Chile is a case in which the treaty's commitments interact with democratic transition and institutional reform. Despite a comparatively long history of democratic governance, Chile is a country whose recent past has been marred by widespread use of torture perpetrated by the military and sanctioned by the highest levels of government. In 1973, a military junta led by General Augusto Pinochet overthrew the government of Salvador Allende and ruthlessly rooted out – tortured and murdered – political opponents and sympathizers with the left. For most of its rule, Pinochet's junta was not formally constrained by international human rights treaties, although throughout the period his government was accused of grave breaches of customary international law related to crimes against humanity and serious human rights abuses. Yet, human rights organizers – and, significantly, the political opposition to the junta – drew to a considerable extent on international law norms and rhetoric to legitimate demands for an end to human rights abuses and torture. The junta ratified the CAT in 1988 – just before the election in which Pinochet would lose his official grasp on government. Not only would the CAT be the legal instrument responsible for Pinochet's extradition to face torture charges, it would also inspire litigation in Chilean courts that would cumulatively contribute to significant improvements in Chilean law and ultimately practice. Torture has not been eradicated from the country, but the CAT has been very useful in bringing attention to the problem, reducing the overt reliance on "states of exception," and reducing torturers' calculations that they will escape responsibility for their actions through amnesty, statutes of limitations, or protection in sympathetic military courts.

The domestic opposition to the repressive tactics of the junta, whose goal was to crush socialism, was led by the moral authority of the outspoken Catholic Church. The church early on had a legal strategy for responding to the crushing repression of Pinochet's military dictatorship.[89] As early as October 1973, a religious-cum-legal alliance against the repression developed under the coleadership of Catholic and Lutheran bishops. They founded the Cooperative Committee for Peace in Chile (COPACHI), which focused initially on providing legal defense in the courts-martial cases as well as in cases of political firings. Expanding from a mere 8 employees to over 100 less than a year after its founding, COPACHI began to investigate a broad range of rights violations. By 1974, when a Mexican newspaper reported that COPACHI was keeping records on fundamental human rights violations,

---

89 The Catholic Church in Chile's role in defending human rights deserves much more attention than can be devoted to it in these pages. In Mara Loveman's words, "The Church as an institution provided a 'moral shield' for human rights work through its domestic influence as a source of legitimacy and its international symbolic, moral, and political weight" (1998:494).

the organization was viewed by the government as in a threatening alliance with the political opposition. That year, COPACHI filed some 1,568 habeas corpus petitions on behalf of persons held in government detention, with the intent of both documenting these cases and delegitimating the government's practices. COPACHI personnel defended the actions of former government officials as nontreasonous and the tensions in Chile as normal political opposition rather than a "state of war."[90] In these ways, COPACHI opposed the junta's most extreme forms of repression and cultivated a counterargument in favor of democratic values.

This legal strategy had little immediate effect within Chile[91] – none of the writs for habeas corpus were successful – but it did serve a broader political purpose: It publicized government violations to both domestic and international audiences. Indeed, Chilean lawyers who participated in the legal work of COPACHI viewed themselves as part of a broader international legal culture, from which they drew inspiration and to which they wished to appeal for further support. According to Rosemarie Bornard, a lawyer associated with COPACHI from its earliest days, "The conception that we lawyers had was that we formed part of an international community . . . we believed that we were part of an international community founded on law. So it was something very natural that we would look to the international arena for help."[92]

This is precisely what COPACHI (disbanded on the orders of Pinochet in 1975) and its successor organization, the Vicariate of Solidarity,[93] did. With data gathered for domestic trials and petitions, by 1979 these organizations had filed an estimated 1,720 petitions to international organizations on behalf of 1,928 individuals missing or held in detention.[94] In the 1970s, however, the international human rights regime was far less developed than it would become toward century's end. To be sure, the UDHR was available, and human rights organizations in Chile made reference to its norms on a regular basis. But in Chile, the status of the ICCPR was contested. ICCPR ratification was one of the last actions taken by Allende's regime before its overthrow. The UN records the date of Chile's ratification as 1972, but the position of the junta was that it had

---

90 Fruhling and Woodbridge 1983:518.
91 The established legal community was in general a very weak voice against the activities of the early junta. An Amnesty International official met with the Chilean Bar Association late in 1973 and didn't seem serious about identifying prisoners. Nor could Amnesty International find allies on the Supreme Court – whose chief justice denied in 1974 that significant human rights violations were going on. See the discussion in Ensalaco 2000:107.
92 Quoted by Hawkins 2002:56.
93 The Vicariate of Solidarity, founded in 1976 under the protection of the Archdiocese of Santiago, played a key role by attempting to record and provide legal services for persons and families of persons detained by the regime. The vicariate itself was made up predominantly of lawyers, social workers, and administrative staff – numbering some 200 persons at its height – and filed thousands of habeas corpus briefs on behalf of political prisoners over the course of its work. For a comprehensive treatment, see Lowden 1996.
94 Hawkins 2002:57.

never been implemented in Chilean law and therefore was not a legally constraining document. Furthermore, the CAT did not exist when Pinochet came to power, though some accounts credit the widespread torture and disappearance under his rule with provoking the international community to address torture specifically. The international legal and institutional environment for human rights was fairly thin in the mid-1970s; still, rights groups appealed to an international audience to apply pressure directly on the Chilean government, as described well by Margaret Keck and Kathryn Sikkink.[95]

That Chile had ratified and implemented in domestic law few international human rights treaties was legally beside the point anyway, since during Pinochet's dictatorship the courts were hardly independent of the government and were largely sympathetic to right-wing ideologies. "During the first seven and a half years of authoritarian rule," according to a recent study by Lisa Hilbink, "the decisions of Chile's high courts overwhelmingly favored the perspectives and policies of the regime's leadership."[96] This is certainly borne out in the crushing defeat most efforts to gain legal attention to rights met in Chile's courts at the time: Of the 2,342 habeas corpus petitions eventually filed by the Vicariate, only 3 succeeded. Most met with convoluted constitutional arguments for rejection.[97] Some scholars have gone even further to suggest that Chile's courts facilitated the authoritarian takeover and consolidation by providing a legal patina for a regime desperate to be perceived as legitimate.[98]

International law could hardly work through a litigation mechanism under these circumstances, but it was not irrelevant to the unfolding of politics in Chile in the latter 1970s. Though no member of the opposition could point to a ratified treaty and claim that the regime had made a legal commitment to live up to international standards for the protection of life and liberty, the UDHR did help to frame the orientation of opposition groups as they groped to articulate principled and programmatic opposition to Pinochet. The year 1978 marked an important turning point in this regard. That year, the Grupo de Estudios Constitucionalistas, or Group of 24, was formed, headed by Patricio Aylwin, who would become Chile's first transitional president of the 1990s. One of the Grupo's most salient member parties, the Christian Democratic Party, began to formulate *Proyecto Alternativo*, or Alternative Project, which recognized as its inspiration the humanism of the UDHR.[99] Despite the fact that specific treaties were not available to support litigation, international human rights law informed the alternative philosophy on which the opposition could begin to build its political alternative to the junta. And there is some evidence

95 Keck and Sikkink 1998.
96 Hilbink 2007:129.
97 Lowden 1996:42.
98 Lowden 1996:30. For a discussion of the split in the legal profession more broadly, see Ensalaco 2000:122–3.
99 Brito 1997:118.

that these ideas were hard to resist. The human rights challenges posed by the newly organizing political opposition – as well as pressure from the public at large and the international community – did encourage the regime to take some liberalizing decisions in 1978.[100] Local liberalization provided further incentives to step up rights demands. As time went on, the opposition became more organized. While few if any human rights organizations existed in Chile before September 1973, by 1985 some 15 local and transnational groups were active.[101]

The Sebastian Acevedo Movement Against Torture was one of the first groups to organize antitorture demonstrations publicly.[102] Demonstrators spearheaded by the Acevedo Movement used international legal instruments to focus their demands for human rights protections just as soon as these were available. In parallel with the UN debate and adoption of the CAT, local activists fastened on torture as the specific focus of their protest. In December 1983, "A peaceful demonstration against torture held by laymen and religious persons" was reported by local radio to have been violently repressed in Santiago. Demonstrators "chant[ed] and pray[ed] . . . demanding an end to torture." They "presented a declaration stating that everyone knows that the CNI [National Information Center] illegally detains persons, . . . and tortures them."[103] According to reports, "pedestrians spontaneously joined the demonstrators in their demand to end torture." *Carabineros* – the uniformed Chilean national police force – responded violently to this and other demonstrations focused on detentions and torture by the CNI. On 29 May 1984, *carabineros* beat antitorture demonstrators, "who were marching in silence . . . against any type of physical and harmful torture."[104] The Sebastian Acevedo Movement Against Torture staged a series of short, spontaneous demonstrations, displaying signs reading "Yes to Life; No to Torture."[105] In August 1984, 100 demonstrators from the Sebastian Acevedo Movement Against Torture demonstrated, reading an open letter addressed to Interior Minister Sergio Onofre Jarpa urging him to publicly state his opposition to torture.[106] Calls by the Alliance for Democracy for the

---

100 Karen DeYoung and John Dinges, "Chile Takes Steps to Liberalize Rule; Chilean Junta Edges Toward More Liberal Government; U.S. Probe in Letelier Death a Catalyst." *The Washington Post,* 17 April 1978.
101 Ensalaco 2000:59.
102 Cleary 1997:15.
103 "Torture Demonstrations 'Violently Repressed,'" Santiago Radio Cooperativa, 14 December 1983; FBIS PY142234. See also "Denunciations of Torture Gain Strength," Paris, AFP; 14 December 1983; FBIS PY160125.
104 "Carabineros 'Beat' Anti-Torture Demonstrators," Santiago Radio Cooperativa, 29 May 1984. FBIS PY292225. See also "Relatives of Missing Detainees March in Santiago," Santiago Radio Cooperativa, 23 May 1984. FBIS PY240242; and "Catholic Episcopate Calls for Halt to Torture," Madrid EFE, 25 April 1985. FFBIS PY260345.
105 "Santiago Demonstration Protests Torture," Santiago Radio Cooperativa, 19 July 1984. FBIS PY1912115.
106 "Demonstrators Protest Torture Near La Moneda," Paris, AFP. 22 August 1984. PY230242. On the significance of the Acevedo movement for Chile's position on torture, see Hawkins 2002:ch. 5.

intervention of the judicial branch to investigate allegations of torture went unheeded.

Activists continued to appeal to whatever international legal instruments were available to them to oppose civil rights violations and brutal treatment by government agents. Almost every December in the 1980s, activists from several rights organizations demonstrated in Santiago to commemorate the anniversary of the UDHR, reading the charter aloud in public and demanding the government's adherence.[107] The Chilean Human Rights Committee, presided over by lawyer Jaime Castillo Velasco, openly criticized the government's decision to banish opponents to Pisagua, a town located 1,900 kilometers north of Santiago, as a violation of "Articles 1 through 13, particularly No. 6, of the Universal Declaration on Human Rights by which every individual has the right to be recognized as a human being with legal rights."[108] The Chilean Human Rights Commission tried to use the ICCPR to argue before the Supreme Court of Chile that the "war councils," which were set up in October 1981 to try "subversives" (especially members of the Movement of the Revolutionary Left, or MIR), violated international law.[109] Their petition was rejected, as was virtually every legal appeal to enforce national and international human rights law during the 1980s and early 1990s.

Human rights laws, whether domestic or international, continued to have no traction in the 1980s because Chilean courts remained under the political influence of the junta. On the few occasions in which courts did try to exert some independent influence, they were ignored by security agencies and other government agents.[110] The courts typically stonewalled legal cases demanding human rights accountability on the part of the government, and when prisoners' family members and others protested, they themselves were sometimes incarcerated.[111] The courts took no action when extralegal banishments took place.[112]

---

107 "Demonstrations Mark Human Rights Day in Santiago," Porto Alegre Radio Guiaba, FBIS PY110149. See also "Human Rights Demonstration Prompts Arrest," Santiago Radio Chilena, 10 December 1985. FBIS PY110135.

108 "Rights Group Condemns 'Reeducation' of Arrested," Santiago Radio Chilena, 31 January 1985. FBIS PY010202.

109 "Chile: Human Rights Commission Objects to 'War Councils,'" IPS-Inter Press Service, 22 February 1985.

110 See the criticism of the judiciary by Archbishop of Santiago Monsignor Juan Francisco Fresno in "Archbishop Reports Human Rights Violation," Santiago Radio Cooperativa, 26 November 1983; translated by FBIS PY262203.

111 In 1985, the Solidarity Vicariate of the Santiago archbishopric requested the Supreme Court of Justice to appoint a judge to investigate the arrest and disappearance of persons between August 1975 and 1976. When relatives of missing persons tried to enter the Court of Justice to express their frustration with the disregard of their request to appoint a special judge to investigate 14 cases of persons who had disappeared between 1975 and 1976, they were themselves arrested. See "Church Requests Investigation of Missing People," Madrid, EFE, 2 January 1985. FBIS PY031315; and "18 Arrested at Court of Justice Building," Santiago Radio Chilena, 10 January 1985. FBIS PY110232.

112 According to the Chilean Human Rights Commission, a total of 127 people were banished to various parts of the country in 1983, yet only 2 of them had been sentenced by the courts. "Rights Group Reports on 1983 Banishments." Madrid EFE, 11 January 1984. FBIS PY111440.

Unsurprisingly, thousands of cases were deterred because litigants anticipated ineffectiveness, inefficiency, or outright reprisals.[113] Several scholars have come to the conclusion that the courts were "structurally incapable of bringing justice to the victims of Pinochet's terror."[114]

But in response to growing internal as well as external demands, the junta (whose members had some important disagreements among themselves regarding how much to concede to human rights groups and the political opposition) did make some gestures toward rights protection. In June 1986, the government created a human rights advisory committee, to be comprised of clergy, lawyers, medical personnel, and military officers, as a step "to pave the way for transition."[115] Pressure began to mount to take action on the new CAT as well. In June 1985, the Sebastian Acevedo Movement Against Torture held "hit-and-run" demonstrations with a massive banner that read, "Why doesn't Chile sign the international Convention Against Torture?" The demonstrators demanded that government authorities explain why Chile had not signed the CAT, which radio commentators announced allows "neither exceptions nor orders . . . [to] justify torture. It also establishes that a torturer can be punished in a foreign country."[116] The CAT therefore offered two things that antitorture activists viewed as very valuable: a legal norm calling for the end to detainment practices that could be "justified" under emergency decree powers (states of exception, states of war) and the potential for torturers to be tried in foreign courts. Both of these aspects of the CAT would become crucial as Chile reformed its courts in the 1990s.

For reasons that scholars have not yet been able to document convincingly, Chile finally did ratify the CAT in September 1988. General Pinochet himself signed the instrument of ratification. Three important reservations were entered upon ratification: that the convention would not be enacted until after 11 March 1990; that it would not be applied retroactively; and that Chile did not recognize the commission's jurisdiction over its internal affairs. Spain and other countries formally objected to these reservations, complaining that they were contrary to the objectives and intention of the international agreement.

Why did a regime infamous for the torture of detainees ratify a convention that bars these practices under all circumstances? No scholar has yet analyzed the ratification specifically, but Darren Hawkins's research implies that it may

---

113   Chilean human rights groups such as CODEPU did try to use judicial intervention on behalf of victims but were quite convinced that judicial institutions were incapable of carrying out justice. See (Chile) 1996:ch. 7. The Chilean Human Rights Commission held that ". . . there are thousands of other cases that have not been submitted to the courts because of legal procedural reasons, because there are no guarantees on the results, or because of fear of reprisals." See "CCDH Report Denounces Human Rights Violations." Madrid EFE, 13 May 1986. FBIS PY141432.

114   Webber 1999:530. See also Ensalaco 2000:222; Hilbink 2007:156.

115   "Human Rights Commission Seen as Part of Transition." Santiago Domestic Service, 27 June 1986. FBIS PY271332.

116   "Anti-Torture Movement Holds Demonstration." Santiago Radio Cooperativa, 20 June 1985. FBIS PY202209.

have been yet another legitimacy-seeking tactic by a junta that was in any case split on how much to concede to its political opposition.[117] The government's public justification was that ratification merely reflected its long-term commitment to human rights. According to the presidential secretary, the decision was "consistent with the principles of the government, maintaining an unchanged policy of preventing and punishing those illegal actions, and with preserving the Constitution and the law."[118] Coming only weeks before the national plebiscite that would determine whether Pinochet would remain in power another eight years, there is a good chance that ratification was a tactic (ultimately unsuccessful) to gain electoral support.[119] Furthermore, the government may have thought that its treaty reservations as well as the national amnesty laws would protect any government or military officials from being held accountable. In any event, at the time – and with attention on the upcoming plebiscite on renewing Pinochet's term as president and passage of the constitution – little was made of the ratification. It merits one factual line in most treatments of Chile's human rights history and its transition to democracy.[120]

It is probably safe to infer that Pinochet's government ratified the CAT anticipating that it would pose no serious threat to his freedom or his mode of governance. If so, his miscalculation began with the results of the plebiscite itself. Despite harassment of the opposition and attacks on the critical media, on 5 October 1988, Pinochet lost the national plebiscite, with nearly 55 percent of Chilean voters rejecting his plan to remain in power. Within weeks, the opposition coalesced around Patricio Aylwin as its candidate for the coming year's presidential elections.

Aylwin was among the leaders of the opposition that as early as 1978 had explicitly built their vision of Chilean political life around the UDHR. The UDHR was integrated into the opposition coalition's platform and represented a clear break with Chile's compromised rights practices.[121] The opposition party proposed several key judicial reforms meant to protect the rights of the detained, including the jurisdiction of ordinary courts in human rights cases,

117 Hawkins 2002:4–5.
118 "Chile: Pinochet Signs OAS and UN Conventions on Torture," BBC Summary of World Broadcasts, 17 September 1988, part 4.
119 This was the view of the Chilean Human Rights Commission, as reported by Shirley Christian. "Violent Scenes as Torture Is Banned," *Sydney Morning Herald* (Australia); source: *New York Times*, 17 September 1988.
120 America's Watch, for example, reported the ratification with practically no comment (U.S.) 1988:106. Five years later, even the 1993 Report of the Chilean National Commission on Truth and Reconciliation neglected to mention that Chile had ratified the CAT in 1988. There is a section on "Norms, Concepts and Criteria" in which torture is mentioned, but the UDHR is the only human rights document cited. The only section that mentions anything Chile has ratified is that on "Laws of War or International Humanitarian Law," referring to Chile's ratification of the 1949 Geneva Conventions. See Berryman 1993:27–9. One reason might be that the CAT requires prosecution, which is not the purpose or strategy of the Truth and Reconciliation Commission.
121 Brito 1997:110.

amnesty for political prisoners, and pardons for those who had not committed blood crimes. They also proposed that ratified international human rights treaties be raised to the status of constitutional law in Chile.[122] In 1989, one of the 54 constitutional changes introduced by the opposition added a line to Article 5 making it a duty of the state to respect and promote the human rights guaranteed by the constitution and by international treaties ratified by Chile.[123] On 30 July 1989, these constitutional reforms were approved by a whopping 85.7 percent of the Chilean electorate.[124]

The electoral success of the opposition did not make the democratic transition easy or human rights unquestionably secure. After all that dissidents had endured, Pinochet was still quite popular in Chile: He had won about 40 percent of the recent vote, and the political right still held the balance of power in the legislature. Moreover, the opposition was faced with an essentially hostile judiciary; the Supreme Court, in particular, was sympathetic to right-wing ideology and to the goals if not all of the methods of the military government.[125] Despite reforms, the new constitution consolidated the authoritarian character of the Supreme Court and continued to protect the independence of the military.[126] One of Pinochet's parting decrees specifically disbarred Juez Rene Garcia Villegas, a prominent human rights judge, from the bench.[127] Despite a frustrating effort to reform the courts further in 1991, they remained extraordinarily conservative and hierarchical, and consistently refused to hear cases or to rule for accountability of those accused of torture.[128]

Several rulings in the 1990s illustrate the refusal of the Supreme Court to alter fundamentally their perspective on accountability for torture. They upheld the national amnesty law, finding that while international treaties had constitutional status in Chilean law, they could not be applied retroactively to extinguish national amnesty protections. Similarly, during the first half of the 1990s, the court refused to allow civilian courts to handle cases accusing military officers, which afforded them the protection of "in-house" military justice. Finally, the court almost always interpreted the national amnesty law as preventing the prosecution of crimes under international law. These positions made it almost impossible for many years to hold perpetrators of torture responsible for their acts.

The watershed year for the litigation of torture cases was 1998. In 1997, the Eduardo Frei government moved to propose and implement a number of reforms, and important shifts in the nature of court decisions began to surface

---

122   Brito 1997:120.
123   Hilbink 2007:179–80, fn 6.
124   Brito 1997:102.
125   Brito 1997:108.
126   Brito 1997:102.
127   Brito 1997:106; Ensalaco 2000:222.
128   Hilbink 2007:181–2.

in a very short time.[129] Most importantly, General Pinochet was arrested in London in 1998 while on a fleeting visit there. He was arrested and held, ironically, only because Chile had in 1988 ratified the CAT, which required either the prosecution or the extradition of alleged torturers to jurisdictions willing to prosecute. As a result of judicial reform and the example of the extraordinary reach of the CAT, litigation in Chilean courts began to change drastically. The number of cases alleging or in some way related to torture increased significantly.[130] Torture cases began appearing in much greater numbers in the Supreme Court and the Appeals Court of Santiago by 2003. In many more cases, the courts are relying on the CAT to make decisions. These trends are clear in Figure 7.2.

Not all cases mention the CAT, but this is because a significant number are about jurisdiction within Chile. The question these cases raised was that of the proper legal venue – military courts versus civilian courts – for trying allegations of torture committed by the military.[131] This is not something the CAT deals with explicitly, and so it is not surprising that the convention is not mentioned in several of the courts' decisions depicted in Figure 7.2.

But the CAT is highly relevant to the question of prosecuting torturers. Hence, the Appeals Court of Santiago cited the CAT in several decisions relating to the national amnesty law. In 1994 the Appeals Court found a way to reduce the amnesty's reach in certain unresolved cases by ruling that kidnapping is a continuing and permanent offense ("qualified kidnapping") until the bodies of the victims are found and, as such, continues past the time limit set by these

---

129 Hilbink 2007:185.
130 Lutz and Sikkink 2001.
131 For a list of the cases on which Figure 7.2 is based, see Appendix 7.3 on my Web site at http://scholar.iq.harvard.edu/bsimmons/mobilizing-for-human-rights. Reflecting its conservative nature, the Supreme Court early on refused to turn these cases over to civilian courts. In 1994, the court found that military jurisdiction was appropriate because the alleged crimes, including torture, were carried out during an armed conflict (or internal war) and because they were perpetrated by military officers in the pursuit of their military duties. Supreme Court, 16 November 1994, Rol 30751; Chile Lexis-Nexis database. Two years later, the same court held that the issue of jurisdiction over crimes including torture committed by military officers in the 1970s was moot, because any responsibility that could have been assigned to these officers had been extinguished by that time. Supreme Court, 8 January 1996; Chile Lexis-Nexis database. The attitude of the court began to change after 2000. That year, it rejected the argument that military officers and CNI operatives who had perpetrated crimes against the civilian population during the military dictatorship should be tried under a military or a civil court. Supreme Court, 1 June 2000, Rol 1.075-00; 11 November 2000, Rol 3.243-2000; 12 November 2000, Rol 3.243-00; 10 March 2003; Chile Lexis-Nexis database. By 2006, the court had firmly established that ordinary courts should have jurisdiction: Military courts could not hear cases involving ordinary crimes against civilians committed by military officers, even if these crimes were perpetrated while they were carrying out their military duties. Supreme Court, 4 January 2006; Rol 5212-2005; Chile Lexis-Nexis database. The CAT was not relevant to this internal decision about jurisdiction over crimes including torture; hence, it was not cited in this cluster of cases, but the Chilean Supreme Court after Pinochet's detainment and extradition had clearly decided that military officers should no longer be protected by the military system of justice.

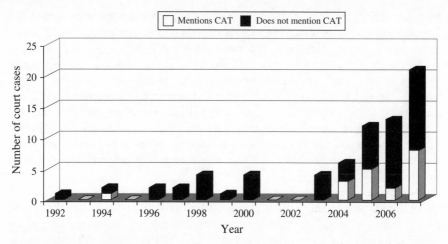

Figure 7.2. Chilean Court Cases on Torture: Supreme Court, Constitutional Tribunal, and Appeals Court of Santiago.

amnesty laws, making such crimes subject to laws and treaties in force at present.[132] In 2007, the Appeals Court rendered an even more significant decision, holding that under the military government there was a systematic pattern of state violence – including torture – that violated fundamental human rights norms. The court held that the state has an affirmative obligation to prosecute and sanction crimes against humanity and cannot grant amnesty to perpetrators of these abuses, as established in multiple human rights documents, among them the Genocide Convention and the CAT.[133] In both of these cases, the CAT was central in supplying the Appeals Court with a clear rationale for setting aside national amnesty laws and establishing judicial principles of accountability.

Only recently has the Supreme Court begun to agree that international legal obligations to which Chile is party make a blanket national amnesty legally untenable. In an important case in 2006, the Supreme Court made explicit use of the CAT to rule that Chile's amnesty law cannot be applied to crimes against humanity.[134] International treaties, including the CAT, were binding in national law, the court held; thus, even if an individual might otherwise be absolved under the national amnesty, these obligations required judicial punishment.[135] The Supreme Court has made use of the CAT as well as general principles of international law to establish the principle that there are no statutory limits in

---

132 Appeals Court of Santiago, 30 September 1994; Chile Lexis-Nexis database.
133 Appeals Court of Santiago, 18 December 2007, Rol 11801-2006; Chile Lexis-Nexis database.
134 Supreme Court, 30 May 2006, Rol 3215-2005; Chile Lexis-Nexis database.
135 Supreme Court, 6 June 2006, Rol 1528-2006 00; Chile Lexis-Nexis database.

the case of grave rights violations such as torture.[136] The CAT has also been used to make the case for compensation to victims or their families for torture committed during the Pinochet era.[137] Overall, the CAT has been especially useful in Chilean law to establish the limits of amnesty and the rules relating to criminal responsibility under the military regime.

The litigation involving allegations of torture has not been exclusively about the past. The CAT has also been used to hold democratically elected governments' agents liable for their alleged torture of persons held in official detention. In 2005, a prisoner who was on a hunger strike alleged that he had been tortured (including insults and multiple beatings) by the prison's guards, who were under direct orders from the superintendent. The Supreme Court made extensive use of the CAT to interpret national legislation, which it called "subservient" to international treaties. In particular, it used the CAT to interpret the meaning of torture within national law.[138] The convention has also been cited in cases of excessive judicial punishment to reduce long prison sentences imposed on debtors.[139]

Chile's Supreme Court has also drawn upon the CAT to hold *foreign* leaders accountable for official torture. Alberto Fujimori appealed to the court to prevent his extradition to Peru to face a multitude of charges, including torture. The court cited the CAT in support of their conclusion that a head of state does not possess criminal immunity against the crime of torture and that Fujimori is therefore not immune to prosecution. The Supreme Court also used the CAT to establish that Fujimori's alleged acts constituted "rational indices of culpability," as required by the extradition treaty.[140] As a result of this ruling, Fujimori was extradited to Peru to face criminal charges in September 2007.[141]

Did the possibility of torture litigation – appealing to the CAT in Chilean courts – have any effect on torture practices in the country? It will never be possible to know the definitive answer to that question. But the evidence is

---

136 Supreme Court, 5 September 2007, Rol 6525-2006; Chile Lexis-Nexis database. In this case, however, the torturer was given an "attenuated sentence," which they held to be permissible under the treaty. Furthermore, in 18 October 2007, Rol 4691-2007 the court seemed to contradict itself, arguing that there is no treaty or general norm of international law that proscribes statutory limits. The minority argued strenuously nevertheless that the state was under an obligation – represented by the CAT and other treaties – to prosecute torturers regardless of the amnesty.

137 Compensation is addressed in Article 14 of the CAT. Such compensation has not been without controversy in Chile. See Kevin G. Hall, "Chilean Torture Victims Demand Compensation, Prosecution." 13 December 2004. http://www.soaw.org/newswire_detail.php?id=642 (accessed 30 June 2008).

138 Supreme Court, 14 December 2005; Rol 5468-2005, Chile Lexis-Nexis database.

139 See, for example, Supreme Court, 4 April 2004, Rol 1179-2004; 15 November 2004, Rol 5185-2004; 6 April 2004, Rol 1179-2004.

140 Supreme Court, 21 September 2007; Rol 3744-2007, Chile Lexis-Nexis database.

141 On the broader significance of the Pinochet case for dictators worldwide see Bosco 2000; Davis 2003.

suggestive. The torture index does begin to improve in Chile in 1999 – just as it becomes clear that the CAT is highly relevant to how international and hence Chilean law is equipped to deal with the atrocities of the Pinochet regime.[142] The most noticeable improvement on the torture scale did not come in the first decade of the country's democratic transition. Rather, it came when the utility of the CAT became clear and the courts had undergone crucial reforms. Under these circumstances, international law became available to Chilean activists to hold their government accountable for torture, past and current.

Israel: An Embattled Democracy

Israel is an interesting case: It is a highly democratic country and a country that the World Bank scores well but not at or near the top of the countries they have rated on their rule of law scale. Israel also faces security threats that make interrogation of terrorist and criminal suspects a serious issue. It is a good case for illustrating the ways in which international treaty commitment can gain traction through the mobilization of activists employing a strategy of litigation. The fact that the Israeli Supreme Court is so easy for individuals to access made the strategy possible. This combination of factors gave the CAT special traction in Israeli domestic politics and institutions, which in turn provided some impetus for revising coercive practices that the international community had described as torture.

Israel is a democracy, and there is no particular reason to think that a treaty banning torture should have much impact in a democratic country, which is far less likely to practice torture in the first place. Israel provides an interesting case study because it is an outlier: a stable democracy with a recent history of harsh interrogation practices that many would describe as torture. It is a good case to compare with those of transitioning and politically unstable regimes. In particular, it is interesting to observe the ways in which ratification of the CAT opened up political as well as legal space within Israel for critics of government practices. Once Israel had ratified the CAT (in 1991), domestic political groups mobilized and made strategic use of Israel's own institutional strengths: relatively independent and competent courts. As a result, Israeli interrogation practices have moderated, though they are still far from perfect.

Israeli law has addressed the issue of torture since passage of the Prevention of Terrorism Act (1948) shortly after the inception of the state. Controversial regulations dating from 1977 permitted "moderate physical pressure" in the interrogation of terrorist suspects, but it was not until 1987 – and the eruption of the intifada – that the government's policies were systematically assessed by

---

142 The torture scale improves from 3 to 2 in 1999, indicating a move from fairly regularized brutality to cases of isolated incidents.

the Landau Commission Report. After an investigation undertaken in response to a five-year prison sentence for a Palestinian man that was based largely on a forced confession, the commission controversially concluded that the use of "moderate physical" and "non-violent psychological" pressure by the General Security Services (Shin Bet) was acceptable against Palestinians suspected of security offences. The report – details of which were never made public – contained interrogation guidelines allowing for "a moderate measure of physical pressure," which nonetheless "must never reach the level of torture."[143]

The report of the Landau Commission was part of a broader effort in the late 1980s to address the limits of permissible practices for interrogating individuals in the custody of public authorities. Israel signed the CAT in 1986, just before the 1987 outbreak of the first intifada. Partially in response to growing internal and external pressures (and despite an uptick in security concerns), the government ratified in October 1991, with some reservations.[144] Two important human rights changes in the Basic Law followed in 1992.[145] These changes provided political and legal opportunities for activists to demand further change in policy and practice. Israel's dualist legal system meant that the CAT itself could not be enforced in national courts in the absence of implementing legislation,[146] but ratification of the CAT became an important point of leverage in the lobbying campaign to bring Israel's penal code into conformity with the nation's public international commitment.[147] Both international and local human rights organizations campaigned in the early 1990s for an amendment to the Israeli Penal Code (Article 277), which allowed physical pressure. The Prohibition of Torture Bill was amended in 1996 to bring its wording into conformity with the CAT, but it would be years before its provisions became law.[148]

Meanwhile, allegations of abusive interrogation practices were becoming a more common feature of the nightly news.[149] In 1993, the evening news told the story of Hassan Zubeidi, a 34-year-old grocer from Anabta on the West Bank, who had allegedly been beaten comatose by Shin Bet. This case and others sent the government into a flurry of activity that it hoped would deflect concern. In

143 For a discussion of the contents of the Landau Commission Report see Grosso 2000.
144 Source: http://www2.ohchr.org/english/law/cat-ratify.htm (accessed 2 July 2008).
145 Laursen 2000:440.
146 Grosso 2000:319. This does not mean that international law has no effects on Israeli law. For a discussion of the possibilities, see Benvenisti 1994.
147 See Ray 2000:46; Clark 2000–1; Grosso 2000; St. Amand 1999–2000.
148 Ray 2000:46.
149 In general, the relative openness of the Israeli political system, with its lack of press censorship, meant that many of the most egregious abuses were in fact fairly easy to document. In 1992, five reports showed that, since the intifada began, between 2,000 and 3,000 detainees had been beaten, hooded, deprived of sleep, or made to stand in boxes no bigger than their bodies for hours. See Caroline Moorehead, "The Court to Rule on Use of Torture in Israel," *The Independent* (London), 21 April 1993; International news, p. 11.

April the government announced that a ministerial committee had tightened up the 1987 Landau Commission guidelines for Shin Bet interrogators. In June a bill banning torture was proposed by several members of parliament, and the justice minister, David Libai, appointed a committee to study the proposal. Public protest was limited, partly because Israelis continued to view Shin Bet as crucial to Israel's security.[150]

While hardly sparking a mass social movement, the human rights issues – raised in stark fashion in the aftermath of the intifada – fueled a burst of organized activism. By one count, only 1 human rights NGO existed in Israel before December 1987, and about 15 of the 25 rights NGOs currently operating in Israel were established in the years immediately following.[151] In the Occupied Territories, only one rights organization existed before the intifada, and about six other rights organizations were established within a very short period following its eruption.[152] One of the most important groups formed was the Public Committee Against Torture, which spearheaded much of the legal activity discussed below. Links with international rights groups were forged, from Amnesty International and Middle East Watch to the International Commission of Jurists and Physicians for Human Rights.[153] International rights discourse peppered their press releases, human rights reports, and correspondence with Israeli authorities (government, military, civil administration).[154]

Israeli activists chose an explicit strategy of legal contestation in their efforts to stamp out their government's practice of what many considered torture. "Politically motivated Palestinian and Israeli lawyers used the legal terrain as a site of resistance to reform or to transform the way the state exercises power," according to one astute observer.[155] This strategy is clearly reflected in the number of cases alleging torture that were brought to the Israeli Supreme Court in the 1990s. Figure 7.3 illustrates this explosion of cases. The first such case was brought to the court the very year the CAT was ratified. The timing of the first torture case is interesting: While one would have thought that the rise of the intifada and the existence of the Landau Commission Report four years prior might have sparked such litigation, it was not until the government had actually completed formal ratification of the CAT that allegations of torture were brought to the Supreme Court. Although the case was dismissed for want of

---

150 Joel Greenberg, "Israel Rethinks Interrogation of Arabs," *New York Times*, Section 1, p. 3, 14 August 1993.
151 Gordon 2004.
152 Hanafi and Tabar 2004.
153 In the summer of 1993, a series of physicians' organizations – including the Israeli Medical Association and the Association of Israeli-Palestinian Physicians for human rights – publicly refused to cooperate with the government in its interrogation practices. See Joel Greenberg, "Israel Rethinks Interrogation of Arabs." *New York Times*, Section 1, p. 3, 14 August 1993.
154 Gordon and Berkovitch n.d.:12.
155 Hajjar 2001:24.

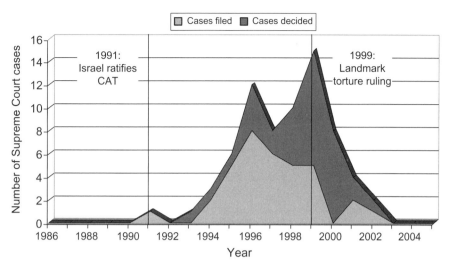

Figure 7.3. Torture Litigation in Israel. *Note*: In all cases, plaintiffs are Palestinians and NGOs on their behalf (mainly the Public Committee against Torture in Israel and the Center for the Defense of the Individual). The defendant is the General Security Service (GSS) (in some cases, the minister of defense and the police were additional defendants). In one case, the defendant was the commander of Israeli Defense Forces in the West Bank. *Source*: Israeli Supreme Court, CD-ROM.

a specific complaint of the use of torture,[156] the barrage of cases that followed alleged again and again that Israel's practices contravened domestic law as well as the nation's international obligations.

Meanwhile, the Israeli government over the course of the 1990s was making a reasonable effort to comply with its obligations under the CAT to report on a regular basis to the Committee Against Torture, the CAT's oversight body, on implementation efforts. The Israeli government is one of a minority of governments that reported promptly, as required by the treaty. The reports were often criticized as inadequate by rights groups, who supplemented the government's characterization of its practices with their own. In 1994 the Committee Against Torture expressed its "great concern" regarding Israel's alleged use of "psychological and physical torture to extract confessions from detainees

156 "The plaintiffs argue, in a nutshell, that the Landau Commission recommendations with regard to the GSS interrogation methods are illegal from the point of view of [Israel's] criminal law.... It has also been argued that these recommendations constitute a permit for torture and contradiction to international law. In his oral argument Mr. Feldman [plaintiff's attorney] argued that the recommendations contradict Basic Law: Human Dignity and Liberty...." Note that the case was filed in 1991, prior to the enactment of the Basic Law in 1992. This is probably why he added the claim about the Basic Law only at the oral argument stage in 1992–3. Case 2581/91, Tadkin legal database [CD-ROM]; translated by Asif Efrat.

and prisoners." Israel's response was both to deny violations of the CAT and to improve supervision of interrogation processes.[157]

Yet, Israel's struggle with terrorism over the course of the 1990s made it hard for the government to eschew completely the continued use of moderate physical pressure against suspects. In September 1994, critics of such practices gained support from some politicians on the right when members of an alleged Jewish terror cell were arrested and some alleged physical or mental violence while under interrogation.[158] After a wave of deadly suicide bombings in 1994, the government was reported to have given Shin Bet permission to use force in interrogations, although the service was required to seek permission from a ministerial commission every three months for the continued use of moderate physical pressure against terrorist suspects.[159] Efforts to codify the conditions under which such pressure could be used were roundly criticized by Amnesty International and other groups as proposals to "legalize torture in Israel and the occupied territories."[160] While the government argued in favor of flexibility under extenuating circumstances, Amnesty International cited the nonderogable nature of the CAT's Article II.[161]

The Israeli government responded to its critics in two ways: necessity and compliance. "The main duty of the government is to protect its citizens," said Uri Dromi, the chief government spokesman in late 1995, "and therefore we have to resort to methods that are not so nice. In other circumstances we would not do it, but we are faced with a very dangerous enemy, and it is the enemy not only of Israel but of the free world."[162] At the same time, the government expressed its desire to comply with the CAT it had ratified five years before. In defending a legislative proposal to set guidelines on the use of physical pressure in interrogations in early 1996, Minister of Justice David Libai noted that "The [proposed] methods used during interrogations will be in line with the International Convention against torture and will not lead to suffering or great pain. . . . This law will give clear regulations on acceptable methods, which will help Shin Bet agents avoid mistaken initiatives."[163] Allegations by Amnesty International and other groups of "the legalization of torture in Israel" were adamant and immediate. The secretary general of Amnesty International, Pierre

157 Abed Jaber, "UN Concerned by Torture in Israel," United Press International, 23 October 1995. For an assessment that Israel practically ignored the UN committee's 1994 report, see *New York Times*, "UN Panel Rules Israel Uses Torture," 10 May 1997, p. A6.
158 *The Economist*, 1 October 1994, p. 58.
159 Agence France Presse, "Israel to Legalise Use of Force Against Palestinian Prisoners," International news, 23 January 1996.
160 United Press International, 23 October 1995, "Amnesty Says Israel to Legalize Torture."
161 Abed Jaber, "UN Concerned by Torture in Israel," United Press International, 23 October 1995. See also Derek Brown, "Making Torture Legal," *The Guardian*, foreign page, p. 9, 23 October 1995.
162 Derek Brown, "Making Torture Legal," *The Guardian*, foreign page, p. 9, 23 October 1995.
163 Agence France Presse, "Israel to Legalise Use of Force Against Palestinian Prisoners," International news, 23 January 1996.

Sane, protested against the draft bill during meetings with Justice Minister Libai and members of the Knesset.[164] The government again tried to reassure both a domestic and an international audience that the proposed bill would not contravene international conventions against torture. "The bill has not yet been submitted to the government or the Knesset (parliament) but we want to inform international opinion that it contains no articles authorizing torture," Foreign Ministry spokesman Yigal Palmor said.[165]

In a short while, the experts comprising the Committee Against Torture were to allege otherwise. Israel's techniques became a target of the committee's concern after a 1996 Israeli Supreme Court ruling gave interrogators more leeway in using physical means to uncover information on terrorism.[166] In May 1997 the committee summoned Israel for an extraordinary hearing to face accusations that its practices did in fact violate the international convention against torture. The committee's position was that the Shin Bet's methods were indisputably torture as defined in international law.[167] The Israeli delegation in Geneva, meanwhile, rejected the charges in a communiqué that denied that "torture or related methods" were used and asserted that the committee's conclusions were based on unsubstantiated allegations.[168] They also pointed to extenuating circumstances, which the committee noted but had also insisted that they provided no excuse to ignore the treaty's nonderogable provisions.[169] According to the *Jerusalem Post*, "The conclusions of the committee were widely expected."[170] A year later, a UN-appointed special rapporteur for Palestine, Hannu Halinen, concluded that interrogation methods used by Israeli agents in Palestine were "breaches of the Convention against Torture and Other Cruel, Inhuman or Degrading Treatment or Punishment – ratified by Israel in 1991."[171]

By 1998, the government and activists in alliance with the UN Committee Against Torture were at an impasse, with the former claiming that specific Israeli practices did not and the latter claiming that they did constitute torture.

164 "We sincerely hope that this bill will never be turned into law because it's a bad law that will set a precedent internationally," Sane said after those talks. Agence France Presse, "Israel Mounts International Campaign to Defend 'Torture Law'," International news, 20 February 1996.

165 Agence France Presse, "Israel Mounts International Campaign to Defend 'Torture Law'." International news, 20 February 1996.

166 *New York Times*, "UN Panel Rules Israel Uses Torture." 10 May 1997, p. A6.

167 Serge Schmemann, "The Use of Force – A Special Report; In Israel, Coercing Prisoners Is Becoming Law of the Land," *New York Times*, 7 May 1997, Section A, p. 1.

168 Gustavo Capdevila, "Human Rights: U.N. Warns Israel, Others Against Use of Torture," Inter-Press Service, 9 May 1997.

169 See Deutsche Presse-Agentur, "Israel Violates Anti-Torture Convention, U.N. Committee Says," International news, 9 May 1997; Serge Schmemann, "The Use of Force – A Special Report; In Israel, Coercing Prisoners Is Becoming Law of the Land," *New York Times*, 7 May 1997, Section A, p. 1.

170 Associated Press, "U.N. Committee: Israel's Interrogation Methods Constitute Torture," *Jerusalem Post*, News, 11 May 1997.

171 Deutsche Presse-Agentur, "U.N. Concern Over Israel's Treatment of Palestinian Detainees," International news, 16 March 1998.

The most decisive way remaining to settle the issue was to apply to the highest legal authority in Israel to decide this very issue. As early as 1994, Israeli human rights organizations spearheaded by a small group of lawyers decided to bring practically every case of suspected torture or ill treatment before the Israeli High Court of Justice,[172] hence the bulge in cases in the 1990s noted in Figure 7.3. Over the course of the 1990s, hundreds of petitions were filed by human rights groups to the Israeli courts, employing international and humanitarian law in their petitions.[173] By most accounts, the effort of the Public Committee against Torture and other Israeli human rights groups to involve the courts was a deliberate strategy to get an authoritative and locally legitimate statement[174] on whether practices of moderate physical pressure constituted torture by international standards (to which Israel by this time was legally committed).

The High Court avoided answering this question for some eight years. One reason was that many on the court, including the chief justice, Aharon Barak, thought that the matter ought to be settled by legislation, and not by a court judgment.[175] Seventeen cases were dismissed because they did not demonstrate, according to the court, that the pressures employed by the GSS constituted torture (see Appendix 7.4 on my Web site at http://scholar.iq.harvard.edu/ bsimmons/mobilizing-for-human-rights). These decisions elicited critical, often outraged reactions from human rights groups in the press.[176] But the flood of cases demanding an answer to this central question finally encouraged the High Court to address it directly.

The landmark case came on 7 September 1999, and the decision was unanimous. The court held that:

> . . . a reasonable investigation is necessarily one free of torture, free of cruel, inhuman treatment of the subject and free of any degrading handling whatsoever. There is a prohibition on the use of "brutal or inhuman means" in the course of an investigation. . . . Human dignity also includes the dignity of the suspect being interrogated. . . . This conclusion is in perfect accord with (various) International Law treaties – to which Israel is a signatory – which prohibit the use of torture, "cruel, inhuman treatment" and "degrading treatment." . . . These prohibitions are

---

172 Grosso 2000:333.
173 Gordon and Berkovitch n.d.:12. See footnote 11: interview with Yossi Schwartz, founder of HaMoked: Center for the Defense of the Individual, 7 August 2003.
174 Observers speculated that "A formal indictment of torture in Israel would be a significant victory for human rights when the use of torture is probably increasing." Caroline Moorehead, "The Court to Rule on Use of Torture in Israel," *The Independent* (London), 21 April 1993, International news, p. 11.
175 Joel Greenberg, "Israel Court Weighs Legality of What Many Call Torture," *New York Times*, 25 January 1999, p. A10.
176 See, for example, Joel Greenberg, "Israel Rethinks Interrogation of Arabs," *New York Times*, 14 August 1993, Section 1 p. 3; Deutsche Presse-Agentur, "Amnesty Accuses Israel of Endangering Human Rights," International news, 15 November 1996; *CNN Today*, 19 November 1996, transcript #96111909V34.

"absolute." There are no exceptions to them and there is no room for balancing. Indeed, violence directed at a suspect's body or spirit does not constitute a reasonable investigation practice.[177]

The court went on to say that particular practices were not permitted according to these prohibitions:

> ... we declare that the GSS does not have the authority to "shake" a man, hold him in the "Shabach" position ..., force him into a "frog crouch" position and deprive him of sleep in a manner other than that which is inherently required by the interrogation.[178]

Initial reactions to the ruling were very optimistic, almost ebullient.[179] The Israeli human rights organization B'Tselem characterized the decision as putting "an end to torture in Israel,"[180] while the Palestinian human rights group LAW declared that the decision "outlawed torture."[181] Once the amazement wore off, reactions to the High Court decision were much more restrained.[182] While certain practices – such as violent shaking, certain painful positions, and prolonged hooding – were declared to be torture by the court, the door was also left open for these issues to be legalized through parliamentary legislation.

It was only a matter of months before conservative members of the Knesset moved to do so. In November 1999 approximately 64 members of the 120-member Israeli parliament introduced a bill specifically authorizing the GSS to use physical pressure in interrogation. The author of the bill acknowledged that the bill would be "introducing torture into the law of the State of Israel" and that the provisions he proposed violated international law and Israel's treaty obligations.[183] As it turns out, however, legislating torture in a democratic forum is politically not very feasible. Antitorture lobbyists turned out in numbers, and the bill did not pass.

---

177 Judgement on the Interrogation Methods applied by the GSS; The Supreme Court of Israel, sitting as the High Court of Justice; Cases H.C. 5100/94, H.C. 4054/95, H.C. 6536/95, H.C. 5188/96, H.C. 7563/97, H.C. 7628/97, H.C. 1043/99, para. 23. Text available at http://www.derechos.org/human-rights/mena/doc/torture.html (accessed 14 August 2008).

178 Id., paragraph 40 (accessed 14 August 2008).

179 "The High Court decision brings an end to an inglorious chapter in Israel's history, in which the state authorized Shin Bet interrogators to use torture methods in their work on the grounds of security needs." *Ha'aretz*, editorial, 7 September 1999. See also Deborah Sontag, "Court Bans Most Use of Force in Interrogations," *New York Times*, 7 September 1999, p. A1.

180 Press Release, B'Tselem, 6 September 1999.

181 LAW, "After 18 Months, Israeli High Court Outlaws Torture," 7 September 1999.

182 St. Amand (1999–2000:683) asserts that the decision was a tiny legal step and notes that there was no explicit reference to the international prohibition contained in the CAT; see also Mandel 1999:313.

183 Aryeh Dayan, "A Ticking Time Bomb in the Knesset: Some 64 MKs Have Signed a Bill Specifically Authorizing the Shin Bet to Use Torture Under Certain Conditions – Despite the Fact That Israel Has Signed an International Treaty Prohibiting It," *Ha'aretz*, 1 November 1999.

What are the larger implications of torture litigation in Israel? The Israeli Supreme Court did not ban torture, as many would have liked to see it do. On the other hand, torture has never been legitimated through a parliamentary decision of the Knesset, despite security threats that might have made it expedient to do so. Activists and monitors continue to criticize certain aspects of Israel's interrogation practices. And yet, even Israel's critics recognize that practices have improved. Peter Burns of the 10-member UN Committee Against Torture told reporters in 2001 that "There is absolutely no question that the high court ruling has had an impact."[184] Now, instead of speaking in terms of flagrant violations, the committee focuses on the ways in which Israel's compliance is incomplete. "In the absence of a defined crime of torture in terms consistent with the Convention we feel there are gaps, [and] that certain types of conduct slip through the net," Burns said. This assessment comports with the evidence used to assess torture practices in this chapter. While their practices have improved one category on the torture scale since 1999, Israel is still a country in which detainee abuse is on balance not uncommon.

International law played a crucial supporting role in this episode. Mobilization in Israel on the issue of the treatment of detainees followed ratification of the CAT, and used the fact and language of that commitment to articulate an undeniable proposition: Israel was obligated by international convention not to engage in torture. The key problem was that the government disagreed that that is what its agents were doing. And here the convention played another crucial role: It bolstered the judgment that particular practices were beyond the pale. Ratification entailed reporting to the Committee Against Torture; reporting spawned counter-reports and eventually a formal decision of the committee that particular practices were in breach of an international commitment. By 1999, a fairly independent High Court felt that it could not avoid a ruling on the legality of the practices in question. While it did not appeal directly to international law in its decision, the court was constrained by the interpretation of the CAT by its authoritative implementation committee. The solution chosen was to declare Israel's practices inconsistent with existing law, which the court acknowledged could be changed by legislative means – a move that itself served to diffuse conservative opposition. Effectively, Israel's voluntarily assumed CAT obligation put normative and legal constraints on Israeli politics and institutions that impacted practices and made wholesale violation of international torture standards untenable.

CONCLUSIONS

The ban on torture is the strongest international legal prohibition contained in any human rights treaty. By ratifying the CAT, governments expressly

---

184 Peter Capella, "UN Panel Urges Israel to Eliminate Torture." Agence France Presse, 23 November 2001. See also Elizabeth Olson, "Citing Some Progress, U.N. Panel on Torture Urges Israel to Take More Steps," *New York Times*, 24 November 2001, p. A8.

acknowledge that there are no conditions under which the use of severe physical or psychological pain by public authorities is justified. Yet, despite such clear prohibitory language, there is little quantifiable evidence that signing a treaty makes it so. Torture is appallingly widespread. Even if we take into account the likelihood that information on torture has improved over the course of the past two decades, and even if we concede that standards of what constitutes torture may be getting tougher, there are still far too many cases in which governments are willing to ignore or even to condone detainee treatment that is illegally harsh.

The initial evidence casts some doubt on the ability of treaty commitments to alter this basic reality. Indicators of torture seem to have gotten worse over time even as the number of CAT signatories increased. The *unconditional* effects of ratifying the CAT were, if anything, negative, indicating that it is quite common for governments to perform *worse* on this scale once they have ratified the CAT. It is important to reiterate the opening observations of this chapter: The decentralized and secretive nature of this offense makes it difficult to study, let alone to stop. Some governments practice torture out of self-constructed "necessity," justifying their practices with references to security and the public or national interest.

It is wrong to conclude, however, that the CAT has failed to improve the treatment of government-held detainees. This chapter revealed the ability of a treaty commitment to influence positively government behavior in moderately democratic and transitional regimes, of which there are many. Chile is a good example of how this can work out in practice. This chapter has also found some impact in countries whose legal systems are at least moderately well equipped to enforce international treaty commitments. Israel is a good example of how this can happen. The main finding of this chapter is that a CAT commitment significantly improves the treatment of detainees in countries with at least moderate levels of public accountability. CAT ratification resonates in those polities; individuals and groups who may have good reason to fear mistreatment of themselves, their families, their countrymen, or other humans by the government have strong incentives to mobilize to implement the international ban in domestic law. The domestic politics that mobilize around the issue are likely key to the treaty's gaining traction in the local polity.

The factors that drive torture are many, and many are far more important than a treaty commitment. The use of torture can become distressingly embedded in a local culture of brutality and can be very difficult to dislodge. Consistently, the most significant explanation for torture in every model in this chapter was practices in past years. Governments often continue their "law enforcement" efforts as they have for decades, unless demands from a mobilized public begin to elicit a reexamination of policy. Then too, governments tend to maintain good practices until a national security threat justifies the rougher handling of detainees. It is clear that many factors conspire to create an environment where torture flourishes, from military conflicts to a gagged press.

As Jack Donnelly has written, ". . . the key to change in state practices probably lies not in any one type or forum of activity but in the mobilization of multiple, complementary channels of influence."[185] A treaty commitment has an important role to play in polities where complementary channels of influence – public demands, foreign pressures, powerful and well-respected courts – come together to demand an end to torture. As this chapter has shown, that is most likely to be the case in polities that have experienced both public accountability and its breach. For many countries over the course of the past three decades, the CAT has provided a focal norm and a stabilizing standard from which vigilant polities have insisted their governments not retreat.

185 Donnelly 1998:85.

8

The Protection of Innocents: Rights of the Child

[W]e do what we do in the realm of international organization because we strive, in our own fashion, to give expression to universal truths. What might these be in so contested an arena as international affairs? I believe that they include the truths of human dignity and fundamental equality, whereby a child born in the smallest village of the poorest land is valued as much as one born on Beacon Hill.

> Kofi A. Annan, commencement address, Massachusetts Institute of Technology, 1997[1]

Modern society has recently recognized the need for special protections for children, and many of these have become enshrined in international legal agreements. The politics of children's rights protection differs from that of adults, because children typically require advocates willing to articulate and press their interests. International law can play an important role in advocacy on behalf of children. One of the most important things international law can do is to provide a rights-based framework at least to supplement the protective framework that has a much longer history in many societies and their constitutions. Moreover, it can provide a lever to give their would-be advocates influence over policies likely to have an important impact on the well-being of those who are not able to organize and speak for themselves.

This chapter explores the extent to which the Convention on the Rights of the Child (CRC)[2] and its Optional Protocol Relating to Children in Armed Conflict (OPCAC)[3] have been important in improving the lot of the world's

---

1 Kofi Annan's commencement address can be found at http://web.mit.edu/newsoffice/nr/97/annansp.html (accessed 16 July 2008).
2 Convention on the Rights of the Child, adopted and opened for signature, ratification, and accession by UNGA resolution 44/25 of 20 November 1989; *entry into force* 2 September 1990.
3 Optional Protocol to the Convention on the Rights of the Child on the Involvement of Children in Armed Conflict, adopted and opened for signature, ratification, and accession by UNGA resolution A/RES/54/263 of 25 May 2000; *entry into force* 12 February 2002.

children. The first section addresses historical mores and practices surrounding the use and abuse of children and then turns to the role of international law in addressing these practices. Many international legal instruments developed in the twentieth century have attempted to address children's rights, but the most important of these – binding, universal, involving oversight, and comprehensive in coverage – is the CRC. The second section examines the use of child labor (involving children between 10 and 14 years old) and explores whether the CRC has had an important influence on the economic exploitation of children. As with the other conventions examined earlier, the strongest correlation between ratification and reductions in child labor occurs in middle-income countries. The third section analyzes the effect ratification of the CRC has had on the provision of basic health services to children – immunization against common diseases in early childhood. Here the evidence of a CRC ratification effect is much weaker. Finally, I examine the role of a very specific legal obligation taken on by many fewer states: the obligation contained in the OPCAC not to recruit persons under 18 years of age into the military. In this case the evidence is only marginally statistically significant, but overall it is much more supportive of a positive role for the CRC than most observers might have expected. CRC ratification is associated with convincing reductions in child labor, and ratification of the OPCAC is associated with increases in the legal age of military recruitment, especially for combat and compulsory service. These are important gains for vulnerable individuals who are least able to defend their own interests. These gains are plausibly linked with the specific political empowerment the CRC has lent to advocates who have mobilized assiduously to improve the lives of the young.

CHILDREN'S RIGHTS

The Rise of Public Protections – and Advocacy for Protection

The idea that children have rights as human beings is fairly modern. The ancient world tended to view children's "rights" (particularly those of babies, who had an especially tenuous right to life) on par with those of animals rather than adult humans.[4] In early modern European societies, childhood resembled adulthood: Long working hours and pervasive abuse were common; legal protection was

---

4 According to Aristotle, children lack all the capabilities that raise a human being over animals. Aristotle's notion of the child is laid out in *Politics* (Aristotle and Reeve 1998:34–8). The killing of a newborn was not considered murder until 374 A.D. First Canonical Letter by Basil the Great (canons 2 and 8) http://www.acs.ucalgary.ca/~vandersp/Courses/texts/cappadoc/basilcep.html. According to Roman law, fathers decided whether their children would stay alive or not. Laid out in the Law of the Twelve Tables, around 450 B.C.E.; available at http://www.constitution.org/sps/sps01_1.htm (accessed 16 July 2008).

practically unknown.[5] Throughout most of the nineteenth century, European families resembled working units rather than the child-centered institutions they have become today.[6] In the late-nineteenth-century United States, child abuse cases had to be prosecuted under laws meant to prevent cruelty to animals because as late as 1874, legislation still did not exist to prevent the abuse of children.[7]

Over the course of the past century and a half, the modern state has become a prime guarantor of children's well-being. One way in which this trend can be seen is in constitutional references to states' responsibilities with respect to children. In the late nineteenth and twentieth centuries, states began to assume a constitutional role in child welfare and the regulation of child labor. While constitutional provisions do not necessarily reflect actual state practice on the ground, these provisions can be thought of as "ideological rules" – if not direct reflections of social organization – governing responsibilities toward children.[8] John Boli-Bennet and John Meyer, who pioneered research in this area in the 1970s, interpret these changes as part of a broader shift in the expansion of states' corporate authority globally. This ideological shift signals recognition that parents are not the sole source of child protection. States have a crucial role to play as well.

Nonetheless, children have lagged in gaining basic human rights because historically they typically have been seen as incapable of exercising them. Matthew Happold notes the widespread assumption that "children, by virtue of their lack of capacity and dependence upon adults, could not be right-holders."[9] Others have argued that the issue should not be cast in terms of children's fundamental rights, but rather in terms of society's fundamental obligations to them.[10] "The best interest of the child" is sometimes counterposed to – and, indeed, substituted for – the idea that children can be rights holders as such.[11] According to Michael Freeman, "Because children have lacked the moral coinage of rights, it has been easy to brush their interests aside in the sweep of consequentialist thinking."[12] The

---

5 According to DeMause, it was common in Europe for children to be abandoned, given away, sold, beaten, abused, mutilated and displayed at fairs, forced into prostitution, or castrated and sent into slavery. On the history of the treatment of children in early to modern Europe, see Ariès 1996; DeMause 1975; Rutschky 1977. For a kinder, gentler view of this history, see Pollock 1983.

6 Happold 2005.

7 A cruel child abuse case drew nationwide attention in 1874, when the founder of the American Society for the Prevention of Cruelty to Animals, Henry Bergh, defended Mary Ellen Wilson, a nine-year-old girl who had been badly mistreated (Shelman and Lazoritz 2005). "Because of the absence of legal protection against such abuse the only solution was the prosecution on the basis that the girl was a member of the animal kingdom" (Van Bueren 1995:xxi).

8 Boli-Bennett and Meyer 1978.

9 Happold 2005:27. See also Farson 1974; Holt 1975.

10 See, for example, O'Neill 1988.

11 Tom Campbell (1992) develops a theory of children's rights based on their interests.

12 Freeman 1992:54.

past 20 years have reflected an important shift in many societies' willingness to embrace the concept of children's rights.[13]

Organized advocacy groups had much to do with spreading the notion of public obligations to protect children. Save the Children was founded at the end of World War I in Geneva. It initially took up the cause of children abandoned and orphaned in the war and took the first steps to create international awareness of children's issues by drafting the 1924 Geneva Declaration on the Rights of the Child.[14] While figures on the exact number of organizations strictly devoted to children's issues are difficult to assemble, it is interesting to note that the greatest NGO growth between 1990 and 2000 has been precisely in those areas likely to have a disproportionate impact on children: social services organizations (which grew from 2,361 to 4,215, or 78.5 percent); health-related NGOs (which grew from 1,357 to 2,036, or 50 percent); and education NGOs (which grew from 1,485 to 1,839, or 23.8 percent).[15] Other groups have taken up high-profile children's issues. The Coalition to Stop the Use of Child Soldiers, formed in 1998, has since established a number of national coalitions, which are presently operating in 35 countries.[16] These figures represent a significant growth in the capacity of nongovernmental groups to put children's issues on the national and international agendas.

The contemporary world has, however, hardly solved the problem of guaranteeing children's basic human rights. The United Nations International Children's Emergency Fund (UNICEF) estimates that some 640 million children do not have adequate shelter, 400 million have no access to safe water, 270 million have no access to health care, and 140 million have never been to school.[17] The World Health Organization reports that of the 3.1 million persons killed by AIDS in 2005,

---

13 See the essays debating the nature, justification for, and extent of children rights in Alston et al. 1992.
14 *Adopted* 26 September 1924, League of Nations O.J. Spec. Supp. 21, at 43 (1924). See Cohen 1990. Save the Children is the world's major NGO on children's issues. It now comprises 27 member organizations and operates in more than 110 countries, with a combined income of about $771 million. For further information, see http://www.savethechildren.net/alliance/index.html (accessed 16 July 2008).
15 All of these figures are from Anheier, Glasius, and Kaldor (2001) in the Human Development Report 2002; replicated in a chart displayed on the Web site of the Global Policy Forum at http://www.globalpolicy.org/ngos/role/intro/growth2000.htm.
16 http://www.child-soldiers.org. The coalition was set up by leading international human rights and humanitarian organizations, including Amnesty International, Human Rights Watch, and the International Save the Children Alliance. There are a number of smaller, mostly locally organized organizations advocating for children's rights, for example the Youth Advocate Program International (YAPI), a Washington, D.C.–based NGO founded in 1994 (the financial power and impact of these organizations cannot compete with those of the main organizations; YAPI disposed of only approximately US$ 180,000 in 2002, for instance). Source: http://www.yapi.org (accessed 16 July 2008).
17 According to UNICEF's 2005 report on The State of the World's Children 2005: "Childhood Under Threat." See http://www.unicef.org/publications/files/SOWC_2005_(English).pdf (accessed 16 July 2008).

over 500,000 were children below 15 years of age.[18] According to the ILO, at least 1 million children are prostitutes, with the greatest numbers in Thailand, India, Taiwan, and the Philippines.[19] Human Rights Watch reports the widespread abuse of children in prisons in northern Brazil;[20] UNICEF reports that in Nepal, 7 percent of girls are married before the age of 10 and 40 percent by age 15;[21] thousands, if not millions, of persons in Pakistan are held in debt bondage, many of them children.[22] At least 35 death penalties have been carried out to punish crimes committed by children in the past decade – 19 of them in the United States.[23]

Children in International Law

The special vulnerabilities of children have been recognized and placed in a human rights context in international law. The first formal international recognition that children have special needs was the Geneva Declaration of the Rights of the Child (1924).[24] In five short sentences, it called for the provision of basic human needs and protection "against every form of exploitation," but it did not raise the more controversial issues of who was obligated to ensure this protection or what age defined childhood. The UNGA addressed children's issues in the (nonbinding) Declaration of the Rights of the Child (1959) and called upon "parents, . . . voluntary organizations, local authorities and national Governments to recognize these rights and strive for their observance by legislative and other measures."[25] Largely hortatory in nature, the 1959 resolution put children on the postwar human rights agenda but still failed to define a child by age. It was not until the passage of the CRC in 1989 that a treaty codified the 18th year as the generally accepted transition point to adulthood.[26]

Over the course of the 1940s and 1950s, the intergovernmental organizational capacity to protect children's well-being developed progressively. In 1946, UNICEF[27] was established to assist children globally in times of need. With an

---

18 According to the World Health Organization, http://www.unaids.org/epi2005/doc/report.html.

19 As reported by TimeAsia, http://www.time.com/time/asia/features/slavery/ (accessed 16 July 2008).

20 Human Rights Watch, http://hrw.org/english/docs/2003/04/10/brazil5573.htm (accessed 16 July 2008).

21 As reported by the BBC, http://news.bbc.co.uk/1/hi/world/1206979.stm (accessed 16 July 2008).

22 Human Rights Watch report, http://www.hrw.org/reports/1995/Pakistan.htm (accessed 16 July 2008).

23 As reported by Amnesty International between 1990 and 2003. See http://web.amnesty.org/library/Index/ENGACT500012004 (accessed 16 July 2008).

24 The declaration of 1924 is available at http://www.arabhumanrights.org/cbased/ga/geneva-child-declaration23e.html (accessed 16 July 2008).

25 Declaration of the Rights of the Child, Proclaimed by UNGA Resolution 1386(XIV) of 20 November 1959. The declaration of 1959 is available at http://www.unhchr.ch/html/menu3/b/25.htm (accessed 16 July 2008).

26 CRC, Article 1, states that ". . . a child means every human being below the age of eighteen years unless under the law applicable to the child, majority is attained earlier." See also Singer 2005.

27 It was later renamed to United Nations Children's Fund (in 1953). Information can be obtained from http://www.unicef.org/.

annual budget of almost $2 billion in 2004,[28] UNICEF remains the most impor-
tant intergovernmental institution devoted to children's issues. Intergovernmental efforts are also reflected in more symbolic ways. Ever since 1954, for
example, November 20th has been celebrated as Universal Children's Day,
which marks the declaration of 1959 and, more recently, the convention of
1989.[29] Similarly, 1979 was proclaimed the "International Year of the Child,"
followed by the first efforts to develop a convention on children's rights.

Within a decade of the 1959 declaration, intergovernmental and nongovernmental child advocacy groups succeeded in one of their central strategic goals:
movement toward the legal articulation of the international regulatory structure
relating to childhood (Figure 8.1). This take-off parallels the development (with
a lag) of the international human rights regime more generally. As Figure 8.1
makes clear, not only has the number of international legal instruments
increased, but the ratio of hard (legally binding) to soft law (declarations, standards guidelines) has increased as well. Legal instruments have come to address a
growing range of humanitarian, social, economic, justice, and military issues
relating to minors.

The Legal Centerpiece: The CRC

The CRC[30] stands as the most important international legal agreement to
address children's rights vis-à-vis their governments, their society, and even
their parents. As the latest addition to the six core treaties studied here, it
opened for signature in 1989 and the first instruments of ratification were deposited with the UN in 1990. At present, there are 192 parties and 140 signatories to
the convention – more than any other human rights convention.[31] The main ideas
are laid out in Articles 2, 3, 6, and 12–15. Article 2 provides that "the child is
protected against all forms of discrimination or punishment on the basis of the
status, activities, expressed opinions, or beliefs of the child's parents, legal
guardians, or family members."[32] Article 3 states that all decisions must be made
in the best interest of the child, requiring that "In all actions concerning children,
whether undertaken by public or private social welfare institutions, courts of law,
administrative authorities or legislative bodies, the best interests of the child shall

---

28 Historical data on UNICEF's spending are somewhat difficult to find. This figure is from
    UNICEF (UK): http://www.unicef.org.uk/faqs/faq_detail.asp?faq=12&submit.x=15&;submit.
    y=16 (accessed 16 July 2008).
29 The UNGA recommended in 1954 (resolution 836 (IX)) that all countries institute a "Universal
    Children's Day," to be observed as a day of worldwide fraternity and understanding between
    children and of activity promoting the welfare of the world's children.
30 The convention is available at http://www.unhchr.ch/html/menu3/b/k2crc.htm (accessed 16
    July 2008).
31 By 7 October 2005. http://www.unhchr.ch/pdf/report.pdf (accessed 16 June 2008).
32 CRC, Article 2, para. 2. See the text of the CRC at http://www.unhchr.ch/html/menu3/b/
    k2crc.htm (accessed 16 July 2008).

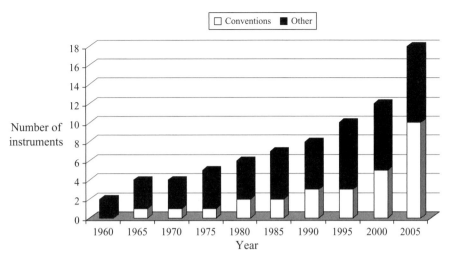

Figure 8.1. Growth in International Legal Instruments Relating to Children's Rights and Protection. Key international conventions (chronological order):

Geneva Declaration of the Rights of the Child of 1924, *adopted* 26 September 1924, League of Nations O.J. Spec. Supp. 21, at 43 (1924).

Declaration of the Rights of the Child, G.A. res. 1386 (XIV), 14 U.N. GAOR Supp. (No. 16) at 19, U.N. Doc. A/4354 (1959).

Convention on Consent to Marriage, Minimum Age for Marriage and Registration of Marriages, 521 U.N.T.S. 231, *entered into force* 9 December 1964.

Recommendation on Consent to Marriage, Minimum Age for Marriage and Registration of Marriages, G.A. res. 2018 (XX), 20 U.N. GAOR Supp. (No. 14) at 36, U.N. Doc. A/6014 (1965).

Declaration on the Protection of Women and Children in Emergency and Armed Conflict, G.A. res. 3318 (XXIX), 29 U.N. GAOR Supp. (No. 31) at 146, U.N. Doc. A/9631 (1974).

Convention concerning Minimum Age for Admission to Employment (ILO No. 138), (1973), 1015 U.N.T.S. 297 (1976), *entered into force* 19 June 1976.

United Nations Standard Minimum Rules for the Administration of Juvenile Justice ("The Beijing Rules"), G.A. res. 40/33, annex, 40 U.N. GAOR Supp. (No. 53) at 207, U.N. Doc. A/40/53 (1985).

United Nations Rules for the Protection of Juveniles Deprived of Their Liberty, G.A. res. 45/113, annex, 45 U.N. GAOR Supp. (No. 49A) at 205, U.N. Doc. A/45/49 (1990).

United Nations Guidelines for the Prevention of Juvenile Delinquency (the Riyadh Guidelines), G.A. res. 45/112, annex, 45 U.N. GAOR Supp. (No. 49A) at 201, U.N. Doc. A/45/49 (1990).

Convention on the Rights of the Child, G.A. res. 44/25, annex, 44 U.N. GAOR Supp. (No. 49) at 167, U.N. Doc. A/44/49 (1989), *entered into force* 2 September 1990.

African Charter on the Rights and Welfare of the Child, OAU Doc. CAB/LEG/24.9/49 (1990), *entered into force* 29 November 1999.

Convention Concerning the Prohibition and Immediate Action for the Elimination of the Worst Forms of Child Labour (ILO No. 182), 38 I.L.M. 1207 (1999), *entered into force* 19 November 2000.

Figure 8.1. (*continued*)

Protocol to Prevent, Suppress and Punish Trafficking in Persons, Especially Women and Children, supplementing the United Nations Convention against Transnational Organized Crime, supplementing the United Nations Convention Against Transnational Organized Crime, G.A. res. 55/25, annex II, 55 U.N. GAOR Supp. (No. 49) at 60, U.N. Doc. A/45/49 (Vol. I) (2001).

Optional protocol to the CRC on the sale of children, child prostitution and child pornography, G.A. res. 54/263, annex II, 54 U.N. GAOR Supp. (No. 49) at 6, U.N. Doc. A/54/49, Vol. III (2000), *entered into force* 18 January 2002.

Optional protocol to the CRC on the involvement of children in armed conflicts, G.A. res. 54/263, annex I, 54 U.N. GAOR Supp. (No. 49) at 7, U.N. Doc. A/54/49, Vol. III (2000), *entered into force* 12 February 2002.

Protocol to Prevent, Suppress and Punish Trafficking in Persons, Especially Women and Children, Supplementing the United Nations Convention Against Transnational Organized Crime, G.A. res. 25, annex II, U.N. GAOR, 55th Sess., Supp. No. 49, at 60, U.N. Doc. A/45/49 (Vol. I) (2001), *entered into force* 25 December 2003.

Convention on contact concerning children (ETS No. 192), Strasbourg, 15.V.2003. UNICEF Guidelines for the Protection of the Rights of Children Victims Trafficking in Southeastern Europe (2003).

Major sources: University of Minnesota Human Rights Library, at http://www1. umn.edu/humanrts/instree/ainstls1.htm; ILO, at http://www.ilo.org/public/english/ standards/norm/whatare/fundam/childpri.htm. Note that this list excludes general human rights instruments, such as the International Covenant on Economic Social, and Cultural Rights, that seek to improve rights and protections of all persons if they do not specify a right or protection specifically for children.

be a primary consideration."[33] Articles 12 through 15 provide for a range of civil rights for children: the right of a child "who is capable of forming his or her own views . . . to express those views freely in all matters affecting the child" – for example, in judicial proceedings (Article 12), the right to free expression (Article 13), freedom of thought, conscience, and religion (Article 14), and freedom of association (Article 15).[34] These provisions signal a move away from an exclusively protective focus and a growing willingness to see children, at least in some circumstances, as partially autonomous agents often able to make decisions and choices on their own. Most ambitiously, Article 27 provides that "States Parties recognize the right of every child to a standard of living adequate for the child's physical, mental, spiritual, moral and social development" and that "States Parties, in accordance with national conditions and within their means, shall take

---

33 CRC, Article 3, para. 1.

34 Some scholars note that these articles provide for something that would not have been possible only a few years before: that "children have rights they can oppose against adults." Happold 2005.

appropriate measures to assist parents and others responsible for the child to imple-ment this right. . . ."[35] While it is phrased conditionally, the treaty does stipulate obligations to improve children's development and life chances.

Like the CEDAW (Chapter 6) but unlike the CAT (Chapter 7), the CRC was meant to be implemented progressively, taking resource constraints into account. Article 4 was drafted explicitly to recognize resource constraints faced by low-income countries: "With regard to economic, social and cultural rights, States Parties shall undertake such measures to the maximum extent of their available resources and, where needed, within the framework of international co-operation."[36] The CRC's guarantee of access to education, for example, is made expressly "with a view to achieving this right progressively . . ."[37] Indeed, the words "progress" or "progressively" appear five times in the text of the CRC, most notably with reference to education and health.[38] In contrast with the non-derogable provisions of the CAT, the CRC was drafted in such as way as, in James Himes's words, "to allay the fears of official representatives that govern-ments would be held responsible for achieving standards of children's well-being that are 'unrealistic' in terms of resource availability and specific time limits, especially in lower-income countries."[39] This drafting of the treaty almost cer-tainly has something to do with states' swift and nearly universal ratification and accession to the main body of the treaty, though a much more cautious approach has been taken to the two optional protocols relating to children in armed con-flict[40] and child trafficking[41] (Figure 8.2). Most states jumped on board the CRC in the first three years in which the text was open for signature; ratification was nearly universal by 1997.

Children themselves possess few of the traditional ways to hold actors accountable for their legal obligations: They have no right to vote, no capacity to lobby or to exert market pressure, and very little independent access to courts in most countries. The CRC tries to remedy this situation by making states accountable to the Committee on the Rights of the Child, which is supposed to consist of experts who have high moral standards and recognized competence in

---

35 CRC, Article 27, paras. 1 and 3.

36 CRC, Article 4. The right to "the highest attainable standard of health," for example, includes a commitment to "undertake to promote and encourage international co-operation" and speci-fies that "particular account shall be taken of the needs of developing countries." CRC, Article 24(4).

37 CRC, Article 28(1).

38 The preamble refers to social progress; Article 24(4) refers to progressive implementation of health care; Article 28(1) refers to progressive implementation of universal access to primary education; and Articles 43(1) and 44(1) refer to reporting on progress in the context of the treaty's oversight mechanisms.

39 Himes 1995:2.

40 UNGA Res. 54/263, Annex I, 54 U.N. GAOR Supp. (No. 49) at 7, U.N. Doc. A/54/49, Vol. III (2000), *entered into force* 12 February 2002.

41 UNGA Res. 54/263, Annex II, 54 U.N. GAOR Supp. (No. 49) at 6, U.N. Doc. A/54/49, Vol. III (2000), *entered into force* 18 January 2002.

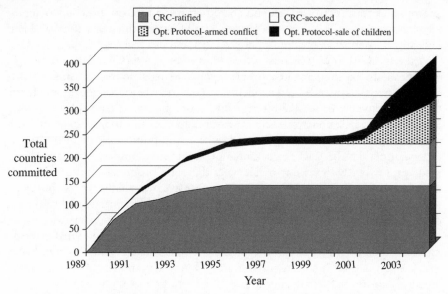

Figure 8.2. Ratification of and Accession to the CRC and Its Optional Protocols. *Source*: Office of the UN High Commissioner for Human Rights http://www.ohchr.org/english/countries/ratification/11.htm.

the field and who serve in their personal capacity (Articles 43 and 44). States are required to report to the committee within two years of ratification and at regular five-year intervals thereafter.[42] Article 44(6) obligates states to make their reports widely available in their own countries.[43] While it is easy to criticize self-reporting as an ineffective way to hold states' feet to the fire,[44] the process of reporting turns out to facilitate political and social mobilization in ways that enhance implementation.

The CRC has garnered a number of important reservations in the process of ratification.[45] The single most frequently reserved article in the convention

42 Articles 44(1)a and 44(1)b.
43 Some think that this may be the most important aspect of the monitoring process. See Lanotte and Goedertier 1996.
44 By my own count, by 2005, more than 200 reports (cumulatively) were due that had not yet been turned in to the committee. Sub-Saharan African state parties were most delinquent, averaging 1.5 reports (or about seven and one-half years) behind, while countries in the Middle East and North Africa were the most prompt, averaging less than 1.0 report in arrears (on average, about five years behind). Furthermore, the quality of the reports is uneven; see Mower 1997:109–15. The committee was also fairly slow in responding, taking two to three years to do so on average; see Simmons and Lamprecht 2006. Verhellen calls monitoring the "Achilles' heel" of the convention (1994:19).
45 For a qualitative discussion, see Schabas 1996. For a graphic description of which particular articles are reserved against by region, see Simmons and Lamprecht 2006.

is Article 14, guaranteeing children's right to free religious thought and conscience. Many governments – and, likely, parents – cannot agree that children are really ready to engage spiritual beliefs and religious thought freely. Likely they have absolutely no interest in recognizing this right, which could in theory threaten parental authority, political control, and societal cohesion. Several of the other widely reserved articles (especially by Middle Eastern and North African governments)[46] touch on family issues that are sensitive in many cultures (Articles 7 on nationality, 21 on adoption, and 9 on separation from parents). Moreover, of all of the six core treaties, the pattern of reservations for the CRC displays the highest degree of *dissensus*. If one were to catalog all of the reservations made to the major human rights agreements, and simply ask, "What are the chances that any two reservations apply to the same treaty article?" the probability would be the *lowest* for the CRC: a 45 percent likelihood compared to a 68 percent likelihood for the ICCPR and a 49 percent likelihood for the ICESCR.[47] Thus, despite its widespread ratification, there may be more underlying disagreement over important normative issues in the case of the CRC than in other human rights accords. Normative divergence on children's issues is probably higher than the ratification data suggest.

What difference has this convention made for the well-being of children? Like the civil and political rights convention and the women's convention, the CRC contains so many obligations that it seems difficult to test compliance with the regime as a whole. Indeed, many of its provisions are clearly aspirational and highly conditioned (to be implemented, as Article 27(3) provides, "in accordance with national conditions and within their means"). Yet, the CRC is expressly obligatory.[48] It is essential to assess whether and by what mechanisms it has in fact ushered in progress for the world's children. The strategy here is to select two provisions that protect children from abuse – restrictions against child labor and prohibitions against the use of child soldiers – and one that requires positive public provisions or at least facilitation (immunization against common childhood illnesses). Whether or not the CRC has done anything to improve children's right to be free from these two forms of exploitation and to enjoy basic good health will now be examined.

---

46 As with the CEDAW, governments of several of the predominantly Islamic countries have also entered exceptionally broad reservations, subordinating CRC obligations to "principles of Islamic laws and values." See Ali and Jamil 1994.

47 Analogous to calculation of the Herfindahl index: the sum of the squares of the proportion of countries that make a reservation on a particular article. See http://risk.ifci.ch/00011677.htm. Note that the index is conditional on making a reservation at all.

48 "Obligation" is mentioned six times in the main body of the treaty text: Article 7(2) relating to nationality; Article 10(1 and 2) relating to family reunification; Article 38(4) relating to humanitarian protection in times of war; and Article 43(1) relating globally to the "obligations undertaken in the present Convention. . . ."

CHILD LABOR

The Problem

Child labor raises real dilemmas for policy: While working long hours limits or precludes the investment in human capital that might increase an individual's lifetime productivity, prohibiting child labor could raise the probability of a family's falling below the poverty level.[49] There are worse outcomes than a child working 10 hours a day – starvation, for example. Nevertheless, the CRC requires governments to take *the individual child's* developmental needs into account. A child has a right to be protected from economic exploitation and to access resources necessary for his or her mental development. If governments are taking this responsibility seriously, we should see a decline in the incidence of child labor and an increase in educational access among CRC signatories.

Child labor has been on the decline for a century and is now close to zero in much of the industrialized world.[50] Economic as well as statutory factors have contributed to this decline. Taking an historical view, increasing wages and technological improvements toward the end of the Industrial Revolution went a long way toward reducing the incidence of children in the workplace.[51] These economic factors were supplemented in a crucial way – notably in the cotton mills of Manchester – by legal restrictions limiting the employment of young children.[52] Legal interventions were especially important in protecting children in the nineteenth-century United States in the relatively low-technology sectors of the economy.[53] More broadly, studies suggest that labor registration and inspection systems, advancing technology, and higher income levels have all contributed to the reduction of children's participation in the formal sector.[54]

Yet, a significant number of children continue to work long hours, sometimes in dangerous conditions, in much of the developing world. A. Glenn Mower notes that when the CRC was drafted, ". . . 25 percent of all children ages 6–11 in low income countries were not in school because they were working and 60 percent of those in the 12–15 year age bracket in these nations were working, not attending school."[55] UNICEF estimates that some 246 million

49 Pigou 1962. See the contemporary case discussions in Schmitz et al. 2004.
50 The decline in child labor is widely recognized and commented on. See, for example, the discussion in Basu 1999. This is not to say that the hazards have been eliminated. For a discussion of the continuing risks associated with child labor in the United States, see Levine 2003.
51 See, for example, Scholliers' (1995) study of Ghent cotton mills.
52 Economic historians have made a good case that legal prohibitions were actually quite important in reducing child labor in the Manchester cotton mills, for example. See Bolin-Hort 1989.
53 See Martin et al. (1992), whose study of the vegetable canning industry in the nineteenth-century United States concludes that technology changes were most important in reducing child labor but that legal prohibitions were crucial in some of the lower-technology industries.
54 Boyden and Rialp 1995:185.
55 Mower 1997:34.

children are engaged in labor worldwide, and believes that about three-quarters of these children can be described as working in hazardous occupations, such as mining, or working with chemicals, pesticides, or dangerous machinery. The vast majority, according to UNICEF, work in the agricultural sector (about 70 percent). The largest number of young workers (127 million below the age of 15) are located in Asia, followed by Africa with 48 million and Latin America and the Caribbean (about 17 million).[56] The primary explanations for the continued use of child workers in many of these countries are exceptionally low wages (hence the need to supplement family incomes); technological underdevelopment (hence a relatively high demand for unskilled labor and a relatively low demand for skilled labor); and a lack of affordable educational opportunities.[57] Under these conditions, families often make the decision to send their children to work instead of school. Children have their own motives to work as well: Work increases their status in the household and the community, elevating them from dependent to provider in a way that, for some, constitutes a positive experience.[58]

For a number of reasons, child labor practices are difficult to change. For starters, it must be noted that there is nowhere near the normative consensus on the child labor issue that there is (at least at the rhetorical level) against torture. Child labor has not, in all times and places, been considered a bad thing. In early modern England, it was somewhat unpleasant but generally a practice thought to be consistent with the interests of the child.[59] In many parts of the world today, child labor is viewed as natural.[60] Moreover, those who employ children in the workplace have a strong vested interest in their continued use.[61] Even if they wanted to, governments could not eliminate the problem on their own: Lowering the dependence on the low-wage labor of children must actually be implemented by civil society and private actors, such as employers, educators, and, not least, parents. As Jo Boyden and Victoria Rialp note, "The challenge for governments, therefore, is to create and sustain coalitions against child labor that are made up of non-statutory, and in some cases even voluntary grass roots bodies, the private sector, and private individuals, none of whom have binding commitments under the CRC."[62]

Child labor has important consequences for the individual child as well as for the society of which he or she is a member. As the CRC explicitly expresses, children have a basic right not to be exploited economically and to have the

---

56 See http://www.unicef.org/protection/index_childlabour.html (accessed 6 May 2006).
57 These factors are reviewed by the World Bank at http://www.worldbank.org/html/extdr/hnp/ hddflash/workp/wp_00056.html#TofC3 (accessed 6 May 2006). See also Canagarajah and Nielsen 2001.
58 Szanton Blanc 1994.
59 Cunningham 1990.
60 See, for example, the discussion in Renteln (1990:59–60), discussing the value many societies place on child and youth labor. For a discussion of Eurocentrism in this context, see Myers 2001.
61 Boyden and Rialp 1995:183.
62 Boyden and Rialp 1995:184.

opportunity to develop their mental, physical, and spiritual capabilities. Working too hard – especially in dangerous and exploitative conditions – makes this impossible. Studies in Latin America confirm that participation in the workforce is a good predictor of educational underachievement,[63] which has negative consequences for the individual child's future autonomy and well-being. Pervasive child labor also contributes to an economy-wide developmental "trap" in which high dependence on children reduces wages, discouraging school attendance, and further depressing the prospects for future economic development.[64] Since poverty is a primary reason for the inability to realize social and economic rights, the appropriate regulation of child labor can have consequences for the human rights of the next generation of children as well.

International Law and Child Labor: From the ILO to the CRC

The ILO, and the international labor movement more generally, spearheaded the first efforts to regulate child labor. Since its founding in 1919, the ILO's approach was to limit the employment of "youths" sector by sector. The Minimum Age Convention (C-138), adopted by the ILO in 1973, was meant to supersede these sectoral regulations and aimed for the "total abolition of child labor" and progressive increases in minimum age standards. C-138 is the first legally binding document in which children were defined specifically: The minimum age for employment is to be no less than the age for compulsory schooling, and in any case not less than 15 (for hazardous work, not less than 18), with 14 years of age set initially for the lowest-income countries.[65] By the mid-1990s only about 50 countries had ratified,[66] but that number reached 144 as of 2005. India and Pakistan – two of the world's most significant sources of child labor – have not yet ratified.[67]

In comparison, the CRC does not seek to ban child labor; instead, the framers sought to prohibit employment that is dangerous or interferes with a young child's development. Article 32(1) states that the "States Parties recognize the right of the child to be protected from economic exploitation and from performing any work that is likely to be hazardous or to interfere with the child's education, or to be harmful to the child's health or physical, mental, spiritual, moral or social development."[68] State parties are required to implement minimum-age laws for

---

63 Psacharopoulos 1997.
64 See the economic analysis in Basu 1999.
65 Convention Concerning Minimum Age for Admission to Employment; International Labor Organization Convention No. 138. *Adopted* 26 June 1973; Session 58, Geneva. *Entry into force* 19 June 1976. Articles 2(3 and 4) and 3(1).
66 Smolin 2000:945.
67 See ratification information at http://www.ilo.org/ilolex/cgi-lex/ratifce.pl?C138 (accessed 17 July 2008).
68 For a general discussion of these obligations, see Detrick 1999:558–79; Mower 1997:34–8.

employment and to regulate the conditions of work.[69] In addition, state parties are obligated to make primary education compulsory, secondary education accessible to all, and vocational and higher education "accessible to all on the basis of capacity by every appropriate means."[70] They are further obligated to "encourage regular attendance at schools" and to take measures to reduce dropout rates.[71] The CRC implicitly recognizes that educational opportunities and child labor are inextricably related. The question is, has such a public legal commitment done much to improve the actual experiences of children?

Data and Methods

This section focuses on what the CRC has contributed to the reduction of child exploitation in the workforce. The dependent variable is the share of children in the 10- to 14-year age group that is in the workforce (World Bank, World Development Indicators). This is not a perfect measure of child labor, since it is possible that children younger than 10 could be working, but the labor of the 10–14 age group is more likely to be productive than that of younger groups and it is a useful proxy for the central hypothesis: that a commitment to the CRC is associated with a reduction in the share of individuals whose labor is exploited at a young age.[72] Unfortunately, the data available globally are very spotty until the 1990s,[73] and in the analyses that follow, it has been necessary to interpolate in order to construct a reasonable time series for analysis. From the data we do have, however, it is clear that in most of the developed world, the share of this age group working is close to zero, and for much of the developing world, the ratio has been on a gradual decline (Figure 8.3).

In order to get an adequate "before and after" picture for the statistical analysis, it is necessary, via interpolation, to extend the data back to 1985. Since it is clear that in all regions of the world child labor has trended down, all statistical tests include a year trend as well as year and country fixed effects to isolate the influence of making a treaty commitment to children. A lagged dependent variable – which accounts for most of the variance in these models – is included such that we are really measuring the acceleration in the rate of reduction over time. The statistical tests are thus designed to test for what a

---

69 CRC, Article 32(2) and (3).
70 CRC, Article 28(1)(a–d).
71 CRC, Article 28(1)(e).
72 The focus here is on the age of workers, not the exact nature of their work. While the latter is clearly important to children's health and safety, employment at a very young age is likely to interfere with education and undermine future economic opportunities. See the discussion in Smolin 2000:976–80.
73 Underreporting of underage workers is a serious problem, even in a country like the United States, where significant resources are devoted to data collection (Kruse and Mahony 2000). Moreover, the lack of a uniform definition of child labor (never clearly defined by the ILO [Smolin 2000]) means that these estimates are likely to contain a very high degree of noise.

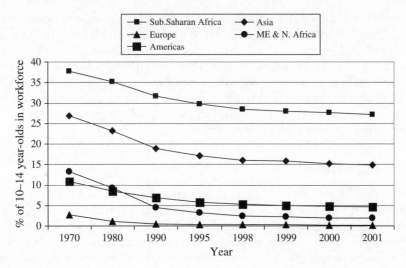

Figure 8.3. Child Labor by Region, 1970–2001. *Source*: World Development Indicators, World Bank.

CRC commitment *adds* to the apparent reduction of child labor around the world. Simultaneous estimations using instrumental variables regression is used to endogenize the treaty commitment itself.

A number of control variables are included to rule out alternative explanations for reductions in child labor. First, the prevalence of child labor could simply be associated with changing economic conditions. Figure 8.3 makes it clear that child labor is related in some way to development, with Africa having the highest rates and Europe the lowest. It is less clear that this effect will show up in a fixed effect model, but several versions presented here test for its significance. The first model compares the effect of ratification of the CRC with a battery of economic variables, including a measure of wealth (log of GDP per capita), GDP growth, and the share of GDP accounted for by international trade. I also control for the share of GDP from agriculture, since agriculture is the sector most likely to employ young children. It is therefore important to control for the natural reduction in child labor as a population shifts from agricultural production to more industrial lifestyles.

Some countries may also have outside incentives to reduce the economic exploitation of children, so the second model focuses on external factors that could influence the employment of children. Development aid could be used as a tool to discourage this practice (indeed, the CRC encourages "international cooperation" in this regard),[74] so a measure of overseas development assistance

---

74 Specifically with respect to provisions for disabled children (Article 23(4)) and education in general (Article 28(3)).

(normalized as a percentage of GDP) is included. The promise of preferential trade could also be a lever to discourage child labor. The total number of a country's preferential trade agreements (PTAs) is included to control for this possibility. If these external inducements are used "effectively,"[75] we should expect them to be associated with a reduction in the share of young children in the workforce. Some studies have found that exposure to external trade and investment alone are associated with a lower incidence of child labor,[76] so I control for trade as a share of GDP. Other external influences could be important as well. If large-scale international military conflicts draw adults out of the workforce and into the military or paramilitary forces, families with children may have an economic opportunity and an enhanced incentive to put their children to work in newly vacated jobs or tasks. If child labor substitutes for adult labor during widespread violent conflicts, then we should expect to see a positive correlation between these wars and the share of children in the workforce.

I control for regional child labor ratios since regions might share cultural traditions or economic conditions that explain employment patterns more broadly. Child labor practices could be the result of trends that are regionally specific but that none of these measures adequately address. Regional economic shocks, evolution of regional culture, common regional political conditions, and regional socialization, learning, or even mimicry could cause the rates across neighboring countries to move together. Since, as I have shown, the regional trends to ratify treaties are quite strong, failure to control for regional practices could lead to the faulty inference that improvements in the ratio are due to treaty ratification rather than these commonly experienced or interdependent regional effects. To address this, I include ratification of ILO conventions relating to child labor, hypothesizing that these might have encouraged some countries to get an early start in reducing dependence on children in the workplace. Additionally, several models include the average regional child labor rate.

Finally, I control for other domestic factors – demographic, political, and institutional – that could account for the patterns of youth employment. It is crucial, for example, to control for the size of the youth population (the share of the population under 14 years of age)[77] since the larger the young demographic group, the smaller the *proportion* of that group that should be expected to be at

---

75 I use the term advisedly since there are good reasons *not* to link trade in a conditional way to child labor practices.

76 Countries that are more open to trade and/or have a higher stock of foreign direct investment also have a lower incidence of child labor (Neumayer and de Soysa 2005). These authors have also found that countries that are more open to trade have fewer rights violations of free association and collective bargaining rights than more closed ones.

77 Additionally, some studies suggest that family size is an important determinant of an older sibling's educational attainment and of the likelihood of participating in the workforce as a child (Patrinos and Psacharopoulos 1997). A large proportion of the population under 14 is a reasonable proxy for family size.

Table 8.1. CRC Commitment and Child Labor

Dependent variable: proportion of 10- to 14-year olds in the labor force
Instrumental variable least squares regression
Coefficients, probabilities based on robust standard errors

Explanatory Variables	Model 1: Economic Factors	Model 2: External Factors	Model 3: Domestic Factors	Model 4: Combined	Model 5: Reduced-Form All Countries	Model 6: Reduced-Form Low-Income Countries	Model 7: Reduced-Form Middle-Income Countries	Model 8: Reduced-Form High-Income Countries
CRC commitment	-.139*** (p = .008)	-.102** (.042)	-.198*** (p = .002)	-.128** (p = .036)	-.133*** (p = .004)	-.064 (p = .230)	-.148** (p = .038)	-.027 (p = .284)
Child labor, $t-1$	1.004*** (p = .000)	1.004*** (p = .000)	1.001*** (p = .000)	1.002*** (p = .000)	1.002*** (p = .000)	.993*** (p = .000)	1.004*** (p = .000)	.775*** (p = .000)
GDP growth	-.00007 (p = .862)	—	—	-.0002 (p = .773)	—	—	—	—
GDP per capita, logged	.071 (p = .118)	—	—	.081 (p = .410)	—	—	—	—
Agriculture share of GDP	.002** (p = .049)	—	—	.002 (p = .409)	—	—	—	—
Trade openness	.0001 (p = .483)	-.00002 (p = .348)	—	.00017 (p = .674)	—	—	—	—
Preferential trade agreements	—	-.029*** (p = .002)	—	-.033* (p = .083)	-.027** (p = .050)	-.046 (p = .211)	-.031 (p = .162)	-.003 (p = .290)
Overseas development assistance/GDP	—	.027 (p = .687)	—	.255** (p = .049)	—	—	—	—
Regional child labor	—	.009 (p = .494)	—	.019 (p = .359)	—	—	—	—
Interstate war	—	-.036 (p = .403)	—	-.046 (p = .259)	—	—	—	—

	(1)	(2)	(3)	(4)	(5)	(6)	(7)	(8)
Ratified ILO 182	—	−.030* (p = .100)	—	−.039 (p = .170)	—	—	—	—
% of population < 14	—	—	−.022** (p = .022)	−.009 (p = .316)	−.020*** (p = .003)	−.027* (p = .087)	−.018 (p = .174)	−.005 (p = .776)
% of population urban	—	—	.005 (p = .400)	.009 (p = .118)	—	—	—	—
Civil war	—	—	−.044 (p = .257)	.003 (p = .930)	—	—	—	—
Female illiteracy rate	—	—	−.0007 (p = .988)	−.004 (p = .356)	—	—	—	—
Compulsory education through age 15	—	—	.109 (p = .877)	.653 (p = .254)	—	—	—	—
Democracy	—	—	−.003 (p = .223)	−.005** (p = .044)	−.006* (p = .053)	—	—	—
Bureaucratic quality	—	—	−.018 (p = .113)	−.016 (p = .108)	−.015 (p = .133)	−.006 (p = .630)	−.020 (p = .148)	.034* (p = .086)
Year	.011*** (p = .004)	.014*** (p = .003)	.011 (p = .313)	.018 (p = .150)	.017*** (p = .009)	−.003 (p = .681)	.016* (p = .060)	.0003 (p = .761)
Country fixed effects?	yes	yes	yes	yes	yes	yes	yes	yes
Year fixed effects?	yes	yes	yes	yes	yes	yes	yes	yes
# of countries	154	158	102	94	165	45 (cases)	76 (cases)	34 (cases)
# of observations	2,157	2,301	1,451	1,248	2,307	557	971	482
R^2	.99	.99	.99	.99	.99	.99	.99	.98

Note: Results are robust when neither country nor year fixed effects are included, but not when country fixed effects are included but year fixed effects are not. Results are robust whether or not the year trend is included. Instrumented: CRC commitment. Instruments: number of years since CRC ratification, regional density of CRC ratification, Common law legal tradition, and three splines.

* Significant at the .10 level; ** significant at the .05 level; *** significant at the .01 level.

work. Political conditions and institutions, including the quality of democratic governance itself, could influence the prevalence of child labor, so Model 3 controls for democracy as well as the quality of the government bureaucracy. If child labor is related to political development, one might expect these conditions to be associated with reductions in the rate of child employment. I also control for urban population and civil war, since child labor could be influenced by broader political disruptions on a scale that could be expected to impact labor markets. Of course, if children are in school, it will be much harder for them to participate in the workforce, so I have collected data on the laws relating to compulsory education in each country, and I control for those whose attendance in school is required through age 15.[78] Because some studies have found that parents who themselves are educated want their own children to go to school rather than to work,[79] I also control for adult female literacy.

The results of several tests of these arguments are presented in Table 8.1. All of the models in the table report the results of two-stage ordinary least squares models, with country and year fixed effects[80] (not reported) and a lagged dependent variable. Unsurprisingly, these variables alone account for the vast bulk of the variance in the rate of children's participation in the labor market. In the first four models, ratification of the CRC does appear to be strongly associated with a reduction in the rate of child labor in the following year. This is true whether we include only those variables that are statistically significant (Model 5) or the full complement of controls described previously (Model 4). According to these results, ratification of the CRC alone is responsible for an acceleration in the reduction in child labor of about a tenth to a fifth of a percentage point in the first year after ratifying (−.102 in Model 2 to −.198 in Model 3).[81]

One of the most interesting findings among the control variables is the apparently significant relationship between PTAs and the reduction of child labor. In every specification, the larger the number of such agreements, the more likely a country was to reduce its dependence on child labor. This is true even

---

78 With respect to legislative interventions, compulsory education is found in some studies to be more effective than prohibiting child labor, since presence in school is more readily monitored than absence from the workplace (Weiner 1991). Studies in India suggest that the availability of good schools alone can do a good deal to draw children out of the workplace to get an education (Dreze and Gazdar 1997). On the other hand, even when schooling is subsidized, it is difficult to get families in very poor countries, such as Bangladesh, to significantly reduce their children's hours of labor (Ravallion and Wodon 2000).

79 Parents who are educated understand the importance of schooling from personal experience. As a result, parental education plays a large role in determining child schooling and employment (Tienda 1979).

80 Note that the results are not robust to a specification that includes the country fixed effects only. Statistically significant results for the CRC require either no fixed effects or fixed effects for both country and year.

81 Models for three and five years out show an accumulation rather than a reduction in this rate over time, so the results presented here are quite conservative.

when we control for the impact of obvious developmental and demographic conditions. Each PTA accelerates the reduction in child labor by about three hundredths of 1 percent each year (−.033 in Model 4). The negotiation of five new PTAs (the maximum in our sample) could therefore have the effect of accelerating the reduction in child labor by about 1.5 percent. The lag structure (observance of the PTA prior to the change in child labor rates) suggests that causation runs from the agreements to the rates, but because PTAs themselves are not endogenized in this model, we may be overlooking important selection effects. Nonetheless, these results strongly suggest that external incentives – in this case, the incentive to form special trading relationships – could have an important impact on a country's willingness to fall in line with what is an apparently significant norm: Children should not be exploited for economic purposes. Note the strength of PTAs' correlation with reduced child labor even when overall trade as a share of GDP has been controlled.

It is quite surprising how weakly many of the other variables performed. The only economic variable that showed any sign of statistical significance in explaining child labor was the share of GDP accounted for by agriculture. As this share increases, child labor tends to increase as well (Model 1). This effect is swamped by other factors, however (Model 4). Among the external influences on child labor, the strongest and most robust is that of PTAs. The share of trade in GDP and the provision of development assistance, on the other hand, had no impact. This suggests an important role for trade conditionality as a tool for addressing child labor. The hypothesis that war could divert labor from the economy to the battlefield and suck children into productive jobs was never supported by the data, but there does seem to be a marginal impact of at least one ILO convention (though this is swamped in the combined model).[82] In contrast to many of the models in previous chapters, average child labor ratios in the region never predicted the ratio of a country within that region.

Model 3 tests additional domestic conditions' ability to explain child labor. The level of democracy and the quality of a country's public bureaucracy are especially significant in this regard (unfortunately, the two are quite closely correlated, so it is difficult for both to be statistically significant in the same model). Popular government and a competent bureaucracy are associated with reductions in child employment. Model 3 also demonstrates the importance of controlling for the youth of the population, although the estimate is somewhat unstable across specifications. The larger the proportion of the population under 14, the smaller the proportion of that group that is likely to be economically active. Even so, ratification of the CRC was highly significant, and in fact the estimate reached its maximum – accelerating the reduction in child labor by

---

82 ILO Convention 138 was also tested but was not found to be statistically significant in any specification and was dropped from the analysis.

about a fifth of a percentage point in the first year after ratification – in this specification.

More interesting still is the incidence of the CRC's most beneficial effects. The CRC has had its weakest effects in countries with an extremely low capacity to address the issue: low-income countries. These countries are highly constrained on two counts. First, and most obviously, families in poorer countries are highly motivated to have at least some of their children work. The fruit of their labor may be the only thing keeping a family from slipping into starvation. Second, these are the countries that are least likely to have the resources to enforce whatever rules may in fact exist to address the exploitation of children. In the poorest countries, child labor is a "stubborn fact," and while ratification of the CRC may contribute on the margins in these countries (the coefficient is negative but not statistically significant), it is not likely a major tool for addressing the problem. Indeed, in these countries, we may need to allow for the fact that child labor is not perceived as a problem at all, but rather as a palliative for dire family poverty.

The CRC also has very weak if any effects in rich countries. With many protections for children already in place, the CRC provides practically no new protections for children as workers. The expected value of using the CRC to mobilize to protect children from economic exploitation is probably quite small in these countries. Groups and the broader public within these countries are likely to have little incentive to wave the CRC in front of public officials or to use it on any significant scale as legal leverage.

The story is apparently quite different in the middle-income countries. In these countries, it is far less likely that a child's labor is the difference between starvation and survival. Not working – and instead investing in an education – is a realistic possibility. Governments have the resources, if they decide to deploy them, to encourage and ensure that students are in school rather than selling cigarettes on the street. In these countries, children's advocates have the motivation to demand compliance with CRC obligations. The CRC can be a resource for advocates to hold governments to their commitments. A comparison of Models 6–8 shows that the CRC apparently has its most significant effect in these middle-income countries, where groups have both the motive and the means to shape children's future by using the CRC as a focal point for their organization and advocacy.

BASIC HEALTH CARE: IMMUNIZATIONS

If the CRC has had an important effect on the prevalence of child labor, it is reasonable to ask whether there is further evidence that it has encouraged governments to work to improve the quality of life for their nation's children. One area in which the CRC imposes fairly clear obligations on governments is with respect to basic provisions for children's health. The convention, for example, requires governments to try to provide the "highest attainable standard of health" (Article 24), which includes an emphasis on primary health care and the encouragement of a "basic knowledge of child health."[83] Article 6, moreover, establishes an obligation on the part of state parties to "ensure to the maximum extent possible" child survival.[84] One way this can be done is for governments to make basic vaccines for childhood diseases – diphtheria, pertussis, tetanus (DPT), measles, polio, and tuberculosis – more widely available. Indeed, immunizations for these common diseases are one of the most cost-effective ways to save children's lives and improve overall health. A study published in *Lancet* in 2003 estimated that vaccinating all babies worldwide against measles alone would have spared the lives of more than 103,000 children under five years of age in 2000.[85] This section tests the proposition that the CRC has had an important effect on the immunization rates of the youngest children, between one and two years of age.

Fortunately for the children of the world, there has been an increase over time in the immunization rates for these diseases. Figure 8.4 demonstrates that some of the sharpest increases in these rates began before the CRC was open for ratification. Clearly, it is possible to boost immunizations without a treaty that creates an obligation to improve the health of children. For example, UNICEF's Universal Childhood Immunization campaign (1985–90) is quite likely responsible, in part, for the steep increase in immunization rates during those pre-CRC years.[86] The question in this section is, what, if anything, has CRC ratification added to the effort to inoculate children for childhood diseases worldwide? The models to be specified try to estimate the treaty effect as distinct from global campaigns and foreign aid (controlled in the models). Year fixed effects are also used to help account for global campaigns that on their own might accelerate immunization rates.

As is the case with every rights provision examined in this study, many factors other than treaty obligations contribute to the realization of rights. Regarding immunization, a vast public health literature has focused on the issue. The majority of these studies are concerned with the question of uptake – when and why do families decide to have their babies inoculated? Most examine single counties (even villages) and are based on micro-level surveys. As I argued in Chapter 6, uptake is not the ideal indicator for this study. Most problematically, it comes closest to confusing treaty compliance with treaty effectiveness. It is easy to imagine conditions under which governments support vaccination while families strongly resist (the same could, of course, be said for child labor,

---

83 CRC, Articles 24(1) and 24(2)(e).
84 CRC, Article 6(2).
85 Jones et al. 2003:68.
86 In 1982 UNICEF initiated the "Child Survival Revolution," which emphasized rehydration and immunization for diseases common to early childhood worldwide, including measles and DPT (Justice 2000).

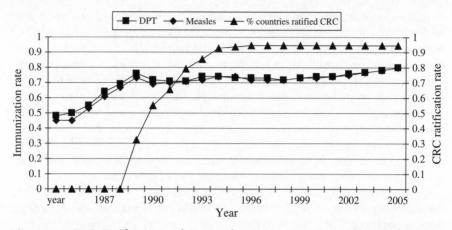

Figure 8.4. CRC Ratification and Rates of One- to Two-Year-Old Immunizations Worldwide. *Source*: World Development Indicators. *Note*: Includes ratifications and accessions.

discussed earlier). But in the absence of any policy or programmatic evidence, I am using immunization rates as a rough proxy for compliance narrowly and treaty effects more generally. The strategy is to control for as many uptake factors as possible and interpret the findings in that light. Factors that are found to be associated in micro-level studies with uptake will be controlled at the national level in the following tests.

Explanations for the decision to have a baby inoculated have focused largely on the maternal, familial, and village settings. One factor of key importance in several studies is the ability of parents to know and to understand the importance of the treatment. Several micro-level studies have pointed to the importance of maternal education in explaining the demand for inoculations. Desai and Alva find that maternal education is a strong predictor of children's immunization status in many countries, even when controlling for a host of other variables.[87] The more mothers know about the protective effects of immunizations, the more likely they are to have their children immunized.[88] Thus, in the

---

87 Desai and Alva 1998. See also Gage et al. (1997), whose intensive study of Niger and Nigeria suggests that maternal education may be even more important than family structure in explaining immunization rates among children in those countries.

88 See Streatfield et al. 1990. Women's education – and empowerment more generally – has been central to a number of studies on immunization uptake. For example, Steele et al. (1996) found that membership of women in Bangladesh in "Women's Savings Groups" set up by Save the Children had a strong positive effect on immunization uptake, evidence that "education" should be understood broadly and need not be formal to be quite effective. For a broad-ranging discussion of conditions influencing vaccination uptake, see Streefland et al. 1999.

tests that follow, I control for the national rate of female illiteracy, as was the case with child labor.

Another key uptake issue is access. Several studies have found that the distance to a health clinic is important in determining whether or not a child is inoculated.[89] The further a family has to travel, the less likely they are to get the health care they need; this is true for immunizations as well. On the assumption that urban areas are better served by health clinics – and that distances tend to be greater in rural areas – it is important to control for how urban each country is. Urbanization should increase the chances of having a clinic nearby and should therefore be associated with increased immunization rates.

The demand for immunization is also likely to be influenced by the cost. The less affordable any medical treatment is, the harder it will be to convince families to pay for the service. Affordability may be an issue at the level of national policy as well. One important predictor of demand for vaccines is their cost relative to the economy.[90] Poor countries are expected to have much lower immunization rates than wealthy ones. While most of this effect will be picked up in the country fixed effects, it may also be that as wealth increases, immunization rates increase as well.

There are, of course, a number of ways in which immunization costs can be mitigated. One is through foreign development assistance, which might subsidize or pay for vaccines directly or might supplement public budgets to make vaccines more broadly available. I therefore control for overseas development assistance as a proportion of GDP. But beyond general aid, it is often crucial for developing countries to have access to international institutional support to address issues not only of cost, but also of information and medical infrastructure.[91] Specific global immunization funds have been set up to increase developing countries' access to vaccines. One such group is the Global Alliance for Vaccines and Immunization (GAVI), a public-private partnership launched in 2000 whose sole aim is to save lives and improve health through childhood immunization.[92] Governments below a certain wealth threshold defined by the group are invited to apply for funds to support particular projects for immunization delivery. The activities of this group may have been inspired by the vision of the CRC, but it operates quite independently. Since it would not be appropriate to attribute higher coverage rates to CRC ratification that might be attributable to funding from this group, I control for whether a country applied for and actually received support from the GAVI fund in a particular year. Since one of the most important factors in immunization rates is the extent to which international and bilateral agencies promote and national governments

---

89 Pebley et al. 1996.
90 Miller and Flanders 2000.
91 Mahoney and Maynard 1999.
92 For a description of GAVI, its organization, membership, goals and activities, see http://www.gavialliance.org/.

appreciate the potential value of new vaccines,[93] the work of this group – with emphasis not only on providing vaccines but also on information and medical infrastructure – is potentially quite important.[94]

A host of other factors can influence a government's willingness and ability to supply access to childhood immunizations.[95] Some regimes have made it a national priority to immunize all children, while others have depended on the parents to make the decision. This might explain the somewhat paradoxical finding that except in very poor countries, democracies have lower coverage rates than autocracies.[96] Other regimes may simply lack the capacity or expertise to organize health care delivery with any appreciable reliability or on any significant scale. Thus, the quality of a country's institutions – its "bureaucratic capacities" – is also expected to be strongly related to immunization rate coverage and vaccine adoption.[97] Furthermore, regions of violent conflict have been especially difficult to bring under disease control, because it is hard to access, monitor, and earn the trust of populations in need of inoculations in these areas.[98] As in the case of child labor, I control for both international and civil wars, with the expectation that these violent conflicts will reduce the likelihood that babies will be inoculated.

The results are reported in Table 8.2. The dependent variables in this table are the proportion of one- to two-year-olds who have been immunized against measles and DPT. These vaccines were chosen because they are in principle widely available and because the consensus in the medical profession is that they are a highly cost-effective way to improve human health.[99] The World Bank has also made these data accessible in a consistent time series. One thing is clear in Table 8.2: Ratification of the CRC is far less consistently related to immunization rates than it is to child labor. According to these results, there is no relationship with DPT coverage at all. In fact, the only factor that seems consistently to influence DPT coverage is violent civil conflict. Not surprisingly, governments have other priorities during such conflicts; with vulnerable populations difficult to reach and monitor, immunization rates do in fact seem to plummet.

For reasons that are not clear, the measles immunization rate is (very weakly) likely to be associated with CRC ratification. This suggests that in the year following ratification, on average the inoculation rate accelerated by about 3 percent. As with DPT, civil conflict is the only other factor to

---

93 Hausdorff 1996.
94 Gauri and Khaleghian (2002) find that "the global policy environment and contact with international agencies" is one of the most important determinants of immunization rates.
95 Gauri and Khaleghian (2002) argue that coverage rates respond more to supply-side than demand effects, at least at the present time.
96 Gauri and Khaleghian 2002.
97 Gauri and Khaleghian 2002.
98 This has been the case, for example, with polio eradication. See Hull and Aylward 2001; Widdus 1999:S10.
99 See Jones et al. 2003.

Table 8.2. CRC Commitment and Child Immunizations

Dependent variable: proportion of 1- to 2-year-olds inoculated for specified disease
Instrumental variable least squares regression
Coefficients, probabilities based on robust standard errors

Explanatory Variables	Development/ Demographic Model		Conflict/Political Model		High-Income Cases Only	Middle-Income Cases Only	Low- and Middle-Income Cases Only
	Measles	DPT	Measles	DPT	Measles	Measles	Measles
CRC commitment	2.79*	.937	1.48	.306	−1.17	3.63*	3.24**
	($p = .092$)	($p = .392$)	($p = .287$)	($p = .771$)	($p = .236$)	($p = .062$)	($p = .049$)
Immunization (measles or DTP), $t - 1$	.581***	.624***	.674***	.732***	.633***	.477***	.574***
	($p = .000$)	($p = .000$)	($p = .000$)	($p = .000$)	($p = .000$)	($p = .000$)	($p = .000$)
Total population, logged	19.85	6.61	—	—	—	—	—
	($p = .169$)	($p = .598$)					
% of population <14, logged	.350	−1.40	—	—	—	—	—
	($p = .957$)	($p = .826$)					
% of population urban, logged	−7.97	−2.71	—	—	—	—	—
	($p = .169$)	($p = .604$)					
Overseas development assistance/GDP	1.24	2.58	—	—	—	—	—
	($p = .842$)	($p = .533$)					
GDP per capita, logged	−18.97	7.38	—	—	—	—	—
	($p = .161$)	($p = .503$)					
GDP, logged	−17.06	−4.81	—	—	—	—	—
	($p = .169$)	($p = .654$)					
Female illiteracy rate	.079	.034					
	($p = .465$)	($p = .734$)					
GAVI award	1.62	1.38	—	—	—	—	2.56**
	($p = .154$)	($p = .335$)					($p = .015$)
Bureaucratic quality	.281	.184	—	—	−1.57	.516	.303
	($p = .451$)	($p = .579$)			($p = .133$)	($p = .310$)	($p = .384$)

(continued)

Table 8.2 (continued)

Explanatory Variables	Development/Demographic Model		Conflict/Political Model		High-Income Cases Only	Middle-Income Cases Only	Low- and Middle-Income Cases Only
	Measles	DPT	Measles	DPT	Measles	Measles	Measles
Civil war	—	—	-2.91*** (p = .001)	-2.14*** (p = .007)	—	-3.41* (p = .086)	-3.36*** (p = .003)
Interstate war	—	—	-1.46 (p = .196)	1.12 (p = .212)	.829 (p = .623)	—	—
Democratic	—	—	-.066 (p = .540)	-.009 (p = .916)	—	—	—
Left executive	—	—	-.273 (p = .619)	.242 (p = .599)	—	—	—
Regional immunization (measles or DTP)	—	—	—	—	.083 (p = .477)	.261*** (p = .000)	.215*** (p = .002)
Year	-.236 (p = .581)	-.040 (p = .855)	.493*** (p = .000)	.254*** (p = .002)	.236 (p = ...)†	-.064 (p = .747)	-.184 (p = .732)
Country fixed effects?	yes	yes	yes	yes	yes	yes	yes
Year fixed effects?	yes	yes	yes	yes	yes	yes	yes
Countries/cases	102	102	153	153	35 cases	76 cases	106 cases
Observations	1,567	1,568	2,608	2,665	554	1,069	1,701
R^2	.88	.91	.90	.93	.86	.83	.89

Note: Results are robust whether or not the year trend is included. Instrumented: CRC commitment. Instruments: number of years since CRC ratification, regional density of CRC ratification, common law legal tradition, and three splines.

In specifications by income category, analysis is by *case* rather than *country*, since countries can shift income categories. There are therefore more cases than countries in the last three models.

* Significant at the .10 level; ** significant at the .05 level; *** significant at the .01 level.

† A *p*-value could not be calculated due to the small number of observations.

systematically influence immunization rates (in the same negative direction). As was the case with child labor, we can also see that the CRC has had its greatest positive impact in middle-income countries. Indeed, when low-income countries alone are analyzed, the only significant explanation for the coverage rate is the rate in the previous year and the coverage rate of other countries in the region. Not even civil war influenced coverage rates in the poorest countries. The positive effects of GAVI support are clear when the middle- and low-income countries are pooled but, perhaps surprisingly, GAVI support has no effect in the poorest countries alone.

The effects of CRC ratification – if they exist in explaining immunizations – are statistically much weaker and less robust than those for child labor. This finding might indicate the difficulty of providing positive rights compared to negative protections. The former involve positive actions on the part of a range of actors, from public officials to private medical personnel. While enforcing prohibitions on child labor is not easy, it might be possible to encourage it with spot checks and occasional monitoring. In order for immunization rates to rise significantly, a health care provider must literally hold every child and insert a needle into his or her little arm, assuming that a parent is willing and able to reach a clinic. In such cases, capacity issues render treaty compliance a much more daunting task. Nonetheless, there is some evidence that in the middle-income countries at least, ratification of the CRC is associated with higher rates of protection against these common childhood diseases.

CHILD SOLDIERS

The Problem

The use of child soldiers in military conflicts has received widespread attention in recent years, but it is hardly a new phenomenon. What seems to have changed since the end of the Cold War, however, may be the extent to which particularly brutal and drawn-out civil wars have been fought near civilian populations with the ready availability of small arms that children find relatively easy to tote. These circumstances have led to conflicts that particularly impact children.[100]

In its Global Report of 2000–1, the UN listed some 36 countries in which very young soldiers were known to be engaged in violent operations. In a few cases, these youths were recruited almost exclusively by governments (Chad, Eritrea, Ethiopia), but in most cases, both governments and opposition groups drew on children to fight their battles (primarily in Africa,[101] but also in Iran,

---

100 The UN report "Impact of Armed Conflict on Children," by Graca Machel, is of particular significance in articulating this view; see Machel 1996a, 1996b. See also Allen 2000; DeWaal 1997; Hick 2001.
101 Angola, Burundi, Republic of Congo, Democratic Republic of Congo, Rwanda, Sudan, and Uganda.

Iraq, Israel and the Occupied Territories, and Myanmar). In a relatively long list of countries, opposition forces include children, but governments have apparently refrained from responding in kind (Peru, Russia, Turkey, Lebanon, Nepal, Pakistan, the Philippines, the Solomon Islands, Sri Lanka, Tajikistan, Papua New Guinea, and Uzbekistan).[102] In a few cases, governments are loosely allied with paramilitary groups that draw on children to fill out their ranks (Colombia, Mexico, the former Yugoslavia, Algeria, India, Indonesia, and East Timor). Where conflict has been most prolonged, children have been recruited by governments, paramilitaries, *and* opposition forces (Sierra Leone, Sudan, Somalia, and Afghanistan).[103] As these cases illustrate, the contexts in which children are used in violent confrontations are often those in which the legitimate rule of the state itself is in question and where law and order have almost completely broken down.[104]

Just why children (most of whom were neither overtly coerced nor abducted) choose to fight is the subject of a growing ethnographic literature. Poverty, education, peer pressure, and identity all are cited as playing an important role.[105] Simply living in a war zone raises the probability that families will be disrupted and children swept into combat. Most children who eventually do take up arms have had little or no education and have little immediate hope of receiving much, if any.[106] In this light, children's involvement in combat should be understood as making the best of a bad situation.[107] Anthropologists and sociologists, through their ethnographic research in Africa, have found that children often develop a fierce pride in their martial activities. Some of this research suggests that participation in war is not a wholly negative experience, and it describes the experience in some cases as empowering for the child. However, on the consequences of military combat at a young age, pediatricians and psychiatrists tend to reach different conclusions.[108]

---

102 For a discussion that focuses on the use of child soldiers primarily by rebel groups, see Briggs 2005.
103 See the UN report at http://www.un.org/works/goingon/soldiers/childsoldiersmap.html (accessed 17 July 2008).
104 Briggs 2005:153; de Berry 2001.
105 Brett and Specht 2004; Cohn and Goodwin-Gill 1994; McCallin 1998.
106 See McCallin (1998:72): "One of the most striking aspects of the Child Soldiers Research Project was the fact that, prior to their recruitment, most of the children had limited or no education, schooling was disrupted or discontinued either as a direct result of the conflict or because the family could not afford it, or families needed the income the child could provide by leaving school and working." Families' economic security is key to avoiding rerecruitment.
107 "In countries where poverty and numbers overwhelm education and job opportunities, militia enrolment is seen by many as a better option than starving on the street. But recruitment also reflects the discovery that children are good fighters" (Peters and Richards 1998:76).
108 Victoria Bernal's (2000) study of women and girls in the Eritrean war suggests that a certain amount of (temporary) empowerment was associated with their involvement. Similarly, Harry West's study of women and girls in Mozambique's liberation front concludes that young female participants often felt "empowered rather than victimized by the war" (2000:180). Compare the views of pediatricians and psychiatrists, who view the experience of participation in armed conflict as overwhelmingly negative (Pearn 2003; Somasundaram 2002).

International Law and Child Soldiers

As a matter of international law, unless a state has ratified the OPCAC, the minimum age for military recruitment is 15 years. The first protocol of the Geneva Convention requires that "The Parties to the conflict shall take all feasible measures in order that children who have not attained the age of fifteen years do not take a direct part in hostilities and, in particular, they shall refrain from recruiting them into their armed forces. . . ."[109] The CRC contains a nearly identical obligation.[110] Furthermore, the International Criminal Court defines the systematic recruitment for combat of youths of age below 15 as a war crime,[111] and the court's first defendant faces this specific charge.[112]

The OPCAC was an explicit effort to nudge the international norm upward toward 18 years, spearheaded by the former foreign minister of Uganda, Olara Otunnu, and spurred on by the Coalition to Stop the Use of Child Soldiers.[113] At the time the OPCAC was negotiated, nearly half of the membership of the UN – the United States included – permitted *voluntary* recruitment below that age. The protocol ended up banning mandatory conscription for youths less than 18 and called for "all feasible measures" to ensure that they do not participate in hostilities.[114] NGOs promptly geared up for a global ratification campaign.[115] Nonetheless, generally, there is little confidence that international law has made significant progress in improving the lot of children with respect to armed conflict in most areas of the world.[116] The world is full of hot spots where pessimism is undoubtedly justified. Yet, there exist no systematic tests, using explicit criteria, concerning the effects of the recent effort to raise the minimum combat age. Has the OPCAC helped in this regard? This is the question explored in the following section.

---

109 Protocol to the Geneva Convention I, Article 77(2); text at http://www.icrc.org/ihl.nsf/7c4d08 d9b287a42141256739003e636b/f6c8b9fee14a77fdc12564100052b079 (accessed 17 July 2008).

110 Article 38(3) of the CRC states: "States Parties shall refrain from recruiting any person who has not attained the age of fifteen years into their armed forces. In recruiting among those persons who have attained the age of fifteen years but who have not attained the age of eighteen years, States Parties shall endeavour to give priority to those who are oldest."

111 Rome Statute of the International Criminal Court, Article VIII states: "1. The Court shall have jurisdiction in respect of war crimes in particular when committed as part of a plan or policy or as part of a large-scale commission of such crimes. 2. For the purpose of this Statute, 'war crimes' means: . . . (b) Other serious violations of the laws and customs applicable in international armed conflict, within the established framework of international law, namely, any of the following acts: . . . (xxvi) Conscripting or enlisting children under the age of fifteen years into the national armed forces or using them to participate actively in hostilities." See the text at http://untreaty.un.org/cod/icc/statute/romefra.htm (accessed 17 July 2008).

112 See the list of "situations" referred to the International Criminal Court's prosecutor at http:// www.icc-cpi.int/cases.html (accessed 17 July 2008).

113 See Gerschutz and Karns 2005:43.

114 Dennis 2000:179.

115 See http://www.child-soldiers.org/document_get.php?id=680.

116 Herbst 2004.

Data and Methods

In some ways, analyzing the effects of the OPCAC on government compliance is easier than gauging the effects of the CRC itself. For one thing, OPCAC is a focused legal requirement: It deals with the age of military service and nothing else. It is therefore easier to infer that if a government signs OPCAC, it is doing so for a specific purpose rather than responding to a vague set of child-friendly exhortations. For another, ratification of OPCAC is not nearly as universal as ratification of the treaty itself. As of May 2006, 107 countries had ratified,[117] allowing for much more observed variance on the ratification of this instrument than on that of the CRC itself.

Analyzing the CRC's OPCAC does raise some difficulties, however. The primary problem is that it was negotiated relatively recently. The first country to ratify was Canada, in July 2000. This was nearly a decade after the CRC itself, and unfortunately, for purposes of quantitative analyses, after some of the most useful datasets end. Because data are limited in time, time series analysis is not very useful in this case. Instead, I use a cross-sectional instrumental variable regression to see whether ratification of the OPCAC has increased the likelihood that a country has raised its minimum legal age for military participation. The dependent variable is *increase in the legal age* between 2000 and 2005, controlling for the observed legal age in 2000. Controlling for the observed legal age in 2000 is important because countries that now bar persons younger than 18 from the military are already in compliance and are unlikely to increase the age further. The dependent variable is coded 1 if there has been any improvement (the legal age has been raised between 2000 and 2005); otherwise, it is coded 0. The variable of primary interest, of course, is whether a country has ratified the OPCAC within this time period (2000–5). In this section, I test the proposition that an OPCAC commitment increases the likelihood that a government will raise its legal age for military participation.

In order to proceed, it was necessary to assemble an original dataset on laws and practices with respect to the age of military service around the world based on government information, CRC reports, and the observations and reports of NGOs.[118] Using and cross-checking a variety of sources, four measures of legal age provisions were coded: (1) the legal minimum age for joining the military; (2)

---

117 Ratification status can be found at http://www.unhchr.ch/html/menu2/6/protocolchild.htm (accessed 17 July 2008).

118 This database was assembled by my research assistant, Eugen Lamprecht, over the course of the summer and fall of 2005. While he did the overwhelming bulk of the data collection, all errors of fact and in the analysis that follow are my responsibility. The primary NGO source is the Coalition to Stop the Use of Child Soldiers, which issues the Child Soldiers Global Reports (published for the first time in 2001). The reports cover military recruitment laws and practices in some 190 countries. The Child Soldiers Report for 2004 can be accessed at http://www.child-soldiers.org. The previous report for 2001 can be obtained directly from the coalition.

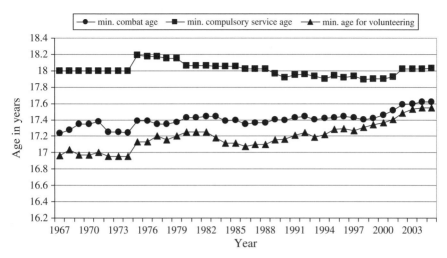

Figure 8.5. Changes in Minimum Age for Military Service, World Averages. *Source*: Author's original database, drawn from UN, NGO, and governmental sources.

the legal minimum age for military conscription (nonvoluntary); (3) the legal minimum age for voluntary enlistment; and (4) the legal age for participation in combat. Figure 8.5 shows that worldwide, the minimum age for compulsory conscription is highest at around 18 years of age. The minimum age for combat and volunteering worldwide is lower but has drifted upward over the past several years. Table 8.3 lists specific counties that increased their minimum age for military service between 2000 and 2005.

While this is probably the best database available on the status of children in the military worldwide, the data admittedly have some important limitations. First, it has not been possible to create a long time series with any confidence for most countries. Good information could be found on minimum-age laws for most countries with a high degree of confidence as far back as 1990, but prior to that time, information is quite spotty and much less reliable.[119] Second, it was not always possible to ascertain a country's laws with respect to all four of the measures defined previously. Some sources refer only to minimum enlistment age and are not specific about the conditions of service (voluntary versus compulsory; combat versus support units; with or without parental permission). Information that could not pin down such specifics was nevertheless included in the first category stated earlier. Third, all information is conditional on a

119 The database codes minimum ages only for those years in which we could document the existing law using a credible source.

Table 8.3. Countries That Increased the Age of Military Service between 2000 and 2005, by Category of Service

Volunteer Age	Combat Age	Compulsory Service Age
Afghanistan	Afghanistan	Angola
Aruba	Angola	Croatia
Belgium	Austria	Israel
Bosnia and Herzegovina	Belgium	Macedonia
Denmark	Bosnia and Herzegovina	Morocco
Estonia	Brazil	Norway
Greece	Croatia	Poland
Iraq	Denmark	
Kazakhstan	Iraq	
Macedonia	Macedonia	
Netherlands	New Zealand	
New Zealand	Norway	
Norway	Rwanda	
Rwanda	Slovak Republic	
Slovak Republic	South Africa	
South Africa	Switzerland	
Spain	Ukraine	
Switzerland		
Ukraine		

Source: Author's original database, drawn from UN, NGO, and governmental sources (see Appendix 1).

country's having a military.[120] Similarly, information on compulsory age is conditional on a regime of compulsory conscription, which is the case for only 94 countries in the dataset.

Demographics, development, and military violence are the primary variables for which it is important to control in this section. Governments might have incentives to use younger citizens in their military forces if young people are readily available, if they (or their families) need income (or at least one less hungry mouth at the table), and if the government demand for forces is high due to a military conflict (whether interstate or civil). Governments might also be influenced by the policies of other governments in their region (whether

---

120 Countries that do not have a military and therefore are never included in any of these analyses are Costa Rica, Dominica, Iceland (which nonetheless has legislation specifying 18 as the minimum age should a military be created), Kiribati, Liechtenstein, Panama (dissolved in 1990), and a number of small island countries that have police forces of a few hundred (including Saints Kitts and Nevis, Lucia, and Vincent, as well as the Solomon Islands, Vanuatu, Western Samoa (defended by New Zealand), and the Marshall Islands and Micronesia (defended by the United States).

because of normative convergence or concerns for military parity), the size and location of their population (it may be easier to recruit in urban areas, for example), and the nature of the regime itself. More autocratic regimes could be expected to ignore law in this area altogether; they are not likely to experience significant civil society pressures to change whatever rules prevailed in 2000.

Does a commitment to the OPCAC significantly increase the probability that a government will raise its minimum military service age? Table 8.4 addresses this question. It reports the results of two-stage instrumental variable regressions for five different measures of military service age.

As discussed previously, the dependent variable is an improvement in the legal age for military service sometime between 2000 and 2005 (coded 1; otherwise, coded 0). In every case, ratification of the OPCAC is associated with a change in the legal age in the expected direction (an increase in the age). In three of the cases (for voluntary military service, combat service, and any increase in military age) the change is mildly statistically significant ($p < .10$). The statistically strongest (though substantively smallest) impact is in the category of compulsory military service. Model 3 tells us that ratification of the OPCAC is associated with nearly a 39 percent greater chance that a state in fact raised the compulsory military service age at some time during the period 2000–5. Overall, these models suggest that the OPCAC has had a statistically detectable effect on the age of service for all categories with the exception of our "catchall" (and noisiest) category, "military service."[121]

The only other variables that have a consistently significant effect on the propensity to raise the minimum age requirement is a country's wealth (measured as GDP per capita) and dummy variables by region. The regional dummies indicate that countries in Sub-Saharan Africa and East Asia and the Pacific were among the most likely to raise their military service ages, in comparison to the Americas and the Middle East (the omitted categories). Countries in these regions were much more likely to raise their legal ages for most forms of military service (with the exception of the minimum age for combat service). These regional effects aside, development level almost certainly predicts an increase in the age threshold. Poorer countries were much less likely to raise their minimum service age than wealthier ones. And unsurprisingly, the higher the legal age in 2000, the less likely were governments to have raised it further by 2005.

What is surprising is what does *not* seem to influence legal change to protect children from military service. Changes in national laws between 2000 and 2005 were not significantly influenced by civil or international wars, either historically

121 It is possible that our decision to code all credible evidence of improvements in military age requirements – even though it is not specific as to conditions of service – has introduced some error into this particular measure. The other three measures – combat age, voluntary service age, and compulsory service age – may by their nature be more precise codings.

Table 8.4. CRC OPCAC Commitment and Increase in the Legal Minimum Age for Military Service

Dependent variable: increase in legal minimum military service age
Instrumental variable least squares regression
Coefficients, probabilities based on robust standard errors

Explanatory Variables	Model 1: Any Military Service		Model 2: Voluntary Military Service Only		Model 3: Compulsory Military Service Only		Model 4: Military Combat Only		Model 5: Any Increase in Age	
CRC OPCAC ratification	.331	$(p = .130)$	.490*	$(p = .064)$	.388**	$(p = .040)$	.594*	$(p = .092)$	.568*	$(p = .097)$
Legal age, 2000	-.083***	$(p = .004)$	-.096***	$(p = .004)$	-.119**	$(p = .016)$	-.246***	$(p = .001)$	-.127***	$(p = .001)$
GDP per capita, logged	.059**	$(p = .017)$	.063**	$(p = .032)$	.098**	$(p = .019)$	.127**	$(p = .024)$	.072**	$(p = .039)$
East and southern Africa	.368***	$(p = .006)$	.316**	$(p = .011)$	.650**	$(p = .043)$	.356	$(p = .235)$	.283*	$(p = .061)$
Eastern Europe	.174**	$(p = .050)$	.280**	$(p = .015)$	.450***	$(p = .005)$	.220	$(p = .246)$	-.431	$(p = .304)$
East Asia and Pacific	.162*	$(p = .069)$	.194*	$(p = .086)$	.564**	$(p = .017)$	.046	$(p = .791)$	.348*	$(p = .095)$
West Africa	.344***	$(p = .010)$	.435***	$(p = .008)$	.581***	$(p = .007)$	.452	$(p = .118)$	.778**	$(p = .036)$
Western Europe	—		—		-.938**	$(p = .011)$	.032	$(p = .925)$	-.978	$(p = .145)$
Regional improvement	.176	$(p = .163)$	.249	$(p = .146)$	1.66***	$(p = .009)$	-.324	$(p = .603)$	3.88*	$(p = .085)$
Constant	.698*	$(p = .098)$	.783	$(p = .141)$	.941	$(p = .232)$	3.01***	$(p = .006)$	.930	$(p = .125)$
# of observations	131		129		74		129		132	
R^2	—		—		.16		.12		—	

Note: Democracy, regional improvements, population, and civil and international war history (1990–7) and status (1998–2002) were never statistically significant and do not affect these results. Log of urban population and log of youth population were statistically significant only in explaining compulsory military service age.

Instrumented: OPCAC ratification. Instruments: all exogenous variables plus the number of years since OPCAC ratification, regional density of OPCAC ratification, common law legal tradition.

* Significant at the .10 level; ** significant at the .05 level; *** significant at the .01 level.

(1990–7) or contemporaneously (1998–2002). Population size never impacted the decision to change the rules, nor did the proportion of the population less than 14 years of age or the urbanization of the population. There is no evidence that popularly elected governments have behaved any differently than autocracies. Increases in the minimum age for military service in a country's region mattered in two of the models (for compulsory age and "any" increase), but the sign flips for combat age. While regions clearly differ from one another (note the importance of the regional dummy variables), regional *improvements* are not an especially compelling explanation for improvements in individual countries.

Ratification of the OPCAC is apparently associated with legal improvements in ratifying countries, but these tests say little about the *actual* use of young soldiers on the ground. Many governments have the political freedom not only to ratify treaties, but to pass domestic legislation that they have no intention of enforcing and with which they have little will to comply. An even more stringent test of the impact of the OPCAC would be to show its association with observed government *practices* in addition to changed national laws. In addition to the information on the legal age regimes described previously, we gathered evidence from NGOs and the UN on the extent to which individuals less than 18 years of age were *actually observed or reported* to be serving in a country's armed forces. "Does the government actually recruit children less than 18 years of age into the armed forces?" was the key question guiding coding of the various reports. We distinguished cases in which such recruitment was "not uncommon" (more than 1 percent of those recruited yearly) from cases in which it was "rare or exceptional" from cases in which no under-18 recruitment was documented.[122] Data were gathered for both 2000 and 2005, and a dependent variable was constructed representing *improvement* (as previously).

It is very difficult to model the *actual* government recruitment of soldiers under 18. The primary reason is that this variable is measured with far more error than the laws themselves. The most serious problem is that it is very difficult for an observer to tell whether an individual is 18. This is difficult enough in developed countries, but in countries in which birth records are unreliable or widely unavailable, even a government wishing to make a good-faith effort to root out youngsters could have a difficult time doing so effectively. It is even more difficult for NGO and UN observers to tell whether the individuals they see toting automatic weapons in the Sudan have reached 18 or not. Nutritional and other differences that vary between regions, ethnic groups, and countries make it tough to tell by observation alone whether a person is less than 18. Nonetheless, many observers have made

---

122 The primary source was http://www.child-soldiers.org/, which was compared to various UN and other reports.

Table 8.5. The CRC OPCAC and Improvements in Compliance with the
18-Year Minimum Age for Military Service

Dependent variable: change between 2000 and 2005 in the extent to which 18-year-olds actually serve in the military
Instrumental variable least squares regression
Regression coefficients, probabilities based on robust standard errors

Explanatory Variable	Model 1		Model 2		Model 3	
CRC OPCAC ratification	.336	$(p = .197)$	.456*	$(p = .076)$	.438*	$(p = .081)$
Observed extent of participation, at age 18, 2000	.213***	$(p = .001)$	.184***	$(p = .005)$	.151**	$(p = .012)$
Civil war (1998–2002)	—		.061	$(p = .143)$	.061*	$(p = .061)$
Population, logged	—		−.038	$(p = .142)$	−.055*	$(p = .084)$
Interstate war (1998–2002)	—		.356	$(p = .375)$	.491	$(p = .219)$
GDP per capita, logged	—		—		.101	$(p = .764)$
Democracy	—		—		.004	$(p = .793)$
Constant	−.235	$(p = .121)$	.275	$(p = .429)$	.466	$(p = .337)$
# of observations	125		125		111	
R^2	.10		.06		.08	

Instrumented: CRC OP ratification.
Instruments: All exogenous variables plus regional ratification of the CRC OPCAC; common law legal heritage, and civil war between 1990 and 1997.
* Significant at the .10 level; ** significant at the .05 level; *** significant at the .01 level.

a good-faith effort to report their best guesses, and we have made our best effort to code them consistently. The results of the analysis are presented in Table 8.5.

Clearly, it is not easy to explain much of the variance with respect to actual government recruitment, but there is some indication that the OPCAC works in the right direction. Once some reasonable controls are introduced, the (endogenized) ratification of OPCAC does seem to have a mild positive effect on moving away from the actual recruitment of very young children into the military. As we would certainly expect, the surest result is that countries that had especially bad policies in 2000 were more likely to improve (they had more *room* for improvement, after all). There is also some evidence in Model 3 that countries that experienced civil wars in the early period (1998–2002) were more likely to improve their recruitment practices by 2005. But with a modest degree of confidence (around 90 percent), we can also say that those that ratified the OPCAC were more likely *actually* to eschew drawing youngsters into the military than were those that did not. If this claim is true, it provides evidence that international legal commitments have an important supporting role to play in improving the lot of some of the world's more vulnerable children.

CONCLUSIONS

The CRC is the first comprehensive statement that children have a broad panoply of rights that their governments are bound to respect and the international community is encouraged to support through international cooperation. The evidence presented in this chapter suggests that, in the aggregate, the focal influence of CRC ratification may have had some positive consequences for children, particularly within those countries in which it was ratified. One of the key functions of the convention has been to empower the demands and participation of children's rights advocates by providing a clear statement of each state's obligations to its children. The treaty has provided a focal point for mobilizing children's advocates, activists, and ordinary citizens to participate in articulating expectations and demands regarding governments' commitment to children. Ratification has stimulated organization and elevated the political stakes in compliance.

While the evidence presented in this chapter has been quantitative, illustrative stories of how the CRC has motivated children's advocates to mobilize to demand attention to children's issues abound. Research on Ghana suggests the crucial role that the CRC played in galvanizing opponents of exploitative child labor and proponents of education to lobby for legislation to address children's issues. Largely due to the mobilization of NGOs, ratification was followed shortly afterward by the Children's Act, which adopts CRC standards with respect to, among other things, the right to education, regulation of child labor, and minimum ages for employment.[123] While there have been some clear difficulties in implementation[124] – Ghana falls in the World Bank's low-income category, although it is also rated as having a moderate degree of bureaucratic competence – the CRC has provided an important focal point for raising the priority given to children and seeking out international assistance to realize the CRC's ideals. Of course, technical and financial capacity remains a crucial issue for a country such as Ghana. In recognition of this fact, the government has

123 Woll 2000:62. A World Bank study based on Ghana concluded that education and child labor were independent and should be addressed in a coordinated fashion. See Canagarajah and Coulombe 1997.

124 On Ghana's difficulty in implementing the Children's Act, which has also been heavily influenced by the British model of social work, see Laird 2002.

applied for and received international assistance to help fulfill its obligations to children, successfully accessing GAVI funds discussed earlier for new rounds of vaccinations. Indeed, Ghana was one of six countries on the basis of which Save the Children concluded that "The Convention has been used by governments and NGOs as an additional tool with which to push for advances for children, in both the developed and developing world."[125] Certainly, international NGOs such as Save the Children have had an important role to play in helping local stakeholders in Ghana to understand, mobilize around, and use the CRC and other legal instruments to affect policy.[126]

To be sure, the CRC has had an impact in less dramatic ways as well. In Chapter 4, I argued that one way in which the ratification of international agreements can have effects on policies and priorities of governments is simply to change the national agenda. The CRC has had consequences in countries that we do not usually think of as rampant violators of children's rights and well-being. The OPCAC's impact in Europe is a case in point. Prior to the negotiation and ratification of the protocol, several European countries still permitted children less than 18 years of age to be recruited into the armed forces. In Austria, for example, before 2001, 17-year-olds could legally see combat. Austria signed the OPCAC in September 2000, and only four months later, the Military Service Act, which raised the legal minimum age for military combat to 18, came into force. Austria then ratified the OPCAC in February 2002. There is little evidence of a movement within Austria to address this issue at all until the international community placed the OPCAC on the table. But once the question of ratification arose, Austria had to make the appropriate changes in order to come into compliance. Indeed, the federal minister for national defense, Herbert Scheibner, proudly linked the amendment in Austrian law directly to the CRC as he introduced the bill: "[W]e are one of the first countries, ladies and gentlemen, which realizes the Convention of the UN on the prohibition of child soldiers." Other representatives echoed the sentiment that it was essential to comply with and then ratify the CRC's OPCAC.[127] It should be emphasized that in this case the changes were hardly controversial. While debate raged over the level of military funding, the tasks of the Federal Army, and political control of the National Defense Council, all

---

125 Woll 2000:26.
126 Woll 2000:121.
127 Representative Walter Murauer, also of the governing Austrian People's Party, emphasized that "An essential point for me is also that it corresponds with the UN convention against child soldiers, and that we comply with the Convention on the Rights of the Child. No young person under the age of 18, that's what it says, may be called up into military combat missions. This is thus... a consequence in the context of the UN convention." Debate in parliament regarding the amendment of the 1990 Military Service Act, 46th session of the National Council of Austria, 21st Legislation Period, Friday, 24 October 2000 (in German; trans.: Eugen Lamprecht).

parties converged on raising the minimum combat age so as to comply with the treaty.[128] This case illustrates that international law can influence national policies in relatively uncontroversial ways simply by placing a new issue on the national agenda.

The CRC is not always so uncontroversial. It may have had a more fundamental, if controversial, influence on the politics of at least some of the countries that have ratified. As noted at the beginning of this chapter, while the notion that children are to be *protected* by society has been accepted for many years, the notion that they have *rights* is relatively radical. The convention can therefore be useful in influencing the way people think about, debate, and justify particular approaches to children's issues. In some countries, it has been important in breaking down abusive forms of paternalism that have traditionally surrounded the care of children. Jean Grugel and Enrique Peruzzotti have detailed the ways in which this has affected the approach to children's issues in Argentina, for example. The CRC had been deployed to oppose police brutality against young persons, to demand a rights-centered Children's Code, to reform the juvenile justice system, and to demand the introduction of universal child benefits. In the case of Argentina, these scholars argue that the CRC "became a legal norm set, the legitimacy of which was difficult to question, that could be used domestically to judge government performance against; it became, as it were, a script for contentious claims and the foundation of activist arguments."[129] Compatible with the argument of this book, these scholars view the CRC as making a fundamental impact on the political mobilization structure in Argentina.[130]

Ratification of the CRC has hardly solved the social and economic problems of the world's children. It is, after all, an extraordinarily ambitious convention, and even wealthy countries have been criticized for their imperfect compliance with all aspects of the CRC.[131] Developing countries in particular face harsh trade-offs in implementing policies to reduce the economic and military exploitation of children.[132] Even sympathetic observers have noted that the impact of

---

128 Representative Loos of the conservative Austrian People's Party summed up the consensus in this way: "I believe one can't say anything negative about it. There, only positive things were made. Even representative Pilz [Green Party representative] discovered positive things about it, even though he only said "Wuff, wuff!" [simulation of a barking dog] yesterday. Today at least he said one sentence: That the thing with the under 18 years is a good thing about this law. Thus everybody found something good about it, and that is as such not so bad." To which representative Pilz replied, "Dear ladies and gentlemen! The UN Convention is okay, everything else not! – thanks." See debate in parliament regarding the amendment of the 1990 Military Service Act, 46th session of the National Council of Austria, 21st Legislation Period, Friday, 24 October 2000 (in German; trans.: Eugen Lamprecht).

129 Grugel and Peruzzotti 2007a:16.

130 See also Grugel and Peruzzotti 2007b.

131 For example, Australia with respect to juvenile justice (Naffine 1992). In fact, the CRC's comprehensive nature can present problems of resource mobilization and measurement of progress in implementation, a point discussed by Himes (1995).

132 Parker 1995:34.

the CRC has been "shallow"; that is, organizational attention has been concentrated at the national level, with only the slightest influence on localities.[133] As this study has emphasized repeatedly, treaty commitments are not magic. They cannot substitute for programs that deal with the tragic consequences of the experiences of children who have been through active combat.[134] They do not undo deeper structural injustices, which some people argue are wrought by the very nature of the international economy itself.[135] Most important perhaps, it is crucial to keep in mind that the category of "rights" itself is not the only relevant ethical category when talking about the well-being of children.[136]

But this chapter has shown that the CRC and its OPCAC have had detectable consequences in the direction envisioned by the treaty. The results suggest that countries that have made a commitment to improve the lot of their children generally have worked to do so. One thing the treaty has done is to *define* childhood, and while this does not automatically end disagreement over its span, it does make it harder to use the age of individuals strategically to advance particular political, ideological, or social ends.[137] The influence of these agreements is detectable in legal shifts in the recruitment regimes of many countries as well as in outcome indicators, including reductions in child labor and children in the military and increases in immunization rates. These results are important given the pressures governments must feel to give in to economic and military interests above children's rights protections. If the treaty has given children and their advocates a way to reduce wanton exploitation and increase the chances for the "protection and harmonious development of the child,"[138] then it has been an important tool indeed.

133 Woll 2000.
134 On programmatic efforts to reintegrate these children into normal civilian life, see Bracken and Petty 1998.
135 "If one is to be outraged by child labor, one must also be outraged by the way in which industrially backward nations are being forced to turn to such forms of extraction in order to cover their debt-servicing arrangements." "Those That Be in Bondage: Child Labor and IMF Strategy in India"; FOIL (Forum of India Leftists) pamphlet #1 (fall 1996), http://www.proxsa.org/economy/labor/chldlbr.html (accessed 17 July 2008). For a compatible perspective see Toor 2001.
136 O'Neill 1992.
137 On the strategic use of age, see Scheper-Hughes and Sargent 1998.
138 CRC, preamble.

9

Conclusion

Eventually, in all human rights work, the question of what fifty years of enactment and activism add up to has to be asked, even if we know it cannot be answered definitively.

Michael Ignatieff[1]

Over 30 years ago, Rosalind Higgins, the first female ever to be appointed to the International Court of Justice, wrote, "There is now a legal yardstick against which the behavior of states may be judged and a point of reference for the individual in the assertion of his claims."[2] The creation of an international legal regime for human rights was one of the most ambitious multilateral projects of the twentieth century. Yet, it is a project whose full significance is hard to appreciate. It is difficult in the first instance to understand why this branch of international law exists at all. What could states ever hope to gain by acceding to an international "legal yardstick" for internal behavior? For many people, it is also difficult to see how a set of rules with weak international enforcement provisions could possibly make much impact on the world. Without sanctions for those countries that do not measure up, it is not obvious how governments can be influenced to take human rights standards seriously.

This study was motivated to shed light on the existence and influence of the international legal regime for human rights that has developed over the past 60 years, even if, as Michael Ignatieff has noted, we can never answer this question definitively. The effort is nonetheless an important one. No other international legal regime has aimed quite so consistently, explicitly, and universally at improving the quality of human existence as has international human rights law. From the sweeping guarantee of a right to life, to freedom of conscience;

---

1 Ignatieff 1999:322.
2 Higgins 1978:11.

from the right to equality before the law to the obligation of governments to address social conditions that give rise to gender discrimination; from the right to be free from torture to the right to the best possible standard of health (within national means), these treaties summarize a breathtaking scope of human aspirations.

And yet, on the 60th anniversary of the UDHR, it is apparent that we do not live in a world where rights can be taken for granted. Genocide in Darfur, the "disappearance" of detainees in the custody of Russian federal forces in Chechnya, bonded child labor in India, and even the U.S. government's refusal to denounce explicitly practices that the international community broadly accepts as torture evince shortcomings in human rights protections. Of course, good news never grabs headlines as greedily as does atrocity. The best way to bias our thinking against the power of international law to protect human rights is to pick up the newspaper.

Perhaps this is why the prevailing sentiment among those who have given the issue much thought is that international law has done very little to improve the rights chances of people around the world. This sentiment has largely developed in an evidentiary vacuum. Anecdotes of noncompliance are typically held up as clear evidence that international law is meaningless for or even dangerous to the realization of human dignity. But even the most horrific anecdotes of international human rights law violations no more prove the absence of effective international law than do headlines about murder on the streets of Boston or Los Angeles prove the absence of effective law here at home. The key question is not whether crime exists – that is an indubitable point. It is, *what* and *how* has international law contributed to the chances that human beings will enjoy their rights more fully than would have been the case in the absence of the major human rights treaties? We should resist the understandable tendency to answer this question by drawing exclusively on the most dramatic rights tragedies of our time. After all, no one believes that international law is the only tool that can or should be used to address these kinds of abuses. But it is crucial to understand also that international law contains powerful norms that can inspire and be effectively wielded by stakeholders, at least under some circumstances. The evidence accumulated in this book suggests that we may have a much more powerful tool in our hands than we may have realized.

The claims in this book should not be misunderstood. International law is not a panacea for all ills. It will not eliminate ruthless dictators, end racial or gender discrimination for all time, or raise all humans to an acceptable standard of living. These international legal commitments are not magic bullets. They have helped but not cured the rights deficit the world so clearly faced and tried to address in 1947. Indeed, we continue to face such a deficit today. The root causes of rights violations – structural inequities, social and psychological dynamics of violence and domination – cannot be directly addressed by these treaties. They are merely a set of principles that individuals should enjoy basic guarantees, but principles of an especially potent nature. The principles espoused in the conventions analyzed in this book have garnered broad official acceptance worldwide. There are disagreements among states over the exact meaning of some of their provisions but also widespread acknowledgment of their authoritative character. These treaties have inspired some of the most significant constitutional changes within countries in the past three decades. They have touched off domestic debates, provoked demands, and raised the expectations of ordinary citizens. They have been used at crucial moments and critical junctures by litigants and judges to shape domestic law, institutions, and practices for the future. In many cases, people are much better off because of international human rights law than they would have been in its absence.

This conclusion has three purposes. The first is to review the major findings of the book and to place them in comparative perspective, especially across issues, across countries, and over time. The second purpose is to situate these findings and my conclusions in the context of more critical scholarly writing on the value of international law. Finally, I will discuss the policy implications of this research, which I take to be significant, but which can be inappropriately oversimplified. While international law has been a useful tool for individuals and groups to press their rights – politically and legally – it is only one of several ways to work toward better rights prospects around the world. Were readers to conclude that all efforts to address poverty, ameliorate international and civil conflict, or support broader processes of democratization can be called off in favor of treaty ratification alone, this book will have caused more harm than good. The message instead is that authoritative principles are a crucial element in empowering individuals to imagine, articulate, and mobilize as rights holders. They deserve at least the rhetorical support of the international community when they try to assert the rights to which that community has assented. Governments, too, deserve the rhetorical and material support of the international community in their good-faith efforts to live up to their commitments. International human rights law is not an alternative to other kinds of action. It should be thought of as a set of principles to help guide when and how various forms of external assistance – and intervention – should be used.

COMMITMENT AND COMPLIANCE: TWIN PUZZLES FOR INTERNATIONAL HUMAN RIGHTS LAW

This study was motivated by the desire to understand how international law could influence outcomes and behaviors that it purports to address. The puzzle that underlies studies of international law is the question of self-binding: Why would a government decide to make a commitment to its peers internationally to behave in certain ways toward its own citizens?

The Development of an International Legal Regime for Human Rights

The crucial starting point for answering this question is the historical context in which international human rights law developed in the first place. The twentieth century was one of important changes for understanding the process of international human rights development. Two century-long trends were crucial: the changing balance of power between civil society and state actors and the elaboration of state accountability in international law more generally. The relentless reduction in transaction costs (communications, literacy) helped to empower the governed relative to governments over the century. The spread of democratic forms of government helped to create a willing constituency for international norms in favoring human rights. International law itself over the course of the twentieth century came to reflect much higher standards of accountability from governments in maintaining their international agreements. Peer-to-peer accountability – mandating reporting, surveillance, monitoring, and dispute settlement – has been thickening for decades in many areas governed by international law, from trade to arms control. The development of an international legal regime for human rights should be understood in this context.

Human rights might never have joined the growing body of international law had it not been for the tragedy of genocide in Europe and the opportunity the postwar peace presented to weave human rights into the new international order. A look at the historical record shows that there was nothing inevitable about this move. It resulted from a coalition of determined actors – individuals like Raphael Lemkin, a Polish émigré who made it his life's goal to have the international community accept and define the concept of genocide and ensconce its prohibition in a universal treaty; coalitions of ethnic groups from Koreans to Jews who testified tirelessly to the UN Human Rights Commission; and individuals such as Eleanor Roosevelt (although she was constrained by American politics in the positions she could take), Canadian John Humphreys, Charles Malik of Lebanon, and Max Sørenson of Denmark, all of whom thought that the UDHR should have binding legal qualities and even some means of enforcement. These actors were joined by emerging leaders in the decolonization movement eager to use notions of self-determination of peoples to oust their European colonizers and gain full-fledged independence. They were also urged on by the voices of minorities within ostensibly democratic countries – civil rights leaders in the United States, for example – who saw the international community as providing hope and support for their own struggles. It is a testament to the tenacity and persuasiveness of these and others that despite the indifference and even opposition of the major powers – the United States, Britain, and the Soviet Union – the general principles of the UDHR were transposed into binding treaties. Moreover, it is largely due to the perseverance of NGOs with a special interest in the content of particular treaties – Amnesty International with respect to the CAT, international women's organizations with respect to the CEDAW, and Save the Children with respect to the CRC – that the process of legalization has continued.

This complex history of legalization has put states in an interesting position. In principle, all independent states have had the right to participate in international law formation, yet none single-handedly controls the fate of this process – not even the United States, which has had such a preponderant imprint on the nature of post–World War II institutions. Certainly, no state has wanted to be seen as an opponent of human rights. Even during the Cold War, when security concerns easily trumped human rights ideals in the foreign policies of the two superpowers, neither wanted to be seen as opposing the development of international human rights law. Indeed, each used international agreements selectively to try to gain the moral high ground, with the Soviets pointing to capitalism's shameful neglect of economic rights and the Americans excoriating the Soviets for denying their people freedom of religion, movement, and authentic political participation. To be sure, some states were avid supporters of at least certain of the agreements – Ghana, Nigeria, and Sierra Leone in the case of the CERD, Sweden and Poland in the case of the CRC – but it is important to recognize that a good deal of the momentum for making the principles of the UDHR legally binding came from individuals and groups that did not directly represent state interests.

Why Commit? The Ratification Decision

Once we understand just how much fuel nonstate actors added to the process of legalization, it becomes easier to understand why ratification is such a dilemma for states. In a world they could fully control, states might have preferred to maintain a conspiracy of silence among themselves on the treatment of their own people, but by mid-century this was no longer a simple option. The process described previously left states with a decision – oppose and obstruct legalization, participate and shape it, or remain aloof. Few wanted to be criticized for obstruction; many felt that their best option was to try to shape the outcome. Some genuinely and passionately supported legalization. But none had the power to create the "perfect" treaty from their own point of view. So, at the end of each new round of multilateral human rights treaty negotiation, each state was faced with a decision: to ratify or not to ratify?

As theory suggests, for the most part, states tend to vote their preferences with respect to treaty ratification. States with strong democratic participation and civil liberties tend to support treaties that reflect those ideals with their early ratification. In fact, one fairly consistent finding is that the more democratic a country is and the more democratic it becomes, the more likely it is to ratify each of the human rights treaties examined in this study. Autocratic regimes have little natural preference for committing themselves to provide expanded rights to their people. China's decision to remain outside of the ICCPR is a case in point. Sincere ratifiers choose to bind themselves because they believe in the treaty's purposes and anticipate minimal adjustment in order to achieve a respectable level of compliance. Sincere nonratifiers do not want or plan to change their behavior to conform to the treaty's obligations. There is nothing especially mysterious about the decisions of these states. Their attitudes and expectations about rights compliance have a strong influence over ratification.

It is much more difficult to divine the motives of states that do the unexpected: fail to ratify when they already have a fairly good rights record (false negatives) and ratify when they appear to have little intention of making necessary improvements (false positives). The theory developed in this study emphasizes the rational calculations governments make in these cases based on the ratification costs and benefits they face and the information they have. Governments hardly consider the ratification problem in an institutional vacuum. The tendency of some of the human rights literature to view governments as homogeneous units that costlessly absorb international norms has elided the significant institutional differences that give rise to quite different ratification calculations. Ratification by the executive alone is fundamentally different from the need to muster a supermajority in the legislature. Federalism raises costs by requiring central governments to lobby localities to get their support for implementation.

The nature of the domestic legal system itself can have a strong impact on the willingness of a government to ratify a human rights treaty. Keeping in mind that treaties create legal obligations, it is crucial to understand how and at what cost human rights treaties are integrated into the domestic legal system. Governments in polities with highly respected independent courts over which judges with broad powers of interpretation preside tend to be cautious before ratifying a treaty that could potentially be used in a suit against the government itself. Furthermore, actors in legal systems based largely on local case law, which has developed organically and incrementally from the bottom up, are more likely to resist the "general principles" approach of treaties. This has been the first study to make this theoretical claim and to document it statistically. The propensity for common law countries to ratify human rights treaties at a much slower and lower rate than civil law countries has been one of the most consistent and original findings of this study.

The group of countries that have concerned policymakers, activists, and scholars most has been those I have labeled false positives – states that ratify international human rights agreements but apparently without any intention of trying to come into compliance with their obligations. On the basis of this type of country, scholars and observers have far too easily concluded that the international human rights regime is worthless, that treaty ratification is little more than cynical expressive support, and that unless the international community is willing to enforce these agreements, they will remain little more than scraps of paper. I have argued in these pages that such ratification is strategic, not especially expressive and not the wholesale adoption of a script of modernity. Governments sometimes ratify human rights treaties because they want to enjoy praise and acceptance and avoid criticism. That is why they often respond to the social pressure to ratify when countries in their region begin to do so. In the short run, this is completely understandable: It is difficult for rights activists to single out one country for criticism when an entire region remains aloof from a treaty regime. Laggards are much easier to target and credibly to shame than are actors that behave like everyone else. This is perhaps why there is such a strong tendency for the decision to ratify to be influenced by ratification patterns within one's own region.

But strategic behavior is far from a general theory of human rights treaty ratification. It is really only a rational strategy in the short run. Mere ratification cannot glean kudos or deflect criticism for long when it becomes obvious that behavior has not improved. The evidence is quite compelling that strategic ratification – following the crowd – takes place in low-information environments and that it was most prevalent in the early years of the human rights regime. There was also some suggestive evidence for the ICCPR that authoritarian governments ratified toward the end of their terms (no such pattern existed in democracies), which could be interpreted as evidence of ratifying with an eye to the near term. Clearly, not every government can accurately forecast the nature and extent of compliance pressure it will eventually face from its own polity. The more unstable the political setting, the more difficult such pressure is to predict. *Some governments calculate – based on imperfect information and with short time horizons – that ratification may be worth the gamble for achieving short-term benefits.* In at least a few cases, the gamble has helped to support much stronger demands for change than the government had bargained for.

Treaty Effects: A Nudge Toward Compliance

Charles Malik, one of the original members of the UNCHR who was instrumental in drafting the UDHR in 1947, noted that ". . . human rights are more subtle and internal than any formal-external international relations which have hitherto been brought under the dominion of so-called 'international law.'"[3] His observation comports with one of the central insights of this study. As an internal matter, no one has a greater stake in how international human rights treaties are observed than the individuals in the ratifying state.

Just as the typical critique of treaty ratification bemoans the insincere ratifier, the typical description of the international regime for human rights centers

---

3 http://www.udhr.org/history/ibrmalik.htm.

on its inherent weakness. Scores of volumes have been written on the inability of the UN to enforce human rights and the unwillingness of the major powers consistently to do so. New research now focuses on the strategic choices that NGOs make in deciding on the kinds of cases they investigate and publicize. Without the power of reciprocity that supports so many other kinds of international cooperation, international human rights treaties are often portrayed as naive aspirations at best and false hopes at worst.

These dominant descriptions do not give enough credit to local stakeholders themselves. I advocate a theoretical focus on how human rights treaties and their ratification interact with and influence domestic politics. I do not argue that transnational actors have not been crucial to the question of compliance, but they are too often presented as the "white knights" that make demands for those who are not often credited with the ability to speak, strategize, litigate, and mobilize for themselves and their society. *Stakeholder agency* is drastically underplayed in most accounts of compliance with human rights treaties. This is less true in anthropological studies, but it is rampant in world polity theories of sociology and statist theories of international relations.

The theoretical focus of this book has been squarely on the domestic consequences of human rights treaty ratification. I assume that no one has a more consistent, intense interest in whether and how a government complies with its human rights commitments than the human beings on the ground in that country. In the context of that polity, the rights in question may be controversial or they may be accepted as a matter of course. But even when treaties are relatively noncontroversial, they are independently consequential. I have argued that treaties and the question of their ratification exogenously introduce a new issue into domestic politics that, but for its international provenance, would not have been on the national agenda at that point in time or possibly at all. Law and practice can change even when compliance looks like an act of national consensus. Austria's ratification of the OPCAC is an example. Across the political spectrum – from the conservative Catholic Party to the Greens – Austrian legislators agreed to raise the age for participation in combat units from 17 to 18 years of age. Yet, it would not have even been on the national agenda were it not for the question of ratifying the OPCAC.

Quite commonly, of course, rights are controversial. The right not to be discriminated against on the basis of race or gender is a good example. Discrimination by its very nature favors certain groups over others, and the right of equal access to jobs, education, and even equality before the law necessarily privileges certain groups who can be expected to resist. Treaties that delegitimize discrimination can be very valuable in such settings. As international legal commitments, they may give rise to domestic implementing legislation that, along with the treaty itself, can be used to fight discrimination in the courts. The CEDAW was quite useful in this regard to Japanese women who were willing to use legal tactics to improve their prospects for better access to promotion in the workplace.

And so, it is important to theorize how and why stakeholders and their allies use treaties to strengthen their rights claims. I have argued that treaties assist in the process of political mobilization of groups who stand to gain from their provisions. In many countries – especially those that are at least partially democratic and are based on the rule of law – ratified treaties provide highly legitimate focal points that help to clarify reasonable demands, support the legitimacy of those demands, and contribute to the political and legal resources stakeholders can bring to bear in the quest to realize treaty rights.

The evidence that treaties may have an effect on outcomes is surprisingly strong. Four treaties that vary significantly in their nature and content were shown by a broad range of tests to have contributed to the rights performance of governments around the world. The ICCPR, for example, has inspired religious groups to seek a greater arena of religious thought and practice, free from the interference of their government. Ratification of the ICCPR has supported these demands. The evidence suggests that governments that ratify are much more likely than those that do not to follow up that legal action by reducing their interference in the free practice of religion within their polity.

Quite clearly, though, the politics of rights differ by the nature of the right, the range of potential violators, and the nature of individuals who might benefit from the right in question. The norms and treaties analyzed in this book interact with domestic politics, and the way in which they interact varies significantly across the kind of right under consideration. From a mobilization perspective, it is easy to understand why an international commitment on freedom of religious practice differs systematically from one on fair trials. The former has a built-in pressure group – organized religious minorities – who are prepositioned to press governments for compliance. For a number of reasons, the mobilization mechanism is bound to be weaker in the case of fair trials. Most obviously, alleged criminals or other kinds of suspects typically are not well positioned to mobilize to demand better treatment by law enforcement authorities and the local court system. With the exception of the case of a well-organized political opposition, the most immediate stakeholders are often isolated individuals who stand accused of criminal activity. Moreover, alleged criminals do not enjoy the natural sympathy of a broad segment of most societies. In fact, it is easy to frame the issue of fair trials as being "soft on crime" or "soft on terrorism" and thereby convince people otherwise sympathetic to strong legal protections to back off from taking a stand for speedy, fair, and public trials. Even in the United States, where the justice system rivals the best in the world, appeals to the dangers posed by those with alleged connections to international terrorism have allowed hundreds of human beings to languish in Guantanamo without access to American or international standards of justice.

Some issues and some constituencies are much easier to rally around than others. Just look at the difference between issues that are perceived to be connected with national (or at least regime) security and those that are not. The use of torture (though governments almost never use that word) is frequently justified by public authorities on the basis of a national emergency or other "necessity." Often such a characterization will lead strong majorities to be quiescent in the face of allegations that torture is in fact taking place. Chile under and even after Pinochet provides an example. Many Chileans may have abhorred torture, but thought that the threat from the left and the ensuing chaos and left-inspired violence required a firm response from their leaders. One reason torture is hard to eradicate is that it is easily framed as a necessity to protect national security.

The contrast with children's issues is stark. If there is any group around whom most societies can mobilize to protect, it is children. Children themselves represent practically no threat to any political regime or to national security. True, they can be used as a tool by rebels and governments to ratchet up civil war violence as child soldiers, but the recruitment of young children into the army typically does much more to change the social than the military dynamics of most conflicts. Thus, as we have seen, the more protective measures for children are fairly uncontroversial in principle. Protection from exploitation in the form of harsh and extensive work – especially when it competes with school – is increasingly viewed even in developing countries as bad for the full development of children. The CRC has helped activists to focus on this issue, and its ratification is strongly associated with reductions in rates of child labor, even when controlling for the economic, developmental, and demographic factors usually associated with the widespread use of children in the workforce. The employment of children has not nearly approached zero – nor should it, for many of the reasons discussed in Chapter 8 – but the awareness of the issues brought into focus most recently by the CRC and the processes of state reporting, justification, and counterjustification by children's activists have assisted in the exposure and reduction of the economic exploitation of children.

Human rights issues vary in other important ways as well. For example, they vary considerably in the extent to which each right can effectively be observed and monitored. Governments are much less likely to violate rights that are centrally administered and easy to observe than rights that are highly decentralized. Compare the use of the death penalty with torture. The former is a public policy about how to punish criminals. It is almost always administered centrally by state authorities, according to particular laws and rituals. It is comparatively straightforward to document the number of capital punishments carried out by the state; usually, it is a matter of public record. Torture, on the other hand, is decentralized and often furtive. Less a policy than a practice, it can be committed by thousands of officials in hundreds of police precincts throughout a country. In contrast to capital punishment, when torture is used, it is often denied and the evidence hidden, sometimes by making the victims of torture themselves disappear. It is therefore not surprising that when a government ratifies an international agreement to end capital punishment, it is very likely to comply with that obligation. Indeed, because noncompliance would be so obvious, many governments changed their national law first and then ratified the ICCPR's optional protocol. Compliance with the CAT, by comparison, is much harder to detect.

There is little doubt that most governments do not have the capacity to implement every aspect of their international legal obligations. Most operate under administrative and resource constraints; these are severe in the poorest countries. In no area is this truer than in the provision of positive rights, such as health care. Treaties alone do not dissolve these constraints. They can help to mobilize an international community to assist in the process of implementation. We have seen in the case of children's immunization, for example, that the poorest countries benefit most certainly from international immunization programs that provide financial, informational, and infrastructural resources. But they have almost certainly benefited from the public commitment governments have made to the international community and to their own public to put a high priority on children's health as a matter of right. At least we can see this for measles immunization, if not for DPT inoculations.

What has the ratification of international human rights treaties added to the broader normative environment surrounding the civil liberties, inappropriateness of torture, equality for women, and the rights of children? Why is the impact of an international treaty on state practices not just a story about international norms, ideas about appropriate behavior, or the influence of scripts of modernity? There is good evidence that ratification of treaties – in combination with certain domestic institutional conditions – can have a unique impact that nonlaw influences cannot adequately capture: They are legal obligations. As such, they can in some cases be used to influence domestic law and can be used as part of a court case, often with the government itself as the defendant. This is why, as we discovered in Chapter 3, governments with strong, independent judges with broad powers of interpretation – two characteristics of common law legal systems – are sometimes reluctant to ratify human rights agreements in the first place.

Moreover, the evidence that international law has mattered for many rights and under certain circumstances is not redundant to broader trends in democratization. Many of the rights examined in this study – the right to not be executed by the government, the right of girls to access education in numbers equal to those of boys, the right of children not to be drafted into the military – simply do not correlate strongly with improvements within countries in participatory democracy. In the statistical tests, the effect of the treaty was forced to compete in most models with yearly democracy trends in each country. In fact, democratization was included in both the selection and the output equations; that is, it was systematically accounted for in the explanation for participation in the treaty regime and treaty compliance thereafter. In many cases, ratification of the human rights treaty has had a significant influence on rights practices, even controlling for changes in democracy within countries from one year to the next. Governments might have improved their human rights anyway because they were on the road to democracy, but treaties have made these improvements even more likely on the margin.

What is especially interesting and very important for understanding the nature of international law's contribution to human rights is the consistently important role it has played in polities in which institutions are changing, evolving, and in flux. In these cases, stakeholders, officials, and/or activists are searching for the right kinds of persuasive examples and focal points to influence the development of their own futures. Colombian women, for example, sought to influence the future institutions of their country by advocating the principles contained in the CEDAW during discussions of constitutional reform. The Chilean opposition insisted on the inclusion of international law's explicit constitutional status during debates over the nature of Chile's governing institutions into the future. The treaties discussed here have had an especially central role when the design of basic institutions in domestic governance was at stake. It is under these conditions that publics have had the motive to mobilize to advocate their vision of the future, and ratified treaties have provided crucial focal points for clarifying their position and making their voices heard.

The importance of an opportunity to influence a country's rights future is supported by the finding that ratified treaties have their strongest effects in countries that are neither stable democracies nor stable autocracies. The findings show, for example, that governments' willingness to reduce interference in the free practice of religion was associated with ratification of the ICCPR, but this effect was especially strong in this large, heterogeneous set of countries. Even more striking, *only* in these partially democratic or transitioning countries did the ICCPR have any effect on provisions for a civil liberty as important as fair trials. Similarly, the CAT has had a significantly bigger positive impact in countries in which democracy has had a tenuous foothold. In all of these cases, this category includes countries that have transitioned to democracy, away from democracy, and have fluctuated somewhere in the middle. In fact, it is a conclusion that holds on average for all countries except those that have been stable democracies or stable autocracies since World War II. It is impossible to put exact numbers on this finding, but it means that for a broad swathe of humankind, the CAT has been associated with a lower chance of being tortured when in government detention than would otherwise have been the case.

The theoretical reason for expecting the most powerful treaty effects in this middle group of countries goes beyond this particular measure of regime type. I have argued that mobilization to demand observance of a human rights obligation can be thought of as a combination of motive and means. On the one hand, if stakeholders and their allies have a motive to organize to demand observance but have no realistic chance of influencing government policy or outcomes, they are unlikely to pay the price to do so. On the other hand, if stakeholders and allies have a realistic chance of influencing government policy but have little motive to do so because they already enjoy a secure package of rights, they are also unlikely to organize to demand treaty compliance. The expected value of mobilization is maximized in polities where people have both the motive and the means to make clear their human rights demands. Treaties are useful because they can convince locals that they may indeed be entitled to think of themselves as rights holders, and because they provide additional political and legal resources for those who are motivated to pursue their rights.

A similar logic may apply to other kinds of institutionally flexible situations as well. Women may be less likely to demand their rights in countries with inhospitable social or political conditions. The finding that the CEDAW could never be shown to have had any effects in polities with a stable official state religion may be interpreted as meaning that this is a setting in which women have little motive to organize to demand equal rights. This could be due to women's own preferences, but it may also be due to their (rational) belief that it would do little good to organize for a right that will be opposed by a coalition as strong as that of the church and state. Indeed, the case of Colombia illustrates the resistance a conservative church can pose to women's rights to modern forms of reproductive health care and birth control. In that case the church was officially disestablished, much of the content of the CEDAW was imported into the Colombian constitution, and women ended up with good access to reproductive health services and, through litigation, to a somewhat liberalized abortion law. It is hard to imagine such changes in a Catholic polity in which church and state are closely allied.

The theoretical logic may even be broadened further to reflect the constraints posed by extreme poverty. The greater the state's responsibility to provide positive rights, the more the capacity actually to do so comes into play. The evidence discussed in Chapter 8 shows that ratification of the CRC was more likely to have positive effects on immunization rates for measles in middle-income countries (high-middle- plus low-middle-income countries, as defined by the World Bank) than in low-income countries. We might be tempted to attribute some of this effect to parental ignorance, but the tests controlled for illiteracy rates, which were not shown consistently to influence immunization rates. Even if parents knew that immunizations could protect their child, how much good would it do to demand immunizations from a health bureaucracy that simply did not have the capacity to provide it? Unsurprisingly, the CRC has not influenced immunization rates in wealthy countries either. The sophistication of health care delivery in these countries raised rates long before most of the richest countries had ratified the CRC. But this leaves a huge middle category, with sufficient resources to reprioritize children's health in ways that newly mobilized children's health advocates have claimed are especially cost effective. A *right* to the best possible attainable health can be a critical tool in the hands of children's activists for making basic health care, such as measles inoculations, more widely available.

International human rights treaties can work through a variety of mechanisms, but what has become clearer through this research has been the importance of their legal status and the potential to be useful in litigation. Often it is difficult to mobilize a politically influential coalition to demand that the government pay attention to the rights of the less powerful members of society. But in many countries, the courts have been a time-honored institution for protecting the rights of minorities, at least where the judiciary is competent and independent of egregious political manipulation. The statistical tests showed that the CAT had practically no effect in countries with the lowest rankings on the World Bank's rule of law scale, but, somewhat surprisingly, the highest-scoring countries on this scale didn't improve much with ratification either. But it was shown that countries with at least a moderate rule of law score are much more likely to improve their torture practices after ratifying the CAT. In both Israel and Chile, the CAT has been used to litigate cases alleging torture. In Israel, the Supreme Court rendered a landmark decision in 1999 that, consistent with international standards, found that many of the security force's interrogation practices were in fact torture, and held that they would have to be changed or specifically made legal by the Knesset. In Chile, a reformed Supreme Court became the venue for a number of cases once Pinochet's extradition demonstrated just how powerful the CAT could be in the hands of human rights lawyers and principled judges.

Litigation was a plausible mechanism in cases of gender discrimination as well. The CEDAW had a much larger effect on the ratio of girls to boys in school and women's share of public employment in higher rule of law countries than in lower rule of law countries. This might be because of the availability of a respectable court system capable of rendering an independent judgment on the merits of a discrimination case. In a country hardly known for its litigious nature, a small minority of women in Japan used the CEDAW first to demand improvements in their own domestic antidiscrimination law and then to enforce it in the courts. In Colombia, women used the CEDAW in courts to achieve a more liberal (though still highly restrictive) national abortion law. This was possible only after Colombian courts were reformed and made widely accessible.

Of course, the ratification of treaties has clear limits. While treaties tend to have positive effects on rights on average, their effects are not universally positive, even in countries undergoing a good deal of institutional fluctuation and regime challenge. It would certainly be possible to select four countries in which ratified treaties never became part of a public discourse for rights. The point of this book has been to document a *tendency* for treaties to be associated with positive rights outcomes, and then to follow up with illustrative cases that demonstrate plausible mechanisms that link the treaty to eventual improvements. This tendency is amplified, the evidence shows, where domestic institutions are in flux, where there is a minimal incentive for local actors to mobilize, where national courts are minimally competent to render independent judgments, and where the state has at least some capacity to address the rights issue at stake.

Beyond Treaties: The Broader Effects of International Law on Human Rights

Any study of international treaties, no matter how comprehensive it claims to be, will be able to speak directly only to a small part of the effect of international law and even more broadly international norms on domestic governmental behavior and rights outcomes. International human rights law is comprised of both custom and treaty law, and there is a debate among legal scholars about which of these sources of obligation are likely to have the strongest positive impact on actual practices. The debate has been difficult to resolve because other than the occasional anecdote, no systematic evidence has been available to show that either source of legal obligation is effective at all, much less somehow more effective than the other. Generations of legal scholars have been able to do little more than debate the relative merits of treaties versus custom, without much empirical grist for their arguments.[4]

While this research clearly speaks to the effects of treaties, there is simply no point in reviving the debate in order to declare it resolved. For one thing, customary international law is too thin in the human rights area to provide much protection for the array of rights discussed in this book. Hopeful claims that the UDHR itself comprises customary international law[5] are unfortunately inconsistent with custom defined as rules of law derived from "a general practice accepted as law."[6] Even if the UDHR were deemed customary international law, it does not in itself establish clear legal obligations. The only individual human right discussed in this book that is broadly accepted as constituting custom is the right to be free from torture. In some cases – for example, women's rights, the death penalty – the norms contained in these treaties work *against* accepted domestic norms. For the rights discussed in this book, it is hard to imagine customary international law doing the work that I have attributed to treaty ratification itself. For even if a legal argument could be made that a broad panoply of rights is covered by international custom, custom suffers in

---

4 Goodman and Jinks 2004:675; Kennedy 2000.
5 Reisman 1990:867.
6 Statutes of the International Court of Justice, Article 38, 1(b); http://www.icc.cpi.int (accessed 18 August 2008).

comparison to a treaty commitment in its ability to focus domestic demands. While international custom can have a direct effect even without implementing legislation, particularly in some common law countries,[7] it would be much harder to mobilize domestic audiences to demand implementation of international custom than a ratified treaty. The act of a government committing in a quite public way to explicit legal provisions is central to the domestic mechanisms discussed in this book. Ratification of a treaty provides at least the color of local ownership of specific human rights obligations. The same cannot be said of international custom.

This research has focused not only on treaty existence, but on treaty *ratification* more specifically. I have argued that ratification stimulates groups to form, to organize, and to make their views known as a government begins to implement the agreement (or not). Ratification debates give rise to publicity that encourages interested citizens and their advocates to think about, strategize, and articulate demands for compliance. Ratification creates an obligation on the part of the States party to report to an oversight committee, and the act of reporting provokes shadow reports by groups, even if the government itself would prefer to submit a whitewash. In some countries – Colombia and Chile, for example – new constitutional provisions make ratification all that is necessary to import international law into the domestic legal system.

Yet, it is quite likely that treaties have effects unrelated to ratification per se. First, a treaty could have existential effects. Its very existence could change global conceptions of what constitutes appropriate behavior of a government toward its own citizens. Governments could become socialized to the norms contained in a specific treaty, yet for a number of reasons – some of which have been discussed in Chapter 3 – find it difficult to ratify a specific agreement. Second, a treaty could have anticipatory effects. Many governments specifically aim to come into compliance with a treaty before ratification.[8] There is pretty clear evidence, for example, that governments abolish the death penalty prior to ratification of the OPDP to the ICCPR. Anticipatory effects can vary by the type of right in question. Since capital punishment is an especially easy-to-monitor practice, governments are encouraged to end it before formally being obligated in international law to do so. Third, treaties can mobilize international assistance to support compliance. The norms contained in certain treaties – for example, the health and education provisions of the CRC – are a delight to the governments of some developing countries, which are encouraged to believe that they have a strong basis to expect technical and infrastructural assistance from international agencies such as ECOSOC, the World Health Organization, and even private donors.[9] Not only did the evidence in Chapter 8 reveal (weak) ratification effects on immunization rates

7　Franck and Fox 1996; Neuman 1997.
8　Simmons and Hopkins 2005:322.
9　See, for example, Articles 23(4) and 28(3) of the CRC.

among developing countries; it revealed as well important positive effects of international programs designed to boost governments' capacity to live up to their obligations for basic health provisions under the CRC.

All of this contributes to an important point: By focusing on treaty ratification, I have quite likely *underestimated* the influence of international law on human rights practices. Estimates of the influence of ratification are diminished by countries that internalize treaty norms but fail to ratify. They are also diminished by countries that insist on complying sometimes years prior to ratification. Nor do my results pick up the indirect effects of treaty ratification on various forms of mobilization of international society, whether for purposes of improving states' capacity to deliver the goods or shaming them into refraining from outright abuses, independent of their ratification decisions. Customary international law might also encourage governments to comply prior to ratification. The evidence presented in this study is therefore a *conservative* estimate of international law's overall effect on governments' behavior.

Legalization and Legalism: The Obsession with Law

The central message of this study – that international law, and specifically treaty ratification, has made a positive contribution to human rights practices around the world – may be unexpected news to political realists and critical legal scholars alike. The former have stressed the irrelevance of international law for important issues in human affairs. The latter have tended to view international law as oversold or, worse, quite detrimental to true human well-being. Both are skeptical that international law should be anyone's answer to the problem of human rights violations.

Since I have reviewed political realists' view of the role of international law in Chapter 4, I will focus here on points made by critical legal scholars. Their insights flow from a willingness to question the very assumptions of the international legal system, especially the perspectives and actors it privileges. David Kennedy, for example, has challenged the assumption that we should focus on international law as a way to address human well-being. "Foregrounding" law demotes a wide range of issues that are not addressed by the international legal system but that surely are important for the broader realization of global justice. Human rights as captured by positive public international law frames the central issues as ones between state and civil society, and loses natural law conceptions of a broad range of duty bearers other than the state itself.[10] Moreover, there is a real risk that "... the legal formalization of rights and the establishment of legal machinery for their implementation [will make] the achievement of these forms an end in itself."[11]

10 Føllesdal and Pogge 2005:16.
11 Kennedy 2004:12.

David Kennedy's warnings about the risks of foregrounding law are useful as cautionary notes but are not an accurate description of the current state of affairs. Public international law is but one tool among many to address broader issues of global justice. True, it is a tool that focuses primarily on government–civil society relationships. It *does not* address broader problems of structural violence: massive gaps between the rich and poor, the vulnerabilities associated with globalization, or persistent and deep-rooted forms of ethnic, religious, or gender discrimination. The CAT was developed to address *public* officials' brutality toward individuals held in detention, not the everyday brutalities experienced by millions of women at the hands of their husbands.

But to say that there are other important problems that public international law does not address very well does nothing to diminish the areas in which it has had some modest success. While it has done little to date to address various forms of private cruelty and inhuman treatment, it is no small thing that the CAT has contributed to a presumption that governments should not inflict excruciating punishments on human beings – to include, thanks to the treaty, psychological pain and suffering. The results in Chapter 7 show clearly that at least in some countries, ratification of the CAT has had a real impact on the probability of actually being tortured in official custody. While much injustice and cruelty remain, it is not convincing to argue that because international law has not solved all problems, it should not be given due credit for those it has begun successfully to address.

The foregrounding of state–society relationships inherent in the public international law frame has not stopped creative thinkers from using international human rights norms to frame new accountability relationships. The Global Compact is a (controversial) way to think about global corporate responsibility with respect to human rights. Some 3,000 companies and 40 national firm networks have participated in this project, which aims to offer a new vision of corporations as duty bearers "within their respective sphere of activity and influence." Many problems remain to be sorted out, and the compact has not been widely accepted by either corporations or the UN Human Rights Council, not least because it has not to date offered clear guidance on the boundaries between corporate and state responsibilities in the rights area. But the compact is at least evidence that the state-centered framework of public international law has not had iatrogenic effects on our ability to think outside the state-centered box.[12]

One point often made by realists and critical legal scholars alike is that the fixation on legalization and especially international prosecutorial modes of justice is an inappropriate way to deal with human rights violations.[13] International

---

12 Ruggie 2007.
13 For the views of a critical legal scholar, see Engle 2005. For the views of two realists see Vinjamuri and Snyder 2004.

tribunals for human rights violations are criticized as expensive[14] and counter-productive. Universal jurisdiction – the idea that any state may claim jurisdiction over individuals alleged to have committed particularly heinous crimes (including egregious human rights violations), regardless of where the crime was committed or the nationality of the victim or alleged perpetrator – has been criticized as subject to political manipulation that would swamp domestic legal systems and ultimately lead to the subversion of justice.[15] For many, the International Criminal Court is the primary example of where a misguided logic of international judicialization has led.

This is not the place to launch into a full analysis of the international prosecution of egregious human rights violations.[16] It is enough for the conclusion of the present study to note that none of the treaties with the exception of the CAT could possibly be enforced through these means. States have made a clear effort to keep disputes arising from these treaties out of legally binding foreign and international venues. Article 29(1) of the CEDAW, which would have state parties submit disputes to the International Court of Justice, is the most reserved-against provision in that treaty. All of the oversight committees for the treaties examined in this study have only optional authority to render "views" – not legally binding decisions – on allegations of state violations of treaty provisions. Moreover, individuals have a private right of standing only after the exhaustion of domestic remedies for alleged violations. Nonetheless, it has taken more than 40 years after opening for signature for the UN Human Rights Council to approve an *optional* protocol giving individuals a chance to lodge allegations of state violations of the ICESCR with that treaty's oversight committee.[17] A real international prosecutorial capacity has been developed only for the most egregious human rights abuses such as genocide and crimes against humanity. Even in these cases, the International Criminal Court is *complementary* to and not a substitute for national investigation and prosecution. International human rights as a whole are not at risk of "overjudicialization." Indeed, as I have argued throughout this book, international enforcement of these agreements was by design and remains weak.

In short, there is little evidence that using international legal instruments has done anything to foreground law in a deleterious fashion. Peacekeeping and

---

14 In 2004 and 2005, the UN spent $329.3 million on the International Tribunal for the former Yugoslavia and $255.9 million on the International Criminal Tribunal for Rwanda out of a total annual budget of about $20 billion. See, for example, http://www.unausa.org/site/pp.asp?c=fvKRI8MPJpF&;b=1813833 and http://www.worldwatch.org/node/5466#notes (accessed 20 August 2008).

15 See, for example, Goldsmith 2003.

16 I have analyzed the International Criminal Court in other publications, finding that patterns of ratification, implementation, and peace negotiations suggest that it will be reasonably successful in its stated goal of reducing the impunity of violations while supporting international peace and stability. See Simmons and Danner 2007.

17 Approved 18 June 2008.

development programs continue to get much more funding at the UN than do human rights programs. Bilateral foreign aid is an order of magnitude larger for economic and social programs than for all human rights programs combined.[18] Only the most cycloptic individuals see only problems that the law addresses and view law as the only tool to deal with them. It is important not to criticize the entire system of international human rights law based on the lack of perspective of a few zealots. To do so would be akin to damning domestic law for the legalistic obsessions of the Inspector Javerts of the world.

As Lisa Hajjar has written in the context of Israel, "Human Rights movements are mobilizations inspired and guided by law."[19] One need not be obsessed with law or legalism to be able to use legal tools when and where they are useful to achieve actors' purposes. This opens the door for the "instrumentalization" of rights – the strategic invocation of rights language to justify preferred political or policy outcomes – but this danger is no greater in the area of human rights than the instrumentalization of other values in international affairs, such as the distinction between war and peace or environmental protection.[20] As authoritative statements of focal values, human rights treaties at least provide the possibility of *stabilizing* boundaries between acceptable and unacceptable practices, making the manipulation of rights less elastic than otherwise might have been possible.

International Human Rights Law, Hegemonic Discourse, and the "New Cosmopolitanism"

Debates over the universality of human rights have persisted for decades, even centuries if we want to retrieve evidence from ancient times.[21] The UN Human Rights Commission knew it would face criticisms about the imposition of Western values when it drafted the UDHR in 1947, and to ward off this impression, they commissioned the ECOSOC to solicit input from various thinkers and writers from a range of political and philosophical traditions of the world. They tried to look at a broad range of religions and cultures for conceptions of basic human rights, fully aware that no declaration could possibly gain broad international legitimacy if it were to draw rights only from the literature of the Western Enlightenment.[22] Although they received 70 responses from scholars and leaders from India to China to Russia to Western Europe, it has not been possible to shake the perception that the international legal regime for human rights reflects a hegemonic discourse emanating from the West.

18   Nielsen 2008. Richard Nielsen's data show that human rights aid of all kinds (including democratic assistance) has been less than 5% of total bilateral aid in recent years.
19   Hajjar 2001:21.
20   Berman 2004–5.
21   Herodotus 1972:219–20.
22   See the discussion in Ishay 2004:218–21.

To some extent, the reaction against the international human rights regime bears a strong similarity to other forms of resistance to globalization. Claims that human rights are universal and indivisible provoke, in Balakrishnan Rajagopal's words, "a culture-based local resistance strategy against the global culture of economic and cultural imperialism of the West."[23] "The New Cosmopolitanism," in his view, is a response that moves "away from uncritical celebration of human rights discourse"[24] and is much more willing to view local particularities and traditions as not only tolerable but often worthy of celebration. And to be clear, it is not only the New Cosmopolitans who are worried about the hegemony of international human rights law. The far-right wing of the political spectrum in the West is wary as well.[25]

There is nothing at all wrong with a healthy skepticism of the contents of human rights treaties and vigilance against the assertion of rights that serve to perpetuate the hegemonic domination of one culture or society over another. The Communist states objected to Article 17 of the UDHR protecting private property; several Islamic countries opposed Article 18, providing for the freedom not only to choose but to change one's religion. African countries – most of which were still not independent when the UDHR was drafted and voted on – had less say than those in most other areas of the world about the contents of the UDHR but were early and enthusiastic supporters of one of the first three multilateral conventions, the CERD.

The hegemonic nature of the international legal system for human rights has been drastically overdrawn. The governments of developing countries have participated broadly in the formation of this regime, and most of them broadly accept the principles set out in the major multilateral treaties. Ultimately, the decision about whether to ratify an agreement or not is one that the sovereign state has a right to make. States also have the right to enter reservations when they decide to ratify. Ironically, as I demonstrated empirically in Chapter 3, the states that have entered the greatest number of reservations tend to be the wealthier hegemons rather than allegedly resistant developing country governments. For developing countries, problems are often related to implementation rather than to the principles themselves. India, for example, officially takes a principled position against child labor[26] but admits to having many difficulties in implementation. No government of which I am aware has justified official torture on the basis of local cultural practices. One might retort that the fact that so many governments apparently accept these rights only reflects the hegemonic

---

23 Rajagopal 2002:152.
24 Rajagopal 2002:151.
25 One example captures this sentiment: "Disturbing and undesirable ideas are being thrust upon us in a deceptive and stealthy manner from an unexpected source known as 'international law'" (Hirsen 1999:5).
26 See official government policy discussed at http://www.indianembassy.org/policy/Child_ Labor/childlabor.htm (accessed 20 August 2008).

nature of the ideas in question. But none of the major powers has been willing to enforce human rights standards on a regular basis. Richard Nielsen's detailed study of aid from OECD countries shows that governments are likely to enforce human rights by manipulating aid flows only when the rights violations are egregious and when they cause negative externalities such as refugee flows.[27] If this is true, this is a soft form of hegemony indeed.

Some people might insist that soft hegemony – the hegemony of beguiling ideas – is the most insidious kind. If Western perspectives dominate discussions of the proper *interpretation* of basic human rights, there is a case for ideational power. The oversight committees for the various treaties discussed in this book have important powers of interpretation, both in dialog with governments submitting their reports and with the broader rights community (domestic and international). Nine of the current expert members of the UN Human Rights Committee, for example, are from the non-Asian OECD countries or Europe, while three are from Latin America and two each are from Sub-Saharan Africa, North Africa or the Middle East, and Asia. Interestingly, however, 14 of the current 18 members of the committee did substantial graduate studies, often relating to human rights, in Western Europe and/or North America.[28] It can reasonably be claimed that this committee – and arguably the oversight committees associated with other multilateral human rights agreements – is the torchbearer for Western rights notions and a conduit for Western values globally.

While treaty oversight does seem to be heavily influenced by Western perspectives, this point should not be exaggerated. For one thing, the real power of the oversight committees is quite limited, as I have emphasized. Second, since the committees typically engage in dialog rather than operate in a judicial mode, it is quite possible that members will learn as much about local values and constraints as they will imbue to state parties. Third, the principle of recognizing variation in meeting treaty obligations – known in the European context as the "margin of appreciation"[29] – has to a certain extent informed the deliberations of the oversight committees.

Finally, hegemony is a double-edged sword. There are many hegemonies, and the rights discussed in this book do indeed reinforce some sources of authority and undercut others. Part of the opposition to these rights at the local level is itself hegemonic in nature. The dominance of authoritarian governments and corrupt officials is challenged by many of the rights in question here. Certain locally hegemonic cultural ideas are as well, such as the notion that women are inferior to men or that the church or mosque is the sole source of

27 Nielsen 2008.
28 For a list of current UNHRC members and their curricula vitae, see http://www2.ohchr.org/english/bodies/hrc/members.htm (accessed 20 August 2008).
29 This concept has been criticized as undercutting the universality of international human rights standards. See, for example, Benvenisti 1999.

truth. For oppressed individuals, it does not matter whether the source of hegemony is local or external. My argument is that they will organize, mobilize, and sometimes litigate in favor of the concepts of human dignity and freedom from which they feel they will most benefit. In many instances, external standards for a fair trial and decent treatment while in government detention will be more important to a political opponent than "justice" in the local style.

The New Cosmopolitanism represents a justified sensitivity to global values that run roughshod over local distinctiveness. In a positive vein, it also helps to account for some of the findings in this study. In Chapter 5, I found that, unsurprisingly, freedom of religion is far more restricted in predominantly Islamic countries. In Chapter 6, the use of religion dummy variables made it clear that access to modern forms of birth control was significantly influenced by the dominant religion of a polity. The case studies on Japan's resistance to equal employment opportunities for women and Colombia's resistance to abortion in order to save a woman's life also attest to various forms of cultural resistance to the norms contained in these treaties. Resistance and backlash are common reactions to the introduction of new ideas and values. In some cases the new ideas will be ignored, in others they will disturb the status quo, and in yet others they will be embraced in time. That's politics. But international legal norms must not be dismissed uniquely as hegemonic. In the struggle against oppression from whatever source, it can be quite useful for one hegemony to be used to challenge another.

Agency: The State and Domestic Civil Society

One of the lessons that follows from the research in this book is the crucial role that domestic actors play in their own human rights fate. Rights stakeholders around the world have actively made decisions about when and how to employ the norms contained in human rights treaties to influence practices on the ground in their countries. Sometimes they have done this with outside help, but the locals are the ones who carry the ball and take the risks. They also make decisions about what is culturally appropriate in their society and how best to deploy limited resources in order to realize the greatest benefits from the promises of the human rights treaties their governments have signed. As in Colombia, they may advocate the principles of the CEDAW at a critical moment in constitutional history; they may decide to establish legal clinics alongside the health clinics that are aimed at giving women and their families a greater say in their reproductive choices. In contrast to a human rights discourse that ". . . portrays victims as passive and innocent, violators as abnormal, and human rights professionals as heroic,"[30] the approach I have taken in this study is to look to

30 Kennedy 2004:14.

domestic stakeholders as agents with the strongest incentives consistently to make demands for compliance with treaty obligations.

A theory that emphasizes the power of international treaty obligations to mobilize domestic groups is a crucial supplement to the mechanisms that exist in the literature. Margaret Keck and Kathryn Sikkink have written about transnational alliances that form to do an end run around highly repressive states.[31] Xinyuan Dai has analyzed a domestic constituency mechanism that works through the ballot box when locals have access to new information provided by external treaty oversight agencies.[32] The first of these may indeed be the only possible compliance mechanism in cases of extremely repressive regimes. The second may be all that is necessary in responsive and highly accountable democracies. But most states are at neither of these two extremes. They are partially democratic, newly democratic, democratizing, and sometimes backsliding toward authoritarianism. Under these circumstances, it is important to examine the variety of ways in which local citizens on the ground actively use international legal agreements to hold governments accountable. Local stakeholders have the incentive to demonstrate, lobby, and sometimes litigate in these countries. A ratified treaty is a useful way to justify and support these tactics.

Human rights practices make international news, but by and large they are not the mainstay of international high politics. State-centric approaches to the study of compliance with human rights treaties typically conclude that international human rights agreements are not enforceable. They are right if, by enforcement, they expect peer pressure for compliance to be very strong. I have argued in Chapter 4 that states generally have little or no incentive to enforce international human rights standards. They may do so exceptionally – when the costs are negligible or when the negative consequences, such as refugees or regional security-threatening instability, are significant. That states could after many years converge on sanctions against the apartheid-based regime of South Africa is virtually the only exception of any consequence, and why governments would eventually agree to coordinated sanctions realism provides no clue. Simply put, realist theories of international relations provide no particular handle on understanding human rights compliance. They correctly predict that *peer* enforcement will be weak and episodic. They wrongly conclude that international human rights law is unenforceable. Cases from Japan to Colombia to Chile to Israel demonstrate otherwise.

Understanding the motivations, institutions, capacities, and politics at the local level is essential in the human rights area because other state-centric approaches are wanting as well. Rational functionalism – which has served quite well the study of international institutions in a range of issues areas, from trade to prisoner-of-war regimes – is largely orthogonal to the problem of compliance

31   Keck and Sikkink 1998.
32   Dai 2007.

with human rights agreements. International human rights agreements are not negotiated by states primarily for mutual gain, which is the underlying assumption of the rational functionalist approach. Chapter 2 demonstrated that the effort to create a legal regime was clearly a normative response to the atrocities of fascism and World War II. The international legalization of human rights was fostered and nurtured largely by nonstate actors, who provided testimony, offered drafts, and whipped up support for a growing number of treaties based on the elaboration of the nonbinding UDHR. It was never a regime designed with contractually based state-to-state reciprocity in mind.

This leaves us with the obvious. Human rights outcomes are highly contingent on the nature of domestic demands, institutions, and capacities. In this highly contingent context, local agents have the motive to use whatever tools may be available and potentially effective to further rights from which they think they may benefit. This is a liberal theory, in the sense that the crucial relationships are indeed those between local stakeholders – civil society – and their governments. International law is not likely to have much effect where domestic actors have little or no incentive to organize; we saw evidence of this result with respect to women's rights in countries with a solid church–state alliance; we also saw it reflected in stable autocracies whose civil liberties practices remained unchanged after ratification. I have emphasized throughout that treaties are not a silver bullet through the heart of the world's dictatorial regimes. Yet, they offer some leverage where repression itself can be contested.

IMPLICATIONS FOR POLICY AND PRACTICE

"What you cannot enforce, do not command."[33] Sophocles's words could be used to critique the entire 60-year project of enshrining human rights in international law. But to do so would miss an opportunity to address human abuse and human well-being in one of the most responsible ways possible: by giving stakeholders a legitimate way to demand, shape, and implement it for themselves.

Human rights are a difficult policy area to address because there are so few good tools at the disposal of the international community to influence internal practices. Certainly, there are few that are actually *policy* instruments per se. The evidence shows that many factors contribute to rights improvements or deterioration. The best policy advice for protecting and improving human rights would be to develop, democratize, and avoid war.[34] The international community has been working on these mega-projects for the past century. They should remain our top priorities. But this section considers specific targeted responses to human rights shortcomings per se. For all but the most egregious rights

33 Sophocles, http://www.quotationspage.com/quote/2664.html.
34 Carey and Poe 2004:8.

violations – possibly, only to include genocide or an equally disastrous humanitarian catastrophe – forcible external intervention is and ought to be off the
table. It ought to stay off the table except in the most exceptional circumstances
because, first, it won't happen and, second, it would be disastrous if it did. As
Thomas Franck and Nigel Rodley wrote over three decades ago, "Nothing
would be a more foolish footnote to man's demise than that his final destruction
was occasioned by a war to ensure human rights."[35]

The use of military intervention is simply not a tool appropriate to ensure
compliance with international human rights standards. There are practically no
circumstances in which military force could be used proportionately – that is, in
a way that could be calibrated to achieve a specific human rights objective
without inflicting much more harm than good. Furthermore, it is not a sustain-
able solution to most right abuses. Getting rid of one repressive dictator hardly
ensures that a liberal democrat will take his or her place. Moreover, there is a
well-known risk that attends any claim of humanitarian motives to achieve
laudable objectives: "Human rights" could become a shibboleth for interventions that have predominantly strategic motivations.[36] The international community has understandably been split on the use of military intervention on
humanitarian, let alone human rights, grounds. This does not mean that a constructive dialog about a "right to protect" should not continue in the UN and
elsewhere. It does mean that military intervention is probably not a viable
response to the everyday repressions described in this study.[37]

Economic incentives of various kinds are another alternative to encourage
the improvement of human rights. The bluntest approach would be to use the
strategic withholding of trade to encourage better rights performance. The
weaknesses of depending on trade sanctions are well known. Political opposition from commercial interests makes sanctions hard to sustain. The larger the
target – think China – the more difficult it is to deny commercial interests
normal trading relationships with a country. It is difficult to target sanctions
in a way that encourages the regime to change its practices without harming civil
society as well, rendering some people double victims. Were countries (implau-
sibly) to agree to sanction Indian products for the widespread use of child labor,
the burden would largely be borne by families at or near the poverty level. There
are significant cooperation problems among sanctioning states themselves, since
defection when others are sanctioning can be quite profitable. No case demonstrated this more clearly than the Carter administration's efforts to sanction the
Soviet Union by withholding U.S. agricultural products. And as we have seen in
the recent case of Iraq, the black market and corruption can overwhelm the
thrust of trade sanctions. For these and other reasons, sanctions are often quite

---

35   Franck and Rodley 1973:300.
36   Forsythe (1993:7) critiques several U.S. invasions with human rights justifications on these
     grounds.
37   For a moral argument against intervention to protect human rights, see Beitz 2004.

ineffective in enforcing human rights standards.[38] Indeed, an argument can be made that economic engagement with the goal of stimulating development constitutes a positive strategy for rights improvement, though it is not a substitute for the clearly articulated principles found in multilateral human rights treaties. The one fairly unambiguous success story for trade sanctions was the bringing down of apartheid in South Africa. Even so, it took over 30 years and involved extraordinary efforts that are not likely to be widely replicable.

Aid might be another useful tool in the bundle of incentives that can be wielded by the international community to encourage human rights practices. Aid incentives may be more politically palatable in donor countries than is trade, as withholding it is generally not very costly (on the contrary). Whether aid is really associated with rights improvements is much debated. Most of the evidence suggests that unless the aid is targeted to specific purposes associated with improving rights practices, it has little positive impact.[39] Richard Nielsen, for example, has found that when aid is targeted narrowly at developing a capacity for institutions that protect human rights, it can sometimes have that effect.[40] Similarly, the evidence in Chapter 8 suggests that aid to support immunization programs is positively associated with increases in those rates. But unless governments and private actors are very cautious about how they tailor their aid, it is unlikely to have a significant effect on rights practices generally.

The crucial policy point is that none of these economic incentives or development programs should be considered substitutes for clear legal rights. This book would be completely misunderstood were readers to conclude that we can set the millennium's development goals, international peacekeeping, and judicious humanitarian efforts aside and do nothing but ratify human rights treaties. These strategies are mutually supportive. A growing literature in international relations stresses the importance of formal agreements in creating focal points to guide the efforts of a range of actors in achieving international cooperation. Without the kind of principled guidance offered in international treaties, efforts could become dissipated, actors could work at cross-purposes, and the coherent message of the priority of rights observance could become garbled. Treaties do not guarantee clarity, and there is much room to disagree on the proper interpretation of their contents, but in their absence, it would be much harder for all actors concerned to target rights aid or condition trade agreements in a coherent way.

---

38 See the discussion in de Feyter 1996, who argues that there is little legal justification or legitimacy in linking labor or other human rights standards with trade agreements. But see also Hafner-Burton (2005), who argues that such a linkage is realistically one of the few reliable ways to enforce rights.

39 "Positive incentives" are a possibility for improving working conditions; Abouhard and Cingranelli (2004) found that countries receiving World Bank and IMF loans tended to have better workers' rights than countries that did not.

40 Nielsen 2008.

Thus, the major policy implication is that international human rights law should be respected, rhetorically and in practice. As Charles Malik, one of the original drafters of the UDHR, argued in 1948, "The need is above everything else for courageous and sustained moral leadership. It is for some one nation so to put its own house in order and so to be fired by a genuine sense of mission as to have its words on fundamental human rights ring with authority."[41] Governments that respect rights should be willing to obligate themselves to the provisions of these treaties, with only minor reservations that guard especially sensitive areas of local particularity. International human rights law deserves far more support from the major powers and global normative leaders, especially the United States, than it has received to date. The world has much more to gain than U.S. citizens remotely have to lose by ratifying the conventions we have refused to accept, such as the CRC, the CEDAW, and the ICESCR. To believe otherwise is to admit that the United States no longer has the moral authority it once did to influence the tenor of values around the world. Tangible and rhetorical support for international human rights agreements could strengthen the legitimacy of the rules and standards people around the world have tried to grasp in their own contestation of various forms of local oppression. The least a major democratic polity can do is show some solidarity – and ratify the multilateral human rights agreements on the table.

Governments everywhere should also be encouraged to ratify. But this research has shown that there is no particular payoff to pressuring stable, highly repressive regimes to do so; at least this should not be a high priority. Attention should instead be focused on supporting ratification in those countries in which the agreements are likely eventually to matter the most. To know which countries these are, it is crucial to understand their history, governing institutions, and culture. Where these are solidly opposed to the rights contained in multilateral treaties, ratification pressures are unlikely to help and could even be counterproductive. This policy implication runs counter to the goals of some organizations that advocate universal ratification of all treaties. This study suggests that resources should be focused instead on ratification in countries with some history of or prospect for liberalization. These are the crucial rights battlegrounds in the medium term.

Another well-advised policy plan may be to concentrate human rights efforts regionally. A regional focus can have a multiplier effect; as Chapter 3 demonstrated, countries are much more likely to ratify human rights agreements when they are surrounded by other countries in the region that have already done so. Being surrounded by and compared to a critical mass of ratifying countries itself encourages ratification, which in turn can provide an opening to domestic groups to demand compliance. Public and private bodies

---

41 Charles Malik, "What Are Human Rights?" originally published in August 1948 by *The Rotarian*. Available at http://www.udhr.org/history/whatare.htm (accessed 24 July 2008).

should emphasize improvements and problems regionally, wherever possible comparing the rights practices of countries not with the West but with their own neighbors. Such an approach could potentially undercut the perception that rights are a game of the West against the rest. It would direct the debate away from cultural relativism and toward varying practices – some more praiseworthy than others – *within* cultures and *within* developmental levels. It would also reveal social camouflage for what it is – a cynical gambit for short-term gain – and bolster progress at the regional level that has some chance of being emulated.

Governments around the world that are dedicated to human rights should also facilitate with real resources the development of local infrastructures where these rights can be enforced. I have stressed capacity limitations in the provision of positive rights, such as health care, but even the domestic ownership of negative rights, such as civil and political rights, can be costly to guarantee without the devotion of resources in that direction. Farrokh Jhabvala, a scholar and attorney from India, has stressed in his work the tremendous legal, administrative, and research capacity that is necessary to enforce domestically a commitment such as the ICCPR.[42] Nonetheless, he rightly concludes that domestic supervision is of far greater and more enduring significance for the promotion and protection of human rights than external machinery.[43]

This research also has implications for advocates and rights workers whose ambition it is to improve human dignity worldwide. At the simplest level, this research suggests that they should think about international law as a concrete tool that could help achieve their goals. They should read the major rights documents and be aware of their contents. If their own government has not ratified one of these treaties, they might add their voice to those calling for ratification. They should think about appropriate ways to make individuals and groups of stakeholders aware that their governments have promised to respect certain rights. One of the most important things that local rights workers can do is to help individuals grasp what international human rights standards can concretely mean to them in their current circumstances. This involves what Sally Engles Merry refers to as translating international norms "into the vernacular,"[44] drawing connections for local stakeholders between global principles and life as they experience it.

Furthermore, human rights workers should consider whether and how an alliance with legal advisers might be warranted. The decision as to whether or not to take a legal turn will depend very much on facts on the ground. The decision in Colombia to site legal clinics next door to family planning health clinics demonstrates a creative linkage that in that country's context did

---

42 Jhabvala 1987:300–2.
43 Jhabvala 1985.
44 Merry 2006:passim.

eventually bear fruit. Human rights advocates might think about forming stra-tegic alliances with "cause lawyers," as they did in Israel, and plan a strategy for litigation. Litigation is expensive and is workable only where domestic courts are reasonably functional and independent, but sometimes the principle won can be priceless, as many believe was the case with the landmark Israeli Supreme Court's 1999 decision about torture standards.

The most important policy advice that comes from this study, however, is domestic ownership. Human rights treaties matter where local groups have taken up the torch for themselves. Without that, transnational and peer pressure will ultimately flag as funders and headline hunters seek new opportunities to make their mark. Human rights work is not that different from development work in this regard. In defending his proposals to end world poverty, Jeffrey Sachs told the press that "I'm not proposing a single global plan dictated by some UN central command. Quite the opposite, I'm proposing that we help people help themselves. This can be done without legions of people rushing over to these countries to build houses and schools. This is what people in their own communities can do if we give them the resources to do it."[45] Some of the most important resouces in the human rights area are the treaties to which govern-ments themselves have publicly committed. Rights are about ideas, and these treaties spell them out in black and white.

Some policy precautions are certainly in order. Even when we talk about rights, we must consider the public policy implications and think through the possible consequences of how specific rights are implemented. The right of children not to be exploited economically provides an example. The principle involved is that children should have the early opportunity to develop their skills and potential as human beings. They should primarily be in school, and should not be subject to hazardous working conditions or extremely long work-ing hours. This does not mean that child labor should be abolished completely. In fact, to do so would have dire consequences for families on the cusp of basic subsistence. Unfortunately, until extreme poverty is eliminated – until "struc-tural violence" itself is rectified – sending relatively young children to work might be the least objectionable choice among dire alternatives. In principle, we can oppose child labor. On the ground, the best way to implement this policy is to regulate hours and working conditions. Perhaps most importantly, study after study shows that the provision of affordable (usually free) and highly relevant education is the best incentive families can be provided to cooperate with the reduction in their children's working hours. This is just one example of how the rights contained in the CRC – in this case, a right to education as well as a right to be free from economic exploitation – are mutually reinforcing. Since

45 Interview with *Mother Jones* (magazine); interviewed by Onnesha Roychoudhuri, 6 May 2005. The text of the interview can be found at http://www.motherjones.com/news/qa/2005/05/jeffrey_sachs.html.

the problem is often one of resources, not necessarily of political will or cultural resistance, the international community can play a crucial role in facilitating children's rights through educational assistance funding and programs.

Implementing other rights discussed in this study can be problematic as well. The ban against torture is a good example. Not only did the evidence show that torture is one of the most difficult issue areas in which to gain compliance with human rights treaties – after all, abuses can take place in thousands of decentralized police stations across a country – it is also one of the most difficult activities to contain. One common complaint about banning torture is that as soon as particular practices come to be understood as prohibited, equally tortuous substitutes are used and often are even harder to detect after the fact. The debate over water-boarding – immobilizing a person on his or her back, head inclined downward, while pouring water over the covered face and into the breathing passages – illustrates the problem of drawing boundaries. Psychological forms of abuse are even more problematic. Indeed, trying to draw legal lines around torture, legitimating certain practices even while banning others, could have the effect of routinizing practices on the cusp of torture, ultimately making them easier to justify.[46] The international community has tended to address this issue by drawing the normative line more and more inclusively so that the definition of torture today is much less tolerant than in previous decades.

Finally, there is no denying that some of the rights discussed in this study will in fact be highly controversial. I have argued that international human rights have the most radical ideational impacts in countries where the rights being introduced are the most foreign. I will not deny that introducing external standards may foment some degree of internal conflict.[47] In many cases, these norms will challenge local ways of doing, being, and believing. Consider the right to religious freedom. If this right is interpreted as a right not only to believe as one sees fit, but also to proselytize freely without government interference, then there is the possibility of real cultural conflict and change. This is the basis of Islam's strong stance against conversion to another faith. We must acknowledge that the freedom to proselytize provides a structural advantage to religious faiths with evangelical philosophies. Makau Wa Mutua decries the violence that an unfettered freedom of Christianity and Islam to proselytize has wrought on African religions and cultures.[48] Conversion is an individual right but also a possible threat to ethnocultural groups.[49] Some people will view this prospect as simply the way that the "marketplace of ideas" works; let the truth prevail. Others are much more skeptical when that ideational marketplace is supplemented with access to health assistance or other humanitarian aid administered by a swelling army of private religious organizations.

46 Felner 2005.
47 Mahbubani 1995.
48 Mutua 1996:418–19.
49 Thomas 2001.

Governments have a right and a responsibility to demand that religious freedom is not practiced in a way that itself forces particular beliefs on others.

CONCLUSION

Sixty years ago, humanity stepped onto a path that many thought could have important consequences for human well-being for decades to come. Upon passage of the UDHR, Charles Malik exclaimed:

> Whoever values man and his individual freedom above everything else cannot fail to find in the present Declaration a potent ideological weapon. If wielded in complete goodwill, sincerity, and truth, this weapon can prove most significant in the history of the spirit.[50]

The intervening decades have shown both the naiveté and the profound insights of this claim. The halting efforts to translate the UDHR into binding legal obligations – often in spite of opposition from very powerful quarters – has produced a set of rules that reflect the aspirations of a broad swath of humanity. Yet, we are only beginning to understand the import of the legal foundations that were set six decades ago.

The finding of this book is that ratification of human rights treaties has had positive consequences for human rights in much of the world. From civil liberties, to women's rights, to the right to be free from torture, to the right of children to realize their potential, under many circumstances these agreements have delivered at least modest benefits to millions. International law is not and never will be a panacea for all human woes. David Kennedy has criticized "law's own tendency to overpromise." But contrary to his concerns, people are not waiting for "a foreign emancipatory friend who does not materialize."[51] They have strong incentives to use law – or whatever tools are available – to enhance the legitimacy of their claims and the prospects for realizing their interests. It should hardly be surprising that governments' solemn commitments to respect rights have been taken seriously by individuals and groups who imagine a better life if these promises are in fact kept.

It is hard to imagine a world in which the UDHR had never been written – a world devoid of authoritative agreements that individuals have rights that their governments must not trample or the provision of which can be indefinitely ignored. It would indeed be a world of very different priorities than the one we inhabit today. Change has been gradual but encouragingly cumulative. As Martin Luther King, Jr., said, "The arc of history is long, but it bends towards justice." International human rights treaties have helped to nudge the human race in the right direction.

50 See http://www.udhr.org/history/Biographies/biocm.htm.
51 Kennedy 2004:22.

Appendix 1: Data Appendix

This appendix describes the nature and source of the data used throughout this study. All variables are listed by chapter. Explanatory variables are listed in the order in which they appear in the tables (first appearance only). Note: all URLs were most recently accessed on 15 January 2009.

CHAPTER 3

Dependent Variables

Ratification (of the ICCPR, ICESCR, CERD, CEDAW, CAT, and CRC). Dichotomous variables (0 = not ratified; 1 = ratified) indicate the year in which each agreement was ratified by the respective government. Throughout, "accession" is coded as "ratification," since the legal obligations are generally indistinguishable. *Source*: Office of the High Commissioner for Human Rights (OHCHR), http://www2.ohchr.org/english/bodies/ratification/.

Reservations (to the ICCPR, ICESCR, CERD, CEDAW, CAT, and CRC). Reservations that were in place as of 2002. Declarations and understandings are included only if they have the effect of altering the nature of a state's obligation. This variable is used in two forms: as the log of the number of articles within a treaty specifically affected by the reservation and as a dichotomous measure indicating whether (1) or not (0) any reservation is in effect at all. *Source*: http://www2.ohchr.org/english/bodies/ratification/.

Types of reservations (to the ICCPR, ICESCR, CERD, CEDAW, CAT, and CRC). A coding of whether each reservation is broad, narrow, relates to a specific provision in the national code, is based on incapacity to implement a provision or provisions of the treaty, or is designed to reduce enforceability of the agreement. (See Table 3.4 for details on coding.) *Source*: http://www2.ohchr.org/english/bodies/ratification/.

ICCPR Article 41 declaration. Whether (1) or not (0), as of 2002, a government had made an Article 41 declaration acknowledging the authority of the Human Rights Committee to render views on complaints of states parties regarding treaty violation. *Source*: OHCHR, http://www2.ohchr.org/english/bodies/ratification/docs/DeclarationsArt41ICCPR.pdf.

ICCPR OPI ratification. Whether (1) or not (0), as of 2002, a government had ratified the first optional protocol to the ICCPR, acknowledging the authority of the Human Rights Committee to render views on complaints of individuals regarding treaty violation. *Source*: OHCHR, http://www2.ohchr.org/english/bodies/ratification/5.htm.

CERD Article 14 declaration. Whether (1) or not (0), as of 2002, a government had made an Article 14 declaration acknowledging the authority of the Committee on the Elimination of Racial Discrimination to render views on complaints of individuals regarding treaty violation. *Source*: OHCHR, http://www2.ohchr.org/english/bodies/ratification/2.htm.

CAT Article 22 declaration. Whether (1) or not (0), as of 2002, a government had made an Article 22 declaration acknowledging the authority of the Committee Against Torture to render views on complaints of individuals regarding treaty violation. *Source*: OHCHR, http://www2.ohchr.org/english/bodies/ratification/9.htm.

CEDAW OPI ratification. Whether (1) or not (0), as of 2002, a government had ratified the optional protocol to the CEDAW, acknowledging the authority of the Committee on the Elimination of Discrimination Against Women to render views on complaints of individuals regarding treaty violation. *Source*: OHCHR, http://www2.ohchr.org/english/bodies/ratification/8_b.htm.

Explanatory Variables

Democracy. A 20 point scale (−10 highly autocratic; 10 highly democratic) meant to capture the extent of democratic institutions in each state. The subindicators of this scale are: regulation of executive recruitment (extent to which there are institutionalized procedures regarding the transfer of executive power); the competitiveness of executive recruitment (extent to which executives are chosen through competitive elections); openness of executive recruitment (extent of opportunities for nonelites to attain executive office); executive constraints (operational or de facto independence of the chief executive); regulation of participation (development of institutional structures for political expression); competitiveness of participation (extent to which nonelites are able to access institutional structures for political expression). *Source*: The Polity IV Project, http://www.systemicpeace.org/polity/polity06.htm.

Democracy^2. The square of the score on the polity scale. See "Democracy."

Protestant. Whether (1) or not (0) the dominant religion practiced in that country is Protestant Christianity. *Sources*: Central Intelligence Agency: *CIA*

World Factbook, https://www.cia.gov/library/publications/the-world-factbook/; Europa Publications Limited 1999; United States Department of State, Office of Media Services 2000.

Catholic. Whether (1) or not (0) the dominant religion practiced in that country is Catholic Christianity. *Sources*: Central Intelligence Agency: *CIA World Factbook*, https://www.cia.gov/library/publications/the-world-factbook/; Europa Publications Limited 1999; United States Department of State, Office of Media Services 2000.

Islam. Whether (1) or not (0) the dominant religion practiced in that country is Sunni or Shi'a Islam. *Sources*: Central Intelligence Agency: *CIA World Factbook*, https://www.cia.gov/library/publications/the-world-factbook/; Europa Publications Limited 1999; United States Department of State, Office of Media Services 2000.

Left executive. From the World Bank's original coding of the chief executive's party as left, right, center, or no information, this variable was recoded to distinguish a "left party" (1) from all other categories (0). *Source*: World Bank Database of Poitical Institutions. For a detailed description of how left is defined, see http://siteresources.worldbank.org/INTRES/Resources/469232-1107449512766/dpi2006_vote_share_variable_definitions.pdf.

Common law legal tradition. Whether (1) or not (0) a country's legal system is based primarily on British common law. Data were collected from two sources: Global Development Network Growth Database, William Easterly and Hairong Yu, World Bank, http://econ.worldbank.org/WBSITE/EXTERNAL/EXTDEC/EXTRESEARCH/0,contentMDK:20701055~pagePK:64214825~piPK:64214943~the Site PK:469382,00.html, and Waguespack and Birnir 2005.

Presidential system. Whether a governing system can be characterized as primarily presidential (0) or primarily parliamentary (2). Ambiguous cases are coded (1). For a detailed description of the criteria used, see the World Bank Database of Political Institutions, http://siteresources.worldbank.org/INTRES/Resources/469232-1107449512766/dpi2006_vote_share_variable_definitions.pdf.

Ratification process. A four-category scale that captures the degree of political difficulty represented by the formal process of ratification. The categories are treaty ratification by individual chief executive or cabinet decision (1); rule or tradition of informing the legislative body of signed treaties (1.5); majority consent of one legislative body (2); supermajority in one body or majority in two separate legislative bodies (3). *Source and detailed description*: Appendix 3.2, my Web site at http://scholar.iq.harvard.edu/bsimmons/mobilizing-for-human-rights.

Ratification barriers in democracies. The interaction of the democracy and ratification process variables. See "Democracy" and "Ratification process" for definitions and sources.

Federalism. A scale ranging from 0 (most centralized) to 6 (most federal) based on the following subindices: whether or not there are autonomous regions (0 or 1); whether municipal governments are locally elected (0–2); whether state or provincial governments are locally elected (0 or 1); whether states/provinces have authority to tax and spend (0 or 1); and whether states/provinces are the constituencies of senators (0 or 1). *Source*: World Bank Database of Political Institutions. For a detailed description, see http://siteresources.worldbank. org/INTRES/Resources/469232-1107449512766/dpi2006_vote_share_variable_ definitions.pdf.

Regional ratifications. The density of ratifications within the region for each of the treaties modeled. Thus, this variable captures the proportion of countries in Western Europe that have ratified the ICCPR when the ICCPR is the dependent variable. The proportion excludes the country itself and is always lagged one period. Classification of countries by region (East and Southern Africa, West Africa, East Asia and Pacific, Central Asia, Eastern Europe, Rest of Europe, Middle East, North Africa, Americas) is based on World Bank categories.

Embeddedness. The extent to which each country participates in other major international agreements. It is the sum of ratifications each year for each country across the following: the Vienna Convention on the Law of Treaties (1969) *Source*: http://treaties.un.org/Pages/ViewDetailsIII.aspx?&src= TREATY&id=468&chapter=23&Temp=mtdsg3&lang=en; Convention Concerning the Protection of World Culture and Natural Heritage (1972) *Source*: http://74.125.95.132/search?q=cache:525scAqQ-uUJ:www.unep.org/gc/gc21/ Documents/gc-21-INF-16/INF16_convention. PDF+wcnh+treaty&;hl=en&ct= clnk&cd=1&gl=us; Vienna Convention on the Protection of the Ozone Layer (1985) *Source*: http://treaties.un.org/Pages/ViewDetails.aspx?src=TREATY&id= 503&chapter=27&lang=en; the total number of preferential trade agreements (Hafner-Burton 2005); Convention on International Trade in Endangered Species of Wild Fauna and Flora (1973). *Source*: http://www.cites.org/eng/disc/ parties/chronolo.shtml.

Average regional political rights. The average score in each of nine World Bank regions (excluding the country under analysis; see regional ratifications) on the Freedom House political rights index. *Source*: http://freedomhouse.org/ template.cfm?page=15.

Regional norm for government role in market. The regional average of a measure of the extent of government involvement in the national economy. The index ranges from 1 to 10, with an observed minimum of 1.7 and an observed maximum of 9.1. Components of this index include: general government consumption spending as a percentage of total consumption; transfers and subsidies as a percentage of GDP; government enterprises and investment as a percentage of GDP; top marginal tax rate (and income threshold to which it applies); top marginal income tax rate (and income threshold at which it applies); top marginal income and payroll tax rate (and income threshold at which it applies). For a detailed description see http://www.freetheworld.com/2008/EFW2008App1.pdf. Data are downloadable at http://www.freetheworld.com.

GDP per capita, logged (wealth). In constant 2000 U.S. dollars. *Source*: World Bank, World Development Indicators, http://devdata.worldbank.org/dataonline/.

GDP logged (size). Log of country GDP measures in constant 2000 U.S. dollars. *Source*: World Bank, World Development Indicators, http://devdata.worldbank.org/dataonline/.

Overseas development assistance/GDP. Official development assistance and official aid, in constant U.S. dollars as a share of GDP. *Source*: World Bank, World Development Indicators, http://devdata.worldbank.org/dataonline/.

Use of IMF credits. A dichotomous variables coded 1 if the country received credits from the IMF in a particular year and 0 otherwise. *Source*: Coded from data obtained from the World Bank, World Development Indicators, http://devdata.worldbank.org/dataonline/.

Democratic since World War I. All countries scoring 8 or above on the polity scale every year since 1917. See "Democracy."

Democratic since World War II. All countries scoring 8 or above on the polity scale every year since 1945 or their post-1945 independence. See "Democracy."

Newly transitioned democracy. The interaction of countries that have scored both above and below 7 on the polity scale but are currently above 7 (highly democratic). See "Democracy."

Density of regional reservations. This variable has two forms analogous to the variable "Reservations": The average number of reservations (logged) in the region; among states that have ratified; and the proportion of states in the region with any reservation among those that have ratified. See "Reservations" and "Regional ratifications."

Density of regional reservations by type. The proportion of states in the region with any reservation of the specific type being modeled among states that have ratified. See "Types of reservations" and "Regional ratifications."

Rule of law. Average rule of law score assigned by the World Bank between 1996 and 2004. This proxy measures "perceptions of the extent to which agents have confidence in and abide by the rules of society, and in particular the quality of contract enforcement, property rights, the police, and the courts, as well as the likelihood of crime and violence." *Source*: World Bank, http://info.worldbank.org/governance/wgi/pdf_country.asp.

World ratifications. The density of ratifications worldwide for each of the treaties modeled. Thus, this variable captures the proportion of countries globally that have ratified the ICCPR when the ICCPR is the dependent variable. The proportion excludes the country itself and is always lagged one period.

CHAPTER 5

Dependent Variables

INGO memberships. The number of INGOs that citizens of a state have membership in, logged, for each state. *Source*: Hafner-Burton and Tsutsui 2005. Original data are from Yearbook of International Organizations, http://www.uia.org/website.htm and http://www.hrweb.org/legal/undocs.html (updated by the author).

Religious freedom. An indicator of "the extent to which the freedom of citizens to exercise and practice their religious beliefs is subject to actual government restrictions." This variable is dichotomous; that is, countries are coded as either "restrictive" (0) or "free" (1). Governmental practices that count as restrictions include prohibitions on proselytizing; prohibitions on clergies' political participation; arrest, detention, or violence toward religious officials; citizen conversions forced by government officials; citizen arrests; harassment and/or intimidation for religious beliefs and practices; and so forth. *Source*: Cingranelli and Richards, http://ciri.binghamton.edu/documentation/ciri_variables_short_descriptions.pdf.

Fair trials. An index based on U.S. State Department reports measuring the extent to which trials are carried out by independent and impartial tribunals; whether an accused person has a right to counsel (and, if necessary, an interpreter) and to present a defense; whether there is a presumption of innocence; whether the trial is held publicly, in a timely fashion, and with a right to appeal; whether there are prohibitions on ex post facto laws; and whether the right exists to have charges presented with prior notice. The original data (1985–97) were coded from 1 (very fair) to 4 (very unfair). *Source*: Hathaway 2002. These were updated by the author, and the scale was inverted for the analyses.

Death penalty, de jure. A measure of existing laws on the death penalty. It indicates whether a country has abolished the death penalty under all circumstances (0), whether the death penalty has been abolished for "ordinary crimes," usually everything but treason (1), and whether the state retains the death penalty for ordinary crimes (2). *Source*: Amnesty International, http://web.amnesty.org/pages/deathpenalty-countries-eng.

Death penalty abolition. The first year (1) in which the death penalty was abolished (year of effective policy change); otherwise 0. *Source*: Amnesty International, http://www.amnesty.org/en/death-penalty/countries-abolitionist-for-all-crimes.

Explanatory Variables

ICCPR commitment. Whether (1) or not (0) a government had ratified or acceded to the ICCPR. *Source*: Office of the High Commissioner for

Human Rights (OHCHR), http://www2.ohchr.org/english/bodies/ratification/4.htm.

Civil liberties. An index ranging from 1 (excellent) to 7 (poor) that measures "freedoms of expression and belief, associational and organizational rights, rule of law, and personal autonomy without interference from the state." *Source*: Freedom House, http://www.freedomhouse.org/template.cfm?page=351&ana_page=341&year=2008.

Change in civil liberties. Change from one year to the next in a country's civil liberties score. See "Civil liberties."

Year trend. A variable (1970, 1971, 1972, etc.) indicating the year.

State religion, 1970–2000. Whether (1) or not (0) a state had an official state religion between 1970 and 2000. Data supplied by Rachel McCleary, used in Barro and McCleary (2005), based on data originally collected by Barrett (1982) and Barrett, Kurian, and Johnson (2001).

Establishing states, 1970–2000. Whether (1) or not (0) states established an official religion between 1970 and 2000. *Source*: see "State religion, 1970–2000."

Disestablishing states, 1970–2000. Whether (1) or not (0) states disestablished an official religion between 1970 and 2000. *Source*: see "State religion, 1970–2000."

Religious fractionalization. An index representing the probability that two randomly selected individuals from a population belong to the same religious group. (One minus the Herfindahl index.) *Source*: Alesina et al. 2003.

GDP growth. Yearly rate of growth in total gross domestic product. *Source*: World Bank, World Development Indicators, http://devdata.worldbank.org/dataonline/.

Trade openness. Total trade (imports plus exports) as a share of GDP. *Source*: World Bank, World Development Indicators, http://devdata.worldbank.org/dataonline/.

Civil war. Whether (1) or not (0) a country experienced a civil war in a particular year. *Source*: http://www.correlatesofwar.org/COW2%20Data/WarData/IntraState/Intra-State%20War%20Format%20(V%203-0).htm. This source was updated with information based on the list of recent civil wars collected by Wikipedia: http://en.wikipedia.org/wiki/List_of_recent_wars.

Interstate war. Whether (1) or not (0) a country was involved in interstate military conflict in a given year. Data collected by Gleditsch, Wallensteen, Eriksson, Sollenberg and Strand, Peace Research Institute, Oslo. The dataset is described in Gleditsch et al. (2002), http://www.prio.no/CSCW/Datasets/Armed-Conflict/.

Regional fair trial average. The regional average of the Fair trial index. See "Fair trials"; see regions defined in "Regional ratification."

Democratic change. First difference in the polity scale from one year to the next. See "Democracy."

Military government. Whether (1) or not (0) the head of state was an active duty military officer in a particular year. *Source*: World Bank Database of Political Institutions. For a detailed description see http://siteresources. worldbank.org/INTRES/Resources/469232-1107449512766/dpi2006_vote_share_ variable_definitions.pdf.

Truth commission. Whether (1) or not (0) a country has had a truth commission look into human rights abuses in a particular year. *Sources*: Bronkhorst 1995; Hayner 1994, 2001; United States Institute of Peace, http://www.usip.org/ library/truth.html#tc.

Criminal trials. Whether (1) or not (1) a country has had one or more domestic human rights trials involving individual criminal responsibility of government agents (of any rank, from police to head of state) for human rights violations in a specific year. Information was coded from the U.S. Department of State Country Reports on Human Rights Practices for all countries from 1979 to 2004. *Source*: Kim and Sikkink 2007. Available at https://www.law. uchicago.edu/files/intlaw-sikkink.pdf.

Ethnic fractionalization. An index representing the probability that two randomly selected individuals from a population belong to the same ethnic group. (One minus the Herfindahl index.) *Source*: Alesina et al. 2003.

Language fractionalization. An index representing the probability that two randomly selected individuals from a population belong to the same linguistic group. (One minus the Herfindahl index.) *Source*: Alesina et al. 2003.

Total fractionalization, logged. Sum of the fractionalization index for religious, ethnic, and linguistic groups for each country, logged. See "Religious [Ethnic, Linguistic] fractionalization." *Source*: Alesina et al. 2003.

Total population, logged. Total population for each country by year, logged. *Source*: World Bank, World Development Indicators, http://devdata. worldbank.org/dataonline/.

Execution year. Whether (1) or not (0) an execution was performed in a specific year. *Source*: Amnesty International, http://www.amnesty.org/en/ death-penalty/countries-abolitionist-for-all-crimes.

Civil war experience. Whether (1) or not (0) a country experienced a civil war at any point in the post–World War II years. See "Civil war."

Years since independence, logged. The log of the number of years since a country's formal independence. Year of independence is from Central Intelligence Agency, *World Factbook*, https://www.cia.gov/library/publications/the- world-factbook/, and Europa Publications Limited 1999.

Membership in Council of Europe. Whether (1) or not (0) a country is a member of the Council of Europe. *Source*: http://www.coe.int/T/E/Com/ About_Coe/Member_states/default.asp. As this is a measure of anticipated membership, the data are for three years into the future.

Regional death penalty density. Proportion of countries within each region that practice the death penalty. See "Regional ratification" for definition of the regions and "Death penalty, de jure" for death penalty data.

Europe. Whether (1) or not (2) a country is located in Europe (east or west).

CHAPTER 6

Dependent Variables

Women's INGO memberships. The number of women's INGOs in which citizens of a state have membership, for each state, logged. *Source*: Berkovitch 1999. Original data were coded from Yearbook of International Organizations, http://www.uia.org/website.htm and http://www.hrweb.org/legal/undocs.html. Data were updated by Christine Min Wotipka and Kiyoteru Tsutsui.

Girls' education. The ratio of girls to boys enrolled in primary and secondary schools. *Source*: World Bank, World Development Indicators, http://devdata. worldbank.org/dataonline/.

Access to modern family planning. Self-reported government policy with respect to women's access to modern forms of birth control, coded as follows: 0 = government limits access; 1 = government provides no support for access; 2 = government provides indirect support; 3 = government provides direct support. *Source*: United Nations Population Division (UNPD), Department of Economic and Social Affairs, http://www.un.org/esa/population/publications/npp2001/doc/nppdownload.htm.

Women's employment. Share of women in total public employment. Total public sector employment covers all general government employment plus employment in publicly owned enterprises and companies owned/operated at all levels of government. It covers all persons employed directly by those institutions, without regard for the particular type of employment contract. *Source*: ILO Public Sector Employment Data Base; ILO Bureau of Statistics, Geneva, Switzerland, http://laborsta.ilo.org/.

Explanatory Variables

CEDAW commitment. Whether (1) or not (0) a government had ratified or acceded to the CEDAW. *Source*: Office of the High Commissioner for Human Rights (OHCHR), http://www2.ohchr.org/english/bodies/ratification/8.htm.

Regional enrollment ratios. The average regional ratio of girls to boys in elementary and secondary schools. See "Regional ratification" for definition of regions and "Girls'education."

% of population urban. Urban population as a share of total population. *Source*: World Bank, World Development Indicators, http://devdata.worldbank.org/dataonline/.

% of population under 14. Share of the population under 14 years of age as a share of total population. *Source*: World Bank, World Development Indicators, http://devdata.worldbank.org/dataonline/.

Child labor. Share of 10- to 14-year-olds who are active in the labor force. *Source*: World Bank, World Development Indicators, http://devdata.worldbank.org/dataonline/.

Initial contraceptive policy. Initial policy reported by governments to the UNPD in 1976. See "Access to modern family planning."

Policy of population increase. Self-reported government policy with respect to overall population control, coded as follows: 0 = government non-intervention; 1 = government policy to reduce population; 2 = government policy to maintain population; 3 = government policy to increase population. Recoded to record whether (1) or not (0) a government's stated policy was to increase its state's population. *Source*: United Nations Population Division, Department of Economic and Social Affairs, http://www.un.org/esa/population/publications/wpp2007/WPPdownload.htm.

Policy of population reduction. Whether (1) or not (0) a government's stated policy goal was to control or reduce its state's population. See "Policy of population increase." *Source*: United Nations Population Division, Department of Economic and Social Affairs, http://www.un.org/esa/population/publications/wpp2007/WPPdownload.htm.

Average regional access to modern family planning. Average regional policies with respect to public support for access to modern forms of birth control. See "Regional ratification" for regions and "Access to modern family planning."

Dominant religion fixed effects (results not reported). See Chapter 6, footnote 86 for the inventory of religions from which "dominant religion" dummies were constructed. *Sources*: Central Intelligence Agency, *CIA World Factbook*, https://www.cia.gov/library/publications/the-world-factbook/; Europa Publications Limited 1999; United States Department of State, Office of Media Services 2000.

Average regional women's employment. Average regional proportions of women in total public employment. See "Regional ratification" for regions and "Women's employment."

CHAPTER 7

Dependent Variable

Torture prevalence. A 5-point scale that captures the prevalence and severity of torture by public officials in each country. Note that higher numbers are improvements (reductions in torture). See Table 7.1. *Source*: Hathaway 2002.

Explanatory Variables

CAT commitment. Whether (1) or not (0) a government had ratified or acceded to the CAT. *Source*: Office of the High Commissioner for Human Rights (OHCHR), http://www2.ohchr.org/english/bodies/ratification/9.htm.

Free press. A categorical variable indicating the extent to which the press within each country is free from government interference. The variable is coded as follows: 0 = not free, 1 = partly free, 2 = free. Where separate scores were given for broadcast and printed press (1979–1992), these were averaged. *Source*: Freedom House, http://www.freedomhouse.org/template.cfm?page=274.

Preferential trade agreements, with HR provisions. The number of new preferential trade agreements with the United States or Europe with human rights provisions negotiated each year. *Source*: Hafner-Burton 2005.

Average regional torture prevalence. Average torture prevalence for the region. See "Regional ratification" for the regions and "Torture prevalence."

PTAs with hard HR conditions. Total number of preferential trade agreements with hard conditionality provisions in force between the country and the United States or the EU. *Source*: Hafner-Burton 2005.

UN 1503 investigation. Whether (1) or not (0) a country was the subject of a 1503 procedure investigation by the UN Human Rights Commission in a particular year. See Appendix 7.1 on my Web site. *Source*: UNHCHR, http://www.unhchr.ch/html/menu2/8/stat1.htm.

UNGA HR resolution. Whether (1) or not (0) there was a resolution passed by the UNGA in that year criticizing a specific country's human rights practices. The country must be named in the resolution. *Source*: http://www.un.org/documents/resga.htm.

Visit, special rapporteur on torture. Whether (1) or not (0) a country had been subject to a visit by the special rapporteur on torture in a given year. *Source*: UNGA and OHCHR, http://www.ohchr.org/english/issues/torture/rapporteur/visits.htm.

Stable democracy. All countries that have been stable democracies (never below 8 on the polity scale) since World War II. Note: this is the union of "Democratic since World War I" and "Democratic since World War II." *Source*: The Polity IV Project, http://www.systemicpeace.org/polity/polity06.htm. See also Appendix 2 for a list of countries.

Never democratic. The country never scored above 5 on the polity scale in the twentieth century. *Source*: The Polity IV Project, http://www.systemicpeace.org/polity/polity06.htm. See also Appendix 2 for a list of countries.

Partial/transitional democracy. All countries other than "Stable democracies" and those that were "Never democratic." This includes countries that are transitioning to democracy, moving toward authoritarianism, and hovering between 5 and 8 on the polity scale. *Source*: The Polity IV Project, http://www.systemicpeace.org/polity/polity06.htm. See also Appendix 2 for a list of countries.

European CPT. Whether (1) or not (0) a country has ratified or acceded to the European Convention for the Prevention of Torture and Inhuman or Degrading Treatment or Punishment (CETS No.: 126). *Source*: Council of Europe, http://conventions.coe.int/Treaty/Commun/ChercheSig.asp?NT=126&CM=8&DF=&CL=ENG.

African charter commitment. Whether (1) or not (0) a country has ratified or declared adherence to the African Charter on Human and People's Rights. *Source*: http://www1.umn.edu/humanrts/instree/ratz1afchr.htm.

Inter-American CPPT. Whether (1) or not (0) a country has ratified or acceded to the Inter-American Convention to Prevent and Punish Torture, OAS Treaty Series No. 67. *Source*: OAS, Department of Legal Affairs and Services, Office of Inter-American Law and Programs, http://www.oas.org/juridico/english/Sigs/a-51.html.

Any regional commitment. Whether (1) or not (0) a country has ratified or acceded to any of the following: the European Convention for the Prevention of Torture and Inhuman or Degrading Treatment or Punishment, the African Charter on Human and People's Rights, or the Inter-American Convention to Prevent and Punish Torture. *Sources*: "European CPT," "African Charter commitment," and "Inter-American CPPT."

Strong rule of law. Any country that scores on average above +1 on the World Bank's "Rule of law" measure. See "Rule of law." See also Appendix 2 for a list of countries.

Moderate rule of law. Any country scoring between −1 and +1 on the World Bank's "Rule of law" measure. See "Rule of law." See also Appendix 2 for a list of countries.

Weak rule of law. Any country scoring below −1 on the World Bank's "Rule of law" measure. See "Rule of law." See also Appendix 2 for a list of countries.

CHAPTER 8

Dependent Variables

Child labor. Proportion of 10- to 14-year-olds in the labor force. See "Child labor" under Explanatory Variables, Chapter 6.

Measles immunization. Proportion of one- and two-year-olds inoculated for measles. *Source*: World Bank, World Development Indicators, http://devdata.worldbank.org/dataonline/.

DPT immunization. Proportion of one- and two-year-olds inoculated for DPT. *Source*: World Bank, World Development Indicators, http://devdata.worldbank.org/dataonline/.

Increase in military age. Increases in the legal minimum military service age, measured in years; for example, a shift in the minimum age from 16 to 18 is coded as 2. Separate indicators are developed for legal changes in the minimum ages for (1) any increase in the minimum military service age; (2) increase in minimum age for military volunteers; (3) minimum age for compulsory service; and (4) minimum age for combat service. *Sources*: The Global Report (2001 and 2004) by the Coalition to Stop the Use of Child Soldiers, http://www.child-soldiers.org/home; Individual State Reports to the UN Committee on the Rights of the Child, based on Article 44 of the CRC from 1990, http://documents. un.org/default.asp; and the Conscription and Conscientious Objection Documentation Project, War Resisters' International, http://www.wri-irg.org/co/ rtba/index.html. Other online sources were used to confirm the data contained in these documents. For countries where a discrepancy between official disclosure and practice was ascertainable or likely, such as Liberia and Colombia, or where sources contradicted each other or information was not clear, the Written Replies by the Country concerning the List of Issues received by the Committee on the Rights of the Child and/or the CRC's Concluding Observations (http:// documents.un.org/default.asp, Official documents of the UN) were also reviewed. Where sources contradicted each other and no further data were available, independent sources were weighed more heavily than a government's official information. If it was possible to locate a law containing the information, this information was used and is documented in the database. See my Web site at http://scholar.iq.harvard.edu/bsimmons/mobilizing-for-human-rights.

Improvements in observed under-age soldiers. Indicates the change between 2000 and 2005 in the extent to which 18-year-olds serve in the military, as reported by nongovernmental sources. The underlying data are coded as follows: 0 = no indications of any persons under 18 in combat units; 1 = rare or exceptional observation of persons under 18 in combat units; and 2 = not uncommon to observe persons under 18 in combat units. The data are recoded to reflect changes from one category to another. *Sources*: see "Increase in military age."

Explanatory Variables

CRC commitment. Whether (1) or not (0) a government had ratified or acceded to the CRC. *Source*: Office of the High Commissioner for Human Rights (OHCHR), http://www2.ohchr.org/english/bodies/ratification/11.htm.

Ratified ILO 182. Whether (1) or not (0) a government had ratified or acceded to the Convention concerning the Prohibition and Immediate Action for the Elimination of the Worst Forms of Child Labour (1999). *Source*: International Labor Organization, http://www.ilo.org/ilolex/cgi-lex/ratifce.pl?C182.

Agriculture share of GDP. The proportion of GDP accounted for by agricultural production. *Source*: World Bank, World Development Indicators, http://devdata.worldbank.org/dataonline/.

Female illiteracy rate. Proportion of females between the ages of 15 and 24 who are illiterate. *Source*: World Bank, World Development Indicators, http://devdata.worldbank.org/dataonline/.

Compulsory education through age 15. Whether (1) or not (0) a country has mandatory education requirements in place for children through age 15. *Source*: UNESCO's Global Monitoring Report 2003/4, http://portal.unesco.org/education/en/ev.php-URL_ID=24188&URL_DO=DO_TOPIC&URL_SECTION=201.html.

Bureaucratic quality. A 6-point scale that measures the extent to which a country's bureaucracy is believed to be very capable (6) or incapable (0) of carrying out a range of administrative tasks. For a full discussion of the conceptualization of this variable, see Knack and Keefer 1995. *Source*: *International Country Risk Guide*, The Political Risk Services Group, http://www.prsgroup.com/.

GAVI award. Whether (1) or not (0) the specific country received an award from the Global Alliance for Vaccines and Immunization for the purpose of increasing the immunization rate. *Source*: GAVI. See the individual country data at http://www.gavialliance.org/performance/country_results/index.php.

Regional immunization rate. The average inoculation rate for countries in the region. See "Regional ratification" for definition of regions and "Measles immunization" and "DPT immunization."

CRC OPCAC commitment. Whether (1) or not (0) a government had ratified or acceded to the Optional Protocol to the Convention on the Rights of the Child on the Involvement of Children in Armed Conflict (2000). *Source*: Office of the High Commissioner for Human Rights (OHCHR), http://www2.ohchr.org/english/bodies/ratification/11_b.htm.

Legal age, 2000. Baseline measure used to control for the initial minimum legal age for military recruits. See "Increase in military age."

Regional improvement. The proportion of countries within the region that have improved (raised) their minimum age for military service. For the definition of regions, see "Regional ratification." See also "Increase in military age."

Observed extent of participation at age 18, 2000. A baseline measure of the extent to which children under the age of 18 were observed in military units in 2000. See "Improvements in observed under-age soldiers."

Civil war (1998–2002). Whether (1) or not (0) a country was involved in a civil war at any time between 1998 and 2002. See "Civil war."

Appendix 2: Regime Type and Rule of Law Categories

Democratic since World War II	Partial/Transitional Democracy	Never Democratic	Strong Rule of Law	Moderately Strong Rule of Law	Moderately Weak Rule of Law	Weak Rule of Law
Australia	Albania	Afghanistan	Australia	Antigua	Albania	Afghanistan
Austria	Argentina	Algeria	Austria	Aruba	Algeria	Angola
Belgium	Armenia	Angola	Bahamas	Bahrain	Argentina	Belarus
Botswana	Bangladesh	Azerbaijan	Belgium	Barbados	Armenia	Cameroon
Canada	Benin	Bahrain	Canada	Belize	Azerbaijan	Comoros Islands
Costa Rica	Bolivia	Belarus	Chile	Botswana	Bangladesh	Congo (Zaire)
Denmark	Brazil	Bhutan	Denmark	Cape Verde	Benin	Congo
Finland	Bulgaria	Burma	Finland	Costa Rica	Bhutan	Equatorial Guinea
Germany	Chile	Burundi	France	Cyprus	Bolivia	Guinea-Bissau
Iceland	Colombia	Cameroon	Germany	Czech Republic	Bosnia	Haiti
Ireland	Czech Republic	Chad	Iceland	Dominica	Brazil	Iraq
Israel	Dominican Republic	China	Ireland	Egypt	Bulgaria	Laos
Italy	Estonia	Comoros Islands	Japan	Estonia	Burkina Faso	Liberia
Jamaica	Ecuador	Cuba	Liechtenstein	Greece	Burundi	Myanmar
Japan	El Salvador	Djibouti	Luxembourg	Grenada	Cambodia	Nigeria
Lithuania	Fiji	Egypt	Netherlands	Hungary	Central African Republic	Solomon Islands
Luxembourg	France	Equatorial Guinea	New Zealand	India	Chad	Somalia
Mauritius	The Gambia	Eritrea	Norway	Israel	China	Sudan
Netherlands	Greece	Ethiopia	Oman	Italy	Colombia	Tajikistan
New Zealand	Guatemala	Gabon	Portugal	Jordan	Croatia	Turkmenistan
Norway	Haiti	Guinea	Qatar	Kiribati	Cuba	Uzbekistan
Papua New Guinea	Honduras	Iran	Singapore	Korea	Djibouti	
Sweden	Hungary	Iraq	Spain	Kuwait	Dominican Republic	
Switzerland	Indonesia	Ivory Coast	Sweden	Latvia	Ecuador	
		Jordan	Switzerland	Lithuania		

(*continued*)

El Salvador
Eritrea
Ethiopia
Fiji
Gabon
The Gambia
Georgia
Ghana
Guatemala
Guinea
Guyana
Honduras
Indonesia
Iran
Ivory Coast
Jamaica
Kazakhstan
Kenya
Kyrgyz Republic
Lebanon
Lesotho
Libya
Macedonia
Madagascar
Malawi
Maldives
Mali
Marshall Islands
Mauritania
Mexico
Micronesia

Malaysia
Malta
Mauritius
Mongolia
Morocco
Namibia
Panama
Poland
San Marino
Saudi Arabia
Slovak Republic
Slovenia
South Africa
Sri Lanka
St. Kitts
St. Lucia
St. Vincent
Thailand
Trinidad and Tobago
Tunisia
Turkey
Uruguay

United Kingdom
United Arab Emirates
United States

Kazakhstan
Kuwait
Laos
Lebanon
Liberia
Libya
Mauritania
Morocco
Oman
Qatar
Rwanda
Saudi Arabia
Sierra Leone
Singapore
Swaziland
Syria
Tajikistan
Tanzania
Togo
Tunisia
Turkmenistan
Uganda
United Arab Emirates
Uzbekistan
Yemen

Korea (Republic of)
Latvia
Lesotho
Madagascar
Malawi
Malaysia
Mali
Moldova
Mongolia
Nepal
Nicaragua
Nigeria
Pakistan
Panama
Paraguay
Peru
Philippines
Poland
Portugal
Romania
Slovak Republic
Somalia
Spain
Sri Lanka
Thailand
Turkey
Ukraine
Uruguay
Venezuela
Zimbabwe

Trinidad and Tobago
United Kingdom
United States

Appendix 2 *(continued)*

Democratic since World War II	Partial/Transitional Democracy	Never Democratic	Strong Rule of Law	Moderately Strong Rule of Law	Moderately Weak Rule of Law	Weak Rule of Law
					Moldova	
					Mozambique	
					Nepal	
					Nicaragua	
					Niger	
					Pakistan	
					Papua New Guinea	
					Paraguay	
					Peru	
					Philippines	
					Romania	
					Russia	
					Rwanda	
					São Tomé and Príncipe	
					Senegal	
					Seychelles	
					Sierra Leone	

Surinam
Swaziland
Syria
Tanzania
Togo
Tonga
Uganda
Ukraine
Vanuatu
Venezuela
Vietnam
Yemen
Yugoslavia
Zambia
Zimbabwe

Democratic since World War II (stable democracies): the country never falls below a score of 8 on the democracy measure of the Polity dataset.

Never democratic: the country never rises above a score of 5 on the democracy measure of the Polity dataset.

Transitional/partial democracies: all other countries.

Strong (high) rule of law countries: score above 1 on the World Bank's rule of law scale.

Weak (low) rule of law countries: score below −1 on the World Bank's rule of law scale.

Moderately high (between 0 and 1) and moderately low (between −1 and 0) are combined in the statistical analysis to constitute the moderate rule of law countries.

See Appendix 1 for definitions and sources of "Democracy" and "Rule of law."

References

Abbott, Kenneth, Robert O. Keohane, Andrew Moravcsik, Anne-Marie Slaughter, and Duncan Snidal. 2000. Legalization and World Politics: An Introduction. *International Organization* 54(3): 385–99.

Abbott, Roderick. 1993. Gatt and the Trade Policy Review Mechanism – Further Reflections on Earlier Reflections. *Journal of World Trade* 27(3): 117–19.

Abouharb, M. Rodwan, and David L. Cingranelli. 2004. Human Rights and Structural Adjustment: The Importance of Selection. In *Understanding Human Rights Violations: New Systematic Studies*, edited by Sabine C. Carey and Steven C. Poe, 127–41. Aldershot, Hants, England; Burlington, Vt.: Ashgate.

Adriaansen, Robert. 1998. Open Forum: At the Edges of the Law: Civil Law V. Common Law: A Response to Professor Richard B. Cappalli. *Temple International and Comparative Law Journal* 12(spring): 107–13.

Agi, Marc. 1979. *René Cassin: Fantassin Des Droits De L'homme*. Paris: Plon.

Ainsworth, M., K. Beegle, and A. Nyamete. 1996. The Impact of Women's Schooling on Fertility and Contraceptive Use: A Study of Fourteen Sub-Saharan African Countries. *World Bank Economic Review* 10(1): 85–122.

Albrecht, H.-J. 2000. The Death Penalty in China from a European Perspective. In *EU–China Human Rights Dialogue: Proceedings of the Second EU–China Legal Expert Seminar Held in Beijing on 19 and 20 October 1998*, edited by Manfred Nowak and Chunying Xin, 95–118. Wien: Verlag Österreich.

Alesina, Alberto, Arnaud Devleeschauwer, William Easterly, Sergio Kurlat, and Romain Wacziarg. 2003. Fractionalization. *Journal of Economic Growth* 8(2): 155–94.

Ali, Mohammed M., John Cleland, and Iqbal Shah. 2003. Trends in Reproductive Behavior among Young Single Women in Colombia and Peru. *Demography* 40(4): 659–73.

Ali, Shaheen Sardar, and Baela Jamil. 1994. *The United Nations Convention on the Rights of the Child, Islamic Law and Pakistan Legislation: A Comparative Study*. Peshawar, Pakistan: Educational Computing Services & Publishers.

Allain, Jean, and Andreas O'Shea. 2002. African Disunity: Comparing Human Rights Law and Practice of North and South African States. *Human Rights Quarterly* 24(1): 86–125.

Allen, Tim. 2000. A World at War. In *Poverty and Development into the 21st Century*, edited by Tim Allen and Alan Thomas, 163–88. Oxford: Oxford University Press.

Almond, Gabriel Abraham, and Sidney Verba. 1963. *The Civic Culture: Political Attitudes and Democracy in Five Nations*. Princeton, N.J.: Princeton University Press.

Alston, Philip, Stephen Parker, and John Seymour, eds. 1992. *Children, Rights, and the Law*. Oxford: Clarendon Press.

Americas Watch Committee (U.S.). 1988. *Chile News in Brief.* New York: Americas Watch Committee.

Ancel, Marc. 1962. *The Death Penalty in European Countries*, edited by the European Committee on Crime Problems. Strasbourg: Council of Europe.

Anckar, Carsten. 2004. *Determinants of the Death Penalty: A Comparative Study of the World*. London, New York: Routledge.

Anderson, Benedict. 1991. *Imagined Communities: Reflections on the Origin and Spread of Nationalism*, rev. ed. London, New York: Verso.

Anderson, Bonnie S. 2000. *Joyous Greetings: The First International Women's Movement, 1830–1860*. Oxford, New York: Oxford University Press.

Anderson, Carol. 2003. *Eyes Off the Prize: The United Nations and the African American Struggle for Human Rights, 1944–1955*. Cambridge: Cambridge University Press.

Anghie, Antony. 2005. *Imperialism, Sovereignty, and the Making of International Law*. Cambridge: Cambridge University Press.

Ankumah, Evelyn A. 1996. *The African Commission on Human and Peoples' Rights: Practice and Procedures*. The Hague: Martinus Nijhoff.

Anon. 1999a. The Hague Forum on the Implementation of the Cairo Program of Action. *Population and Development Review* 25(1): 196–202.

       1999b. The United Nations on the Implementation of the Cairo Program of Action. *Population and Development Review* 25(3): 613–34.

Antoun, Richard T. 2001. *Understanding Fundamentalism: Christian, Islamic, and Jewish Movements*. Walnut Creek, Calif.: AltaMira Press.

Apodaca, Claire. 1998. Measuring Women's Economic and Social Rights Achievement. *Human Rights Quarterly* 20(1): 139–72.

       2001. Global Economic Patterns and Personal Integrity Rights after the Cold War. *International Studies Quarterly* 45(4): 587–602.

Arat, Zehra F. Kabasakal. 2002. The Women's Convention and State Reservations: The Lack of Compliance by Muslim States. Paper presented at the 43rd annual convention of the International Studies Association, New Orleans, March 23–7, 2002. Purchase College, State University of New York.

Ariès, Philippe. 1996. *Centuries of Childhood*. London: Pimlico.

Aristotle. 1998. *Politics* (translated, with an introduction and notes, by C.D.C. Reeve). Indianapolis: Hackett.

Aron, Raymond. 1981. *Peace and War: A Theory of International Politics*. Malabar, Fla.: Krieger.

Ashworth, Georgina. 1999. Political Perspectives on the Civil and Political Rights of Women. In *Women and International Human Rights Law*, edited by Kelly Dawn Askin and Dorean M. Koenig, 245–56. Ardsley, N.Y.: Transnational Publishers.

Asian Human Rights Commission. 2000. *Decline of Fair Trial in Asia: Papers from an Asian Seminar on Fair Trial, 7–12 November 1999, Kwoloon, Hong Kong*. Hong Kong: Asian Human Rights Commission.

Atwell, Mary Welek. 2004. *Evolving Standards of Decency: Popular Culture and Capital Punishment.* New York: P. Lang.

Augusto Cancado, Antonio. 1997. The Right to a Fair Trial under the American Convention on Human Rights. In *The Right to a Fair Trial in International and Comparative Perspective,* edited by Andrew Byrnes, 4–12. Hong Kong: Centre for Comparative and Public Law University of Hong Kong.

Azzam, Fateh. 1993. Non-Governmental Organizations and the UN World Conference on Human Rights. *The Review (International Commission of Jurists)* 50:89–105.

Badawi El-Sheikh, Ibrahim Ali. 1997. Preliminary Remarks on the Right to a Fair Trial under the African Charter on Human and People's Rights. In *The Right to a Fair Trial,* edited by David S. Weissbrodt and Rüdiger Wolfrum, 327–40. Berlin, New York: Springer.

Baehr, P. R. 1989. The General Assembly: Negotiating the Convention on Torture. In *The United Nations in the World Political Economy: Essays in Honour of Leon Gordenker,* edited by David P. Forsythe and Leon Gordenker, 36–53. Basingstoke, England: Macmillan.

Baker, R. 1992. Psychological Consequences for Tortured Refugees Seeking Asylum and Refugee Status in Europe. In *Torture and Its Consequences: Current Treatment Approaches,* edited by Metin Basoglu, 83–106. Cambridge: Cambridge University Press.

Bantekas, Ilias, and Peter Hodgkinson. 2000. Capital Punishment at the United Nations: Recent Developments. *Criminal Law Forum* 11(1): 23–34.

Banton, Michael P. 1996. *International Action against Racial Discrimination.* Oxford: Clarendon Press.

Barkun, Michael. 1968. *Law without Sanctions: Order in Primitive Societies and the World Community.* New Haven, Conn.: Yale University Press.

Barratt, Bethany. 2004. Aiding or Abetting: British Foreign Aid Decisions and Recipient Country Human Rights. In *Understanding Human Rights Violations: New Systematic Studies,* edited by Sabine C. Carey and Steven C. Poe, 43–62. Aldershot, Hants, England; Burlington, Vt.: Ashgate.

Barrett, David B. 1982. *World Christian Encyclopedia.* Oxford: Oxford University Press.

Barrett, David B., George T. Kurian, and Todd M. Johnson. 2001. *World Christian Encyclopedia,* 2nd ed. Oxford: Oxford University Press.

Barro, Robert J., and Rachel M. McCleary. 2005. Which Countries Have State Religions? *Quarterly Journal of Economics* 120(4): 1331–70.

Basoglu, Metin. 1993. Prevention of Torture and Care of Survivors: An Integrated Approach. *Journal of the American Medical Association* 270(5): 606–11.

Basu, Kaushik. 1999. Child Labor: Cause, Consequence, and Cure, with Remarks on International Labor Standards. *Journal of Economic Literature* 38:1083–119.

Baumer, Eric P., Steven F. Messner, and Richard Rosenfeld. 2003. Explaining Spatial Variation in Support for Capital Punishment: A Multilevel Analysis. *American Journal of Sociology* 108(4): 844–75.

Beccaria, Cesare. 1963. *On Crimes and Punishment* Indianapolis: Bobbs-Merrill.

Becker, Lawrence C., and Charlotte B. Becker. 2001. *Encyclopedia of Ethics,* 2nd ed. New York: Routledge.

Beigbeder, Yves. 1994. *International Monitoring of Plebiscites, Referenda and National Elections: Self-Determination and Transition to Democracy.* Dordrecht, Boston: Martinus Nijhoff.

Beitz, Charles R. 2004. Human Rights and the Law of Peoples. In *The Ethics of Assistance: Morality and the Distant Needy,* edited by Deen K. Chatterjee, 193–214. Cambridge: Cambridge University Press.

Benvenisti, Eyal. 1994. The Influence of International Human Rights Law on the Israeli Legal System: Present and Future. *Israel Law Review* 28(1): 136–53.

———. 1999. Margin of Appreciation, Consensus and Universal Standards. *New York University Journal of International Law and Politics* 31(4): 843–54.

Berkovitch, Nitza. 1999. *From Motherhood to Citizenship: Women's Rights and International Organizations*. Baltimore: Johns Hopkins University Press.

Berkowitz, Beth A. 2006. *Execution and Invention: Death Penalty Discourse in Early Rabbinic and Christian Cultures*. New York: Oxford University Press.

Berman, Nathaniel. 2004–5. Privileging Combat – Contemporary Conflict and the Legal Construction of War. *Columbia Journal of Transnational Law* 43(1): 1–72.

Berman, William C. 1970. *The Politics of Civil Rights in the Truman Administration*. Columbus: Ohio State University Press.

Bernal, Victoria. 2000. Equality to Die For?: Women Guerrilla Fighters and Eritrea's Cultural Revolution. *PoLAR: Political and Legal Anthropology Review* 23(2): 61–76.

Berryman, Phillip. 1993. *Report of the Chilean National Commission on Truth and Reconciliation*. South Bend, Ind.: Notre Dame University Press.

Beyer, Peter. 2003. Constitutional Privilege and Constituting Pluralism: Religious Freedom in National, Global, and Legal Context. *Journal for the Scientific Study of Religion* 42(3): 333–9.

Blacker, Coit, and Gloria Duffy, eds. 1984. *International Arms Control: Issues and Agreements*, 2nd ed. Stanford, Calif.: Stanford University Press.

Blackhurst, Richard. 1988. Strenthening the GATT Surveillance of Trade-Related Policies. In *The New GATT Round of Multilateral Trade Negotiations: Legal and Economic Aspects*, edited by Meinhard Hilf and Ernst-Ulrich Petersmann, 123–55. Deventer, the Netherlands: Kluwer.

Blanton, Shannon Lindsey. 2005. Foreign Policy in Transition? Human Rights, Democracy, and U.S. Arms Exports. *International Studies Quarterly* 49(4): 647–68.

Block, Brian P., and John Hostettler. 1997. *Hanging in the Balance: A History of the Abolition of Capital Punishment in Britain*. Winchester, England: Waterside Press.

Bobbio, Norberto. 1996. *The Age of Rights*. Cambridge: Polity Press.

Bodenhamer, David J. 1992. *Fair Trial: Rights of the Accused in American History, Bicentennial Essays on the Bill of Rights*. New York: Oxford University Press.

Bogdan, Michael. 1994. *Comparative Law*. Deventer, the Netherlands: Kluwer.

Boli, John, and George M. Thomas, eds. 1999. *Constructing World Culture: Internationl Nongovernmental Organizations since 1975*. Stanford, Calif.: Stanford University Press.

Boli-Bennett, John, and John W. Meyer. 1978. The Ideology of Childhood and the State. *American Sociological Review* 43:797–812.

Bolin-Hort, Per. 1989. Work, Family and the State: Child Labour and the Organization of Production in the British Cotton Industry, 1780–1920. *Bibliotheca Historica Lundensis, 66*. Lund, Sweden: Lund University Press.

Bolton, John. 2000. Is There Really "Law" in International Affairs? *Transnational Law and Contemporary Problems* 10:1–48.

Booth, Ken, and Russell B. Trood. 1999. *Strategic Cultures in the Asia-Pacific Region*. New York: Macmillan.

Borgwardt, Elizabeth. 2005. *A New Deal for the World: America's Vision for Human Rights*. Cambridge, Mass.: Belknap Press of Harvard University Press.

Bork, Robert H. 1989/90. The Limits of "International Law." *The National Interest* 18:3–10.

Bosco, David. 2000. Dictators in the Dock. *The American Prospect*: 14 August 2000, 26–9.

Boulanger, Christian, and Austin Sarat. 2005. Putting Culture into the Picture: Toward a Comparative Analysis of State Killing. In *The Cultural Lives of Capital Punishment: Comparative Perspectives*, edited by Austin Sarat and Christian Boulanger, 1–45. Stanford, Calif.: Stanford University Press.

Boulesbaa, Ahcene. 1999. *The U.N. Convention on Torture and the Prospects for Enforcement.* International Studies in Human Rights, V. 51. The Hague: Martinus Nijhoff.

Bowers, William J., Glenn L. Pierce, and John F. McDevitt. 1984. *Legal Homicide: Death as Punishment in America, 1864–1982.* Boston: Northeastern University Press.

Boyden, Jo, and Victoria Rialp. 1995. Children's Right to Protection from Economic Exploitation. In *Implementing the Convention on the Rights of the Child: Resource Mobilization in Low-Income Countries*, edited by James R. Himes, 183–221. The Hague: Martinus Nijhoff.

Boyle, Francis A. 1980. The Irrelevance of International Law. *California Western International Law Journal* 10:193–219.

Boyle, Peter G. 1993. *American–Soviet Relations: From the Russian Revolution to the Fall of Communism.* London, New York: Routledge.

Bracken, Patrick, and Celia Petty, eds. 1998. *Rethinking the Trauma of War.* London, New York: Free Association Books.

Bravo, German A. 1973. Population Policy in Colombia – Holistic Approach. *International Journal of Health Services* 3(4): 737–44.

Brems, Eva. 2006. *Article 14: The Right to Freedom of Thought, Conscience, and Religion: A Commentary on the United Nations Convention on the Rights of the Child.* Leiden, Boston: Martinus Nijhoff.

Brett, Rachel, and Irma Specht. 2004. *Young Soldiers: Why They Choose to Fight.* Boulder, Colo.: Lynne Rienner.

Brewster, Rachel. 2003. Domestic Origins of International Agreements. *Virginia Journal of International Law* 44(2): 1–42.

Briggs, Jimmie. 2005. *Innocents Lost: When Child Soldiers Go to War.* New York: Basic Books.

Brito, Alexandra Barahona de. 1997. *Human Rights and Democratization in Latin America: Uruguay and Chile.* Oxford, New York: Oxford University Press.

Bronkhorst, Daan. 1995. *Truth and Reconciliation: Obstacles and Opportunities for Human Rights.* Amsterdam: Amnesty International, Dutch Section.

Brown, Martin, Jens Christiansen, and Peter Philips. 1992. The Decline of Child Labor in the U.S. Fruit and Vegetable Canning Industry: Law or Economics? *The Business History Review* 66(4): 723–70.

Brown-Nagin, Tomiko. 2005. Elites, Social Movements, and the Law: The Case of Affirmative Action. *Columbia Law Review* 105(5): 1436–1528.

Buckley, Sandra. 1994. A Short History of the Feminist Movement in Japan. In *Women of Japan and Korea: Continuity and Change*, edited by Joyce Gelb and Marian Lief Palley, 150–88. Philadelphia: Temple University Press.

Buena de Mesquita, Bruce, Feryal Marie Cherif, George W. Downs, and Alastair Smith. 2005. Thinking Inside the Box: A Closer Look at Democracy and Human Rights. *International Studies Quarterly* 49(3): 439–58.

Bull, Hedley. 1977. *The Anarchical Society: A Study of Order in World Politics.* New York: Columbia University Press.

Bulterman, Mielle K., and Martin Kuijer, eds. 1996. *Compliance with Judgments of International Courts.* The Hague: Martinus Nijhoff.

Burgerman, Susan D. 1998. Mobilizing Principles: The Role of Transnational Activists in Promoting Human Rights Principles. *Human Rights Quarterly* 20(4): 905–23.

Burgers, Jan Herman. 1989. An Arduous Delivery: The United Nations Convention against Torture. In *Effective Negotiation: Case Studies in Conference Diplomacy*, edited by Johan Kaufmann, 45–52. Dordrecht, the Netherlands: Martinus Nijhoff.

———. 1992. The Road to San-Francisco – the Revival of the Human-Rights Idea in the 20th Century. *Human Rights Quarterly* 14(4): 447–77.

Burgers, Jan Herman, and Hans Danelius. 1988. *The United Nations Convention Against Torture: A Handbook on the Convention Against Torture and Other Cruel, Inhuman, or Degrading Treatment or Punishment.* Dordrecht, the Netherlands: Martinus Nijhoff.

Burstein, Paul. 1991. Legal Mobilization as a Social Movement Tactic: The Struggle for Equal Employment Opportunity. *The American Journal of Sociology* 96(5): 1201–25.

Burstein, Paul, and Kathleen Monaghan. 1986. Equal Employment Opportunity and the Mobilization of Law. *Law & Society Review* 20(3): 355–88.

Busch, Marc L., and Eric Reinhardt. 2000. Geography, International Trade, and Political Mobilization in U.S. Industries. *American Journal of Political Science* 44(4): 703–19.

Bzdera, Andre. 1993. Comparative Analysis of Federal High Courts: A Political Theory of Judicial Review. *Canadian Journal of Political Science* 26(1): 3–29.

Caldwell, John C., James F. Phillips, and Barkat-e-Khuda. 2002. The Future of Family Planning Programs. *Studies in Family Planning* 33(1): 1–10.

Cameron, Samuel. 1993. The Demand for Capital Punishment. *International Review of Law and Economics* 13(1): 47–59.

Campbell, Tom D. 1992. The Rights of the Minor: As Person, as Child, as Juvenile, as Future Adult. In *Children, Rights, and the Law*, edited by Philip Alston, Stephen Parker, and John Seymour, 1–23. Oxford: Clarendon Press.

Canagarajah, Sudharshan, and Harold Coulombe. 1997. Child Labor and Schooling in Ghana. *World Bank Policy Research Working Paper No. 1844.*

Canagarajah, Sudharshan, and Helena Skyt Nielsen. 2001. Child Labor in Africa: A Comparative Study. *The Annals of the American Academy of Political and Social Science* 575(1): 71–91.

Cantwell, Nigel. 1992. The Origins, Development, and Significance of the United Nations Convention on the Rights of the Child. In *The United Nations Convention on the Rights of the Child: A Guide to The "Travaux Préparatoires,"* edited by Sharon Detrick, Jaap E. Doek, and Nigel Cantwell, 19–30. Dordrecht, the Netherlands: Martinus Nijhoff.

Cappalli, Richard B. 1997. *The American Common Law Method.* Irvington-on-Hudson, N.Y.: Transnational Publishers.

———. 1998. Open Forum: At the Point of Decision: The Common Law's Advantage Over the Civil Law. *Temple International and Comparative Law Journal* 12(spring): 87–105.

Carey, Sabine C., and Steven C. Poe. 2004. *Understanding Human Rights Violations: New Systematic Studies, Ethics and Global Politics.* Aldershot, Hants, England; Burlington, Vt.: Ashgate.

Carleton, David, and Michael Stohl. 1985. The Foreign Policy of Human Rights: Rhetoric and Reality from Jimmy Carter to Ronald Reagan. *Human Rights Quarterly* 7(2): 205–29.

———. 1987. The Role of Human Rights in U.S. Foreign Assistance Policy: A Critique and Reappraisal. *American Journal of Political Science* 31(4): 1002–18.

Carozza, Paolo G. 2003. Subsidiarity as a Structural Principle of International Human Rights Law. *American Journal of International Law* 97:38–79.

Carr, Edward Hallett. 1964. *The Twenty Years' Crisis, 1919–1939: An Introduction to the Study of International Relations.* New York: Harper & Row.

Carter, Kim S. 1998. New Crimes against Peace? The Application of International Humanitarian Law Compliance and Enforcement Mechanisms to Arms Control and Disarmament Treaties. In *Treaty Compliance: Some Concerns and Remedies,* edited by Canadian Council on International Law, 1–20. London: Kluwer Law International.

Cassese, Antonio. 1996. *Inhuman States: Imprisonment, Detention and Torture in Europe Today.* Oxford: Polity Press.

Charlesworth, Hilary, Christine Chinkin, and Shelley Wright. 1991. Feminist Approaches to International Law. *American Journal of International Law* 85(4): 613–45.

Charney, Jonathan I. 1996. The Implications of Expanding International Dispute Settlement Systems: The 1982 Convention on the Law of the Sea. *American Journal of International Law* 90(1): 69–75.

Charnovitz, Steve. 1997. Two Centuries of Participation: NGOs and International Governance. *Michigan Journal of International Law* 18: 183–286.

Chayes, Abram, and Antonia Handler Chayes. 1993. On Compliance. *International Organization* 47(2): 175–205.

   1995. *The New Sovereignty: Compliance with International Regulatory Agreements.* Cambridge, Mass.: Harvard University Press.

Checkel, Jeffrey. 1997. International Norms and Domestic Politics: Bridging the Rationalist–Constructivist Divide. *European Journal of International Relations* 3(4): 473–95.

   2001. Why Comply? Social Learning and European Identity Change. *International Organization* 55(3): 553–88.

Chibundu, Maxwell O. 1999. Making Customary International Law through Municipal Adjudication: A Structural Inquiry. *Virginia Journal of International Law* 39(4): 1069–150.

Chinkin, Christine. 2000. Human Rights and the Politics of Representation: Is There a Role for International Law? In *The Role of Law in International Politics,* edited by Michael Byers, 131–48. Oxford: Oxford University Press.

Cingranelli, David L., and Thomas E. Pasquarello. 1985. Human Rights Practices and the Distribution of U.S. Foreign Aid to Latin American Countries. *American Journal of Political Science* 29(3): 539–63.

Cingranelli, David L., and David L. Richards. 1999a. Measuring the Level, Pattern, and Sequence of Government Respect for Physical Integrity Rights. *International Studies Quarterly* 43(2): 407–18.

   1999b. Respect for Human Rights after the End of the Cold War. *Journal of Peace Research* 36(5): 511–34.

Clark, Ann Marie. 2001. *Diplomacy of Conscience: Amnesty International and Changing Human Rights Norms.* Princeton, N.J.: Princeton University Press.

Clark, Belinda. 1991. The Vienna Convention Reservations Regime and the Convention on Discrimination against Women. *American Journal of International Law* 85(2): 281–321.

Clark, Melissa. 2000–1. Israel's High Court of Justice Ruling on the General Security Service Use of "Moderate Physical Pressure": An End to the Sanctioned Use of Torture? *Indiana Comparative and International Law Review* 11(1): 145–82.

Clark, Roger S. 2000. How International Human Rights Law Affects Domestic Law. In *Human Rights: New Perspectives, New Realities,* edited by Adamantia Pollis and Peter Schwab, 185–207. Boulder, Colo.: Lynne Rienner.

Claude, Inis L. 1955. *National Minorities: An International Problem.* Cambridge, Mass.: Harvard University Press.

Claude, Richard P., and Thomas B. Jabine. 1986. Symposium on Statistical Issues in the Field of Human Rights: Introduction. *Human Rights Quarterly* 8(4): 551–66.

Claude, Richard Pierre, and Burns H. Weston. 1992. *Human Rights in the World Community: Issues and Action,* 2nd ed. Philadelphia: University of Pennsylvania Press.

Cleary, Edward L. 1997. *The Struggle for Human Rights in Latin America.* Westport, Conn.: Praeger.

Cmiel, Kenneth. 1999. The Emergence of Human Rights Politics in the United States. Available at http://www.historycooperative.org/journals/jah/86.3/cmiel.html (accessed 8 December 2005).

Coccia, Massimo. 1985. Reservations to Multilateral Treaties on Human Rights. *California Western International Law Journal* 15:1–51.

Coglianese, Cary. 2001–2. Social Movements, Law, and Society: The Institutionalization of the Environmental Movement. *University of Pennsylvania Law Review* 150:85–119.

Cohen, Cynthia Price. 1990. The Role of Nongovernmental Organizations in the Drafting of the Convention on the Rights of the Child. *Human Rights Quarterly* 12(1): 137–47.

Cohen, Cynthia Price., Stuart N. Hart, and Susan M. Kosloske. 1996. Monitoring the United Nations Convention on the Rights of the Child – the Challenge of Information Management. *Human Rights Quarterly* 18(2): 439–71.

Cohn, Ilene, and Guy S. Goodwin-Gill. 1994. *Child Soldiers: The Role of Children in Armed Conflict.* Oxford: Clarendon Press.

Comité de Defensa de los Derechos del Pueblo (Chile). 1996. *Crímenes e Impunidad: La Experiencia del Trabajo Médico, Psicológico, Social y Jurídico en la Violación del Derecho a La Vida: Chile 1973–1996: VII Región Del Maule, IX Región de La Araucana, X Región de Los Lagos, Serie Verdad y Justicia, V. 6.* Santiago, Chile: Codepu: Dit-T.

Connor, Cormac T. 2001. Human Rights Violations in the Information Age. *Georgetown Immigration Law Journal* 16:207–35.

Cook, Rebecca J., and Bernard M. Dickens. 2003. Human Rights Dynamics of Abortion Law Reform. *Human Rights Quarterly* 25(1): 1–59.

Cook, Rebecca J., Bernard. M. Dickens, and Laura E. Bliss. 1999. International Developments in Abortion Law from 1988 to 1998. *American Journal of Public Health* 89(4): 579–86.

Cook, Rebecca J. 1993a. International Human Rights and Women's Reproductive Health. *Studies in Family Planning* 24(2): 73–86.

1993b. Women's International Human Rights Law: The Way Forward. *Human Rights Quarterly* 15(2): 230–61.

Coomaraswamy, R. 1996. Reinventing International Law: Women's Rights as Human Rights in the International Community. *Bulletin of Concerned Asian Scholars* 28(2): 16–26.

Cortell, Andrew P., and James W. Davis, Jr. 1996. How Do International Institutions Matter? The Domestic Impact of International Rules and Norms. *International Studies Quarterly* 40: 451–78.

Council of Europe, European Commission for Democracy through Law, ed. 2000. *The Right to a Fair Trial.* Collection Science and Technique of Democracy, No. 28. Strasbourg: Council of Europe.

Crockatt, Richard. 1995. *The Fifty Years War: The United States and the Soviet Union in World Politics, 1941–1991.* London, New York: Routledge.

Cross, Frank B. 1999. The Relevance of Law in Human Rights Protection. *International Review of Law and Economics* 10(1): 87–98.

Cunningham, Hugh. 1990. The Employment and Unemployment of Children in England c. 1680–1851. *Past and Present* 126:115–50.

Curzon Price, Victoria. 1991. GATT's New Trade Policy Review Mechanism. *The World Economy* 14(2): 227–38.

Dai, Xinyuan. 2005. Why Comply? The Domestic Constituency Mechanism. *International Organization* 59(2): 363–98.

   2007. *International Institutions and National Policies*. Cambridge: Cambridge University Press.

Damaska, Mirjan R. 1986. *The Faces of Justice and State Authority: A Comparative Approach to the Legal Process*. New Haven, Conn.: Yale University Press.

Danilenko, Gennady M. 1994. The New Russian Constitution and International Law. *The American Journal of International Law* 88(3): 451–70.

Danilenko, Gennady M., and William Burnham. 2000. *Law and Legal System of the Russian Federation*, 2nd ed. Yonkers, N.Y.: Juris.

Danner, Mark. 2004. *Torture and Truth: America, Abu Ghraib, and the War on Terror*. New York: New York Review of Books.

Darbyshire, Penny, and Keith James Eddey. 2001. *Eddey and Darbyshire on the English Legal System*, 7th ed. London: Sweet & Maxwell.

David, René, and John E. C. Brierley. 1978. *Major Legal Systems in the World Today: An Introduction to the Comparative Study of Law*, 2nd ed. London: Stevens.

Davis, Christina L. 2004. International Institutions and Issue Linkage: Building Support for Agricultural Trade Liberalization. *American Political Science Review* 98(1): 153–69.

Davis, David Brion. 1957. The Movement to Abolish Capital Punishment in America, 1787–1861. *The American Historical Review* 63(1): 23–46.

Davis, Derek H. 2002. The Evolution of Religious Freedom as a Universal Human Right: Examining the Role of the 1981 United Nations Declaration on the Elimination of All Forms of Intolerance and of Discrimination Based on Religion or Belief. *Brigham Young University Law Review* 2002:217–36.

Davis, Madeleine. 2003. *The Pinochet Case: Origins, Progress and Implications*, edited by the University of London. London: Institute of Latin American Studies.

de Berry, Jo. 2001. Child Soldiers and the Convention on the Rights of the Child. *Annals of the American Academy of Political and Social Science* 575(1): 92–105.

de Feyter, Koen. 1996. The Prohibition of Child Labor as a Social Clause in Multilateral Trade Agreements. In *Monitoring Children's Rights*, edited by Eugeen Verhellen, 431–44. The Hague: Martinus Nijhoff.

De Neufville, Judith Innes. 1986. Human Rights Reporting as a Policy Tool – an Examination of the State Department Country Reports. *Human Rights Quarterly* 8(4): 681–99.

De Vries, Margaret Garritsen, and J. Keith Horsefield. 1969. *The International Monetary Fund, 1945–1965: Twenty Years of International Monetary Cooperation*. Washington, D.C.: International Monetary Fund.

De Zayas, Alfred M. 1997. The United Nations and the Guarantees of a Fair Trial in the International Covenant on Civil and Political Rights and the Convention Against Torture and Other Cruel, Inhuman or Degrading Treatment or Punishment. In *The Right to a Fair Trial*, edited by David S. Weissbrodt and Rüdiger Wolfrum, 669–96. Berlin, New York: Springer.

De Zayas, Alfred M., Jakob Moller, and Torkel Opsahl. 1985. Application of the ICCPR Under the Optional Protocol by the Human Rights Committee. *German Yearbook of International Law* 28:9–64.

DeJong, Jocelyn. 2000. The Role and Limitations of the Cairo International Conference on Population and Development. *Social Science & Medicine* 51(6): 941–53.

DeMause, Lloyd. 1975. *The History of Childhood.* New York: Harper & Row.

Dennis, Michael J. 2000. Newly Adopted Protocols to the Convention on the Rights of the Child. *American Journal of International Law* 94(4): 789–96.

Desai, Sonalde, and Soumya Alva. 1998. Maternal Education and Child Health: Is There a Strong Causal Relationship? *Demography* 35(1): 71–81.

Detrick, Sharon. 1999. *A Commentary on the United Nations Convention on the Rights of the Child.* The Hague, Boston: Martinus Nijhoff.

DeWaal, Alex. 1997. Contemporary Warfighting in Africa. In *Restructuring the Global Military Sector,* edited by Mary Kaldor and Basker Vashee, 287–322. London, New York: Pinter.

Dezalay, Yves, and Bryant Garth. n.d. Law, Lawyers, and Empire: From the Foreign Policy Establishment to Technical Legal Hegemony. Available at http://www.law.berkeley.edu/institutes/csls/Garthcenterpaper.pdf (accessed 8 June 2009).

2006. From the Cold War to Kosovo: The Rise and Renewal of the Field of International Human Rights. *Annual Review of Law and Social Science* 2(1): 231–55.

Diaz, Soledad. 1998. Contraceptive Technology and Family Planning Services. *International Journal of Gynecology & Obstetrics* 63:S85–S90.

Diehl, Paul F. 1996. The United Nations and Peacekeeping. In *Coping with Conflict after the Cold War,* edited by Edward Kolodziej and Roger Kanet, 147–65. Baltimore: Johns Hopkins University Press.

Disability, National Council on. 2002. Understanding the Role of an International Convention on the Human Rights of People with Disabilities: A White Paper. Available at http://www.ncd.gov/newsroom/publications/2002/unwhitepaper_05-23-02.htm (accessed 12 August 2005).

Dix, Robert H. 1987. *The Politics of Colombia.* New York: Praeger.

Donnelly, Jack. 1986. International Human Rights: A Regime Analysis. *International Organization* 40(3): 599–642.

1998. *International Human Rights,* 2nd ed. Boulder, Colo.: Westview Press.

Donnelly, Jack, and Rhoda E. Howard. 1988. Assessing National Human Rights Performance: A Theoretical Framework. *Human Rights Quarterly* 10:214–48.

Donner, Laura A. 1993–4. Gender Bias in Drafting International Discrimination Conventions: The 1979 Women's Convention Compared with the 1965 Racial Convention. *California Western International Law Journal* 24:241–54.

Dower, John W. 1999. *Embracing Defeat: Japan in the Wake of World War II.* New York: W.W. Norton/ New Press.

Downs, George W., and Michael A. Jones. 2002. Reputation, Compliance, and International Law. *Journal of Legal Studies* 33(1 [part 2]): S95–S114.

Downs, George W., David M. Rocke, and Peter N. Barsoom. 1996. Is the Good News About Compliance Good News About Cooperation? *International Organization* 50(3): 379–406.

Drèze, Jean P., and Haris Gazdar. 1997. Uttar Pradesh: The Burden of Inertia. In *Indian Development: Selected Regional Perspectives,* edited by Jean Drèze and Amartya Kumar Sen, 33–108. Delhi, New York: Oxford University Press.

Drèze, Jean, and Amartya Kumar Sen. 2002. *India: Development and Participation*, 2nd ed. Oxford, New York: Oxford University Press.

Dudziak, Mary L. 2000. *Cold War Civil Rights: Race and the Image of American Democracy, Politics and Society in Twentieth-Century America*. Princeton, N.J.: Princeton University Press.

Duffy, Michael. 1992. Practical Problems of Giving Effect to Treaty Obligation – the Cost of Consent. *Australian Yearbook of International Law* 12:16–21.

Dunér, Bertil, ed. 1998. *An End to Torture: Strategies for Its Eradication*. London, New York: Zed Books; St. Martin's Press.

Dunér, Bertil, and Hanna Geurtsen. 2002. The Death Penalty and War. *International Journal of Human Rights* 6(4): 1–28.

Dupuy, Trevor N., and Gay M. Hammerman, eds. 1973. *A Documentary History of Arms Control and Disarmament*. New York: R. R. Bowker.

Duraisamy, P. 2002. Changes in Returns to Education in India, 1983–94: By Gender, Age-Cohort and Location. *Economics of Education Review* 21(6): 609–22.

Durham, W. Cole, Jr., and Lauren B. Homer. 1998. Russia's 1997 Law on Freedom of Conscience and Religious Associations: An Analytical Appraisal. *Emory International Law Review* 12(1): 101–246.

Editorial. 1998. Religious Persecution in Today's Germany: Old Habits Renewed. *Journal of Church and State* 40(4): 741.

Eglitis, Daina Stukuls. 2000. Mother Country: Gender, Nation, and Politics in the Balkans and Romania. *East European Politics and Society* 14(3): 693–702.

Ehrlich, Isaac. 1975. The Deterrent Effect of Capital Punishment: A Question of Life and Death. *The American Economic Review* 65(3): 397–417.

Eide, Asbjorn. 1998. The Historical Significance of the Universal Declaration. *International Social Science Journal* 50(4): 475–97.

Einhorn, Barbara, and Charlotte Sever. 2003. Gender and Civil Society in Central and Eastern Europe. *International Feminist Journal of Politics* 5(2): 163–91.

Eisenhower, Dwight D. 1963. *Mandate for Change, 1953–1956: The White House Years*. Garden City, N.Y.: Doubleday.

Ekirch, A. Roger. 1987. *Bound for America: The Transportation of British Convicts to the Colonies, 1718–1775*. Oxford: Clarendon Press.

Ellmann, Stephen. 1998. Cause Lawyering in the Third World. In *Cause Lawyering: Political Commitments and Professional Responsibilities*, edited by Austin Sarat and Stuart A. Scheingold, 349–430. New York: Oxford University Press.

Emery, Cyril Robert. 2005. Treaty Solutions from the Land Down Under: Reconciling American Federalism and International Law. Available at http://ssrn.com/abstract=695621 (accessed 24 October 2005).

Encyclopaedia Britannica. 2007. *Human Rights*. Encyclopaedia Britannica Online. Available at http://www.search.eb.com.ezp-prod1.hul.harvard.edu/eb/article-9106289 (accessed 17 December 2008).

Endres, Anthony M., and Grant A. Fleming. 2002. *International Organizations and the Analysis of Economic Policy, 1919–1950*. Cambridge: Cambridge University Press.

Engle, Karen. 2005. Liberal Internationalism, Feminism, and the Suppression of Critique: Contemporary Approaches to Global Order in the United States. *Harvard International Law Journal* 46(2): 427–41.

Ensalaco, Mark. 2000. *Chile under Pinochet: Recovering the Truth*. Philadelphia: University of Pennsylvania Press.

Eskridge, William N., Jr. 2001–2. Channeling: Identity-Based Social Movements and Public Law. *University of Pennsylvania Law Review* 150:419–525.

Estreicher, Samuel. 2003. Rethinking the Binding Effect of Customary International Law. *Virginia Journal of International Law* 44:5–18.

Europa Publications Limited. 1999. *The Europa World Year Book.* 40th ed. London: Europa Publications.

Evans, Carolyn M. 2002. Chinese Law and the International Protection of Religious Freedom. *Journal of Church and State* 44(4): 749–74.

Evans, Malcolm, and Rodney Morgan. 1997. The European Convention for the Prevention of Torture: 1992–1997. *The International and Comparative Law Quarterly* 46(3): 663–75.

Evans, Malcolm, and Rachel Murray. 2002. *The African Charter on Human and Peoples' Rights: The System in Practice, 1986–2000.* Cambridge: Cambridge University Press.

Evans, Peter B., Harold Karan Jacobson, and Robert D. Putnam. 1993. *Double-Edged Diplomacy: International Bargaining and Domestic Politics. Studies in International Political Economy, V. 25.* Berkeley: University of California Press.

Evans, Tony. 1996. *U.S. Hegemony and the Project of Universal Human Rights.* New York: St. Martin's Press.

ed. 1998. *Human Rights Fifty Years On: A Reappraisal.* Manchester, England: Manchester University Press.

2001. *The Politics of Human Rights: A Global Perspective.*; London, Sterling, Va.: Pluto Press.

Ewick, Patricia, and Susan S. Silbey. 1998. *The Common Place of Law: Stories from Everyday Life, Language and Legal Discourse.* Chicago: University of Chicago Press.

Farber, Daniel A. 2002. Rights as Signals. *Journal of Legal Studies* 31(1) (Part 1): 83–98.

Farer, Tom J. 1988. *The Grand Strategy of the United States in Latin America.* New Brunswick, N.J.: Transaction Books.

Farson, Richard Evans. 1974. *Birthrights.* New York: Macmillan.

Faundez, Julio. 2005. Democratization through Law: Perspectives from Latin America. *Democratization* 12(5): 749–65.

Fawn, Rick. 2001. Death Penalty as Democratization: Is the Council of Europe Hanging Itself? *Democratization* 8(2): 69–96.

Fearon, James D. 1997. Signaling Foreign Policy Interests: Tying Hands versus Sinking Costs. *The Journal of Conflict Resolution* 41(1): 68–90.

Fein, Helen. 1995. More Murder in the Middle: Life-Integrity Violations and Democracy in the World, 1987. *Human Rights Quarterly* 17(1): 170–91.

Felice, William. 2003. *The Global New Deal: Economic and Social Human Rights in World Politics.* Lanham, Md.; Oxford: Rowman & Littlefield.

Felner, Eitan. 2005. Torture and Terrorism: Painful Lessons from Israel. In *Torture: Does It Make Us Safer? Is It Ever OK? A Human Rights Perspective,* edited by Kenneth Roth, Minky Worden, and Amy D. Bernstein, 28–43. New York: New Press.

Fields, A. Belden. 2003. *Rethinking Human Rights for the New Millennium.* New York: Palgrave Macmillan.

Fijalkowski, Agata. 2005. Capital Punishment in Poland: An Aspect of the "Cultural Life" of Death Penalty Discourse. In *The Cultural Lives of Capital Punishment: Comparative Perspectives,* edited by Austin Sarat and Christian Boulanger, 147–68. Stanford, Calif.: Stanford University Press.

Finnemore, Martha. 1993. International Organizations as Teachers of Norms: The United Nations Educational, Scientific, and Cutural Organization and Science Policy. *International Organization* 47(4): 565–97.

Finnemore, Martha, and Kathryn Sikkink. 1998. International Norm Dynamics and Political Change. *International Organization* 52(4): 887–918.

Fischer, Dana D. 1982. Decisions to Use the International Court of Justice: Four Recent Cases. *International Studies Quarterly* 26(2): 251–77.

Fisher, Roger. 1981. *Improving Compliance with International Law*. Charlottesville: University of Virginia Press.

Flowers, Petrice Ronita. 2002. "International Norms and Domestic Policies in Japan: Identity, Legitimacy and Civilization." Ph.D. thesis, University of Minnesota.

Føllesdal, Andreas, and Thomas Winfried Menko Pogge, eds. 2005. *Real World Justice: Grounds, Principles, Human Rights, and Social Institutions*. Dordrecht, the Netherlands: Springer.

Forsythe, David P. 1985. The United Nations and Human Rights. *Political Science Quarterly* 100(2): 249–69.

1989. *Human Rights and World Politics*. Lincoln: University of Nebraska Press.

1993. *Human Rights and Peace: International and National Dimensions, Human Rights in International Perspective, V. 1*. Lincoln: University of Nebraska Press.

Fox, Jonathan. 2004. The Rise of Religious Nationalism and Conflict: Ethnic Conflict and Revolutionary Wars, 1945–2001. *Journal of Peace Research* 41(6): 715–31.

Franck, Thomas M. 1990. *The Power of Legitimacy among Nations*. New York: Oxford University Press.

Franck, Thomas M., and Gregory H. Fox, eds. 1996. *International Law Decisions in National Courts*. Irvington-on-Hudson, N.Y.: Transnational Publishers.

Franck, Thomas M., and Nigel S. Rodley. 1973. After Bangladesh: The Law of Humanitarian Intervention by Military Force. *The American Journal of International Law* 67(2): 275–305.

Freedman, Lynn P., and Stephen L. Isaacs. 1993. Human Rights and Reproductive Choice. *Studies in Family Planning* 24(1): 18–30.

Freeman, Jo. 1979. Resource Mobilization and Strategy. In *The Dynamics of Social Movements: Resource Mobilization, Social Control, and Tactics*, edited by Mayer N. Zald and John D. McCarthy, 167–89. Cambridge, Mass.: Winthrop.

Freeman, Marsha A., and Arvonne S. Fraser. 1994. Women's Human Rights: Making the Theory a Reality. In *Human Rights: An Agenda for the Next Century*, edited by Louis Henkin and John Lawrence Hargrove, 103–35. Washington, D.C.: American Society of International Law.

Freeman, Michael D. A. 1992. Taking Children's Rights More Seriously. In *Children, Rights, and the Law*, edited by Philip Alston, Stephen Parker, and John Seymour, 52–71. Oxford: Clarendon Press.

Friedman, Elisabeth J., Kathryn Hochstetler, and Ann Marie Clark. 2005. *Sovereignty, Democracy, and Global Civil Society: State–Society Relations at UN World Conferences*. Albany: State University of New York Press.

Friedman, Thomas L. 2001. The Impact of Globalization on World Peace. In *Arnold C. Harberger Distinguished Lecture Series, 31*. Los Angeles: Burkle Center for International Relations.

Froese, Paul. 2004. After Atheism: An Analysis of Religious Monopolies in the Post-Communist World. *Sociology of Religion* 65(1): 57–75.

Fruhling, Hugo, and Frederick Woodbridge, Jr. 1983. Stages of Repression and Legal Strategy for the Defense of Human Rights in Chile: 1973–1980. *Human Rights Quarterly* 5(4): 510–33.

Frymer, Paul. 2003. Acting When Elected Officials Won't: Federal Courts and Civil Rights Enforcement in U.S. Labor Unions, 1935–85. *American Political Science Review* 97(3): 483–99.

Fu, Hua Ling. 1997. The Right to a Fair Trial in China: The New Criminal Procedure Law. In *The Right to a Fair Trial in International and Comparative Perspective*, edited by Andrew Byrnes, 78–88. Hong Kong: Centre for Comparative and Public Law University of Hong Kong.

Gage, Anastasia J., A. Elisabeth Sommerfelt, and Andrea L. Piani. 1997. Household Structure and Childhood Immunization in Niger and Nigeria. *Demography* 34(2): 295–309.

Gal, Susan, and Gail Kligman. 2000. *The Politics of Gender after Socialism: A Comparative-Historical Essay.* Princeton, N.J.: Princeton University Press.

Galey, Margaret E. 1984. International Enforcement of Women's Rights. *Human Rights Quarterly* 6:463–90.

1999. Women and Education. In *Women and International Human Rights Law*, edited by Kelly Dawn Askin and Dorean M. Koenig, 402–39. Ardsley, N.Y.: Transnational Publishers.

Gamson, William A., and David S. Meyer. 1996. Framing Political Opportunity. In *Comparative Perspectives on Social Movements: Political Opportunities, Mobilizing Structures and Cultural Framings*, edited by Doug McAdam, John D. McCarthy, and Mayer N. Zald, 275–90. Cambridge: Cambridge University Press.

Gandhi, Mahatma. 1957. *An Autobiography: The Story of My Experiments with Truth.* Beacon Paperbacks, No. 35. Boston: Beacon Press.

Garland, David. 2001. *The Culture of Control: Crime and Social Order in Contemporary Society.* Oxford, New York: Oxford University Press.

Garland, David W. 2002. The Cultural Uses of Capital Punishment. *Punishment & Society* 4(4): 459–87.

Garthoff, Raymond L. 1994. *Detente and Confrontation: American–Soviet Relations from Nixon to Reagan*, rev. ed. Washington, D.C.: Brookings Institution.

Gatrell, Vic A. C. 1994. *The Hanging Tree: Execution and the English People 1770–1868.* Oxford, New York: Oxford University Press.

Gauri, Varun, and Peyvand Khaleghian. 2002. Immunization in Developing Countries: Its Political and Organizational Determinants. *World Development* 30(12): 2109–32.

Gelb, Joyce. 2002. *Feminism, NGOs, and the Impact of the New Transnationalisms.* University of California International and Area Studies Digital Collection. New York: City University of New York.

Gelber, Katharine. 1999. Treaties and Intergovernmental Relations in Australia: Political Implications of the Toonen Case. *Australian Journal of Politics and History* 45(3): 330–45.

2001. Human Rights Treaties in Australia – Empty Words? *Australian Review of Public Affairs Digest.* Available at http://www.australianreview.net/digest/2001/04/gelber.html (accessed 12 April 2001).

Gerschutz, Jill Marie, and Margaret P. Karns. 2005. Transforming Visions into Reality: The Convention on the Rights of the Child. In *Children's Human Rights: Progress and Challenges for Children Worldwide*, edited by Mark Ensalaco and Linda C. Majka, 31–51. Lanham, Md.: Rowman & Littlefield.

Ghandhi, P. R. 1986. The Human Rights Committee and the Right of Individual Communication. In *British Year Book of International Law*, 201–51. Oxford: Clarendon Press.

Ginsburg, Tom, Zachary Elkins, and Svitlana Chernykh. 2006. *Commitment and Diffusion: How and Why National Constitutions Incorporate International Law.* Champaign-Urbana, Ill.

Gleditsch, Nils Petter, Peter Wallensteen, Mikael Eriksson, Margareta Sollenberg, and Håvard Strand. 2002. Armed Conflict 1946–2001: A New Dataset. *Journal of Peace Research* 39(5):615–637.

Glendon, Mary Ann. 1998. Knowing the Universal Declaration of Human Rights. *Notre Dame Law Review* 73:1153–90.

2001. *A World Made New: Eleanor Roosevelt and the Universal Declaration of Human Rights*. New York: Random House.

2003. The Forgotten Crucible: The Latin American Influence on the Universal Human Rights Idea. *Harvard Human Rights Journal* 16:27–39.

Glendon, Mary Ann, Christopher Osakwe, and Michael W. Gordon. 1982. *Comparative Legal Traditions in a Nutshell. Nutshell Series*. St. Paul, Minn.: West.

Glennon, Robert Jerome. 1991. Role of Law in the Civil Rights Movement: The Montgomery Bus Boycott, 1955–1957. *Law and History Review* 9(1): 59–111.

Gold, Joseph. 1983. Strengthening the Soft International Law of Exchange Arrangements. *American Journal of International Law* 77:443–89.

Goldblat, Jozef. 1982. *Agreements for Arms Control: A Critical Survey*, edited by the Stockholm International Peace Research Institute. London: Taylor and Francis.

Goldsmith, Jack, and Stephen D. Krasner. 2003. The Limits of Idealism. *Daedalus* 132(winter): 47–63.

Goldsmith, Jack, and Eric A. Posner. 2002. Moral and Legal Rhetoric in International Relations: A Rational Choice Perspective. *Journal of Legal Studies* 31, part 2: S115–S140.

2005. *The Limits of International Law*. Oxford, New York: Oxford University Press.

Goldstein, Judith. 1986. The Political Economy of Trade: Institutions of Protection. *American Political Science Review* 80(1): 161–84.

Goldstein, Robert J. 1986. The Limitations of Using Quantitative Data in Studying Human Rights Abuses. *Human Rights Quarterly* 8(4): 607–27.

Goodliffe, Jay, and Darren G. Hawkins. 2006. Explaining Commitment: States and the Convention Against Torture. *The Journal of Politics* 68(2): 358–71.

Goodman, Ryan. 2002. Human Rights Treaties, Invalid Reservations, and State Consent. *American Journal of International Law* 96(3): 531–60.

Goodman, Ryan, and Derek Jinks. 2003. Measuring the Effects of Human Rights Treaties. *European Journal of International Law* 13:171–83.

2004. How to Influence States: Socialization and International Human Rights Law. *Duke Law Journal* 54:621–701.

Gordon, Neve, ed. 2004. *From the Margins of Globalization: Critical Perspectives on Human Rights*. Lanham, Md.: Lexington Books.

Gordon, Neve, and Nitza Berkovitch. n.d. The Appearance of Human Rights Discourse in Domestic Settings: Israel as a Case Study. Available at http://burdacenter.bgu.ac.il/publications/finalReports2003-2004/BerkovitzGordon.pdf (accessed 8 December 2005).

Gray, Christine, and Benedict Kingsbury. 1992. Developments in Dispute Settlement: Interstate Arbitration since 1945. In *British Year Book of International Law*, edited by James Crawford and Vaughan Lowe. 97–134. Oxford: Clarendon Press.

Gray, Mark M., Miki Caul Kittilson, and Wayne Sandholtz. 2006. Women and Globalization: A Study of 180 Countries, 1975–2000. *International Organization* 60(2): 293–333.

Grieves, Forest L. 1969. *Supranationalism and International Adjudication*. Urbana: University of Illinois Press.

Grosso, Catherine M. 2000. International Law in the Domestic Arena: The Case of Torture in Israel. *Iowa Law Review* 86:305–37.

Grugel, Jean, and Enrique, Peruzzotti. 2007a. Globalisation, Human Rights and Domestic Advocacy: Mobilising for Children's Rights in Argentina after the Convention of the Rights of the Child. Paper presented at the 2007 annual convention of the American Political Science Association, Chicago, 30 August–2 September 2007.

2007b. Claiming Rights Under Global Governance: Children's Rights in Argentina. *Global Governance* 13(2): 199–216.

Gupta, Dipak K., Albert J. Longman, and Alex P. Schmid. 1994. Creating a Composite Index for Assessing Country Performance in the Field of Human Rights – Proposal for a New Methodology. *Human Rights Quarterly* 16(1): 131–62.

Gurr, Ted Robert. 1986. The Political Origins of State Violence and Terror: A Theoretical Analysis. In *Government Violence and Repression: An Agenda for Research*, edited by Michael Stohl and George A. Lopez, 45–71. New York: Greenwood Press.

Gusfield, Joseph R. 1968. The Study of Social Movements. In *International Encyclopedia of the Social Sciences*, edited by David L. Sills, 445–52. New York: Macmillan.

Guzman, Andrew T. 2002. International Law: A Compliance Based Theory. *California Law Review* 90:1823.

Haas, Michael. 1994. *Improving Human Rights*. Westport, Conn.: Praeger.

Hafner-Burton, Emilie M. 2005. Trading Human Rights: How Preferential Trade Agreements Influence Government Repression. *International Organization* 59(3): 593–629.

Hafner-Burton, Emilie M., and Kiyoteru Tsutsui. 2005. Human Rights in a Globalizing World: The Paradox of Empty Promises. *American Journal of Sociology* 110(5): 1373–1411.

Hajjar, Lisa. 2001. Human Rights in Israel/Palestine: The History and Politics of a Movement. *Journal of Palestine Studies* 30(4): 21–38.

Halberstam, Malvina. 1999. U.S. Ratification of the Convention on the Elimination of All Forms of Discrimination against Women. In *Women and International Human Rights Law*, edited by Kelly Dawn Askin and Dorean M. Koenig, 141–63. Ardsley, N.Y.: Transnational Publishers.

Halberstam, Malvina, and Elizabeth F. DeFeis. 1987. *Women's Legal Rights: International Covenants an Alternative to ERA?* Dobbs Ferry, N.Y.: Transnational Publishers.

Hall, John R. 2003. Religion and Violence: Social Processes in Comparative Perspective. In *Handbook of the Sociology of Religion*, edited by Michele Dillon, 359–81. Cambridge: Cambridge University Press.

Hamburg, David. 2000. Human Rights and Warfare: An Ounce of Prevention Is Worth a Pound of Cure. In *Realizing Human Rights: Moving from Inspiration to Impact*, edited by Samantha Power and Graham T. Allison, 321–36. New York: St. Martin's Press.

Hanafi, Sari, and Linda Tabar. 2004. Donor Assistance, Rent-Seeking and Elite Formation. In *State Formation in Palestine: Viability and Governance During a Social Transformation*, edited by Mushtaq H. Khan, 215–38. London, New York: Routledge.

Handler, Joel F. 1978. *Social Movements and the Legal System: A Theory of Law Reform and Social Change*. New York: Academic Press.

Hannum, Hurst. 1991. Contemporary Developments in the International Protection of the Rights of Minorities. *Notre Dame Law Review* 66: 1431–50.

Happold, Matthew. 2005. *Child Soldiers in International Law*. Manchester, England: Manchester University Press.

Harding, Timothy W. 1989. Prevention of Torture and Inhuman or Degrading Treatment: Medical Implications of a New European Convention. *Lancet* 27(1): 1191–3.

Hartlyn, Jonathan, and John Dugas. 1999. Colombia: The Politics of Violence and Democratic Transformation. In *Democracy in Developing Countries: Latin America*, edited by Larry Jay Diamond, 249–307 Boulder, Colo.: Lynne Rienner.

Hathaway, Oona. 2002. Do Human Rights Treaties Make a Difference? *Yale Law Journal* III: 1935–2042.

Hausdorff, William P. 1996. Prospects for the Use of New Vaccines in Developing Countries: Cost Is Not the Only Impediment. *Vaccine* 14(13): 1179–86.

Hawkins, Darren G. 2002. *International Human Rights and Authoritarian Rule in Chile: Human Rights in International Perspective, V. 6*. Lincoln: University of Nebraska Press.

2004. Explaining Costly International Institutions: Persuasion and Enforceable Human Rights Norms. *International Studies Quarterly* 48(4): 779–804.

Hawkins, Darren G., and Melissa Humes. 2002. Human Rights and Domestic Violence. *Political Science Quarterly* 117(2): 231–58.

Hayner, Priscilla B. 1994. Fifteen Truth Commissions – 1974 to 1994: A Comparative Study. *Human Rights Quarterly* 16(4): 597–655.

2001. *Unspeakable Truths: Confronting State Terror and Atrocity*. New York: Routledge.

Heffernan, Liz. 1997. A Comparative View of Individual Petition Procedures Under the European Convention on Human Rights and the International Covenant on Civil and Political Rights. *Human Rights Quarterly* 19(1): 78–112.

Heimburger, Angela, Caudia Gras, and Alessandra Guedes. 2003. Expanding Access to Emergency Contraception: The Case of Brazil and Colombia. *Reproductive Health Matters* 11(21): 150–60.

Helfer, Laurence R. 1999. Forum Shopping for Human Rights. *University of Pennsylvania Law Review* 148(2): 285.

2002. Overlegalizing Human Rights: International Relations Theory and the Commonwealth Caribbean Backlash Against Human Rights Regimes. *Columbia Law Review* 102:1832–44.

Helfer, Laurence R., and Anne-Marie Slaughter. 1997. Toward a Theory of Effective Supranational Adjudication. *Yale Law Journal* 107(2): 273–391.

Helzner, Judith E. 2002. Transforming Family Planning Services in the Latin American and Caribbean Region. *Studies in Family Planning* 33(1): 49–60.

Hendry, James McLeod. 1955. *Treaties and Federal Constitutions*. Washington, D.C.: Public Affairs Press.

Henkin, Louis. 1979. *How Nations Behave: Law and Foreign Policy*. New York: Council on Foreign Relations.

1995. *International Law: Politics and Values*. Dordrecht, the Netherlands: Martinus Nijhoff.

Herbst, Jeffrey. 2004. International Laws of War and the African Child: Norms, Compliance, and Sovereignty. In *International Law and Organization: Closing the Compliance Gap*, edited by Michael W. Doyle and Edward C. Luck, 185–204. Lanham, Md.: Rowman & Littlefield.

Hernandez-Truyol, Berta Esperanza. 1999. Human Rights through a Gendered Lens: Emergence, Evolution, Revolution. In *Women and International Human Rights Law*, edited by Kelly Dawn Askin and Dorean M. Koenig, 3–39. Ardsley, N.Y.: Transnational Publishers.

Herodotus. 1972. *The Histories*, translated by Aubrey De Sélincourt. New York: Penguin Books.

Heyns, Cristof, and Frans Viljoen. 2001. The Impact of the United Nations Human Rights Treaties on the Domestic Level. *Human Rights Quarterly* 23(3): 483–535.

Hick, Steven. 2001. The Political Economy of War-Affected Children. *Annals of the American Academy of Political and Social Science* 575(1): 106–21.

Higgins, Rosalyn. 1978. Conceptual Thinking About the Individual in International Law. *British Journal of International Studies* 4(1): 1–19.

Hilbink, Lisa. 2007. *Judges Beyond Politics in Democracy and Dictatorship: Lessons from Chile.* Cambridge: Cambridge University Press.

Himes, James R. 1995. Introduction. In *Implementing the Convention on the Rights of the Child: Resource Mobilization in Low-Income Countries,* edited by James R. Himes, 1–32. The Hague: Martinus Nijhoff.

Hirsen, James L. 1999. *The Coming Collision: Global Law vs. U.S. Liberties.* Lafayette, La.: Huntington House.

Ho, Virgil K.Y. 2005. What Is Wrong with Capital Punishment? Official and Unofficial Attitudes Toward Capital Punishment in Modern and Contemporary China. In *The Cultural Lives of Capital Punishment: Comparative Perspectives,* edited by Austin Sarat and Christian Boulanger, 274–90. Stanford, Calif.: Stanford University Press.

Hodgson, Dorothy Louise. 2003. Women's Rights as Human Rights: Women in Law and Development in Africa. *Africa Today* 49(2): 3–26.

Hoffmann, Stanley. 1956. The Role of International Organization: Limits and Possibilities. *International Organization* 10(3): 357–72.

Holt, John Caldwell. 1975. *Escape from Childhood: The Needs and Rights of Children.* Harmondsworth, England: Penguin Books.

Hood, Roger. 2001. Capital Punishment: A Global Perspective. *Punishment & Society* 3(3): 331–54.

Howland, Courtney W. 1999. Women and Religious Fundamentalism. In *Women and International Human Rights Law,* edited by Kelly Dawn Askin and Dorean M. Koenig, 533–621. Ardsley, N.Y.: Transnational Publishers.

Htun, Mala. 2003. *Sex and the State: Abortion, Divorce, and the Family Under Latin American Dictatorships and Democracies.* Cambridge: Cambridge University Press.

Hudec, Robert E. 1999. The New WTO Dispute Settlement Procedure. *Minnesota Journal of Global Trade* 8:1–24.

Hull, Harry F., and R. Bruce Aylward. 2001. Progress Towards Global Polio Eradication. *Vaccine* 19(31): 4378–84.

Humphrey, John P. 1984. Political and Related Rights. In *Human Rights in International Law: Legal and Policy Issues,* edited by Theodor Meron, 171–203. Oxford: Clarendon Press.

Humphrey, John P., A. John Hobbins, and Louisa Piatti. 1994. *On the Edge of Greatness: The Diaries of John Humphrey, First Director of the United Nations Division of Human Rights.* Montreal: McGill University Libraries.

Hunt, Alan. 1990. Rights and Social Movements: Counter-Hegemonic Strategies. *Journal of Law and Society* 17(3): 309–28.

Huntington, Samuel P. 1991. The Third Wave: Democratization in the Late Twentieth Century. *The Julian J. Rothbaum Distinguished Lecture Series, V. 4.* Norman: University of Oklahoma Press.

Husarska, Anna. 2000. "Conscience Trigger": The Press and Human Rights. In *Realizing Human Rights: Moving from Inspiration to Impact,* edited by Samantha Power and Graham T. Allison, 337–50. New York: St. Martin's Press.

Ibhawoh, Bonny. 2000. Between Culture and Constitution: Evaluating the Cultural Legitimacy of Human Rights in the African State. *Human Rights Quarterly* 22(3): 838–60.

Ignatieff, Michael. 1999. Human Rights. In *Human Rights in Political Transitions: Gettysburg to Bosnia*, edited by Carla Alison Hesse and Robert Post, 313–24. New York: Zone Books.

———. 2001. Human Rights as Politics. In *Human Rights as Politics and Idolatry*, edited by Michael Ignatieff and Amy Gutmann, 3–52. Princeton, N.J.: Princeton University Press.

Inglehart, Ronald, and Pippa Norris. 2003. *Rising Tide: Gender Equality and Cultural Change around the World*. Cambridge: Cambridge University Press.

Irr, Caren. 2003. Who Owns Our Culture? Intellectual Property, Human Rights and Globalization. In *Constructing Human Rights in the Age of Globalization*, edited by Mahmood Monshipouri, Neil Englehart, and Andrew J. Nathan, 3–33. Armonk, N.Y.: M.E. Sharpe.

Ishay, Micheline. 1997. *The Human Rights Reader: Major Political Writings, Essays, Speeches, and Documents from the Bible to the Present*. New York: Routledge.

———. 2004. *The History of Human Rights: From Ancient Times to the Globalization Era*. Berkeley: University of California Press.

Iwasawa, Yuji. 1998. *International Law, Human Rights, and Japanese Law: The Impact of International Law on Japanese Law*. Oxford: Clarendon Press.

Jacobs, David, and Jason T. Carmichael. 2002. The Political Sociology of the Death Penalty: A Pooled Time-Series Analysis. *American Sociological Review* 67(1): 109–31.

———. 2004. Ideology, Social Threat, and the Death Sentence: Capital Sentences Across Time and Space. *Social Forces* 83(1): 249–78.

Jacobs, David, and Ronald Helms. 1997. Testing Coercive Explanations for Order: The Determinants of Law Enforcement Strength Over Time. *Social Forces* 75(4): 1361–92.

James, Harold. 1995. The Historical Development of the Principle of Surveillance. *International Monetary Fund Staff Papers* 42(4): 762–91.

Jayawickrama, Nihal. 1997. The Right to a Fair Trial Under the International Covenant on Civil and Political Rights. In *The Right to a Fair Trial in International and Comparative Perspective*, edited by Andrew Byrnes, 37–67. Hong Kong: Centre for Comparative and Public Law University of Hong Kong.

Jayne, Susan H., and David K. Guilkey. 1998. Contraceptive Determinants in Three Leading Countries. *Population Research and Policy Review* 17(4): 329–50.

Jenkins, J. Craig. 1983. Resource Mobilization Theory and the Study of Social Movements. *Annual Review of Sociology* 9(1): 527–53.

Jennings, M. Kent. 1999. Political Responses to Pain and Loss. *American Political Science Review* 92(113): 1–13.

Jenson, Jane. 1996. Representation of Difference: The Varieties of French Feminism. In *Mapping the Women's Movement: Feminist Politics and Social Transformation in the North*, edited by Mónica Threlfall, 73–114. London, New York: Verso.

Jessup, Philip C. 1959. *The Use of International Law: Five Lectures Delivered at the University of Michigan, February 27, 28, March 3, 6, and 7, 1958*. The Thomas M. Cooley Lectures, 8th Ser. Ann Arbor: University of Michigan Law School.

Jhabvala, Farrokh. 1985. Domestic Implementation of the Covenant on Civil and Political Rights. *Netherlands International Law Review* 32:461–86.

———. 1987. On Human Rights and the Socio-Economic Context. In *Third World Attitudes toward International Law: An Introduction*, edited by Frederick E. Snyder and Sathirathai Surakiart, 293–320. Dordrecht, the Netherlands: Martinus Nijhoff.

Joachim, Jutta. 2003. Framing Issues and Seizing Opportunities: The UN, NGOs, and Women's Rights. *International Studies Quarterly* 47(2): 247–74.

Johnson, David T. 2006. Where the State Kills in Secret: Capital Punishment in Japan. *Punishment & Society* 8(3): 251–85.

Johnston, Alastair Iain. 2002. The Social Effects of International Institutions on Domestic (Foreign Policy) Actors. In *Locating the Proper Authorities: The Interaction of Domestic and International Institutions*, edited by Daniel Drezner, 145–96. Ann Arbor: University of Michigan Press.

Johnston, Douglas M. 1997. *Consent and Commitment in the World Community: The Classification and Analysis of International Instruments*. Irvington-on-Hudson, N.Y.: Transnational Publishers.

Jones, Gareth, Richard W. Steketee, Robert E. Black, Zulfiqar A. Bhutta, and Saul S. Morris. 2003. How Many Child Deaths Can We Prevent This Year? *Lancet* 362:65–71.

Juergensmeyer, Mark. 1993. *The New Cold War? Religious Nationalism Confronts the Secular State*. Berkeley: University of California Press.

Justice, Judith. 2000. The Politics of Child Survival. In *Global Health Policy, Local Realities: The Fallacy of the Level Playing Field*, edited by Linda M. Whiteford and Lenore Manderson, 23–28. Boulder, Colo.: Lynne Rienner.

Kamiya, Masako. 1995. A Decade of the Equal Employment Act in Japan: Has It Changed Society? *Law in Japan* 25:40–83.

Kamminga, Menno T. 1992. *Inter-State Accountability for Violations of Human Rights*. Philadelphia: University of Pennsylvania Press.

Kane, Hal, and Jane A. Peterson. 1995. *The Hour of Departure: Forces That Create Refugees and Migrants*. Worldwatch Paper 125. Washington, D.C.: Worldwatch Institute.

Kaufman, Natalie Hevener. 1990. *Human Rights Treaties and the Senate: A History of Opposition*. Chapel Hill: University of North Carolina Press.

Kaufman, Natalie Hevener, and Maria Luisa Blanco. 1999. Drafting and Interpreting Article 27. In *Implementing the U.N. Convention on the Rights of the Child: A Standard of Living Adequate for Development*, edited by Arlene Bowers Andrews and Natalie Hevener Kaufman, 17–31. Westport, Conn.: Praeger.

Kaufman, Natalie Hevener, and David Whiteman. 1988. Opposition to Human Rights Treaties in the United States: The Legacy of the Bricker Amendment. *Human Rights Quarterly* 10(3): 309–37.

Kaufmann, Daniel, Aart Kraay, and Massimo Mastruzzi. 2008. *Governance Matters VII: Aggregate and Individual Governance Indicators, 1996–2007*. Washington, D.C.: World Bank. Available at http://papers.ssrn.com/sol3/papers.cfm?abstract_id=1148386 (accessed 8 June 2009).

Keck, Margaret E., and Kathryn Sikkink. 1998. *Activists Beyond Borders: Advocacy Networks in International Politics*. Ithaca, N.Y.: Cornell University Press.

Keith, Linda Camp. 1999. The United Nations International Covenant on Civil and Political Rights: Does It Make a Difference in Human Rights Behavior? *Journal of Peace Research* 36(1): 95–118.

——— 2002. Constitutional Provisions for Individual Human Rights (1977–1996): Are They More Than Mere "Window Dressing?" *Political Research Quarterly* 55(1): 111–43.

Kennan, George Frost. 1951. *American Diplomacy, 1900–1950*. Charles R. Walgreen Foundation Lectures. New York: New American Library.

Kennedy, David. 2000. When Renewal Repeats: Thinking Against the Box. *New York University Journal of International Law & Politics* 32:335–500.

——— 2004. *The Dark Sides of Virtue: Reassessing International Humanitarianism*. Princeton, N.J.: Princeton University Press.

Kent, Ann. 1999. *China, the United Nations, and Human Rights*. Philadelphia: University of Pennsylvania Press.

Keohane, Robert O. 1983. Sovereignty, Interdependence, and International Institutions. In *Ideas and Ideals: Essays on Politics in Honor of Stanley Hoffmann*, edited by Linda B. Miller and Michael Joseph Smith, 91–107. Boulder, Colo.: Westview Press.

————. 1984. *After Hegemony: Cooperation and Discord in the World Political Economy*. Princeton, N.J.: Princeton University Press.

————. 1997. International Relations and International Law: Two Optics. *Harvard International Law Journal* 38(2): 487–502.

Keohane, Robert O., Andrew Moravcsik, and Anne-Marie Slaughter. 2000. Legalized Dispute Resolution: Interstate and Transnational. *International Organization* 54(3): 457–88.

Kessler, J. Christian. 1995. *Verifying Nonproliferation Treaties: Obligation, Process, and Sovereignty*, edited by the Institute for National Strategic Studies. Washington, D.C.: National Defense University.

Kim, Hunjoon, and Kathryn Sikkink. 2007. Do Human Rights Trials Make a Difference? Presented at the 2007 annual meeting of the American Political Science Association, Chicago.

King, Jeff, and A. John Hobbins. 2003. Hammarskjöld and Human Rights: The Deflation of the UN Human Rights Programme 1953–1961. *Journal of the History of International Law* 5(2): 337–86.

Kishimoto, Koichi. 1988. *Politics in Modern Japan: Development and Organization*, 3rd ed. Tokyo: Japan Echo.

Klabbers, Jan. 2000. Accepting the Unacceptable? A New Nordic Approach to Reservations to Multilateral Treaties. *Nordic Journal of International Law* 69:179–93.

Klein, Eckart 1998. *The Monitoring System of Human Rights Treaty Obligations: Colloquium, Universität Potsdam, 22, 23 November 1996*. Berlin: Berlin Vlg. A. Spitz.

Klotz, Audie. 1995. *Norms in International Relations: The Struggle against Apartheid*. Ithaca, N.Y.: Cornell University Press.

Knack, Stephen, and Philip Keefer. 1995. Institutions and Economic Performance: Cross-Country Tests Using Alternative Institutional Measures. *Economics and Politics* 7(3): 207–27.

Knapp, Kiyoko Kamio. 1995. Still Office Flowers: Japanese Women Betrayed by the Equal Employment Opportunity Law. *Harvard Women's Law Journal* 18:83–137.

————. 1999. Don't Awaken the Sleeping Child: Japan's Gender Equality Law and the Rhetoric of Gradualism. *Columbia Journal of Gender and Law* 8:143–96.

Knowles, Stephen, Paula K. Lorgelly, and P. Dorian Owen. 2002. Are Educational Gender Gaps a Brake on Economic Development? Some Cross-Country Empirical Evidence. *Oxford Economic Papers – New Series* 54(1): 118–49.

Kobayashi, Yoshie. 2004. *A Path Toward Gender Equality: State Feminism in Japan*. New York: Routledge.

Koh, Harold H. 1991. Transnational Public Law Litigation. *Yale Law Journal* 100:2347.

————. 1999. How Is International Human Rights Law Enforced? *Indiana Law Journal* 74(4): 1397–417.

Kokott, Juliane B. 1997. Fair Trial – the Inter-American System. In *The Right to a Fair Trial*, edited by David S. Weissbrodt and Rüdiger Wolfrum, 133–62. Berlin, New York: Springer.

Kolodner, Eric. 1994. Religious Rights in China: A Comparison of International Human Rights Law and Chinese Domestic Legislation. *Human Rights Quarterly* 16:455–90.

Korey, William. 1998. *NGOs and the Universal Declaration of Human Rights: A Curious Grapevine*. New York: St. Martin's Press.

Korpi, Walter. 1974. Conflict, Power and Relative Deprivation. *American Political Science Review* 68(4): 1569–78.

Koskenniemi, Martii. 2000. Carl Schmitt, Hans Morgenthau, and the Image of Law in International Relations. In *The Role of Law in International Politics: Essays in International Relations and International Law*, edited by Michael Byers, 17–34. Oxford, New York: Oxford University Press.

——— 2002. *The Gentle Civilizer of Nations: The Rise and Fall of International Law, 1870–1960*. Hersch Lauterpacht Memorial Lectures. Cambridge: Cambridge University Press.

Krasner, Stephen. 1993. Sovereignty, Regimes, and Human Rights. In *Regimes Theory and International Relations*, edited by Volcker Rittberger and Peter Mayer, 139–67. Cambridge: Cambridge University Press.

——— 1999. *Sovereignty: Organized Hypocrisy*. Princeton, N.J.: Princeton University Press.

Krenn, Michael L. 1998. *Race and U.S. Foreign Policy During the Cold War*. New York: Garland.

Kruse, Douglas L., and Douglas Mahony. 2000. Illegal Child Labor in the United States: Prevalence and Characteristics. *International Labor Relations Review* 54:17–40.

Ku, Charlotte. 2001. *Global Governance and the Changing Face of International Law*. Paper presented at the annual meeting of the Academic Council on the United Nations System, Puebla, New Mexico.

Küng, Hans, and Jürgen Moltmann. 1990. *The Ethics of World Religions and Human Rights*. London: SCM Press.

La Porta, Rafael, Florencio Lopez-de-Silanes, Cristian Pop-Eleches, and Andrei Schleifer. 2002. The Guarantees of Freedom. In *Harvard Institute of Economic Research Discussion Paper Series, 1–30*. Cambridge, Mass.

——— 2004. Judicial Checks and Balances. *Journal of Political Economy* 112(2): 445–70.

Laird, Siobhan. 2002. The 1998 Children's Act: Problems of Enforcement in Ghana. *British Journal of Social Work* 32:893–905.

Lakoff, George. 1996. *Moral Politics: What Conservatives Know That Liberals Don't*. Chicago: University of Chicago Press.

Lam, Alice C. L. 1992. *Women and Japanese Management: Discrimination and Reform*. London, New York: Routledge.

Landa, Janet T. 1981. A Theory of the Ethnically Homogeneous Middleman Group: An Institutional Alternative to Contract Law. *The Journal of Legal Studies* 10(2): 349–62.

Landes, William M., and Richard A. Posner. 1975. The Independent Judiciary in an Interest-Group Perspective. *Journal of Law and Economics* 18:875–901.

Landman, Todd. 2005. *Protecting Human Rights: A Comparative Study*. Washington, D.C.: Georgetown University Press.

Landsberg-Lewis, Ilana. 1998. *Bringing Equality Home: Implementing the Convention on the Elimination of All Forms of Discrimination against Women, CEDAW*, edited by the United Nations Development Fund for Women and the United Nations Committee on the Elimination of Discrimination Against Women. New York: United Nations Development Fund for Women.

Lane, Sandra D. 1994. From Population Control to Reproductive Health: An Emerging Policy Agenda. *Social Science & Medicine* 39(9): 1303–14.

Langley, Winston. 1988. *Human Rights, Women, and Third World Development*. Boston: William Monroe Trotter Institute.

Lanotte, Johan Vande, and Geert Goedertier. 1996. Monitoring Human Rights: Formal and Procedural Aspects. In *Monitoring Children's Rights*, edited by Eugeen Verhellen, 73–111. The Hague: Martinus Nijhoff.

Laugier, Henri. 1950. Statement by Henri Laugier, Assistant Secretary-General for the United Nations Department of Social Affairs on the Covenant of Human Rights. *International Organization* 4(3): 553–9.

Lauren, Paul Gordon. 1998. *The Evolution of International Human Rights: Visions Seen.* Philadelphia: University of Pennsylvania Press.

Laursen, Andreas. 2000. Israel's Supreme Court and International Human Rights Law: The Judgement on Moderate Physical Pressure. *Nordic Journal of International Law* 69(4): 413–47.

Lauterpacht, Hersch. 1950. *International Law and Human Rights.* New York: Praeger.

Leary, Virginia A. 1979. A New Role for Non-Governmental Organizations in Human Rights: A Case Study of Non-Governmental Participation in the Development of Norms of Torture. In *UN Law/Fundamental Rights*, edited by Antonio Cassese, 197–210. Alphen aan den Rijn, the Netherlands: Sitjhoff & Noordhoff.

LeBlanc, Lawrence J. 1995. *The Convention on the Rights of the Child: United Nations Lawmaking on Human Rights.* Lincoln: University of Nebraska Press.

Legro, Jeffrey W. 1997. Which Norms Matter? Revisiting the "Failure" of Internationalism. *International Organization* 51(1): 31–63.

Leigh, Leonard H. 1997. The Right to a Fair Trial and the European Convention on Human Rights. In *The Right to a Fair Trial*, edited by David S. Weissbrodt and Rüdiger Wolfrum, 645–68. Berlin, New York: Springer.

Lerner, Natan. 1996. Religious Human Rights Under the United Nations. In *Religious Human Rights in Global Perspective: Legal Perspectives*, edited by Johan D. Van der Vyver and John Witte, 79–134. The Hague: Martinus Nijhoff.

2000. *Religion, Beliefs, and International Human Rights.* Maryknoll, N.Y.: Orbis Books.

2006. *Religion, Secular Beliefs, and Human Rights: 25 Years After the 1981 Declaration.* Leiden, Boston: Martinus Nijhoff.

Lester, Anthony. 1984. Fundamental Rights: The United Kingdom Isolated? In *1984 Public Law*, edited by Graham Zellick, 46–72. London: Stevens and Sons.

Levine, Daniel H. 1981. *Religion and Politics in Latin America: The Catholic Church in Venezuela and Colombia.* Princeton, N.J.: Princeton University Press.

Levine, Marvin J. 2003. *Children for Hire: The Perils of Child Labor in the United States.* Westport, Conn.: Praeger.

Lijnzaad, Liesbeth. 1995. *Reservations to UN Human Rights Treaties: Ratify and Ruin?* edited by T.M.C. Asser Instituut. Dordrecht, the Netherlands: Martinus Nijhoff.

Lillich, Richard B. 1984. Civil Rights. In *Human Rights in International Law: Legal and Policy Issues*, edited by Theodar Meron, 115–70. Oxford: Clarendon Press.

Linebaugh, Peter. 1991. *The London Hanged: Crime and Civil Society in the 18th Century.* London: Allen Lane: The Penguin Press.

Lippman, Matthew. 1994. The Development and Drafting of the United Nations Convention Against Torture and Other Cruel, Inhuman or Degrading Treatment or Punishment. *Boston College International and Comparative Law Review* 17:275–335.

Lipset, Seymour Martin. 1960. *Political Man: The Social Bases of Politics.* Garden City, N.Y.: Doubleday.

Lipson, Charles. 1991. Why Are Some International Agreements Informal? *International Organization* 45(4): 495–538.

Little, David. 1996. Studying "Religious Human Rights": Methodological Foundations. In *Religious Human Rights in Global Perspective: Legal Perspectives*, edited by Johan D. Van der Vyver and John Witte, 45–77. The Hague: Martinus Nijhoff.

Liu, Dongxiao, and Elizabeth Heger Boyle. 2001. Making the Case: The Women's Convention and Equal Employment Opportunity in Japan. *International Journal of Comparative Sociology* 42(4): 389–404.

Livezey, Lowell W. 1989. U.S. Religious Organizations and the International Human Rights Movement. *Human Rights Quarterly* 11(1): 14–81.

Lopez, George A., and Michael Stohl, eds. 1989. *Dependence, Development, and State Repression*, edited by Bernard K. Johnpoll. New York: Greenwood Press.

Loth, Wilfried. 1988. *The Division of the World, 1941–1955*. New York: St. Martin's Press.

Loveman, Mara. 1998. High-Risk Collective Action: Defending Human Rights in Chile, Uruguay, and Argentina. *The American Journal of Sociology* 104(2): 477–525.

Lowden, Pamela. 1996. *Moral Opposition to Authoritarian Rule in Chile, 1973–90*. New York: St. Martin's Press.

Luke, Nancy, and Susan C. Watkins. 2002. Reactions of Developing-Country Elites to International Population Policy. *Population and Development Review* 28(4): 707–33.

Lukes, Steven. 2006. Liberal Democratic Torture. *British Journal of Political Science* 36:1–16.

Lush, Louisiana, John Cleland, Kelley Lee, and Gill Walt. 2000. Politics and Fertility: A New Approach to Population Policy Analysis. *Population Research and Policy Review* 19(1): 1–28.

Lutz, Ellen L., and Kathryn Sikkink. 2000. International Human Rights Law and Practice in Latin America. *International Organization* 54(3): 633–59.

——— 2001. The Justice Cascade: The Evolution and Impact of Foreign Human Rights Trials in Latin America. *Chicago Journal of International Law* 2(1): 1–33.

MacBride, Roger Lea. 1955. *Treaties versus the Constitution*. Caldwell, Idaho: Caxton Printers.

Machel, Graça. 1996a. Children in War. *Development: Journal of the Society for International Development* 42(1): 42–5.

——— 1996b. *Impact of Armed Conflict on Children*. New York: United Nations Department of Public Information.

Mahbubani, Kishore. 1995. The Pacific Impulse. *Survival* 37(1): 105–20.

Mahoney, Paul G. 2001. The Common Law and Economic Growth: Hayek Might Be Right. *Journal of Legal Studies* 30(2 part 1): 503–25.

Mahoney, Richard T., and James E. Maynard. 1999. The Introduction of New Vaccines into Developing Countries. *Vaccine* 17(7–8): 646–52.

Malinowski, Tom. 2005. Banned State Department Practices. In *Torture: Does It Make Us Safer? Is It Ever OK? A Human Rights Perspective*, edited by Kenneth Roth, Minky Worden, and Amy D. Bernstein, 139–44. New York: New Press.

Mandel, Michael. 1999. Democracy and the New Constitutionalism in Israel. *Israel Law Review* 33(2): 259–321.

Manela, Erez. 2001. The Wilsonian Moment and the Rise of Anticolonial Nationalism: The Case of Egypt. *Diplomacy & Statecraft* 12(4): 99–122.

——— 2006. Imagining Woodrow Wilson in Asia: Dreams of East–West Harmony and the Revolt Against Empire in 1919. *American Historical Review* 111(5): 1327–51.

Mangone, Gerard J. 1954. *A Short History of International Organization*. New York: McGraw-Hill.

Maran, Rita. 1989. *Torture: The Role of Ideology in the French–Algerian War*. New York: Praeger.

Marshall, Anna-Maria. 2003. Injustice Frames, Legality, and the Everyday Construction of Sexual Harassment. *Law and Social Inquiry* 28(3): 659–90.

Martin, Francisco Forrest. 2001. *Challenging Human Rights Violations: Using International Law in U.S. Courts*. Ardsley, N.Y.: Transnational Publishers.

Martin, Lisa L. 1992. *Coercive Cooperation: Explaining Multilateral Economic Sanctions*. Princeton, N.J.: Princeton University Press.

2000. *Democratic Commitments: Legislatures and International Cooperation*. Princeton, N.J.: Princeton University Press.

Martin, William. 1999. The Christian Right and American Foreign Policy. *Foreign Policy* (114): 66–80.

Mathews, Jessica T. 1997. Power Shift. *Foreign Affairs* 76(1): 50–66.

Matscher, Franz. 2000. The Right to a Fair Trial in the Case Law of the Organs of the European Convention on Human Rights. In *The Right to a Fair Trial*, edited by the European Commission for Democracy through Law Council of Europe, 10–23. Strasbourg: Council of Europe.

Mavroidis, Petros. 1992. Surveillance Schemes: The GATT's New Trade Policy Review Mechanism. *Michigan Journal of International Law* 13(2): 374–414.

Mayer, Ann Elizabeth. 1995. Rhetorical Strategies and Official Policies on Women's Rights: The Merits and Drawbacks of the New World Hypocrisy. In *Faith and Freedom: Women's Human Rights in the Muslim World*, edited by Mahnaz Afkhami, 104–32. Syracuse, N.Y.: Syracuse University Press.

1999. Religious Reservations to the Convention on the Elimination of All Forms of Discrimination Against Women. In *Religious Fundamentalisms and the Human Rights of Women*, edited by Courtney W. Howland, 105–16. New York: St. Martin's Press.

McCallin, Margaret. 1998. Community Involvement in the Social Reintegration of Child Soldiers. In *Rethinking the Trauma of War*, edited by Patrick Bracken and Celia Petty, 60–75. London, New York: Free Association Books.

McCann, Michael W. 1986. *Taking Reform Seriously: Perspectives on Public Interest Liberalism*. Ithaca, N.Y.: Cornell University Press.

1994. *Rights at Work: Pay Equity Reform and the Politics of Legal Mobilization, Language and Legal Discourse*. Chicago: University of Chicago Press.

2004. Law and Social Movements. In *The Blackwell Companion to Law and Society*, edited by Austin Sarat, 506–22. Malden, Mass.: Blackwell.

2006. Law and Social Movements: Contemporary Perspectives. *Annual Review of Law and Social Science* 2:17–38.

McCarthy, John D., and Mayer N. Zald. 1977. Resource Mobilization and Social Movements: A Partial Theory. *The American Journal of Sociology* 82(6): 1212–41.

McCormick, James M., and Neil J. Mitchell. 1997. Human Rights Violations, Umbrella Concepts, and Empirical Analysis. *World Politics* 49:510–25.

McGoldrick, Dominic. 1991. *The Human Rights Committee*. Oxford: Clarendon Press.

McKean, Warwick A. 1983. *Equality and Discrimination Under International Law*. Oxford: Clarendon Press.

McKinlay, R. D., and A. S. Cohan. 1975. Comparative Analysis of Political and Economic Performance of Military and Civilian Regimes – Cross-National Aggregate Study. *Comparative Politics* 8(1): 1–30.

1976. Performance and Instability in Military and Non-Military Regime Systems. *American Political Science Review* 70(3): 850–64.

Mearsheimer, John. 1994–5. The False Promise of International Institutions. *International Security* 19(3): 5–26.

Meron, Theodor. 2000. The Humanization of Humanitarian Law. *American Journal of International Law* 94(2): 239–78.

Merry, Sally Engle. 2006. *Human Rights and Gender Violence: Translating International Law into Local Justice.* Chicago: University of Chicago Press.

Meyer, John W., John Boli, George M. Thomas, and Francisco O. Ramirez. 1997. World Society and the Nation-State. *American Journal of Sociology* 103(1): 144–81.

Meyer, William H. 1998. *Human Rights and International Political Economy in Third World Nations: Multinational Corporations, Foreign Aid, and Repression.* Westport, Conn.: Praeger.

Miethe, Terance D., Hong Lu, and Gini R. Deibert. 2005. Cross-National Variability in Capital Punishment: Exploring the Sociopolitical Sources of Its Differential Legal Status. *International Criminal Justice Review* 15(2): 115–30.

Miller, Kate, and Allan Rosenfield. 1996. Population and Women's Reproductive Health: An International Perspective. *Annual Review of Public Health* 17:359–82.

Miller, Mark A., and W. Dana Flanders. 2000. A Model to Estimate the Probability of Hepatitis B- and *Haemophilus influenzae* Type B-Vaccine Uptake into National Vaccination Programs. *Vaccine* 18(21): 2223–30.

Milner, Helen V. 1997. *Interests, Institutions, and Information: Domestic Politics and International Relations.* Princeton, N.J.: Princeton University Press.

Minow, Martha. 2002. Instituting Universal Human Rights Law: The Invention of Tradition in the Twentieth Century. In *Looking Back at Law's Century*, edited by Austin Sarat, Bryant G. Garth, and Robert A. Kagan, 58–77. Ithaca, N.Y.: Cornell University Press.

Mirow, Matthew C. 2000. The Power of Codification in Latin America: Simon Bolivar and the *Code Napoleon. Tulane Journal of International and Comparative Law* 8:83–116.

Mitchell, Neil J., and James M. McCormick. 1988. Economic and Political Explanations of Human Rights Violations. *World Politics* 40(4): 476–98.

Moghadam, Valentine M. 2005. *Globalizing Women: Transnational Feminist Networks.* Baltimore: Johns Hopkins University Press.

Mohamad, Maznah. 2002. Towards a Human Rights Regime in Southeast Asia: Charting the Course of State Commitment. *Contemporary Southeast Asia: A Journal of International and Strategic Affairs* 24(2): 230.

Molony, Barbara. 1995. Japan's 1986 Equal Employment Law and the Changing Discourse on Gender. *Signs* 20(winter): 268–301.

Moravcsik, Andrew. 1997. Taking Preferences Seriously: A Liberal Theory of International Politics. *International Organization* 51(4): 513–53.

2000. The Origins of Human Rights Regimes: Democratic Delegation in Postwar Europe. *International Organization* 54(2): 217–52.

Morgan, Martha I. 1998. Taking Machismo to Court: The Gender Jurisprudence of the Colombian Constitutional Court. *The University of Miami InterAmerican Law Review* 30:253–342.

Morgenthau, Hans. 1985. *Politics among Nations: The Struggle for Power and Peace*, 6th ed. New York: Knopf.

Morrow, James D. 2002. The Laws of War, Common Conjectures, and Legal Systems in International Politics. *Journal of Legal Studies* 33(1, part 2): S41–S60.

Morsink, Johannes. 1999. *The Universal Declaration of Human Rights: Origins, Drafting, and Intent.* Philadelphia: University of Pennsylvania Press.

Moskowitz, Moses. 1974. *International Concern with Human Rights.* Dobbs Ferry, N.Y.: Oceana.

Mower, A. Glenn. 1997. *The Convention on the Rights of the Child: International Law Support for Children.* Westport, Conn.: Greenwood Press.

Muller, Edward N. 1985. Income Inequality, Regime Repressiveness, and Political Violence. *American Sociological Review* 50(1): 47–61.

Muller, Edward N., and Mitchell A. Seligson. 1994. Civic Culture and Democracy – the Question of Causal Relationships. *American Political Science Review* 88(3): 635–52.

Mullerson, Rein A. 1997. *Human Rights Diplomacy.* London, New York: Routledge.

Muntarbhorn, Vitit. 1998. Asia, Human Rights, and the New Millenium. *Transnational Law and Contemporary Problems* 8:407–21.

Muthu, Sankar. 2003. *Enlightenment Against Empire.* Princeton, N.J.: Princeton University Press.

Mutua, Makau Wa. 1996. Limitations on Religious Rights: Problematizing Religious Freedom in the African Context. In *Religious Human Rights in Global Perspective: Legal Perspectives,* edited by Johan D. Van der Vyver and John Witte, 417–40. The Hague: Martinus Nijhoff.

2000. Politics and Human Rights: An Essential Symbiosis. In *The Role of Law in International Politics,* edited by Michael Byers, 149–76. Oxford: Oxford University Press.

2001. Savages, Victims, and Saviors: The Metaphor of Human Rights. *Harvard International Law Journal* 42(1): 201–46.

Myers, William E. 2001. The Right Rights? Child Labor in a Globalizing World. *Annals of the American Academy of Political and Social Science* 575(1): 38–55.

Myullerson, Rein. 1992. Monitoring Compliance with International Human Rights Standards: Experience of the UN Human Rights Committee. In *Canadian Human Rights Yearbook, 1991–1992,* edited by Caroline Andrew, Yolande Grise, Danielle Letocha, France Morrissette, and J. Yvon Theriault, 105–18. Ottawa: University of Ottawa Human Rights Research and Education Centre.

Naffine, Ngaire. 1992. Children in the Children's Court: Can There Be Rights without a Remedy? In *Children, Rights, and the Law,* edited by Philip Alston, Stephen Parker, and John Seymour, 76–97. Oxford: Clarendon Press.

Nair, Sumati. 1992. Population Policies and the Ideology of Population Control in India. *Issues in Reproductive and Genetic Engineering–Journal of International Feminist Analysis* 5(3): 237–52.

Nantwi, Emmanuel K. 1966. *The Enforcement of International Judicial Decisions and Arbitral Awards in Public International Law.* Leyden, the Netherlands: Sijthoff.

Naples, Nancy A., and Manisha Desai. 2002. *Women's Activism and Globalization: Linking Local Struggles and Transnational Politics.* New York: Routledge.

Neier, Aryeh. 1998. *War Crimes: Brutality, Genocide, Terror, and the Struggle for Justice.* New York: Times Books.

Neuman, Gerald L. 1997. Sense and Non-Sense About Customary International Law: A Response to Professors Bradley and Goldsmith. *Fordham Law Review* 66: 371–92.

Neumayer, Eric. 2005. Do International Human Rights Treaties Improve Respect for Human Rights? *Journal of Conflict Resolution* 49(6): 925–53.

Neumayer, Eric, and Indra de Soysa. 2005. Trade Openness, Foreign Direct Investment and Child Labor. *World Development* 33(1): 43–63.

2006. Globalization and the Right to Free Association and Collective Bargaining: An Empirical Analysis. *World Development* 34(1): 31–49.

Nielsen, Richard. 2008. "Foreign Aid for Human Rights." Cambridge, Mass.: Harvard University. Unpublished ms.

Nielson, Daniel L., and Matthew S. Shugart. 1999. Constitutional Change in Colombia – Policy Adjustment through Institutional Reform. *Comparative Political Studies* 32(3): 313–41.

Nippold, Otfried, and Amos Shartle Hershey. 1923. *The Development of International Law after the World War* Oxford, London, New York: Clarendon Press.

Nkrumah, Kwame. 1957. *The Autobiography of Kwame Nkrumah*. Edinburgh, New York: Thomas Nelson.

Norris, Pippa. 2001. *Digital Divide: Civic Engagement, Information Poverty, and the Internet Worldwide*. Cambridge: Cambridge University Press.

North, Charles M., and Carl R. Gwin. 2004. Religious Freedom and the Unintended Consequences of State Religion. *Southern Economic Journal* 71(1): 103–17.

Nussbaum, Arthur. 1954. *A Concise History of the Law of Nations*, rev. ed. New York: Macmillan.

Nussbaum, Martha Craven. 2001. *Women and Human Development: The Capabilities Approach*. Cambridge: Cambridge University Press.

O'Brien, Kevin J. 1996. Rightful Resistance. *World Politics* 49(1): 31–55.

O'Donnell, Guillermo A., Philippe C. Schmitter, and Laurence Whitehead. 1986. *Transitions from Authoritarian Rule*. Baltimore: Johns Hopkins University Press.

O'Hare, Ursula A. 1999. Realizing Human Rights for Women. *Human Rights Quarterly* 21(2): 364–402.

O'Neill, Onora. 1988. Children's Rights and Children's Lives. *Ethics* 98:445–63.

    1992. Children's Rights and Children's Lives. In *Children, Rights, and the Law*, edited by Philip Alston, Stephen Parker, and John Seymour, 24–42. Oxford: Clarendon Press.

Odio Benito, Elizabeth. 1989. Elimination of All Forms of Intolerance and Discrimination Based on Religion or Belief, edited by United Nations Centre for Human Rights. Human Rights Study Series, 2. New York: United Nations.

Ohlin, Jens David. 2005. Applying the Death Penalty to Crimes of Genocide. *The American Journal of International Law* 99(4): 747–77.

Ollila, Eeva, Meri Koivusalo, and Elina Hemminki. 2000. International Actors and Population Policies in India, with Special Reference to Contraceptive Policies. *International Journal of Health Services* 30(1): 87–110.

Olsen, Frances. 1992. Children's Rights: Some Feminist Approaches to the United Nations Convention on the Rights of the Child. In *Children, Rights, and the Law*, edited by Philip Alston, Stephen Parker, and John Seymour, 192–220. Oxford: Clarendon Press.

Olson, Lynne, and Stanley Cloud. 2003. *A Question of Honor: The Kosciuszko Squadron: Forgotten Heroes of World War II*. New York: Knopf. Distributed by Random House.

Oosterveld, Valerie L. 1999. Women and Employment. In *Women and International Human Rights Law*, edited by Kelly Dawn Askin and Dorean M. Koenig, 367–402. Ardsley, N.Y.: Transnational Publishers.

Opolot, James S. E. 1981. *World Legal Traditions and Institutions*, rev. ed. Jonesboro, Tenn.: Pilgrimage.

Orend, Brian. 2002. *Human Rights: Concept and Context*. Peterborough, Ontario; Orchard Park, N.Y.: Broadview Press.

Orentlicher, Diane F. 1994. Addressing Gross Human Rights Abuses: Punishment and Victim Compensation. In *Human Rights: An Agenda for the Next Century*, edited by Louis Henkin and John Lawrence Hargrove, 425–73. Washington, D.C.: American Society of International Law.

Osofsky, Hari M. 1997. Domesticating International Criminal Law: Bringing Human Rights Violators to Justice. *Yale Law Journal* 107(1): 191–226.

Ott, Emiline Royco. 1977. Population Policy Formation in Colombia – Role of Ascofame. *Studies in Family Planning* 8(1): 2–10.

Otterbein, Keith F. 1986. *The Ultimate Coercive Sanction: A Cross-Cultural Study of Capital Punishment.* New Haven, Conn.: HRAF Press.

Otto, Diane. 1996. Nongovernmental Organizations in the United Nations System: The Emerging Role of International Civil Society. *Human Rights Quarterly* 18(1): 107–41.

  1999. A Post-Beijing Reflection on the Limitations and Potential of Human Rights Discourse for Women. In *Women and International Human Rights Law*, edited by Kelly Dawn Askin and Dorean M. Koenig, 115–35. Ardsley, N.Y.: Transnational Publishers.

Pace, John P. 1998. The Development of Human Rights Law in the United Nations, Its Control and Monitoring Machinery. *International Social Science Journal* 50(4): 499.

Pais, Marta Santos. 1994. Rights of Children and the Family. In *Human Rights: An Agenda for the Next Century*, edited by Louis Henkin and John Lawrence Hargrove, 183–202. Washington, D.C.: American Society of International Law.

Palmer, John P., and John Henderson. 1998. The Economics of Cruel and Unusual Punishment. *European Journal of Law and Economics* 5(3): 235–45.

Parker, David. 1995. Resources and Child Rights: An Economic Perspective. In *Implementing the Convention on the Rights of the Child: Resource Mobilization in Low-Income Countries*, edited by James R. Himes, 33–54. The Hague: Martinus Nijhoff.

Parkinson, Loraine. 1989. Japan's Unequal Employment Opportunity Law: An Alternative Approach to Social Change. *Columbia Law Review* 89:604–866.

Parrado, Emilio A. 2000. Social Change, Population Policies, and Fertility Decline in Colombia and Venezuela. *Population Research and Policy Review* 19(5): 421–57.

Partsch, Karl Josef. 1981. Freedom of Conscience and Expression and Political Freedoms. In *The International Bill of Rights: The Covenant on Civil and Political Rights*, edited by Louis Henkin, 209–45. New York: Columbia University Press.

Patrinos, Harry Anthony, and George Psacharopoulos. 1997. Family Size, Schooling and Child Labor in Peru – an Empirical Analysis. *Journal of Population Economics* 10(4): 387–405.

Pearn, John. 2003. Children and War. *Journal of Paediatrics and Child Health* 39(3): 166–72.

Pebley, Anne R., Noreen Goldman, and German Rodriguez. 1996. Prenatal and Delivery Care and Childhood Immunization in Guatemala: Do Family and Community Matter? *Demography* 33(2): 231–47.

Peck, Connie. 1996. *The United Nations as a Dispute Settlement System.* The Hague: Kluwer Law International.

Pedriana, Nicholas. 2004. Help Wanted Now: Legal Resources, the Women's Movement, and the Battle over Sex-Segregated Job Advertisements. *Social Problems* 51(2): 182–201.

Perritt, Henry H. 1998. Symposium on the Internet and Legal Theory: The Internet Is Changing International Law. *Chicago-Kent Law Review* 73:997–1054.

Perry, Michael J. 2007. *Toward a Theory of Human Rights: Religion, Law, Courts.* Cambridge: Cambridge University Press.

Peters, Anne. 1999. *Women, Quotas, and Constitutions: A Comparative Study of Affirmative Action for Women under American, German, EC and International Law.* The Hague, Boston: Kluwer Law International.

Peters, Krijn, and Paul Richards. 1998. Fighting with Eyes Open: Youth Combatants Talking About War in Sierra Leone. In *Rethinking the Trauma of War*, edited by Patrick Bracken and Celia Petty, 76–111. London, New York: Free Association Books.

Pevehouse, Jon C. 2002. Democracy from the Outside In? International Organizations and Democratization. *International Organization* 56(3): 515–49.

Phillips, Damon J., and Ezra W. Zuckerman. 2001. Middle-Status Conformity: Theoretical Restatement and Empirical Demonstration in Two Markets. *American Journal of Sociology* 107(2): 379–429.

Pietilä, Hilkka, and Jeanne Vickers. 1994. *Making Women Matter: The Role of the United Nations*, rev. and updated ed. London: Zed Books.

Pigou, Arthur C. 1962. *The Economics of Welfare*, 4th ed. London: Macmillan.

Plata, Maria Isabel, and Samantha Guy. 2000. Addressing Reproductive Health Needs among Colombia's Internally Displaced. *Sexual Health Exchange* 2:6–7. Available at http://www.popline.org/docs/1350/152653.html (accessed 8 June 2009).

Poe, Steven C. 1992. Human-Rights and Economic-Aid Allocation under Ronald Reagan and Jimmy Carter. *American Journal of Political Science* 36(1): 147–67.

Poe, Steven C., and C. Neal Tate. 1994. Repression of Human Rights to Personal Integrity in the 1980s: A Global Analysis. *American Political Science Review* 88(4): 853–72.

Poe, Steven C., Neal Tate, and Linda Camp Keith. 1999. Repression of the Human Right to Personal Integrity Revisited: A Global Crossnational Study Covering the Years 1976–1993. *International Studies Quarterly* 43:291–315.

Poe, Steven C., Dierdre Wendel-Blunt, and Karl Ho. 1997. Global Patterns in the Achievement of Women's Human Rights to Equality. *Human Rights Quarterly* 19(4): 813–35.

Pogge, Thomas Winfried Menko. 2002. *World Poverty and Human Rights: Cosmopolitan Responsibilities and Reforms.* Malden, Mass.: Blackwell.

Polletta, Francesca. 2000. The Structural Context of Novel Rights Claims: Southern Civil Rights Organizing, 1961–1966. *Law & Society Review* 34(2): 367–406.

Pollock, Linda A. 1983. *Forgotten Children: Parent–Child Relations from 1500 to 1900.* Cambridge: Cambridge University Press.

Port, Kenneth L. 1991. The Japanese International Law Revolution – International Human Rights Law and Its Impact in Japan. *Stanford Journal of International Law* 28(1): 139–72.

Posner, Michael H. 1994. The Establishment of the Right of Nongovernmental Human Rights Groups to Operate. In *Human Rights: An Agenda for the Next Century*, edited by Louis Henkin and John Lawrence Hargrove, 405–23. Washington, D.C.: American Society of International Law.

Potter, Harry. 1993. *Hanging in Judgment: Religion and the Death Penalty in England.* New York: Continuum.

Potter, Pitman B. 2003. Belief in Control: Regulation of Religion in China. *The China Quarterly* 174:317–37.

Powell, Emilia J., and Jeffrey K. Staton. 2007. *Domestic Judicial Institutions and Human Rights Treaty Violation.* Statesboro, Ga., and Tallahassee, Fla. Available at http://papers/ssrn.com/s013/papers.cfm?abstract_id=1028672

Power, Samantha. 2002. *"A Problem from Hell": America and the Age of Genocide*. New York: Basic Books.

Power, Samantha, and Graham T. Allison, eds. 2000. *Realizing Human Rights: Moving from Inspiration to Impact*. New York: St. Martin's Press.

Pruden, Caroline. 1998. *Conditional Partners: Eisenhower, the United Nations, and the Search for a Permanent Peace*. Baton Rouge: Louisiana State University Press.

Psacharopoulos, George. 1994. Returns to Investment in Education – a Global Update. *World Development* 22(9): 1325–43.

1997. Child Labor versus Educational Attainment: Some Evidence from Latin America. *Journal of Population Economics* 10(4): 377–86.

Puhar, Eva. 2005. The Abolition of the Death Penalty in Central and Eastern Europe: A Survey of Abolition Processes in Former Communist Countries. In *Occasional Papers Series, Vol. II. Centre for Capital Punishment Studies*. London: University of Westminster Press.

Putnam, Robert D., Robert Leonardi, and Raffaella Nanetti. 1993. *Making Democracy Work: Civic Traditions in Modern Italy*. Princeton, N.J.: Princeton University Press.

Quarterman, John. 1999. Internet Growth Rates. *SunExpert Magazine:* 39–40.

Qureshi, Asif H. 1990. The New GATT Trade Policy Review Mechanism: An Exercise in Transparency or Enforcement. *Journal of World Trade* 24(3): 147–60.

Radzinowicz, Leon. 1999. *Adventures in Criminology*. London, New York: Routledge.

Rajagopal, Balakrishnan. 2002. From Modernization to Democratization: The Political Economy of the "New" International Law. In *Reframing the International: Law, Culture, Politics*, edited by Richard A. Falk, Lester Edwin J. Ruiz, and R. B. J. Walker, 136–62. New York: Routledge.

Ramirez, Francisco O., Yasemin Soysal, and Suzanne Shanahan. 1997. The Changing Logic of Political Citizenship: Cross-National Acquisition of Women's Suffrage Rights, 1890 to 1990. *American Sociological Review* 62(5): 735–45.

Ratner, Steven R. 2004. Overcoming Temptations to Violate Human Dignity in Times of Crisis: On the Possibilities for Meaningful Self-Restraint. *Theoretical Inquiries in Law (Online Edition)* 5(1): Article 3. Available at http://www.bepress.com/til/default/vol5/iss1/art3 (accessed 8 June 2009).

Ratner, Steven R., and Jason S. Abrams. 2001. *Accountability for Human Rights Atrocities in International Law: Beyond the Nuremberg Legacy*, 2nd ed. Oxford, New York: Oxford University Press.

Ravallion, Martin, and Quentin Wodon. 2000. Does Child Labour Displace Schooling? Evidence on Behavioural Responses to an Enrollment Subsidy. *The Economic Journal* 110(462): C158–C75.

Ray, June. 2000. Human Rights Protection and the Rule of Law: Case Studies in Israel and Egypt. In *The Rule of Law in the Middle East and the Islamic World: Human Rights and the Judicial Process*, edited by Eugene Cotran and Mai Yamani, 43–50. London, New York: I. B. Tauris.

Rehof, Lars Adam. 1993. *Guide to the Travaux Préparatoires of the United Nations Convention on the Elimination of All Forms of Discrimination against Women*. Boston: Kluwer Academic.

Reidy, David A., and Mortimer N. S. Sellers, eds. 2005. *Universal Human Rights: Moral Order in a Divided World*. Lanham, Md.: Rowman & Littlefield.

Reisman, W. Michael. 1990. Sovereignty and Human Rights in Contemporary International Law. *American Journal of International Law* 84(4): 866–76.

1992. *Systems of Control in International Adjudication and Arbitration: Breakdown and Repair*. Durham, N.C.: Duke University Press.

Renteln, Alison Dundes. 1990. *International Human Rights: Universalism versus Relativism.* Newbury Park, Calif.: Sage.

Reus-Smit, Christian, ed. 2004. *The Politics of International Law.* Cambridge: Cambridge University Press.

Richards, David L., Ronald D. Gelleny, and David H. Sacko. 2001. Money with a Mean Streak? Foreign Economic Penetration and Government Respect for Human Rights. *International Studies Quarterly* 45(2): 219–39.

Riis, Ole. 1999. Modes of Religious Pluralism Under Conditions of Globalisation. *International Journal on Multicultural Societies* 1(1): 20–34.

Risse, Thomas, and Kathryn Sikkink. 1999. The Socialization of International Human Rights Norms into Domestic Practice: Introduction. In *The Power of Human Rights: International Norms and Domestic Change,* edited by Thomas Risse, Steve C. Ropp, and Kathryn Sikkink, 1–38. Cambridge: Cambridge University Press.

Roan, Michael. 1996. The Role of Secular Non-Governmental Organizations in the Cultivation and Understanding of Religious Human Rights. In *Religious Human Rights in Global Perspective: Legal Perspectives,* edited by Johan D. Van der Vyver and John Witte, 135–59. The Hague: Martinus Nijhoff.

Robertson, Arthur H., and J. G. Merrills. 1993. *Human Rights in Europe: A Study of the European Convention on Human Rights,* 3rd ed. Manchester, England; New York: Manchester University Press.

Robertson, Geoffrey. 1999. *Crimes Against Humanity: The Struggle for Global Justice.* London: Allen Lane.

Robertson, Robert E. 1994. Measuring State Compliance with the Obligation to Devote the "Maximum Available Resources" to Realizing Economic, Social, and Cultural Rights. *Human Rights Quarterly* 16:693–714.

Robin, Marie-Monique. 2005. Counterinsurgency and Torture. In *Torture: Does It Make Us Safer? Is It Ever OK? A Human Rights Perspective,* edited by Kenneth Roth, Minky Worden, and Amy D. Bernstein, 44–54. New York: New Press. Distributed by W. W. Norton.

Rodley, Nigel S. 1986. United Nations Action Procedures Against Disappearances, Summary or Arbitrary Executions, and Torture. *Human Rights Quarterly* 8(4): 700–30.

———. 1999. *The Treatment of Prisoners Under International Law,* 2nd ed. New York: Oxford University Press.

Romano, Cesare. 1999. The Proliferation of International Judicial Bodies: The Pieces of the Puzzle. *New York University Journal of International Law and Politics* 31(summer): 709–51.

Ron, James, Howard Ramos, and Kathleen Rodgers. 2005. Transnational Information Politics: NGO Human Rights Reporting, 1986–2000. *International Studies Quarterly* 49(3): 557–88.

Roosevelt, Eleanor D. 1947. Statements by E. Roosevelt. *Department of State Bulletin* 17, Dec. 19:867.

Rosenberg, Gerald N. 1991. *The Hollow Hope: Can Courts Bring About Social Change?* Chicago: University of Chicago Press.

———. 1992. Hollow Hopes and Other Aspirations: A Reply to Feeley and McCann. *Law & Social Inquiry* 17(4): 761–78.

Rosenne, Shabtai. 1989. *The World Court: What It Is and How It Works,* 4th ed. Dordrecht, the Netherlands: Martinus Nijhoff.

Ross, James. 2005. A History of Torture. In *Torture: Does It Make Us Safer? Is It Ever OK? A Human Rights Perspective*, edited by Kenneth Roth, Minky Worden, and Amy D. Bernstein, 3–17. New York: New Press. Distributed by W. W. Norton.

Ross, John A., and William L. Winfrey. 2002. Unmet Need for Contraception in the Developing World and the Former Soviet Union: An Updated Estimate. Available at http://sparky.agi-usa.org/pubs/archives/nr_280302.html (accessed 28 July 2003).

Roth, Kenneth. 2000. The Charade of U.S. Ratification of International Human Rights Treaties. *Chicago Journal of International Law* 1:347–54.

Rouner, Leroy S., ed. 1988. *Human Rights and the World's Religions*. Notre Dame, Ind.: University of Notre Dame Press.

Rovine, Arthur. 1981. Defense of Declarations, Reservations, and Understandings. In *U.S. Ratification of the Human Rights Treaties with or without Reservations?* edited by Richard B. Lillich, 54–67. Charlottesville: University Press of Virginia.

Royston, Erica, and Sue Armstrong. 1989. *Preventing Maternal Deaths*. Geneva: World Health Organization.

Ruddell, Rick. 2005. Social Disruption, State Formation and Minority Threat: A Crossnational Study of Imprisonment. *Punishment & Society* 7:7–28.

Ruddell, Rick, and Martin G. Urbana. 2004. Minority Threat and Punishment: A Cross-National Analysis. *Justice Quarterly* 21(4): 903–31.

Rueschemeyer, Dietrich, Evelyne Huber Stephens, and John D. Stephens. 1992. *Capitalist Development and Democracy*. Cambridge: Polity Press.

Ruggie, John Gerard. 1998. What Makes the World Hang Together? Neo-Utilitarianism and the Social Constructivist Challenge. *International Organization* 52(4): 855–86.

——— 2007. Business and Human Rights: The Evolving National Agenda. *American Journal of International Law* 101(4): 819–40.

Rupp, Leila J. 1997. *Worlds of Women: The Making of an International Women's Movement*. Princeton, N.J.: Princeton University Press.

Rutschky, Katharina. 1977. *Schwarze Pädagogik: Quellen Zur Naturgeschichte Der Bürgerlichen Erziehung, Ullstein Buch; Nr. 3318*. Frankfurt/Main: Ullstein GmbH.

Sadana, Ritu. 2002. Definition and Measurement of Reproductive Health. *Bulletin of the World Health Organization* 80(5): 407–9.

Sai, Fred T. 1993. Political and Economic Factors Influencing Contraceptive Uptake. *British Medical Bulletin* 49(1): 200–9.

Sangroula, Yubaraj. 2000. Fair Trial: Still a Long Way to Achieve in Nepal. In *Decline of Fair Trial in Asia: Papers from an Asian Seminar on Fair Trial, 7–12 November 1999*, Kowloon, Hong Kong, edited by the Asian Human Rights Commission and Danske Menneskerettighedscenter, 195–215. Hong Kong: Asian Human Rights Commission.

Santa-Cruz, Arturo. 2005. Constitutional Structures, Sovereignty, and the Emergence of Norms: The Case of International Election Monitoring. *International Organization* 59(3): 663–93.

Sarat, Austin, and Stuart A. Scheingold. 1998. Cause Lawyering and the Reproduction of Professional Authority. In *Cause Lawyering: Political Commitments and Professional Responsibilities*, edited by Austin Sarat and Stuart A. Scheingold, 3–28. New York: Oxford University Press.

Schabas, William A. 1996. Reservations to the Convention on the Rights of the Child. *Human Rights Quarterly* 18(2): 472–91.

2002. *The Abolition of the Death Penalty in International Law*, 3rd ed. Cambridge: Cambridge University Press.

Schachter, Oscar. 1991. *International Law in Theory and Practice.* Dordrecht, the Netherlands: Martinus Nijhoff.

1998. The Decline of the Nation-State and Its Implications for International Law. *Columbia Journal of Transnational Law* 36:7.

Scheingold, Stuart A. 1974. *The Politics of Rights: Lawyers, Public Policy, and Political Change.* New Haven, Conn.: Yale University Press.

Schenker, Joseph G., and Vered H. Eisenberg. 1997. Ethical Issues Relating to Reproduction Control and Women's Health. *International Journal of Gynecology and Obstetrics* 58(1): 167–76.

Scheper-Hughes, Nancy, and Carolyn Fishel Sargent. 1998. Introduction: The Cultural Politics of Childhood. In *Small Wars: The Cultural Politics of Childhood*, edited by Nancy Scheper-Hughes and Carolyn Fishel Sargent, 1–33. Berkeley: University of California Press.

Schmitz, Cathryne L., Elizabeth Kim, Jin Traver, and Desi Larson. 2004. *Child Labor: A Global View, A World View of Social Issues.* Westport, Conn.: Greenwood Press.

Schneider, Elizabeth M. 1986. The Dialectic of Rights and Politics: Perspectives from the Women's Movement. *New York University Law Review* 61(4): 589–652.

Scholliers, Peter. 1995. Grown-Ups, Boys and Girls in the Ghent Cotton Industry: The Voortman Mills, 1835–1914. *Social History* 20(2): 201–18.

Schou, Nina. 2000. Instances of Human Rights Regimes. In *Delegating State Powers: The Effect of Treaty Regimes on Democracy and Sovereignty*, edited by Thomas M. Franck, 209–54. Ardsley, N.Y.: Transnational Publishers.

Schoultz, Lars. 1981. U.S. Foreign Policy and Human Rights Violations in Latin America: A Comparative Analysis of Foreign Aid Distributions. *Comparative Politics* 13(2): 149–70.

Shuster, Milan R. 1973. *The Public International Law of Money.* Oxford: Clarendon Press.

Scott, Douglas S., and Walter A. Dorn. 1998. The Compliance Regime Under the Chemical Weapons Convention: A Summary and Analysis. In *Treaty Compliance: Some Concerns and Remedies*, edited by the Canadian Council on International Law and the Markland Group, 87–132. London, Boston: Kluwer Law International.

Sen, Amartya Kumar. 1999. *Development as Freedom.* New York: Knopf.

Shany, Yuval. 2006. How Supreme Is the Supreme Law of the Land? Comparative Analysis of the Influence of International Human Rights Treaties Upon the Interpretation of Constitutional Texts by Domestic Courts. *Brookings Journal of International Law* 31(2): 341–404.

Shapiro, Steven R. 1993. *Human Rights Violations in the United States: A Report on U.S. Compliance with the International Covenant on Civil and Political Rights.* New York: Human Rights Watch and the American Civil Liberties Union.

Sharif, Adel Omar. 2000. The Rule of Law in Egypt from a Judicial Perspective: A Digest of the Landmark Decisions of the Supreme Constitutional Court. In *The Rule of Law in the Middle East and the Islamic World: Human Rights and the Judicial Process*, edited by Eugene Cotran and Mai Yamani, 1–34. London: I.B. Tauris.

Shelman, Eric A., and Stephen Lazoritz. 2005. *The Mary Ellen Wilson Child Abuse Case and the Beginning of Children's Rights in 19th Century America.* Jefferson, N.C.: McFarland.

Shelton, Dinah. 1983. State Practice on Reservation to Human Rights Treaties. *Canadian Human Rights Yearbook*, edited by Jean-Denis Archambault and R. Paul Nedin-Davis, 205–34. Toronto: Carswell.

1994. The Participation of Non-Governmental Organizations in International Judicial Proceedings. *American Journal of International Law* 88(4): 611–42.

1997. Compliance with International Human Rights Soft Law. In *International Compliance with Nonbinding Accords*, edited by Edith Brown Weiss, 119–43. Washington, D.C.: American Society of International Law.

Shepard, George W. 1981. Transnational Development of Human Rights: The Third World Crucible. In *Global Human Rights*, edited by Ved P. Nanda, James R. Scarritt, and George W. Shepard. Boulder, Colo.: Westview Press.

Sieghart, Paul. 1983. *The International Law of Human Rights*. Oxford: Clarendon Press.

Sigmund, Paul E. 1996. Religious Human Rights in Latin America. In *Religious Human Rights in Global Perspective: Legal Perspectives*, edited by Johan D. Van der Vyver and John Witte, 467–81. The Hague: Martinus Nijhoff.

Sikkink, Kathryn. 1993. Human Rights, Principled Issue Networks, and Sovereignty in Latin America. *International Organization* 47(3): 411–41.

Silverstein, Helena. 1996. *Unleashing Rights: Law, Meaning, and the Animal Rights Movement*. Ann Arbor: University of Michigan Press.

Simmons, Beth A. 2000. International Law and State Behavior: Commitment and Compliance in International Monetary Affairs. *American Political Science Review* 94(4): 819–35.

Simmons, Beth A., and Allison Marston Danner. forthcoming. Credible Commitments and the International Criminal Court. *International Organization*.

Simmons, Beth A., and Zachary Elkins. 2004. The Globalization of Liberalization: Policy Diffusion in the International Political Economy. *American Political Science Review* 98(1): 171–89.

Simmons, Beth A., and Daniel J. Hopkins. 2005. The Constraining Power of International Treaties: Theory and Methods. *American Political Science Review* 99(4): 623–31.

Simmons, Beth A., and Eugen Lamprecht. 2006. "Regulating Childhood: Child Labor and Child Soldiers as an International Regulatory Issue." Cambridge, Mass.

Singer, Peter W. 2005. *Children at War*. New York: Pantheon Books.

Singh, Susheela, and Gilda Sedgh. 1997. The Relationship of Abortion to Trends in Contraception and Fertility in Brazil, Colombia and Mexico. *International Family Planning Perspectives* 23(1): 4–14.

Sironi, Francoise, and Raphaelle Branche. 2002. Torture and the Borders of Humanity. *International Social Science Journal* 54(174): 539–48.

Skeen, Andrew. 2000. The Right to a Fair Trial in South African Law. In *The Right to a Fair Trial*, edited by the European Commission for Democracy through Law, Council of Europe, 110–29. Strasbourg: Council of Europe.

Skjelsbaek, Kjell. 1971. The Growth of International Nongovernmental Organization in the Twentieth Century. *International Organization* 25(3): 420–42.

Slaughter, Anne-Marie. 1995. A Typology of Transjudicial Communication. *University of Richmond Law Review* 29:99.

Slaughter, Joseph. 1997. A Question of Narration: The Voice in International Human Rights Law. *Human Rights Quarterly* 19(2): 406–30.

Smith, Jackie, Ron Pagnucco, and George A. Lopez. 1998. Globalizing Human Rights: The Work of Transnational Human Rights NGOs in the 1990s. *Human Rights Quarterly* 20(2): 379–412.

Smolin, David M. 2000. Strategic Choices in the International Campaign Against Child Labor. *Human Rights Quarterly* 22(4): 942–87.

Snyder, Jack L., and Leslie Vinjamuri. 2003–4. Trials and Errors: Principle and Pragmatism in Strategies of International Justice. *International Security* 28(3): 5–44.

Solomon, Aaron. 2001. The Politics of Prosecutions Under the Convention Against Torture. *Chicago Journal of International Law* 20(2): 309–13.

Somasundaram, Daya. 2002. Child Soldiers: Understanding the Context. *British Medical Journal* 324:1268–71.

Soss, Joe, Laura Langbein, and Alan R. Metelko. 2003. Why Do White Americans Support the Death Penalty? *Journal of Politics* 65(2): 397–421.

Spirer, Herbert F. 1990. Violations of Human Rights: How Many? The Statistical Problems of Measuring Such Infractions Are Tough, but Statistical Science Is Equal to It. *American Journal of Economics and Society* 49:199–210.

Spohr, Chris. A. 2003. Formal Schooling and Workforce Participation in a Rapidly Developing Economy: Evidence From "Compulsory" Junior High School in Taiwan. *Journal of Development Economics* 70(2): 291–327.

Spriggs, James F., II. 1996. The Supreme Court and Federal Administrative Agencies: A Resource-Based Theory and Analysis of Judicial Impact. *American Journal of Political Science* 40(4): 1122–51.

St. Amand, Matthew G. 1999–2000. Public Committee Against Torture in *Israel v. The State of Israel et al.*: Landmark Human Rights Decision by the Israeli High Court of Justice or Status Quo Maintained? *North Carolina Journal of International and Comparative Regulation* 25:655–84.

Steele, Fiona, Ian Diamond, and Sajeda Amin. 1996. Immunization Uptake in Rural Bangladesh: A Multilevel Analysis. *Journal of the Royal Statistical Society. Series A (Statistics in Society)* 159(2): 289–99.

Steigerwald, David. 1999. The Reclamation of Woodrow Wilson? *Diplomatic History* 23(1): 79–99.

Stetson, Dorothy McBride. 1995. Human Rights for Women: International Compliance with a Feminist Standard. *Women & Politics* 15(3): 71–95.

Stohl, Michael, David Carleton, George A. Lopez, and Stephen Samuels. 1986. State Violation of Human Rights: Issues and Problems of Measurement. *Human Rights Quarterly* 8(4): 592–606.

Stohl, Michael, and George A. Lopez. 1984. *The State as Terrorist: The Dynamics of Governmental Violence and Repression.* Westport, Conn.: Greenwood Press.

1986. *Government Violence and Repression: An Agenda for Research.* New York: Greenwood Press.

Stone, Geoffrey R. 2005. *Constitutional Law*, 5th ed. New York: Aspen.

Stone, Julius. 1966. *Law and the Social Sciences in the Second Half Century.* Minneapolis: University of Minnesota Press.

Streatfield, Kim, Masri Singarimbun, and Ian Diamond. 1990. Maternal Education and Child Immunization. *Demography* 27(3): 447–55.

Streefland, Pieter, A. M. R. Chowdhury, and Pilar Ramos-Jimenez. 1999. Patterns of Vaccination Acceptance. *Social Science & Medicine* 49(12): 1705–16.

Sullivan, Donna J. 1988. Advancing the Freedom of Religion or Belief through the UN Declaration on the Elimination of Religious Intolerance and Discrimination. *The American Journal of International Law* 82(3): 487–520.

Sundstrom, Lisa McIntosh. 2002. "International Rights Regimes and Resistant Domestic Norms: Russia and Women's Rights." Paper prepared for delivery at the 43rd annual convention of the International Studies Association, New Orleans, 24–27 March 2002. Vancouver: University of British Columbia.

Sung, Hung-En. 2006. Democracy and Criminal Justice in Cross-National Perspective: From Crime Control to Due Process. *The Annals of the American Academy of Political and Social Science* 605(1): 311–37.

Sussman, Leonard R. 2000. Censor Dot Gov: The Internet and Press Freedom 2000. *Journal of Government Information* 27(5): 537–45.

Sutton, John R. 2000. Imprisonment and Social Classification in Five Common-Law Democracies, 1955–1985. *American Journal of Sociology* 106(2): 350–86.

Swaine, Edward T. 2003. Does Federalism Constrain the Treaty Power? *Columbia Law Review* 103(3): 403–533.

Swidler, Leonard J. 1990. *After the Absolute: The Dialogical Future of Religious Reflection.* Minneapolis: Fortress Press.

Swinarski, Christophe. 1997. On the Right to a Fair Trial Under International Humanitarian Instruments. In *The Right to a Fair Trial in International and Comparative Perspective*, edited by Andrew Byrnes, 26–36. Hong Kong: Centre for Comparative and Public Law, University of Hong Kong.

Szanton Blanc, Cristina. 1994. *Urban Children in Distress: Global Predicaments and Innovative Strategies.* Yverdon, Switzerland: Gordon and Breach.

Szasz, Paul C. 1999. *Administrative and Expert Monitoring of International Treaties.* Ardsley, N.Y.: Transnational Publishers.

Tahzib, Bahiyyih G. 1996. *Freedom of Religion or Belief: Ensuring Effective International Legal Protection.* The Hague: Martinus Nijhoff.

Talbi, Mohamed. 1986. Religious Liberty: A Muslim Perspective. In *Religious Liberty and Human Rights in Nations and in Religions*, edited by Leonard J. Swidler, 175–87. Philadelphia: Ecumenical Press.

Tananbaum, Duane. 1988. *The Bricker Amendment Controversy: A Test of Eisenhower's Political Leadership.* Ithaca, N.Y.: Cornell University Press.

Tardu, Maxime. 1980. United Nations Responses to Gross Violations of Human Rights: The 1503 Procedure. *Santa Clara Law Review* 20:559.

Taylor, Paul M. 2005. *Freedom of Religion: UN and European Human Rights Law and Practice.* Cambridge: Cambridge University Press.

Teitel, Ruti G. 2000. *Transitional Justice.* Oxford, New York: Oxford University Press.

Teklehaimanot, Kibrom I. 2002. Using the Right to Life to Confront Unsafe Abortion in Africa. *Reproductive Health Matters* 10(19): 143–50.

Telser, Lester G. 1987. *A Theory of Efficient Cooperation and Competition.* Cambridge: Cambridge University Press.

Tetley, William. 1999–2000. Mixed Jurisdictions: Common Law vs. Civil Law (Codified and Uncodified). Available at http://www.cisg.law.pace.edu/cisg/biblio/tetley.html (accessed 5 September 2002).

Thomas, Daniel C. 2001. *The Helsinki Effect: International Norms, Human Rights, and the Demise of Communism.* Princeton, N.J.: Princeton University Press.

Thomas, George Marta. 2001. Religions in Global Civil Society. *Sociology of Religion* 62(4): 515–33.

Tibi, Bassam. 1994. Islamic Law/Shari'a, Human Rights, Universal Morality and International Relations. *Human Rights Quarterly* 16(2): 277–99.

Tienda, Marta. 1979. Economic Activity of Children in Peru: Labor Force Behavior in Rural and Urban Contexts. *Rural Sociology* 44:370–91.

Tolley, Howard. 1987. *The U.N. Commission on Human Rights.* Boulder, Colo.: Westview Press.

———. 1989. Popular Sovereignty and International Law – ICJ Strategies for Human Rights Standard Setting. *Human Rights Quarterly* 11(4): 561–85.

———. 1991. Interest Group Litigation to Enforce Human Rights. *Political Science Quarterly* 105(4): 617–38.

———. 1994. *The International Commission of Jurists: Global Advocates for Human Rights.* Philadelphia: University of Pennsylvania Press.

Toor, Saadia. 2001. Child Labor in Pakistan: Coming of Age in the New World Order. *Annals of the American Academy of Political and Social Science* 575(1): 194–224.

Trebilcock, Anne. 1999. ILO Conventions and Women Workers. In *Women and International Human Rights Law,* edited by Kelly Dawn Askin and Dorean M. Koenig, 301–18. Ardsley, N.Y.: Transnational Publishers.

Tshosa, Onkemetse. 2001. *National Law and International Human Rights Law: Cases of Botswana, Namibia and Zimbabwe.* Aldershot, England; Burlington, Vt.: Ashgate.

Tunc, Andre. 1976. Methodology of the Civil Law in France. *Tulane Law Review* 50:459–654.

Turk, Austin T. 1976. Law as a Weapon in Social Conflict. *Social Problems* 23(3): 276–91.

Turrell, Robert Vicat. 2004. *White Mercy: A Study of the Death Penalty in South Africa.* Westport, Conn.: Praeger.

United States Department of State, Office of Media Services. 2000. *Countries of the World and Their Leaders.* Detroit: Gale Research Co.

Upham, Frank. 1987. *Law and Social Change in Postwar Japan.* Cambridge, Mass.: Harvard University Press.

Uprimny, Rodrigo. 2003. The Constitutional Court and Control of Presidential Extraordinary Powers in Colombia. *Democratization* 10(4): 46–69.

USIP. 2001a. *U.S. Human Rights Policy toward Africa.* Washington, D.C.: United States Institute of Peace.

———. 2001b. *U.S. Human Rights Policy toward Latin America.* Washington, D.C.: United States Institute of Peace.

Valencia-Weber, Gloria, and Robert J. Weber. 1986. El-Salvador: Methods Used to Document Human-Rights Violations. *Human Rights Quarterly* 8(4): 731–70.

Van Alstine, Michael P. 2004. Federal Common Law in an Age of Treaties. *Cornell Law Review* 89(4): 892–992.

van Boven, Theo. 1989–1990. The Role of Non-Governmental Organizations in International Human Rights Standard Setting: A Prerequisite of Democracy. *California Western International Law Journal* 20(2): 207–25.

Van Bueren, Geraldine. 1995. The International Law on the Rights of the Child. *International Studies in Human Rights, V. 35.* Dordrecht, the Netherlands: Martinus Nijhoff.

Van Bueren, Geraldine, and Deirdre Fottrell. 1999. The Potential of International Law to Combat Discrimination Against Girls in Education. In *Religious Fundamentalisms and the Human Rights of Women,* edited by Courtney W. Howland, 129–39. New York: St. Martin's Press.

van Dijk, Pieter. 1983. *The Right of the Accused to a Fair Trial Under International Law.* The Netherlands: Studieen Informatiecentrum Mensenrechten.

Verhellen, Eugeen. 1994. *Convention on the Rights of the Child: Background, Motivation, Strategies, Main Themes.* Leuven, Belgium: Garant.

Vermulst, Edwin, and Bart Driessen. 1995. An Overview of the WTO Dispute Settlement System and Its Relationship with the Uruguay Round Agreements. *Journal of World Trade* 29:131–61.

Vincent, R. John. 1986. *Human Rights and International Relations*. Cambridge: Cambridge University Press.

Vinjamuri, Leslie, and Jack Snyder. 2004. Advocacy and Scholarship in the Study of International War Crime Tribunals and Transitional Justice. *Annual Review of Political Science* 7:345–62.

Viotti, Maria Luiza Ribeiro. 1987. *Implementation of the Declaration on the Elimination of All Forms of Intolerance and of Discrimination Based on Religion or Belief*, UN Doc. E/CN.4/1987/ 35. New York: United Nations.

von Stein, Jana. 2005. Do Treaties Constrain or Screen? Selection Bias and Treaty Compliance. *American Political Science Review* 99(4): 611–22.

Waguespack, David M., and Johanna K. Birnir. 2005. Foreignness and the Diffusion of Ideas. *Journal of Engineering and Technology Management* 22(1–2): 31–50.

Walker, Scott, and Steven C. Poe. 2002. Does Cultural Diversity Affect Countries' Respect for Human Rights? *Human Rights Quarterly* 24(1): 237–63.

Waltz, Kenneth Neal. 1979. *Theory of International Politics*. Reading, Mass.: Addison-Wesley.

Waltz, Susan. 2001. Universalizing Human Rights: The Role of Small States in the Construction of the Universal Declaration of Human Rights. *Human Rights Quarterly* 23(1): 44–72.

Wantchekon, Leonard, and Andrew Healy. 1999. The "Game" of Torture. *Journal of Conflict Resolution* 43(5): 596–609.

Wapner, Paul. 1995. Politics Beyond the State: Environmental Activism and World Civic Politics. *World Politics* 47(3): 331–40.

Watts, Ronald L. 1998. Federalism, Federal Political Systems, and Federations. *Annual Review of Political Science* 1:117–37.

Weathers, Charles. 2005. In Search of Strategic Partners: Japan's Campaign for Equal Opportunity. *Social Science Japan Journal* 8:69–89.

Webber, Frances. 1999. The Pinochet Case: The Struggle for the Realization of Human Rights. *Journal of Law and Society* 26(4): 523–37.

Weeramantry, Lucian G. 2000. *The International Commission of Jurists: The Pioneering Years*. The Hague, Boston: Kluwer Law International.

Weiner, Myron. 1991. *The Child and the State in India: Child Labor and Education Policy in Comparative Perspective*. Princeton, N.J.: Princeton University Press.

Weisburd, Arthur M. 1999. Implications of International Relations Theory for the International Law of Human Rights. *Columbia Journal of Transnational Law* 38(1): 45–112.

Weissbrodt, David. 1986. The Three Theme Special Rapporteurs of the UN Commission on Human Rights. *American Journal of International Law* 80(3): 685–99.

2001. *The Right to a Fair Trial Under the Universal Declaration of Human Rights and the International Covenant on Civil and Political Rights*. The Hague: Martinus Nijhoff.

Weissbrodt, David, and Mattias Hallendorff. 1999. Travaux Préparatoires of the Fair Trial Provisions – Articles 8 to 11 – of the Universal Declaration of Human Rights. *Human Rights Quarterly* 21(4): 1061–96.

Welch, Claude Emerson. 1995. *Protecting Human Rights in Africa: Roles and Strategies of Non-Governmental Organizations*. Philadelphia: University of Pennsylvania Press.

Wenar, Leif. 2005. The Nature of Human Rights. In *Real World Justice: Grounds, Principles, Human Rights, and Social Institutions*, edited by Andreas Føllesdal and Thomas Winfried Menko Pogge, 285–93. Dordrecht, the Netherlands: Springer.

West, Harry G. 2000. Girls with Guns: Narrating the Experience of War of Frelimo's "Female Detachment." *Anthropological Quarterly* 73(4): 180–94.

Westlake, John. 1894. *Chapters on the Principles of International Law.* Cambridge: Cambridge University Press.

Weston, Burns. 1999. The Universality of Human Rights in a Multi-Cultured World: Toward Respectful Decision-Making. In *The Future of International Human Rights,* edited by Burns Weston and Stephen P. Marks, 65–99. Ardsley, N.Y.: Transational Publishers.

Whitman, James Q. 2003. *Harsh Justice: Criminal Punishment and the Widening Divide between America and Europe.* Oxford, New York: Oxford University Press.

Widdus, Roy. 1999. The Potential to Control or Eradicate Infectious Diseases through Immunisation. *Vaccine* 17(Supplement 2): S6–S12.

Wiesberg, Laurie S., and Harry M. Scoble. 1981. Recent Trends in the Expanding Universe of NGOs Dedicated to the Protection of Human Rights. In *Global Human Rights: Public Policies, Comparative Measures, and NGO Strategies,* edited by Ved P. Nanda, James R. Scarritt, and George W. Shepard, 229–60. Boulder, Colo.: Westview Press.

Wils, Annababette, and Anne Goujon. 1998. Diffusion of Education in Six World Regions, 1960–90. *Population and Development Review* 24(2): 357–68.

Wilson, William J. 1973. *Power, Racism, and Privilege: Race Relations in Theoretical and Sociohistorical Perspectives.* New York: Macmillan.

Winikoff, Beverly, and Maureen Sullivan. 1987. Assessing the Role of Family Planning in Reducing Maternal Mortality. *Studies in Family Planning* 18(3): 128–43.

Woll, Lisa. 2000. *The Convention on the Rights of the Child Impact Study.* Stockholm: Save the Children Sweden.

Wolpin, Kenneth I. 1978. Capital Punishment and Homicide in England: A Summary of Results. *The American Economic Review* 68(2): 422–27.

Wood, E. Thomas, and Stanislaw M. Jankowski. 1994. *Karski: How One Man Tried to Stop the Holocaust.* New York: Wiley.

Worden, Minky. 2005. Torture Spoken Here: Ending Global Torture. In *Torture: Does It Make Us Safer? Is It Ever OK? A Human Rights Perspective,* edited by Kenneth Roth, Minky Worden, and Amy D. Bernstein, 79–105. New York: New Press.

Wotipka, Christine Min, and Francisco O. Ramirez. 2008. World Society and Human Rights: An Events History Analysis of the Convention on the Elimination of All Forms of Discrimination Against Women. In *The Global Diffusion of Markets and Democracy,* edited by Beth A. Simmons, Frank Dobbin, and Geoffrey Garrett, 303–43. Cambridge: Cambridge University Press.

Wyman, James H. 1997. Vengeance Is Whose? The Death Penalty and Cultural Relativism in International Law. *Journal of Transnational Law & Policy* 6(2): 543–70.

Wynarczyk, Peter. 1999. The Political Economy of Capital Punishment. *Economic Affairs* 19(1): 43–7.

Yamani, Mai. 2000. Muslim Women and Human Rights in Saudi Arabia: Aspirations of a New Generation. In *The Rule of Law in the Middle East and the Islamic World: Human Rights and the Judicial Process,* edited by Eugene Cotran and Mai Yamani, 137–43. London, New York: I. B. Tauris.

Yamashita, Yasuko. 1993. The International Movement toward Gender Equality and Its Impact on Japan. *U.S.-Japan Women's Journal English Supplement* 5:69–86.

Zald, Mayer N., and John D. McCarthy, eds. 1979. *The Dynamics of Social Movements: Resource Mobilization, Social Control, and Tactics*. Cambridge, Mass.: Winthrop.

Zemans, Frances Kahn. 1983. Legal Mobilization: The Neglected Role of the Law in the Political System. *American Political Science Review* 77(3): 690–703.

Zimring, Franklin E. 2003. *The Contradictions of American Capital Punishment*. Oxford, New York: Oxford University Press.

Zirakzadeh, Cyrus Ernesto. 2006. Social Movements in Politics: A Comparative Study. In *Perspectives in Comparative Politics*, expanded ed. New York: Palgrave Macmillan.

Zweigert, Konrad, and Hein Kötz. 1987. *Introduction to Comparative Law*, 2nd rev. ed. Oxford: Clarendon Press.

Index